UNIX System Programming Using C++

Terrence Chan

To join a Prentice Hall PTR internet mailing list:
point to http://www.prenhall.com

Prentice Hall PTR
Upper Saddle River, New Jersey 07458

http://www.prenhall.com.

Library of Congress Cataloging-in-Publication Data

Chan, Terrence

UNIX system programming using C++ / Terrence Chan.

p.   cm.

Includes bibliographical references and index.

ISBN 0-13-331562-2

1. C++ (Computer program language) 2. UNIX (Computer file)

I. Title.

QA76.73.C153C46 1997

005.13'3--dc20   96-30559

                                                                    CIP

Editorial/Production Supervisor: Nicholas Radhuber
Manufacturing Manager: Alexis Heydt
Acquisitions Editor: Greg Doench
Editorial Assistant: Leabe Berman
Cover Design: Lundgren Graphics, Ltd.
Cover Design Direction: Jerry Votta

 © 1997 by Prentice Hall PTR
Prentice-Hall, Inc.
A Simon & Schuster Company
Upper Saddle River, New Jersey 07458

The publisher offers discounts on this book when ordered in bulk quantities.
For more information, contact:

Corporate Sales Department
PTR Prentice Hall
1 Lake Street
Upper Saddle River, NJ 07458

Phone: 800-382-3419, Fax: 201-236-7141
E-mail: dan_rush@prenhall.com

Printed in the United States of America
10 9 8 7 6 5 4 3 2 1

ISBN 0-13-331562-2

Prentice-Hall International (UK) Limited, London
Prentice-Hall of Australia Pty. Limited, Sydney
Prentice-Hall Canada Inc., Toronto
Prentice-Hall Hispanoamericana, S.A., Mexico
Prentice-Hall of India Private Limited, New Delhi
Prentice-Hall of Japan, Inc., Tokyo
Simon & Schuster Asia Pte. Ltd., Singapore
Editora Prentice-Hall do Brasil, Ltda., Rio de Janeiro

Table of Contents

Preface

The content of this book is derived from my several years of teaching Advanced UNIX Programming with C and C++ at two University of California Extensions (Berkeley and Santa Cruz). The objectives of the courses were to teach students advanced programming techniques using UNIX system calls and the ANSI C and C++ programming languages. Specifically, students who took the courses learned the following:

- Advanced ANSI C and C++ programming techniques, such as how to use function pointers and create functions that accept variable numbers of arguments
- The ANSI C library functions and C++ standard classes, and how to use them to reduce development time and to maximize portability of their applications
- Familiarity with the UNIX kernel structure and the system calls. These allow users to write sophisticated applications to manipulate system resources (e.g., files, processes, and system information), and to design new operating systems
- How to create network-based, multitasking, client/server applications which run on heterogenous UNIX platforms

The objective of this book is to convey to readers the techniques and concepts stated above. Furthermore, this book provides more detailed explanations and comprehensive examples on each topic than can be done in a course. Thus, readers can gain a better understanding of the subject matter and can learn at their own pace. This book also describes the latest advanced UNIX programming techniques on remote procedure calls and multithreaded programs. These techniques are important for the development of advanced distributed client/server applications in a symmetrical multiprocessing and network-based computing environment.

All the aforementioned information will be described in the C++ language. This is because in the last few years more and more advanced software developers are using C++ in applications development. This is due to the fact that the C++ language provides much stronger type-checking and includes object-oriented programming constructs than other procedural programming languages. These features are very useful in facilitating large-scale, complex UNIX system applications development and management.

This book covers the C++ programming language based on the draft version of the ANSI/ISO C++ standard [1, 2, 3]. Most of the latest C++ compilers provided by various computer vendors (e.g., Sun Microsystems Inc., Microsoft Corporation, Free Software Foundation, etc.) are compliant with this standard.

In addition to the C++ language, some significant C library functions, as defined by the ANSI C standard [4], are also described in this book. These functions are not covered by the C++ standard classes or by the UNIX application program interface. Thus, it is important that users be familiar with these to increase their knowledge base and choices of library functions.

The UNIX operating systems covered in this book include: UNIX System V.3, UNIX System V.4, BSD UNIX 4.3 and 4.4, Sun OS 4.1.3, and Solaris 2.4. The last two operating systems belong to SUN Microsystems, where Sun OS 4.1.3 is based on BSD 4.3 with UNIX System V.3 extensions, and Solaris 2.4 is based on the UNIX System V.4.

Although the primary focus of this book is on UNIX system programming, the IEEE (Institute of Electrical and Electronics Engineering) POSIX.1, POSIX.1b, and POSIX.1c standards are also covered in detail. This is to aid system programmers to develop applications that can be readily ported to different UNIX systems, as well as to POSIX-compliant systems (e.g., VMS and Windows-NT). This is important as most advanced commercial software products must run on heterogenous platforms by various computer vendors. Thus, the POSIX and ANSI standards can help users create highly platform-independent applications.

Target Audience

The book is targeted to benefit experienced software engineers and managers who are working on advanced system applications development in a UNIX environment. The products they develop may include advanced network-based client/server applications, distributed database systems, operating systems, compilers, or computer-aided design tools.

The readers should be familiar with the C++ language based on the AT&T version 3.0 (or the latest) and should have developed some C++ application programs on their own in the past. Moreover, the readers should be familiar with at least one version of UNIX system (e.g.,

UNIX System V). Specifically, the readers should know the UNIX file system architecture, user accounts assignment and management, file access control, and jobs control methods. Readers who need to brush up on UNIX system knowledge may consult any text book covering an introduction to the UNIX system.

Book Content

Although this book covers the ANSI C++ and C library functions and UNIX APIs extensively, the primary focus in describing these functions is to convey the following information to readers:

- Purposes of these functions
- Conformance of these functions to standard(s)
- How to use these functions
- Examples of their uses
- Where appropriate, how these functions are implemented in a UNIX system
- Any special considerations (e.g., conflict between the UNIX and POSIX standards) in using these functions

It is not the intention of the author to make this book a UNIX system programmer's reference manual. Thus, the function prototypes and header files required to use the ANSI library and UNIX API functions are described, but the detailed error codes that may be returned by these functions and the archive or shared libraries needed by users' programs will not be depicted. This type of information may be obtained via either the man pages of the functions or the programmer's reference manuals from the users' computer vendors.

The general organization of this book is:

- Chapter 1 describes the history of the C++ programming language and various UNIX systems. It also describes the ANSI/ISO C, ANSI/ISO C++, IEEE POSIX.1, POSIX.1b, and POSIX.1c standards
- Chapters 2 and 3 review the draft ANSI/ISO C++ programming language and object-oriented programming techniques. The C++ I/O stream classes, template functions, and exception handlings are also depicted in detail
- Chapter 4 describes the ANSI C library functions
- Chapter 5 gives an overview of the UNIX and POSIX APIs. Special header files and compile time options, as required by various standards, are depicted.
- Chapters 6 and 7 describe UNIX and POSIX.1 file APIs. These depict APIs that can be used to control various types of files in a system. They also describe file-locking techniques used to synchronize files in a multiprocessing environment

- Chapter 8 describes UNIX and POSIX.1 process creation and control methods. After reading this chapter, readers can write their own multiprocessing applications, such as a UNIX shell
- Chapter 9 describes UNIX and POSIX.1 signal handling methods
- Chapter 10 describes UNIX and POSIX.1b interprocess communication methods. These techniques are important in creating distributed client/server applications.
- Chapter 11 describes advanced network programming techniques using UNIX sockets and TLI
- Chapter 12 describes remote procedure call. This is important for development of network transport protocol-independent client/server application development on heterogenous UNIX platforms
- Chapter 13 describes multithreaded programming techniques. These techniques allow applications to make efficient use of multiprocessor resources available on any machines on which they run

Note that although this book is based on C++, the focus on this book is not object-oriented programming techniques. This is because some readers are expected to be new to UNIX system programming and/or C++ language, thus it may be difficult for these readers to learn both object-oriented and system programming techniques at the same time. However, this book includes many useful C++ classes for interprocess communication, sockets, TLI, remote procedure call, and multithreaded programming. These classes encapsulate the low-level programming interface to these advanced system functions, and can be easily extended and incorporated into user applications to reduce their development efforts, time, and costs.

Example Programs

Throughout the book extensive example programs are shown to illustrate uses of the C++ classes, library functions, and system APIs. All the examples have been compiled by a Sun Microsystems C++ (version 4.0) compiler and tested on a Sun SPARC-20 workstation running Solaris 2.4. These examples are also compiled and tested using the Free Software Foundation GNU g++ compiler (version 2.6.3) on a Sun SPARC-20 workstation. Since the GNU g++ compilers can be ported to various hardware platforms, the examples presented in this book should run on different platforms (e.g., Hewlett Packadd's HP-UX and International Business Machines's AIX) also.

Readers are encouraged to try out the example programs on their own systems to get more in-depth familiarity of this subject matter. Users may download an electronic copy of the example programs via anonymous ftp to *ftp.prenhall.com*. The directory that stores the example tar file is */pub/ptr/professional_computer_science.w-0.22/chan/unixsys*. There are README files in the tar file that describe the programs and their cross references to chapters in the book. Finally, readers are welcome to send Emails to the author at *twc@netcom.com*.

Acknowledgments

I would like to thank Peter Collinson, Jeff Gitlin, Chi Khuong, Frank Mitchell, and my wife Jessica Chan for their careful reviewing of the book manuscript. Much of their valuable input has been incorporated in the final version of this book. Furthermore, I would like to extend my appreciation to Greg Doench, Nick Radhuber, and Brat Bartow for their valuable assistance in helping me through the preparation and publication process of this book.

Finally, I am grateful to my former students at the University of California Santa Cruz Extension who took my Advanced UNIX System Calls course and gave me valuable feedback in the refinement of the course material, much of which is used throughout this book.

References

[1].   Margaret A. Ellis and Bjarne Stroustrup, *The Annotated C++ Reference Manual*, Addison-Wesley, 1990.

[2].   Andrew Koenig, *Working Paper for Draft Proposed International Standard for Information Systems -- Programming Language C++ (Committees: WG21/N0414, X3J16/94-0025)*, January 1994.

[3].   Bjarne Stroustrup, *Standardizing C++. The C++ Report. Vol. 1. No. 1*, 1989.

[4].   American National Standard Institute, *American National Standard for Information Systems - Programming Language C, X3.159 - 1989*, 1989.

UNIX and ANSI Standards

Since the invention of UNIX in the late 1960s, there has been a proliferation of different versions of UNIX on different computer systems. Recent UNIX systems have developed from AT&T System V and BSD 4.x UNIX. However, most computer vendors often add their own extensions to either the AT&T or BSD UNIX on their systems, thus creating the different versions of UNIX. In late 1980, AT&T and Sun Microsystems worked together to create the UNIX System V release 4, which is an attempt to set a UNIX system standard for the computer industry. This attempt was not totally successful, as only a few computer vendors today adopt the UNIX System V.4.

However, in the late 1980s, a few organizations proposed several standards for a UNIX-like operating system and the C language programming environment. These standards are based primarily on UNIX, and they do not impose dramatic changes in vendors' systems; thus, they are easily adopted by vendors. Furthermore, two of these standards, ANSI C and POSIX (which stands for Portable Operating System Interface), are defined by the American National Standard Institute (ANSI) and by the Institute of Electrical and Electronics Engineers (IEEE). They are very influential in setting standards in the industry; thus, most computer vendors today provide UNIX systems that conform to the ANSI C and POSIX.1 (a subset of the POSIX standards) standards.

Most of the standards define an operating system environment for C-based applications. Applications that adhere to the standards should be easily ported to other systems that conform to the same standards. This is especially important for advanced system programmers who make extensive use of system-level application program interface (API) functions (which include library functions and system calls). This is because not all UNIX systems provide a uniform set of system APIs. Furthermore, even some common APIs may be implemented differently on different UNIX systems (e.g., the *fcntl* API on UNIX System V can be used to lock and unlock files, something that the BSD UNIX version of *fcntl* API does not support). The ANSI C and POSIX standards require all conforming systems to provide a uniform set of standard libraries and system APIs, respectively; the standards also define the signatures (the data type, number of arguments, and return value) and behaviors of these functions on all systems. In this way, programs that use these functions can be ported to different systems that are compliant with the standards.

Most of the functions defined by the standards are a subset of those available on most UNIX systems. The ANSI C and POSIX committees did create a few new functions on their own, but the purpose of these functions is to supplement ambiguity or deficiency of some related constructs in existing UNIX and C. Thus, the standards are easily learned by experienced UNIX and C developers, and easily supported by computer vendors.

The objective of this book is to help familiarize users with advanced UNIX system programming techniques, including teaching users how to write portable and easily maintainable codes. This later objective can be achieved by making users familiar with the functions defined by the various standards and with those available from UNIX so that users can make an intelligent choice of which functions or APIs to use.

The rest of this chapter gives an overview of the ANSI C, draft ANSI/ISO C++, and the POSIX standards. The subsequent chapters describe the functions and APIs defined by these standards and others available from UNIX in more detail.

1.1   The ANSI C Standard

In 1989, the American National Standard Institute (ANSI) proposed C programming language standard X3.159-1989 to standardize the C programming language constructs and libraries. This standard is commonly known as the *ANSI C standard,* and it attempts to unify the implementation of the C language supported on all computer systems. Most computer vendors today still support the C language constructs and libraries as proposed by Brian Kernighan and Dennis Ritchie (commonly known as *K&R C*) as default, but users may install the ANSI C development package as an option (for an extra fee).

The major differences between ANSI C and K&R C are as follows:

- Function prototyping
- Support of the *const* and *volatile* data type qualifiers
- Support wide characters and internationalization
- Permit function pointers to be used without dereferencing

Although this book focuses on the C++ programming technique, readers still need to be familiar with the ANSI C standard because many standard C library functions are not covered by the C++ standard classes, thus almost all C++ programs call one or more standard C library functions (e.g., get time of day, or use the *strlen* function, etc.). Furthermore, for some readers who may be in the process of porting their C applications to C++, this section describes some similarities and differences between ANSI C and C++, so as to make it easy for those users to transit from ANSI C to C++.

ANSI C adopts C++ function prototype technique where function definition and declaration include function names, arguments' data types, and return value data types. Function prototypes enable ANSI C compilers to check for function calls in user programs that pass invalid numbers of arguments or incompatible argument data types. These fix a major weakness of the K&R C compilers: Invalid function calls in user programs often pass compilation but cause programs to crash when they are executed.

The following example declares a function *foo* and requires that *foo* take two arguments: the first argument *fmt* is of *char** data type, and the second argument is of *double* data type. The function *foo* returns an *unsigned long* value:

```
unsigned long foo ( char* fmt, double data )
{
        /* body of foo */
}
```

To create a declaration of the above function, a user simply takes the above function definition, strips off the body section, and replaces it with a semicolon character. Thus, the external declaration of the above function *foo* is:

```
unsigned long foo ( char* fmt, double data );
```

For functions that take a variable number of arguments, their definitions and declarations should have "..." specified as the last argument to each function:

```
int printf( const char* fmt, ...);
```

```
int printf( const char* fmt, ... )
{
        /* body of printf */
}
```

The *const* key word declares that some data cannot be changed. For example, the above function prototype declares a *fmt* argument that is of a *const char** data type, meaning that the

3

function *printf* cannot modify data in any character array that is passed as an actual argument value to *fmt*.

The *volatile* key word specifies that the values of some variables may change asynchronously, giving a hint to the compiler's optimization algorithm not to remove any "redundant" statements that involve "volatile" objects. For example, the following statements define an *io_Port* variable that contains an address of an I/O port of a system. The two statements that follow the definition are to wait for two bytes of data to arrive from the I/O port and retain only the second byte of data:

```
char get_io()
{
        volatile char* io_Port = 0x7777;
        char ch = *io_Port;                    /* read first byte of data */
        ch = *io_Port;                         /* read second byte of data */
}
```

In the above example, if the *io_Port* variable is not declared to be "volatile," when the program is compiled, the compiler may eliminate the second *ch = *io_Port* statement, as it is considered redundant with respect to the previous statement.

The *const* and *volatile* data type qualifiers are also supported in C++.

ANSI C supports internationalization by allowing C programs to use wide characters. Wide characters use more than one byte of storage per character. These are used in countries where the ASCII character set is not the standard. For example, the Korean character set requires two bytes per character. Furthermore, ANSI C also defines the *setlocale* function, which allows users to specify the format of date, monetary, and real number representations. For example, most countries display the date in <day>/<month>/<year> format, whereas the US displays the date in <month>/<day>/<year> format.

The function prototype of the *setlocale* function is:

```
#include <locale.h>

char setlocale ( int category, const char* locale );
```

The *setlocale* function prototype and possible values of the *category* argument are declared in the <locale.h> header. The *category* values specify what format class(es) is to be changed. Some possible values of the *category* argument are:

category value	Effect on standard C functions/macros
LC_CTYPE	Affects the behaviors of the <ctype.h> macros
LC_TIME	Affects the date and time format as returned by the *strftime, ascftime* functions, etc.
LC_NUMERIC	Affects the number representation formats via the *printf* and *scanf* functions
LC_MONETARY	Affects the monetary value format returned by the *localeconv* function
LC_ALL	Combines the effects of all the above

The *locale* argument value is a character string that defines which locale to use. Possible values may be C, POSIX, en_US, etc. The C, POSIX, en_US locales refer to the UNIX, POSIX, and US locales. By default, all processes on an ANSI C or POSIX compliant system execute the equivalent of the following call at their process start-up time:

```
setlocale( LC_ALL, "C" );
```

Thus, all processes start up have a known locale. If a *locale* value is NULL, the *setlocale* function returns the current *locale* value of a calling process. If a *locale* value is "" (a null string), the *setlocale* function looks for an environment variable LC_ALL, an environment variable with the same name as the *category* argument value, and, finally, the LANG environment variable - in that order - for the value of the *locale* argument.

The *setlocale* function is an ANSI C standard that is also adopted by POSIX.1.

ANSI C specifies that a function pointer may be used like a function name. No dereference is needed when calling a function whose address is contained in the pointer. For example, the following statements define a function pointer *funcptr,* which contains the address of the function *foo*:

```
extern void foo ( double xyz, const int* lptr );
void (*funcptr)(double, const int*) = foo;
```

The function *foo* may be invoked by either directly calling *foo* or via the *funcptr.* The following two statements are functionally equivalent:

```
foo (12.78, "Hello world");
funcptr (12.78, "Hello world");
```

The K&R C requires *funcptr* be dereferenced to call *foo*. Thus, an equivalent statement to the above, using K&R C syntax, is:

```
(*funcptr)(12.78, "Hello world");
```

Both the ANSI C and K&R C function pointer uses are supported in C++.

In addition to the above, ANSI C also defines a set of *cpp* (C preprocessor) symbols which may be used in user programs. These symbols are assigned actual values at compile time:

cpp symbol	Use
__STDC__	Feature test macro. Value is 1 if a compiler is ANSI C conforming, 0 otherwise
__LINE__	Evaluated to the physical line number of a source file for which this symbol is reference
__FILE__	Value is the file name of a module that contains this symbol
__DATE__	Value is the date that a module containing this symbol is compiled
__TIME__	Value is the time that a module containing this symbol is compiled

The following *test_ansi_c.c* program illustrates uses of these symbols:

```
#include <stdio.h>
int main()
{
#if __STDC__ == 0
        printf("cc is not ANSI C compliant\n");
#else
        printf(" %s compiled at %s:%s. This statement is at line %d\n",
                __FILE__, __DATE__, __TIME__, __LINE__);
#endif
        return 0;
}
```

Note that C++ supports the __LINE__, __FILE__, __DATE__, and __TIME__ symbols, but not __STDC__.

Finally, ANSI C defines a set of standard library functions and associated headers. These headers are the subset of the C libraries available on most systems that implement K&R C. The ANSI C standard libraries are described in Chapter 4.

1.2   The ANSI/ISO C++ Standard

In early 1980s, Bjarne Stroustrup at AT&T Bell Laboratories developed the C++ programming language. C++ was derived from C and incorporated object-oriented constructs, such as classes, derived classes, and virtual functions, from simula67 [1].The objective of developing C++ is "to make writing good programs earlier and more pleasant for individual programmer" [2]. The name C++ signifies the evolution of the language from C and was coined by Rick Mascitti in 1983.

Since its invention, C++ has gained wide acceptance by software professionals. In 1989, Bjarne Stroustrup published *The Annotated C++ Reference Manual* [3]. This manual became the base for the draft ANSI C++ standard, as developed by the X3J16 committee of ANSI. In early 1990s, the WG21 committee of the International Standard Organization (ISO) joined the ANSI X3J16 committee to develop a unify ANSI/ISO C++ standard. A draft version of such a ANSI/ISO standard was published in 1994 [4]. However, the ANSI/ISO standard is still in the development stage, and it should become an official standard in the near future.

Most latest commercial C++ compilers, which are based on the AT&T C++ language version 3.0 or later, are compliant with the draft ANSI/ISO standard. Specifically, these compilers should support C++ classes, derived classes, virtual functions, operator overloading. Furthermore, they should also support template classes, template functions, exception handling, and the iostream library classes.

This book will describe the C++ language features as defined by the draft ANSI/ISO C++ standard.

1.3   Differences Between ANSI C and C++

C++ requires that all functions must be declared or defined before they can be referenced. ANSI C uses the K&R C default function declaration for any functions that are referenced before their declaration and definition in a user program.

Another difference between ANSI C and C++ is given the following function declaration:

```
int foo ();
```

ANSI C treats the above function as an old C function declaration and interprets it as declared in the following manner:

```
int foo (...);
```

which means *foo* may be called with any number of actual arguments. However, for C++, the same declaration is treated as the following declaration:

```
int foo ( void );
```

which means *foo* may not accept any argument when it is called.

Finally, C++ encrypts external function names for type-safe linkage. This ensures that an external function which is incorrectly declared and referenced in a module will cause the link editor (*/bin/ld*) to report an undefined function name. ANSI C does not employ the type-safe linkage technique and, thus, does not catch these types of user errors.

There are many other differences between ANSI C and C++, but the above items are the more common ones run into by users (For a detailed documentation of the ANSI C standard, please see [5]).

The next section describes the POSIX standards, which are more elaborate and comprehensive than are the ANSI C standard for UNIX system developers.

1.4   The POSIX Standards

Because many versions of UNIX exist today and each of them provides its own set of application programming interface (API) functions, it is difficult for system developers to create applications that can be easily ported to different versions of UNIX. To overcome this problem, the IEEE society formed a special task force called POSIX in the 1980s to create a set of standards for operating system interfacing. Several subgroups of the POSIX such as POSIX.1, POSIX.1b and POSIX.1c are concerned with the development of a set of standards for system developers.

Specifically, the POSIX.1 committee proposes a standard for a base operating system application programming interface; this standard specifies APIs for the manipulation of files and processes. It is formally known as the IEEE standard 1003.1-1990 [6], and it was also adopted by the ISO as the international standard ISO/IEC 9945:1:1990. The POSIX.1b committee proposes a set of standard APIs for a real-time operating system interface; these include interprocess communication. This standard is formally known as the IEEE standard

1003.4-1993 [7]. Lastly, the POSIX.1c standard [8] specifies multithreaded programming interface. This is the newest POSIX standard and its details are described in the last chapter of this book.

Although much of the work of the POSIX committees is based on UNIX, the standards they proposed are for a generic operating system that is not necessarily a UNIX system. For example, VMS from the Digital Equipment Corporation, OS/2 from International Business Machines, and Windows-NT from the Microsoft Corporation are POSIX-compliant, yet they are not UNIX systems. Most current UNIX systems, like UNIX System V release 4, BSD UNIX 4.4, and computer vendor-specific operating systems (e.g., Sun Microsystem's Solaris 2.x, Hewlett Packard's HP-UX 9.05 and 10.x, and IBM's AIX 4.1.x, etc.) are all POSIX.1-compliant but they still maintain their system-specific APIs.

This book will discuss the POSIX.1, POSIX.1b and POSIX.1c APIs, and also UNIX system-specific APIs. Furthermore, in the rest of the book, unless stated otherwise, when the word *POSIX* is mentioned alone, it refers to both the POSIX.1 and POSIX.1b standards.

To ensure a user program conforms to the POSIX.1 standard, the user should either define the manifested constant _POSIX_SOURCE at the beginning of each source module of the program (before the inclusion of any headers) as:

```
#define _POSIX_SOURCE
```

or specify the -D_POSIX_SOURCE option to a C++ compiler (CC) in a compilation:

```
%    CC -D_POSIX_SOURCE *.C
```

This manifested constant is used by *cpp* to filter out all non-POSIX.1 and non-ANSI C standard codes (e.g., functions, data types, and manifested constants) from headers used by the user program. Thus, a user program that is compiled and run successfully with this switch defined is POSIX.1-conforming.

POSIX.1b defines a different manifested constant to check conformance of user programs to that standard. The new macro is _POSIX_C_SOURCE, and its value is a time-stamp indicating the POSIX version to which a user program conforms. The possible values of the _POSIX_C_SOURCE macro are:

_POSIX_C_SOURCE value	Meaning
198808L	First version of POSIX.1 compliance
199009L	Second version of POSIX.1 compliance
199309L	POSIX.1 and POSIX.1b compliance

Each _POSIX_C_SOURCE value consists of the year and month that a POSIX standard was approved by IEEE as a standard. The *L* suffix in a value indicates that the value's data type is a long integer.

The _POSIX_C_SOURCE may be used in place of the _POSIX_SOURCE. However, some systems that support POSIX.1 only may not accept the _POSIX_C_SOURCE definition. Thus, readers should browse the *unistd.h* header file on their systems and see which constants, or both, are used in the file.

There is also a _POSIX_VERSION constant that may be defined in the <unistd.h> header. This constant contains the POSIX version to which the system conforms. The following sample program checks and displays the _POSIX_VERSION constant of the system on which it is run:

```
/* show_posix_ver.C */
#define _POSIX_SOURCE
#define _POSIX_C_SOURCE        199309L
#include <iostream.h>
#include <unistd.h>
int main()
{
#ifdef _POSIX_VERSION
    cout << "System conforms to POSIX: "
            << _POSIX_VERSION << endl;
#else
    cout << "_POSIX_VERSION is undefined\n";
#endif
    return 0;
}
```

In general, a user program that must be strictly POSIX.1- and POSIX.1b-compliant may be written as follows:

```
#define _POSIX_SOURCE
#define _POSIX_C_SOURCE   199309L
#include <unistd.h>
/* include other headers here */
int main()
{
    ...
}
```

1.4.1   The POSIX Environment

Although POSIX was developed based on UNIX, a POSIX-compliant system is not necessarily a UNIX system. A few UNIX conventions have different meanings, according to the POSIX standards. Specifically, most standard C and C++ header files are stored under the */usr/include* directory in any UNIX system, and each of them is referenced by the:

        #include <header_file_name>

This method of referencing header files is adopted in POSIX. However, for each name specified in a *#included* statement, there need not be a physical file of that name existing on a POSIX-conforming system. In fact the data that should be contained in that named object may be builtin to a compiler, or stored by some other means on a given system. Thus, in a POSIX environment, included files are called simply *headers* instead of *header files*. This "headers" naming convention will be used in the rest of the book. Furthermore, in a POSIX-compliant system, the */usr/include* directory does not have to exist. If users are working on a non-UNIX but POSIX-compliant system, please consult the C or C++ programmer's manual to determine the standard location, if any, of the headers on the system.

Another difference between POSIX and UNIX is the concept of *superuser*. In UNIX, a superuser has privilege to access all system resources and functions. The superuser user ID is always zero. However, the POSIX standards do not mandate that all POSIX-conforming systems support the concept of a superuser, nor does the user ID of zero require any special privileges. Furthermore, although some POSIX.1 and POSIX.1b APIs require the functions to be executed in "special privilege," it is up to an individual conforming system to define how a "special privilege" is to be assigned to a process.

1.4.2   The POSIX Feature Test Macros

Some UNIX features are optional to be implemented on a POSIX-conforming system. Thus, POSIX.1 defines a set of feature test macros, which, if defined on a system, means that the system has implemented the corresponding features.

These feature test macros, if defined, can be found in the <unistd.h> header. Their names and uses are:

Feature test macro	Effects if defined on a system
_POSIX_JOB_CONTROL	The system supports the BSD-style job control
_POSIX_SAVED_IDS	Each process running on the system keeps the saved set-UID and set-GID, so that it can change its effective user ID and group ID to those values via the *seteuid* and *setegid* APIs, respectively

11

Feature test macro	Effects if defined on a system
_POSIX_CHOWN_RESTRICTED	If the defined value is -1, users may change ownership of files owned by them. Otherwise, only users with special privilege may change ownership of any files on a system. If this constant is undefined in <unistd.h> header, users must use the *pathconf* or *fpathconf* function (described in the next section) to check the permission for changing ownership on a per-file basis
_POSIX_NO_TRUNC	If the defined value is -1, any long path name passed to an API is silently truncated to NAME_MAX bytes; otherwise, an error is generated. If this constant is undefined in the <unistd.h> header, users must use the *pathconf* or *fpathconf* function to check the path name truncation option on a per-directory basis
_POSIX_VDISABLE	If the defined value is -1, there is no disabling character for special characters for all terminal device files; otherwise, the value is the disabling character value. If this constant is undefined in the <unistd.h> header, users must use the *pathconf* or *fpathconf* function to check the disabling character option on a per-terminal device file basis

The following sample program prints the POSIX-defined configuration options supported on any given system:

```
/* show_test_macros.C */
#define _POSIX_SOURCE
#define _POSIX_C_SOURCE     199309L
#include <iostream.h>
#include <unistd.h>
int main()
{
#ifdef _POSIX_JOB_CONTROL
      cout << "System supports job control\n";
#else
      cout << "System does not support job control\n";
#endif
```

```
#ifdef _POSIX_SAVED_IDS
    cout << "System supports saved set-UID and saved set-GID\n";
#else
    cout << "System does not support saved set-UID and "
        << " saved set-GID\n";
#endif

#ifdef _POSIX_CHOWN_RESTRICTED
    cout << "chown_restricted option is: " <<
            _POSIX_CHOWN_RESTRICTED << endl;
#else
    cout << "System does not support chown_restricted option\n";
#endif

#ifdef _POSIX_NO_TRUNC
    cout << "Pathname trunc option is: " <<  _POSIX_NO_TRUNC
        << endl;
#else
    cout << "System does not support system-wide pathname"
        << " trunc option\n";
#endif

#ifdef _POSIX_VDISABLE
    cout << "Disable char. for terminal files is: "
        << _POSIX_VDISABLE << endl;
#else
    cout << "System does not support _POSIX_VDISABLE\n";
#endif
    return 0;
}
```

1.4.3   Limits Checking at Compile Time and at Run Time

POSIX.1 and POSIX.1b define a set of system configuration limits in the form of manifested constants in the <limits.h> header. Many of these limits are derived from the UNIX systems and they have the same manifested constant names as their UNIX counterparts, plus the _POSIX_ prefix. For example, UNIX systems define the constant CHILD_MAX, which specifies the maximum number of child processes a process may create at any one time. The corresponding POSIX.1 constant is _POSIX_CHILD_MAX. The reason for defining these constants is that although most UNIX systems define a similar set of constants, their values vary substantially from one UNIX system to another. The POSIX-defined constants specify the minimum values for these constants for all POSIX-conforming systems; thus, it facilitates application programmers to develop programs that use these system configuration limits.

The following is a list of POSIX.1-defined constants in the <limits.h> header:

Compile time limit	Min. value	Meaning
_POSIX_CHILD_MAX	6	Maximum number of child processes that may be created at any one time by a process
_POSIX_OPEN_MAX	16	Maximum number of files that may be opened simultaneously by a process
_POSIX_STREAM_MAX	8	Maximum number of I/O streams that may be opened simultaneously by a process
_POSIX_ARG_MAX	4096	Maximum size, in bytes, of arguments that may be passed to an *exec* function call
_POSIX_NGROUP_MAX	0	Maximum number of supplemental groups to which a process may belong
_POSIX_PATH_MAX	255	Maximum number of characters allowed in a path name
_POSIX_NAME_MAX	14	Maximum number of characters allowed in a file name
_POSIX_LINK_MAX	8	Maximum number of links a file may have
_POSIX_PIPE_BUF	512	Maximum size of a block of data that may be atomically read from or written to a pipe file
_POSIX_MAX_INPUT	255	Maximum capacity, in bytes, of a terminal's input queue
_POSIX_MAX_CANON	255	Maximum size, in bytes, of a terminal's canonical input queue
_POSIX_SSIZE_MAX	32767	Maximum value that can be stored in a *ssize_t*-typed object
_POSIX_TZNAME_MAX	3	Maximum number of characters in a time zone name

The following is a list of POSIX.1b-defined constants:

Compile time limit	Min. value	Meaning
_POSIX_AIO_MAX	1	Number of simultaneous asynchronous I/O
_POSIX_AIO_LISTIO_MAX	2	Maximum number of operations in one listio
_POSIX_TIMER_MAX	32	Maximum number of timers that can be used simultaneously by a process
_POSIX_DELAYTIMER_MAX	32	Maximum number of overruns allowed per timer
_POSIX_MQ_OPEN_MAX	2	Maximum number of message queues that may be accessed simultaneously per process
_POSIX_MQ_PRIO_MAX	2	Maximum number of message priorities that can be assigned to messages
_POSIX_RTSIG_MAX	8	Maximum number of real-time signals
_POSIX_SIGQUEUE_MAX	32	Maximum number of real time signals that a process may queue at any one time
_POSIX_SEM_NSEMS_MAX	256	Maximum number of semaphores that may be used simultaneously per process
_POSIX_SEM_VALUE_MAX	32767	Maximum value that may be assigned to a semaphore

Note that the POSIX-defined constants specify only the minimum values for some system configuration limits. A POSIX-conforming system may be configured with higher values for these limits. Furthermore, not all these constants must be specified in the <limits.h> header, as some of these limits may be indeterminate or may vary for individual files.

To find out the actual implemented configuration limits system-wide or on individual objects, one can use the *sysconf, pathconf*, and *fpathconf* functions to query these limits' values at run time. These functions are defined by POSIX.1; the *sysconf* is used to query general system-wide configuration limits that are implemented on a given system; *pathconf* and *fpathconf* are used to query file-related configuration limits. The two functions do the same thing; the only difference is that *pathconf* takes a file's path name as argument, whereas *fpathconf* takes a file descriptor as argument. The prototypes of these functions are:

```
#include <unistd.h>

long sysconf ( const int limit_name );
long pathconf ( const char* pathname, int flimit_name );
long fpathconf ( const int fdesc, int flimit_name );
```

The *limit_name* argument value is a manifested constant as defined in the <unistd.h> header. The possible values and the corresponding data returned by the *sysconf* function are:

Limit value	*sysconf* return data
_SC_ARG_MAX	Maximum size, in bytes, of argument values that may be passed to an *exec* API call
_SC_CHILD_MAX	Maximum number of child processes that may be owned by a process simultaneously
_SC_OPEN_MAX	Maximum number of opened files per process
_SC_NGROUPS_MAX	Maximum number of supplemental groups per process
_SC_CLK_TCK	The number of clock ticks per second.
_SC_JOB_CONTROL	The _POSIX_JOB_CONTROL value
_SC_SAVED_IDS	The _POSIX_SAVED_IDS value
_SC_VERSION	The _POSIX_VERSION value
_SC_TIMERS	The _POSIX_TIMERS value
_SC_DELAYTIMER_MAX	Maximum number of overruns allowed per timer
_SC_RTSIG_MAX	Maximum number of real time signals
_SC_MQ_OPEN_MAX	Maximum number of message queues per process
_SC_MQ_PRIO_MAX	Maximum priority value assignable to a message
_SC_SEM_MSEMS_MAX	Maximum number of semaphores per process
_SC_SEM_VALUE_MAX	Maximum value assignable to a semaphore
_SC_SIGQUEUE_MAX	Maximum number of real time signals that a process may queue at any one time
_SC_AIO_LISTIO_MAX	Maximum number of operations in one listio
_SC_AIO_MAX	Number of simultaneous asynchronous I/O

As can be seen in the above, all constants used as a *sysconf* argument value have the _SC_ prefix. Similarly, the *flimit_name* argument value is a manifested constant defined in the <unistd.h> header. These constants all have the _PC_ prefix. The following lists some of these constants and their corresponding return values from either *pathconf* or *fpathconf* for a named file object:

Limit value	*pathconf* return data
_PC_CHOWN_RESTRICTED	The _POSIX_CHOWN_RESTRICTED value
_PC_NO_TRUNC	Return the _POSIX_NO_TRUNC value
_PC_VDISABLE	Return the _POSIX_VDISABLE value
_PC_PATH_MAX	Maximum length, in bytes, of a path name
_PC_LINK_MAX	Maximum number of links a file may have
_PC_NAME_MAX	Maximum length, in bytes, of a file name
_PC_PIPE_BUF	Maximum size of a block of data that may be auto-

	matically read from or written to a pipe file
_PC_MAX_CANON	Maximum size, in bytes, of a terminal's canonical input queue
_PC_MAX_INPUT	Maximum capacity, in bytes, of a terminal's input queue

These variables parallel their corresponding variables as defined on most UNIX systems (the UNIX variable names are the same as those of POSIX, but without the _POSIX_ prefix). These variables may be used at compile time, such as the following:

```
char pathname [ _POSIX_PATH_MAX + 1];
for (int i=0; i < _POSIX_OPEN_MAX; i++)
    close (i);                              // close all file descriptors
```

The following *test_config.C* program illustrates the use of *sysconf, pathconf,* and *fpathconf:*

```
#define _POSIX_SOURCE
#define _POSIX_C_SOURCE 199309L
#include <stdio.h>
#include <iostream.h>
#include <unistd.h>
int main()
{
    int res;
    if ((res=sysconf(_SC_OPEN_MAX))==-1)
        perror("sysconf");
    else cout << "OPEN_MAX: " << res << endl;

    if ((res=pathconf("/",_PC_PATH_MAX))==-1)
        perror("pathconf");
    else cout << "Max path name: " << (res+1) << endl;

    if ((res=fpathconf(0,_PC_CHOWN_RESTRICTED))==-1)
        perror("fpathconf");
    else
        cout << "chown_restricted for stdin: " << res << endl;
    return 0;
}
```

1.5   The POSIX.1 FIPS Standard

FIPS stands for Federal Information Processing Standard. The POSIX.1 FIPS standard was developed by the National Institute of Standards and Technology (NIST, formerly, the National Bureau of Standards), a department within the US Department of Commerce. The latest version of this standard, FIPS 151-1, is based on the POSIX.1-1988 standard. The POSIX.1 FIPS standard is a guideline for federal agencies acquiring computer systems. Specifically, the FIPS standard is a restriction of the POSIX.1-1988 standard, and it requires the following features to be implemented in all FIPS-conforming systems:

- Job control; the _POSIX_JOB_CONTROL symbol must be defined
- Saved set-UID and saved set-GID; the _POSIX_SAVED_IDS symbol must be defined
- Long path name is not supported; the _POSIX_NO_TRUNC should be defined - its value is not -1
- The _POSIX_CHOWN_RESTRICTED must be defined - its value is not -1. This means only an authorized user may change ownership of files, system-wide
- The _POSIX_VDISABLE symbol must be defined - its value is not equal to -1
- The NGROUP_MAX symbol's value must be at least 8
- The read and write API should return the number of bytes that have been transferred after the APIs have been interrupted by signals
- The group ID of a newly created file must inherit the group ID of its containing directory

The FIPS standard is a more restrictive version of the POSIX.1 standard. Thus, a FIPS 151-1 conforming system is also POSIX.1-1988 conforming, but not vice versa. The FIPS standard is outdated with respect to the latest version of the POSIX.1, and it is used primarily by US federal agencies. This book will, therefore, focus more on the POSIX.1 standard than on FIPS.

1.6   The X/Open Standards

The X/Open organization was formed by a group of European companies to propose a common operating system interface for their computer systems. The organization published the *X/Open Portability Guide,* issue 3 (XPG3) in 1989, and issue 4 (XPG4) in 1994. The portability guides specify a set of common facilities and C application program interface functions to be provided on all UNIX-based "open systems." The XPG3 [9] and XPG4 [10] are based on ANSI-C, POSIX.1, and POSIX.2 standards, with additional constructs invented by the X/Open organization.

In addition to the above, in 1993 a group of computer vendors (e.g., Hewlett-Packard, International Business Machines, Novell, Open Software Foundation, and Sun Microsystems, Inc.) initiated a project called *Common Open Software Environment* (COSE). The goal of the project was to define a single UNIX programming interface specification that would be supported by all the vendors. This specification is known as *Spec 1170* and has been incorporated into XPG4 as part of the X/Open Common Application Environment (CAE) specifications.

The X/Open CAE specifications have a much broader scope than do the POSIX and ANSI-C standards. This means applications that conform to ANSI-C and POSIX also conform to the X/Open standards, but not necessarily vice versa. Furthermore, though most computer vendors and independent software vendors (ISVs) adopted POSIX and ANSI-C, some of them have yet to conform to the X/Open standards. Thus, this book will focus primarily on the common UNIX system programming interface and the ANSI-C and POSIX standards. Readers may consult more detailed publications [4,5] for further information on the X/Open CAE specifications.

1.7   Summary

This chapter gave an overview of the various standards that are applicable to UNIX system programmers. The objective is to familiarize readers with these standards and to help readers understand the benefits they provide. The details of these standards and their corresponding functions and APIs, as provided on most UNIX systems, are described in the rest of the book.

1.8   References

[1].   O-J. Dahl, B. Myrhaug, and K. Nygaard, *SIMULA Common Base Language,* 1970.

[2].   Bjarne Stroustrup, *The C++ Programming Language,* Second Edition, 1991.

[3].   Margaret A. Ellis and Bjarne Stroustrup, *The Annotated C++ Reference Manual,* Addison-Wesley, 1990.

[4].   Andrew Koenig, *Working Paper for Draft Proposed International Standard for Information Systems -- Programming Language C++ (Committees: WG21/N0414, X3J16/94-0025),* 1994.

[5].   American National Standard Institute, *American National Standard for Information Systems - Programming Language C, X3.159 - 1989*, 1989.

[6].   Institute of Electrical and Electronics Engineers, *Information Technology - Portable Operating System Interface (POSIX) Part 1: System Application Program Interface (API) [C language], IEEE 1003.1.* 1990.

[7].   Institute of Electrical and Electronics Engineers, *Information Technology - Portable Operating System Interface (POSIX) Part 1: System Application Program Interface (API) [C language] - Amendment: Real-Time Extension, IEEE 1003.1b.* 1993.

[8].   Institute of Electrical and Electronics Engineers, *Information Technology - Portable Operating System Interface (POSIX) Part 1: System Application Program Interface (API) [C language] - Amendment: Thread Extension, IEEE 1003.1c.* 1995.

[9].   X/Open, *X/Open Portability Guide,* Prentice Hall, 1989.

[10].   X/Open, *X/Open CAE Specification, Issue 4*, Prentice Hall, 1994.

C++ Language Review

This chapter reviews the essential constructs of the C++ language, which is based on the draft ANSI/ISO C++ standard [1]. The readers are assumed to be familiar with the C++ language, at least at the beginner's level. This chapter gives a quick review of the C++ programming techniques, so as to refresh the reader's memory. It also describes the template classes and exception handling. These latter subjects are new features to the C++ language and defined by the ANSI/ISO C++ standard. Readers who need a more detailed reference on the C++ language programming may consult [2,3].

Besides describing the C++ language constructs, this chapter also covers the C++ standard I/O classes and object-oriented design techniques. The standard I/O classes are powerful and rich in functionality. They essentially replace the C stream I/O functions and the strings function. It is important for readers to know these I/O classes to maximize code reuse and to reduce their application development time and costs.

Object-oriented programming techniques enable users to move from algorithmic program designs to object-based program designs. When doing object-oriented programming, users are more concerned with the types of objects that their programs have to deal with, the properties of these objects, and how they interact with each other and with users. Object-oriented programming techniques are valuable for database and GUI applications and are also useful in encapsulating low-level network communication protocol to provide a higher level interface for network-based application developers. The latter chapters in this book will show how this is done.

2.1   C++ Features for Object-Oriented Programming

C++ supports class declarations. Classes are used to construct user-defined data types. Each class encapsulates the data storage and legal operations of any object of that data type. Thus, C++ programs spend less time in the traditional algorithmic design for their applications but put more effort in designing classes and management of class objects and their interactions.

A class provides data hiding such that the internal data can be classified as "public," "private," and "protected." Class "public" data are accessible by any user functions which are not defined inside the class. Class "private" data cannot be accessed by anyone except member functions defined in the same class. Finally, class "protected" data are "private" to all user functions, but "public" to all its own and subclasses' member functions. The elaborate scheme of classifying class data is to allow developers to control the access and manipulation of class objects' data. This prevents class objects' data being changed anywhere in user programs. Furthermore, any changes to a class private and protected data will have minimum impact on user functions, provided the member functions used to access those data remain the same.

Furthermore, a class imposes a well-defined interface for objects of that type to interact with the rest of the world. This allows users to change the internal implementation of any class while maintaining the working order of the rest of the program (as long as the interface of the class remains unchanged). This renders well-designed C++ programs that are easy to maintain or change.

Another advantage of classes is that they promote code sharing. Specifically, a new class may be "derived" from one or more existing classes, and the new class contains all the data storage and functions of its derived class(es). Furthermore, the new class may define additional data and functions that are unique to objects of that new type, and it may even redefine the functions it inherits from its base class(es). Thus, class inheritance provides maximum flexibility in generating new classes that are similar, but not identical, to existing classes.

Like other object-oriented languages, C++ supports *constructor* and *destructor* functions for classes. These ensure that objects are properly initialized when created and that data is cleaned up when being discarded. Moreover, C++ defines the *new* and *delete* operators for objects to allocate and deallocate dynamic memory. However, unlike other object-oriented languages, there is no built-in garbage collection to manage dynamic memory used by objects, and *constructor* and *destructor* functions are not mandated for all defined classes. These relaxations are done to reduce the overhead of C++ programs' run-time performance but require developers to be disciplined in crafting their programs.

ANSI/ISO C++ supports template classes and functions. These allow users to create and debug some generic classes and functions. Once these are done, they may safely derive real classes and functions that work with different data types. This saves substantial program development and debug time. In addition to this, C++ defines a formal method of exception handling. This maintains consistent methods for all C++ applications to handle exceptions that may occur in their programs.

All in all, object-oriented programming strives to achieve the following goals:

- Data abstraction to ensure a well-defined interface for all objects
- Class inheritance to promote code reuse
- Polymorphism such that classes derived from other classes may have different data and functions
- Modeling of objects and their interactions after real-life situations

All the above objectives are supported by C++, and it is also backward-compatible with C. Thus it allows C programmers to start using C++ with their C programs, then migrate toward using C++ and object-oriented constructs in their programs at a pace at which they are comfortable.

2.2   C++ Class Declaration

A C++ class represents an abstract data type. It consists of data members and functions. These, in turn, may be classified as private, public, and protected. Private data members and functions are accessible via the same class member functions only, whereas public data members and functions are accessible by any other objects. These public data members and functions form the external interface to the world for objects of the class. Protected data members and functions are like their private counterparts but are also accessible to subclasses' member functions.

When a class data member or function is referenced anywhere outside the class declaration, the "::" scope resolution operator should be used to qualified their names. Specifically, the name appearing on the left of the "::" operator is a class name, and the name appearing on the right is a variable or function defined in the class. For example, *menu::num_fields* refers to the *num_fields* data member of the class *menu*. In addition to this, if no name appears on the left of a "::", it means that the name specified on the right is a global variable or function. For example, if there is a global variable called *x*, and in a class declaration there is also a data member called *x*, the member functions of that class may reference the global variable *x* by *::x*, and the data member *x* by either *x* or *<class_name>::x*.

The following *menu.h* header declares a class called *menu*:

```
#ifndef MENU_H
#define MENU_H
```

```
class menu
{
    private::
        char* title;
    protected:
        static int num_fields;
    public:
        // constructor function
        menu( const char* str )
        {
            title = new char[strlen(str)+1];
            strcpy (title, str );
            num_fields = 0;
        };
        // constructor function
        menu()
        {
            title = 0;
            num_fields = 0;
        };
        // destructor function
        ~menu()
        {
            delete title;
        };
        void incr_field( int size=1 )
        {
            num_fields+= size
        };
        static int fields()
        {
            return num_fields;
        };
        char* name()
        {
            return title;
        };
};
#endif           /* menu.h */
```

In the above, *menu::num_fields* and *menu::fields()* are declared as static. Unlike non-static data members where each object of a class has its own private copy of those members, there is only one instance of each static data member for all objects. Static data members are used like global variables by all objects of the same type. The accessibility of static data members by objects of other classes is determined by whether the data members are declared as private, protected, or public.

Static data members must be defined in a source module if they are being used in a program. For example, the following module defines the *menu::num_fields* data member with an initial value of zero:

```
// module name: a.C
#include <string.h>
#include "menu.h"
int menu::num_fields = 0;
int main() {                    {... }
```

Note that in the above example, although *menu::num_fields* is a protected data member, it is legal to define and initialize it in a program scope. However, further modification of that variable in user programs must be done only via the *menu* class member functions, subclass functions, or friend functions. The same also applies for private static data members.

Static member functions can access only static data members in a class. Thus in the *menu* class, the *menu::fields()* cannot access the *menu::title* data member. Whereas nonstatic member functions must be called via objects of a class, static functions have no such restriction:

```
menu abc ("Example");
abc.incr_field( 5 );
cout << "static func. called independent of objects: "
        << menu::fields() << endl;
cout << "Static func. can also be called via object: "
        << abc.fields() << endl;
```

Static data members and functions are commonly used to track how many objects of a class have been created as well as other general statistics, They can also be used to manage dynamic memory created by all objects of a class and to do garbage collection.

The *menu::menu* functions are constructors. A constructor function is called when an object of a class is created, and it initializes the data members of a newly created object. A constructor function may be overloaded, which means multiple constructor functions with

different signatures may be defined in a same class. For example, the following object definitions use different constructor functions:

```
menu abc;                    // use menu::menu()
menu xyz ("Example");        // use menu::menu( const char* str )
```

The *menu()::~menu()* is a destructor function. It is called when an object of a class is
going out of scope to ensure proper cleanup of the object's data (e.g., deallocate dynamic
memory used by the object). A destructor function cannot be overloaded, and it accepts no
argument.

In the menu class example, all member function definitions are placed in the class declaration. This means these member functions are to be used as inline functions, or like macros, in C terminology. The advantage of using inline functions is to improve program
performance by eliminating the overhead of function calls. The disadvantage of inline functions is that any changes made in an inline function require source modules that reference the
function to be recompiled.

A user may declare class member functions as non-inline by placing their definitions in
a separate source module. For example, *menu.h* may be changed to the following:

```
#ifndef MENU_H
#define MENU_H
class menu
{
    private:
        char* title;
    protected:
        static int num_fields;
    public:
        // constructor function
        menu( const char* str );
        menu();
        // destructor function
        ~menu();
        void incr_field( int size=1 );
        static int fields();
        char* name() ;
};
#endif
```

Then a separate C++ module, for example, *menu.C,* must be created to define the actual member functions:

```cpp
// source file name: menu.C
#include <string.h>
#include "menu.h"
// a constructor with an argument
menu::menu ( const char* str )
{
      title = new char[strlen(str)+1];
      strcpy (title, str );
      num_fields = 0;
}
// a constructor with no argument
menu::menu()
{
      title = 0;
      num_fields = 0;
}
// a destructor
menu::~menu()
{
      delete title;
}
// Note:the siz argument cannot have default value here
void menu::incr_field ( int size )
{
      num_fields += size;
}
// a static member function
int menu::fields()
{
      return num_fields;
}
// another non-static member function.
char*menu:: name()
{
      return title;
}
```

Any program that uses the menu class must be compiled with *menu.C* to create an executable object. For example, given the following *test_menu.C* file:

```
// source test_menu.C
#include <iostream.h>
#include "menu.h"
int menu::num_fields = 0;
int main()
{
        menu abc ("Test");
        cout << abc.name() << endl;
        return menu::fields();
}
```

the *test_menu.C* is compiled as shown below to create an executable program *a.out*:

```
%    CC test_menu.C menu.C
%    a.out
Test
```

Finally, notice that the *menu::incr_field* function declaration in the *menu.h* has a default value for the *size* argument, but in the *menu.C* file the *menu::incr_field* function definition is not allowed to specify a default value for the *size* argument. In C++ 1.0, this was allowed, but it may lead to inconsistency in assigning default values to function arguments. Thus, this practice is no longer allowed.

2.3   Friend Functions and Classes

The friend construct in C++ allows designated functions and member functions of other classes to directly access private and protected data members of a class. This is for special occasions where it is more efficient for a function to directly access an object's private data than to go through its class member function. For example, the << operator function is commonly declared as a friend function to classes so that one can print objects of these classes as if they were of the basic data types (e.g., *int, double*).

Since friend functions can directly access and change private data of objects of a class, the compiler must be told that these are special, authorized functions. Thus, their names must be listed as *friend* in the class declaration. Furthermore, it serves as a reminder to users that whenever the class declaration is changed, all of its friend functions may require modification accordingly.

The following example illustrates the use of a friend function and a friend class:

```
// source module: friend.C
#include <iostream.h>
int year;
class foo;
class dates
{
        friend ostream& operator<<(ostream&,dates&);
        int year, month, day;
    public:
        friend class foo;
        dates() { year=month=day = 0; };
        ~dates() {};
        int sameDay(int d) const { return d==day; };
        void set(int y) const { ::year = y; };
        void set(int y) { year = y; };
};

class foo
{
    public:
        void set(dates& D, int  year) {D.year = year; };
};

ostream& operator<<(ostream& os, dates& D)
{
    os << D.year << " ," << D.month << " ," << D.day;
    return os;
}

int main()
{
        dates Dobj;
        foo Fobj;
        Fobj.set(Dobj, 1998);
        clog << "Dobj: " << Dobj << '\n';
}
```

In the above example, the $<<$ operator and class *foo* are declared as friends of the class *dates*. This means that the $<<$ function and class *foo*'s member functions can access the private data members of any objects of class *dates*. The compilation and sample output of the program is:

```
%    CC friend.C
%    a.out
Dobj: 1998, 0, 0
```

2.4   Const Member Functions

Const member functions are special member functions that cannot modify any data members in their class. They are designed to accommodate class objects that are defined as *const*. Specifically, a const object can invoke only its class's const member functions. This guarantees that the object's data is not being modified.

The C++ compiler flags an error when a const object invokes a nonconst member function. The only exception to this is that nonconst constructors and destructors may be applied to const objects. Finally, const and nonconst member functions with the same signatures may be overloaded.

The following example illustrates the definition of const member functions and their usage:

```
// source module: const.C
static int year = 0;
class dates
{
        int year, month, day;
    public:
        dates() { year=month=day = 0; };
        ~dates() {};
        void set(int y) { year = y; };
        // const member functions
        void print( ostream& = cerr ) const;
        int sameDay(int d) const { return d==day; };
        // note: this function is overloaded
        void set(int y) const { ::year = y; };
};
```

```
void dates::print( ostream& os ) const
{
        os << year << "," << month << "," << day << '\n';
}

int main()
{
        const dates foo;              // const object
        dates foo1;                   // non-const object
        foo.set(1915);                // ::year = 1915
        foo.print();                  // year=0, month=0, day=0
        foo1.set(25);                 // foo1.year=25
        foo1.print();                 // year=25,month=0,day=0

}
```

In the above example, *foo* is a const object and *foo1* is a nonconst object. Both objects are initialized via the *dates::dates* constructor. The *foo.set(1915)* statement invokes the const member function *dates::set*, whereas the *foo1.set(25)* statement invokes the nonconst member function *dates::set*. The *foo.print()* and *foo1.print()* statements both invoke the const member function *dates::print*. This is fine, as nonconst objects can always invoke const member functions, but not vice versa.

The compilation and sample output of the program is:

```
%     CC const.C
%     a.out
0, 0, 0
25, 0, 0
```

2.5   C++ Class Inheritance

Class inheritance allows a class to be derived from one or more existing classes. The new class is called a subclass, and the class(es) it derived from is called a *base class* or *super class*.

A subclass inherits all data members and functions of its base class(es), and it may access all protected and public data members and functions of its base class. Furthermore, a subclass may define additional data members and functions that are unique to itself.

The following *window.h* header declares a *window* class, which is a subclass of *menu*:

```
#ifndef WINDOW_H
```

```
#define WINDOW_H
#include "menu.h"
#include <iostream.h>
class window : public menu
{
      private:
            int xcord, ycord;
      public:
            // constructor function
            window( const int x, const int y, const char* str ) : menu(str)
            {
                  xcord = x;
                  ycord = y;
            };
            // destructor
            ~window() {};
            // window-specific function
            void show (ostream& os )
            {
                  os << xcord << ',' << ycord << " => " << name() << endl;
            };
};
#endif
```

In a subclass declaration, a base class name may be preceded by a "public" or "private" key word, which means that the base class public data members and functions are to be treated as "public" or "private," respectively, in the subclass. If no such key word is specified, the default is "private."

A subclass member function can directly access only the protected and public data members of its base class(es). A subclass can explicitly mark selected "public" or "protected" data members and/or functions of "private" base classes to be "public" or "protected," respectively, in the subclass.

For example, the following *class window2* makes all the menu data members and functions it inherits private except the *menu::num_fields*, which is treated as protected in this subclass:

```
class window2 : private menu
{
      private:
```

```
            int xcord, ycord;
        protected:
            menu::num_fields;           // make menu::num_field protected
        public:
            ...
    };
```

When an object of a subclass is defined, the calling sequence of the subclass and base class(es) constructor function is in the order shown below:

- Base class constructors, in the order listed in the subclass declaration
- Data member constructors, in the order declared in the subclass
- Subclass constructors

For example, given the following subclass declaration:

```
    class a, b;
    class base1, base2;
    class sub : public base1, private base2
    {
        a var1;
        b var2;
    public:
        ...
    };
    sub foo;
```

the invocation order of constructor functions for the variable *foo* is: *base1::base1, base2::base2, a::a, b::b,* and, finally, *sub::sub.*

When an object of a subclass is out of scope, the calling sequence of the subclass and base class(es) destructor functions is in the order shown below:

- Subclass destructor
- Data member destructors, in reverse order as to that declared in the subclass
- Base class destructors, in the reverse order to that listed in the subclass declaration

In the above example, if the variable *foo* is going out of scope, the invocation order of destructor functions for it is: *sub::~sub, b::~b, a::~a, base2::~base2*, and, finally, *base1::~base1*.

When a subclass's constructor is called, the data to be passed on to its base classes' constructors and its data members' constructors are specified in a subclass constructor's initialization list. The list is specified after the subclass constructor function argument list but before the function body definition:

```
<subclass>::<subclass> ( <arg_list> ) : <initialization list>
{
      /* body */
}
```

and <initlialization list> is:

```
<class_name> ( <arg> ) [ , <class_name> ( <arg> ) ]+
```

For example, the *class sub* constructor function may be written as:

```
sub::sub( int x, int y, int z ) : base1(a), base2(b), a(z), b(z=1)
{
      /* body */
}
```

An initialization list can be specified only in a subclass constructor function definition, not at its declaration. Furthermore, one can skip specifying a base class or a data member name in an initialization list if that class does not have a constructor defined or it has a constructor defined that does not take any argument.

2.6   Virtual Functions

A class member function may be declared with a "virtual" key word. This means that any sub-classes of this class may redefine this virtual function. This is C++'s way of supporting polymorphism in object-oriented programming. A subclass may or may not redefine virtual functions that it inherits from its base classes. If it does redefine any virtual function, it cannot change the signature of these functions.

Virtual functions are used to define common operations for a set of related classes. The interface of these operations is the same for all of those classes, but the actual behavior (or implementation) of these operations may be changed per class. For example, a base class menu may define a draw operation that draws a form on a console, and its subclass window may redefine the draw operation to draw a window and then a menu on a console.

Constructor functions may not be declared as virtual functions. Destructor and over-loaded operator functions can and should be declared as virtual.

The following example illustrates uses of virtual functions:

```
// source module: virtual.C
#include <iostream.h>
class date
{
      int year, month, day;
   public:
      date(int y, int m, int d)  { year=y; month=m; day=d; };
      virtual ~date() {};
      virtual void print() {cerr << year << '/' << month << '/'
                                   << day << "\n";};
      virtual void set (int a, int b, int c) { year=a;  month=b;  day=c; };
};
class derived : public date
{
      int x;
   public:
      derived (int a,int b,int c,int d): date(a,b,c), x(d) {};
      ~derived() {};
      void print() { date::print(); cout << "derived: x=" << x << "\n"; };
      virtual void set(int a, int b, int c) {x=a;};
};

int main()
{
      date foo(1991,5,4);
      derived y(1,2,3,4);
      date* p = &y;
      p->print();                     // derived::print()
      p = & foo;
      p->print();                     // date::print()
}
```

In the above example, the *date::~date, date::print*, and *date::set* are all declared as virtual functions. The *class derived* redefines the *print* and *set* virtual functions. In the *main* function, when the variable *p* is pointing to *y*, the *p->print()* statement actually invokes the *derived::print* function, and when *p* is pointing to *foo*, the *p->print()* statement invokes the *date::print* function. Had the *date::print* function not been declared as virtual, then both the *p->print()* statements in the *main* function would have invoked only the *date::print* function, and the *derived::print* function would have been treated as an overloaded function of the *date::print* function.

The compilation and sample output of the program is:

```
%     CC virtual.C
%     a.out
1/2/3
derived: x=4
1991/5/4
```

2.7   Virtual Base Classes

Assume that a class *A* and a class *B* are both derived from a class *Base*. If then a class *C* is derived from both class *A* and class *B*, each object of class *C* has two copies of data members of class *Base*, and this may not be desirable for an application. To ensure, in such a multiple inheritance situation, that only one copy of class *Base* data members are kept for every object of class *C*, class *Base* must be declared as "virtual" in both class *A* and class *B* declarations, as illustrated below:

```
class Base
{
      int x;
      ...
};


class A : virtual public Base
{
      int y;
      ...
};


class B: virtual public Base
{
      int z;
```

```
            ...
     };

     class C : public A, private B
     {
            int w;
            ....
     };
```

A layout of the storage of an object (for example *foo*) of class *C* is similar to the following:

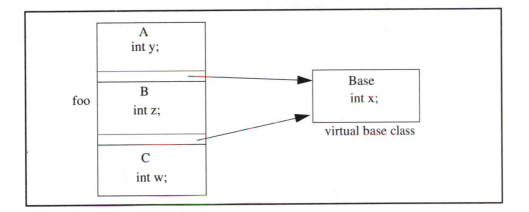

A virtual base class must define a constructor function that either takes no argument or has default values for all its arguments. A virtual base class is initialized by its most derived class (e.g., class *Base* is initialized via class *C*, not by class *A* or by class *B*). If the most derived class does not explicitly initialize the virtual base class, then the virtual base class's constructor, which does not require function arguments, is invoked to initialize objects of the most derived class. Furthermore, virtual base class constructors are invoked before nonvirtual base class constructors, and virtual base class destructors are invoked after nonvirtual base class destructors.

If there is a public virtual base class and a private virtual base class in a subclass, then the virtual base class is treated as public in the most derived class. For example, the class *Base* is treated as a public base class in class *C* in the above example.

The following shows the calling sequences of virtual and nonvirtual base class constructor and destructor functions, and the invocation of a virtual base class function (*base::print*) in a most derived class object:

```
// source module: virtual_base.C
#include <stream.h>

class base
{
    public:
        int x;
        base(int xa=0) : x(xa) { cerr << "base(" << xa << ") called\n"; };
        virtual void print()     { cerr << "x=" << x << "\n"; };
        virtual ~base()          {cerr << "~base() called\n";}
};

class d1 : virtual public base
{
    public:
        int y;
        d1(int xa, int ya) : base(xa)
        {
            cerr<<"d1("<<xa<<","<<ya<<") called\n";   y = ya;
        };
        ~d1()                    { cerr << "~d1() called\n"; };
        void print()             { cerr << "y=" << y << "\n"; };
};

class d2 : virtual public base
{
    public:
        int z;
        d2(int xa, int za) : base(xa)
        {
            cerr<<"d2("<<xa<<","<<za<<") called\n";   z = za;
        };
        ~d2()                    { cerr << "~d2() called\n"; };
};


class derived : public d1, public d2
{
    public:
```

```
            int all;
            derived(int a, int b, int c, int d) : base(a), d1(a,b), d2(a,c), all(d)
                                      {   cerr << "derived(" << all << ") called\n";};
            void prints()             {  base::print();cerr << "all=" << all << "\n";};
    };

    int main()
    {
            derived foo(1,2,3,4);
            foo.prints();
    }
```

The compilation and sample output of the program is:

```
    %    CC virtual_base.C
    %    a.out
    base(1) called
    d1(1,2) called
    d2(1,3) called
    derived(4) called
    x=1
    all=4
    ~d2() called
    ~d1() called
    ~base() called
```

2.8   Abstract Classes

An abstract class is designed to be a framework for derivation of subclasses. It has an incomplete specification of its operations; thus, no objects should be defined for any abstract class. The C++ compiler enforces such an restriction.

An abstract class declares one or more pure virtual functions; these functions have no definitions, and all sub-classes of the abstract class must redefine these functions. A pure virtual function is declared as shown below:

```
    class abstract_base
    {
            public:
```

```
        virtual void draw() = 0;          // a pure virtual function
};
```

An abstract class must contain at least one pure virtual function declaration. Users may define abstract class-typed pointer or reference variables, but these variables must reference subclass objects only.

The following example illustrates the uses of an abstract class. The program is an inter-active program that displays a menu for the user to select operations. Each operation is encap-sulated by one *menu_obj*-typed object. The *menu_obj* class is derived from the *abstract_base* class. The latter is an abstract base class and contains two pure virtual functions: *info* and *opr*. These pure virtual functions are re-defined in the *menu_obj* class, and the *info* function is called to display the use of a *menu_obj* class object, while the *opr* function is called to actu-ally execute the function of a *menu_obj*-typed object.

In the example, there are three *menu_obj* class objects defined: one is to display a local date/time, the second one is to display Greenwich Mean Time date/time, and the last one is to terminate the program. These objects are stored in a dispatch table called *menu*. The *main* function iteratively calls the *menu_obj::info* functions of all objects stored in *menu* to display a menu to console. It then gets an input selection from a user and invokes the *menu_obj::opr* function of a corresponding object. Note that the program is extensible, in that users may define more *menu_obj* class objects and store them in *menu*, and the program will automati-cally include those objects in action:

```
// source module: abstract.C
#include <iostream.h>
#include <time.h>
#include <string.h>
typedef void (*PF)();

class abstract_base              // abstract base class
{
   protected:
      PF       fn_ptr;
      char    *info_msg ;        // for displaying information
   public:
      abstract_base(PF fn=0, char* msg=0) {fn_ptr=fn,  info_msg=msg; };
      virtual void info(int) =0;
      virtual void opr() =0;
};
```

```
class menu_obj : public abstract_base // derived class
{
   public:
      menu_obj(PF fn, char *msg) : abstract_base(fn,msg) {};
      void info(int menu_idx)
      {
            cout << menu_idx << ": " << info_msg << "\n";
      };
      void opr()            { this->fn_ptr(); };
};

inline void fn0()
{
      long tim = time(0);
      cerr<<"Local: "<<asctime(localtime(&tim))<<"\n";
}

inline void fn1()
{
      long tim = time(0);
      cerr<<"GMT: "<<asctime(gmtime(&tim))<<"\n";
}

inline void fn2()            { exit(0); }

// dispatch table
 menu_obj menu[] =
{
      menu_obj(fn0, "Local data:time"),
      menu_obj(fn1,"GMT date:time"),
      menu_obj(fn2,"Exit program")
};

#define    MENU_SIZ      sizeof(menu)/sizeof(menu[0])

inline void display_menu()
{
      for (int i=0; i<MENU_SIZ; i++) menu[i].info(i);
}
```

```
int main()
{
      for (int idx; 1; )
      {
            display_menu();
            cout << "Select (0-" << (MENU_SIZ-1) << ")> ";
            cin>>idx;
            if (idx >=0 && idx<MENU_SIZ)
                menu[idx].opr();
            else cerr << "Illegal input: " << idx << "\n";
      }
}
```

The compilation and sample output of the program is:

```
%     CC abstract_base.C
%     a.out
0: Local date:time
1: GMT date:time
2: Exit Program
Select (0-2): 0
Local: Fri Apr 12 19:38:21 1991

0: Local date:time
1: GMT date:time
2: Exit Program
Select (0-2): 1
GMT: Sat Apr 13 02:38:22 1991

0: Local date:time
1: GMT date:time
2: Quit
Select (0-2): 2
```

2.9   The *new* and *delete* Operators

C++ defines the *new* and *delete* operators for dynamic memory management. These operators are supposed to be more efficient than the C *malloc, calloc*, and *free* functions for dynamic memory management.

The argument to a *new* operator is a data type (or class) name and, optionally, a paren-theses-enclosed initialization data list for the new object's constructor function. If no initial-ization data is specified, either the new object's constructor function, which does not take argument, is invoked -- if it is defined, or the new object is not initialized.

For example, given the following class declaration:

```
class date {
      int year, month, day;
   public:
      date( int a, int b, int c ) { year=a, month=b, day=c; };
      date() { year = month = day = 0; };
      ~date() {};
};
```

The following two statements use two different *class date* constructors:

```
date *date1p = new date (1995,7,1);    // use date::date(int,int,int);
date *date2p = new date;               // use date::date();
```

An array of objects may be allocated via the *new* operator. This is done by specifying a class name followed by the number of objects in the array and enclosing that number in brackets. For example, the following statement allocates an array of ten *class date*-type objects:

```
date *dateList = new date [ 10 ];
```

To initialize objects in an array that are allocated via *new*, the object's class should have a constructor that requires no arguments, and this constructor is used to initialize every object in the array. If no such constructor is defined, the objects in the array are not initialized.

There is a global variable, *_new_handler,* defined in the standard C++ library. If this *_new_handler* variable is set to a user-defined function, then whenever the *new* operator fails, it calls this routine to do user-defined error recovery actions. It then returns a NULL pointer value to its caller. If the *_new_handler* is set as its default value NULL, then when the *new* operator fails, it simply returns a NULL pointer to its caller.

The *_new_handler* declaration is defined in the <new.h> header as:

```
extern void (*_new_handler)();
```

It can be set either by direct assignment in users' programs or by the *set_new_handler* macro, as defined in the <new.h>:

```
#include <new.h>
extern void error_handler();                    // user-defined function
main()
{
        _new_handler = error_handler;           // direct assignment
        set_new_handler ( error_handler );      // assigned via a macro
}
```

Finally, the *new* operator may be instructed to use a preallocated memory region to place "dynamic" objects on it. In this case, a user takes over the memory allocation task, and the *new* operator is used to initialize the new objects that are placed on the user-specified memory region. The following example shows how this is done:

```
#include <new.h>
#include "date.h"

const NUM_OBJ = 1000;
date *pool = new char[sizeof(DATE) * NUM_OBJ];
int main()
{
        date *p = new (pool) date [NUM_OBJ];
        delete [NUM_OBJ] p;
}
```

In the above example, a user allocates a memory region pointed to by the *pool* variable. The user then "allocates" NUM_OBJ objects of *class date*. This array is placed in the memory region referenced by *pool,* and the variable *p* points to the array. Finally, the array is deallocated via the *delete* operator.

A dynamic object allocated via the *new* operator should be deallocated via the *delete* operator. For example, to delete a *date* class object whose address is pointed to by a variable called *p*:

```
date *p = new date;
...
delete p;
```

If the object to be deleted is an array, the *delete* operator should be followed by a specification of the number of entries in the array, and then the array name. For example:

```
date *arrayP = new date[10];
...
delete [10] arrayP;
```

The above syntax is needed, as it causes the destructor function of objects in the array to be invoked for each of the objects. If the above array is deallocated as:

```
delete arrayP;
```

Then the destructor function is called for the first object in the array only.

The *new* and *delete* operators may be overloaded in a class; then, whenever an object of such a class is allocated via the *new* and deallocated via the *delete* operators, the class instance of these operators is used instead.

The overloaded *new* and *delete* operators must be declared as class member functions. They are treated as static member functions, in that they cannot modify any data member of objects in their classes.

The following example illustrates the declaration of overloaded *new* and *delete* operators in the *class date*:

```
class date
{
        int year, month, day;
    public:

        date( int a, int b, int c )   { year=a, month=b, day=c; };

        ~date() {};

        // overloaded new operator
        void* operator new (size_t siz )
        {
                return ::new char [siz ];
        };
};
```

```
// overloaded delete operator
void operator delete (void* ptr )
{
        ::delete ptr;
};
};
```

An overloaded *new* member function must take a *size_t*-type argument, which specifies the size, in bytes, of an object to be allocated. The function then returns the address of newly allocated object.

An overloaded *delete* member function must take a *void** argument, which points to an object to be deallocated. The function does not return any value.

Users are free to implement the body of the *new* and *delete* member functions in any way they like.

2.10   Operator Overloading

C++ allows users to define standard built-in operators to work on classes. This enables class objects to be used as if they were of the built-in data type. The built-in '+', '-', '*', and "[]" operators have no meaning to class objects, unless users explicitly overload these operators in their classes.

+	-	*	/	%	^	&	|
~	!	,	=	<	>	<=	>=
++	--	<<	>>	==	!=	&&	||
+=	-=	/=	%=	^=	&=	|=	<<=
>>=	[ ]	( )	->	->*	new	delete	

The C++ operators that may be overloaded in classes are shown in the above table. Specifically, the meanings, precedence, and arity of operators cannot be overridden by overloading. This means that the "+", "-", "*" and "&" operators may be defined as unary or binary operators. Furthermore, overloading treats all prefix and suffix instances of "++" and "--" operators as prefix operators.

All overloaded operator functions must take at least one class object as argument. They may be declared as friend or member functions. However, operators such as "<<" and ">>," which do not require a left operand to be a class object, should be defined as friend functions, and operators such as "[]", '=', "->", "()" and "+=," which require a left operand to be a class object, should be declared as member functions.

The following example illustrates the use of operator overloading:

```
// source module: overload.c
#include <iostream.h>
#include <string.h>
class sarray
{
    int num;
    char *data;
  public:
    sarray( const char* str )                // constructor
    {
        num = strlen(str)+1;
        data = new char[num];
        strcpy( data, str );
    };

    ~sarray() { delete data; };

    char& operator[] (int idx )              // destructor
    {
        if (idx>=0 && idx < num)
            return data[idx];
        else
        {
            cerr << "Invalid index: " << idx << endl;
            return data[0];
        };
    };
};
```

```
const char* operator=( const char* str )
{
    if (strlen(str))
    {
        delete data;
        num = strlen(str)+1;
        data = new char[num];
        strcpy (data, str );
    }
    return str;
};

const sarray& operator=( const sarray& obj )
{
    if (strlen(obj.data))
    {
        delete data;
        num = strlen(obj.data)+1;
        data = new char[num];
        strcpy (data, obj.data );
    }
    return obj;
};

int operator == ( const char* str )
{
    return (str && data) ?  strcmp(data,str) : -1;
};

int operator < ( const char* str)
{
    return (strcmp(data,str) < 0) ? 1 : 0;
};

int operator > ( const char* str )
{
    return (strcmp(data,str) > 0) ? 1 : 0;
};
```

```
                friend ostream& operator << (ostream& os, sarray& obj)
                {
                        return os << (obj.data ? obj.data : "Nil") ;
                };
        };

        int main()
        {
            sarray A("Hello"), B("world");
            cout << "A: " << A << endl;              // << operator
            A = "Bad";                               // = operator
            A[0] = 'T';                              // [] operator
            cout << "A: " << A << endl;
            A = B;                                   // = array& operator
            cout << "A: " << A[1] << endl;
            cout << "A < B: " << (A < "Two") << endl;
            return 0;
        }
```

The above example defines a class *sarray*, which manages a character array per its object. The advantage of using the class is that each of its objects adjusts its buffer dynamically to fit any character string stored in it. Furthermore, the objects can be operated on using the "<<", "[]", "=," and "<" operators, due to the declaration of the overloaded operator functions. All of these make the *sarray* objects more intuitive to understand and use, and they hide the low-level array manipulation coding from users.

The compilation and sample output of the program is:

```
% CC overload.c
% a.out
A: Hello
A: Tad
A: o
A < B: 0
```

2.11   Template Functions and Template Classes

Template functions and template classes enable users to create generic functions and classes that work with different data types and classes. After these functions and classes are coded and tested, users can create different instances of these functions and classes for specific data types and/or classes. Thus, template functions and classes significantly save application development time. Another advantage of these is the reduction, per program, of unique functions and class names that require definition. This speeds up the compilation process and reduces potential name conflicts in users' programs.

A template function or a template class is instantiated when it is first used or when its address is being taken. These instances have no names, and they last only as long as they are in use.

2.11.1 Template Functions

The formal syntax of a template function declaration is:

```
template <formal param. list> <return_value> <function_name>
    ( <arg_list> )
{
    <body>
}
```

For example, to declare a template function that swaps the content of two objects:

```
template <class T> void swap ( T& left, T& right )
{
    T temp = left;
    left = right;
    right = tenp;
}
```

Once the above template function is declared, users can create objects of specialized instances of that class for various data types. The following example shows how this is done:

```
main()
{
    int a = 1, b = 2;
    swap (a, b) ;          // creates s awap(int,int) instance
    double aa = 101.0, bb = 25.0;
```

```
        swap( aa, bb );          // creates a swap(double,double) instance
    }
```

A formal parameter list is enclosed by the "<" and ">" characters. The list consists of a comma separated list of formal type parameters. The list cannot be empty. Each formal type parameter begins with a *class* key word and is followed by a type identifier. For example, the following declaration is correct:

```
    template <class T, class U>  void foo( T*, U);
```

whereas the following declaration is wrong, as the type U does not have the *class* key word preceding it:

```
    template <class T, U> void foo1(T&);          // Error. Must be "class U"
```

A type parameter may appear only once in a formal type parameter list. Thus, the following declaration is incorrect, as it specifies class *T* twice:

```
    template <class T, class T> void foo1(T&);        // Error
```

Each type parameter must appear at least once in a template function argument list. Thus, the following declaration is incorrect, as the type *U* is not used in the function argument list:

```
    template <class T, class U> U  foo1(T&);        // Error
```

A correct version of the declaration is to use type *U* in the function argument list, such as the following:

```
    template <class T, class U> U foo1(T&,U*);       // OK.
```

A template function can be declared *extern, static,* or *inline.* The specifier is placed after the formal parameter list and before the return value type specification. The following examples declare an inline function and an external function:

```
        template <class T> inline void foo( T* tobj, int size) { ... }
        template <class T> extern int fooA( T&  tobj) ;
```

A template function can be overloaded, provided that the signature of each declaration is distinguished, either by argument type or by number. For example, the following declarations are all legal:

```
template <class T> T min(T  t1, T t2);
template <class T> T min(T* t1, T t2, T t3);
template <class T> T min(T  t1, int t2);
```

However, the two declarations below are incorrect, as type parameter identifiers cannot be used to differentiate overloaded template functions:

```
template <class T> T min(T  t1, T t2);
template <class U> U min(U t1, U t2);                    // Error!
```

Finally, specialized template functions can be defined. Specialized functions are used in higher precedence than are generic template functions in resolving function references. For example, in the following program, the first invocation of *min* in the *main* function uses the specialized version of *min* that takes *char**-typed arguments, and the second invocation of *min* creates an instance of the template function *min* for the double data type:

```
template <class T> T min(T t1, T t2)
{
        return (t1 < t2) ? t1 : t2;
}
// specialized version of min()
char * min(char* t1, char* t2)
{
        return (strcmp(t1,t2) < 0) ? t1 : t2;
}

int main()
{
        char* ptr = min ("C++","UNIX");          //  min(char*,char*)
        double x = min(2.0, 3.0);                // min(T,T)
}
```

2.11.2 Template Classes

The formal syntax of a template class declaration is:

```
template <formal parameter list> class <class_name>
{
        <declaration>
}
```

In a template class declaration, the *template* key word is followed by a formal parameter list, then a class name and its body. A formal parameter list is enclosed by the "<" and ">" characters. The list consists of a comma-separated list of formal parameters. A formal parameter may be a type parameter or a constant expression parameter. The following is an example of a template class declaration:

```
template <class T, int len> class foo
{
        T  list[len];
        ...
};
```

As in a template function declaration, each parameter declared in a formal parameter list should be used at least once in the associated template class declaration. Moreover, whenever a template class name is referenced, it must always be specified along with its parameter list enclosed by angle brackets, except inside the class declaration. The following example depicts a declaration of a template class *Array,* which contains an array of type *T* with *len* entries. The *T* and *len* are parameters to be supplied when the template class instances are created. Note also that the constructor function definition has the class name and parameter list specified:

```
template <class T, int len>   class Array
{
    public:
        Array();
        ~Array() {};
    protected:
        T  list[len];
};


template <class TT, int len> inline
Array<TT,len> :: Array()
{
        ...
}
```

To create an object for a specialized instance of a template class, users specify the class name, followed by the actual data for the parameter list enclosed in "<" and ">." Thus to create an object of the *Array* class that contains an integer array with 100 entries, the object definition is:

```
Array<int, 100> foo;                         // foo is an object
```

Template classes can be derived from template or nontemplate base classes. The type/subtype relationship between derived and public base template classes holds, provided they are of the same actual parameter types.

The following example declares a template subclass *Array_super* which is derived from the template classes *b1* and *b2*. The *foo* variable is defined as the int-instance of the *Array_super* class, and *ptr* is a pointer to the int-instance of the class *b1*. *S*ince *b1<int>* and *Array_super<int>* have the same parameter type, they are compatible and, thus, *ptr* can be assigned the address of *foo*. However, *b1<double>* and *Array_super<int>* are incompatible; thus, it is an error to assign the address of *foo* to *ptr2*.

```
template <class Type>
        class Array_super :  public b1<Type>, public b2<Type> {...};
Array_super<int> foo;
b1<int> *ptr = &foo;                    // Correct
b1<double> *ptr2 = &foo;                // Error
```

Friend functions and classes can be declared inside template classes. Each of these friend functions and classes may be one of the following:

- Nontemplate function or class
- Template function or class
- Specialized instance of a template function or class

If a friend function or class is a general template, this means that all instances of that function or class are friends to the template class. On the other hand, if a friend function or class is a specialized instance of a template, only that instance is a friend to the template class being declared. The following example illustrates these concepts:

```
template <class U> class Container
{
        // general template friend class
        template <class T> friend class general_class;
```

```
            // general template friend function
            template <class UT> friend general_func ( <UT&, int );

            // Only the same type U instance of class Array is friend
            friend class Array<U>;

            // Only the same type U instance of the function is friend
            friend ostream& operator<< (ostream&, Container<U>&);

            // non-template friend class
            friend class dates;

            // non-template friend function
            friend void foo ();
    };
```

In the above example, the template class *Container* has a formal parameter of type *U*. The *Container* class has a few friend functions and classes; of these, class *dates* and *foo* are friends for all specialized instances of the *Container* class. The template *Array* class and the overloaded operator "<<" are friends for specialized instances of the *Container* class as long as they use the same parameter type. Thus, *Array<int>* is a friend class for the *Container<int>*, but *Array<double>* is not a friend for the *Container<int>*. Finally, all specialized instances of the template *general_class* class and *general_func* function are friends for all specialized instances of the *Container* class.

Specialized member functions or template classes may be defined for a template class. However, all these specialized instances can be defined only after the template class is declared. Furthermore, a specialized template class must define all member functions of a template class on which it is based. The following shows an example of a declaration of a template class *Array*, then a specialized constructor of *Array* for the *double* data type, and, lastly, a definition of a specialized class *Array* for the *char** type:

```
        template <class T> class Array
        {
            public:
                Array(int sz) { ar=new T[size=sz]; };
                ~Array() { delete [siz] ar; };
                T& operator[](int i) { return ar[i]; };
            protected:
                T* ar;
```

```
        int size;
    };


// Specialized constructor for double type
Array<double>::Array( int size ) { ... }

// Specialized Array class definition
class Array<char*>
{
    public:
        Array(int sz)          { ar=new char[size=sz]; };
        ~Array()               { delete [] ar; };
        char& operator[](int i) { return ar[i]; };
    protected:
        char* ar;
        int size;
    };
```

A template class can declare static data members. Each specialized instance of the template class has its own set of static data members. The following example declares a template *Array* class with two static data members: *Array<T>::pool* and *Array<T>::pool_sz*. These static variables are defaulted to be initialized to 0 and 100, respectively, for all specialized instances of class *Array*:

```
        template <class T> class Array
        {
            public:
                Array(int sz)          { ar=new char[size=sz]; };
                ~Array()               { delete [sz] ar; };
                void *operator new(size_t);
                void operator delete(void*,size_t);
            protected:
                char*           ar;
                int             size;
                static Array *  pool;
                static const int pool_sz;
            };
        template <class T> Array<T>* Array<T>::pool = 0;
        template<class T> const int Array<T>::pool_size = 100;
```

One can define a specialized instance of static class data members and specify unique initial values for them. Thus one can define the *Array<char>::pool* and *Array<char>::pool_sz* variables for the *char* instance of the class *Array* as:

```
Array<char>* Array<char>::pool = new char[1000];
Array<char>* Array<char>::pool_sz = 1000;
```

In addition to all the above, static class data members of a template class can be accessed only through a specialized instance of the class. Thus the first statement below, which directly references the *Array<T>::pool,* is illegal, whereas the references of *Array<char>::pool* and *Array<int>::pool_sz* are correct:

```
cout << Array<T>::pool << endl;            // Error
Array<char>* ptr = Array<char>::pool;      // Correct
int x = Array<int>::pool_sz;               // Correct
```

Finally, a nontemplate function can manipulate objects of specialized instances of template classes, whereas a template function can use objects of either a specific instance or of a general parameterized template class. In the following, *foo* is a nontemplate function; thus, it may work with objects of a specialized instance (in this case, *Array<int>*) of the class *Array.* On the other hand, *foo2* is a template function and it can manipulate objects of any instance of the class *Array,* as long they have the same parameter type (i.e., *foo2<int>* function can take a *Array<int>* type object as argument):

```
 void foo( Array<int>& Aobj, int size )
{
      Array<int> *ptr = &Aobj;
         ...
}

template <class T> extern void foo2 ( Array<T>&, Array<int>& );
```

2.12   Exception Handling

ANSI/ISO C++ provides a standard exception handling method for all applications to respond to run-time program anomalies. This simplifies application development efforts and ensures consistency in behavior of applications.

An exception is an error condition detected in a program at run time. An exception is "raised" via a *throw* statement, and an exception handler function is "caught" by a user-defined *catch*-block, which is in the same program. If a catch-block does not terminate the program, the program control flow continues at the code right after the catch-block and is not after the *throw* statement. Furthermore, only by code executed directly or indirectly within a *try* block can exception be thrown. Thus, exception handling requires special structuring of users' C++ program to anticipate code region where exception may occur and to specify one or more catch-blocks to handle exception.

C++ exception handling mechanisms are synchronous, in that exceptions are triggered in users' applications via the explicit *throw* statements. This differs from asynchronous exceptions caused by events like keyboard interruptions from users. The latter exceptions are unpredictable as to when and where they will occur, and they can be handled via the *signal* function (see the chapter on Signals).

The following example illustrates a simple exception handling in C++:

```
// source module: simple_exception.C
#include <iostream.h>
main( int argc, char* argv[])
{
    try {
        if (argc==1) throw "Insufficient no. of argument";
        while (--argc > 0)
            cout << argc << ": " << argv[argc] << endl;
        cout << "Finish " << argv[0] << endl;
        return 0;
    }
    catch (const char* msg ) {
        cerr << "exception: " << msg << endl;
    }
    catch (int unused ) {
        cerr << "This catch block is un-used\n";
        return 99;
    }
    cout << "main: continue here after exception\n";
    return 1;
}
```

In the above example, the normal function code for *main* is enclosed in the try block. In this block, a test is made on the *argc* value. If its value is 1, an exception occurs and the throw statement is executed to raise an exception. However, if *argc* value is greater than 1, the *while* loop is executed to dump out all command line arguments, in reverse order, and the program terminates via the *return 0* statement.

The syntax of a *throw* statement is:

```
throw <expression> ;
```

where <expression> is any C++ expression that evaluates to a C++ basic data type value or a class object. The <expression> value is used to select a catch-block that the "argument" type matches or that is compatible with the <expression> data type. If a *throw* statement is executed, the rest of the statements in the same *try* block are skipped, and the program flow continues in a selected catch-block.

One or more catch-blocks may be specified in a function. The catch-blocks must be specified right after a try block. Each catch block begins with the catch key word, followed by a object tag specification enclosed in "(" and ")". After that, one or more statements for the block are enclosed in "{" and "}". Note that although a catch-block looks like a function definition, it is not a function. It is really just a set of C++ statements collected together and given an object tag. The object tag is used by a *throw* statement to select which catch-block to execute, and the object contains the <expression> value of the *throw* statement. This value usually conveys more information about an exception that was raised.

After a catch-block is executed, if it does not terminate the program, the program flow continues at the statement after the catch-blocks.

In the above example, a sample compilation and sample run of the program, with no exceptions, are:

```
%     CC simple_exception.C
%     a.out hello
1: hello
Finish a.out
```

If the program is rerun without any argument, an exception occurs and the program's output is:

```
%     a.out
exception: Insufficient no. of argument
main: continue here after exception
```

Note that in the above run, the *throw* statement includes a *char** expression, thus the *catch (const char* msg)* block is selected, but not the *catch(int unused)* block. However, if users add a statement like *throw 5* in the *try* block, this *new* statement, if executed, selects the *catch(int unused)* block only.

A *throw* statement can also specify a class object name as argument. This allows it to pass more information to a catch-block for better error diagnostics and reporting. The following program is a revised version of the previous example:

```
// source module: simple2.C
#include <iostream.h>

// special class for error reporting
class errObj
{
   public:
      int line;
      char* msg;
      // constructor function
      errObj( int lineNo, char* str )
      {
         line = lineNo;
         msg = str;
      };
      // destructor function
      ~errObj() {};
};

main( int argc, char* argv[])
{
      try {
         if (argc==1) throw errObj(__LINE__,
                                 "Insufficient no. of arguments");
         while (--argc > 0)
               cout << argc << ": " << argv[argc] << endl;
         cout << "Finish " << argv[0] << endl;
         return 0;
      }
      catch (errObj& obj )   {
         cerr  << "exception at line: " << obj.line << ", msg: "
```

```
                << obj.msg << endl;
        }
        cout << "main: continue here after exception\n";
        return 1;
    }
```

The compilation and sample run of the program, with an exception, are:

```
%    CC simple2.C
%    a.out
exception at line: 23, msg: Insufficient no. of arguments
main: continue here after exception
```

If an exception is raised but no catch-blocks in the same function match the *throw* statement's argument, then the function is "returned" to its calling function(s), and the catch-blocks in each of these functions are searched for a match to the *throw*'s argument. The process stops when either a catch-block is matched and the program flow continues in that block and in the code after that, or no match is found and the built-in function *terminate* is called. The *terminate* function in turns calls the *abort* function, which aborts the program.

When a function returns to its caller(s) due to a *throw* statement, any objects local to an exiting function are deallocated via their destructors, and the run-time stack is rewound to deallocate the stack frame reserved for the exiting function.

The following example illustrates these concepts:

```
// source module: simple3.C
#include <iostream.h>
void f2 ( int x )
{
        try    {
                switch (x) {
                    case 1: throw "exception from f2.";
                    case 2: throw 2;
                }
                cout << "f2: got " << x << " arguments.\n";
                return;
        }
        catch (int no_arg ) {
```

```
            cerr << "f2 error: need at least " << no_arg << " arguments\n";
        }
        cerr << "f2 returns after an exception\n";
    }

    main( int argc, char* argv[])
    {
        try        {
            f2(argc);
            cout << "main: f2 returns normally\n";
            return 0;
        }
        catch (const char* str ) {
            cerr << "main: " << str << endl;
        }
        cerr << "main: f2 returns via an exeception\n";
        return 1;
    }
```

In the above example, if the program is invoked with no argument, the *f2* function executes the *throw "exception from f2"* statement and this causes the *catch (const char* str)* block in *main* to be executed. The program output is:

```
%    CC simple3.C
%    a.out
main: exception from f2.
main: f2 returns via an execution
```

If, however, the program is invoked with one argument (and *argc* value is 2), the *f2* function executes the *throw 2* statement and this causes the *catch(int no_arg)* block in *f2* to be executed. The program output for this is:

```
%    a.out hello
f2 error: need at least 2 arguments
f2 returns after an exception
main: f2 returns normally
```

Finally, if the program is invoked with two or more arguments, then no exception is raised by *f2*, and the program output is:

```
%    a.out hello world
f2: got 3 arguments.
main: f2 returns normally
```

2.12.1 Exceptions and Catch-Blocks Matching

When a *throw* statement with an argument of data type T is executed, the following rules are used to match a catch-block to catch the exception. Assuming the data type of a catch block is of type C, then the catch-block is selected if any one of the following conditions is true:

- T is same as C
- T is a const or volatile of C, or vice versa
- C is a reference of T, or vice versa
- C is a public or protected base class of T
- Both C and T are pointers, and T can be converted to C by a standard pointer conversion

2.12.2 Function Declarations with Throw

A function declaration may optionally specify a set of exceptions that it directly or indirectly will throw by providing a *throw list*. For example, the following statement declares an external function *funct*, which may throw exceptions with data tag of *const char** or *int*.

```
extern void funct (char * ar)  throw(const char*, int);
```

A throw list may be empty, which means that a function will not throw any exceptions. The following statement declares *funct2* not raise any exception, either directly or indirectly:

```
extern void funct2(char * ar)  throw();
```

However, if the above *funct2* does invoke a throw statement, the built-in *unexpected* function is called. The *unexpected* function, by default, calls the *abort* function to terminate the program.

A throw list is not part of a function type. Thus, it cannot be used to overload functions. For example, the following two function declarations are treated the same by the C++ compiler:

```
extern void funct3 (char * ar)  throw(char*);
extern void funct3 (char * ar=0);
```

2.12.3 The Terminate and Unexpected Functions

The *terminate* function is called when a *throw* statement is executed but no matching catch-block is found. By default, the *terminate* function invokes the *abort* function to abort the program. However, users may install their functions in place of *abort* in *terminate* via the *set_terminate* function, as follows:

```
extern void user_terminate( void );
void (*old_handler)(void);
old_handler = set_terminate ( user_terminate );
```

In the above sample statement, the *user_terminate* is a user-defined function to be called when *terminate* is invoked. The *user_terminate* function is installed via the *set_terminate* function, and the *old_handler* variable holds the old function installed in the *terminate* function.

The *unexpected* function is called when a *throw* statement is executed in a function that is declared with an empty throw list. By default, the *unexpected* function invokes the *terminate* function to abort the program. However, users may install their functions in place of *terminate* in *unexpected* via the *set_unexpected* function as follows:

```
extern void user_unexpected ( void );
void (*old_handler)(void);
old_handler = set_unexpected ( user_unexpected );
```

In the above sample statement, the *user_unexpected* is a user-defined function to be called when *unexpected* is invoked. The *user_unexpected* function is installed via the *set_unexpected* function, and the *old_handler* variable holds the old function installed in the *unexpected* function.

Since the *terminate* and *unexpected* functions are assumed to never return to their caller, any user-installed functions to be invoked by either *terminate* or *unexpected* should terminate the program at their completion.

Actually, the *terminate* and *unexpected* functions should rarely be called in a well-designed program, as they really signal that users programs have not accounted for all possible exceptions raised in their programs, and this is not a good programming practice. The only exception to this is the use of third-party C++ libraries, which raises undocumented exceptions. In this case, users should report the problems to their vendors and install the handler for *terminate* and/or *unexpected* only as a short-term work-around.

2.13   Summary

This chapter covers the object-oriented program design and the draft ANSI/ISO C++ language features. As discussed in the chapter, C++ is derived from C and has added constructs to support an object-oriented programming style. These new constructs include classes declaration, classes inheritance, polymorphism via virtual functions, and template functions and classes. Finally, the C++ exception handling method is also discussed. Extensive examples are depicted to illustrate the uses of these concepts.

These C++ features are discussed here to refresh users' memories of the C++ programming techniques so that they can understand the rest of the book. Furthermore, some readers may not be familiar with the new features of ANSI/ISO C++. This chapter describes those new features in more detail.

The next chapter discusses the C++ I/O stream libraries. These libraries are used extensively by all C++ applications, but their full features are not always understood by readers. The next chapter should help users refresh their memories and learn some new features.

2.14   References

[1].   Andrew Koenig, *Working Paper for Draft Proposed International Standard for Information Systems -- Programming Language C++ (Committees: WG21/N0414, X3J16/94-0025)*, January 1994.

[2].   Margaret A. Ellis and Bjarne Stroustrup, *The Annotated C++ Reference Manual*, Addison-Wesley, 1990.

[2].   Bjarne Stroustrup, *The C++ Programming Language*, Addison-Wesley, 1991.

C++ I/O Stream Classes

This chapter reviews the C++ I/O stream classes. These classes are defined in the draft ANSI/ISO C++ standard. They enable users to perform I/O operations with the standard input and output streams, disk files, and character buffers. They essentially eliminate the needs of users to use the C stream I/O functions, string functions, and the *printf* class functions. The advantage of using the C++ I/O stream classes is that they allow the compiler do more type-checking on the actual arguments supplied to these classes. They can also be extended to support user-defined classes.

There are three major headers for the I/O stream classes. The <iostream.h> header declares the *istream, ostream,* and *iostream* classes for the standard input and output stream I/O operations. It also declares the *cout, cin, cerr*, and *clog* objects that are used in most C++ programs. The <fstream.h> header declares the *ifstream, ofstream*, and *fstream* classes for disk file I/O operations. Finally, the <strstream.h> header declares the *istrstream, ostrstream,* and *strstream* classes for in-core data formatting with character buffers.

Although C++ I/O stream classes, especially the *cout, cin*, and *cerr* objects, are widely used in most C++ applications, not all users know the detailed features of these classes, nor are they being described fully by many textbooks on C++ programming. The rest of this chapter gives a comprehensive description of these I/O stream classes.

3.1   The I/O Stream Classes

The <iostream.h> header declares three classes for the standard input and output streams I/O: *istream, ostream*, and *iostream*. The *istream* class is for data input from an input stream, the *ostream* class is for data output to an output stream, and the *iostream* class is for data input and output within a stream. Besides these classes, the <iostream.h> header also declares four objects:

Stream object	Function
cin	An *istream* class object tied to the standard input
cout	An *ostream* class object tied to the standard output
cerr	An *ostream* class object tied to the standard error, providing unbuffered output
clog	An *ostream* class object tied to the standard error, providing buffered output

Note that the *cin, cout, clog*, and *cerr* objects do not use the same file descriptors as do the C *stdin, stdout*, and *stderr* stream pointers. However, users may force *cin* and *stdin* to use the same file descriptor; *cout* and *stdout* to use another file descriptor; and *cerr, clog,* and *stderr* to use a third file descriptor; via the static function:

        ios::sync_with_stdio();

The above function should be called in a user program before any stream I/O operation is performed.

3.1.1   The istream Class

The *istream* class is used to extract data from an input stream. The *cin* object is of this data type. The user-visible operations that are defined for the *istream* class are:

Operation	Function
>>	Extracts white space delimited data (of any standard data type) from an input stream
istream& get(char c) , int get()	Extracts a character from an input stream. White spaces are treated as legal characters
istream& read(char* buf, int size)	Extracts *size* bytes of data from an input stream and puts it into *buf*

Operation	Function
istream& getline(char* buf, int limit, char delimiter='\n')	Extracts from an input stream at most *limit*-1 byte of data, or when the delimiter character or *EOF* (end-of-file) is encountered. The extracted data are put into *buf*. The delimiter character, if found, is not included in *buf*
int gcount()	Returns the number of bytes extracted by the last call of *read* or *getline*
istream& putback(char c)	Puts the specified character *c* back into an input stream
int peek()	Returns the next character in an input stream but does not extract it
istream& ignore(int limit=1, int delimiter=EOF)	Discards up to *limit* characters in an input stream, or if the delimiter character or *EOF* are encountered
streampos tellg()	Returns the current stream marker byte offset from the beginning of the stream
istream& seekg(streampos offset, seek_dir d=ios::beg)	Repositions the stream marker to *offset* bytes from the beginning of the file (if *d*=ios::beg), current stream marker position (if *d*=ios::cur), or *EOF* (if *d*=ios::end)

The following is a UNIX *wc*-like program that illustrates the use of *istream* class operations. Specifically, the program counts the number of lines, words, and characters found in the standard input stream:

```
/* source module: wc.C */
#include <iostream.h>
#include <ctype.h>

int main()
{
      int ch, lineno=0, charno = 0, wordno = 0;
      for (int last=0; cin && (ch = cin.get()) != EOF; last=ch)
         switch (ch)   {
            case '\n':  lineno++, wordno++;
                        break;
```

```
case '/':    if (cin.peek()=='/')      {        // don't count comments
                 cin.ignore(10000,'\n');
                 lineno++;
             }
             else charno++;
             break;
default:     charno++;
             if (isspace(ch) && last!=ch) wordno++;
}
cout << charno << " "  << wordno << " " << lineno << "\n" << flush;
}
```

The compilation and sample run of this program are:

```
%    CC wc.C
%    a.out < /etc/passwd
557  23    14
```

The ">>" operator may be overloaded as a friend function for each user-defined class. This enables users to extract class object data in the same manner as they do for the standard C++ data type objects. The overloaded ">>" function should be defined in the following manner:

```
class X                          // user-defined class
{      ...
    public:
        friend istream& operator >> (istream& is, X& xObj)
        {
            is >> <class X data members>;
            return is;
        };
        ...
};
```

3.1.2   The ostream Class

The *ostream* class is used to insert data to an output stream. The *cout, cerr,* and *clog* objects are of this data type. The user-visible operations that are defined for the *ostream* class are:

Operation	Function
<<	Inserts the value of any standard data type to an output stream
ostream& put(char ch)	Inserts a character *ch* to an output stream
ostream& write(const char*buf, int size)	Inserts *size* byte of data contained in *buf* to an output stream
typedef streampos long; streampos tellp()	Returns the current stream marker byte offset from the beginning of the stream
ostream& seekp(streampos offset, seek_dir d=ios::beg)	Repositions the stream marker to *offset* bytes from the beginning of the file (if *d*=ios::beg), current stream marker position (if *d*=ios::cur), or *EOF* (if *d*=ios::end)
ostream& flush()	Forces flushing of data to an output stream

The following statements illustrate the use of *ostream* class operations:

```
cout << "x=" << x << ",y=" << y << "\n";
cout.put('\n').write("Hello world",11).put('\n');
```

The "<<" operator may be overloaded as a friend function for each user-defined class. This enables users to print class objects' data in the same manner as they do for the standard C++ data type objects. The overloaded "<<" function should be defined in the following manner:

```
class X                      // user-defined class
{
    ...
    public:
        friend ostream& operator << (ostream& os, X& xObj)
        {
            os <<<class X data members>;
            return os;
        };
    ...
};
```

3.1.3   The iostream Class

The *iostream* class is derived from the *istream* and *ostream* classes. It contains all the properties of its two base classes. This class is used primarily as a base class for the *fstream* class, and the latter is commonly used for defining objects to read/write disk files.

3.1.4   The ios Class

The *istream, ostream,* and *iostream* classes contain a virtual base class *ios*. The *ios* class records an error state and a format state for each I/O stream class object. Specifically, the *ios* class declares the following operations:

Operation	Function
int eof()	Returns 1 if *EOF* has been encountered in a stream
int bad()	Returns 1 if an invalid operation (e.g., seeking pass *EOF*) has been detected
int fail()	Returns 1 if an I/O operation is unsuccessful or bad() is true
int good()	Returns 1 if all previous I/O operations have been successful
int rdstate()	Returns the error state of a stream
void clear(bits=0)	Sets the error state's bit vector to the value given in *bits*. If *bits* is 0, resets the error state to 0
int width(int len)	Sets the field width to *len* for the next data to be inserted, or sets the buffer limit to *len-1* for character string extraction. This routine returns the previous field width
char fill(char ch)	Sets the fill (padding) character to *ch*. Returns the previous fill character
int precision(int)	Sets the number of significant digits to be displayed for real number insertion. Returns the previous precision value
long setf(long bitFlag)	Adds the format bit(s) as specified in *bitFlag* to the existing format state for insertion. Returns the old format state value. Possible values for *bitFlag* may be:

ios::showbase		Displays numeric base
ios::showpoint		Displays trailing decimal point and zero
ios::showpos		Displays sign character for numeric values
ios::uppercase		Uses "X" for hexadecimal number display (when *ios::showbase* is set), and "E"to print floating point numbers in scientific notation

long setf(long bitFlag long bitField)

Sets/resets (as according to *bitFlag*) the format bits as specified in *bitField* for insertion. Returns the old format state value. Possible values for *bitField/ bitFlag* may be:

ios::basefield	ios::hex	Sets the numeric base to hexadecimal
	ios::oct	Sets the numeric base to octal
	ios::dec	Sets the numeric base to decimal (the default)
ios::floatfield	ios::fixed	Displays real numbers in decimal notation
	ios::scientific	Displays real numbers in scientific notation
ios::adjustfield	ios::left	Left-justifies the next argument by inserting fill characters after the value
	ios::right	Right justifies the next argument by inserting fill characters before the value
	ios::internal	Fill characters are added after any leading sign or base indication, but before the value
ios::skipws	0	Extraction will not skip white spaces
	ios::skipws	Extraction will skip white spaces (default)

All I/O operations of a stream object are aborted if its error state is not zero. Users can check the error state of a stream object via the *ios::bad* or *ios::fail* function, or by using the overloaded "!" operator. The following sample statements illustrate how this is done:

```
if (!cin || !cout) cerr << "I/O error detected";
if (!(cout << x) || x<0) cout.clear(ios::badbit | cout.rdstate());
if (cout.fail()) clog << "cout fails\n";
```

A stream object's error state can be reset via the *ios::clear* function:

```
if (!cin) cin.clear();
```

Besides dealing with error states, the *ios* class functions are also used to set data formatting options of stream objects. The data formatting features provided by the *ios* class are as powerful as those provided by the C *printf* class functions.

The following example program illustrates the use of these *ios* functions:

```
// source module: ios.C
#include <iostream.h>
int main()
{
        int x = 1024;
        double y= 200.0;
        static char str[80] = "Hello";
        cout.setf( ios::showbase I ios::showpos I ios::uppercase );
        cout.setf( ios::scientific, ios::floatfield );
        cout.precision(8);
        cout << "'";
        cout.width(10);
        cout.fill('*');
        cout  << x << "', y='" << y << "'\n";
        cout << "'";
        cout.width(7);
        cout.setf(ios::left,ios::adjustfield);
        cout.setf(ios::fixed, ios::floatfield );
        cout << x << "', y='" << y << "'\n";
        cout << "'";
        cout.width(8);
        cout.setf(ios::right,ios::adjustfield);
        cout << str << "'\n";
}
```

In the above example, the *ios::setf (ios::scientific, ios::floatfield)* and the *ios::precision(8)* set the display format for floating point data in scientific notation with a precision of eight, respectively. The *ios::setf (ios::fixed, ios::floatfield)* statement, on the other hand, sets the display format for floating point value to be fixed point notation. Note that once a display format is set for an object, the setting is unchanged until it is overridden by the next *ios::setf* call.

The rest of the example should be quite self-explanatory. The compilation and sample output of the program is:

```
%     CC ios.C -o ios; ios
'*****+1024', y='+2.00000000E+02'
'+1024**', y='+200.00000000'
'***Hello'
```

3.2   The Manipulators

A manipulator is a function that can be included in an I/O stream class operation to cause some special effects. For example, the flush manipulator is commonly used with *ostream* class objects to force flushing of buffered data held in these objects:

```
cout << "A big day" << flush;
```

A simple manipulator is a function that takes an *istream&* or *ostream&* argument, operates on it in some way, and returns a reference of the object. The following example illustrates the definitions of two manipulators, *tab* and *fld*. The *tab* manipulator inserts a TAB character to an output stream, and the *fld* manipulator sets the display format of an output stream to display integer data in octal format and with the *O* prefix. Furthermore, the minimum field width for displaying a value is 10:

```
ostream& tab(ostream& os)
{
              return os << '\t';
}

ostream& fld(ostream& os)
{
              os.setf(ios::showbase,ios::showbase);
              os.setf( ios::oct, ios:basefiled);
              os.width(10);
              return os;
}
```

The following statements show how to use the manipulators:

```
int x = 50, y = 234;
cout << fld << x << tab << y << '\n';
```

The <iomanip.h> header file declares a set of system-supplied manipulators that are commonly used with stream class objects. Some of these manipulators are:

Manipulator	Function
flush	Forces flushing of data to an output stream
setw(int width)	Sets the minimum field width for the next argument to be inserted and the maximum buffer limit (*width-1*) for the next character string extraction
resetiosflags(long bitFlag) setiosflags(long bitFlag)	Resets or sets the specified format bits in the stream's format state
setprecision(int p)	Sets the precision to *p* for the next real number to be inserted

The following statements show the sample uses of some of these system-supplied manipulators:

```
cout << x << setw(5) << y << flush;        // force flushing of cout
cin   >> resetiosflags(ios::skipws)        // No white spaces skipping
      >> c
      >> setiosflags(ios::skipws);         // Skip white spaces
cout <<  setprecision(8) << Dval;          // set precision
```

3.3   The File I/O classes

The <fstream.h> header declares the *ifstream, ofstream*, and *fstream* classes for file manipulation. These classes provide functionality that is equivalent to the *fopen, fread, fwrite*, and *fclose*, etc. C stream files functions.

Specifically, the *ifstream* class is derived from the *istream* class, and it enables users to access files and read data from them. The *ofstream* class is derived from the *ostream* class, and it enable users to access files and write data to them. Finally, the *fstream* class is derived from both the *ifstream* and *ofstream* classes. It enable users to access files for both data input and output.

The constructors of the *ifstream* and *ofstream* classes are defined in the <fstream.h> header as:

```
ifstream::ifstream();
ifstream::ifstream( const char* name, int open_mode=ios::in,
                        int prot = filebuf::openprot /* 0644 */);
ofstream::ofstream();
ofstream::ofstream( const char* name, int open_mode=ios::out,
                        int prot = filebuf::openprot);
```

The possible values of the *open_mode* argument and their meanings are:

Open mode	Meaning
ios::in	Opens a file for read
ios::out	Opens a file for write
ios::app	Appends new data to end of file. This implies *ios::out*
ios::ate	A seek to the end of file is performed after the file is opened. This does not imply *ios::out*
ios::nocreate	Returns an error if the file does not exist
ios::noreplace	Returns an error if the file already exists
ios::trunc	If a file exists, truncates its previous content. This mode is implied with *ios::out* if it is not specified with *ios::app* or *ios::ate*

The *prot* argument specifies the default access permission to be assigned to a file if it is created by the constructor function. The default value *filebuf::openprot* is 0644, which means read-write for a file owner, and read-only for anyone else. This argument value is not used when a file to be opened by the constructor already exists.

The following sample statements illustrate the use of the *ifstream* and *ofstream* classes. In the example, a file called *from* is opened for read, and another file called *to* is opened for write. If both files are opened successfully, the content of the *from* file is copied to that of the *to* file. If either file cannot be opened successfully, an error is flagged:

```
ifstream source ("from");
ofstream target("to");
if (!source || !target)
    cerr << "Error: File 'from' or 'to' open failed\n";
else for (char c=0; target && source.get(c); )
    target.put(c);
```

Besides the member functions inherited from the *iostream* classes, the *ifstream, ofstream,* and *fstream* classes also define their own specific functions:

Function	Meaning
void open(const char* fname, int mode, int prot=openprot)	Attaches the stream object to the named file
void close()	Closes the file to which the stream object is attached
void attach(int fd)	Attaches the stream object to the stream referenced by the file descriptor *fd*
filebuf* rdbuf()	Returns a *filebuf* array associated with the stream object

The following is a simple program to illustrate the use of the *open, close,* and *attach* functions that are unique to the *fstream* classes:

```
#include <iostream.h>
#include <fstream.h>
int main(int argc, char *argv[])
{
    ifstream source;
    if (argc ==1 || *argv[1]=='-')
        source.attach(0);                    // attach to stdin
    else source.open(argv[1],ios::in);
    ...
    if (source.rdbuf()->is_open)
        source.close();                      // Close the file if it is opened
}
```

Finally, random file I/O may be performed using the *seekg* and *tellg* functions that the *fstream* classes inherited from the *iostream* classes. The following example statements illustrate how these functions are used:

```
fstream tmp("foo",ios::inlios::out);
streampos pos = tmp.tellg();        // remember file location
...
tmp.seekg(pos);                     // return to previous location
...
tmp.seekg(-10, ios::end);           // Goto 10 bytes from EOF
tmp.seekg(0, ios::beg);             // Rewind to beginning of file
tmp.seekg (20, ios::cur);           // Move 20 byte ahead
```

3.4   The strstream Classes

The <strstream.h> header defines the *istrstream, ostrstream,* and *strstream* classes for incore formatting. These classes provide functions that are equivalent to the *sprintf* and *sscanf* C library functions. The advantages of using these classes over the *sprintf* and *sscanf* functions are that these classes may be overloaded to work with user-defined classes and they allow the C++ compiler to do type-checking on programs at compile time.

The *istrstream* class is derived from the *istream* class, and it enables users to extract formatted data from a character buffer. The *ostrstream* class is derived from the *ostream* class, and it enables users to insert formatted data into a character buffer. Finally, the *strstream* class is derived from both the *istrstream* and *ostrstream* classes. It enables users to extract and insert format data with a character buffer.

The *istrstream, ostrstream,* and *strstream* classes do not declare any member functions that are unique to their classes. The following is an example of incore formatting using these *strstream* classes:

```
// source module: strstream.C
#include <iostream.h>
#include <strstream.h>
main()
{
        double dval;
        int ival;
        char wd[20];
        static char buf[32] = "45.67 99 Hello";

        // dval= 45.67, ival=99, wd="Hello"
        istrstream(buf) >> dval >> ival >> wd;
        ostrstream(buf,sizeof(buf)) << ival << " <- " << dval
                << ',' << wd << '\0';
        cout << buf << endl;                    // "99 <- 45.67,Hi"
}
```

In the above example, the *47.67, 99,* and *Hello* data are extracted from the *buf* variable and assigned to the *dval, ival,* and *wd* variables, respectively, via the i*strstream* class. This is similar to using the C *sscanf* function. In the statement, a temporary *istrstream* class object is created, and it uses *buf* as its internal buffer to perform data extraction.

The *dval, ival,* and *wd* variables values are assigned to *buf* again in a different format, via the *ostrstream* class. This is similar to using the C *sprintf* function. Note that a temporary *ostrstream* class object is created by the statement, and it uses *buf* as its internal buffer for data insertion. Finally, the terminating "\0" character in the statement is needed so that the format string stored in *buf* is NULL-terminated.

The compilation and sample output of the program is:

```
%    CC strstream.C
%    a.out
99 <- 45.67,Hi
```

If no buffer is supplied to an *ostrstream* object's constructor, the object keeps an internal dynamic array to store the input data. Users can access this array by invoking the *ostrstream::str* function. However, once the *ostrstream::str* function is called, the dynamic array is "frozen," which means that no more data can be inserted into the array via the *strstream* object, and the users are responsible for deallocating the array when done.

The following example illustrate the uses of the *ostrstream::str* function:

```cpp
// source module: strstream.C
#include <iostream.h>
#include <fstream.h>
#include <strstream.h>

int main(int argc, char *argv[])
{
    fstream source;
    if (argc ==1 || *argv[1]=='-')
        source.attach(0);                    // attach to stdin
    else source.open(argv[1],ios::in);

    // Read the input stream and store into internal array
    ostrstream str;
    for (char c=0; str && source.get(c); )
        str.put(c);


    // Get the internal array
    char *ptr = str.str();
```

```
        // Doing something to the data in the array
        ...

        // Deallocate the array
        delete ptr;

        // Close the input stream
        source.close();                          // Close the file
    }
```

3.5   Summary

This chapter reviews the C++ I/O stream classes. These classes and their system-defined objects (*cin, cout, cerr,* and *clog*) are used extensively in most C++ programs because they offer more type-checking and are extensible in supporting user-defined classes. Thus, it is advantageous to know the basic, as well as advanced, features of these classes.

The next chapter is a review of some advanced standard C library functions. These functions are not covered by the C++ standard classes or by the UNIX and POSIX application program interface functions, but they are very useful to know and should help users in development of advanced system applications.

Standard C Library Functions

C defines a set of library functions that have no direct correspondence in C++ standard classes or in UNIX and POSIX APIs. These functions provide the following services:

- Data manipulation, conversion, and encryption
- Enabling definition of variable argument functions by users
- Dynamic memory management
- Date and time processing
- Obtaining system information

The major advantages of using the standard C library functions are portability and low maintenance of users' applications. This is because most systems (UNIX or others) that support C provide the same set of standard C library functions. These functions should have the same function prototypes and behave the same on different systems. Furthermore, these library functions do not change constantly; thus, programs that use them are easy to maintain. Finally, ANSI C has standardized some of these library functions, further ensuring the availability of these functions on all ANSI C-compliant systems. Thus, C library functions should be used where applicable to reduce application development time and costs.

This chapter depicts the major ANSI C-defined library functions and a few library functions that are non-ANSI C standard but are widely available on all UNIX systems. The objective of describing these functions is to make users aware of them so that they can make use of these functions to reduce their applications development time and improve the portability and maintenance of their programs.

If portability and maintenance are major concerns of your applications, it is recommended that readers use the C++ standard classes and standard C library functions as much as possible, and use the system APIs only when necessary. However, if your applications are time-critical or require extensive kernel interfacing, use the system APIs more often than the C++ standard classes and standard C library functions.

The standard C library functions are declared in a set of header files that are commonly placed in the */usr/include* directory on UNIX systems. The archive and shared libraries that contain the object code of these library functions are the *libc.a* and *libc.so*, respectively. These libraries are commonly placed in the */usr/lib* directory on UNIX systems.

The next few sections describe the ANSI C library functions as defined in the following header files:

- <stdio.h>
- <stdlib.h>
- <string.h>
- <memory.h>
- <malloc.h>
- <time.h>
- <assert.h>
- <stdarg.h>
- <getopt.h>
- <setjmp.h>

Besides the above, the following headers are not defined in ANSI C but are available on most UNIX systems:

- <pwd.h>
- <grp.h>
- <crypt.h>

These header files declare functions which aid users in accessing UNIX systems' user and group account information, and they are defined in the *libc.a* library on UNIX systems. These headers are also described in this chapter, in case users find them useful in application development.

4.1   <stdio.h>

The <stdio.h> header declares the FILE data type that is used to reference stream files in C programs. There are also a set of macros and functions to support the manipulation of stream files. Examples of these macros and functions, which should already be familiar to readers are:

Stream function/macro	Uses
fopen	Opens a stream file for read and/or write
fclose	Closes a stream file
fread	Reads a block of data from a stream file
fgets	Reads a line of text from a stream file
fscanf	Reads formatted data from a stream file
fwrite	Writes a block of data to a stream file
fputs	Writes a line of text to a stream file
fprintf	Writes formatted data to a stream file
fseek	Re-positions the next read or write location in a stream file
ftell	Returns the current location in a stream file where the next read or write will occur. The return value is the number of bytes offset from the beginning of the file
freopen	Re-uses a stream pointer to reference a new file
fdopen	Converts a file descriptor to a stream pointer
feof	A macro which returns a non-zero value if end-of-file is found in a given stream file, or a zero value otherwise
ferror	A macro which returns a non-zero value if an error or end-of-file has been encountered in a given stream file, or a zero value otherwise
clearerr	A macro which clears the error and end-of-file flags of a given stream file
fileno	A macro which returns the file descriptor associated with a given stream file.

The *freopen* function is often used to redirect the standard input or standard output of an executed program. The function prototype is:

FILE* *freopen* (**const char*** file_name, **const char*** mode, **FILE*** old_stream);

The *file_name* argument is a path name of a new stream to be opened. The *mode* argument specifies the new stream is to be opened for read and/or write. This is the same argument as that used in *fopen*, and the new stream must be opened for access consistent with that of the stream, as referenced by the *old_stream* argument. For example, if an old stream is opened for read-only, so must the new stream be opened. The same is true if the old stream is write-only or read-write. The function attempts to open the new stream of the specified access mode. If the new stream is opened successfully, the old stream is closed, and the stream pointer *old_stream* is set to reference the new stream. If the new stream cannot be opened, the *old_stream* is closed regardless. The function returns the *old_stream* value if it succeeds, or a NULL value if it fails.

The following example program emulates the UNIX *cp* (copy file) command. The program takes two file path names as arguments, and it copies the content of the file specified by the first argument (*argv[1]*) to the file specified in the second argument (*argv[2]*). Note that instead of using two stream pointers to reference the two files, the *stdin* and *stdout* stream pointers are set to reference the source and destination files, respectively, via the *freopen* function. Then, data in the source file is read via the *gets* library function and is written to the destination file via the *puts* library function:

```
#include <stdio.h>
int main( int argc, char* argv[] )
{
    if ( argc !=3 )    {
        cerr << "usage: " << argv[0] << " <src> <dest>\n";
        return 1;
    }
    (void)freopen( argv[1], "r", stdin );      // stdin references source file
    (void)frepen( argv[2],"w",stdout );        // stdout references dest. file
    for ( char buf[256]; gets( buf ); )
        puts( buf );
    return 0;
}
```

The *fdopen* function converts a file descriptor to a stream pointer. File descriptors are used in UNIX APIs to access files. Unlike stream pointers, they do not provide data buffering services. If users wish to do I/O data buffering, they may use this function to convert a file descriptor to a stream pointer. The *fdopen* function prototype is:

FILE* *fdopen* (**const int** file_desc, **const char*** mode);

The *file_desc* argument is a file descriptor to be converted. The *mode* argument specifies the access mode of the new stream pointer to be created. The possible *mode* values are the same as those for the *fopen* call and must be consistent with the way the *file_desc* descriptor was opened. Specifically, if a given file descriptor is opened for read-only, the *mode* value should be *"r."* Similarly, if a given file descriptor is for write-only, the *mode* value should be *"w."* The function returns a new stream pointer if it succeeds or a NULL pointer if it fails. One possible cause of failure is the *mode* argument value is inconsistent with the a *file_desc* descriptor access mode.

The following sample function illustrates one possible implementation of the *fopen* function by using *fdopen*:

```
FILE* fopen ( const char* file_name, const char* mode )
{
        int fd, access_mode;
        /* convert mode to integer valued access_mode */
        if (( fd = open( file_name, access_mode, 0666 )) < 0 )
            return NULL;
        return fdopen ( fd, mode );
}
```

In the above example, the character string mode argument is converted to an integer-valued access mode flag. The *open* API is then called to open a file that is named by the *file_name* argument, and the returned file descriptor is stored in *fd*. The function converts *fd* to a stream pointer via the *fdopen* call and returns that stream pointer as the return value.

The *fdopen* call is also used in other situations, such as the implementation of the *popen* function. This will be depicted in Chapter 8.

Finally, the <stdio.h> header also declares the *popen* and *pclose* functions. These functions are used to execute a shell command within a user program. This is very useful in enabling user programs to perform system functions conveniently, and some of these functions cannot be done via any standard library function or system API.

The function prototypes of the *popen* and *pclose* functions are:

```
FILE* popen ( const char shell_cmd, const char* mode );
int pclose ( FILE* stream_ptr );
```

The *shell_cmd* argument of the *popen* function is a user-defined shell command. It can be any command that can be executed on a command line by a shell. Users may specify input redirection, output redirection, or command pipes in the command. In UNIX, the function invokes a Bourne shell to execute the command. Furthermore, the *mode* argument value may be *"r"* or *"w"*, which specifying the function to return a stream pointer for users to read the standard input data or to write data to the standard output, respectively, of the to-be-executed command. The function returns NULL if the command cannot be executed, or a stream pointer if it succeeds. Note that the *popen* function creates an *unnamed pipe* for passing data between a process calling *popen* and the executed command. Unnamed pipes are discussed in Chapter 7.

The *pclose* function is called to close a stream pointer that is obtained from *popen*. It also makes sure the executed command is terminated properly. The implementation of the *popen* and *pclose* function is explained in Chapter 8, when the UNIX process APIs are discussed.

The following example program, *ps.C*, displays all executing processes on a UNIX system that are owned by the user *root*:

```
#include <stdio.h>
int main ()
{
        /* execute the command */
        FILE * cmdp = popen( "ps -ef | grep root","r" );
        if ( !cmdp )    {
           perror ( "popen" );
           return 1;
        }
        char result [256] ;
        /* now read the "grep" command outputs */
        while ( fgets( result, sizeof(result), cmdp ) )
           fputs( result, stdout );              // echo each line read

        pclose( cmdp );                          // close the stream
        return 0;
}
```

4.2   <stdlib.h>

The <stdlib.h> header declares a set of functions for data conversion, random number generation, get and set shell environment variables, program execution control, and execution of shell commands. These functions were traditionally declared in the <stdio.h> header, but because they do not involve stream manipulation, they are grouped into a separate header by the ANSI C standard.

The *system* function declared in the <stdlib.h> header performs a function similar to the *popen* function, except that users can access the standard output or standard input of the executed command. The function prototype of the *system* function is:

```
int system ( const char* shell_cmd );
```

The *shell_cmd* argument is a character string that contains a user-defined shell command. The command may be anything that is legally entered on a shell command line of a given system. Furthermore, input redirection, output redirection, and command pipes may be specified in a *shell_cmd*. In UNIX, the function invokes a Bourne-shell to execute the command. The function returns a zero value if it succeeds and a nonzero value if the execution of a given command fails. For example, the following statement executes the shell commands: *cd /bin ; ls -l | sort -b | wc > /tmp/wc.out*:

```
if (system ( "cd /bin; ls -l | sort -b | wc > /tmp/wc.out" ) == -1)
        perror( "system ");
```

This executes the commands in the same manner as if they were entered in a UNIX console. Note that because the *system* function invokes Bourne shell as a subshell to execute a *shell_cmd*, any definition of shell variables or change of work directory in a *shell_cmd* is not effective when the *system* function call returns.

The following *mini-shell.C* program emulates a UNIX shell. It takes one or more lines of commands from a user. For each input command line, it calls *system* to execute the command. The program terminates when end-of-file is encountered in the standard input:

```
#include <iostream.h>
#include <stdlib.h>
int main()
{
        char  cmd[256];
        for ( ; ; )        {
                /* show a mini-shell prompt */
                cout << "*> " << flush;
                /* Get a user's input. Quit if EOF */
                if ( !cin.getline( cmd, 256 ) ) break;

                /* Execute the user command */
                if ( system( cmd ) == -1 ) perror( cmd );
        }
```

```
            return 0;
    }
```

The following functions are defined in the <stdlib.h> header and convert data from character strings to other C data values, such as double, long, int, etc.:

```
int       atoi (const char* str_val );
double    atof ( const char str_val );
long      atol ( const char* str_val );
double    strtod( const char* str_val, char ** endptr );
long      strtol ( const char* str_val, char** endptr, int radix );
unsigned long strtoul (const char* str_val, char**endptr, int radix );
```

Each of the above functions converts a numerical string specified in *str_val* into its actual data value (float, double, long, or unsigned long) and returns that value. If the *endptr* argument is present and its value is an address of a character pointer, that pointer is set to point to a location in *str_val* where the conversion ends. If the conversion fails, the pointer is set to *str_val,* and the function returns a zero value. The *radix* argument specifies the base of the numerical string stored in *str_val*.

C and C++ provide the *sscanf* function and the *istrstream* class, respectively, to perform operations similar to the above conversion functions. For example, the *atol* function can be written as any one of the following:

```
/* C method */
#include <stdio.h>
long atol ( const char* str_val )
{
    long x;
    if (sscanf( str_val, "%ld", &x ) ==1 )
        return x;
    else return 0;
}

/* C++ method */
#include <strstream.h>
long atol ( const char* str_val )
{
    long x;
    istrstream( str_val,strlen(str_val)+1 ) >> x;
```

```
            return x;
      }
```

The *rand* and *srand* functions, as declared in the <stdlib.h> header, perform random number generation. Their function prototypes are:

```
      int rand ( void );
      void srand ( unsigned int seed );
```

The *srand* function obtains a *seed* number from the user and sets a starting point for a new sequence of pseudorandom numbers to be returned on each subsequent call of *rand*. The sequence of pseudorandom numbers returned by *rand* may be repeated if *srand* is called again with the same *seed* value. If *rand* is called before *srand*, the default *seed* value is 1. The integer numbers returned by *rand* are in the range of 0 to 2^{15} - 1. If a user wishes to restrict the pseudo-random numbers returned to be in the range of 1 to N (where N is any arbitrary positive integer value), the *rand* call may be modified as:

```
      int    random_num = rand() % N + 1;
```

The following example function returns a random number that is unique on each call:

```
      #include <time.h>
      int get_rand()
      {
            srand( (unsigned)time( 0 ) );
            return rand();
      }
```

In the above example, the *time* function is declared in the <time.h> header. It returns an integer that is the number of seconds elapsed since January 1, 1970 up to the current moment. (This function is described in more detail in a later section when the <time.h> header is discussed). Because the *time* function's return value is unique per call (assuming at least a one-second interval between any two consecutive calls), the *seed* to the *srand* function is also unique and is, thus, the returned random number from *rand*. Random numbers are used extensively in programs that do statistical sampling and analysis.

In addition to the above functions, the <stdlib.h> also declares the following functions that are used in the termination of executed programs:

---

void *exit* (**int** status_code);

int *atexit* (**void** (*cleanup_fnptr)(**void**));

void *abort* (**void**);

The *exit* function should be familiar to readers, as it is used to terminate a user's program (a process) and returns an integer exit status code to a calling shell. By UNIX convention, a *status_code* value of 0 means that the program's execution was successful. Otherwise, the *status_code* value is nonzero.

The *atexit* function may be called to register a user-defined function. This function takes no argument and does not return any value. The function is called by the *exit* function and is supposed to do clean-up work before the calling process is terminated. Multiple functions may be registered in a process via multiple *atexit* function calls, and these functions are invoked, in an order reversed from that registered, when the containing process calls exit.

The *abort* function is called when a process is in a panic state. The function terminates the process, and in UNIX it causes a *core* file to be generated. A *core* file is useful in aiding users to debug an aborted process.

Finally, the *getenv* function is declared in the <stdlib.h> header. This function allows a process to query a shell environment variable value. There is also a *putenv* function that allows a process to define a shell environment variable. However, the *putenv* function is not defined in ANSI C, even though it is available on most UNIX systems. The function prototypes of the *getenv* and *putenv* functions are:

---

char* *getenv* (**const char*** env_name);

int *putenv* (**const char***env_def);

The *env_name* argument value to a *getenv* call is a character string of a shell environment variable name. The function returns a NULL value if a given environment variable is undefined.

The *env_def* argument value to a *putenv* call is a character string that contains an environment variable name, an equal character, and the value to be assigned to the variable. The function returns a zero value if it succeeds, a nonzero value otherwise.

The following statements show the value of the PATH shell environment variable, then sets an environment variable *CC* to have the value of *c++*:

```
char* env = getenv( "PATH" );
cout << "\"PATH\" value is: " << env << '\n';
if ( putenv( "CC=c++" ) )   cerr << "putenv of CC failed\n";
```

2.3   <string.h>

The <string.h> header declares a set of functions for character string manipulations. These functions are well known to C and C++ programmers and are used in almost every C program that deals with character strings. The commonly used string functions are:

```
int     strlen    (const char* str );
int     strcmp   ( const char* str1, const char* str2);
int     strncmp ( const char* str1, const char* str2, const int n);
char*   strcat   (char* dest, const char* src);
char*   strncat  ( char* dest, const char* src, const int n);
char*   strcpy   ( char* dest, const char* src);
char*   strncpy  ( char* dest, const char* src, const int n);
char*   strchr   ( const char* str, const char ch);
char*   strrchr  ( const char* str, const char ch);
char*   strstr   ( const char* str, const char* key);
char*   strpbrk  ( const char* str1, const char* delimit);
```

The uses of these string functions are:

Function	Use
strlen	Returns the number of characters of the NULL-terminated *str* argument. The NULL character is not counted in the return value
strcmp	Compares the equality of the *str1* and *str2* arguments. This function returns zero if the two strings are the same, nonzero otherwise
strncmp	Compares up to *n* characters of the *str1* and *str2* argument strings for equality. The function returns zero if the result is a match, nonzero otherwise
strcat	Concatenates the *src* argument string to the *dest* argument string. The resultant *dest* string is appended a NULL character. The function returns the address of the *dest* argument string
strncat	Concatenates up to *n* characters of the *src* argument string to the *dest* argument string. The result-

	ant *dest* string is NULL-terminated. The function returns the address of the *dest* argument string
strcpy	Overrides the content of the *dest* argument string by the *src* argument string, including the terminating NULL character. The function returns the address of the *dest* argument string
strncpy	Overrides the first *n* characters of the *dest* argument string by the *src* argument string. If the *src* argument string's size is equal to or larger than *n,* the NULL character is not copied over. The function returns the address of the *dest* argument string
strchr	Searches the *str* argument for the first occurrence of the *ch* character. The function returns the address of the *ch* character in the *str* string, or NULL if *ch* is not found
strrchr	Searches the *str* argument for the last occurrence of the *ch* character. The function returns the address of the *ch* character in the *str* string or NULL if *ch* is not found
strstr	Searches the *str* argument for the first occurrence of the *key* character string. The function returns the address of the *key* string in *str* sting or NULL if the *key* string is not found
strpbrk	Searches the *str* argument for the occurrence of any character as specified in the *delimit* argument. The function returns the address of the matched character in the *str* string or NULL if there is no match

Besides the above functions, the following sections describe a few useful functions that are not commonly known by C and C++ programmers:

4.3.1   strspn, strcspn

The *strspn* and *strcspn* function prototypes are:

```
const char*  strspn ( char*str, const char* delimit);
const char*  strcspn ( char*str, const char* delimit);
```

The *strspn* function returns the number of leading characters in *str* that are specified in the *delimit* argument. This function is useful in skipping leading delimiting characters in a string. The following example returns the address of the next nonwhite space character in the input argument *buf*:

```
#include <string.h>
char* skip_spaces ( char* buf )
{
      return buf + strspn( buf, "   \t\n" );
}
```

The *strcspn* function returns the number of leading characters in *str* that are not speci-fied in the *delimit* argument. This function is useful in finding the next delimiting character in a character string. The following example returns the next white-space delimited token in the input argument *buf*:

```
#include <string.h>
char* get_token ( char* buf )
{
      char* ptr = buf + strspn( buf," \n\t" );        // find beginning of a token
      char *endptr = ptr + strcspn( ptr," \n\t" );   // find delimiter after token
      if ( endptr > ptr ) *endptr = '\0';
      if ( *ptr )
            return ptr;                                // return token
      else return NULL;                                // end of string. No token
}
```

4.3.2   strtok

The *strtok* function prototype is:

```
const char* strtok ( char*str, const char* delimit);
```

This function breaks the *str* argument into one or more tokens. Each token is delimited by characters as specified in the *delimit* argument. If the *str* argument is an address of a char-acter string, the *strtok* function returns the first token in the string. If, however, the *str* argu-ment is a NULL value, the function returns the next token in a previously given string.

This function returns NULL if there are no more tokens to be returned from a string.

The following example breaks a string into tokens that are delimited by white-space characters. Each token obtained is printed to the standard output:

```cpp
#include <iostream.h>
#include <string.h>
int main ( int argc, char* argv[] )
{
    while ( --argc > 0 )
        for ( char* tok; tok = strtok( argv[argc], "  \n\t" ); argv[argc]= 0 )
            cout << "tok: " << tok << endl;
}
```

Note that the *strtok* function modifies the input *str* argument by replacing delimiting characters after tokens in *str* with the NULL character. Users who wish to reuse character strings to be parsed by *strtok* should make a copy of these strings so that they can use the copied strings later.

The following example illustrates a possible implementation of the *strtok* function. Note that the function has a static pointer, *lptr,* to remember where to parse the next token in either a new or an old string. Furthermore, if the function finds a delimiting character after a token, it replaces the delimiter by a NULL character. Thus, the function modifies the input character string as it extracts tokens from it.

```cpp
#include <string.h>
char* my_strtok ( char* str, const char* delimit )
{
    static char* lptr;
    if ( tr )   {                               // start parsing a new string
        str += strspn( str,delimit );           // skip leading delimiters
        if (!*str ) return NULL;                // done if it is a NULL string
        lptr = str;
    }
    else ( !lptr )                              // continue to parse old string
        return NULL;                            // return if no more token

    char* tokn = lptr + strspn( lptr, "  \t\n" );   // skip leading delimiter
    lptr = tokn + strcspn( tokn,"   \t\n" );        // find next delimiter
    if ( *tokn && lptr > tokn )
        *lptr++ = '\0';                             // NULL-terminate token
```

```
        else lptr = NULL;                    // find last token in a string
        return *tokn ? tokn : NULL;          // return token, if any
}
```

4.3.3   strerror

The *strerror* function prototype is:

```
        const char*  strerror ( int errno );
```

This function can be used to get a system diagnostic message. The *errno* argument value may be any error code as defined in the <sys/errno.h> header file, or may be the global *errno* variable. The global *errno* variable is set whenever a system API is called, and its value is zero if the API execution is successful, nonzero otherwise.

The return character string is read-only and should not be deallocated by users.

The *perror* function may be called to print a system diagnostic message if any system API call fails. The *strerror* function allows users to define their own version of the *perror* function.

The following example depicts one possible implementation of the *perror* function using *strerror:*

```
        #include <iostream.h>
        #include <string.h>

        void my_perror ( const char* msg_header )
        {
            if (msg_header && strlen(msg_header)) // print if it is defined by a user
                cerr << msg_header << ": " << strerror( errno ) << endl;
            else cerr << strerror(errno ) << endl;
        }

        /* test program for my_perror function */
        int main( int argc, char* argv[] )
        {
            FILE *fp;
            while ( --argc > 0 )                 // for each cmd line argument
```

```
            if ( (fp = fopen( *++argv, "r" )) )      // fp=0 if open fails
                my_perror( *argv );                  // print a diagnostic
            else fclose ( fp );                      // close file if is opened OK
        return 0;
    }
```

4.4   <memory.h>

The <memory.h> header declares a set of functions for byte stream manipulations. These functions are more similar to the string functions, except that they have a more general purpose and can be used for noncharacter string object manipulation. For example, one can use these functions to initialize, compare, and copy struct-typed objects.

The functions declared in the <memory.h> header are:

```
void*    memset   (const void* memp, int ch, size_t len );
int      memcmp   ( const void* mem1, const void* mem2, size_t len );
void*    memcpy   (void* dest, const void* src, size_t len );
void*    memccpy  ( void* dest, const void* src, const int ch, size_t len);
void*    memchr   ( const void* memp, const int ch, size_t len );
```

The *memset* function initializes the first *len* bytes of a memory region pointed to by *memp*. The memory is initialized with the *ch* byte throughout. The function returns the address of *memp*.

The following statements illustrate the initialization of a *struct stat*-typed variable to contain all NULL data:

```
struct stat *statp = new stat;
if (statp)
    (void)memset( (void*)statp, NULL, sizeof( struct stat ) );
```

The *bzero* function in BSD UNIX initializes a memory region to all zero bytes. This function may be implemented via the *memset* function as:

```
void bzero ( char *memp, int len )
{
    (void) memset( memp, NULL,(size_t)len );
}
```

The *memcmp* function compares the equality of the first *len* bytes of two memory regions pointed to by *mem1* and *mem2*. The function returns zero if the two memory regions are identical in the first *len* bytes, a positive value if the *mem1* region contains data that are lexicographically greater than those of *mem2*, or a negative value if the *mem1* region contains data that are lexicographically less than those of *mem2*.

The following statements compare the equality of two *struct stat*-typed variables:

```
int cmpstat ( struct stat* statp1, struct stat* statp2 )
{
        return memcmp( (void*)statp1, (void*)statp2, sizeof( struct stat ) );
}
```

The *strcmp* function may be implemented via the *memcmp* function as follows:

```
int my_strcmp (const char* str1, const char* str2 )
{
        int len1 = strlen( str1 ), len2 = strlen( str2 );
        if ( len1 > len2 ) len1 = len2;
        return memcmp( (void*)str1, (void*)str2, len1 );
}
```

Furthermore, the BSD UNIX *bcmp* function may also be implemented via the *memcmp* function:

```
#define bcmp ( s1, s2, n )    memcmp( (void*)s1, (void*)s2, (size_t)n )
```

The *memcpy* function copies the first *len* bytes of data from the memory region pointed to by *src* to the memory region pointed to by *dest*. The function returns the address of the *dest* memory region.

The BSD UNIX *bcopy* function may also be implemented via the *memcpy* function:

```
#define bcopy ( src, dest, n ) memcpy( (void*)dest, (void*)src, (size_t)n )
```

Note that the *bcopy, bcmp,* and *bzero* functions are not defined in the ANSI C standard, but they are widely used in UNIX system programs.

The *memcpy* function may be used to implement the *strcpy* function:

```
#define strcpy( dest, src )    \
        memccpy( (void*)dest, (void*)src, '\0', (size_t)strlen( src ) )
```

The *memccpy* function copies data from a memory region pointed to by *src* to a memory region pointed to by *dest*. The function either copies the first *len* bytes of data from *src* to *dest* or wait until the *ch* byte that is found within the first *len* byte of *src* is copied to *dest*.

The *memccpy* function may be used to implement the *strncpy* function:

```
#define strncpy( dest, src, n ) \
        memccpy ( (void*)dest, (void*)src, '\0', (size_t)n )
```

Finally, the *memchr* function searches the first *len* byte of a memory region pointed to by *memp* and returns the address of the first occurrence of *ch* in that region, or NULL if there is no match. The *memchr* function may be used to implement the *strchr* function:

```
#define strchr(str,ch)      memchr( (void*)str, ch, (size_t)strlen( str ) )
```

4.5   <malloc.h>

The <malloc.h> header declares a set of functions for dynamic memory allocation and disposal. These functions are not used extensively by C++ programmers, as they use the *new* and *delete* operators to perform the same functions. However, the *realloc* function declared in the <malloc.h> header can be used to adjust the size of any dynamic memory, and this feature is not provided by the C++ *new* operator. This section explains in detail the use of *realloc*.

The functions declared in the <malloc.h> header are:

```
void*    malloc (const size_t size );
void*    calloc ( const size_t num_record, const size_t size_per_record );
void     free   ( void* memp );
void*    realloc ( void* old_memp, const size_t new_size );
```

The uses of *malloc, calloc*, and *free* should be familiar to users already. Specifically, the following statements both allocate a dynamic memory of size 1048 bytes:

```
char* mem1 = (char*)malloc( 1048 ) );        // C style
```

```
    char* nem2 = new char [ 1048 ];              // C++ style
```

The *calloc* function is similar to *malloc*, except that it guarantees that the allocated memory is initialized with the zero byte.

The *free* function is similar to the *delete* operator, and they both deallocate dynamic memory. For example, the following statement discards dynamic memory referenced by a variable called *mem1*:

```
    free ( mem1 );
```

The *realloc* function is used to adjust the size of any dynamic memory allocated by *malloc* or *calloc*. It is very useful in managing a dynamic array that may change size in the course of a process execution. For example, a program that stores any user input from the standard input has no way of knowing ahead of time how many lines of data will be obtained from a user. A dynamic array may be used in this situation to allocate just the exact amount of memory, via the *realloc* function, to store the user input at any time.

Note that in the above example, the process may also use a linked-list or a fixed-size array to store the user's input. The drawbacks of the linked-list approach, as compared to using an array (static or dynamic), are: Because each linked-list record requires storage for a next pointer, it consumes more memory that does an array with the same number of entries. Furthermore, linked-lists setup and traversal are generally more time-consuming that are accessing data from arrays. The drawback of using a fixed-size array as compared to using a dynamic array is that it requires preallocation of all the memory to store the maximum allowed input data; thus, it is not as efficient in memory usage as dynamic arrays. Moreover, this approach imposes a maximum amount of input data allowed and may be too restrictive to users. Using a dynamic array, no such limit is necessary. In summary, dynamic arrays are preferred over linked-lists when the data stored are accessed frequently and when the order of the stored data does not change. Also dynamic arrays are preferred over static arrays if the size of an array may change (increase or decrease) over time and if it is not practical to set an upper limit on the size of an array.

The *realloc* function takes two arguments.The first argument, *old_memp*, contains an address of a dynamic memory region previously allocated. The second argument, *new_size*, is the size, in bytes, of a new dynamic memory region to be returned. The *new_size* value may be larger or smaller than the size of the old memory region as referenced by *old_memp*. The *realloc* function attempts to adjust the old dynamic memory region size to be *new_size*. If this cannot be achieved, a new dynamic memory region of size *new_size* is allocated. The function then copies data from the old memory region to the new memory region, up to the maximum size of the old or the new memory region (whichever is less), and the old memory region is deallocated by the function. If the new memory region size is larger than the old one, the content of the memory in the new one that is not initialized by the old memory data is undefined.

The following *malloc.C* program depicts the use of *realloc* to store a user's input data from the standard input:

```cpp
#include <iostream.h>
#include <string.h>
#include <malloc.h>
int main()
{
        char** inList = 0, buf[256];
        int numIn = 0, max_size = 0;
        /* get all input lines from a user */
        while (cin.getline(buf, sizeof(buf) )) {
           if ( ++numIn > max_size )  {
               max_size += 2;
               if ( !inList )
                   inList = (char**)calloc( max_size,sizeof(char*) );
               else
                   inList = (char**)realloc( inList,sizeof(char*)*max_size );
           }
           /* store an input line */
           inList[numIn-1] = (char*)malloc( strlen( buf )+1 );
           strcpy( inList[numIn-1], buf );
        }
        /* now print back all input lines from a user */
        while ( --numIn >= 0 )    {
           cout << numIn << ": " << inList[numIn] << endl;
           free( inList[numIn] );
        }
        free ( inList );
        return 0;
}
```

The above sample program reads input lines from the standard input. As it reads each input line it stores it into the *inList* array. The size of the *inList* array is adjusted dynamically based on the actual number of input lines read. The *max_size* and *numIn* variables contain the current size of the *InList* array and the number of input lines actually read, respectively. If the *numIn* value is the same as that of *max_size* and a new input line is read, the *max_size* value is increased by two, and the *inList* array size is enlarged by two more entries via the *realloc* function call.

After all input lines are read and end-of-file is encountered from the standard input, the sample program prints all saved lines to the standard output, in an order reverse to that found and deallocates all dynamic memory along the way.

Note that in the sample program, when the *inList* variable is first allocated, it is done via a *calloc* call. This is because if one attempts to allocate dynamic memory via *realloc* as:

```
char* memp = (char*)realloc( 0, new_size );
```

on some UNIX systems the *realloc* function will segmentation fault (e.g., Sun OS 4.1.x), whereas on other systems the function will work. Thus, to ensure portability, one should avoid assigning a NULL as the first argument value to any *realloc* call.

Finally, the dynamic memory allocated via *malloc, calloc,* and *realloc* may be managed differently than that allocated by the *new* operator. This means that memory allocated by *malloc, calloc,* or *realloc* should be deallocated via the *free* function only, and that allocated by the *new* operator should be discarded by the *delete* operator.

4.6   <time.h>

The <time.h> header declares a set of functions for system clock query. They can be used to obtain the local and the Universal Standard Time (UTC) date/time, as well as statistics of cpu (central processing unit) uses of processes.

The functions declared in the <time.h> header are:

time_t	*time*	(**time_t*** timv);
const char*	*ctime*	(**const time_t*** timv);
struct tm*	*localtime*	(**const time_t*** timv);
struct tm*	*gmtime*	(**const time_t*** timv);
const char*	*asctime*	(**const tm*** tm_p);
time_t	*mktime*	(**struct tm*** tm_p);
clock_t	*clock*	(**void**);

The *time* function returns the number of seconds elapsed since the official birthday of UNIX: January 1, 1970. The *time_t*-typed result is passed via the *timv* argument and via the function's return value if it is not NULL.

The c*time* function returns the local date and time in the following example format:

"Sun Sept. 16 01:03:52 1995\n"

The *ctime* function is almost always used with the *time* function to obtain the local date/time:

```
time_t timv = time( 0 );
cout << "local time: " << ctime ( &timv );
```

The *localtime* and *gmtime* functions take an address of a *time_t*-typed variable and returns an address of a read-only *struct tm*-typed record. The *time_t*-typed input variable should be set by a prior time function call, and the returned *struct tm*-typed record contains the local and UTC date/time information, respectively. The *struct tm*-typed record may be passed to the *asctime* function to obtain a character string of the time stamp in the same format as that of the *ctime* returned value. The *struct tm* data type is defined in the <time.h> header.

The following statements illustrate the use of these functions:

```
#include <time.h>
time_t timv = time( 0 );
struct tm *local_tm = localtime( &timv );
struct tm *gm_tm = gmtime( &timv );
cout << "local time stamp: " << asctime( local_tm );
cout << "UTC time stamp: " << asctime ( gm_tm );
```

The following function returns the time stamp of any number of hours before or after the current time:

```
const char* time_stamp( long offset_hours )
{
        time_t timv = time ( 0 );               // get current time
        timv += offset_hours * 60 * 60;         // covert offset to sec
        return ctime( & timv );                 // return offset time stamp
}
```

The *mktime* function is the inverse of the *localtime* and *gmtime* functions. It takes an address of a *struct tm*-typed record and returns a *time_t* value for it. Furthermore, the *mktime* functions normalize the data in the input argument to make them within range. The function is useful in getting the time stamp of any arbitrary date from 00:00:00 UTC, January 1, 1970 to 03:14:07 UTC, January 19, 2038, inclusively.

For example, the following program depicts the day of the week for April 5, 1999:

```cpp
#include <iostream.h>
#include <time.h>
static struct tm time_str;                    // initializes all fields to 0
main()
{
        time_t tmv;
        time_str.tm_year    = 1999 - 1900;     // year = 1999
        time_str.tm_mon     = 4 - 1;           // mon = April
        time_str.tm_mday    = 5;               // day = 5
        if ( ( tmv=mktime(&time_str )) != -1 )    {
                timv[3] = NULL;
                cout << timv << endl;          // should print "Mon"
        }
}
```

The definition of the *clock* function's return value may vary on different systems. The ANSI C standard defines the *clock* function returns the number of microseconds elapsed since a calling process started executing. However, on some UNIX systems, the *clock* function's return value is the number of microseconds elapsed since the process first called the *clock* function. Users should consult their system programmer's reference manual or the *clock* man page on their system for the exact definition.

However, the following *clock.C* program illustrates the correct use of the *clock* function to monitor process executing time, regardless of how the function is implemented on a given system:

```cpp
#include <iostream.h>
#include <time.h>

main()
{
        time_t clock_tick = CLOCKS_PER_SECOND;
        clock_t start_time = clock();          // start timer

        /* do the normal work of the process ...*/
```

```
        clock_t elapsed_time = clock() - start_time;
        cout << "Run time: " << (elapsed_time / clock_tick) << endl;
}
```

4.7   <assert.h>

The <assert.h> header declares a macro that can be used to assert some conditions in a process that should always be true. If, however, an assertion error occurs during a process execution, the macro flags an error message to the standard error port and indicates that physical line in which the source file assertion failed. After that, the macro aborts the process.

Thus, the *assert* macro can be a substantial time saver in helping users to debug their programs for checking "should not have occurred" conditions. Furthermore, the assert macros can be taken out in a released product just by specifying the -DNDEBUG switch when compiling the source code of the product.

The following a*ssert.C* example statements illustrate the use of the *assert* macro:

```
#include <fstream.h>
#include <string.h>
#include <assert.h>
int main( int argc, char* argv[] )
{
        assert ( argc > 1 );                        // should have 1 arg
        ifstream ifs( argv[1] );
        assert( ifs.good() );                       // should be opened OK
        char *nam = new char[strlen(argv[1])+1];
        assert( nam );                              // should not be NULL
}
```

When the *assert.C* program is compiled and run with no argument, the console output is:

```
%    cc assert.C -o assert ; assert
Assertion failed: file "assert.C", line 5
```

The *assert* macro is defined in the <assert.h> as:

```
#ifndef NDEBUG
#define assert(ex) { if (!(ex)) { \
        fprintf(stderr,"Assertion failed: file: \"%s\", line %d\n", \
                __FILE__, __LINE__ ); exit(1); }
#endif
```

Note that in the above the *assert* is a macro and can be compiled away from users' program by defining the *NDEBUG* manifested constant.

4.8   <stdarg.h>

The <stdarg.h> header declares a set of macros that users may use to define variable argument functions. Examples of variable argument functions are *printf* and *scanf* in C. These functions may be called with one or more actual arguments, and the functions must get all those arguments to function correctly. This is accomplished by making use of the macros defined in the <stdarg.h> header.

The <stdarg.h> header defines the following macros:

```
#define va_start(ap,parm) (ap) = (char*)(&(parm) + 1)
#define va_arg(ap,type) ((type*)((char*)(ap) += sizeof(type)))[-1]
#define va_end(ap)
```

To use the above macros, a function must have one well-defined argument in its prototype. The *va_start* macro is called to set the *ap* argument to contain the location of the run-time stack where the next argument value after *parm* (which is the last known argument of the calling function) resides. The macro does that by taking the address of *parm* and adding the byte offset of the data to which *parm* points. This gives the address of the next function argument value after *parm*.

The *va_arg* is called to extract the next argument value in the run-time stack. For this to work, the caller must know the data type of the next argument on the stack. The *va_arg* macro does two things for each call:

- Advances *ap* to point to a stack location after the next argument to be returned
- Returns the next argument on the stack

For the first task, the operation:

$$(char*)(ap) += sizeof(type)$$

typecasts *ap* to be a character pointer, then adds the size of the next argument data. This, in effect, advances *ap* to point to the address of the argument after the one to be fetched.

The second task is accomplished via the operation:

$$((type*)((char*)(ap) += sizeof(type)))[-1]$$

The above operation typecasts the *ap* that has been newly advanced to be an array of *type*. The *-1* index causes the next argument data on the stack to be returned to the caller. The following diagram illustrates the operations of *va_arg*; the next argument to be returned is assumed to be of type double:

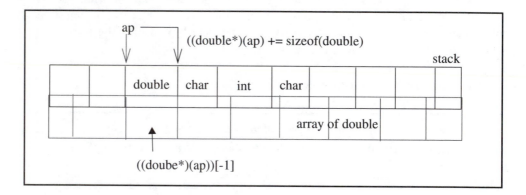

The *va_end* is currently an NOP macro. It is defined to match the *va_start* macro and as a place-holder for any future extension of the *stdarg.h* functionality.

The following *pritnf.C* program contains the *my_printf* function, which emulates the *printf* function:

```
#include <iostream.h>
#include <stdio.h>
#include <stdarg.h>
#include <string.h>
#include <floatingpoint.h>

#define SHOW(s) fputs(s,stdout), cnt+=strlen(s)
```

```
/* my version of printf */
int my_printf ( const char* format, ...)
{
     char *tokp, ifmt[256], *hdr = ifmt, buf[256];
     int  cnt = 0;
     va_list pa;
     strcpy(ifmt,format);              // use local copy of the input text
     va_start(pa,format);              // pa points to args on stack

     while ( tokp=strchr( hdr,'%' ) )     {  // search for the '%' character
         *tokp++ = '\0';
         SHOW( hdr );                  // show leading text up to '%'
         if ( strchr( "dfgeisc%",*tokp )) {  // do if a legal format spec
            switch (*tokp)     {
               case 'd':                        // %i, %d
               case 'i':
                       gconvert( (double)va_arg(pa,int),sizeof(buf),0,buf );
                       break;
               case 's':                 // %s
                       strcpy( buf,va_arg(pa,char*) );
                       break;
               case 'c':                 // %c
                       buf[0] = va_arg( pa,char );
                       buf[1] = '\0';
                       break;
               case 'f':                 // %f
                       gconvert( va_arg( pa,double),8,1,buf );
                       break;
               case 'g':                 // %g
                       gconvert( va_arg( pa,double ),8,0,buf );
                       break;
               case '%':                 // %%
                       strcpy( buf,"%" );
                       break;
            }
            SHOW(buf);                // show the extracted argument
         }
         else     {                   // Show the character as is
              putchar( *tokp );
```

```
                        cnt++;
                 }
                 hdr = tokp + 1;
          }
          SHOW(hdr);                          // show any last trailing text
          va_end( pa );
          return cnt;                         // return the no. of char. printed
   }

   int main()
   {
          int cnt = my_printf( "Hello %% %s %zZZ\n", "world" );
          cout << "No. char: " << cnt << endl;
          cnt = my_printf( "There are %d days in %c year\n", 365, 'A' );
          cout << "No. char: " << cnt << endl;
          cnt = my_printf( "%g x %i = %f\n", 8.8, 8, 8.8*8 );
          cout << "No. char: " << cnt << endl;
          return 0;
   }
```

In the above program, the *gconvert* function converts a double-type value to a character string format. This is a non-ANSI C standard function but is commonly available on most UNIX systems. The function prototype of *gconvert* is:

> char* ***gconvert*** (**double** dval, **int** ndigits, **int** trailing, **char*** buf);

The *dval* argument to *gconvert* contains the double-type value to be converted, and the *buf* argument specifies a user-defined buffer where the converted character string is placed. The *ndigits* argument defines the maximum number of significant digits that the *buf* argument may hold, and the *trailing* argument value may be 0 or 1, which determines whether or not any trailing decimal point or zero should be discarded. The function returns the buffer address as referenced in the *buf* argument.

The compilation and sample output of this test program is:

```
%      cc printf.c -o printf
%      printf
Hello % world zZZ
```

No. of char: 18
There are 365 days in A year
No. of char: 29
8.8 x 8 = 70.400000
No. of char: 20

Associated with the *va_arg* macros are the *vfprintf, vsprint,* and *vprintf* functions. These are similar to the *fprintf, sprintf,* and *printf* functions, respectively, except that they take *ap* as a pointer to the actual arguments of callers. These functions' prototypes are:

int	***vprintf***	*(**const char*** format, **va_list** ap);*
int	***vsprintf***	*(**char*** buf, **const char*** format, **va_list** ap);*
int	***vfprintf***	*(**FILE*** fp, **const char*** format, **va_list** ap);*

These functions can be used to write a general message-reporting function:

```
/* source file: test_vfprintf.c */
#include <stdio.h>
#include <stdlib.h>
#include <stdarg.h>
typedef enum { INFO, WARN, ERROR, FATAL } MSG_TYPE_ENUM;
static int numErr, numWarn, numInfo;

void msg ( const MSG_TYPE_ENUM mtype, const char* format, ... )
{
    switch (mtype)      {
      case INFO:   numInfo++;
                    break;
      case WARN: numWarn++;
                    fputs( "Warning: ",stderr );
                    break;
      case ERROR:numErr++;
                    fputs( "Error: ",stderr );
                    break;
      case FATAL: fputs( "Fatal: ", stderr );
                    break;
    }
    va_list pa;
    va_start( format, ap );
```

```
        vfprintf( stderr, format, pa );
        va_end( ap );
        if (mtype == FATAL ) exit( 2 );
}
/* Tets program for the msg function */
int main()
{
        msg( INFO, "Hello %% %s %%\n", "world" );
        msg( WARN, "There are %d days in %c year\n", 265, "A" );
        msg ( ERROR, "%g x %i = %f\n", 8.8, 8, 8.8*8 );
        msg( FATAL, "Bye-bye\n" );
}
```

The compilation and execution of this test program are:

```
%       cc test_vfprintf.c -o test_vfprintf
%       test_vfprintf
Hello % world %
Warning: There are 365 days in A year
Error: 8.8 x 8 = 70.400000
Fatal: Bye-bye
```

4.9   Command Line Arguments and Switches

The *getopt* function that is declared in the <stdlib.h> header may be used to implement programs that accept UNIX-style command line switches and arguments. Specifically, such programs' invocation syntax must be:

<program_name> [-<switch> ...] [<argument> ...]

All switches (or options) to a program must each begin with a "-" character and then a single letter (e.g., *-o*). Switch letters are case-sensitive. Multiple switches may be stacked such that: *-a -b* switches may be specified as *-ab* or *-ba*. A switch may be followed by an optional argument (e.g., *-o a.out*). If two or more switches are stacked, only the last switch specified may accept an argument. For example: *-o a.out -O* may be specified as *-Oo a.out*, but not as *-oO a.out*.

No switches may be specified after nonswitch arguments to a program. Thus the following invocation is incorrect, as the nonswitch argument */usr/prog/test.c* is specified before the *-o* switch.

```
%    a.out   -l    /usr/prog/test.c -o abc
```

If a program's invocation follows the above rules, the program may use the *getopt* function to extract switches and any of their associated arguments from the command line. The use of this is shown later on.

The *getopt* function and its associated global variables *opterr, optarg,* and *optind* are declared in the <stdlib.h> header:

```
extern int      optind, opterr;
extern char*    optarg;

int getopt ( int argc, char *const* argv[], const char* optstr);
```

The first two arguments to a *getopt* function call are the *argc* and *argv* variables of the *main* function, respectively. The *optstr* argument contains a list of switch letters that are legal to the program. The function scans the *argv* vector and looks for switches that are defined in *optstr*. For each call of *getopt*, the function returns a switch letter that is found in *argv* and is defined in *optstr*. If a switch is specified as *<switch_letter>:* in *optstr,* then the switch, if specified, must be accompanied by an argument, and that argument can be obtained via the *optarg* global pointer.

If a switch is found in *argv* but is not listed in *optstr*, the *getopt* function will flag an error message to the standard error port, and the function returns the "?" character. However, if a user sets the *opterr* global variable to be nonzero before calling *getopt*, the function will be silent for subsequent illegal switches found in *argv*.

Finally, when no more switches are found in *argv*, the *getopt* function returns the EOF value, and *optind* is set to point to the entry in *argv* where the first non-switch command line argument is stored. If *optind* is same as *argc*, there are no nonswitch arguments to a program.

The following *test_getopt.C* program accepts the *-a, -b,* and *-o* switches. If the *-o* switch is specified, there should also be a file name specified with it:

```
#include <iostream.h>
#include <stdio.h>
#include <stdlib.h>
#include <string.h>
static char* outfile;
static int a_flag, b_flag;
```

```
int main( int argc, char* argv[] )
{
     int ch;
     while ( (ch=getopt( argc, argv,"o:ab" )) != EOF )
        switch ( ch )       {
           case 'a':     a_flag = 1;              // found -a
                         break;
           case 'b':     b_flag = 1;              // found -b
                         break;
           case 'o':     outfile = new char[strlen(optarg)+1];
                         strcpy(outfile,optarg);    // found -o <file>
                         break;
           case '?':     /* let getopt flags an eror message */
           default:      break;                   // an illegal switch
        }
     /* no more switches. Scan the rest of non-switch arguments */
     for ( ; optind < argc; optind++ )
        cout << " non-switch argument: " << argv[optind] << endl;

     return 0;
}
```

The compilation and sample runs of the *test_getopt.C* programs are:

```
%    CC   test_getopt.c   -o     test_getopt
%    test_getopt
%    test_getopt   -abo    xyz     /etc/hosts
non-switch argument: /etc/hosts
%    test_getopt   -xay    -bz     /usr/lib/libc.a
a.out: illegal option -- x
a.out: illegal option -- y
a.out: illegal option -- z
 non-switch argument: /usr/lib/libc.a
```

The limitations of *getopt* are: (1) switches must use single letter only; (2) switches must either have associated arguments or none; users cannot define switches that may optionally accept argument; (3) the function does not check the data type of switch arguments; (4) users may not specify mutually exclusive switches.

Despite the above limitations, *getopt* is valuable in saving users program development and debug time, and ensuring that users' programs follow the UNIX invocation convention

4.10   **<setjmp.h>**

The <setjmp.h> header declares a set of functions that allow a process to do *goto* from one function to another. Recalling a C *goto* statement only allows a process to transfer pro-cess flow from one statement to another within the same function. The functions defined in the <setjmp.h> header eliminate this restriction. These functions should be used sparingly. For example, if an error is detected in a deeply recursive function, it makes sense to report the error and then do a *goto* to the main function, so as to start the processing over again. This is what a UNIX shell does if an error is detected in one of its subshells. In this circumstance, the <setjmp.h> functions offer efficient error recovery and save users from adding layers and lay-ers of error-checking code for error recovery. However, like the problem of using *goto*, if these functions are used without discipline in a program, it will become difficult for users to track program flow.

The <setjmp.h> header defines the following functions:

```
int setjmp ( jmp_buf loc );
void longjmp ( jmp_buf loc, int val );
```

The *setjmp* function records a location in a program code where the future *goto* (via the *longjmp* call) will return. The *jmp_buf* data type is defined in the <setjmp.h> header, and the *loc* argument records the location of the *setjmp* statement. If a user wishes to define multiple locations in a program where the future *longjmp* call can return, each location must be recorded in a *jmp_buf*-typed variable and is set by a *setjmp* call.

The *setjmp* function always returns zero when it is called directly in a process.

The *longjmp* function is called to transfer a program flow to a location that was stored in the *loc* argument. The program code marked by *loc* must be in a function that is among the callers of the current function. When the process is "jumping" to that target function, all the stack space used by the current function and its callers up to the target function are discarded by the *longjmp* function. The process resumes execution by reexecuting the *setjmp* statement in the target function that is marked by *loc*. The return value of the *setjmp* function is the *val* value, as specified in the *longjmp* function call. The *val* value should be nonzero (if it is zero, it is set to one by the *setjmp* function) so that it can be used to indicate where and why the *longjmp* function was invoked, and a process can do error-handling accordingly.

The following *test_setjmp.C* program illustrates the use of *setjmp* and *longjmp* functions:

```
/* source file name: test_setjmp.C */
#include <iostream.h>
#include <setjmp.h>
static jmp_buf loc;
int main()
{
        int retcode, foo();

        if ( (retcode=setjmp( loc )) != 0 )     {          // error recovery
            cerr << "Get here from longjmp. retcode=" << retcode << endl;
            return 1;
        }
        /* normal flow of program */
        cout << "Program continue after setting loc via setjmp...\n";
        foo();
        cout << "Should never get here ....\n";
        return 1;
}
int foo()
{
        cout << "Enter foo. Now call longjmp....\n";
        longjmp (loc, 5);
        cout << "Should never gets here....\n";
        return 2;
}
```

The compilation and output of the *test_setjmp.C* program are:

```
%      cc test_setjmp.c    -o test_setjmp
%      test_setjmp
Program continue after setting loc via setjmp...
Enter foo. Now call longjmp....
Get here from longjmp. retcode=5
```

4.11   <pwd.h>

The <pwd.h> defines a set of functions for users to obtain user accountant information, as specified in the UNIX */etc/passwd* file. The functions defined in the <pwd.h> header are:

---

const struct passwd* *getpwnam* (**const char*** user_name);

const struct passwd* *getpwuid*(**const int** uid);

int *setpwent* (**void**);

const struct passwd* *getpwent* (**void**);

int *endpwent* (*void*);

const struct passwd* *fgetpwent* (**FILE** * fptr);

The *struct passwd* data type is defined in the <pwd.h> as:

```
struct passwd
{
        char*           pw_name;           // user's login name
        char*           pw_passwd:         // encrypted password
        int             pw_uid;            // user's user ID
        int             pw_gid;            // user's group ID
        char*           pw_age;            // password aging info
        char*           pw_comment;        // general user's info
        char*           pw_dir;            // user's home directory
        char*           pw_shell;          // user's login shell
};
```

Each *struct passwd* record contains data from one line of the */etc/password* file. This contains the account information of one user on a UNIX system. Specifically, the information consists of a user's login name, assigned user ID, group ID, login shell, home directory, and login password (in encrypted form), etc.

The *getpwnam* function takes a user login name as argument and returns a pointer to a *struct passwd*-typed record that contains that user's information if the user is defined on the system on which this function call is made. Conversely, it returns a NULL pointer if the given user name is invalid.

The following statement depicts the home directory of a user name *joe*:

```
struct passwd *pwd = getpwnam( "joe" );
if ( !pwd )
        cerr << "'joe' is not a valid user on this system\n";
else
        cout << pwd->pw_name << ", home=" << pwd->pw_dir << endl;
```

The *getpwuid* function takes a user *UID* as argument, and returns a pointer to a *struct passwd*-typed record that contains the user's information if the user is defined on the system on which this function call is made. Again, it returns a NULL pointer if the given user *UID* is invalid.

The following statement depicts the user name and login shell of a user whose *UID* is 15:

```
struct passwd *pwd = getpwuid( 15 );
if ( !pwd )
        cerr << "'15' is not a valid UID on this system\n";
else
        cout << pwd->pw_name << ", shell=" << pwd->pw_shell << endl;
```

The *setpwent* function resets an internal file pointer to point to the beginning of the */etc/passwd* file. The *getpwent* function returns a pointer to a *struct passwd*-type record, which contains the next entry of the */etc/passwd* file. When all entries in a */etc/passwd* are scanned by the *getpwent* function, it returns a NULL pointer to indicate end-of-file. The *endpwent* function is called to close the internal file pointer, which references the */etc/passwd* file.

The following *test_pwd.C* program dumps out all defined users and their *UID* and *GID* information to the standard output:

```
#include <iostream.h>
#include <pwd.h>
int main()
{
        setpwent();
        for ( struct passwd *pwd; pwd=getpwent(); )
            cout << pwd->pw_name << ", UID: " << pwd->pw_uid
                << ", GID: " << pwd->pw_gid << endl;
        endpwent();
        return 0;
}
```

Finally, the *fgetpwent* function is like the *getpwent*, except here users supply a file pointer that references a file having the same syntax of the */etc/passwd* file. The function returns an user accountant data at the next entry in the given file. The *setpwent* and *endpwent* functions are not used with this *fgetpwent* function.

4.12   <grp.h>

The <grp.h> defines a set of functions for users to obtain group accountant information as specified in the UNIX */etc/group* file. The functions defined in the <group.h> header are:

```
const struct group*    getgrnam ( const char* group_name);
const struct group* getgrgid( const int gid );
int setgrent ( void );
const struct group* getgrent ( void );
int endgrent ( void );
const struct group* fgetgrent ( FILE * fptr );
```

The *struct group* data type is defined in the <grp.h> header as:

```
struct group
{
      char*          gr_name;         // group name
      char*          gr_passwd:       // group encrypted password
      int            gr_gid;          // group ID
      char**         gr_comment;      // group member names
};
```

Each *struct group* record contains data from one line of the */etc/group* file. This contains the account information of one group on a UNIX system. Specifically, the information consists of a group name, assigned group ID, and a list of those user names that are members of the group.

The *getgrnam* function takes a group name as argument and returns a pointer to a *struct group*-typed record that contains that group's information if the group is defined on the system on which this function call is made. It returns a NULL pointer if the given group name is invalid.

The following statement depicts the group ID of a group name *developer*:

```
struct group *grp = getgrnam( "developer" );
if ( !grp )
        cerr << "'developer' is not a valid group on this system\n";
else
        cout << grp->gr_name << ", GID=" << grp->gr_gid << endl;
```

The *getgrgid* function takes a group ID as argument and returns a pointer to a *struct group*-typed record that contains that group's information if the group is defined on the system on which this function call is made. On the contrary, it returns a NULL pointer if the given group ID is invalid.

The following statement depicts the group members of a group whose *GID* is 200:

```
struct group *grp = getgrgid( 200 );
if ( !grp )
        cerr << "'200' is not a valid GID on this system\n";
else for ( int i=0; grp->pw_comment && grp->pw_comment[i]; i++ )
        cout << grp->gr_comment[i] << endl;
```

The *getgrent* function resets an internal file pointer to point to the beginning of the */etc/group* file. The *getgrwent* function returns a pointer to a *struct group*-type record that contains information at the next entry of the */etc/group* file. When all entries in a */etc/group* are scanned by the *getgrwent* function, it returns a NULL pointer to indicate end-of-file. The *endgrent* function is called to close the internal file pointer, which references the */etc/group* file.

The following *test_grp.C* program dumps all defined groups and their *GID* information to the standard output:

```
#include <iostream.h>
#include <grp.h>
int main()
{
      setgrent();
      for ( struct group*grp; grp=getgrent(); )
          cout  << grp->gr_name << ", GID: " << grp->gr_gid << endl;
      endgrent();
      return 0;
}
```

Finally, the *fgetgrent* function is like the *getgrent*, except here users supply a file pointer that references a file having the same syntax of the */etc/group* file. The function returns a group accountant data at the next entry in the given file. The *setgrent* and *endgrent* functions are not used with this *fgetgrent* function.

4.13   <crypt.h>

The <crypt.h> header declares a set of functions for data encryption and decryption. These are important functions for maintaining system security. For example, user passwords and system data files that need high security must be encrypted so that no unauthorized person can easily find out what they are. Furthermore, authorized persons must know the secret keys to decrypt these objects so that they can read and modify them.

The <crypt.h> header declares the following functions:

char*	***crypt***	(**const char*** key, const char* salt);
void	***setkey***	(**const char** salt[64]);
void	***encrypt***	(**char** key[64], **const int** flag);

The *crypt* function is used on UNIX systems to encrypt user passwords and to check for user login password validity. The function takes two arguments. The first argument, *key,* is a user-defined password. The second argument, *salt,* is used to encode the resultant encrypted string. The *salt* argument value consists of two characters from the following character set:

'a' to 'z', 'A' to 'Z', '0' to '9', or '/'

If the function is called by the *password* process on UNIX to encode a new user password, the process supplies a randomly generated *salt* value. The resultant encoded string is in the format of:

<salt><encrypted password string>

Then, when a user attempts to login to a system by supplying a user name and a password, the login process checks the authentication of the user as follows:

```
#include <iostream.h>
#include <crypt.h>
#include <pwd.h>
#include <string.h>
```

```
int check_login( const char* user_name, const char* password )
{
    struct passwd* pw;
    if ( !(pw=getpwnam( user_name )) ) {
        cerr << "Invalid login name: " << user_name << endl;
        return 0;                              // authentication fails
    }
    char* new_pw = crypt( password,pw->pw_passwd );
    if ( strcmp( new_pw,pw->pw_passwd ) ) {
        cerr << "Invalid password: " << password << endl;
        return 0;                              // authentication fails
    }
    /* both user name and password are valid */
    return 1;
}
```

In the above example, the function is called to ensure that the given user login name and password are valid. The function returns 1 if they are valid, 0 otherwise. The function calls the *getpwnam* function to convert a given user name to a pointer to the *struct passwd*-typed record. If the user name is valid, the *getpwnam* function returns a non-NULL value, otherwise, it returns NULL value, and the *check_login* function returns a failure status.

After a *struct passwd*-typed record is obtained, the *check_login* function calls *crypt* to encrypt the given password. The *salt* supplied to the *crypt* call is the *pw_passwd* field of the *struct passwd*-type record. This is the encrypted password of the user, and the first two characters of this string are the *salt* that was used to generate the encrypted password. The return value of *crypt* is an encrypted password string, and it is compared against the *pw_passwd* value. If they match, the given password is valid, otherwise, the *check_login* function returns a failure status.

As can be seen from the above example, the *crypt* function does not decrypt strings. However, it can be used to encrypt a new string and then compare that against an old string to verify the old string content. It is important to note that the first two characters of the old encrypted string are the *salt* used to generate it. If the new string is the same as the old one prior to encryption and is encrypted with a different salt value, the resultant encrypted new string will be different than the old one.

The *setkey* and *encrypt* functions perform a function similar to *crypt*, except they use the National Bureau of Standards (NBS) data encryption standard (DES) algorithm, which is more secure than the algorithm used by *crypt*. The *setkey* function argument is a character array of 64 entries. Each of these entries should contain an integer value of either 1 or 0, which is one bit of an eight byte *salt* value. The *encrypt* function first argument *key* is a character array of 64 entries, each of these entries contains one bit of an eight byte *key* value to be encrypted (if the third argument *flag* value is 0) or decrypted (if the *flag* value is 1). The resultant encrypted or decrypted string is passed back to the caller in the same *key* argument. The *encrypt* function can process up to only eight characters on each call.

4.14   Summary

This chapter described the ANSI C library functions and some UNIX-specific C library functions. These functions are not covered by the C++ standard classes or by the UNIX and POSIX APIs. Thus, by knowing these functions, users may make use of them to save application development time and to ensure high portability and low maintenance of their end products. Examples were included in this chapter to illustrate the uses of some of these C library functions.

As mentioned in the beginning of the chapter, the limitations of these C library functions are that they do not provide enough functions for users to develop system-level applications. Users must use UNIX and POSIX APIs to create such applications. The remainder of the book is devoted to describing the UNIX and POSIX APIs and the advanced usage of them for system-level programming. In addition to that, examples will be shown on how to use these APIs to implement some of the standard C library functions described in this chapter.

UNIX and POSIX APIs

Unix systems provide a set of application programming interface functions (commonly known as *system calls*) which may be called by users' programs to perform system-specific functions. These functions allow users' applications to directly manipulate system objects such as files and processes that cannot be done by using just standard C library functions. Furthermore, many of the UNIX commands, C library functions, and C++ standard classes (e.g., the iostream class) call these APIs to perform the actual work advertised. Thus, users may use these APIs directly to by-pass the overhead of calling the C library functions and C++ standard classes, or to create their own versions of the UNIX commands, C library functions and C++ classes.

Most UNIX systems provide a common set of APIs to perform the following functions:

- Determine system configuration and user information
- Files Manipulation
- Processes creation and control
- Interprocess communication
- Network communication

Most UNIX APIs access their UNIX kernel's internal resources. Thus, when one of these APIs is invoked by a process (a process is a user's program under execution), the execution context of the process is switched by the kernel from a user mode to a kernel mode. A user mode is the normal execution context of any user process, and it allows the process to access its process-specific data only. A kernel mode is a protective execution environment that allows a user process to access kernel's data in a restricted manner. When the API execu-

125

tion completes, the user process is switched back to the user mode. This context switching for each API call ensures that processes access kernel's data in a controlled manner, and minimizes any chance of a run-away user application may damage an entire system. In general, calling an API is more time-consuming than calling a user function due to the context switching. Thus, for those time-critical applications, users should call their system APIs only if it is absolute necessary.

5.1   The POSIX APIs

Most POSIX.1 and POSIX.1b APIs are derived from UNIX APIs. However, the POSIX committees do create their own APIs when there is perceived deficiency of the UNIX APIs. For example, the POSIX.1b committee creates a new set of APIs for interprocess communication using messages, shared memory, and semaphores. There are equivalent constructs for messages, shared memory, and semaphores in System V UNIX, but the latter constructs use a nonpathname-naming scheme to identify these IPC facilities, and processes cannot use these IPCs to communicate across a LAN. Thus, the POSIX.1b committee created a different version of messages, shared memory, and semaphores that eliminated these short-coming.

In general, POSIX APIs uses and behaviors are similar to those of UNIX APIs. However, users' programs should define the _POSIX_SOURCE (for POSIX.1 APIs) and/or _POSIX_C_SOURCE (for both POSIX.1 and POSIX.1b APIs) in their programs to enable the POSIX APIs declarations in header files that they include.

5.2   The UNIX and POSIX Development Environment

The <unistd.h> header declares some commonly used POSIX.1 and UNIX APIs. There is also a set of API-specific headers placed under the <sys> directory (on a UNIX system it is the /usr/include/sys directory). These <sys/...> headers declare special data types for data objects manipulated by both the APIs and by users' processes. In addition to these, the <stdio.h> header declares the *perror* function, which may be called by a user process whenever an API execution fails. The *perror* function prints a system-defined diagnostic message for any failure incurred by the API.

Most of the POSIX.1, POSIX.1b, and UNIX API object code is stored in the *libc.a* and *libc.so* libraries. Thus, no special compile switch need be specified to indicate which archive or shared library stores the API object code. However, some network communication APIs' object code is stored in special libraries on some systems (e.g., the socket APIs are stored in *libsocket.a* and *libsocket.so* libraries on Sun Mircosystems Solaris 2.x system). Thus, users should consult their system programmer's reference manuals for the special header and library needed for the APIs they use on their systems.

5.3   **API Common Characteristics**

Although the POSIX and UNIX APIs perform diverse system functions on behalf of users, most of them returns an integer value which indicates the termination status of their execution. Specifically, if a API returns a -1 value, it means the API's execution has failed, and the global variable *errno* (which is declared in the <errno.h> header) is set with an error code. A user process may call the *perror* function to print a diagnostic message of the failure to the standard output, or it may call the *strerror* function and gives it *errno* as the actual argument value, the *strerror* function returns a diagnostic message string and the user process may print that message in its preferred way (e.g., output to a error log file).

The possible error status codes that may be assigned to *errno* by any API are defined in the <errno.h> header. When a user prints the man page of a API, it usually shows the possible error codes that may be assigned to *errno* by the API, and the reason why. Since this information is readily available to users and they may be different on different systems, this book will not describe the *errno* values for individual API in any details. However, the following is a list of commonly occur error status codes and their meanings:

Error status code	**Meaning**
EACCESS	A process does not have access permission to perform an operation via a API
EPERM	A API was aborted because the calling process does not have the superuser privilege
ENOENT	An invalid file name was specified to an API
BADF	A API was called with an invalid file descriptor
EINTR	A API execution was aborted due to a signal interruption (see Chapter 9 for the explanation of signal interruption)
EAGAIN	A API was aborted because some system resource it requested was temporarily unavailable. The API should be called again later.
ENOMEM	A API was aborted because it could not allocate dynamic memory
EIO	I/O error occurred in a API execution
EPIPE	A API attempted to write data to a pipe which has no reader
EFAULT	A API was passed an invalid address in one of its arguments
ENOEXEC	A API could not execute a program via one of the exec API
ECHILD	A process does not have any child process which it can wait on

If an API execution is successful, it returns either a zero value or a pointer to some data record where user-requested information is stored.

5.4   Summary

This chapter gives an overview of UNIX and POSIX APIs and describes the common uses and characteristics of these APIs. These APIs are powerful, and they enable users to develop advanced system programs that manipulate system objects (e.g., files and processes) in more ways than can be done via the standard C library functions and C++ classes alone. Furthermore, users may use these APIs to create their own library or C++ classes or their own versions of shell commands to augment those supplied by a system. However, most of these APIs involve context switching of user processes between user mode and kernel mode; thus, this is a time penalty in using these APIs.

The rest of the book examines the UNIX and POSIX APIs in more detail. The APIs are for file manipulation, process manipulation, interprocess communication, and remote procedure call. Examples will be shown on how to use these APIs to construct user's own versions of C library functions and UNIX shell commands, and also to create C++ classes to make abstract data types for system objects such as processes and for system functions like interprocess communication.

UNIX Files

$\mathbf{F}$iles are the building blocks of any operating system, as most operations in a system invariably deal with files. When you execute a command in UNIX, the UNIX kernel fetches the corresponding executable file from a file system, loads its instruction text to memory, and creates a process to execute the command on your behalf. Furthermore, in the course of execution, a process may read from or write to files. All these operations involve files. Thus, the design of an operating system always begins with an efficient file management system.

Files in UNIX and POSIX systems cover a wide range of file types. These include text files, binary files, directory files, and device files. Furthermore, UNIX and POSIX systems provide a set of common system interfaces to files, such that they can be handled in a consistent manner by application programs. This, in turn, simplifies the task of developing application programs on those systems.

This chapter will explore the various file types in UNIX and POSIX systems and will show how they are created and used. Moreover, there is a set of common file attributes that an operating system keeps for each file in the system -- these attributes and their uses are explained in detail. Finally, the UNIX System V kernel and process-specific data structures used to support file manipulation are described to tie in the system call interface for files. The UNIX and POSIX.1 system calls for file handling are discussed in the next chapter.

6.1   File Types

A file in a UNIX or POSIX system may be one of the following types:

- Regular file
- Directory file
- FIFO file
- Character device file
- Block device file

A *regular file* may be either a text file or a binary file. UNIX and POSIX systems do not make any distinction between these two file types, and both may be "executable", provided that the execution rights of these files are set and that these files may be read or written to by users with the appropriate access permission.

Regular files may be created, browsed through, and modified by various means such as text editors or compilers, and they can be removed by specific system commands (e.g., *rm* in UNIX).

A *directory file* is like a file folder that contains other files, including subdirectory files. It provides a means for users to organize their files into some hierarchical structure based on file relationship or uses. For example, the UNIX */bin* directory contains all system executable-programs, such as *cat, rm, sort*, etc.

A directory may be created in UNIX by the *mkdir* command. The following UNIX command will create the */usr/foo/xyz* directory if it does not exist:

```
mkdir    /usr/foo/xyz
```

A UNIX directory is considered empty if it contains no other files except the "." and ".." files, and it may be removed via the *rmdir* command. The following UNIX command removes the */usr/foo/xyz* directory if it exists:

```
rmdir    /usr/foo/xyz
```

The content of a directory file may be displayed in UNIX by the *ls* command.

A *block device file* represents a physical device that transmits data a block at a time. Examples of block devices are hard disk drives and floppy disk drives. A *character device file,* on the other hand, represents a physical device that transmits data in a character-based manner. Examples of character devices are line printers, modems, and consoles. A physical device may have both block and character device files representing it for different access methods. For example, a character device file for a hard disk is used to do raw (nonblocking) data transfer between a process and the disk.

An application program may perform read and write operations on a device file in the same manner as on a regular file, and the operating system will automatically invoke an appropriate device driver function to perform the actual data transfer between the physical device and the application.

Note that a physical device may have both a character and a block device file refer to it, so that an application program may choose to transfer data with that device by either a character-based (via the character device file) or block-based (via the block device file) method.

A device file is created in UNIX via the *mknod* command. The following UNIX command creates a character device file with the name */dev/cdsk0*, and the major and minor numbers of the device file are 115 and 5, respectively. The argument *c* specifies that the file to be created is a character device file:

```
mknod    /dev/cdsk    c    115    5
```

A major device number is an index to a kernel table that contains the addresses of all device driver functions known to the system. Whenever a process reads data from or writes data to a device file, the kernel uses the device file's major number to select and invoke a device driver function to carry out the actual data transfer with a physical device. A minor device number is an integer value to be passed as an argument to a device driver function when it is called. The minor device number tells the device driver function what actual physical device it is talking to (a driver function may serve multiple physical device types), and the I/O buffering scheme to be used for data transfer.

Device driver functions are supplied either by physical device vendors or by operating system vendors. Whenever a device driver function is installed to a system, the operating system kernel will require reconfiguration. This scheme allows an operating system to be extended at any customer site to handle any new device type preferred by users.

A block device file is also created in UNIX by the *mknod* command, except that the second argument to the *mknod* command will be *b* instead of *c*. The *b* argument specifies that the file to be created is a block device file. The following command creates a */dev/bdsk* block device file with the major and minor device numbers of 287 and 101, respectively:

```
mknod    /dev/bdsk    b    287    101
```

In UNIX, *mknod* must be invoked through superuser privileges. Furthermore, it is conventional in UNIX to put all device files in either the */dev* directory or a subdirectory beneath it.

A *FIFO file* is a special pipe device file which provides a temporary buffer for two or more processes to communicate by writing data to and reading data from the buffer. Unlike regular files, however, the size of the buffer associated with a FIFO file is fixed to PIPE_BUF. (PIPE_BUF and its POSIX.1 minimum value, _POSIX_PIPE_BUF, are defined in the <limits.h> header). A process may write more than PIPE_BUF bytes of data to a FIFO file, but it may be blocked when the file buffer is filled. In this case the process must wait for a reader process to read data from the pipe and make room for the write operation to complete. Finally, data in the buffer is accessed in a first-in-first-out manner, hence the file is called a FIFO.

The buffer associated with a FIFO file is allocated when the first process opens the FIFO file for read or write. The buffer is discarded when all processes which are connected to the FIFO close their references (e.g., stream pointers) to the FIFO file. Thus the data stored in a FIFO buffer is temporary; they last as long as there is one process which has a direct connection to the FIFO file for data access.

A FIFO file may be created in UNIX via the *mkfifo* command. The following command creates a FIFO file called */usr/prog/fifo_pipe* if it does not exist:

mkfifo   /usr/prog/fifo_pipe

In some early versions of UNIX (e.g., UNIX System V.3), FIFO files were created via the *mknod* command. The following UNIX command creates the */usr/prog/fifo_pipe* FIFO file if it does not exist:

mknod   /usr/prog/fifo_pipe   p

The UNIX System V.4 supports both the *mknod* and *mkfifo* commands, whereas BSD UNIX supports only the *mkfifo* command to create FIFO files.

A FIFO file may be removed like any regular file. Thus FIFO files can be removed in UNIX via the *rm* command.

Beside the above file types, BSD UNIX and UNIX System V.4 also define a *symbolic link file* type. A symbolic link file contains a path name which references another file in either the local or a remote file system. POSIX.1 does not yet support symbolic link file type, although it has been proposed to be added to the standard in a future revision.

A symbolic link may be created in UNIX via the *ln* command. The following command creates a symbolic link */usr/mary/slink* which references the file */usr/jose/original*. The *cat* command which follows will print the content of the */usr/jose/original* file:

```
ln    -s    /usr/jose/original    /usr/mary/slink
cat   -n    /usr/mary/slink
```

The path name referenced by a symbolic link may be depicted in UNIX via the *ls -l* command on the symbolic link file. The following command will show that */usr/mary/slink* is a symbolic link to the */usr/jose/original* file:

```
%   ls   -l    /usr/mary/slink
sr--r--r--   1    terry      20 Aug 20, 1994    slink -> /usr/jose/original
%
```

It is possible to create a symbolic link to reference another symbolic link. When symbolic links are supplied as arguments to the UNIX commands *vi, cat, more, head, tail*, etc., these commands will dereference the symbolic links to access the actual files that the links reference. However, the UNIX commands *rm, mv*, and *chmod* will operate only on the symbolic link arguments directly and not on the files that they reference.

6.2   The UNIX and POSIX File Systems

Files in UNIX or POSIX systems are stored in a tree-like hierarchical file system. The root of a file system is the root directory, denoted by the "/" character. Each intermediate node in a file system tree is a directory file. The leaf nodes of a file system tree are either empty directory files or other types of files.

The absolute path name of a file consists of the names of all the directories, specified in the descending order of the directory hierarchy, starting from "/," that are ancestors of the file. Directory names are delimited by the "/" characters in a path name. For example, if the path name of a file is */usr/xyz/a.out*, it means that the file *a.out* is located in a directory called *xyz*, and the *xyz* directory is, in turn, stored in the *usr* directory. Furthermore, the *usr* directory is in the "/" directory.

A relative path name may consist of the "." and ".." characters. These are references to the current and parent directories, respectively. For example, the path name *../../.login* denotes a file called *.login,* which may be found in a directory two levels up from the current directory. Although POSIX.1 does not require a directory file to contain "." and ".." files, it does specify that relative path names with "." and ".." characters be interpreted in the same manner as in UNIX.

A file name may not exceed NAME_MAX characters, and the total number of characters of a path name may not exceed PATH_MAX. The POSIX.1-defined minimum values for

NAME_MAX and PATH_MAX are _POSIX_NAME_MAX and _POSIX_PATH_MAX, respectively. These are all defined in the <limits.h> header.

Furthermore, POSIX.1 specifies the following character set is to be supported by all POSIX.1-compliant operating systems as legal file name characters. This means application programs that are to be ported to POSIX.1 and UNIX systems should manipulate files with names in the following character set only:

> A to Z   a to z   0 to 9   _   -   .

The path name of a file is called a *hard link*. A file may be referenced by more than one path name if a user creates one or more hard links to the file using the UNIX *ln* command. For example, the following UNIX command creates a new hard link */usr/prog/new/n1* for the file */usr/foo/path1*. After the *ln* command, the file can be referenced by either path name.

> ln   /usr/foo/path1   /usr/prog/new/n1

Note that if the *-s* option is specified in the above command, the /usr/prog/n1 will be a symbolic link instead of a hard link. The differences between hard and symbolic links will be explained in Chapter 7.

The following files are commonly defined in most UNIX systems, although they are not mandated by POSIX.1:

File	Use
/etc	Stores system administrative files and programs
/etc/passwd	Stores all user information
/etc/shadow	Stores user passwords (For UNIX System V only)
/etc/group	Stores all group information
/bin	Stores all the system programs like cat, rm, cp, etc.
/dev	Stores all character and block device files
/usr/include	Stores standard header files
/usr/lib	Stores standard libraries
/tmp	Stores temporary files created by programs

6.3   The UNIX and POSIX File Attributes

Both UNIX and POSIX.1 maintain a set of common attributes for each file in a file system. These attributes and the data they specify are:

Attribute	Value meaning
file type	Type of file
access permission	The file access permission for owner, group, and others
Hard link count	Number of hard links of a file
UID	The file owner user ID
GID	The file group ID
file size	The file size in bytes
last access time	The time the file was last accessed
last modify time	The time the file was last modified
last change time	The time the file access permission, UID, GID, or hard link count was last changed
inode number	The system inode number of the file
file system ID	The file system ID where the file is stored

Most of the above information can be depicted in UNIX by the *ls -l* command on any files.

The above attributes are essential for the kernel to manage files. For example, when a user attempts to access a file, the kernel matches the user's UID and GID against those of the file to determine which category (user, group, or others) of access permission should be used for the access privileges of the user. Furthermore, the last modification time of files is used by the UNIX *make* utility to determine which source files are newer than their corresponding executable files and require recompilation.

Although the above information is stored for all file types, not all file types make use of the information. For example, the file size attribute has no meaning for character and block device files.

In addition to the above attributes, UNIX systems also store the major and minor device numbers for each device file. In POSIX.1, the support of device files is implementation-dependent; thus, it does not specify major and minor device numbers as standard attributes for device files.

All the above attributes are assigned by the kernel to a file when it is created. Some of these attributes will stay unchanged for the entire life of the file, whereas others may change as the file is being used. The attributes that are constant for any file are:

- File type
- File inode number

- File system ID
- Major and minor device number (for device files on UNIX systems only)

The other attributes are changed by the following UNIX commands or system calls:

UNIX command	System call	Attributes changed
chmod	chmod	Changes access permission, last change time
chown	chown	Changes UID, last change time
chgrp	chown	Changes GID, last change time
touch	utime	Changes last access time, modification time
ln	link	Increases hard link count
rm	unlink	Decreases hard link count. If the hard link count is zero, the file will be removed from the file system
vi, emac	-	Changes file size, last access time, last modification time

6.4   Inodes in UNIX System V

Two of the file attributes which were mentioned but not explained in the above are the inode number and the file system ID. One may also notice that file names are not part of the attributes which an operating system keeps for files. This section will use UNIX System V as the context to give answers to all these puzzles.

In UNIX System V, a file system has an inode table which keeps tracks of all files. Each entry of the inode table is an inode record which contains all the attributes of a file, including an unique inode number and the physical disk address where the data of the file is stored. Thus if a kernel needs to access information of a file with an inode number of, say 15, it will scan the inode table to find an entry which contains an inode number of 15, in order to access the necessary data. Since an operating system may have access to multiple file systems at one time (they are connected to the operating system via the *mount* system command, and each is assigned an unique file system ID), and an inode number is unique within a file system only, a file inode record is identified by a file system ID and an inode number.

An operating system does not keep the name of a file in its inode record, because the mapping of file names to inode numbers is done via directory files. Specifically, a directory file contains a list of names and their respective inode numbers for all files stored in that directory. For example, if a directory *foo* contains files *xyz, a.out,* and *xyz_ln1*, where *xyz_ln1* is a hard link of *xyz*, the content of the directory *foo* is shown in Figure 6.1 (most implementation-dependent data is omitted).

To access a file, for example /usr/joe, the UNIX kernel always knows the "/" directory inode number of any process (it is kept in a process U-area and may be changed via the *chdir* system call). It will scan the "/" directory file (via the "/" inode record) to find the inode number of the *usr* file. Once it gets the *usr* file inode number, it checks that the calling process has permission to search the *usr* directory and accesses the content of the *usr* file. It then looks for the inode number of the *joe* file.

Whenever a new file is created in a directory, the UNIX kernel allocates a new entry in the inode table to store the information of the new file. Moreover, it will assign a unique inode number to the file and add the new file name and inode number to the directory file that contains it.

inode number	file name
115	.
89	..
201	xyz
346	a.out
201	xyz_ln1

Figure 6.1 A sample directory file content

Inode numbers and file system IDs are defined in POSIX.1, but the uses of these attributes are implementation-dependent. Inode tables are kept in their file systems on disk, but the UNIX kernel maintains an in-memory inode table to contain a copy of the recently accessed inode records.

6.5   Application Program Interface to Files

Both UNIX and POSIX systems provide an application interface similar to files, as follows:

- Files are identified by path names
- Files must be created before they can be used. The UNIX commands and corresponding system calls to create various types of files are:

File type	UNIX command	UNIX and POSIX.1 system call
Regular files	vi, ex, etc.	open, creat
Directory files	mkdir	mkdir, mknod
FIFO files	mkfifo	mkfifo, mknod
Device files	mknod	mknod
Symbolic links	ln -s	symlink

- Files must be opened before they can be accessed by application programs. UNIX and POSIX.1 define the *open* API, which can be used to open any files. The *open* function returns an integer file descriptor, which is a file handle to be used in other system calls to manipulate the open file

- A process may open at most OPEN_MAX files of any types at any one time. The OPEN_MAX and its POSIX.1-defined minimum value _POSIX_OPEN_MAX are defined in the <limits.h> header

- The *read* and *write* system calls can be used to read data from and write data to opened files

- File attributes can be queried by the *stat* or *fstat* system call

- File attributes can be changed by the *chmod*, *chown*, *utime*, and *link* system calls

- File hard links can be removed by the *unlink* system call

To facilitate the query of file attributes by application programs, UNIX and POSIX.1 define a *struct stat* data type in the <sys/stat.h> header. A *struct stat* record contains all the user-visible attributes of any file being queried, and it is assigned and returned by the *stat* or *fstat* function. The POSIX.1 declaration of the *struct stat* type is:

```
struct stat
{
        dev_t      st_dev;       /* file system ID */
        ino_t      st_ino;       /* File inode number */
        mode_t     st_mode;      /* Contains file type and access flags */
        nlink_t    st_nlink;     /* Hard link count */
        uid_t      st_uid;       /* File user ID */
        gid_t      st_gid;       /* File group ID */
        dev_t      st_rdev;      /* Contains major and minor device numbers */
        off_t      st_size;      /* File size in number of bytes */
        time_t     st_atime;     /* Last access time */
        time_t     st_mtime;     /* Last modification time */
        time_t     st_ctime;     /* Last status change time */
};
```

If the path name (or file descriptor) of a symbolic link file is passed as an argument to a *stat* (or *fstat*) system call, the function will resolve the link reference and show the attributes of the actual file to which the link refers. To query the attributes of a symbolic link file itself, one can use the *lstat* system call instead. Because symbolic link files are not yet supported by POSIX.1, the *lstat* system call is also not a POSIX.1 standard.

6.6   UNIX Kernel Support for Files

In UNIX System V.3, the kernel has a file table that keeps track of all opened files in the system. There is also an inode table that contains a copy of the file inodes most recently accessed.

When a user executes a command, a process is created by the kernel to carry out the command execution. The process has its own data structure which, among other things, is a file descriptor table. The file descriptor table has OPEN_MAX entries, and it records all files opened by the process. Whenever the process calls the *open* function to open a file for read and/or write, the kernel will resolve the path name to the file inode. If the file inode is not found or the process lacks appropriate permissions to access the inode data, the *open* call fails and returns a -1 to the process. If, however, the file inode is accessible to the process, the kernel will proceed to establish a path from an entry in the file descriptor table, through a file table, onto the inode for the file being opened. The process for that is as follows:

1. The kernel will search the process file descriptor table and look for the first unused entry. If an entry is found, that entry will be designated to reference the file. The index to the entry will be returned to the process (via the return value of the *open* function) as the file descriptor of the opened file.

2. The kernel will scan the file table in its kernel space to find an unused entry that can be assigned to reference the file.

   If an unused entry is found, the following events will occur:

   a. The process's file descriptor table entry will be set to point to this file table entry.
   b. The file table entry will be set to point to the inode table entry where the inode record of the file is stored.
   c. The file table entry will contain the current file pointer of the open file. This is an offset from the beginning of the file where the next read or write operation will occur .
   d. The file table entry will contain an open mode that specifies that the file is opened for read-only, write-only, or read and write, etc. The open mode is specified from the calling process as an argument to the *open* function call.
   e. The reference count in the file table entry is set to 1. The reference count keeps

track of how many file descriptors from any process are referencing the entry.

f. The reference count of the in-memory inode of the file is increased by 1. This count specifies how many file table entries are pointing to that inode.

If either (1) or (2) fails, the *open* function will return with a -1 failure status, and no file descriptor table or file table entry will be allocated.

Figure 6.2 shows a process's file descriptor table, the kernel file table, and the inode table after the process has opened three files: *xyz* for read-only, *abc* for read-write, and *abc* again for write-only.

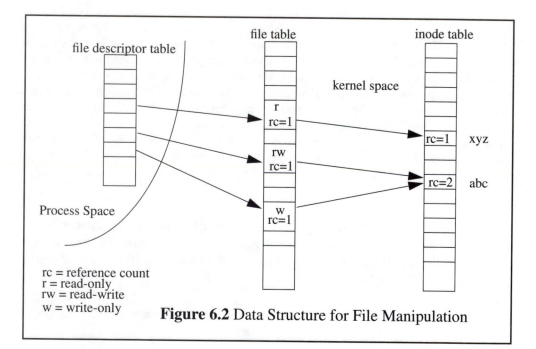

Figure 6.2 Data Structure for File Manipulation

Note that the reference count of an allocated file table entry is usually 1, but a process may use the *dup* (or *dup2*) function to make multiple file descriptor table entries point to the same file table entry. Alternatively, the process may call the *fork* function to create a child process, such that the child and parent process file table entries are pointing to corresponding file table entries at the same time. All these will cause a file table entry reference count to be larger than 1. The *dup, dup2*, and *fork* functions and their uses will be explained in more detail in Chapter 8.

The reference count in a file inode record specifies how many file table entries are pointing to the file inode record. If the count is not zero, it means that one or more processes are currently opening the file for access.

Once an *open* call succeeds, the process can use the returned file descriptor for future reference. Specifically, when the process attempts to read (or write) data from the file, it will use the file descriptor as the first argument to the *read* (or *write*) system call. The kernel will use the file descriptor to index the process's file descriptor table to find the file table entry of the opened file. It then checks the file table entry data to make sure that the file is opened with the appropriate mode to allow the requested read (or write) operation.

If the read (or write) operation is found compatible with the file's open mode, the kernel will use the pointer specified in the file table entry to access the file's inode record (as stored in the inode table). Furthermore, it will use the file pointer stored in the file table entry to determine where the read (or write) operation should occur in the file. Finally, the kernel checks the file's file type in the inode record and invokes an appropriate driver function to initiate the actual data transfer with a physical device.

If a process calls the *lseek* system call to change the file pointer to a different offset for the next read (or write) operation, the kernel will use the file descriptor to index the process file descriptor table to find the pointer to the file table entry. The kernel then accesses the file table entry to get the pointer to the file's inode record. It then checks that the file is not a character device file, a FIFO file, or a symbolic link file, as these files allow only sequential read and write operations. If the file type is compatible with *lseek*, the kernel will change the file pointer in the file table entry according to the value specified in the *lseek* arguments.

When a process calls the *close* function to close an opened file, the sequence of events are as follows:

1. The kernel sets the corresponding file descriptor table entry to be unused.

2. It decrements the reference count in the corresponding file table entry by 1. If the reference count is still non-zero, go to 6.

3. The file table entry is marked as unused.

4. The reference count in the corresponding file inode table entry is decrement by one. If the count is still nonzero, go to 6.

5. If the hard-link count of the inode is not zero, it returns to the caller with a success status. Otherwise it marks the inode table entry as unused and deallocates all the physical disk storage of the file, as all the file path names have been removed by some process.

6. It returns to the process with a 0 (success) status.

6.7 Relationship of C Stream Pointers and File Descriptors

C stream pointers (FILE*) are allocated via the *fopen* C function call. A stream pointer is more efficient to use for applications doing extensive sequential read from or write to files, as the C library functions perform I/O buffering with streams. On the other hand, a file descriptor, allocated by an *open* system call, is more efficient for applications that do frequent random access of file data, and I/O buffering is not desired. Another difference between the two is stream pointers is supported on all operating systems, such as VMS, CMS, DOS, and UNIX, that provide C compilers. File descriptors are used only in UNIX and POSIX.1-compliant systems; thus, programs that use stream pointers are more portable than are those using file descriptors.

To support stream pointers, each UNIX process has a fixed-size stream table with OPEN_MAX entries. Each entry is of type FILE and contains working data from an open file. Data stored in a FILE record includes a buffer for I/O data buffering, the file I/O error status, and an end-of-file flag, etc. When *fopen* is called, it scans the calling process FILE table to find an unused entry, then assigns this entry to reference the file and returns the address of this entry (FILE*) as the stream pointer for the file. Furthermore, in UNIX, the *fopen* function calls the *open* function to perform the actual file opening, and a FILE record contains a file descriptor for the open file. One can extract the file descriptor associated with a stream pointer via the *fileno* macro, which is declared in the <stdio.h> header:

int *fileno* (**FILE*** stream_pointer);

Thus, if a process calls *fopen* to open a file for access, there will be an entry in the process FILE table and an entry in the process's file descriptor table being used to reference the file. If the process calls *open* to open the file, only an entry in the process's file descriptor table is assigned to reference the file. However, one can convert a file descriptor to a stream pointer via the *fdopen* C library function:

FILE* *fdopen* (**int** file_descriptor, **char** * open_mode);

The *fdopen* function has an action similar to the *fopen* function, namely, it assign a process FILE table entry to reference the file, records the file descriptor value in the entry, and returns the address of the entry to the caller.

After either the *fileno* or *fdopen* call, the process may reference the file via either the stream pointer or the file descriptor. Other C library functions for files also rely on the operating system APIs to perform the actual functions. The following lists some C library functions and the underlying UNIX APIs they use to perform their functions:

C Library function	UNIX system call used
fopen	open
fread, fgetc, fscanf, fgets	read
fwrite, fputc, fprintf, fputs	write
fseek, ftell, frewind	lseek
fclose	close

6.8   Directory Files

A directory is a record-oriented file. Each record contains the information of a file residing in that directory. The record data type is *struct dirent* in UNIX System V and POSIX.1, and *struct direct* in BSD UNIX. The record content is implementation-dependent, but in UNIX and POSIX systems they all contain two essential member fields: a file name and an inode number. The usage of directory files is to map file names to their corresponding inode numbers so that an operating system can resolve any file path name to locate its inode record.

Although an application can use the *open, read, write, lseek,* and *close* system calls to manipulate directory files, UNIX and POSIX.1 define a set of portable functions to open, browse, and close directory files. They are built on top of the *open, read, write,* and *close* system calls and are defined in <dirent.h> for UNIX System V and POSIX.1-compliant systems or in <sys/dir.h> for BSD UNIX:

Directory function	Purpose
opendir	Opens a directory file
readdir	Reads the next record from file
closedir	Closes a directory file
rewinddir	Sets file pointer to beginning of file

The *opendir* function returns a handle of type DIR*. It is analogous to the FILE* handle for a C stream file. The handle is used in the *readdir, rewinddir,* and *closedir* function calls to specify which directory file to manipulate.

Besides the above functions, UNIX systems also define the *telldir* and *seekdir* functions for random access of different records in a directory file. These functions are not POSIX.1 standard, and they are analogous to the *ftell* and *fseek* C library functions, respectively.

If a process adds or deletes a file in a directory file while another process has opened the file via the *opendir*, it is implementation-dependent as to whether the latter process will see the new changes via the *readdir* function. However, if the latter process does a *rewinddir* and then reads the directory via the *readdir*, according to POSIX.1, it should read the latest content of the directory file.

6.9   Hard and Symbolic Links

A hard link is a UNIX path name for a file. Most UNIX files have only one hard link. However, users may create additional hard links for files via the *ln* command. For example. the following command creates a new link call */usr/joe/book.new* for the file */usr/mary/ fun.doc*:

> ln   /usr/mary/fun.doc   /usr/joe/book.new

After the above command, users may refer to the same file by either */usr/joe/book.new* or */ usr/mary/fun.doc*.

Symbolic links can be created in the same manner as hard links, except that you must specify the *-s* option to the *ln* command. Thus, using the above example, you can create */usr/ joe/book.new* as a symbolic link instead of a hard link with the following command:

> ln   -s /usr/mary/fun.doc   /usr/joe/book.new

Symbolic links or hard links are used to provide alternative means of referencing files. For example, you are at the */usr/jose/proj/doc* directory, and you are constantly browsing the file */usr/include/sys/unistd.h*. Thus, rather than specifying the full path name */usr/include/sys/ unistd.h* every time you reference it, you could define a link to that file as follows:

> ln   /usr/include/sys/unistd.h   uniref

From now on, you can refer to that file as *uniref*. Thus links facilitate users in referencing files.

ln differs from the *cp* command in that *cp* creates a duplicated copy of a file to another file with a different path name, whereas *ln* primarily creates a new directory entry to reference a file. For example, given the following command:

> ln   /usr/jose/abc   /usr/mary/xyz

the directory files */usr/jose* and */usr/mary* will contain:

inode number	filename		inode number	filename
115	.		515.	.
89	..		989	..
201	**abc**		**201**	**xyz**
346	a.out		146	fun.c
/usr/jose			/usr/mary	

Note that both the */usr/jose/abc* and */usr/mary/xyz* refer to the same inode number, 201. Thus there is no new file created. If, however, we use the *ln -s* or the *cp* command to create the */usr/mary/xyz* file, a new inode will be created, and the directory files of */usr/jose* and */usr/mary* will look like the following:

inode number	file name		inode number	file name
115	.		515	.
89	..		989	..
201	**abc**		**345**	**xyz**
346	a.out		146	fun.c
/usr/jose			/usr/mary	

If the */usr/mary/xyz* file was created by the *cp* command, its data content will be identical to that of */usr/jose/abc*, and the two files will be separate objects in the file system. However, if the */usr/mary/xyz* file was created by the *ln -s* command, then the file data will consist only of the path name */usr/mary/abc*.

Thus, *ln* helps save disk space over *cp* by not creating duplicated copies of files. Moreover, whenever a user makes changes to a link (hard or symbolic) of a file, the changes are visible from all the other links of the file. This is not true for files created by *cp*, as the duplicated file is a separate object from the original.

Hard links are used in all versions of UNIX. The limitations of hard links are:

* Users cannot create hard links for directories, unless they have superuser (root) privileges. This is to prevent users from creating cyclic links in a file system. An example of a cyclic link is like the following command:

         ln   /usr/jose/text/unix_link   /usr/jose

If this command succeeds, then whenever a user does a *ls -R /usr/jose*, the *ls* command will run into an infinite loop in displaying, recursively, the subdirectory tree of */usr/jose*. UNIX allows the superuser to create hard links on directories with the assumption that a supervisor will not make this kind of mistake

* Users cannot create hard links on a file system that references files on a different system. This is because a hard link is just a directory entry (in a directory file that stores the new link) to reference the same inode number as the original link, but inode numbers are unique only within a file system (hard links cannot be used to reference files on remote file systems)

To overcome the above limitations, BSD UNIX invented the symbolic link concept. A symbolic link can reference a file on any file system because its data is a path name, and an operating system kernel can resolve path names to locate files in either local or remote file systems. Furthermore, users are allowed to create symbolic links to directories, as the kernel can detect cyclic directories caused by symbolic links. Thus, there will be no infinite loops in directory traversal. Symbolic links are supported in the UNIX System V.4, but not by POSIX.1.

The following table summarizes the differences between symbolic and hard links:

Hard Link	Symbolic Link
Does not create a new inode	Create a new inode
Can not link directories, unless this is done by root	Can link directories
Can not link files across file systems	Can link files across file systems
Increase the hard link count of the linked inode	Does not change the hard link count of the linked inode

6.10   Summary

This chapter describes the UNIX and POSIX file systems and the different file types in the systems. It also depicts how these various files are created and used. Furthermore, the UNIX System V system-wide and per-process data structures that are used to support file manipulation and the application program interfaces for files are covered. The objective of this chapter is to familiarize readers with the UNIX file structures so that they can understand why the UNIX and POSIX system calls were created, how they work, and what their applications for users are.

The next chapter will describe the UNIX and POSIX file APIs in more detail.

UNIX File APIs

T his chapter describes how the UNIX and POSIX applications interface with files. After reading this chapter, readers should be able to write programs that perform the following functions on any type of files in a UNIX or POSIX system:

- Create files
- Open files
- Transfer data to and from files
- Close files
- Remove files
- Query file attributes
- Change file attributes
- Truncate files

To illustrate the application of UNIX and POSIX.1 APIs for files, some C++ programs are depicted to show the implementation of the UNIX commands *ls, mv, chmod, chown*, and *touch* based on these APIs. Furthermore, this chapter defines a C++ class called *file*. This *file* class inherits all the properties of the C++ *fstream* class, and it has additional member functions to create objects of any file type, as well as to display and change file object attributes.

Readers are assumed to have read the last chapter to become familiar with the UNIX and POSIX file structures, as they are fundamental to a sound understanding of the use and application of the file APIs described in this chapter.

7.1   General File APIs

As explained in the last chapter, files in a UNIX or POSIX system may be one of the following types:

- Regular file
- Directory file
- FIFO file
- Character device file
- Block device file
- Symbolic link file

There are special APIs to create these different types of files. These APIs will be described in later sections. However, there is a set of generic APIs that can be used to manipulate more than one type of files. These APIs are:

API	Use
open	Opens a file for data access
read	Reads data from a file
write	Writes data to a file
lseek	Allows random access of data in a file
close	Terminates the connection to a file
stat, fstat	Queries attributes of a file
chmod	Changes access permission of a file
chown	Changes UID and/or GID of a file
utime	Changes last modification and access time stamps of a file
link	Creates a hard link to a file
unlink	Deletes a hard link of a file
umask	Sets default file creation mask

These general APIs are explained as follows.

7.1.1   open

The *open* function establishes a connection between a process (a process is an application program under execution) and a file. If can be used to create brand new files. Furthermore, after a file is created any process can call the *open* function to get a file descriptor to refer to the file. The file descriptor is used in the *read* and *write* system calls to access the file content.

The prototype of the *open* function is:

```
#include <sys/types.h>
#include <fcntl.h>

int open ( const char *path_name, int access_mode, mode_t permission );
```

The first argument *path_name* is the path name of a file. This may be an absolute path name (a character string begins with the "/" character) or a relative path name (a character string does not begin with the "/" character). If a given *path_name* is a symbolic link, the function will resolve the link reference (and recursively, if the symbolic link refers to another symbolic link) to a nonsymbolic link file to which the link refers.

The second argument *access_mode* is an integer value that specifies how the file is to be accessed by the calling process. The *access_mode* value should be one of the following manifested constants as defined in the <fcntl.h> header:

Access mode flag	Use
O_RDONLY	Opens the file for read-only
O_WRONLY	Opens the file for write-only
O_RDWR	Opens the file for read and write

Furthermore, one or more of the following modifier flags can be specified by bitwise-ORing them with one of the above access mode flags to alter the access mechanism of the file:

Access modifier flag	Use
O_APPEND	Appends data to the end of the file
O_CREAT	Creates the file if it does not exist
O_EXCL	Used with the O_CREAT flag only. This flag causes *open* to fail if the named file already exists
O_TRUNC	If the file exists, discards the file content and sets the file size to zero bytes
O_NONBLOCK	Specifies that any subsequent read or write on the file should be nonblocking
O_NOCTTY	Specifies not to use the named terminal device file as the calling process control terminal

To illustrate the use of the above flags, the following example statement opens a file called */usr/xyz/textbook* for read and write in append mode:

int fdesc = open ("/usr/xyz/textbook",O_RDWR|O_APPEND, 0);

If a file is to be opened for read-only, the file should already exist and no other modifier flags can be used.

If a file is opened for write-only or read-write, any modifier flags can be specified. However, O_APPEND, O_TRUNC, O_CREAT, and O_EXCL are applicable to regular files only, whereas O_NONBLOCK is for FIFO and device files only, and O_NOCTTY is for terminal device files only.

The O_APPEND flag specifies that data written to a named file will be appended at the end of the file. If this is not specified, data can be written to anywhere in the file.

The O_TRUNC flag specifies that if a named file already exists, the *open* function should discard its content. If this is not specified, current data in the file will not be altered by the *open* function.

The O_CREAT flag specifies that if a named file does not exist, the *open* function should create it. If a named file does exist, the O_CREAT flag has no effect on the *open* function. However, if the named file does not exist and the O_CREAT file is not specified, *open* will abort with a failure return status. The O_EXCL flag, if used, must be accompanied by the O_CREAT flag. When both the O_CREAT and O_EXCL flags are specified, the *open* function will fail if the named file exists. Thus, the O_EXCL flag is used to ensure that the *open* call creates a new file.

The O_NONBLOCK flag specifies that if the *open* and any subsequent *read* or *write* function calls on a named file will block a calling process, the kernel should abort the functions immediately and return to the process with a proper status value. For example, a process is normally blocked on reading an empty pipe (*pipe* is described in Section 7.5) or on writing to a pipe that is full. The O_NONBLOCK flag may be used to specify that such read and write operations are nonblocking. In System V.3, O_NDELAY is defined instead of O_NONBLOCK; the two flags have similar uses, but their behaviors are not identical. These are covered in more detail in Section 7.5.

The O_NOCTTY flag is defined in POSIX.1. It specifies that if a process has no controlling terminal and it opens a terminal device file, that terminal will not be the controlling terminal of the process. If this flag is not set, it is implementation-dependent as to whether the terminal will become the process controlling terminal. Note that in UNIX System V.3 where the O_NOCTTY is undefined, if a process has no controlling terminal, the *open* call will automatically establish the first terminal device file opened as the controlling terminal.

The *permission* argument is required only if the O_CREAT flag is set in the *access_mode* argument. It specifies the access permission of the file for its owner, group member, and all other people. Its data type is *int* in UNIX System V (V.3 and earlier), and its value is usually specified as an octal integer literal, such as 0764. Specifically, the left-most, middle, and right-most digits of an octal value specify the access permission for owner, group, and others, respectively. Furthermore, in each octal digit, the left-most, middle, and right-most bits specify the read, write, and execute permission, respectively. The value of each bit is either 1, which means a right is granted, or zero, for no such right. Thus, the 0764 value manes that the new file's owner has read-write-execute permission, group members have read-write permission, and others have read-only permission.

POSIX.1 defines the *permission* data type as *mode_t,* and its value should be constructed based on the manifested constants defined in the <sys/stat.h> header. These manifested constants are aliases to the octal integer values used in UNIX System V. For example, the 0764 *permission* value should be specified as:

S_IRWXU | S_IRGRP | S_IWGRP | S_IROTH

Actually, a *permission* value specified in an *open* call is modified by its calling process *umask* value. An umask value specifies some access rights to be masked off (or taken away) automatically on any files created by the process. A process umask is inherited from its parent process, and its value can be queried or changed by the *umask* system call. The function prototype of the *umask* API is:

```
mode_t     umask ( mode_t     new_umask );
```

The *umask* function takes a new umask value as an argument. This new umask value will be used by the calling process from then on, and the function returns the old umask value. For example, the following statement assigns the current umask value to the variable *old_mask*, and sets the new umask value to "no execute for group" and "no write-execute for others":

mode_t   old_mask = umask (S_IXGRP | S_IWOTH | S_IXOTH);

The *open* function takes its *permission* argument value and bitwise-ANDs it with the one's complement of the calling process umask value,. Thus, the final access permission to be assigned to any new file created is:

actual_permission = permission & ~umask_value

Thus bits which are set in an umask value mean that the corresponding access rights are to be taken off of any newly created files. For example, if *open* is called in System V.3 to create a file called */usr/mary/show_ex* with a permission of 0557, and the umask of the calling process is 031, then the actual access permission assigned to the newly created file is:

actual_permission = 0557 & (~031) = 0546

The return value of the *open* function is -1 if the API fails and *errno* contains an error status value. If the API succeeds, the return value is a file descriptor that can be used to reference the file in other system calls. The file descriptor value should be between 0 and OPEN_MAX-1, inclusively.

7.1.2   creat

The *creat* system call is used to create new regular files. Its prototype is:

```
#include <sys/types.h>
#include <unistd.h>
int creat ( const char* path_name, mode_t mode );
```

The *path_name* argument is the path name of a file to be created. The *mode* argument is the same as that for the *open* API. However, since the O_CREAT flag was added, the *open* API can be used to both create and open regular files. Thus, the *creat* API has become obsolete. It is retained for backward-compatibility with early versions of UNIX. The *creat* function can be implemented using the *open* function as:

```
#define creat(path_name,mode)        \
        open (path_name, O_WRONLY|O_CREAT|O_TRUNC, mode)
```

7.1.3   read

The *read* function fetches a fixed size block of data from a file referenced by a given file descriptor. The function prototype of the *read* function is:

```
#include <sys/types.h>
#include <unistd.h>
ssize_t read ( int fdesc, void* buf, size_t size );
```

The first argument, *fdesc,* is an integer file descriptor that refers to an opened file. The second argument, *buf,* is the address of a buffer holding any data read. The third argument, *size,* specifies how many bytes of data are to be read from the file. The *size_t* data type is defined in the <sys/types.h> header and should be the same as *unsigned int.*

Note that *read* can read text or binary files. This is why the data type of *buf* is a universal pointer (*void**). For example, the following code fragment reads, sequentially, one or more record of *struct sample*-typed data from a file called *dbase*:

```
struct sample { int x; double y; char* z; } varX;
int fd = open ("dbase", O_RDONLY);
while (read(fd,&varX,sizeof(varX)) > 0)
            /* process data stored in varX*/
```

The return value of *read* is the number of bytes of data successfully read and stored in the *buf* argument. It should normally be equal to the *size* value. However, if a file contains less than *size* bytes of data remaining to be read, the return value of *read* will be less than that of *size*. Furthermore, if end-of-file is reached, *read* will return a zero value.

Because *ssize_t* is usually defined as *int* in the <sys/types.h> header, users should not set *size* to exceed INT_MAX in any *read* function call. This ensures that the function return value can reflect the actual number of bytes read.

If a *read* function call is interrupted by a caught signal (signals are explained in Chapter 9) and the operating system does not restart the system call automatically, POSIX.1 allows two possible behaviors of the *read* function. The first one is the same as in UNIX System V.3, where the *read* function will return a -1 value, *errno* will be set to EINTR, and all the data read in the call will be discarded (hence, the process cannot recover the data). The second behavior is mandated by the POSIX.1 FIPS standard, which specifies that the *read* function will return the number of bytes of data read prior to the signal interruption. This allows a process to continue reading the file.

In BSD UNIX where the kernel automatically restarts any system call after a signal interruption, the return value of *read* will be the same as that in a normal execution. In UNIX System V.4, the user can specify, on a per-signal basis, whether the kernel will restart any system call that is interrupted by each signal. Thus, the *read* function behavior may be similar to that of BSD UNIX for restartable signals, or to that of either UNIX System V.3 or POSIX.1 FIPS systems for nonrestartable signals.

The *read* function may block a calling process execution if it is reading a FIFO or a device file and data is not yet available to satisfy the read request. Users may specify the O_NONBLOCK or O_NDELAY flags on a file descriptor to request nonblocking read operations on the corresponding file. The behavior of the *read* function on these special files will be described in detailed in the FIFO and device file API sections.

7.1.4   write

The *write* function puts a fixed size block of data to a file referenced by a given file descriptor. Its operation is opposite to that of the *read* function. Its prototype is:

```
#include <sys/types.h>
#include <unistd.h>

ssize_t write ( int fdesc, const void* buf, size_t size );
```

The first argument, *fdesc,* is an integer file descriptor that refers to an opened file. The second argument, *buf,* is the address of a buffer which contains data to be written to the file. The third argument, *size,* specifies how many bytes of data are in the *buf* argument.

Like the *read* API, *write* can write text or binary files. This is why the data type of *buf* is a universal pointer (*void**). For example, the following code fragment writes ten records of *struct sample*-typed data to a file called *dbase2*:

```
struct sample { int x; double y; char* z; } varX[10 ];
int fd = open ( "dbase2", O_WRONLY );

/* initialize varX array here... */

write( fd, (void*)varX, sizeof varX );
```

The return value of *write* is the number of bytes of data successfully written to a file. It should normally be equal to the *size* value. However, if the write will cause the file size to exceed a system imposed limit or if the file system disk is full, the return value of *write* will be the actual number of bytes written before the function was aborted.

The handling of signal interruption by the *write* function is the same as that for the *read* function: If a signal arrives during a *write* function call and the operating system does not restart the system call automatically, the *write* function may either return a -1 value and set *errno* to EINTR (the System V method) or return the number of bytes of data written prior to the signal interruption. The latter behavior is mandated by the POSIX.1 FIPS standard.

Like the *read* function, in UNIX System V.4 a user can specify, on a per-signal basis, whether the kernel will restart any system call that is interrupted by each signal. Thus, the *write* function behavior may be similar to that of BSD UNIX for restartable signals (and the *write* function return value is the same as that in a normal execution) or to that of either UNIX System V.3 or POSIX.1 FIPS systems for nonrestartable signals.

Finally, the *write* function may perform nonblocking operation if the O_NONBLOCK or O_NDELAY flags are set on the *fdesc* argument to the function. This is the same for the *read* function.

7.1.5   close

The *close* function disconnects a file from a process. The function prototype of the *close* function is:

```
#include <unistd.h>
int close ( int fdesc );
```

The argument *fdesc* is an integer file descriptor that refers to an opened file. The return value of *close* is zero if the call succeeds, or -1 if it fails, and *errno* contains an error code.

The *close* function frees unused file descriptors so that they can be reused to reference other files. This is important, as a process may open up to OPEN_MAX files at any one time, and the *close* function allows a process to reuse file descriptors to access more than OPEN_MAX files in the course of its execution.

Furthermore, the *close* function will deallocate system resources (e.g., file table entries and memory buffer allocated to hold read/write file data) that are dedicated to support the operation of file descriptors. This reduces the memory requirement of a process.

If a process terminates without closing all the files it has opened, the kernel will close those files for the process.

The *iostream* class defines a *close* member function to close a file associated with an iostream object. This member function may be implemented using the *close* API as follows:

```
#include <iostream.h>
#include <sys/types.h>
#include <unistd.h>

int iostream::close() {return close(this->fileno());}
```

7.1.6   fcntl

The *fcntl* function helps a user to query or set access control flags and the *close-on-exec* flag of any file descriptor. Users can also use *fcntl* to assign multiple file descriptors to reference the same file. The prototype of the *fcntl* function is:

```
#include <fcntl.h>

int fcntl ( int fdesc, int cmd, ... );
```

The *cmd* argument specifies which operations to perform on a file referenced by the *fdesc* argument. A third argument value, which may be specified after *cmd,* is dependent on the actual *cmd* value. The possible *cmd* values are defined in the <fcntl.h> header. These values and their uses are:

cmd value	Use
F_GETFL	Returns the access control flags of a file descriptor *fdesc*
F_SETFL	Sets or clears access control flags that are specified in the third argument to *fcntl*. The allowed access control flags are O_APPEND and O_NONBLOCK (or O_NDELAY in non-POSIX-compliant UNIX)
F_GETFD	Returns the *close-on-exec* flag of a file referenced by *fdesc*. If a return value is zero, the flag is off; otherwise, the return value is nonzero and the flag is on. The *close-on-exec* flag of a newly opened file is off by default
F_SETFD	Sets or clears the *close-on-exec* flag of a file descriptor *fdesc*. The third argument to *fcntl* is an integer value, which is 0 to clear the flag, or 1 to set the flag
F_DUPFD	Duplicates the file descriptor *fdesc* with another file descriptor. The third argument to *fcntl* is an integer value which specifies that the duplicated file descriptor must be greater than or equal to that value. The return value of *fcntl,* in this case, is the duplicated file descriptor

The *fcntl* function is useful in changing the access control flag of a file descriptor. For example, after a file is opened for blocking read-write access and the process needs to change the access to nonblocking and in write-append mode, it can call *fcntl* on the file's descriptor as:

```
int cur_flags = fcntl(fdesc, F_GETFL);
int rc = fcntl (fdesc, F_SETFL, cur_flag | O_APPEND | O_NONBLOCK);
```

The *close-on-exec* flag of a file descriptor specifies that if the process that owns the descriptor calls the *exec* API to execute a different program, the file descriptor should be closed by the kernel before the new program runs (if the flag is on) or not (if the flag is off). The *exec* API and the *close-on-exec* flag are explained in more detail in Chapter 8. The following example reports the *close-on-exec* flag of a file descriptor *fdesc*, sets it to on afterward:

```
       cout << fdesc << " close-on-exec: " << fcntl( fdesc, F_GETFD ) << endl;
;      (void)fcntl( fdesc, F_SETFD, 1);              // turn-on close-on-exec flag
```

The *fcntl* function can also be used to duplicate a file descriptor *fdesc* with another file descriptor. The results are two file descriptors referencing the same file with the same access mode (read and/or write, blocking or nonblocking access, etc.) and sharing the same file pointer to read or write the file. This is useful in the redirection of the standard input or output to reference a file instead. For example, the following statements change the standard input of a process to a file called *FOO*:

```
       int fdesc = open("FOO", O_RDONLY);              // open FOO for read
       close(0);                                        // close standard input
       if (fcntl(fdesc,F_DUPFD, 0)==-1) perror("fcntl");  // stdin from FOO now
       char buf[256];
       int rc = read(0,buf,256);                         // read data from FOO
```

The *dup* and *dup2* functions in UNIX perform the same file duplication function as *fcntl*. They can be implemented using *fcntl* as:

```
       #define    dup(fdesc)           fcntl(fdesc,F_DUPFD,0)
       #define    dup2(fdesc1, fd2)    close(fd2), fcntl(fdesc,F_DUPFD,fd2)
```

The *dup* function duplicates a file descriptor *fdesc* with the lowest unused file descriptor of a calling process. The *dup2* function will duplicate a file descriptor *fdesc* using a *fd2* file descriptor, regardless of whether *fd2* is used to reference another file.

File duplication and standard input or output redirection are described in more detail in the next chapter.

The return value of *fcntl* is dependent on the *cmd* value, but it is -1 if the function fails. Possible failures may be due to the specification of an invalid *fdesc* or *cmd*.

7.1.7   lseek

The *read* and *write* system calls are always relative to the current offset within a file. The *lseek* system call can be used to change the file offset to a different value. Thus, *lseek* allows a process to perform random access of data on any opened file. *Lseek* is incompatible with FIFO files, character device files, and symbolic link files.

The prototype of the *lseek* function is:

```
#include <sys/types.h>
#include <unistd.h>

off_t lseek ( int fdesc, off_t pos, int whence );
```

The first argument, *fdesc,* is an integer file descriptor that refers to an opened file. The second argument, *pos,* specifies a byte offset to be added to a reference location in deriving the new file offset value. The reference location is specified by the *whence* argument. The possible values of *whence* and the corresponding file reference locations are:

whence value	Reference location
SEEK_CUR	Current file pointer address
SEEK_SET	The beginning of a file
SEEK_END	The end of a file

The SEEK_CUR, SEEK_SET, and SEEK_END are defined in the <unistd.h> header. Note that it is illegal to specify a negative *pos* value with the *whence* value set to SEEK_SET, as this will cause the function to assign a negative file offset. Furthermore, if an *lseek* call will result in a new file offset that is beyond the current end-of-file, two outcomes possible are: If a file is opened for read-only, *lseek* will fail; if, however, a file is opened for write access, *lseek* will succeed, and it will extend the file size up to the new file offset address. Furthermore, the data between the end-of-file and the new file offset address will be initialized with NULL characters.

The return value of *lseek* is the new file offset address where the next read or write operation will occur, or -1 if the *lseek* call fails.

The *iostream* class defines the *tellg* and *seekg* functions to allow users to do random data access of any iostream object. These functions may be implemented using the *lseek* API as follows:

```
#include <iostream.h>
#include <sys/types.h>
```

```
#include <unistd.h>

streampos iostream::tellg()
{
        return (streampos)lseek( this->fileno(), (off_t)0, SEEK_CUR );
}

iostream&iostream::seekg( streampos pos, seek_dir ref_loc )
{
        if (ref_loc == ios::beg )
             (void)lseek( this->fileno(), (off_t)pos, SEEK_SET);
        else if ( ref_loc == ios::cur )
             (void)lseek( this->fileno(), (off_t)pos, SEEK_CUR );
        else if ( ref_loc == ios::end )
             (void)lseek( this->fileno(), (off_t)pos, SEEK_END );
        return *this;
}
```

The *iostream::tellg* simply calls *lseek* to return the current file pointer associated with an iostream object. The file descriptor of an iostream object is obtained from the *fileno* member function. Note that *streampos* and *off_t* are the same as the *long* data type.

The *iostream::seekg* also relies on *lseek* to alter the file pointer associated with an iostream object. The arguments to *iostream::seekg* are a file offset and a reference location for the offset. There is a one-to-one mapping of the *seek_dir* values to the *whence* values used by *lseek*:

seek_dir value	lseek whence value
ios::beg	SEEK_SET
ios::cur	SEEK_CUR
ios::end	SEEK_END

Thus, the *iostream::seekg* function simply converts a *seek_dir* value to an *lseek whence* value and calls *lseek* to change an iostream object file pointer according to the *pos* value. The file descriptor of an iostream object is obtained from the *fileno* member function.

7.1.8   link

The *link* function creates a new link for an existing file. This function does not create a new file. Rather, it creates a new path name for an existing file.

The prototype of the *link* function is:

```
#include <unistd.h>
int link ( const char* cur_link, const char* new_link );
```

The first argument, *cur_link,* is a path name of an existing file. The second argument, *new_link,* is a new path name to be assigned to the same file. If this call succeeds, the hard link count attribute of the file will be increased by 1.

In UNIX, *link* cannot be used to create hard links across file systems. Furthermore, *link* cannot be used on directory files unless it is called by a process that has superuser privileges.

The UNIX *ln* command is implemented using the *link* API. A simple version of the *ln* program, that does not support the *-s* (for creating a symbolic link) option, is as follows:

```
/* test_ln.C */
#include <iostream.h>
#include <stdio.h>
#include <unistd.h>

int main ( int argc, char* argv[] )
{
   if ( argc!=3 ) {
      cerr << "usage: " << argv[0] << " <src_file> <dest_file>\n";
      return 0;
   }
   if ( link ( argv[1], argv[2 ] ) == -1 )  {
      perror( "link" );
      return 1;
   }
   return 0;
}
```

7.1.9   unlink

The *unlink* function deletes a link of an existing file. This function decreases the hard link count attributes of the named file, and removes the file name entry of the link from a directory file. If this function succeeds, the file can no longer be reference by that link. A file is removed from the file system when its hard link count is zero and no process has any file descriptor referencing that file.

The prototype of the *unlink* function is:

```
#include <unistd.h>
int unlink ( const char* cur_link );
```

The argument *cur_link* is a path name that references an existing file. The return value is 0 if the call succeeds or -1 if it fails. Some possible causes of failure may be that the *cur_link* is invalid (no file exists with that name), the calling process lacks access permission to remove that path name, or the function is interrupted by a signal.

In UNIX, *unlink* cannot be used to remove a directory file unless the calling process has the superuser privilege.

ANSI C defines the *remove* function which does the similar unlink operation. Furthermore, if the argument to the *remove* function is an empty directory, it will remove that directory. The prototype of the *rename* function is:

```
#include <stdio.h>
int rename ( const char* old_path_name, const char* new_path_name );
```

Both the *link* and the *rename* functions fail when the new link to be created is in a different file system (or disk partition) than the original file.

The UNIX *mv* command can be implemented using the *link* and *unlink* APIs. A simple version of the *mv* program is as follows:

```
#include <iostream.h>
#include <unistd.h>
#include <string.h>

int main ( int argc, char* argv[] )
{
    if (argc!=3 || !strcmp( argv[1], argv[2]) )
        cerr << "usage: " << argv[0] << " <old_link> <new_link>\n";
    else if (link (argv[1], argv[2])==0)
        return unlink(argv[1]);
    return -1;
}
```

The above program takes two command line arguments: *old_link* and *new_link*. It first checks that *old_link* and *new_link* are different path names; otherwise, the program will simply exit, as there is nothing to change. The program calls *link* to set up *new_link* as a new reference to *old_link*. If *link* fails, the program will return -1 as an error status; otherwise, it will call *unlink* to remove the *old_link,* and its return value is that of the *unlink* call.

7.1.10   stat, fstat

The *stat* and *fstat* functions retrieve the file attributes of a given file. The difference between the two functions is that the first argument of *stat* is a file path name, whereas the first argument of *fstat* is a file descriptor. The prototypes of the *stat* and *fstat* functions are:

```
#include <sys/stat.h>
#include <unistd.h>

int stat (const char* path_name, struct stat* statv);
int fstat (const int fdesc, struct stat* statv);
```

The second argument to *stat* and *fstat* is the address of a *struct stat*-typed variable. The *struct stat* data type is defined in the <sys/stat.h> header,. Its declaration, which is similar in UNIX and POSIX.1, is as follows:

```
struct stat
{
    dev_ts    t_dev;      /* file system ID */
    ino_t     st_ino;     /* File inode number */
    mode_t    st_mode;    /* Contains file type and access flags */
    nlink_t   st_nlink;   /* Hard link count */
    uid_t     st_uid;     /* File user ID */
    gid_t     st_gid;     /* File group ID */
    dev_t     st_rdev;    /* Contains major and minor device numbers */
    off_t     st_size;    /* File size in number of bytes */
    time_t    st_atime;   /* Last access time */
    time_t    st_mtime;   /* Last modification time */
    time_t-   st_ctime;   /* Last status change time */
};
```

The return value of both functions is 0 if they succeed or -1 if they fail, and *errno* contains an error status code. Possible failures of these functions may be that a given file path name (for *stat*) or file descriptor (for *fstat*) is invalid, the calling process lacks permission to access the file, or the functions are interrupted by a signal.

If a path name argument specified to *stat* is a symbolic link file, *stat* will resolve the link(s) and access the nonsymbolic link file that is being pointed at. This is the same behavior as the *open* API. Thus, *stat* and *fstat* cannot be used to obtain attributes of symbolic link files themselves. To remedy this problem, BSD UNIX invented the *lstat* API. The *lstat* function prototype is the same as that of *stat*:

```
int        lstat ( const char* path_name, struct stat* statv );
```

Lstat behaves just like *stat* for nonsymbolic link files. However, if a *path_name* argument to *lstat* is a symbolic link file, *lstat* will return the symbolic link file attributes, not the file it refers to. *Lstat* is also available in UNIX System V.3 and V.4, but undefined by POSIX.1.

The UNIX *ls* command is implemented based on the *stat* API. Specifically, the *-l* option of *ls* depicts the *struct stat* data of any file to be listed. The following *test_ls.C* program emulates the UNIX *ls -l* command:

```
/* test_ls.C: program to emulate the UNIX ls -l command */
#include <iostream.h>
#include <sys/types.h>
#include <sys/stat.h>
#include <unistd.h>
#include <pwd.h>
#include <grp.h>

static char xtbl[10] = "rwxrwxrwx";
#ifndef  MAJOR
#define    MINOR_BITS      8
#define    MAJOR(dev)      ( (unsigend)dev >> MINOR_BITS )
#define    MINOR(dev)      ( dev & MINOR_BITS )
#endif

/* Show file type at column 1 of an output line */
static void display_file_type ( ostream& ofs, int st_mode )
{
    switch (st_mode&S_IFMT)    {
        case S_IFDIR:    ofs << 'd'; return;        /* directory file */
        case S_IFCHR:    ofs << 'c'; return;        /* character device file */
        case S_IFBLK:    ofs << 'b'; return;        /* block device file */
        case S_IFREG:    ofs << '-'; return;        /* regular file */
        case S_IFLNK:    ofs << 'l'; return;        /* symbolic link file */
        case S_IFIFO:    ofs << 'p'; return;        /* FIFO file */
    }
}
```

```c
/* Show access perm for owner, group, others, and any special flags */
static void display_access_perm ( ostream& ofs, int st_mode )
{
    char amode[10];
    for (int i=0, j= (1 << 8); i < 9; i++, j>>=1)
            amode[i] = (st_mode&j) ? xtbl[i] : '-';          /* set access perm */
    if (st_mode&S_ISUID) amode[2] = (amode[2]=='x') ? 'S' : 's';
    if (st_mode&S_ISGID) amode[5] = (amode[5]=='x') ? 'G' : 'g';
    if (st_mode&S_ISVTX) amode[8] = (amode[8]=='x') ? 'T' : 't';
    ofs << amode << ' ';
}

/* List attributes of one file */
static void long_list (ostream& ofs, char* path_name)
{
    struct stat statv;
    struct group*gr_p;
    struct passwd*pw_p;

    if (lstat(path_name,&statv))   {
        cerr << "Invalid path name: " << path_name << endl;
        return;
    }

    display_file_type( ofs, statv.st_mode );
    display_access_perm( ofs, statv.st_mode );
    ofs << statv.st_nlink;                              /* display hard link count */

    gr_p = getgrgid(statv.st_gid);               /* GID to group name */
    pw_p = getpwuid(statv.st_uid);               /* convert UID to user name */
    ofs   << ' ' << ( pw_p->pw_name ? pw_p->pw_name : statv.st_uid )
          << ' ' << ( gr_p->gr_name ? gr_gr_name : statv.st_gid ) << ' ';

    if ((statv.st_mode&S_IFMT) == S_IFCHR ||
          ( statv.st_mode&S_IFMT)==S_IFBLK )
        ofs << MAJOR( statv.st_rdev ) << ',' << MINOR( statv.st_rdev );
    else  ofs << statv.st_size;                    /* show file size or major/minor no. */

    ofs << ' ' << ctime( &statv.st_mtime ); /* print last modification time */
    ofs << ' ' << path_name << endl;       /* show file name */
}

/* Main loop to display file attributes one file at a time */
int main ( int argc, char* argv[] )
{
    if ( argc==1 )
```

```
                cerr << "usage: " << argv[0] << " <file path name> ...\n";
        else while (--argc >= 1)  long_list( cout, *++argv );
        return 0;
    }
```

The above program takes one or more file path names as arguments. For each path name it calls *long_list* to display the attributes of the named file in the UNIX *ls -l* format. Specifically, each file attributes are depicted in one physical line with the following data:

- The first field (column 1) is a one-character code to depict the file type
- The second field (columns 2-4) has owner read, write, and execute access rights
- The third field (columns 5-7) has group read, write, and execute access rights
- The fourth field (columns 8-10) has other read, write, and execute access rights
- The fifth field is the file hard link count
- The sixth field is the file user name
- The seventh field is the file group name
- *The eighth field is the file size in number of bytes, or the major and minor device numbers, if this is a character or block device file
- The ninth field is the file last modification time stamp
- The tenth field is the file name

The *st_mode* variable in a *struct stat* record stores several attributes: file type, owner access rights, group access rights, other access rights, a *set-UID* flag, a *set-GID* flag, and a *sticky bit*. There are manifested constants defined in the <sys/stat.h> header to aid the extraction of these various fields, as shown in the above program.

The encoding of a file type to a single character code follows the UNIX *ls -l* convention: *d* stands for a directory file type, *c* stands for a character device file type, *b* stands for a block device file type, - stands for a regular file type, *p* stands for a FIFO file type, and *l* stands for a symbolic link file type.

The access permission for any category of people is always depicted in the read, write, and execute order, and by the *r*, *w* and *x* characters, respectively. A - in place of any *r*, *w*, or *x* character means that there is no read, write, or execute right for a category of people.

The *set-UID, set-GID,* and *sticky* flags are UNIX-specific. If the *set-UID* flag of an executable file is on, the effective user ID of any process created by executing that file will be the same as the file user ID. Thus, if a file user ID is zero (the superuser ID in UNIX), the corresponding process will have the superuser privileges. Similarly, if a file *set-GID* flag is on then the effective group ID of any process created by executing that file will be the same as the file group ID. The effective user ID and group ID of a process are used to determine the access permission of the process to any file. Specifically, the kernel first checks a process effective user ID against a file user ID. If they match, the process will be given the file owner access permission. If the process effective user ID does not match a file user ID but its effective group ID matches that of the file, then the file group access rights are applied to the process. Finally, if neither match, the "others" access permission will be used.

The *set-UID* and *set-GID* flags are useful on some UNIX programs, such as the *passwd*. Processes of these programs need to have a superuser privilege to perform their jobs (for *passwd* to alter the */etc/passwd* or */etc/shadow* file to change user password). Thus, by setting the *set-UID* flag of these programs, users who execute these programs can get their work done as if the superuser were there to help them.

The effective user ID and effective group ID are also used when a process creates a file: The file user ID will be assigned that of the process, and its group ID will be assigned in some system-dependent means: In UNIX System V.3, the file group ID will be assigned that of the process; but in BSD UNIX, the file group ID will be set to the group ID of the directory which contains that file. POSIX.1 permits both System V.3 and BSD methods of assigning file group ID. In UNIX System V.4, a new file group ID is assigned the group ID of the directory that contains it (BSD method) if the *set-GID* flag of the directory is on. Otherwise, the file is assigned the effective group ID of the process that creates it (System V.3 method).

If a *sticky* flag of an executable file is set, after a process of that program terminates, its text (instruction code) will stay resident in the computer's swap memory. Consequently, next time the program is executed, the kernel can start up the process faster. The *sticky* flag is reserved for frequently used programs, such as the UNIX shell or *vi* (the visual editor) programs. A *sticky* flag can be set or reset on files by the superuser only.

The user and group names of any file are supported in UNIX but not required by POSIX.1. The function *getpwuid* converts a user ID to a user name. Similarly, the *getgrgid* converts a group ID to a group name. These two functions are defined in the <pwd.h> and <grp.h> headers, respectively.

The file size is depicted for files, directories, and named pipes. For a device file, the *long_list* function shows the major and minor device numbers of the file. These device numbers are extracted from the *st_rdev* field of the *struct stat* record. Some UNIX systems supply macros called **MAJOR** and **MINOR** (defined in the <sys/stat.h> header) to render portable access of these two numbers. If they are not defined by the system, the sample program defines them explicitly. The MINOR_BITS is the number of least significant bits in the *st_rdev* field used to store the minor device number (most UNIX systems use 8 bits), and the rest of higher order bits in the *st_rdev* field store the major device number.

The last two fields are the last modification time stamp and the file name. These are obtained from the *st_mtime* field of *statv* and the *path_name* arguments, respectively.

A sample output of the above program is:

```
% a.out      /etc/motd  /dev/fd0   /usr/bin
-rw-r-xrwx   1    joe       unix      25    July 5, 1994    /etc/motd
crw-r--r-x   2    mary      admin     30    June 25, 1994   /dev/fd0
drwxr-xr--   1    terry     sharp     15    Oct. 16, 1993   /usr/bin
%
```

7.1.11 access

The *access* function checks the existence and/or access permission of user to a named file. The prototype of the *access* function is:

```
#include <unistd.h>

int access ( const char* path_name, int flag );
```

The *path_name* argument is the path name of a file. The *flag* argument contains one or more of the following bit-flags, which are defined in the <unistd.h> header:

Bit flag	Use
F_OK	Checks whether a named file exists
R_OK	Checks whether a calling process has read permission
W_OK	Checks whether a calling process has write permission
X_OK	Checks whether a calling process has execute permission

The *flag* argument value to an *access* call is composed by bitwise-ORing one or more of the above bit-flags. For example, the following statement checks whether a user has read and write permissions on a file called */usr/foo/access.doc*:

```
int   rc = access( "/usr/foo/access.doc", R_OK|W_OK );
```

If a *flag* value is *F_OK*, the function returns 0 if the *path_name* file exists and -1 otherwise.

If a *flag* value is any combination of *R_OK, W_OK*, and *X_OK*, the *access* function uses the calling process real user ID and real group ID to check against the file user ID and group ID. This determines the appropriate category (owner, group, or others) of access permissions in checking against the actual value of *flag*. The function returns 0 if all the requested permission is permitted, and -1 otherwise.

The following *test_access.C* program uses *access* to determine, for each command line argument, whether a named file exists. If a named file does not exist, it will be created and initialized with a character string *"Hello world."* However, if a named file does exists, the program will simply read data from the file:

```
#include <sys/types.h>
#include <unistd.h>
#include <fcntl.h>

int main ( int argc, char* argv[] )
{
    char  buf[256];
    int    fdesc, len;
    while ( --argc > 0) {
        if (access( *++argv, F_OK ) ) {                    // a brand new file
            fdesc = open( *argv, O_WRONLY|O_CREAT, 0744 );
            write( fdesc, "Hello world\n", 12 );
        } else    {                                        // file exists, read data
            fdesc = open( *argv, O_RDONLY );
            while ( len=read( fdesc, buf, 256 ) )
                write( 1, buf, len );
        }
        close ( fdesc );
    }  /* for each command line argument */
}
```

The above simple program may be used as a base for a database management program: If a new database is to be created, the program will initialize the database file with some startup bookkeeping data; whereas if a database file already exists, the program will read some startup data from the file to check for version compatibility between the program and the database file, etc.

7.1.12　chmod, fchmod

The *chmod* and *fchmod* functions change file access permissions for owner, group, and others, as well as the *set-UID, set-GID,* and *sticky* flags. A process that calls one of these functions should have the effective user ID of either the superuser or the owner of the file. The UNIX *chmod* commands is implemented based on the *chmod* API.

The prototypes of the *chmod* and *fchmod* functions are:

```
#include <sys/types.h>
#include <sys/stat.h>
#include <unistd.h>

int chmod ( const char* path_name, mode_t flag );
int fchmod ( int fdesc, mode_t flag );
```

The *path_name* argument of *chmod* is the path name of a file, whereas the *fdesc* argument of *fchmod* is the file descriptor of a file. The *flag* argument contains the new access permission and any special flags to be set on the file. The *flag* value is the same as that used in the *open* API: It can be specified as an octal integer value in UNIX, or constructed from the manifested constants defined in the <sys/stat.h> header. For example, the following function turns on the *set-UID* flag, removes group write permission and others read and execute permission on a file named */usr/joe/funny.book*:

```
/* chmod.C */
#include <sys/types.h>
#include <sys/stat.h>
#include <unistd.h>

void change_mode()
{
    struct stat      statv;
    int              lag = ( S_IWGRP | S_IROTH | S_IXOTH );
    if (stat( "/usr/joe/funny.book", &statv ))
        perror("stat");
    else {
        flag = (statv.st_mode & ~flag) | S_ISUID;
        if (chmod ( "usr/joe/funny.book", flag ))
            perror("chmod");
    }
}
```

The above program first calls *stat* to get the file */usr/joe/funny.book* current access permission, then it masks off group write permission and others read and execute permission from the *statv.st_mode*. Then it sets the *set-UID* flag in the *statv.st_mode*. All the other existing flags are unmodified. The final *flag* value is passed to *chmod* to carry out the changes on the file. If either the *chmod* or *stat* call fails, the program will call *perror* to print a diagnostic message.

Note that, unlike the *open* API, the access permission specified in the *flag* argument of *chmod* is not modified by the calling process umask.

7.1.13   chown, fchown, lchown

The *chown* and *fchown* functions change the user ID and group ID of files. They differ only in their first argument which refer to a file by either a path name or a file descriptor. The UNIX *chown* and *chgrp* commands are implemented based on these APIs. The *lchown* function is similar to the *chown* function, except that when the *path_name* argument is a symbolic link file, the *lchown* function changes the ownership of the symbolic link file, whereas the *chown* function changes the ownership of the file to which the symbolic link refers.

The function prototypes of these functions are:

```
#include <unistd.h>
#include <sys/types.h>

int chown ( const char* path_name, uid_t uid, gid_t gid );
int fchown ( int fdesc, uid_t uid, gid_t gid );
int lchown ( const char* path_name, uid_t uid, gid_t gid );
```

The *path_name* argument is the path name of a file. The *uid* argument specifies the new user ID to be assigned to the file. The *gid* argument specifies the new group ID to be assigned to the file. If the actual value of the *uid* or *gid* argument is -1, the corresponding ID of the file is not changed.

In BSD UNIX, only a process with superuser privilege can use these functions to change any file user ID and group ID. However, if a process effective user ID matches a file user ID and its effective group ID or one of its supplementary group IDs match the file group ID, the process can change the file group ID only.

In UNIX System V, a process whose effective user ID matches either the user ID of a file or the user ID of a superuser can change the file user ID and group ID.

POSIX1. specifies that if the _POSIX_CHOWN_RESTRICTED variable is defined with a non -1 value, *chown* should behave as in BSD UNIX. However, if the _POSIX_CHOWN_RESTRICTED variable is undefined, *chown* should behave as in UNIX System V.

If *chown* is called by a process that has no superuser privileges and it succeeds on a file, it will clear the file *set-UID* and *set-GID* flags. This is to prevent users from creating programs with ownership assigned to someone else (e.g., the superuser) and then executing those programs with the new owner's privileges.

If *chown* is called by a process with the effective UID of a superuser it is implementation-dependent as to how *chown* will treat the *set-UID* and *set-GID* flags of files it modifies. In UNIX System V.3 and V.4, those flags are kept intact.

The following *test_chown.C* program implements the UNIX *chown* program:

```
#include <iostream.h>
#include <sys/types.h>
#include <sys/stat.h>
#include <unistd.h>
#include <pwd.h>

int main (int argc, char* argv[])
{
    if (argc < 3)  {
        cerr << "Usage: " << argv[0] << " <usr_name> <file> ...\n";
        return 1;
    }

    struct passwd *pwd = getpwuid( argv[1] );   /* convert user name to UID */
    uid_t           UID = pwd ? pwd->pw_uid : -1;
    struct  stat    statv;

    if (UID == (uid_t)-1)
        cerr<< "Invalid user name\n";

    else for (int i=2; i < argc; i++)                    /* do for each file specified */
        if (stat(argv[i],&statv)==0)  {
            if (chown( argv[i], UID, statv.st_gid ) )
                perror( "chown" );
        } else perror( "stat" );

    return 0;
}
```

This program takes at least two command line arguments: the first one is a user name to be assigned to files, and the second and any subsequent arguments are file path names. The program first converts a given user name to a user ID via the *getpwuid* function. If that succeeds, the program processes each named file as follows: it calls *stat* to get the file group ID, then calls *chown* to change the file user ID. If either the *stat* or *chown* API fails, *perror* will be called to print a diagnostic message.

7.1.14 utime

The *utime* function modifies the access and modification time stamps of a file. The prototype of the *utime* function is:

```
#include <sys/types.h>
#include <unistd.h>
#include <utime.h>

int utime ( const char* path_name, struct utimbuf* times );
```

The *path_name* argument is the path name of a file. The *times* argument specifies the new access time and modification time for the file. The *struct utimbuf* is defined in the <utime.h> header as:

```
struct utimbuf
{
    time_t    actime;              /* access time */
    time_t    modtime              /* modification time */
};
```

POSIX.1 defines the *struct utimbuf* in the <utime.h> header, whereas UNIX System V defines it in the <sys/types.h> header. The *time_t* data type is the same as *unsigned long*, and its data is the number of seconds elapsed since the birthday of UNIX: 12 AM, January 1, 1970 UTC (Universal Time Coordinate).

If *times* is specified as 0, the API will set the named file access time and modification time to the current time. This requires that the calling process have write access to the named file, its effective user ID match either the file user ID or that of the superuser.

If *times* is an address of a variable of type *struct utimbuf*, the API will set the file access time and modification time according to the values specified in the variable. This requires that the calling process effective UID either match the file UID or be the same as a superuser.

The return value of *utime* is 0 if it succeeds or -1 if it fails. Possible failures of the API may be: The *path_name* argument is invalid, the process has no access permission and ownership to a named file, or the *times* argument has an invalid address.

The following *test_touch.C* program uses the *utime* function to change the access and modification time stamps of files. The time stamp to set is also defined by users:

```
/* Usage: a.out <offset in seconds> <file> ... */
#include <iostream.h>
#include <stdio.h>
#include <sys/types.h>
#include <utime.h>
#include <time.h>

int main ( int argc, char* argv[] )
{
    struct utimbuf    times;
    int               offset;

    if (argc < 3 || sscanf( argv[1], "%d", &offset) != 1) {
        cerr << "usage: " << argv[0] << " <offset> <file> ...\n";
        return 1;
    }

    /* new time is current time + offset in seconds */
    times.actime = times.modtime = time( 0 ) + offset;

    for ( -i=1; i < argc; i ++)                    /* touch each named file */
        if ( utime ( argv[i], &times ) ) perror( "utime" );
    return 0;
}
```

The above program defines a variable called *times* of type *struct utimbuf* and initializes it with the current time value (as obtained from the *time* function call) plus a user-specified offset time (in seconds). The subsequent command line arguments to the program should be one or more file path names. For each of these files, the program will call *utime* to update the file access time and modification time. If any *utime* call fails, the program will call *perror* to print a diagnostic message.

7.2   File and Record Locking

UNIX systems allow multiple processes to read and write the same file concurrently. This provides a means for data sharing among processes, but it also renders difficulty for any process in determining when data in a file can be overridden by another process. This is especially important for applications like a database manager, where no other process can write or read a file while a process is accessing a database file. To remedy this drawback, UNIX and POSIX systems support a file-locking mechanism. File locking is applicable only for regular files. It allows a process to impose a lock on a file so that other processes can not modify the file until it is unlocked by the process.

Specifically, a process can impose a write lock or a read lock on either a portion of a file or an entire file. The difference between write locks and read locks is that when a write lock is set, it prevents other processes from setting any overlapping read or write locks on the locked region of a file. On the other hand, when a read lock is set, it prevents other processes from setting any overlapping write locks on the locked region of a file. It does, however, allow overlapping read locks to be set on the file by other processes. Thus, the intention of a write lock is to prevent other processes from both reading and writing the locked region while the process that sets the lock is modifying the region. A write lock is also known as an exclusive lock. The use of a read lock is to prevent other processes from writing to the locked region while the process that sets the lock is reading data from the region. Other processes are allowed to lock and read data from the locked regions. Hence, a read lock is also called a *shared lock*.

Furthermore, file locks are mandatory if they are enforced by an operating system kernel. If a mandatory exclusive lock is set on a file, no process can use the *read* or *write* system calls to access data on the locked region. Similarly, if a mandatory shared lock is set on a region of a file, no process can use the *write* system call to modify the locked region. These mechanisms can be used to synchronize reading and writing of shared files by multiple processes: If a process locks up a file, other processes that attempts to write to the locked regions are blocked until the former process releases its lock. However, mandatory locks may cause problems: If a runaway process sets a mandatory exclusive lock on a file and never unlocks it, no other processes can access the locked region of the file until either the runaway process is killed or the system is rebooted. System V.3 and V.4 support mandatory locks, but BSD UNIX and POSIX systems do not.

If a file lock is not mandatory, it is an advisory lock. An advisory lock is not enforced by a kernel at the system call level. This means that even though a lock (read or write) may be set on a file, other processes can still use the *read* or *write* APIs to access the file. To make use of advisory locks, processes that manipulate the same file must cooperate such that they follow this procedure for every read or write operation to the file:

- Try to set a lock at the region to be accessed. If this fails, a process can either wait for the lock request to become successful or go do something else and try to lock the file again later
- After a lock is acquired successfully, read or write the locked region
- Release the lock

By always attempting to set an advisory lock on a region of a file to be worked on, a process will not violate any lock protection set by other processes on the same area, and other processes will not modify that area while the lock in imposed. A process should always release any lock that it imposes on a file as soon as it is done, so that other processes can access the now unlocked region. An advisory lock is considered safe, as no runaway processes can lock up any file forcefully, and other processes can go ahead and read or write to a file after a fixed number of failed attempts to lock the file.

The drawback of advisory locks are that programs that create processes to share files must follow the above file locking procedure to be cooperative. This may be difficult to control when programs are obtained from different sources (e.g., from different software vendors). All UNIX and POSIX systems support advisory locks.

UNIX System V and POSIX.1 use the *fcntl* API for file locking. Specifically, the API can be used to impose read or write locks on either a segment or an entire file. The *fcntl* API in BSD UNIX 4.2 and 4.3 does not support the file locking option. The prototype of the *fcntl* API is:

```
#include <fcntl.h>

int fcntl ( int fdesc, int cmd_flag, ... );
```

The *fdesc* argument is a file descriptor for a file to be processed. The *cmd_flag* argument defines which operation is to be performed. The possible *cmd_flag* values are defined in the <fcntl.h> header. The specific values for file locking and their uses are:

cmd_flag	Use
F_SETLK	Sets a file lock. Do not block if this cannot succeed immediately
F_SETLKW	Sets a file lock and blocks the calling process until the lock is acquired
F_GETLK	Queries as to which process locked a specified region of a file

For file locking, the third argument to *fcntl* is an address of a *struct flock*-typed variable. This variable specifies a region of a file where the lock is to be set, unset, or queried. The *struct flock* is declared in the <fcntl.h> as:

```
struct flock
{
    short    l_type;      /* what lock to be set or to unlock file */
    short    l_whence;    /* a reference address for the next field */
    off_t    l_start;     /* offset from the l_whence reference address */
    off_t    l_len;       /* how many bytes in the locked region */
    pid_t    l_pid;       /* PID of a process which has locked the file */
};
```

The *l_type* field specifies the lock type to be set or unset. The possible values, which are defined in the <fcntl.h> header, and their uses are:

l_type value	Use
F_RDLCK	Sets a a read (shared) lock on a specified region
F_WRLCK	Sets a write (exclusive) lock on a specified region
F_UNLCK	Unlocks a specified region

The *l_whence, l_start,* and *l_len* define a region of a file to be locked or unlocked. This is similar to the *lseek* API, where the *l_whence* field defines a reference address to which the *l_start* byte offset value is added. The possible values of *l_whence* and their uses are:

l_whence value	Use
SEEK_CUR	The *l_start* value is added to the current file pointer address
SEEK_SET	The *l_start* value is added to byte 0 of the file
SEEK_END	The *l_start* value is added to the end (current size) of the file

The *l_len* specifies the size of a locked region beginning from the start address as defined by *l_whence* and *l_start*. If *l_len* is a positive number greater than 0, it is the length of the locked region in number of bytes. If *l_len* is 0, the locked region extends from its start address to a system-imposed limit on the maximum size of any file. This means that as the file size increases, the lock also applies to the extended file region. The *l_len* cannot have a negative value.

A *struct flock*-typed variable is defined and set by a process before it is passed to a *fcntl* call. If the *cmd_arg* of the *fcntl* call is F_SETLK or F_SETLKW, the variable defines a region of a file to be locked or unlocked. If, however, the *cmd_arg* is F_GETLK, the variable is used as both an input and a return variable. Specifically, when *fcntl* is called, the variable specifies a region of a file where lock status is queried. Then, when *fcntl* returns, the variable contains the region of the file that is locked and the ID of the process that owns the locked region. The process ID is returned via the *l_pid* field of the variable.

Note that if a process sets a read lock on a file, for example from address 0 to 256, then sets a write lock on the file from address 0 to 512, the process will own only one write lock on the file from 0 to 512. The previous read lock from 0 to 256 is now covered by the write lock, and the process does not own two locks on the region from 0 to 256. This process is called *lock promotion*. Furthermore, if the process now unlocks the file from 128 to 480, it will own two write locks on the file: one from 0 to 127 and the other from 481 to 512. This process is called *lock splitting*.

A lock set by the *fcntl* API is an advisory lock. POSIX.1 does not support mandatory locks. UNIX System V.3 and V.4, however, permit users to set mandatory locks via *fcntl*. This is achieved by setting the following attributes of a file, and thereafter any locks set by *fcntl* on that file will be mandatory locks:

- Turn on the *set-GID* flag of the file
- Turn off the group execute right of the file

Alternatively, the *chmod* command in UNIX System V.3 and V.4 may also be used to specify that any read or write locks set on a file are mandatory. The *chmod* command syntax is:

chmod   a+l   <file_name>

All file locks set by a process will be unlocked when the process terminates. Furthermore, if a process locks a file and then creates a child process via *fork* (the *fork* API is explained in the next chapter), the child process will not inherit the file lock.

The return value of *fcntl* is 0 if it succeeds or -1 if it fails. Possible causes of failure may be that the file descriptor is invalid, the requested region to be locked or unlocked conflicts with locks set by another process, the third argument contains invalid data, or the system-tunable limit on the maximum number of record locks per file has been reached.

The following *file_lock.C* program illustrates a use of *fcntl* for file locking:

```
#include <iostream.h>
#include <stdio.h>
#include <sys/types.h>
#include <fcntl.h>
#include <unistd.h>

int main (int argc, char* argv[])
{
    struct flock            fvar;
    int                     fdesc;
    while (--argc > 0) {                            /* do the following for each file */
        if (( fdesc=open(*++argv,O_RDWR ))==-1 ) {
            perror("open"); continue;
        }
        fvar.l_type         = F_WRLCK;
        fvar.l_whence       = SEEK_SET;
        fvar.l_start        = 0;
        fvar.l_len          = 0;
        /* Attempt to set an exclusive (write) lock on the entire file */
        while (fcntl(fdesc, F_SETLK,&fvar)==-1) {
            /* Set lock fails, find out who has locked the file */
            while (fcntl(fdesc,F_GETLK,&fvar)!=-1 &&
```

```
                     fvar.l_type!=F_UNLCK) {
                     cout << *argv << " locked by " << fvar.l_pid
                                  << " from " << fvar.l_start << " for "
                                  << fvar.l_len << " byte for " <<
                                  (fvar.l_type==F_WRLCK ? 'w' : 'r') << endl;
                     if (!fvar.l_len) break;
                     fvar.l_start    += fvar.l_len;
                     fvar.l_len      = 0;
                 }   /* while there are locks set by other processes */
             }   /* while set lock un-successful */

             /* Lock the file OK. Now process data in the file */
             ...
             /* Now unlock the entire file */
             fvar.l_type         = F_UNLCK;
             fvar.l_whence       = SEEK_SET;
             fvar.l_start        = 0;
             fvar.l_len          = 0;
             if (fcntl(fdesc, F_SETLKW,&fvar)==-1) perror("fcntl");
         }
         return 0;
     }   /* main */
```

The above program takes one or more path names as arguments. For each file specified, the program attempts to set an advisory lock on the entire file via *fcntl*. If the *fcntl* call fails, the program scans the file to list all lock information to the standard output. Specifically, for each locked region, the program reports:

- The file path name
- The process ID that locks that region
- The start address of the locked region
- The length of the locked region
- Whether the lock is exclusive (*w*) or shared (*r*)

The program loops repeatedly until a *fcntl* call succeeds in locking the file. After that, the program will process the file in some way, then it calls *fcntl* again to unlock the file.

7.3   Directory File APIs

Directory files in UNIX and POSIX systems are used to aid users in organizing their files into some structure based on the specific use of files (e.g., a user may store all C++ source of a program under the */usr/<program_name>/C* directory). They are also used by the operating system to convert file path names to their inode numbers.

Directory files are created in BSD UNIX and POSIX.1 by the *mkdir* API:

```
#include <sys/stat.h>
#include <unistd.h>

int mkdir ( const char* path_name, mode_t mode );
```

The *path_name* argument is the path name of a directory file to be created. The *mode* argument specifies the access permission for the owner, group, and others to be assigned to the file. Like in the *open* API, the *mode* value is modified by the calling process umask.

The return value of *mkdir* is 0 if it succeeds or -1 if it fails. Possible causes of failure may be: The *path_name* is invalid, the calling process lacks permission to create the specified directory, or the *mode* argument is invalid.

UNIX System V.3 uses the *mknod* API to create directory files. UNIX System V.4 supports both the *mkdir* and *mknod* APIs for creating directory files. The difference between the two APIs is that a directory created by *mknod* does not contain the "." and ".." links; thus, it is not usable until those links are explicitly created by a user. On the other hand, a directory created by *mkdir* has the "." and ".." links created in one atomic operation, and it is ready to be used. In general, *mknod* should not be used to create directories. Furthermore, on systems that do not support the *mkdir* API, one can still create directories via the *system* API:

```
char      syscmd[ 256 ];
sprintf( syscmd, "mkdir     %s", <directory_name> );
if ( system ( syscmd ) == -1)     perror( "mkdir");
```

A newly created directory has its user ID set to the effective user ID of the process that creates it, and the directory group ID will be set to either the effective group ID of the calling process or the group ID of the parent directory that hosts the new directory (in the same manner as for regular files).

A directory file is a record-oriented file, where each record stores a file name and the inode number of a file that resides in that directory. However, the directory record structure is different on different file systems. For example, UNIX system V directory records are fixed-size, whereas BSD UNIX directory records are of variable size. To allow a process to scan directories in a file system-independent manner, a directory record is defined as *struct dirent* in the <dirent.h> header for UNIX System V and POSIX.1, and as *struct direct* in the <sys/dir.h> header in BSD UNIX 4.2 and 4.3. The *struct dirent* and *struct direct* data types have one common field, *d_name,* which is a character array that contains the name of a file resid-

179

ing in a directory. Furthermore, the following portable functions are defined for directory file browsing. These functions are defined in both the <dirent.h> and <sys/dir.h> headers.

```
#include <sys/types.h>
#if defined (BSD) && !_POSIX_SOURCE
    #include <sys/dir.h>
    typedef struct direct Dirent;
#else
    #include <dirent.h>
    typedef struct dirent Dirent;
#endif

DIR* opendir (const char* path_name);
Dirent* readdir (DIR* dir_fdesc);
int closedir (DIR* dir_fdesc);
void rewinddir (DIR* dir_fdesc);
```

The uses of these functions are:

Function	Use
opendir	Opens a directory file for read-only. Returns a file handle DIR* for future reference of the file
readdir	Reads a record from a directory file referenced by *dir_fdesc* and returns that record information
closedir	Closes a directory file referenced by *dir_fdesc*
rewinddir	Resets the file pointer to the beginning of the directory file referenced by *dir_fdesc*. The next call to *readdir* will read the first record from the file

The *opendir* function is analogous to the *open* API. It takes a directory file path name as an argument and opens the file for read-only. The function returns a DIR* file handler which has a use similar to that of FILE* value returned from *fopen*. The DIR data structure is defined in the <dirent.h> or <sys/dir.h> header.

The *readdir* function reads the next directory record from a directory file referenced by the *dir_fdesc* argument. The *dir_fdesc* value is the DIR* return value from an *opendir* call. The function returns the address of a *struct dirent* or *struct direct* record, which stores the file name of a file entry in the directory. When *readdir* is called after the *opendir* or *rewinddir* API, it will return the first data record from the file, on the next call it will return the second data record in the file, etc. When *readdir* has scanned all records in a directory file, it will return a zero value to indicate that end-of-file has been reached. Note that a data type called *Dirent* was defined to be either *struct dirent* (for POSIX and System V UNIX) or *struct direct* (for BSD UNIX in non-POSIX conformance mode). In this way, any application that calls *readdir* can treat the return value uniformly as *Dirent* in any system.

The *closedir* function is analogous to the *close* API. It terminates the connection between the *dir_fdesc* handler and a directory file.

The *rewinddir* function resets a file pointer associated with a *dir_fdesc*, so that if *readdir* is called again, it will scan the directory file (referenced by the *dir_fdesc*) from the beginning.

UNIX systems (System V and BSD UNIX) have defined additional functions for random access of directory file records. These functions are not supported by POSIX.1:

Function	**Use**
telldir	Returns the file pointer of a given *dir_fdesc*
seekdir	Changes the file pointer of a given *dir_fdesc* to a specified address

Directory files are removed by the *rmdir* API. Users may also use the *unlink* API to remove directories, provided they have superuser privileges. These APIs require that the directories to be removed be empty, in that they contain no files other than the "." and ".." links. The prototype of *rmdir* function is:

```
#include <unistd.h>

int rmdir (const char* path_name);
```

The following *list_dir.C* program illustrates uses of the *mkdir, opendir, readdir, closedir,* and *rmdir* APIs:

```
#include <iostream.h>
#include <stdio.h>
#include <sys/types.h>
#include <unistd.h>
#include <string.h>
#include <sys/stat.h>
#if defined (BSD) && !_POSIX_SOURCE
    #include <sys/dir.h>
    typedef struct direct Dirent;
#else
    #include <dirent.h>
    typedef struct dirent Dirent;
#endif
```

```
int main ( int argc, char* argv[] )
{
   Dirent*     dp;
   DIR*        dir_fdesc;

   while ( --argc > 0 ) {                          /* do the following for each file */
      if ( !(dir_fdesc = opendir( *++argv ) )) {
         if (mkdir( *argv, S_IRWXU|S_IRWXG|S_IRWXO ) == -1 )
            perror( "opendir" );
         continue;
      }

      /* scan each directory file twice */
      for ( int i=0; i < 2; i++ ) {
         for ( int cnt=0; dp=readdir( dir_fdesc ); ) {
            if (i) cout << dp->d_name << endl;
            if (strcmp( dp->d_name, "." ) && strcmp( dp->d_name, ".." ) )
                  cnt++;                            /* count how many files in directory*/
         }
         if (!cnt) { rmdir( *argv ); break; }  /* empty directory */
         rewinddir( dir_fdesc );                   /* reset pointer for second round */
      }
      closedir( dir_fdesc );
   }                                                /* for each file */
}                                                   /* main */
```

The above program takes one or more directory file path names as arguments. For each argument, the program opens it via the *opendir* and stores the file handler in the *dir_fdesc* variable. If the *opendir* call fails, the program assumes the directory does not exist and attempts to create it via the *mkdir* API. If, however, the *opendir* succeeds, the program scans the directory file using the *readdir* API and determines the number of files, excluding "." and ".." files, in the directory. After this is done, it removes the directory, via the *rmdir* API, if it is empty. If a directory is not empty, the program resets the file pointer associated with the *dir_fdesc* via the *rewinddir*, it then scans the directory file a second time and echoes all file names in that directory to the standard output. When the second round of directory scanning is completed, the program closes the *dir_fdesc* with the *closedir* API.

7.4   Device File APIs

Device files are used to interface physical devices (e.g, console, modem, floppy drive) with application programs. Specifically, when a process reads or writes to a device file, the kernel uses the major and minor device numbers of a file to select a device driver function to carry out the actual data transfer. Device files may be character-based or block-based.

Device file support is implementation-dependent. POSIX.1 does not specify how device files are to be created. UNIX systems define the *mknod* API to create device files:

```
#include <sys/stat.h>
#include <unistd.h>

int mknod (const char* path_name, mode_t mode, int device_id);
```

The *path_name* argument is the path name of a device file to be created. The *mode* argument specifies the access permission, for the owner, group, and others, to be assigned to the file, as well as the S_IFCHR or S_IFBLK flag. The latter flag is used to indicate whether this is a character or block device file. Access permission is modified by the calling process umask. Finally, the *device_id* contains the major and minor device numbers and is constructed in most UNIX systems as follows: The lowest byte of a *device_id* is set to a minor device number and the next byte is set to the major device number. For example, to create a block device file called *SCSI5* with major and minor numbers of 15 and 3, respectively, and access rights of read-write-execute for everyone, the *mknod* system call is:

mknod("SCSI5", S_IFBLK|S_IRWXU|S_IRWXG|S_IRWXO, (15<<8) | 3);

Note that in UNIX System V.4, the major and minor device numbers are extended to fourteen and eighteen bits, respectively. The major and minor device numbers are used as follows: When a process reads from or writes to a device file, the file's major device number is used to locate and invoke a device driver function that does the actual data transmission with the physical device. The minor device number is an argument being passed to the device driver function when it is invoked. This is needed because a device driver function may be used for different types of device, and the minor device number specifies the parameters (e.g. buffer size) to be used for a particular device type.

The *mknod* API must be called by a process with superuser privileges. The user ID and group ID attributes of a device file are assigned in the same manner as for regular files. The file size attribute of any device file has no meaningful use.

The return value of *mknod* is 0 if it succeeds or -1 if it fails. Possible failures include: The path name specified is invalid, the process lacks permission to create a device file, or the *mode* argument is invalid.

Once a device file is created, any process may use the *open* API to connect to the file. It can then use *read, write, stat,* and *close* APIs to manipulate the file. *lseek* is applicable to block device files but not to character device files. A device file may be removed via the *unlink* API.

When a process calls *open* to establish connection with a device file, it may specify the O_NONBLOCK and O_NOCTTY flags that are defined by POSIX.1. Uses of these flags are depicted in the following.

In UNIX, if a calling process has no controlling terminal and it opens a character device file, the kernel will set this device file as the controlling terminal of the process. However, if the O_NOCTTY flag is set in the *open* call, such action will be suppressed.

The O_NONBLOCK flag specifies that the *open* call and any subsequent *read* or *write* calls to a device file should be nonblocking to the process.

Only privileged users (e.g., the superuser in UNIX) may use the *mknod* API to create device files. All other users may read and write device files as if they were regular files, subjected to the access permissions set on those device files.

The following *test_mknod.C* program illustrates use of the *mknod, open, read, write*, and *close* APIs on a block device file.

```
#include <iostream.h>
#include <stdio.h>
#include <stdlib.h>
#include <sys/types.h>
#include <unistd.h>
#include <fcntl.h>
#include <sys/stat.h>

int main( int argc, char* argv[] )
{
   if ( argc != 4 ) {
      cout << "usage: " << argv[0] << " <file> <major no> <minor no>\n";
      return 0;
   }
   int major = atoi( argv[2]), minor = atoi( argv[3] );
   (void)mknod( argv[1], S_IFCHR|S_IRWXU|S_IRWXG|S_IRWXO,
          ( major <<8 ) | minor );

   int rc=1, fd = open( argv[1], O_RDWR|O_NONBLOCK|O_NOCTTY );
   char buf[256];

   while ( rc && fd != -1 )
      if (( rc = read( fd, buf, sizeof( buf )) ) < 0 )
           perror( "read" );
      else if ( rc ) cout << buf << endl;
   close(fd);
} /* main */
```

This program takes three arguments: the first one is a device file name, the second one a major device number, and the last one a minor device number. The program will use these arguments to create a character device file via *mknod*. The program opens the file for read-write and sets the O_NONBLOCK and NO_CTTY flags. It then reads data from the device file and echoes data to the standard output. When end-of-file is encountered, the program closes the file descriptor associated with the device file and terminates.

Users should notice that the treatment of device files is almost identical to that of regular files, the only differences are the ways device files are created and the fact that *lseek* is not applicable for character device files.

7.5   FIFO File APIs

FIFO files are also known as *named pipes*. They are special *pipe device* files used for interprocess communication. Specifically, any process can attach to a FIFO file to read, write, or read-write data. Data written to a FIFO file are stored in a fixed-size (PIPE_BUF, as defined in the <limits.h> header) buffer and are retrieved in a first-in-first-out (FIFO) order.

BSD UNIX and POSIX.1 define the *mkfifo* API to create FIFO files:

```
#include <sys/types.h>
#include <sys/stat.h>
#include <unistd.h>

int mkfifo ( const char* path_name, mode_t mode );
```

The *path_name* argument is the path name of a FIFO file to be created. The *mode* argument specifies the access permission, for user, group, and others, to be assigned to the file, as well as the S_IFIFO flag to indicate that this is a FIFO file. Access permission is modified by the calling process umask. The user ID and group ID attributes of a FIFO file are assigned in the same manner as for regular files.

For example, to create a FIFO file called *FIFO5* with access permission of read-write-execute for everyone, the *mkfifo* call is:

mkfifo("FIFO5", S_IFIFO | S_IRWXU | S_IRWXG | S_IRWXO);

The return value of *mkfifo* is 0 if it succeeds or -1 if it fails. Possible failures may be: The path name specified is invalid, a process lacks permission to create the file, or an invalid *mode* argument is specified.

UNIX System V.3 uses the *mknod* API to create FIFO files. However, UNIX System V.4 supports the *mkfifo* API.

Once a FIFO file is created, any process may use the *open* API to connect to the file,. It can then use *read, write*, *stat*, and *close* APIs to manipulate the file. *lseek* is not applicable to FIFO files. A FIFO file may be removed via the *unlink* API.

When a process opens a FIFO file for read-only, the kernel will block the process until there is another process that opens the same file for write. Similarly, if a process opens a FIFO for write, it will be blocked until another process opens the FIFO file for read. This provides a method for processes synchronization. Furthermore, if a process writes to a FIFO that is full, the process will be blocked until another process has read data from the FIFO to make room for new data in the FIFO. Conversely, if a process attempts to read data from a FIFO that is empty, the process will be blocked until another process writes data to the FIFO.

If a process does not desire to be blocked by a FIFO file, it can specify the O_NONBLOCK flag in the *open* call to the FIFO file. With this flag, the *open* API will not block the process even though there is no process attached to the other end of the FIFO file. Furthermore, if the process subsequently calls the *read* or *write* API on the FIFO file and data is not ready for transfer, these functions will return immediately with a -1 value, and set error to EAGAIN. Thus, the process can continue to do something else and try these operations later. UNIX System V defines the O_NDELAY flag which has is similar to the O_NONBLOCK flag. The difference with the O_NDELAY flag is that the *read* and *write* functions will return a zero value when they are supposed to block a process. In this case it is difficult to differentiate between an end-of-file condition and an empty one (where there is the possibility of more being written). UNIX System V.4 supports both the O_NDELAY and O_NONBLOCK flags.

Another special thing about FIFO files is that if a process writes to a FIFO file that has no other process attached to it for read, the kernel will send a SIGPIPE signal (signals are described in Chapter 9) to the process to notify it of the illegal operation. Furthermore, if a process reads a FIFO file that has no process attached to its write end, the process will read the remaining data in the FIFO and then an end-of-file indicator. Thus, if two processes are to communicate via a FIFO file, it is important that the writer process closes its file descriptor when it is done, so that the reader process can see the end-of-file condition.

It is possible for a process to open a FIFO file for both read and write. POSIX.1 does not specify how the kernel should handle this, but in UNIX systems the process will not be blocked by the *open* call. The process can use the file descriptor returned from the *open* API to read and write data with the FIFO file.

The following *test_fifo.C* example illustrates use of *mkfifo, open, read, write*, an *close* APIs for a FIFO file:

```
#include <iostream.h>
#include <stdio.h>
```

```
#include <sys/types.h>
#include <unistd.h>
#include <fcntl.h>
#include <sys/stat.h>
#include <string.h>
#include <errno.h>

int main( int argc, char* argv[] )
{
   if ( argc != 2 && argc != 3 ) {
      cout << "usage: " << argv[0] << " <file> [<arg>]\n";
      return 0;
   }
   int      fd;
   char     buf[256];
   (void)mkfifo( argv[1], S_IFIFO|S_IRWXU|S_IRWXG|S_IRWXO );
   if (argc==2) {                               /* reader process */
        fd = open( argv[1],O_RDONLY|O_NONBLOCK );
        while ( read( fd, buf, sizeof( buf ) )==-1 && errno==EAGAIN )
            sleep( 1 );
        while ( read( fd, buf, sizeof( buf ) ) > 0 )
            cout << buf << endl;
   } else   {                                   /* writer process */
        fd = open( argv[1], O_WRONLY );
        write( fd, argv[2], strlen( argv[2] ) );
   }
   close(fd);
}
```

The above program takes one or two arguments. The first argument is the name of a FIFO file to be used. The program calls *mkfifo* to create the FIFO file if it does not exist. It then checks whether it has one or two arguments. If it has one argument, it will open the FIFO file for read-only. It will then read all data from the FIFO file and echo them to the standard output. However, if the process has two arguments, it will open the FIFO file for write and will write the second argument to the FIFO file. Thus, this program can be run twice to create two processes that communicate through a FIFO file. Assuming the program has been compiled into an executable file call *a.out,* the sample run of this program is:

```
%    a.out FF64                    # create a reader process
%    a.out FF64 "Hello world"      # create a writer process
Hello world                        # reader process output
```

Another method to create FIFO files for interprocess communication is to use the *pipe* API:

```
#include <unistd.h>

int pipe ( int fds[2] );
```

The *pipe* API creates the same FIFO file as does *mkfifo*. However, the FIFO file created by the *pipe* API is transient: There is no file created in a file system to associate with the FIFO file, and it will be discarded by the kernel once all processes close their file descriptors that reference the FIFO. The uses of the *fds* argument are: *fds[0]* is a file descriptor to read data from the FIFO file, and *fds[1]* is a file descriptor to write data to the FIFO file. Because the FIFO file cannot be referenced by a path name, its use is restricted to processes that are related: The FIFO file is created by a parent process, which then creates one or more child processes; these child processes inherit the FIFO file descriptors from the parent, and they can communicate among themselves, and with the parent, via the FIFO file. The restrictive use of FIFO files created by the *pipe* API caused the invention of named pipes, so that unrelated processes can communicate using FIFO files.

7.6   Symbolic Link File APIs

Symbolic links are defined in BSD UNIX 4.2 and used in BSD 4.3, System V.3 and V.4. Symbolic links are developed to overcome several shortcomings of hard links:

- Symbolic links can link files across file systems
- Symbolic links can link directory files
- Symbolic links always reference the latest version of the files to which they link

The last point is the major advantage of symbolic links over hard links. For example, suppose a user creates a file called */usr/go/test1* and a hard link to it called */usr/joe/hdlnk*:

        ln   /usr/go/test1   /usr/joe/hdlnk

If the user deletes the */usr/go/test1*, the file is now referenced by */usr/joe/hdlnk* only. However, if the user then creates a file called */usr/go/test1,* which is a file totally different than */usr/joe/hdlnk,* the */usr/joe/hdlnk* will still refer to the old file, whereas the */usr/go/test1* now refers to the new file. Thus, hard links can be broken by removal of one or more links.

In the above example if a symbolic link is used instead, the link will not be broken. Specifically, after a symbolic link called */usr/joe/synlnk* is created as:

        ln   -s   /usr/go/test1   /usr/joe/symlnk

If the user deletes the */usr/go/test1,* the */usr/joe/symlnk* will refer to a nonexistent file, and any operations on that link (*cat, more, sort,* etc.) will fail. However, if the user creates the new */usr/go/test1,* the */usr/joe/symlnk* will automatically refer to this new file, and the link is reestablished again.

Symbolic links are being proposed to be included the POSIX.1 standard. BSD UNIX defines the following APIs for symbolic links manipulation:

```
#include <sys/types.h>
#include <sys/stat.h>
#include <unistd.h>

int symlink ( const char* org_link, const char* sym_link );
int readlink ( const char* sym_link, char* buf, int size );
int lstat ( const char* sym_link, struct stat* statv );
```

The *org_link* and *sym_link* arguments to a *symlink* call specify the original file path name and the symbolic link path name to be created. For example, to create a symbolic link called */usr/joe/lnk* for a file called */usr/go/test1*, the *symlink* call will be:

```
symlink ( "/usr/go/test1", "usr/joe/lnk" );
```

This syntax is the same as that of the *link* API. The return value of *symlink* is 0 if it succeeds or -1 if it fails. Possible causes of failure are: The path name specified is illegal, the *sym_link* file already exists, or the calling process lacks permission to create the new file.

To query the path name to which a symbolic link refers, users must use the *readlink* API. This is necessary because the *open* API automatically resolves any symbolic link to the actual file to which a link refers, and it will connect a calling process to the actual nonlink file. The arguments to the *readlink* API are: *sym_link* is the path name of a symbolic link, *buf* is a character array buffer that holds the return path name referenced by the link, and *size* specifies the maximum capacity (in number of bytes) of the *buf* argument. The return value of *readlink* is -1 if it fails or the actual number of characters of a path name that is placed in the *buf* argument. Possible causes of failure for *readlink* are: The *sym_link* path name is not a symbolic link, the *buf* argument is an illegal address, or a calling process lacks permission to access the symbolic link file.

The following function takes a symbolic link path name as argument, and it will call *readlink* repeatedly to resolve all links to the file. The *while* loop terminates when *readlink* returns -1, and the *buf* variable contains the nonlink file path name, which is then printed to the standard output:

```
#include <iostream.h>
#include <sys/types.h>
#include <unistd.h>
#include <string.h>

int resolve_link( const char* sym_link )
{
    char*    buf[256], tname[256];
    strcpy(tname,sym_link);
    while ( readlink( tname, buf, sizeof( buf ) ) > 0 )
        strcpy( tname, buf );
    cout <<sym_link << " => " <<buf << endl;
}
```

The *lstat* function is used to query the file attributes of symbolic links. This is needed as the *stat* and *fstat* functions show only nonsymbolic link file attributes. The function prototype and return values of *lstat* are the same as those of *stat*. Furthermore, *lstat* can be used on non-symbolic link files, and it behaves like *stat*. The UNIX *ls -l* command uses *lstat* to display information of all file type, including symbolic links.

The following *test_symln.C* program emulates the UNIX *ln* command. The main function of the program is to create a link to a file. The names of the original file and new link are specified as the arguments to the program, and if the *-s* option is not specified, the program will create a hard link. Otherwise, it will create a symbolic link:

```
#include <iostream.h>
#include <sys/types.h>
#include <unistd.h>
#include <string.h>

/* Emulate the UNIX ln command */
int main (int argc, char* argv[])
{
    char*    buf[256], tname[256];
    if ((argc< 3 && argc > 4) || (argc==4 && strcmp(argv[1],"-s"))) {
        cout << "usage: " << argv[0] << " [-s] <orig_file> <new_link>\n";
        return 1;
    }
    if (argc==4)
        return symlink( argv[2], argv[3]);/* create a symbolic link */
    else
        return link(argv[1], argv[2]);/* create a hard link */
}
```

7.7   General File Class

The C++ *fstream* class can be used to define objects that represent files in a file system. Specifically, the *fstream* class contains member functions like *open, close, read, write, tellg*, and *seekg,* which are based on the *open, read, write*, and *lseek* APIs. Thus, any application program can define *fstream* class objects associated with files for read and write.

However, *fstream* does not provide any means for users to perform *stat, chmod, chown, utime*, and *link* functions on its objects. It also does not create any files other than regular files. Thus *fstream* does not encapsulate the complete POSIX and UNIX systems file object functions.

To remedy the *fstream* class deficiency, a new *filebase* class is defined below, which incorporates the *fstream* class properties and additional functions to allow users to get or change object file attributes and to create hard links:

```
/* filebase.h r*/
#ifndef FILEBASE_H
#define FILEBASE_H

#include   <iostream.h>
#include   <fstream.h>
#include   <sys/types.h>
#include   <sys/stat.h>
#include   <unistd.h>
#include   <utime.h>
#include   <fcntl.h>
#include   <string.h>

typedef enum {   REG_FILE='r', DIR_FILE='d', CHAR_FILE='c',
                 BLK_FILE='b', PIPE_FILE='p', SYM_FILE='s',
                 UNKNOWN_FILE='?'}    FILE_TYPE_ENUM;

/* A base class to encapsulate POSIX and UNIX file objects' properties */
class filebase:     public fstream
{
   protected:
     char*filename;
         friend ostream& operator<<( ostream& os, filebase& fobj )
      {
          /* display file attributes in UNIX ls -l command output format */
          return os;
      };
   public:
     filebase()              { filename = 0; };
```

```
        filebase( const char* fn, int flags, int prot=filebuf::openprot )
            : fstream( fn, flags, prot )
        {
            filename = new char[strlen(fn)+1];
            strcpy(filename,fn);
        };
        virtual ~filebase()   { delete filename; };
        virtual int create( const char* fn, mode_t mode )
                            {       return ::creat ( fn, mode );                        };
        int fileno()        {       return rdbuf()->fd();                              };
        int chmod( mode_t mode )
                            {       return ::chmod ( filename, mode );      };
        int chown( uid_t uid, gid_t gid )
                            {       return ::chown( filename, uid, gid );   };
        int utime( const struct utimbuf *timbuf_Ptr )
                            {       return ::utime( filename,timbuf_Ptr ); };
        int link( const char* new_link )
                            {       return ::link( filename, new_link );    };
        virtual int remove( ){   return ::unlink( filename );                       };

        // Query a filebase object's file type
        FILE_TYPE_ENUM file_type()
        {
            struct statstatv;
            if (stat( filename,&statv )==0 )
                switch ( statv.st_mode & S_IFMT) {
                    case S_IFREG: return REG_FILE;          // regular file
                    case S_IFDIR:  return DIR_FILE;          // directory file
                    case S_IFCHR: return CHAR_FILE;         // char device file
                    case S_IFIFO:  return PIPE_FILE;         // block device file
                    case S_IFLNK:  return SYM_FILE;          // symbolic link file
                }
            return UNKNOWN_FILE;
        };
    };
#endif   /* filebase.h */
```

The *filebase* constructor passes its arguments to its *fstream* superclass constructor for connection with an object to a file named by *fn* with the specified access mode. It then allocates a dynamic buffer to hold the *fn* path name in a *filename* private variable. The *filename* variable is used in other member functions like *chmod*, *link*, and *remove*, etc.

The *filebase* destructor deallocates the *filename* dynamic buffer. It then uses its *fstream* destructor to disconnect an object from a file named by *filename*.

The *fileno* member function returns the file descriptor of a file managed by a filebase object.

The *chmod* member function aids users in changing access permission of a file connected to a *filebase* object. The argument *mode* is the same as that for the POSIX.1 *chmod* function and the *filename* variable specifies which file access permission is to be changed.

The *chown* member function aids users in changing the user ID and group ID of a file connected to a *filebase* object. The arguments *uid* and *gid* are the same as that for the POSIX.1 *chown* function, and the *filename* variable specifies which file user IDs and group IDs are to be changed.

The *utime* member function helps users change the access and modification time stamps of a file connected to a *filebase* object. The argument *timbuf_Ptr* is the same as that for the POSIX.1 *utime* function, and the *filename* variable specifies which file access and modification time stamps are to be changed.

The *link* member function allows users to create a hard link to a file connected to a *filebase* object. The argument *new_link* contains the new link name. The original link of a file connected to an object is obtained from the *filename* variable of the object. This function calls the POSIX.1 *link* function to create a new hard link.

The *create* member function creates a file with a given name. This function calls the *creat* API to create a named file in a file system, and it is applicable only for regular files.

The *remove* member function removes a link referenced by the *filename* variable of an object. If this call succeeds, no processes can reference the file with that path name.

The overloaded "<<" operator of *ostream* is used to display the file attributes of a file connected to a *filebase* object. The function may call the *long_list* function (as depicted in Section 7.1.10) to query and display the file properties named by the *filename* private variable.

The *file_type* function determines the file type of any *filebase* object. It calls the *stat* API on a given *filename* and determine the file type of a corresponding object. The function returns an enumerator based on the FILE_TYPE_ENUM data type. If a *stat* call fails or the file type of an object is undetermined, the function returns an UNKNOWN_FILE value. Otherwise, it returns one of the REG_FILE, DIR_FILE, etc. enumerators as return value.

To illustrate the use of the *filebase* class, the following *test_filebase.C* program defines a *filebase* object called *rfile,* to be associated with a file called */usr/text/unix.doc* for read. Furthermore, the program displays object file attributes to the standard output and changes the file user ID and group ID to 15 and 30, respectively. Furthermore, it changes the file access and modification times to the current time, and then creates a hard link called */home/jon/ hdlnk*. Finally, it removes the original link, */usr/text/unix.doc*. The *test_filebase.C* program is:

```
#include "filebase.h"
int main()
{                                                    // Example for filebase
    filebase    rfile("/usr/text/unix.doc",ios::in);  // define an object
    cout << rfile << endl;                           // display file attributes
    rfile.chown(15, 30);                             // change UID and GID
    rfile.utime(0);                                  // touch time stamp
    rfile.link("/home/jon/hdlnk");                   // create a hard link
    rfile.remove();                                  // remove the old link
}
```

The *filebase* class defines generic functions for all POSIX and UNIX file types. However, it does not provide means for creating nonregular files or supporting file type-specific operations (e.g., file locking). To remedy these drawbacks, the following sections describe new subclasses of *filebase* class which provide complete data encapsulation for different UNIX and POSIX file types.

7.8   *Regfile* Class for Regular Files

The *filebase* class encapsulates most of the properties and functions needed to represent regular file objects in POSIX and UNIX systems except file locking. The *regfile* class is defined as a subclass of *filebase,* but also contains file locking functions. Thus, objects of this *regfile* class can do all regular file operations permitted in POSIX and UNIX systems.

The *regfile* class is defined as follows:

```
#ifndef REGFILE_H                    /* This is regfile.h header */
#define REGFILE_H
#include "filebase.h"
/* A class to encapsulate POSIX and UNIX regular file objects' properties */
class regfile  :   public filebase
{
    public:
        regfile ( const char* fn, int mode, int prot ) : filebase( fn, mode, prot )
                                {};
        ~regfile()              {};
        int lock( int lck_type, off_t len, int cmd = F_SETLK )
                            {   struct flock flck;
                                if (( lck_type&ios::in ) == ios::in )
                                    flck.l_type = F_RDLCK;
                                else if ((lck_type &
                                        ios::ou t ) ==ios::out )
```

194

```
                                                      flck.l_type = F_WRLCK;
                                                  else return -1;
                                                  flck.l_whence = SEEK_CUR;
                                                  flck.l_start = (off_t)0;
                                                  flck.l_len = len;
                                                  return fcntl( fileno(), cmd, &flck );
                                    };
          int lockw( int lck_type, off_t len )
                                         {        return
                                                    lock( lck_type, len, F_SETLKW );
                                    };
          int unlock( off_t len )        {        struct flock flck;
                                                  flck.l_type = F_UNLCK;
                                                  flck.l_whence = SEEK_CUR;
                                                  flck.l_start = (off_t)0;
                                                  flck.l_len = len;
                                                  return fcntl(fileno(),F_SETLK,&flck );
                                    };
          int getlock( int lck_type, off_t len, struct flock& flck )
                                         {        if ( ( lck_type&ios::in ) == ios::in )
                                                      flck.l_type = F_RDLCK;
                                                  else if (( lck_type &
                                                          ios::out)==ios::out )
                                                      flck.l_type = F_WRLCK;
                                                  else return -1;
                                                  flck.l_whence = SEEK_CUR;
                                                  flck.l_start = (off_t)0;
                                                  flck.l_len = len;
                                                  return fcntl(fileno(),F_GETLK,&flck );
                                    };
      };
      #endif                 /* regfile.h */
```

The *regfile::lock* function can set read lock (*lck_type* is *ios::in*) or write lock (*lck_type* is *ios::out*) on a region of a file associated with a *regfile* object. The starting address of a lock region is the current file pointer of a file and can be set by the *fstream::seekg* function. The size of a lock region, in number of bytes, is specified via the *len* argument. The *regfile::lock* function is nonblocking by default. If users specify the *cmd* argument as F_SETLKW or if it is called from the *regfile::lockw* function, the function is blocking. The return value of *regfile::lock* is the same as that of *fcntl* in file locking operation.

The *regfile::lockw* function is a wrapper over the *regfile::lock* function, and it locks files in blocking mode. The return value of *regfile::lockw* function is the same as that of the *regfile::lock* function.

The *regfile::unlock* function unlocks a region of a file associated with a *regfile* object. The starting address of an unlock region is the current file pointer of a file and can be set by the *fstream::seekg* function. The size of an unlock region, in number of bytes, is specified via the *len* argument. The *regfile::unlock* function is nonblocking and its return value is the same as that of *fcntl* in file unlocking mode.

The *regfile::getlock* function queries lock information for a region of a file associated with a *regfile* object. The *lck_type* argument specifies whether read lock (*lck_type* is *ios::in*) or write lock (*lck_type* is *ios::out*) information is sought. The starting address of a region is the current file pointer of a file and can be set by the *fstream::seekg* function. The size of the lock region to be queried, in number of bytes, is specified via the *len* argument. The *regfile::getlock* function is nonblocking, and its return value is the same as that of *fcntl*. If a *regfile::getlock* function call succeeds, the *flck* argument will contain the lock information of a file region.

The *regfile* class provides a complete encapsulation of all UNIX and POSIX regular files functions. It also simplifies the file locking and unlocking APIs such that users need to know only the *fstream* class interface to use the *regfile::lock, regfile::unlock,* and *regfile::getlock* functions. The following *test_regfile.C* program illustrates how to use a *regfile* object to create a temporary file called *foo*, locks the entire file for write, initializes its content with data from the */etc/passwd* file, unlocks the first 10 bytes of the file, and then removes the file:

```
#include "regfile.h"
int main()
{                                           // Example for regfile
    ifstream ifs ("/etc/passwd");
    charbuf[256];
    regfilerfile("foo",ios::out | ios::in);   // define a regfile object
    rfile.lock(ios::out,0);                   // set write lock for entire file
    while (ifs.getline(buf,256)) rfile << buf << endl;
    rfile.seekg(0,ios::beg);                  // set file pointer to beginning of file
    rfile.unlock(10);                         // unlock the first ten byte of file
    rfile.remove();                           // remove the file
}
```

7.9   *dirfile* Class for Directory Files

The *dirfile* class is defined to encapsulate all UNIX and POSIX directory file functions. Specifically, the *dirfile* class defines the *create, open, read, tellg, seekg, close,* and *remove* functions that use the UNIX and POSIX directory file-specific APIs.

The *dirfile* class definition is:

```
#ifndef DIRFILE_H                      /* This is dirfile.h header */
#define DIRFILE_H
#include  <dirent.h>
#include  <string.h>
class dirfile
{
    DIR      *dir_Ptr;
    char     *filename;
  public:
    dirfile( const char* fn )
                            {       dir_Ptr = opendir( fn );
                                    filename = strdup(fn);
                            };
    ~dirfile()              {       if (dir_Ptr) close();
                                    delete(filename);
                            };
    int close()             {       if (dir_Ptr) closedir( dir_Pt r);        };
    int create( const char* fn, mode_t prot )
                            {       return mkdir( fn, prot );                };
    int open( const char* fn )  {   dir_Ptr=opendir( fn );
                                    return dir_Ptr ? 0 : -1;
                            };
    int read( char* buf, int size )
                            {
                                    struct dirent *dp = readdir( dir_Ptr );
                                    if (dp)
                                        strncpy( buf, dp->d_name,size );
                                    return dp ? strlen( dp->d_name ) : -1;
                            };
    off_t tellg()           {       return telldir( dir_Ptr );               };
    void seekg( streampos ofs, seek_dir d )
                            {       seekdir( dir_Ptr, ofs );                 };
    int remove()            {       return rmdir( filename );                };
};
#endif                  /* dirfile.h */
```

The *dirfile* class uses the *mkdir* API to create directory files. Furthermore, it uses the *opendir* and *readdir* API to open and read directory files, respectively. To users, a *dirfile* object can be treated similarly to a regular file object. The only difference is that a *dirfile* object does nothing for write operations. The *dirfile::tellg* and *dirfile::seekg* functions use the UNIX-specific *telldir* and *seekdir* APIs to support random access of any entry in directory files. Finally, the *dirfile::close* function uses *closedir* to close a directory file, and the *dirfile::remove* function uses the *rmdir* API to remove a directory file from a file system.

The following *test_dirfile.C* program creates the */usr/lck/dir.ex* directory using the *dirfile* class. It then opens the */etc* directory and echoes all files in that directory:

```
#include "dirfile.h"
int main()
{                                            // Example for dirfile
    dirfile ndir, edir( "/etc" );            // create a dirfile object to /etc
    ndir.create( "/usr/lck/dir.ex" );        // create /usr/lck/dir.ex
    char buf[ 256 ];
    while ( edir.read( buf, 256 ) )          // echo files in the /etc dir
        cout << buf << end;
    edir.close();                            // close a directory file
}
```

7.10   FIFO File Class

A FIFO file object differs from a *filebase* object in that a FIFO file is created, and the *tellg* and *seekg* functions are invalid for FIFO file objects. The following *pipefile* class encapsulates all the FIFO file type properties:

```
#ifndef PIPEFILE_H    /* This is pipefile.h */
#define PIPEFILE_H
#include "filebase.h"

/* A class to encapsulate POSIX and UNIX FIFO file objects' properties */
class pipefile :   public filebase
{
   public:
       pipefile( const char* fn, int flags, int prot ) : filebase( fn, flags, prot )
                                     {};
       int create( const char* fn, mode_t prot )
                                     {      return mkfifo( fn, prot );          };
       streampos tellg()            {      return ( streampos ) - 1;           };
};
#endif            /* pipefile.h */
```

The following *test_pipefile.C* program creates a FIFO file called *FIFO*, opens it for read (if *argc* is 1) or write (if *argc* is greater than 1). It reads or writes data via the FIFO file, then closes the FIFO file:

```
#include "pipefile.h"

int main( int argc, char* argv[] )
{                                                       // Example for pipefile
    pipefile nfifo( "FIFO", argc==1 ? ios::in : ios::out, 0755 );
    if ( argc > 1 )      {                              // writer process
            cout << "writer process write: " << argv[1] << endl;
            nfifo.write( argv[1],strlen(argv[1])+1 ); // write data to FIFO
    } else {                                            // reader process
            char buf[256];
            nfifo.read(buf,256);                        //read data from FIFO
            cout << "read from FIFO: " << buf << endl;
    }
    nfifo.close();                                      // close FIFO file
}
```

The program can be run twice to create two processes that communicate through the FIFO file. Specifically, one program is run with no command line argument and creates a reader process. Then the program is run again with a command line argument that creates a writer process. When both processes are created, the writer process will write its command line argument to the FIFO file, and the reader process will read that argument from the FIFO file and echo it to standard output. The following is a sample execution of the program, assuming that the program has been compiled to a file called *test_pipefile*:

```
%    CC -o test_pipefile test_pipefile.C
%    test_pipefile &                 # create a reader process
%    est_pipefile "hello"            # create a writer process
     writer process write: hello     # output from the writer process
     read from FIFO: hello           # output from the reader process
```

7.11   Device File Class

A device file object has most of the properties of a regular file object except in the way that the device file object is created. Also the *tellg*, *seekg*, *lock*, *lockw*, *unlock*, and *getlock* functions are invalid for any character-based device file objects. The following *devfile* class encapsulates all the UNIX device files' properties:

```
#ifndef DEVFILE_H              /* This is devfile.h header */
#define DEVFILE_H
#include "regfile.h"
```

```
class devfile  :   public regfile
{
    public:
        devfile( const char* fn, int flags, int prot) : regfile(fn,flags,prot )   {};
        int create( const char* fn, mode_t prot, int major_no, int minor_no,
                        char type='c' )
        {      if (type=='c')
                    return mknod( fn, S_IFCHR | prot,
                                    (major_no << 8) | minor_no );
                else  return mknod( fn, S_IFBLK | prot,
                                    (major_no << 8) | minor_no );
        };
        streampos tellg()              {      if (file_type()==CHAR_FILE)
                                                  return (streampos)-1;
                                              else return fstream::tellg();
                                       };
        istream seekg( streampos ofs, seek_dir d )
                                       {      if (file_type()!=CHAR_FILE)
                                                  fstream::seekg( ofs,d );
                                              return *this;
                                       };
        int lock( int lck_type, off_t len, int cmd=F_SETLK )
                                       {      if (file_type()!=CHAR_FILE)
                                                  return
                                                      regfile::lock( lck_type,len,cmd );
                                              else return -1;
                                       };
        int lockw( int lck_type, off_t len )
                                       {      if (file_type()!=CHAR_FILE)
                                                  return
                                                      regfile::lockw( lck_type,len );
                                              else return -1;
                                       };
        int unlock( off_t len )        {      if (file_type()!=CHAR_FILE)
                                                  return regfile::unlock( len );
                                              else return -1;
                                       };
        int getlock( int lck_type, off_t len, struct flock& flck )
                                       {      if (file_type()!=CHAR_FILE)
                                                  return
                                                      regfile::getlock( lck_type,len,flck );
                                              else return -1;
                                       };
};
#endif                    /* devfile.h */
```

The *devfile::create* function creates a device file via the *mknod* API. The *type* argument specifies that a character (*type* value is *c*) or a block (*type* value is *b*) device file is to be created. The major and minor device numbers, access permission, and the file name of a device file are also specified via the *major_no, minor_no, prot,* and *fn* arguments. The return value of the *devfile::create* function is that of the *mknod* API.

After a device file is created, it can be opened, read, written to, or closed like regular files. Thus, *devfile* inherits all the *fstream* functions for data access to its objects. However, random data access is illegal for character device files. Thus, the *devfile::tellg* and *devfile::seekg* functions work for block device files only.

The following *test_devfile.C* program creates a character device file called */dev/tty* with major and minor device numbers of 30 and 15, respectively. It then opens it for write., writes data to it, and, finally, closes the file.

```
#include "devfile.h"
int main()
{                                              // Example for devfile
    devfile ndev]("/dev/tty", ios::out,0777); // open the device file for write
    ndev << "This is a sample output string\n";// write data to the file
    ndev.close();                              // close the device file
}
```

7.12   Symbolic Link File Class

A symbolic link file object differs from a *filebase* object in the way it is created. Also, a new member function called *ref_path* is provided to depict the path name of a file to which the symbolic link object refers. The following *symfile* class encapsulates all UNIX symbolic link file type properties:

```
#ifndef SYMFILE_H                  /* This is symfile.h header */
#define SYMFILE_H
#include "filebase.h"
/* A class to encapsulate UNIX symbolic link file objects' properties */
class symfile :   public filebase
{
    public:
        symfil()                       {};
        ~symfile()                     {};
```

```
      int setlink( const char* old_link, const char* new_link )
                                    {       filename=new
                                                    char[strlen(new_link)+1];
                                            strcpy(filename,new_link);
                                            return symlink(old_link,new_link);
                              };
      void open( int mode )         {       fstream::open(filename,mode);   };
      const char* ref_path()        {       static char buf[256];
                                            if (readlink(filename,buf,256))
                                                    return buf;
                                            else return (char*)-1;
                              };
};
#endif                            /* symfile.h */
```

The *symfile::create* function creates a symbolic link file via the *symlink* API. The *new_link* argument is a new symbolic link file path name to be created, and the *old_link* is the path name of the original link. The return value of the *symfile::create* function is that of the *symlink* API.

After a symbolic link file is created, it can be opened, read, written to, or closed like any regular files. Thus, *symfile* inherits all the *fstream* functions for data access to its objects. However, all these operations occur on the nonlink file to which the symbolic link refers. Furthermore, the *symfile::ref_path* function is defined for users to query the path name of a nonlink file to which a *symfile* object references.

The following *test_symfile.C* program creates a symbolic link file call */usr/xyz/sym.lnk* that references a file called */usr/file/chap10*. It opens the symbolic link file and reads it content. Then, it echoes the link reference path name, and closes the file:

```
#include "symfile.h"
int main()
{                                               // Example for symfile
      char        buf[256];
      symfile nsym;
      nsym.setlink("/usr/file/chap10","/usr/xyz/sym.lnk");
      nsym.open( ios:in );
      while(nsym.getline(buf,256))
            cout << buf << endl;                // read /usr/file/chap10
      cout << nsym.ref_path() << endl;          // echo "/usr/file/chap10"
      nsym.close();                             // close the symbolic link file
}
```

7.13   File Listing Program

An an example to illustrate the use of the *filebase* class and its subclasses, the following *lstdir.C* program reimplements the UNIX *ls* command to list file attributes of all path name arguments specified for the program. Furthermore, if an argument is a directory the program will list the file attributes of all files in that directory and any subdirectories underneath it. If a file is a symbolic link, the program will echo the path name to which the link refers. Thus, the program behaves like the UNIX *ls -lR* command.

```
#include "filebase.h"
#include "symfile.h"
#include "dirfile.h"

void show_list( ostream& ofs, const char* fname, int deep);

/* this is defined in test_ls.C. Section 7.1.10 */
extern void long_list( ostream& ofs, char* fn );

/* program to implement the UNIX ls -lR command */
void show_dir( ostream& ofs, const char* fname )
{
        dirfile        dirObj(fname);
        char           buf[256];
        ofs << "\nDirectory: " << fname << ":\n";
        while (dirObj.read(buf,256))                    // show all files in a directory
                  show_list(ofs, buf,0);
        dirObj.seekg(0);                                // reset file pointer to beginning
        while (dirObj.read(buf,256))        {           // Look for directory files
              filebase fObj(buf,ios::in,0755);          // define a filebase object
              if (fObj.file_type==DIR_FILE)             // show sub-dir info
                      show_dir(ofs,buf);
              fObj.close();
        }
        dirObj.close();
}

void show_list( ostream& ofs, const char* fname, int deep)
{
        long_list( ofs, fname);
```

```
            filebase    fobj(fname,ios::in,0755);
            if (fobj.file_type()==SYM_FILE)     {          // symbolic link file
                symfile *symObj = (symfile*)fobj;          // define a symfile object
                ofs << " -> " << symObj->ref_path() << endl;// show reference path
            }
            else if (fobj.file_type() == DIR_FILE && deep)// directory file
                show_dir( ofs, fname );                    // show directory content
        }

        int main( int argc, char* argv[])
        {
            while (--argc > 0) show_list( cout , *++argv, 1);
            return 0;
        }
```

The above program is similar to the program in Section 7.1.10, except that it echoes symbolic link references and lists directory contents recursively. The *main* function processes each command line argument by calling the *show_file* function to display file attributes of each argument to the standard output. The *deep* argument of *show_file* specifies, if its value is nonzero, that when a *fname* argument is a directory file, *show_file* should call the *show_dir* function to list the directory content. When *show_file* is called from *main,* the actual value of *deep* is set to 1.

The *show_dir* function is called to display the content of a directory file. It first creates a *dirfile* object to be associated with a directory whose name is specified by *fname*. It then calls *show_file* to list the file attributes of each file in that directory. Note that in this first pass, *show_file* is called with the actual argument of *deep* set to zero, so that *show_file* will not traverse any subdirectory by calling *show_dir*. After the first pass has completed, *show_dir* will scan a given directory a second time and looks for subdirectory files. For each subdirectory file found, *show_dir* will call itself recursively to list the content of the sub-directory. This is the same behavior as the UNIX *ls -lR* command.

For example, look at the following directory structure:

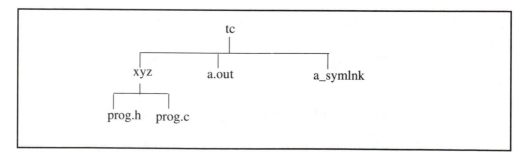

Assuming the above program has been compiled to an executable file called *lstdir*, the following commands and their expected output are:

```
%    CC -o lstdir lstdir.C
%    lstdir    tc
-r-x-r-xr--x   1  util       class      1234 Dec 8, 1993  a.out
prwxrwxrwx 1  util       class      122  Apr 11, 1994 a_symlink
-> /usr/dsg/unix.lnk
drwxr-x--x   1  util       class      234   Jan 17, 1994 xyz

Directry: xyz
-rw-r--r--     1  util       class      814   Dec 18, 1993prog.c
prwxrwxrwx 1  util       class      112   May 21, 1994prog.h
```

7.14   Summary

This chapter depicts the UNIX and POSIX file APIs. These APIs are used to create, open, read, write, and close all types of files in a system: regular, directory, device, FIFO, and symbolic link files. Furthermore, a set of C++ classes are defined to encapsulate the properties and functions of all file types, so that users can use these classes to manipulate files with the same interface as the *iostream* class. These classes are portable on all UNIX and POSIX systems, except for the symbolic link file class (*symfile*), which is not yet defined in the POSIX.1 standard

The inheritance hierarchy of all the file classes defined in the chapter is:

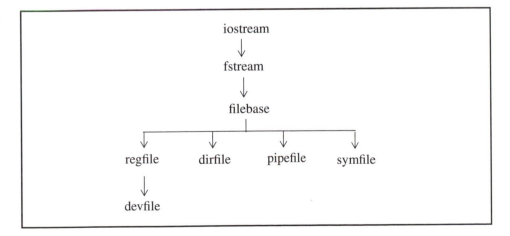

File objects are manipulated by processes in an operating system. The UNIX and POSIX APIs for process creation and control are described in the next chapter.

UNIX Processes

Aprocess is a program (e.g., *a.out*) under execution in a UNIX or POSIX system. For example, a UNIX shell is a process that is created when a user logs on to a system. Moreover, when a user enters a command *cat foo* to a shell prompt, the shell creates a new process. In UNIX terminology, this is a child process, which executes the *cat* command on behalf of the user. When a process creates a *child process,* it becomes the parent process of the child. The child process inherits many attributes from its parent process, and it is scheduled by the UNIX kernel to run independently from its parent.

By being able to create multiple processes that run concurrently, an operating system can serve multiple users and perform multiple tasks concurrently. Thus, process creation and management are the cornerstone of a multiuser and multitasking operating system such as UNIX. Furthermore, the advantages of allowing any process to create new processes in its course of execution are:

1. Any user can create multitasking applications.

2. Because a child process executes in its own virtual address space, its success or failure in execution will not affect its parent. A parent process can also query the exit status and run-time statistics of its child process after it has terminated.

3. It is very common for a process to create a child process that will execute a new program (e.g., the *spell* program). This allows users to write programs that can call on any other program to extend their functionality without the need to incorporate any new source code.

This chapter will explain the UNIX kernel data structures that support process creation and execution, the system call interface for process management, and a set of examples to demonstrate multitasking programs in UNIX.

8.1   UNIX Kernel Support for Processes

The data structure and execution of processes are dependent on operating system implementation. In the following, the process data structure and operating system support in the UNIX System V will be described as an illustration.

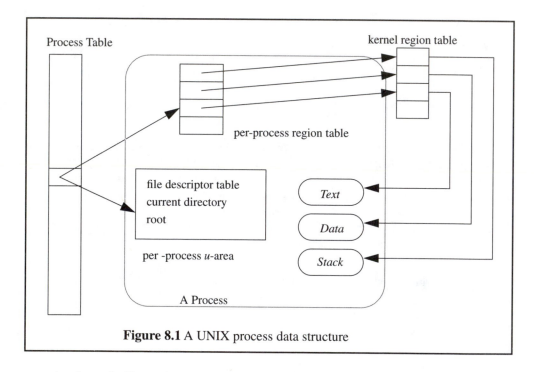

Figure 8.1 A UNIX process data structure

As shown in Figure 8.1, a UNIX process consists minimally of a text segment, a data segment, and a stack segment. A segment is an area of memory that is managed by the system as a unit. A text segment contains the program text of a process in machine-executable instruction code format. A data segment contains static and global variables and their corresponding data. A stack segment contains a run-time stack. A stack provides storage for function arguments, automatic variables, and return addresses of all active functions for a process at any time.

A UNIX kernel has a Process Table that keeps track of all active processes. Some of the processes belong to the kernel. They are called *system processes*. The majority of processes are associated with the users who are logged in. Each entry in the Process Table contains pointers to the text, data, stack segments and the *U*-area of a process. The *U*-area is an extension of a Process Table entry and contains other process-specific data, such as the file descriptor table, current root and working directory inode numbers, and a set of system-imposed process resource limits, etc.

All processes in a UNIX system, except the very first process (process 0) which is created by the system boot code, are created via the *fork* system call. After a *fork* system call, both the parent and child processes resume execution at the return of the *fork* function.

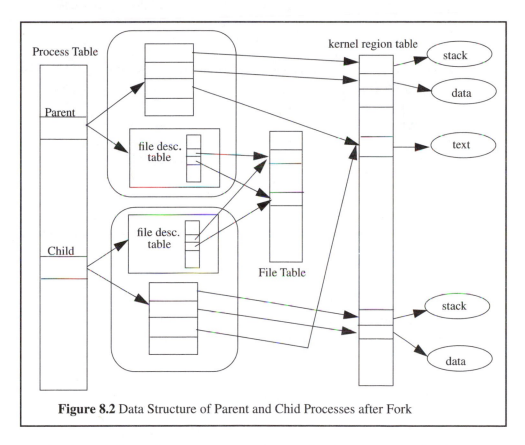

Figure 8.2 Data Structure of Parent and Chid Processes after Fork

As shown in Figure 8.2, when a process is created by *fork,* it contains duplicated copies of the text, data, and stack segments of its parent. Also, it has a file descriptor table that contains references to the same opened files as its parent, such that they both share the same file pointer to each opened file. Furthermore, the process is assigned the following attributes which are either inherited from its parent or set by the kernel:

- A real user identification number (rUID): the user ID of a user who created the parent process. This is used by the kernel to keep track of who creates which processes on a system

- A real group identification number (rGID): the group ID of a user who created the parent process. This is used by the kernel to keep track of which group creates which processes on a system
- An effective user identification number (eUID): this is normally the same as the real UID, except when the file that was executed to create the process has its *set-UID* flag turned on (via the *chmod* command or API). In that case, the process eUID will take on the UID of the file. This allows the process to access and create files with the same privileges as the program file owner
- An effective group identification number (eGID): this is normally the same as the real GID, except when the file which was executed to create the process has its *set-GID* flag turned on (via the *chmod* command or API). In that case, the process eGID will take on the GID of the file. This allows the process to access and create files with the same privileges as the group to which the program file belongs
- *Saved set-UID* and *saved set-GID*: these are the assigned eUID and eGID, respectively, of the process
- Process group identification number (PGID) and session identification number (SID): these identify the process group and session of which the process is member
- Supplementary group identification numbers: this is a set of additional group IDs for a user who created the process
- Current directory: this is the reference (inode number) to a working directory file
- Root directory: this is the reference (inode number) to a root directory file
- Signal handling: the signal handling settings. See the next chapter for an explanation of signals
- Signal mask: a signal mask that specifies which signals are to be blocked
- Umask: a file mode mask that is used in creation of files to specify which accession rights should be taken out
- Nice value: the process scheduling priority value
- Controlling terminal: the controlling terminal of the process

In addition to the above attributes, the following attributes are different between the parent and child processes:

- Process identification number (PID): an integer identification number that is unique per process in an entire operating system
- Parent process identification number (PPID): the parent process PID
- Pending signals: the set of signals that are pending delivery to the parent process. This is reset to none in the child process
- Alarm clock time: the process alarm clock time (as set by the *alarm* system call) is reset to zero in the child process
- File locks: the set of file locks owned by the parent process is not inherited by the child process

After *fork*, a parent process may choose to suspend its execution until its child process terminates by calling the *wait* or *waitpid* system call, or it may continue execution independently of its child process. In the latter case, the parent process may use the *signal* or *sigaction* function (as described in Chapter 9) to detect or ignore the child process termination.

A process terminates its execution by calling the *_exit* system call. The argument to the *_exit* call is the exit status code of the process. By convention, an exit status code of zero means that the process has completed its execution successfully, and any nonzero exit code indicates failure has occurred.

A process can execute a different program by calling the *exec* system call. If the call succeeds, the kernel will replace the process's existing text, data, and stack segments with a new set that represents the new program to be executed. However, the process is still the same process (the process ID and parent process ID are the same), and its file descriptor table and opened directory streams remain mostly the same (except that those file descriptors which have their *close-on-exec* flag set via the *fcntl* system call will be closed upon *exec*'ing). Thus, calling *exec* is like a person changing jobs. After the change, the person still has the same name and personal identifications, but is now working on a different job than before.

When the *exec*'ed program completes its execution, it terminates the process. The exit status code of the program may be polled by the process's parent via the *wait* or *waitpid* function.

fork and *exec* are commonly used together to spawn a subprocess to execute a different program. For example, an UNIX shell executes each user command by calling *fork* and *exec* to execute the requested command in a child process. The advantages of this method are:

- A process can create multiple processes to execute multiple programs concurrently
- Because each child process executes in its own virtual address space, the parent process is not affected by the execution status of its child process

Two or more related processes (parent to child, or child to child with the same parent) may communicate with others by setting up unnamed pipes among them. For unrelated processes, they can communicate using named pipe or interprocess communication methods, as described in Chapter 10.

8.2   Process APIs

8.2.1   fork, vfork

The *fork* system call is used to create a child process. The function prototype of *fork* is:

```
#ifdef _POSIX_SOURCE
#include <sys/stdtypes.h>
#else
#include <sys/types.h>
#endif


pid_t              fork ( void );
```

The *fork* function takes no arguments, and it returns a value of type *pid_t* (defined in <sys/types.h>). The result of the call may be one of the following:

- The call succeeds. A child process is created, and the function returns the child process ID to the parent. The child process receives a zero return value from *fork*
- The call fails. No child process is created, and the function sets *errno* with an error code and returns a -1 value

The common causes of *fork* failure and the corresponding *errno* values are:

Errno value	Meaning
ENOMEM	There is insufficient memory to create the new process
EAGAIN	The number of processes currently existing in a system exceeds a system-imposed limit, so try the call again later

There are system-turnable limits on the maximum number of processes that can be created by a single user (CHILD_MAX) and the maximum number of processes that can exist concurrently system-wide (MAXPID). If either of these limits is exceeded when *fork* is called, the function will return a failure status. The MAXPID and CHILD_MAX symbols are defined in the <sys/param.h> and <limits.h> headers, respectively. Furthermore, a process may obtain the CHILD_MAX value via the *sysconf* function:

```
int child_max = sysconf ( _SC_CHILD_MAX );
```

If a *fork* call succeeds, a child process is created. The data structure of the parent and child processes after *fork* are shown in Figure 8.2. Both the child and the parent process will be scheduled by the UNIX kernel to run independently, and the order of which process will run first is implementation-dependent. Furthermore, both processes will resume their execution at the return of the *fork* call. After the *fork* call, the return value is used to distinguish whether a process is the parent or the child. In this way, the parent and child processes can do different tasks concurrently.

The following *test_fork.C* program illustrates the use of *fork*. The parent process invokes *fork* to create a child process. If *fork* returns -1, the system call fails, and the parent process calls *perror* to print a diagnostic message to the standard error. On the other hand, if *fork* succeeds, the child process, when executed, will print the message *Child process created* to the standard output. It then terminates itself via the *return* statement. Meanwhile, the parent will print the message *Parent process after fork* and will then quit.

```
#include <iostream.h>
#include <stdio.h>
#include <unistd.h>
int main()
{
    pid_t    child_pid;
    cout << "PID: " << getpid() << ", parent: " << getppid() << endl;
    switch (chidl_pid=fork()){
        case (pid_t)-1:
                perror("fork");              /* fork fails */
                break;
        case (pid_t)0:
                cout << "Child created: PID: " << getpid()
                        << ", parent: " << getppid() << endl;
                exit(0);
        default: cout << "Parent after fork. PID: " << getpid()
                        << ", child PID: " << child_pid << endl;
    }
    return 0;
}
```

The sample outputs of this program, when executed, may be:

```
%    CC -o test_fork test_fork.C
%    test_fork
PID: 234, parent: 123
Child created: PID: 645, parent: 234
Parent after fork. PID: 234, child PID: 645
```

An alternative API to *fork* is *vfork*, which has the same signature as does *fork*:

```
pid_t     vfork      (void);
```

vfork has the similar function as *fork,* and it returns the same possible values as does *fork.* It is available in BSD UNIX and System V.4. However, it is not a POSIX.1 standard. The idea of *vfork* is that many programs call *exec* (in child processes) right after *fork.* Thus, it will improve the system efficiency if the kernel does not create a separate virtual address space for the child process until *exec* is executed. This is what happens in *vfork*: After the function is called, the kernel suspends the execution of the parent process while the child process is executing in the parent's virtual address space. When the child process calls *exec* or *_exit*, the parent will resume execution, and the child process will either get its own virtual address space after *exec* or will terminate via the *_exit* call.

vfork is unsafe to use, because if the child process modifies any data of the parent (e.g., closes files or modifies variables) before it calls *exec* or *_exit*, those changes will remain when the parent process resumes execution. This may cause unexpected behavior in the parent. Furthermore, the child should not call *exit* or return to any calling function, because this will cause the parent's stream files being closed or modify the parent run-time stack, respectively.

The latest UNIX systems (e.g., System V.4) have improved on the efficiency of *fork* by allowing parent and child processes to share a common virtual address space until the child calls either the *exec* or *_exit* function. If either the parent or the child modifies any data in the shared virtual address space, the kernel will create new memory pages that cover the virtual address space modified. Thus, the process that made changes will reference the new memory pages with the modified data, whereas the counterpart process will continue referencing the old memory pages. This process is called *copy-on-write,* and it renders *fork* execution efficiency comparable to that of *vfork.* Thus, *vfork* should be used in porting old applications to the new UNIX systems only.

8.2.2   _exit

The *_exit* system call terminates a process. Specifically, the API will cause the calling process data segment, stack segments, and *U*-area to be deallocated and all the open file descriptors to be closed. However, the Process Table slot entry for this process is still intact so that the process exit status and its execution statistics (e.g., total execution time, number of I/O blocks transferred, etc.) are recorded therein. The process is now called a *zombie process,* as it can no longer be scheduled to run. The data stored in the Process Table entry can be retrieved by the process parent via the *wait* or *waitpid* system call. These APIs will also deallocate the child Process Table entry.

If a process *fork*s a child process and terminates before the child, the child process will be assigned by the kernel to be adopted by the *init* process (this is the second process created after a UNIX system is booted. Its process ID is always 1). When the child process terminates, its Process Table slot will be cleaned up by the *init process.*

The function prototype of the _exit function is:

```
#include <unistd.h>

void          _exit          (int exit_code);
```

The integer argument to _exit is a process exit status code. Only the lower 8 bits of the exit code are passed to a parent process. By convention, an exit status of zero indicates that the process terminated successfully, and a nonzero exit status indicates a failed termination. In some UNIX systems, the manifested constants EXIT_SUCCESS and EXIT_FAILURE are defined in the <stdio.h> header and can be used as actual arguments to _exit for the success and failure exit status values, respectively.

The _exit function never fails, and there is no return value.

The C library function exit is a wrapper over _exit. Specifically, exit will first flush and close all opened streams of the calling process. It will then call any functions that were registered via the atexit function (in an order reverse to that in which functions were registered via the atexit function) and, finally call _exit to terminate the process.

The following test_exit.C program illustrates the use of _exit. When the program is run, it declares its existence and then terminates itself via the _exit call. It passes a 0 exit status value to indicate that its execution has been completed successfully.

```
#include <iostream.h>
#include <unistd.h>
int main()
{
    cout << "Test program for _exit" << endl;
    _exit(0);
}
```

After this program is run, users can test the exit status of this program via the *status* (in C shell) or *$?* (in Bourne shell) shell variable. The output of this program may be:

```
%      CC -o test_exit test_exit.C ; test_exit
Test program for _exit
%      echo $status
0
```

8.2.3   wait, waitpid

The *wait* and *waitpid* system calls are used by a parent process to wait for its child process to terminate and to retrieve the child exit status (assigned by the child via *_exit*). Furthermore, these calls will deallocate the Process Table slot of the child process, so that the slot can be reused by a new process. The prototypes of these functions are:

```
#include <sys/wait.h>

pid_t      wait       (int *status_p);
pid_t      waitpid    (pid_t child_pid, int* status_p, int options);
```

The *wait* function will suspend the parent process until either a signal is sent to the process or one of its child processes terminates or is stopped (and its status has not yet been reported). If a child process has already terminated or has been stopped prior to a *wait* call, *wait* returns immediately with the child exit status (via *status_p*), and the function return value is the child PID. If, however, a parent has no unwaited-for child processes or if it is interrupted by a signal while executing *wait*, the function will return a -1 value, and *errno* will contain an error code. Note that if a parent process has spawned more than one child process, the *wait* call will wait for any one of these child processes to terminate.

The *waitpid* function is a more general function than is *wait*. Like *wait*, *waitpid* will collect a child process exit code and PID upon its termination. However, with *waitpid,* the caller has an option to specify which child process to wait for by specifying one of the following values for the *child_pid* argument:

Actual value for *child_pid*	Meaning
A child process ID	Waits for the child with that PID
-1	Waits for any child
0	Waits for any child in the same process group as the parent
A negative value but not -1	Waits for any child whose process group ID is the absolute value of *child_pid*

Furthermore, the caller can direct *waitpid* to be either blocking or nonblocking and to wait for any child that is or is not stopped due to job control. These are specified via the *options* argument. Specifically, if the WNOHANG flag (defined in <sys/wait.h>) is set in an *options* value, the call will be nonblocking (that is, the function will return immediately if there is no child that satisfies the wait criteria). Otherwise, the call is blocking and the parent will be suspended as in a *wait* call. Furthermore, if the WNOTRACED flag is set in the *options* value, the function will also wait for a child that is stopped (but its status has not been reported before) due to job control.

If the actual value to a *status_p* argument of either a *wait* or *waitpid* call is NULL, no child exit status is to be queried. However, if the actual value is an address of an integer-typed variable, the function will assign an exit status code (specified via the *_exit* API) to this variable. The parent can then check the exit status code with the following macros as defined in <sys/wait.h>:

Macro	Use
WIFEXITED(*status_p)	Returns a nonzero value if a child was terminated via an *_exit* call, and zero otherwise
WEXITSTATUS(*status_p)	Returns a child exit code that was assigned to an *_exit* call. This should be called only if WIFEXITED returns a nonzero value
WIFSIGNALED(*status_p)	Returns a nonzero value if a child was terminated due to signal interruption
WTERMSIG(*status_p)	Returns the signal number that had terminated a child process. This should be called only if WIFSIGNALED returns a nonzero value
WIFSTOPPED(*status_p)	Returns a nonzero value if a child process has been stopped due to job control
WSTOPSIG(*status_p)	Returns the signal number that had stopped a child process. This should be called only if WIFSTOPPED returns a nonzero value

In some versions of UNIX, where the above macros are undefined, the above information can be obtained directly from *status_p*. Specifically, the seven least significant bits (bit 0 to bit 6) of *status_p* are zero if a child was terminated via *_exit* or a signal number that terminated the child. The eighth bit of *status_p* is 1 if a core file has been generated due to signal interruption of the child, or 0 otherwise. Furthermore, if the child was terminated via *_exit,* bit 8 to bit 15 of *status_p* is the child exit code that was passed via *_exit*. The following figure illustrates the use of the *status_p* data bits:

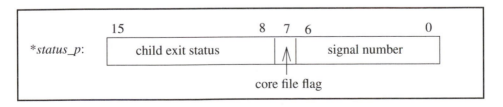

In BSD UNIX, the *status_p* argument is of type *union wait**, where *union wait* is defined in <sys/wait.h>. It is a union of an integer variable and a set of bit-fields. The bit-fields are used to extract the same status information as the above macros.

If the return value of either *wait* or *waitpid* is a positive integer value, it is the child PID. Otherwise, it is *(pid_t)-1* and signifies that either no child satisfied the wait criteria or the function was interrupted by a caught signal. Here, *errno* may be assigned one of the following values:

Errno value	Meaning
EINTR	*Wait* or *waitpid* returns because the system call was interrupted by a signal
ECHILD	For *wait*, it means the calling process has no unwaited-for child process
	For *waitpid*, it means either the *child_pid* value is illegal or the process cannot be in a state as defined by the *options* value
EFAULT	The *status_p* argument points to an illegal address
EINVAL	The *options* value is illegal

Both *wait* and *waitpid* are POSIX.1 standard. *waitpid* is not available in BSD UNIX 4.3, System V.3 and their older versions.

The following *test_waitpid.C* program illustrates use of the *waitpid* API:

```
#include <iostream.h>
#include <stdio.h>
#include <sys/types.h>
#include <sys/wait.h>
#include <unistd.h>

int main()
{
    pid_t        child_pid, pid;
    int          status;
    switch (child_pid=fork())  {
        case (pid_t)-1:perror("fork");              /* fork fails */
                    break;
        case (pid_t)0:cout << "Child process created\n";
                    _exit(15);                      /* terminate child */
        default:     cout << "Parent process after fork\n";
```

```
                        pid = waitpid(child_pid,&status,WNOTRACED);
        }
        if WIFEXITED(status))
            cerr << child_pid << " exits: " <<WEXITSTATUS(status) << endl;
        else if WIFSTOPPED(status))
            cerr << child_pid << " stopped by: " <WSTOPSIG(status)
                  << endl;
        else if WIFSIGNALED(status))
            cerr << child_pid << " killed by: " <<WTERMSIG(status) << endl;
        else perror("waitpid");
        _exit(0);
}
```

This simple program forks a child process that acknowledges its creation and then terminates with an exit status of 15. Meanwhile, the parent suspends its execution via the *waitpid* call. The parent process resumes execution after the child has terminated and the *status* and *child_pid* variables of the parent process are assigned the child's exit code and process ID. The parent uses the macros defined in <sys/wait.h> to determine the execution status of the child in the following order:

- If WIFEXITED returns a nonzero value, the child was terminated via the *_exit* call, and the parent extracts the child's exit code (which is 15 in this example) via the WEXITSTATUS macro. It then prints the value to standard error port

- If WIFEXITED returns a zero value and WIFSTOPPED returns a nonzero value, the child was stopped by a signal. The parent extracts the signal number via the WSTOPSIG macro and prints the value to standard error port

- If both WIFEXITED and WIFSTOPPED return a zero value and WIFSIGNALED returns a nonzero value, the child was terminated by an uncaught signal. The parent extracts the signal number via the WTERMSIG macro and prints the value to standard error port

- If WIFEXITED, WIFSTOPPED, and WIFSIGNALED all return a zero value, either the parent has no child processes or the *waitpid* call was interrupted by a signal. Thus, the parent calls the *perror* function to print detailed diagnostics for the failure

The output of this program may be:

```
%      CC -o test_waitpid test_waitpid.C
%      test_waitpid
```

Child process created
Parent process after fork
1354 exits: 15
%

8.2.4   exec

The *exec* system call causes a calling process to change its context and execute a different program. There are six versions of the *exec* system call. They all have the same function but they differ from each other in their argument lists.

The prototypes of the *exec* functions are:

```
#include <unistd.h>

int    execl     (const char* path, const char* arg, ...);
int    execlp    (const char* file, const char* arg, ...);
int    execle    (const char* path, const char* arg, ..., const char** env);
int    execv     (const char* path, const char** argv, ...);
int    execvp    (const char* file, const char** argv, ...);
int    execve    (const char* path, const char** argv, ..., const char **env);
```

The first argument to the function is either the path name or a file name of a program to be executed. If the call succeeds, the calling process instruction and data memory are overlaid with the new program instruction text and data. The process starts execution at the beginning of the new program. Furthermore, when the new program completes execution, the process is terminated and its exit code will be passed back to its parent process. Note that, whereas *fork* creates a child process that runs independently of its parent, *exec* does not create a new process, but rather it changes the calling process context to execute a different program.

An *exec* call may fail if the program to be executed cannot be accessed or has no execution rights. Furthermore, the program named in the first argument of an *exec* call should be an executable file (i.e., in *a.out* format). However, it is possible in UNIX to specify a shell script name to the *execlp* and *execvp* calls, so that the UNIX kernel will execute a Bourne shell (*/bin/sh*) to interpret the shell script. Because POSIX.1 does not have the notion of shells, it is illegal to use *execlp* or *execvp* to execute shell scripts. This is really not a problem, as users can always *exec* a shell and supply it with the name of a shell script that he or she wishes to execute.

The *p* suffix of *execlp* and *execvp* specifies that if the actual value of a *file* argument does not begin with a "/", the functions will use the shell PATH environment variable to search for the file to be executed. For all the other *exec* functions, the actual value of their first argument should be the path name of any file to be executed.

The *arg* or *argv* arguments are arguments for an *exec*'ed program. They are mapped to the *argv* variable of the *main* function of the new program. For the *execl, execlp,* and *execle* functions, the *arg* argument is mapped to *argv[0]*, the value after *arg* will be mapped to *argv[1]*, and so on. The argument list specified in the *exec* call must be terminated by a NULL value to tell the function where to stop looking for argument values. For the *execv, execvp,* and *execve* functions, the *argv* argument is a vector of character strings, each string being one argument value. The *argv* argument is mapped directly to the *argv* variable of the *main* function of the new program. Thus, the *l* character in an *exec* function name specifies that the argument values are listed in each call, whereas the *v* character in an *exec* function name signifies that the arguments are passed in a vector format.

Note that one must supply at least two argument values to each *exec* call. The first value (*arg* or *argv[0]*) is the name of a program to be *exec*'ed and is mapped to *argv[0]* of the *main* function of the new program. The second mandatory argument is the NULL value that terminates the argument list (for *execl, execlp* and *execle*) or the argument vectors (for *execv, execvp* and *execve*).

The *e* suffix of an *exec* function (*execle* or *execve*) specifies that the last argument (*env*) to a function call is a vector of character strings. Here, each string defines one environment variable and its value in a Bourne shell format:

<environment_variable_name>=<value>

The last entry of *env* must be a NULL value to signal the end of a vector list. In non-ANSI C environment, *env* will be assigned to the third parameter of the *main* function in the *exec*'ed program. In an ANSI C environment, the *main* function can have only two arguments (namely, *argc* and *argv*), and *env* will be mapped to the *environ* global variable of the *exec*'ed program. For the *execl, execlp, execv,* and *execvp* functions, the *environ* global variable is unchanged in the process by the *exec* call (note that the *environ* variable may be updated using the *putenv* function).

If an *exec* call succeeds, the original process text, data, and stack segments are replaced by new segments for an *exec*'ed program. However, the file descriptor table of the process remains unchanged. Those file descriptors whose *close-on-exec* flags were set (by the *fcntl* system call) will be closed before a new program runs. Furthermore, the following process attributes may be changed when the process executes an *exec*'ed program:

- Effective UID: this is changed if an *exec*'ed program file has its *set-UID* flag set
- Effective GID: this is changed if an *exec*'ed program file has its *set-GID* flag set
- Saved set-UID: this is changed if an *exec*'ed program file has its *set-UID* flag set

- Signal handling: signals that are set up to be caught in a process are reset to accept their default actions when the process *exec*'ed a new program. The user-defined signal handler functions are not present in the *exec*'ed program

Most programs call *exec* in a child process because it is desirable to continue a parent process execution after an *exec* call. However, *fork* and *exec* are implemented as two separate functions for the following reasons:

- It is simpler to implement *fork* and *exec* separately
- It is possible for a program to call *exec* without *fork*, or *fork* without *exec*. This renders flexibility in the use of these functions
- Many programs will do some operations in child processes, such as redirect standard I/O to files, before they call *exec*. This is made possible by separating the *fork* and *exec* APIs

The following *test_exec.C* program illustrates use of the *exec* API:

```
#include <iostream.h>
#include <stdio.h>
#include <stdlib.h>
#include <errno.h>
#include <sys/types.h>
#include <sys/wait.h>
#include <unistd.h>

int System( const char *cmd)          // emulate the C system function
{
    pid_t    pid;
    int      status;
    switch (pid=fork())      {
        case -1:      return -1;
        case 0:       execl("/bin/sh", "sh", "-c", cmd, 0);
                      perror("execl");
                      exit(errno);
    }
    if (waitpid(pid,&status,0)==pid && WIFEXITED(status))
        return WEXITSTATUS(status);
    return -1;
}
```

```
int main()
{
        int          rc = 0;
        char         buf[256];
        do {
                     cout << "sh> " << flush;
                     if (!gets(buf)) break;
                     rc = System(buf);
        } while (!rc);
        exit(rc);
}
```

The above program is a simple UNIX shell program. It prompts users to enter shell commands from standard input and executes each command via the *System* function. The program terminates when either user enters end-of-file (<ctrl-D>) at a "shell" prompt or the return status of a *System* call is nonzero. The program differs from a UNIX shell in that its does not support the *cd* command and manipulation of shell variables.

The *system* function emulates the C library function *system*. Specifically, the *system* function prototype is:

```
    int      system   (const char* cmd);
```

Both functions invoke a Bourne shell (*/bin/sh*) to interpret and execute a shell command that is specified via the argument *cmd*. A command may consist of a simple shell command or a series of shell commands separated by semicolons or pipes. Furthermore, input and/or output redirections may be specified with the commands.

The *System* function calls *fork* to create a child process. The child process, in turn, calls *execlp* to execute a Bourne shell program (*/bin/sh*) with the -c and *cmd* as arguments. The -c option instructs the Bourne shell to interpret and execute the *cmd* arguments as if they were entered at the shell level. After *cmd* is executed, the child process is terminated and the exit status of the Bourne shell is passed to the parent process, which calls the *System* function.

Note that the *System* function calls *waitpid* to specifically wait for the child that it forked. This is important, as the *System* function may be called by a process that forked a child process before calling *System*; thus, the *System* function would wait only for child processes forked by it and not those created by the calling process.

When the *waitpid* returns, the *System* function checks that: (1) the return PID matches that of the child process that it forked; and (2) the child was terminated via *_exit*. If both conditions are true, the *System* function returns the child exit code. Otherwise, it returns a -1 to indicate failure status.

The *system* library function is similar to the *System* function, except that the former will include signal handling and set the *errno* variable with an error code when the *waitpid* call fails.

The sample output of the program may be:

```
%    CC -o test_exec test_exec.C
%    test_exec
sh>  date; pwd
Sat Jan 15 18:09:53 PST 1994
/home/terry/sample
sh> echo "Hello world"  |  wc > foo;  cat foo
1    2    12
sh> ^D
```

8.2.5   pipe

The *pipe* system call creates a communication channel between two related processes (for example, between a parent process and a child process, or between two sibling processes with a same parent). Specifically, the function creates a pipe device file that serves as a temporary buffer for a calling process to read and write data with another process. The pipe device file has no assigned name in any file system; thus, it is called an *unnamed pipe*. A pipe is deallocated once all processes close their file descriptors referencing the pipe.

```
#include <unistd.h>

int          pipe      ( int      fifo[2] );
```

The *fifo* argument is an array of two integers that are assigned by the *pipe* API. On most UNIX systems, a pipe is unidirectional in that *fifo[0]* is a file descriptor that a process can use to read data from the pipe, and *fifo[1]* is a different file descriptor that a process can use to write data to the pipe. However, in UNIX System V.4, a pipe is bidirectional and both the *fifo[0]* and *fifo[1]* descriptors may be used for reading and writing data via the pipe. POSIX.1 supports both the traditional UNIX and System V.4 pipe models by not specifying the exact uses of the pipe descriptors. Applications that desire portability on all UNIX and POSIX systems should use pipes as if they were unidirectional only.

Data stored in a pipe is accessed sequentially in a first-in-first-out manner. A process cannot use *lseek* to do random data access of a pipe. Data is consumed from a pipe once it is read.

•

The common method is to set up a communication channel between processes via *pipe*:

- *Parent and child processes*: the parent calls *pipe* to create a pipe, then forks a child. Since the child has a copy of the parent file descriptors, the parent and child can communicate through the pipe via their respective *fifo[0]* and *fifo[1]* descriptors

- *Sibling child processes*: the parent calls *pipe* to create a pipe, then forks two or more child processes. The child processes can communicate through the pipe via their respective *fifo[0]* and *fifo[1]* descriptors

Because the buffer associated with a pipe device file has a finite size (PIPE_BUF), a pipe already filled with data when a process tries to write to it will be blocked by the kernel until another process reads sufficient data from the pipe to make room for the blocked process to succeed in the write operation. Conversely, if a pipe is empty and a process tries to read data from a pipe, it will be blocked until another process writes data into the pipe. These blocking mechanisms can be used to synchronize the execution of two (or more) processes.

There is no limit on how many processes can concurrently attach to either end of a pipe. However, if two or more processes are writing data to a pipe simultaneously, each process can write, at most, PIPE_BUF bytes of contiguous data into the pipe at a time. Consider that when a process (for example, A) writes X bytes of data into a pipe, there is no room for Y bytes in the pipe. If X is larger than Y only the first Y bytes of data are written into the pipe, and the process is blocked. Another process (for example, B) runs and there is room in the pipe (due to a third process reading data from the pipe), and B writes data into the pipe. Then, when process A resumes running, it writes the remaining X-Y bytes of data into the pipe. The end result is that data in the pipe is interlaced between the two processes. Similarly, if two (or more) processes attempt to read data from a pipe concurrently, it may happen that each process reads only a portion of the desired data from the pipe.

To avoid the above drawbacks, it is conventional to set up a pipe as unidirectional communication channel between only two processes, such that one process will be designated as the sender of the pipe and the other process designated as the receiver of the pipe. If two processes, fro example, A and B, need a bidirectional communication channel, they will create two pipes: one for process A to write data to process B, and vice versa.

If there is no file descriptor in the process to reference the write-end of a pipe, the pipe write-end is considered "close" and any process attempts to read data from the pipe will receive the remaining data. However, once all data in the pipe is consumed, a process that attempts to read more data from the pipe will receive an end-of-file (the *read* system call returns a 0 return value) indicator. On the other hand, if no file descriptor references the read-end of a pipe, and the process attempts to write data into the pipe, it will receive the SIGPIPE (broken pipe) signal from the kernel. This is because no data written to the pipe can be retrieved by the process; thus, the write operation is considered illegal. The process that does the write will be penalized by the signal (the default action of the signal is to abort the process).

pipe is used by the UNIX shell to implement the command pipe ("|") for connecting the standard output of one process to the standard input of another process. It is also used in implementation of the *popen* and *pclose* C library functions. The implementation of the *popen* and *pclose* functions is described in the next section.

The return value of *pipe* may be 0 if the call succeeds or -1 if it fails. The possible *errno* values assigned by the API and their meanings are:

Errno value	Meaning
EFAULT	The fifo argument is illegal
ENFILE	The system file table is full

The following *test_pipe.C* program shows the use of *pipe*:

```
#include <iostream.h>
#include <stdio.h>
#include <stdlib.h>
#include <string.h>
#include <sys/types.h>
#include <sys/wait.h>
#include <unistd.h>
int main()
{
      pid_t child_pid;
      int    fifo[2], status;
      char   buf[80];

      if ( pipe(fifo) == -1 ) perror( "pipe" ), exit( 1 );
      switch ( child_pid = fork() ) {
         case -1:        perror( "fork" );
                         exit( 2 );
         case 0:         close( fifo[0] );               /* child process */
                         sprintf( buf, "Child %d executed\n", getpid() );
```

```
                              write( fifo[1], buf, strlen(buf)) ;
                              close( fifo[1] );
                              exit(0);
        }
        close( fifo[1 ] );                                      /* parent process */
        while ( read( fifo[0], buf, 80) ) cout << buf << endl;
        close( fifo[0] );
        if ( waitpid(child_pid,&status,0)==child_pid && WIFEXITED(status) )
              return WEXITSTATUS( status );
        return 3;
}
```

This program shows a simple use of *pipe*. The parent process calls *pipe* to allocate a pipe device file. It then calls *fork* to create a child process. Both the parent and child processes can access the pipe via their own copy of the *fifo* variable.

In the example, the child process is designated as the sender of message to the parent, writing the message *Child <child_pid> executed* to the pipe via the *fifo[1]* descriptor. The *getpid* system call returns the child PID value. After the write, the child terminates via *exit* with a zero exit code.

The parent process is designated the receiver of the pipe, and it reads the child's message from the pipe via the *fifo[0]* descriptor. Note that in the parent process, it first closes the *fifo[1]* descriptor before it goes into a loop to read data from the pipe. This is to ensure that when the child process closes its *fifo[1]* descriptor (after a write), the write end of the pipe will be closed. The parent will eventually receive the end-of-file indicator after if has read all messages from the child process. If the parent does not close *fifo[1]* before it does the read loop, the parent will eventually be suspended in the *read* system call once it has read all data from the pipe (the pipe's write end is still opened as referenced by the parent's *fifo[1]*, and the end-of-file indicator will not be seen).

As a general rule, the reader process should always close the pipe write-end file descriptor before it reads data from the pipe. Similarly, the sender process should always close the pipe write-end descriptor after it finishes writing data to the pipe. This renders the reader process to detect the end-of-file situation.

After the parent process exits from the read loop, it calls *waitpid* to collect the child exit status and terminates with either the child exit code (if the child has terminated via *_exit*) or a failure exit code of 3.

The output of the program may be:

```
%    CC test_pipe.C -o test_pipe;    test_pipe
Child 1234 executed
```

8.2.6   I/O Redirection

In UNIX, a process can use the C library function *freopen* to change its standard input and/or standard output ports to refer to text files instead of the console. For example, the following statements will change the process standard output to the file *foo*, so that the *printf* statement will write the message *Greeting message to foo* to the file:

```
FILE *fptr = freopen("foo","w",stdout);
printf("Greeting message to foo\n");
```

Similarly, the following statements will change the process standard input port to the file *foo*, dumping the entire file content to the standard output:

```
char buf[256];
FILE *fptr = freopen("foo","r",stdin);
while (gets(buf)) puts (buf);
```

The *freopen* function actually relies on the *open* and *dup2* system calls to do redirection of either standard input or output. Thus, to redirect the standard input of a process from the file *src_stream*, the following can be done:

```
#include <unistd.h>
int fd = open("src_stream",O_RDONLY);
if (fd!=-1) dup2(fd,STDIN_FILENO), close(fd);
```

The above statements first open the *src_stream* file for read-only, and the *fd* file description references the opened file. If the *open* call succeeds (*fd* value is not -1), the *dup2* function is called to force the STDIN_FILENO (which is defined in *<unistd.h>* header, and is the standard input file descriptor value) to reference the *src_stream* file, then the *fd* descriptor is discarded via the *close* system call. The result of all this is that the *src_stream* file is now referenced by the STDIN_FILENO descriptor of the process.

Similar system calls can also be used to change the standard output of a process to a file:

```
#include <unistd.h>
int fd = open("dest_stream",O_WRONLY | O_CREAT | O_TRUNC,0644);
if (fd!=-1) dup2(fd,STDOUT_FILENO), close(fd);
```

After the above statements, any data written to the process' standard output, via the STDOUT_FILENO, will be written to the file *dest-file*.

The *freopen* function can be implemented as follows:

```
FILE * freopen (const char* file_name, const char *mode,
                    FILE *old_fstream)
{
    if (strcmp(mode,"r") && strcmp(mode,"w"))
        return NULL;                               /* invalid mode */
    int fd = open(file_name,*mode=='r' ? O_RDONLY :
                    O_WRONLY|O_CREAT | O_TRUNC,0644);
    if (fd == -1) return NULL;
    if (!old_stream) return fdopen(fd, mode);
    fflush(old_fstream);
    int fd2 = dup2(fd, fileno(old_fstream));
    close(fd);
    return (fd2 == -1) ? NULL : old_fstream;
}
```

In the above function, if the *mode* argument value is not *"r"* or *"w"* the function returns a NULL stream pointer, as the function does not support other access modes. Furthermore, if the file named by the *file_name* argument cannot be opened with the specified mode, the function will also return a NULL stream pointer. If the *open* call succeeds and the *old_fstream* argument is NULL, there is no old stream to redirect. The function will just convert the *fd* file descriptor to a stream pointer via the *fdopen* function and return it to the caller.

If, however, the *old_fstream* is not NULL, the function will first flush all data stored in that stream's I/O buffer via the *fflush* function call, then it will use *dup2* to force the file descriptor associated with the *old_fstream* to refer to the opened file. Note that it is invalid to use *fclose* to flush and close the *old_fstream* here. *Freopen* needs to reuse the FILE record referenced by *old_fstream* for the new file, but *fclose* will deallocate the FILE record. The *file*no macro is defined in the <stdio.h> header. It returns a file descriptor associated with a given stream pointer.

After *dup2*, the function closes *fd,* as it is no longer needed, and returns either the *old_fstream,* which now references the new file, or NULL, if the *dup2* call fails.

8.2.6.1 UNIX I/O Redirection

The UNIX shell input redirection (<) and output redirection (>) constructs can be implemented with the same concept as the above, except that the redirection operation will be done before a child process calls *execs* to a shell executing a user command. For example, the following program implements the UNIX shell command:

```
%    sort <  foo > results
```

The following program illustrates a mean for standard input and output redirection:

```
#include <unistd.h>
int main()
{
        int fd, fd2;
        switch ( fork() )  {
            case -1:        perror( "fork" ), break;

            case 0:         if ( (fd = open("foo", O_RDONLY))==-1 ||
                                    (fd2=open("results", O_WRONLY
                                     O_CREAT| O_TRUNC ,0644)) == -1 ) {
                                perror( "open" );
                                _exit( 1 );
                            }

                            /* set standard input from "foo" */
                            if ( dup2(fd,STDIN_FILENO) == -1 ) _exit( 5 );

                            /* set standard output to "result" */
                            if ( dup2(fd2,STDOUT_FILENO) == -1 ) _exit( 6 );

                            close( fd );
                            close( fd2 );
                            execlp( "sort", "sort", 0 );
                            perror( "execlp" ;
                            _exit( 8 );
        }
        return 0;
}
```

The above program forks a child process to execute the *sort* command. After the child process is created, it redirects its standard input to be from the file *foo* and its standard output to the file *results*. If both *open* calls succeed, the child process calls *exec* to execute the *sort* command. Because there is no argument specified to the *sort* command, it will take data from its standard input (the file *foo*). The sorted data are written to the process standard output, which is now the *result* file.

It is possible to redirect standard input and/or output ports in a parent process before *fork* and *exec*. The difference in a child process is that after *fork,* the parent will not use the redirected port(s) or restore the redirected port(s) to its original source (e.g., */dev/tty*). It can then be used in the same way as before *fork*. It is, therefore, easier to redirect standard input and/or output in a child process just before an *exec* system call.

8.2.6.2 UNIX Command Pipes

The UNIX shell command pipes execute multiple commands concurrently, such that the standard output of one command (specified to the left of a "|" symbol) is connected directly to the standard input of the next command (specified to the right of a "|" symbol). For example, given the following command:

```
%     ls   -l   |    sort -r
```

the UNIX shell forks two child processes. One executes the *ls -l* command and the other executes the *sort* command. Furthermore, the standard output data of the child process executing the *ls -l* command will be directed to the standard input port of the one executing the *sort* command. The output of these two commands is a sorted list of the current directory content.

The following *command_pipe.C* program illustrates how to execute two commands concurrently with a command pipe:

```c
#include <stdio.h>
#include <stdlib.h>
#include <unistd.h>
#include <sys/types.h>
#include <sys/wait.h>
#define CLOSE_ALL()            close(fifo[0]), close(fifo[1])

int main( int argc, char* argv[])
{
        int fifo[2];
        pid_tpid1, pid2;

        if(pipe(fifo)) perror("pipe"), _exit(2); /* create a command pipe */

        switch (pid1=fork())  {       /* execute command to the left of pipe */
            case -1:      perror("fork"), exit(3);
            case 0:       if (dup2(fifo[1],STDOUT_FILENO)==-1)
                              perror("dup2"), exit(4);
                          CLOSE_ALL();
                          if (execlp("/bin/sh","sh","-c",argv[1],0)==-1)
                              perror("execl"), exit(5);
        }

        switch (pid2=fork())  {       /* execute command to the right of pipe */
            case -1:      perror("fork"), exit(6);
            case 0:       if (dup2(fifo[0],STDIN_FILENO)==-1)
                              perror("dup2"), exit(7);
                          CLOSE_ALL();
```

```
                          if (execlp("/bin/sh","sh","-c",argv[2],0)==-1)
                                perror("execl"), exit(8);
              }

              CLOSE_ALL();
              if (waitpid(pid1,&fifo[0],0)!=pid1 || waitpid(pid2,&fifo[1],0)!=pid2)
                  perror("waitpid");
              return fifo[0]+fifo[1];
        }
```

This program takes two command line arguments. Each argument specifies a shell command to be executed. If a shell command includes arguments, the command and its arguments must be enclosed by a pair of quotation marks so that the UNIX shell will pass them as one argument to the program. For example, if the following shell command is specified, the *argv[1]* of the program will be *ls -l*, and the *argv[2]* of the program will be *sort -r*.

        %   a.out   "ls -l"   "sort -r"

When the program is run, it creates an unnamed pipe to connect the standard input and output ports of the two commands to be executed. If the *pipe* system call fails, the program calls *perror* to print a diagnostic message and then exits.

After a pipe is created, the program forks a child process to *exec* the shell command specified in *argv[1]*. However, before the *execl* call, the child process redirects its standard output port to the pipe's write end, then closes its copy of the pipe file descriptor. Thus, when the *argv[1]* shell command is executed, the standard output data will be directed into the pipe.

The program also forks another child process to *exec* a Bourne shell that executes the shell command specified in *argv[2]*. However, before the *execl* call the child process redirects its standard input port to the pipe's read end and closes its copy of the pipe file descriptor. Thus, when the Bourne shell executes *argv[2]*, the standard input data will be from the pipe.

After creating two child processes, the parent process closes the file descriptors of the pipe. This is to ensure that when the first child process (which executes *argv[1]*) terminate, there will be no file descriptor referencing the pipe's read end, and the second child process (which executes *argv[2]*) will eventually read the end-of-file indicator from the pipe and know when to terminate itself. The parent process waits for the two child processes to terminate and checks their exit status.

The above program is not POSIX.1-compliant, as the Bourne shell is not defined in POSIX.1. However, it is compliant to POSIX.2, where shells and command pipes are defined.

The sample output of the program may be:

```
%    CC -o command pipe command_pipe.C
%    command_pipe    "ls -l"    wc
52   410    3034
%    command_pipe    pwd    cat
/home/book/chapter10
%    command_pipe    cat    "sort -r"
Hello world
Bye-Bye
^D
Bye-Bye
Hello world
%
```

The above program can be further enhanced to accept an arbitrary number of shell commands and pipes. Thus, if the new program is run with the following command:

```
%    command_pipe    "ls -l"    "sort -r"    "wc"    "cat"
```

it is similar to the following shell command:

```
%    ls -l    |    sort -r    |    wc    |    cat
```

As a general rule, if a UNIX command contains N "|" symbols, the shell must create N pipes (created via the *pipe* API) and $N+1$ child processes. Because each pipe call consumes two file descriptors and because a process may use, at most, OPEN_MAX file descriptors at any one time, a shell process must recycle its file descriptors. This enables the setting up of unnamed pipes to handle an unlimited number of command pipes.

The new program shows how to handle arbitrary numbers of command pipes and shell commands:

```
/* command_pipe2.C */
#include <stdio.h>
#include <stdlib.h>
#include <sys/types.h>
#include <sys/wait.h>
#include <unistd.h>
#define CLOSE(fd)  if (fd < -1) close(fd), fd=-1
static int fifo[2][2] = { -1, -1, -1, -1 }, cur_pipe=0;
```

```
int main( int argc, char* argv[])
{
      for (int i=1; i < argc; i++)     {
          if (pipe(fifo[cur_pipe])) perror("pipe"), _exit(2);
          switch (fork())    {               /* execute command to the left of pipe */
            case -1:      perror("fork"), exit(3);
            case 0:       if (i > 1)    {                    /* not first command */
                             dup2(fifo[1-cur_pipe][0],STDIN_FILENO);
                             CLOSE(fifo[1-cur_pipe][0]);
                          }
                          if (i < argc-1)     {      /* not the last command */
                             dup2(fifo[cur_pipe][1],STDOUT_FILENO);
                             CLOSE(fifo[cur_pipe][0]);
                             CLOSE(fifo[cur_pipe][1]);
                          }
                          if (execlp("/bin/sh","sh","-c",argv[i],0)==-1)
                             perror("execl"), exit(5);
          }
          CLOSE(fifo[1-cur_pipe][0]);
          CLOSE(fifo[cur_pipe][1]);
          cur_pipe = 1 - cur_pipe;
      }
      CLOSE(fifo[1-cur_pipe][0]);
      while (waitpid(-1,0,0))
          ;
      return 0;
}
```

The above program creates an unique pipe between every two consecutive commands. All commands except the very first one will get the standard input data from their pipe's read end (the first command standard input is from the console). Similarly, all commands except the very last one will send their standard output data to the write end of the next command pipe (the last one will send its standard output to the console). The only difficult part here is that the parent process must close all the unnecessary pipe descriptors after each child is created. This is to ensure that it does not use up all the allowable file descriptors and that no unnecessary file descriptors are used up in the new child process. Furthermore, the parent process must make sure only one child process has a file descriptor referencing one end of a pipe at any time. The end-of-file indicator will eventually be passed from the first command process to the next, and so on, until all the child processes receive it and terminate properly.

The sample output of the program may be:

```
%    CC command_pipe2.C
%    a.out    ls    sort    wc
150 50 724
```

```
%    a.out   date
Sun Jan 16 13:0:0 PST 1994
%    a.out   date    wc
1  6  29
%    a.out pwd sort cat
/home/book/chapter11
```

8.2.6.3 The popen and pclose Functions

This section depicts more advanced examples on the usage of *fork, exec,* and *pipe.* Specifically, it will show how to use these APIs to implement the C library functions *popen* and *pclose.*

The *popen* function is used to execute a shell command within a user program. The function prototype of the *popen* function is:

FILE*   ***popen*** (**const char*** shell_cmd, **const char*** mode);

The first argument *shell_cmd* is a character string that contains any shell command a user may execute in a Bourne shell. The function will invoke a Bourne shell to interpret and execute that command.

The second argument *mode* is either *"r"* or *"w."* It specifies that the stream pointer that is returned from the function can be used to either read data from the standard output (if *mode* is *"r"*) or to write data to the standard input (if *mode* is *"w"*) to the Bourne shell process that executes the *shell_cmd.*

popen returns a NULL value if the *shell_cmd* cannot be executed. Possible causes of failure may be that the *shell_cmd* is invalid or that the process lacks permission to execute the command.

The *pclose* function accepts a stream pointer that is returned from a *popen* function call. It will close the stream associated with the stream pointer and then wait for the corresponding Bourne shell process to terminate. The function prototype of the *pclose* function is:

int   ***pclose*** (**FILE** *fstream);

pclose returns the exist status of the command being executed if it succeeds or a -1 if it fails. Possible cause of failure may be that the *fstream* actual value is invalid or not defined by a *popen* call.

The *popen* function is implemented by calling *fork* to create a child process, which in turn will *exec* a Bourne shell (*/bin/sh*) to interpret and execute the *shell_cmd*. Additionally, the parent process will call *pipe* to establish a connection between either the pipe read end and the child standard output (if *mode* is "*r*"), or between the pipe write end and the child standard input (if *mode* is "*w*"). The file descriptor of the pipe other end is converted to a stream pointer, via the *fdopen* function, and is returned to the caller of the *popen* function.

The *popen* function may be implemented as the following:

```
#include <stdio.h>
#include <stdlib.h>
#include <unistd.h>
#include <sys/types.h>
#include <sys/wait.h>
#include <string.h>
#include <limits.h>

struct sh_rec
{
      pid_t    sh_pid;
      FILE*    stream;
}              sh_info[OPEN_MAX];
static int     num_sh;

FILE* popen(const char* shell_cmd, const char* mode)
{
      int fifo[2];
      if ((strcmp(mode,"r") && strcmp(mode,"w")) || pipe(fifo)==-1)
         return 0;

      switch (sh_info[num_sh].sh_pid=fork())      {
         case -1:     perror("fork"); return 0;
         case 0:      (*mode=='r') ?  dup2(fifo[1],STDOUT_FILENO) :
                                      dup2(fifo[0],STDIN_FILENO);
                      close(fifo[0]);
                      close(fifo[1]);
                      execl("/bin/sh", "sh", "-c", shell_cmd, 0);
                      exit(5);
      }
      if (*mode=='r')   {
         close(fifo[1]);
         return (sh_info[num_sh++].stream=fdopen(fifo[0],mode));
```

```
    } else   {
       close(fifo[0]);
       return (sh_info[num_sh++].stream=fdopen(fifo[1],mode));
    }
}
```

Note that each child process PID and its corresponding stream pointer from each *popen* call are recorded in a global array *sh_info*. The *sh_info* array has OPEN_MAX-1 entries, as a process can, at most, call *popen* OPEN_MAX-1 times to allocate stream pointers referencing *exec*'ed shell commands. The data stored in the *sh_info* array is used by the *pclose* function in the following manner: When *pclose* is called, it finds an entry in the *sh_info* array that *stream* value matches with the *fstream* argument value. If there is no match, the *fstream* value is invalid, and the *pclose* function will return a -1 failure value. If there is a match, the *pclose* function will close the stream (a pipe end) referenced by *fstream,* then wait for the corresponding child process (whose PID is given by the *sh_pid* variable in the *sh_info* entry) to terminate before the function returns a zero success value.

The *pclose* function may be implemented as follows:

```
int pclose (FILE *fstream )
{
    int i, status, rc=-1;
    for (i=0; i < num_sh; i++)
        if (sh_info[i].stream==fstream) break;
    if (i == num_sh) return -1;        /* invalid fstream value */
    fclose(fstream);
    if (waitpid(sh_info[i].sh_pid,&status,0)==sh_info[i].sh_pid ||
                                WIFEXITED(status))
        rc = WEXITSTATUS(status);
    for (i++; i < num_sh; i++) sh_info[i-1] = sh_info[i];
    num_sh--;
    return rc;
}
```

The *popen* and *pclose* functions are defined in POSIX.2, but not in POSIX.1. The following *test_popen.C* program illustrates the use of the *popen* and *pclose* functions:

```
#include <stdio.h>
#include <unistd.h>

int main (int argc, char* argv[])
{
    charbuf[256], *mode= (argc>2) ? "w" : "r";
```

237

```
        FILE*fptr;

        if (argc>1 && (fptr = popen(argv[1],mode)))     {
            switch (*mode)  {
                case 'r':   while (fgets(buf,256,fptr)) fputs(buf,stdout);
                            break;
                case 'w':   fprintf(fptr,"%s\n",argv[2]);
            }
            return pclose(fptr);
        }
        return 5;
    }
```

The test program invocation syntax is:

```
    %    a.out <shell_cmd> [ <data to write to shell_cmd> ]
```

If the test program is invoked with a shell command only (that is, one argument), the program will call *popen* to execute the command and print the *exec*'ed command's standard output data to the console. If, however, the program is invoked with a shell command and second argument, the program will execute the shell command, via *popen*, and supply the second argument as data to the standard input port of the *exec*'ed command.

The program calls *pclose* to terminate the *popen* call. The sample output of the test program may be:

```
    %    CC test_popen.C
    %    a.out date
    Sat Jan 15 21:42:22 PST 1994
    %    a.out    "Hello world"    wc
    1    2        11
```

8.3   Process Attributes

A discussion of process will not be complete without mentioning the various APIs to query and set some of the process attributes. This section will depict the process attribute inquiry APIs that are common for both POSIX.1 and UNIX. The next section will depict the POSIX.1 and UNIX APIs that change process attributes.

```
#include <sys/types.h>
#include <unistd.h>

pid_t       getpid       (void);
pid_t       getppid      (void);
pid_t       getpgrp      (void);
uid_t       getuid       (void);
uid_t       geteuid      (void);
gid_t       getgid       (void);
gid_t       getegid      (void);
```

Note that in older versions of UNIX all the above APIs return values that are of type *int*. The *pid_t, uid_t,* and *gid_t* types are defined in the <sys/types.h> header.

The *getpid* and *getppid* APIs return the calling process PID and its parent process ID, respectively. No arguments are needed for these system calls.

The *getpgrp* API returns the calling process's process group ID. Every process in a UNIX or POSIX system belongs to a process group. When a user logs onto a system, the login process becomes a session leader and a process group leader. The session ID and the process group ID of a session leader is the same as its process ID. If the login process creates new child processes to execute jobs, these child processes will be in the same session and process group as the login process. However, if the login process moves some jobs to the background, the process associated with each background job will be assigned a different process group ID. Furthermore, if a background job is executed by more than one process, then the process that created all the other processes for the job will become the process group leader of the job.

The *getuid* and *getgid* system calls return the real user ID and real group ID of the calling process, respectively. The real user-ID and group-ID are the UID and GID of a person who created the process. For example, when you login to a UNIX system, the login shell's real UID and real GID are your UID and GID, respectively. All the child processes created by this login shell will also have your real UID and GID. The real UID and real GID are used by the UNIX kernel to keep track of which user created a process in the system.

The *geteuid* and *getegid* system calls return the effective user ID and effective group ID of the calling process. The effective user ID and group ID are used by the kernel to determine the access permission of the calling process in accessing files. These attributes are also assigned to the UID and GID attributes of files created by the process. In normal situations, a process effective UID is the same as its real UID. However, if the *set-UID* flag of the executable file is set, the process effective user ID will take on the executable file UID. This gives the process the access privileges of the user who owns the executable file. A similar mecha-

239

nism applies to the effective GID, where a process effective GID is different from its real GID if the corresponding executable file *set-GID* flag is set.

An example of the *set-UID* flag use is the */bin/passwd* command. This command aids users changing their passwords in the */etc/passwd* file. Since the */etc/passwd* file is read-only for all users, the process created by executing the */bin/passwd* program must have superuser privileges to be able to write data to the */etc/passwd* file. Thus, the */bin/passwd* file's UID is the superuser user ID, and its *set-UID* flag is ON. A process created by executing the program */bin/passwd* will have the effective UID of the superuser, and it has the privilege to modify the */etc/passwd* file in the course of its run.

The *set-UID* and *set-GID* flags of an executable file may be changed via either the *chmod* UNIX command or the *chmod* API.

The following *getproc.C* program illustrates how to obtain process attributes:

```
#include <iostream.h>
#include <sys/types.h>
#include <unistd.h>

int main ( )
{
        cout << "Process PID: " << (int)getpid() << endl;
        cout << "Process PPID: " << (int)getppid() << endl;
        cout << "Process PGID: " << (int)getpgrp() << endl;
        cout << "Process real-UID: " << (int)getuid() << endl;
        cout << "Process real-GID: " << (int)getgid() << endl;
        cout << "Process effective-UID: " << (int)geteuid() << endl;
        cout << "Process effective-GID: " << (int)getegid() << endl;
}
```

The output of the program may be:

```
%     CC getproc.C
%     a.out
Process PID: 1254
Process PPID: 200
Process PGID: 50
Process real-UID:751
Process real-GID: 77
Process effective-UID: 205
Process effective-GID: 77
%
```

8.4   Change Process Attributes

This section depicts the POSIX.1 and UNIX APIs that change process attributes. Note that some of the process attributes, such as PID and parent PID, can be queried but not changed, whereas some attributes, such as a process session ID, cannot be queried but can be changed.

```
#include <sys/types.h>
#include <unistd.h>

int        setsid        (void);
int        setpgid       (pid_t pid, pid_t pgid);
int        setuid        (uid_t uid);
int        seteuid       (uid_t uid);
int        setgid        (gid_t gid);
int        setegid       (gid_t gid);
```

The *setsid* API sets the calling process to be a new session leader and a new process group leader. The session ID and the process group ID of the process are the same as its PID. The process will also be disassociated with its controlling terminal. This API is commonly called by a daemon process after it is created, so that it can run independently from its parent process. This is a POSIX.1-specific API.

The *setpgid* API sets the calling process to be a new process group leader. The process group ID of the process is the same as its PID. The process will be the only member in the new group. This call will fail if the calling process is already the session leader of a process session. In UNIX System V, the *setpgrp* API is the same as the *setpgid* API.

If the effective UID of a process is a superuser, the *setuid* system call will set the real-UID, effective-UID, and the saved set-UID attributes of the process to the *uid* argument value. If, however, the calling process does not have the effective UID of a superuser, then if *uid* is either the real-UID or saved set-UID value, the API will change the effective UID of the process to *uid*. Otherwise, the API will return a -1 failure status.

If the effective GID of a process is a superuser, the *setgid* system call will set the real-GID, effective-GUID, and the saved set-GID attributes of the process to the *gid* argument value. If, however, the calling process does not have the effective UID of a superuser and *gid* is either the real-GID or saved set-GUID value, the API will change the effective GID of the calling process to *gid*. Otherwise, the API will return a -1 failure status.

The *seteuid* API changes the calling process effective UID to *uid*. If the process has no superuser privilege, the *uid* value must be either the real UID or the saved set-UID of the process. If, on the other hand, the process has superuser privileges, the *uid* may be any value.

The *setegid* API changes the calling process effective GID to *gid*. If the process has no superuser privilege the *gid* must be either the real GID or the saved set-GID of the process. If, on the other hand, the process has superuser privileges, the *gid* may be any value.

8.5   A Minishell Example

To illustrate the use of process APIs, this section depicts a simple UNIX shell program that can create processes which execute any number of UNIX commands, either serially or concurrently. Specifically, the minishell program can execute any user-specified commands with optional input and/or output redirection and can also execute commands in the background and/or foreground. The only limitation of this minishell program is that it does not support any shell variables or metacharacters.

The design of the minishell program is as follows: A simple UNIX command consists of a command name, optional switches, and any number of arguments. Furthermore, input and output redirections may be specified with any command, command pipes may be specified to chain multiple simple commands together, and "&" may be specified to execute a command in the background. The following are examples of UNIX commands that are acceptable by the minishell program:

```
%    pwd > foo                    # a simple command with output redirection
%    sort-r /etc/passwd &         # a command executed in background
%    cat -n < abc > foo           # a command with input/output redirection
%    ls -l | sort-r | cat -n      # two command pipes with three commands
%    cat foo; date; pwd > zz      # three commands executed in sequence
%    (spell /etc/motd | sort ) > xx; date    # execute two cmds in a sub-shell
```

To capture these commands to be executed, a CMD_INFO class is defined, where each of its objects store simple command information. The definition of the CMD_INFO class is:

```
class CMD_INFO
{
   public:
      char**        argv;       // command and argument list
      char*         infile;     // std input re-directed file
      char*         outfile;    // std. output re-directed file
      int           backgrnd;   // 1 if cmd to run in background
      CMD_INFO*     pSubcmd;    // cmds to be run in a sub-shell
      CMD_INFO*     Pipe;       // next command after '|'
      CMD_INFO*     Next;       // next command after ';'
};
```

Specifically, the *argv* variable stores a command and its switches and arguments in a vector of character strings. Thus, given a command as follows:

%   sort -r   /etc/motd > foo &

the *argv* variable of a CMD_INFO object that executes this command will be:

```
argv[0]   =    "sort"
argv[1]   =    "-r"
argv[2]   =    "/etc/motd"
argv[3]   =    0;
```

The *infile* and *outfile* variables store the file names of any input and output redirection files, respectively, that are specified in a command. For the *sort* command example above, the *infile* and *outfile* variables of the CMD_INFO object are:

```
infile    =    0;
outfile   =    "foo"
```

The *backgrnd* variable specifies whether a command is to be executed in foreground or background. The variable by default is 0 which means the corresponding command is to be executed in foreground. However, if "&" is specified in a command, the *backgrnd* variable of that command is set to 1. The *backgrnd* variable of the CMD_INFO object of the *sort* command is:

backgrnd = 1;

The *Next* variable is used to link another CMD_INFO object whose command is executed by the same shell process after the current object command. This allows users to execute multiple commands in a command line by delimiting commands with the ";" character. The command line is as follows:

%   ls -l ;   cat < /etc/passwd ;   date > foo&

The CMD_INFO objects that execute the three UNIX commands are:

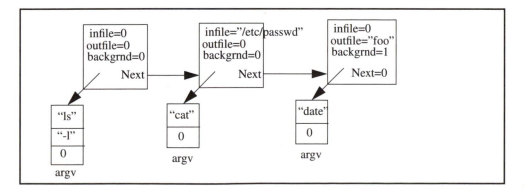

If the *Pipe* variable is not NULL, it specifies that when the current CMD_INFO object command is executed, its standard output data are piped to the standard input of the CMD_INFO object (pointed to by the *Pipe* variable). Furthermore, the commands of both the current object and the one pointed to by the *Pipe* variable will be executed concurrently by the same shell process. Thus, given the following command line:

%   cat -n < /etc/motd | sort -r &; date

the CMD_INFO objects that execute these commands are:

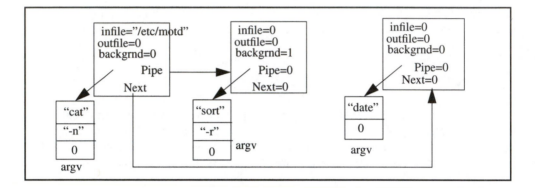

Finally, the *pSubcmd* is used to point to a linked list of CMD_INFO objects whose commands are executed in a separate subshell process from the current shell process. If the *pSubcmd* is not NULL, the *argv* variable of the same object must be NULL, as the current shell's job for this command is to create a subshell to execute the objects pointed to by the *pSubcmd*. Thus, given the following command:

%   date;   (ls -l | cat -n) > foo &;   pwd

The CMD_INFO objects that execute these commands are:

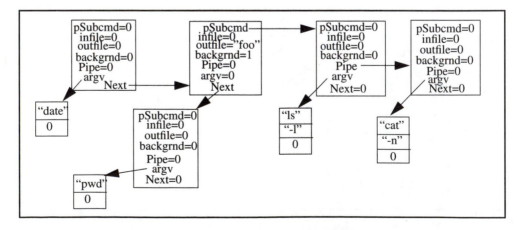

The following *shell.h* header declares the CMD_INFO class and its member functions:

```
/* This is the shell.h header file, which declares the CMD_INFO class */
#ifndef    SHELL_H
#define    SHELL_H

#include <iostream.h>
#include <string.h>
#include <assert.h>
#include <malloc.h>

/* check IO redirection and command pipe conflict */
#define CHECK_IO(fn) if (fn) { \
    cerr << "Invalid re-direct: " << fn << endl; delete fn; fn = 0; }

class CMD_INFO
{
    public:
        char**          argv;       // command and argument list
        char*           infile;     // std input re-directed file
        char*           outfile;    // std. output re-directed file
        int             backgrnd;   // 1 if cmd to run in backgrnd
        CMD_INFO*       pSubcmd;    // cmds to be run in a sub-shell
        CMD_INFO*       Pipe;       // next command after 'l'
        CMD_INFO*       Next;       // next command after ';'

        CMD_INFO()
        {
            argv = 0;
            infile = outfile = 0;
            backgrnd = 0;
            pSubcmd = Pipe = Next = 0;
        };

        ~CMD_INFO()
        {
            if (infile) delete infile;
            if (outfile) delete outfile;
            for (int i=0; argv && argv[i]; i++) free( argv[i] );
            free( argv );
        };

        // Add one argument string to argv list
        void add_arg( char* str )
        {
```

```
        int len = 1;
        if (!argv)
           argv = (char**)malloc(sizeof(char*)*2);
        else {
           while (argv[len]) len++;
           len++;
           argv = (char**)realloc(argv,sizeof(char*)*(len+1));
        }
        assert(argv[len-1] = strdup(str));
        argv[len] = 0;
    };

    // Add a standard input or output redirect file name
    void add_iofile( char*& iofile, char* fnm )
    {
        if (iofile)
           cerr << "Multiple in-direct: " << iofile << " vs " << fnm << endl;
        else iofile = fnm;
    };

    // Add a command pipe
    void add_pipe ( CMD_INFO* pCmd )
    {
        if (Pipe)
           Pipe->add_pipe(pCmd);
        else {
           CHECK_IO(outfile);
           CHECK_IO(pCmd->infile);
           Pipe = pCmd;
        }
    };

    // Add a next command stage
    void add_next( CMD_INFO* pCmd )
    {
        if (Next)
           Next->add_next(pCmd);
        else Next = pCmd;
    };
};    /* CMD_INFO */

/* function is defined in exec_cmd.C */
extern void exec_cmd ( CMD_INFO * cmdp );

#endif
```

The CMD_INFO::CMD_INFO constructor function initializes all variables of a newly created object to be zero.

The ~CMD_INFO::CMD_INFO destructor function deallocates any dynamic memory used by the *argv, infile*, and *outfile* variables of the object to be deleted.

The *CMD_INFO::add_arg* function is called to add word tokens that constitute a shell command to the *argv* variable of an object. This function uses the dynamic memory allocation functions *malloc* and *realloc* to adjust the size of the *argv* according to the actual number of word tokens present in a shell command.

The *CMD_INFO::add_iofile* function is called to add a file name (specified via the *fnm* argument) to either the *infile* or *outfile* variable (specified via the *iofile* argument) of an object. This file is used to redirect the standard input or output of a process that will be created to execute the object's command.

The *CMD_INFO::add_next* function adds a CMD_INFO object to the end of the *Next* linked list of an object. The *Next* linked list specifies a set of commands to be executed in the order of the records present in the list.

The *CMD_INFO::add_pipe* function adds a CMD_INFO object to the end of the *Pipe* linked list of an object. The *Pipe* linked list specifies a set of commands to be executed concurrently, with the standard output of one command piped to the standard input of the next command in the linked list. Moreover, the function checks that a CMD_INFO object cannot pipe data to a pipe and have its standard output redirected to a file at the same time. Similarly, a CMD_INFO object cannot receive data from a pipe and have its standard input redirected from a file at the same time.

With the CMD_INFO class defined, the minishell program will parse each command input line and build up one or more CMD_INFO object linked-lists to represent the corresponding shell commands of an input line. The parsing function of the minishell program is made up of a lexical analyzer and a parser that is created by using *lex* and yacc. Specifically, the lexical analyzer that recognizes command line tokens is constructed from a *lex* source file, as follows:

```
%{/* shell.l:minishell lexical analyzer lex source file */
#include <string.h>
#include "shell.h"
#include "y.tab.h"
%}
%%
;[ \t\v]*\n          return '\n';                  /* skip ';' at end of line */
^[ \t\v]*\n          ;                             /* skip blank lines */
```

```
^#[^\n]\n          ;                                 /* skip comment lines */
#[^\n]*            ;                                 /* skip in-line comment s*/
[ \t\v]            ;                                 /* skip white space */
[A-Za-z_0-9/,.-]+{   yylval.s = strdup(yytext);
                     return NAME;                    /* return a chracter token */
                  }
.                  |                                 /* a single char token */
\n                    return yytext[0];
%%

/* scanner wrap up routine */
int yywrap(){ return 1; }
```

The primary function of the lexical analyzer is to collect NAME tokens and special characters like "<," "<," "|," "(," ")," and ";" which constitute one or more shell commands in each command input line.

A NAME token consists of one or more alphanumeric characters,"-," ".," "_," ",," and "/" characters. It can be a shell command name, a command switch, or an argument to a shell command. When a NAME token is found, the lexical analyzer will return the token character string to the parser via the *yylval* global variable, and the NAME token ID which is defined in the y.tab.h (created from the yacc source file). Punctuation characters like "<," "<," "|," "(," and ")" are returned to the parser as they are.

In addition to the above, the lexical analyzer also ignores comments (a comment begins with a "#" character and is terminated by a newline character), white spaces, blank lines, and the optional ";" at the end of an input line.

Finally, the *yywrap* function is defined as required by *lex*. This function is called when the lexical analyzer encounters end-of-file in its input stream. The function instructs the scanner to stop scanning the input stream by returning one value, so that the parser and, hence, the minishell program, will halt.

The minishell parser expects its entire input data to consist of one or more command lines. Each command line is terminated by a newline character, and the parser will invoke a child process to execute that command line. Furthermore, a command line may consist of one or more shell commands delimited by ";" characters. These shell commands will be executed by the child process sequentially, in the order that they are specified, and any of these commands may be executed in the background if the "&" character is specified at the end of the commands. These syntax rules may be specified as:

```
<input_stream> ::=    [ <cmd_line> '\n' ]+
<cmd_line>     ::=    <shell> ['&'] [';' <shell> ['&'] ]+
```

A shell command may be a basic command, a pipe command, or a complex command:

        `<shell>          ::=    <basic> | <pipe> | <complex>`

A basic command consists of a command name, optional switches and arguments, and any input and/or output redirection. The formal syntax of a basic command is:

        `<basic>      ::= <cmd> [ <switch> ]* [<arg>]* ['<' <file>] ['>' <file>]`

The following are two examples of basic commands:

```
ls -l /etc/passwd
cat -n < srcfile > destfile
```

A pipe command consists of a set of basic and/or complex commands linked together by command pipes ("|"). The formal syntax of a pipe command is:

        `<pipe>       ::= [ <basic> | <complex> ] [ '|' <basic> | <complex> ]+`

The following is an example of a pipe command:

```
ls -l /etc/passwd    |    sort -r  |    cat -n > foo
```

A complex command is one or more shell commands (simple, pipe, and/or complex) enclosed in parentheses and with optional input and output redirection. The formal syntax of a complex command is:

        `<complex>   ::= '(' <shell> [';' <shell> ]* ')' ['<' <file>] ['>' <file>]`

The following is an example of a complex command:

```
( cat < /etc/passwd | sort -r | wc; pwd ) > foo
```

Putting all the above syntax rules together, the *yacc* source file for the minishell parser is as follows:

```
%{      /* shell.y:The minishell program parser */
#include <iostream.h>
#include <stdio.h>
#include <string.h>
#include <assert.h>
```

```
#include <sys/types.h>
#include <sys/wait.h>
#include <unistd.h>
#include <fcntl.h>
#include "shell.h"
static CMD_INFO *    pCmd = 0;
%}

%union
{
    char*           s;
    CMD_INFO *     c;
}
%token <s> NAME

%%
input_stream :  cmd_line '\n'
                    {   exec_cmd($<c>1); }
             |      input_stream cmd_line '\n'
                    {   exec_cmd($<c>2); }
             |      error '\n'
                    {   yyerrok; yyclearin; }

             ;
cmd_line     :      shell backgrnd
                    {   $<c>$ = $<c>1;    }
             |      cmd_line ';' shell backgrnd
                    {   $<c>1->add_next($<c>3);
                        $<c>$ = $<c>1;
                    }

             ;
shell        :      basic
                    {   $<c>$ = $<c>1;    }
             |      complex
                    {   $<c>$ = $<c>1;    }
             |      shell '|' basic
                    {   $<c>1->add_pipe($<c>3);
                        $<c>$ = $<c>1;
                    }
             |      shell '|' complex
                    {   $<c>1->add_pipe($<c>3);
                        $<c>$ = $<c>1;
                    }

             ;
basic        :      cmd_spec io_spec
                    {   $<c>$ = $<c>1;    }

             ;
```

```
complex    :      '(' cmd_line ')'
                      {   pCmd = new CMD_INFO;
                          pCmd->pSubcmd = $<c>2;
                      }
                  io_spec
                      {   $<c>$ = pCmd;      }

               ;
cmd_spec :        NAME
                      {   $<c>$ = pCmd = add_vect(0,$<s>1); }
             |    cmd_spec NAME
                      {   $<c>$ = add_vect($<c>1,$<s>2); }

               ;
io_spec    :      /* empty */
             |    io_spec redir

               ;
redir      :      '<' NAME
                      {   pCmd->add_iofile(pCmd->infile, $<s>2); }
             |    '>' NAME
                      {   pCmd->add_iofile(pCmd->outfile,$<s>2); }

               ;
backgrnd  :       /* empty */
             |    '&'
                      {   pCmd->backgrnd = 1; }

               ;
%%
/* parser error reporting routine */
void yyerror(char* s)  {cerr << s << endl; }

/* add a cmd or arg to vector list */
CMD_INFO *add_vect (CMD_INFO* pCmd, char* str)
{
    int len = 1;
    if (!pCmd) assert(pCmd = new CMD_INFO);
    pCmd->add_arg(str);
    return pCmd;
}
```

In the *shell.y* file, the *cmd_spec* grammar rule recognizes a command name and any optional switches and arguments. When this rule matches, it will create a CMD_INFO object to contain the command data via the *add_vect* function and set the global *pCmd* pointer to point to this newly created object.

The *io_spec* rule collects the file names for any input and/or output redirection and adds these data to the current CMD_INFO object (pointed to by the *pCmd* pointer) via the *CMD_INFO::add_iofile* function.

The *basic* rule is made up of the *cmd_spec* and *io_spec* rules, and it represents one basic shell command specified by a user. It passes the CMD_INFO object that was created by the *cmd_spec* rule to the *shell* rule.

A *shell* rule may be matched by a *basic* rule, a *complex* rule, or *pipe* rule, which consists of a set of *basic* and/or *complex* rules that are separated by the "|" token. For the *pipe* rule the parser will link the CMD_INFO objects, via their *CMD_INFO::Pipe* pointer, that were created by the basic and complex rules through the *CMD_INFO::add_pipe* function. The *shell* rule returns to the *cmd_line* rule either a CMD_INFO object created by the *basic* or *complex* rule or a *Pipe* linked list of CMD_INFO objects.

The *cmd_line* rule is matched by one or more *shell* rules, each of which may be terminated with an optional "&" character and delimited by the ";" character. The parser will link the CMD_INFO objects returned from the *shell* rules together, via their *CMD_INFO::Next* pointer, into a *Next* linked list through the *CMD_INFO::add_next* function. The *cmd_line* rule represents one command input line to the minishell program and returns the first CMD_INFO object in a *Next* linked list (which is constructed to the *input_stream* or *complex* rule).

The *complex* rule is made up of a *cmd_line* rule that is specified in between a matching pair of parentheses characters. Furthermore, input and or output redirection maybe specified after the ')' character. The *complex* rule represents a set of shell commands to be executed in a separate subshell process. The parser will create a special CMD_INFO object to capture this complex rule. In this CMD_INFO object, the *CMD_INFO::argv* argument is NULL, the *CMD_INFO::pSubcmd* pointer will point to the CMD_INFO object (which may be a *Next* linked list) returned from the *cmd_line* rule, and any input and/or output redirection is recorded in the object *CMD_INFO::infile* and *CMD_INFO::outfile* variables. The *complex* rule returns the CMD_INFO object it created to the shell rule.

Finally, the *input_stream* rule is made up of one or more *cmd_line* rules, each terminated by the "\n" character. For each *cmd_line* rule that is matched, the parser will call the *exec_cmd* function to execute the shell commands associated with the CMD_INFO objects returned by the *cmd_line* rule. The *exec_cmd* function is depicted in the following:

```
/* exec_cmd.C: Functions to execute one shell command input line */
#include <iostream.h>
#include <stdio.h>
#include <stdlib.h>
#include <unistd.h>
#include <fcntl.h>
#include <sys/wait.h>
#include "shell.h"
```

```
/* change the standard I/O port of a process */
void chg_io( char* fileName, mode_t mode, int fdesc )
{
   int fd= open(fileName,mode,0777);
   if (fd==-1)
     perror("open");
   else {
     if (dup2(fd,fdesc)==-1) perror("dup2");
     close(fd);
   }
}

/* execute one or more command pipe */
void exec_pipes( CMD_INFO *pCmd )
{
   CMD_INFO *ptr;
   int     fifo[2][2];
   int     bg=0, first=1, cur_pipe = 0;
   pid_t pid;
   while (ptr=pCmd)  {
     pCmd = ptr->Pipe;
     if (pipe(fifo[cur_pipe])==-1)     {
        perror("pipe"); return;
     }
     switch(fork())     {
        case -1:   perror("fork");
                   return;
        case 0:    if (!first)     {                        // not the first cmd
                      dup2(fifo[1-cur_pipe][0],0);
                      close(fifo[1-cur_pipe][0]);
                   }
                   else if (ptr->infile)
                      chg_io(ptr->infile,O_RDONLY,0);
                   if (pCmd)                                // not the last cmd
                      dup2(fifo[cur_pipe][1],1);
                   else if (ptr->outfile)
                      chg_io(ptr->outfile,
                             O_WRONLY|O_CREAT|O_TRUNC,1);
                   close(fifo[cur_pipe][0]);
                   close(fifo[cur_pipe][1]);
                   execvp(ptr->argv[0],ptr->argv);
                   cerr << "Execute '" << ptr->argv[0] << "' fails\n";
                   exit(4);
     }
     if (!first) close(fifo[1-cur_pipe][0]);
     close(fifo[cur_pipe][1]);
```

```
                    cur_pipe = 1 - cur_pipe;
                    bg = ptr->backgrnd;
                    delete ptr;
                    first = 0;
            }
            close(fifo[1-cur_pipe][0]);
            while (!bg && (pid=waitpid(-1,0,0))!=-1) ;
    }

    /* execute one shell command line */
    void exec_cmd( CMD_INFO *pCmd )
    {
        pid_t prim_pid, pid;
        CMD_INFO *ptr = pCmd;

        // create a sub-shell to process one command line
        switch( prim_pid = fork())   {
            case -1:   perror("fork"); return;
            case 0:    break;
            default:   if (waitpid(prim_pid,0,0)!=prim_pid) perror("waitpid");
                       return;
        }
        while (ptr=pCmd)  {            // execute each command stage
            pCmd = ptr->Next;
            if (ptr->Pipe)
                exec_pipes(ptr);        // execute one stage which has pipe
            else  {
                // sub-process to execute one command stage
                switch (pid=fork()) {
                    case -1:   perror("fork"); return;
                    case 0:    break;
                    default:   if (!ptr->backgrnd && waitpid(pid,0,0)!=pid)
                                   perror("waitpid");
                               delete ptr;
                               continue;
                }
                if (ptr->infile)
                    chg_io(ptr->infile,O_RDONLY,0);
                if (ptr->outfile)
                    chg_io(ptr->outfile,O_WRONLY|O_CREAT|O_TRUNC,1);
                if (ptr->argv)   {
                    execvp(ptr->argv[0], ptr->argv);
                    cerr << "Execute '" << ptr->argv[0] << "' fails\n";
                    exit(255);
                } else {
                    exec_cmd(ptr->pSubcmd);
```

```
                    exit(0);
                }
            }
        }
        exit(0);
    }
```

The *exec_cmd* function emulates the UNIX shell in that it forks a child process to execute each shell command input line. Specifically, the function is called with a pointer to a CMD_INFO object, which represents one or more shell commands to be executed. The function first calls *fork* to create a child process, and the parent will call *waitpid* to wait for that child process to terminate. The child is the subshell process, and it scans through the given CMD_INFO object linked-list and executes each command associated with a CMD_INFO object as follows: If the command is a pipe command, it will call the *exec_pipe* command to execute the commands specified via the *Pipe* linked list of that object. If the command is a complex command or basic command, the subshell process will call *fork* to create a new child process to execute the command in the following manner:

If standard input and/or output redirection is specified in the CMD_INFO object, the new child process will change its standard input and/or output to the specified files via the *chg_io* function. If the command is a basic command, the new child process will call *exec* to execute the command specified in the *CMD_INFO::argv* of the object. However, if the command is a complex command (the *CMD_INFO::pSubcmd* of the object is not NULL), the new child process will call the *exec_cmd* function recursively to create a separate child process to execute the complex commands in a different context.

The subshell process will wait for the new child process to terminate before it processes the next CMD_INFO object (unless the *CMD_INFO::backgrnd* flag is set in the current object). This means the new child process is to be run in the background, and the subshell process will not call *waitpid* for the new child process.

If the *CMD_INFO::Pipe* pointer of a CMD_INFO object is not NULL, the object carries a pipe command, and the subshell process will call the *exec_pipe* function to create unnamed pipes and new child processes to execute the corresponding pipe commands.

The *main* function of the minishell program is:

```
/* shell.c:The minishell main program */
#include <iostream.h>
#include <stdio.h>
extern "C" int yyparse();
extern FILE* yyin;
```

```
int main(int argc, char* argv[])
{
   if (argc > 1)  {
      while (--argc > 0)
         if (yyin=fopen(*++argv,"r"))
            yyparse();
         else cerr << "Can't open file: " << *argv << endl;
   } else
      yyparse();
   return 0;
}
```

The main function will call the *yyparse* function to parse the input stream. The *yyparse* function is generated by *yacc* when the *shell.y* is translated by *yacc* to the *y.tab.h* file. The input stream to the minishell program may be the standard input if there is no command line argument to the program (hence, the *argc* value is 1) or it may one or more text files (shell scripts), which are named specifically by a user when the program is invoked. For the latter case, the *main* function will open each shell script file and direct the *yyparse* function to read from that file via the *yyin* global stream pointer.

The minishell program may be compiled as follows:

```
%   yacc -d   shell.y        # create y.tab.c and y.tab.h
%   lex   shell.l            # create lex.yy.c
%   CC -o shell shell.C exec_cmd.C lex.yy.c y.tab.c
```

The sample output of the program is depicted below. The user input commands are highlighted in italic to distinguish them from the minishell program outputs:

```
/export/home/terry/test1 7 > shell
date
Sat Aug 6 11:53:03 PDT 1994
cat -n /etc/motd
   Welcome to T.J. Systems
ls -l  |  cat -n  |  sort -r  |  wc
   10    93      635
pwd;   date;   ls |  wc ;   ps
/export/home/terry/test1
Sat Aug 6 11:54:21 PDT 1994
    9    9     69
PID    TTY    TIME      COMD
351    pts/2  0:00      shell
269    pts/2  0:00      csh
341    pts/2  0:00      shell
```

```
   356      pts/2     0:01        ps
   pwd &;  (ls -l  |   cat -n    |   sort -r   |   wc) > xyz;     cat xyz
   /export/home/terry/test1
      11    103     700
   (ls -l  |   cat -n   |   sort -r   |   wc;  pwd) &;     date
   Sat Aug 6 11:56:03 PDT 1994
      11    103        700
```

8.6   Summary

This chapter depicted the UNIX and POSIX APIs for process creation, control, communication between parent and child processes, and process attribute queries and changes. Furthermore, the methods used to change processes' standard input and output with files, establishing command pipelines, and executing shell commands in a user program are demonstrated. The final minishell example was a simplified UNIX shell program that put all the concepts described in the chapter together and illustrated the applications of those APIs.

One important aspect of process control is signal handling, which deals with the interaction between a process and an operating system kernel in handling asynchronous events. This is the main subject of the next chapter.

Signals

S ignals are triggered by events and are posted on a process to notify it that something has happened and requires some action. An event can be generated from a process, a
user, or the UNIX kernel. For example, if a process performs a divide-by-zero mathematical
operation, or dereferences a NULL pointer, the kernel will send the process a signal to interrupt it. Furthermore, if a user hits the <Delete> or <Ctrl-C> key at the keyboard, the kernel
will send the foreground process a signal to interrupt it. Finally, a parent and its child processes can send signals to each other for process synchronization. Thus, signals are the software version of hardware interrupts. Just as there are several levels of hardware interrupts on
any given system, there are also different types of signals defined for different events that
may occur in a UNIX system.

Signals are defined as integer flags, and the <signal.h> header depicts the list of signals
defined for a UNIX system. The table below lists the POSIX-defined signals that are commonly found in most UNIX systems.

Signal name	Use	Core file gener-ated at default
SIGALRM	Alarm timer time-outs. Can be generated by the alarm() API	No
SIGABRT	Abort process execution. Can be generated by the abort() API	Yes
SIGFPE	Illegal mathematical operation	Yes
SIGHUP	Controlling terminal hang-up	No
SIGILL	Execution of an illegal machine instruction	Yes
SIGINT	Process interruption. Commonly generated by the <Delete> or <ctrl-C> keys	No
SIGKILL	Sure kill a process. Can be generated by the *kill -9 <process_id>* command	Yes

Signal name	Use	Core file generated at default
SIGPIPE	Illegal write to a pipe	Yes
SIGQUIT	Process quit. Commonly generated by a control-\ keys	Yes
SIGSEGV	Segmentation fault. Can be generated by de-referencing a NULL pointer	Yes
SIGTERM	Process termination. Can be generated by the "kill <process_id>" command	Yes
SIGUSR1	Reserved to be defined by users	No
SIGUSR2	Reserved to be defined by users	No
SIGCHLD	Sent to a parent process when its child process has terminated	No
SIGCONT	Resume execution of a stopped process	No
SIGSTOP	Stop a process execution	No
SIGTTIN	Stop a background process when it tries to read from its controlling terminal	No
SIGTSTP	Stop a process execution by the control-Z keys	No
SIGTTOU	Stop a background process when it tries to write to its controlling terminal	No

When a signal is sent to a process, it is *pending* on the process to handle it. The process can react to pending signals in one of three ways:

- Accepts the default action of the signal, which for most signals will terminate the process
- Ignore the signal. The signal will be discarded and it has no effect whatsoever on the recipient process
- Invoke a user-defined function. The function is known as a signal handler routine and the signal is said to be *caught* when this function is called. If the function finishes its execution without terminating the process, the process will continue execution from the point it was interrupted by the signal

A process may set up per signal handling mechanisms, such that it ignores some signals, catches some other signals, and accepts the default action from the remaining signals. Furthermore, a process may change the handling of certain signals in its course of execution. For example, a signal may be ignored in the beginning, then set to be caught, and after being caught, set to accept the default action. A signal is said to have been *delivered* if it has been reacted to by the recipient process.

The default action for most signals is to terminate a recipient process (exceptions are the SIGCHLD and SIGPWR signals). Furthermore, some signals will generate a core file for the aborted process so that users can trace back the state of the process when it was aborted. These signals are usually generated when there is an implied program error in the aborted process. For example, the SIGSEGV signal is generated when a process tries to de-reference a NULL pointer. Thus if the process accepts the default action of SIGSEGV, a core file is generated when the process is aborted and the user can use the core file to debug the program.

Most signals can be ignored or caught except the SIGKILL and SIGSTOP signals. The SIGKILL signal can be generated by a user via the *kill -9 <process ID>* command in a UNIX shell. The SIGSTOP signal halts a process execution. For example, when you type <ctrl-Z> at the keyboard, the kernel will send the SIGSTOP signal to the foreground process to stop it. A companion signal to SIGSTOP is SIGCONT, which resumes a process execution after it has been stopped. SIGSTOP and SIGCONT signals are used for job control in UNIX.

A process is allowed to ignore certain signals so that it is not interrupted while doing certain mission-critical work. For example, when a database management process is updating a database file, it should not be interrupted until it is finished, otherwise, the database file will be corrupted. Thus, this process should specify that all common interrupt signals (e.g., SIG-INT and SIGTERM) are to be ignored before it starts updating the database file. It should restore signal handling actions for these signals afterward.

Because most signals are generated asynchronously to a process, a process may specify a per signal handler function. These functions are called when their corresponding signals are caught. A common practice of a signal handler function is to clean up a process work environment, such as closing all input and output files, before terminating the process gracefully.

9.1   The UNIX Kernel Supports of Signals

In UNIX System V.3, each entry in the kernel Process Table slot has an array of signal flags, one for each signal defined in the system. When a signal is generated for a process, the kernel will set the corresponding signal flag in the Process Table slot of the recipient process. Furthermore, if the recipient process is asleep (for example, it is waiting for a child process to terminate or is executing the *pause* API), the kernel will awaken the process by scheduling it as well. When the recipient process runs, the kernel will check the process *U*-area that contains an array of signal handling specifications, where each entry of the array corresponds to a signal defined in the system. The kernel will consult the array to find out how the process will react to the pending signal. If the array entry for the signal contains a zero value, the process will accept the default action of the signal. If the array entry contains a 1 value, the process will ignore the signal, and the kernel will discard it. Finally, if the array entry contains any other value, it is used as the function pointer for a user-defined signal handler routine. The kernel will set up the process to execute that function immediately, and the process will return to its current point of execution (or to someplace else if the signal handler does a long jump) if the signal handler function does not terminate the process.

If there are different signals pending on a process, the order in which they are sent to a recipient process is undefined. Furthermore, if multiple instances of a signal are pending on a process, it is implementation-dependent on whether a single instance or multiple instances of the signal will be delivered to the process. In UNIX System V.3, each signal flag in a Process Table slot records only whether a signal is pending, but not how many of them are present.

The way caught signals are handled by UNIX System V.2 and by earlier versions has been criticized as unreliable. Subsequently, BSD UNIX 4.2 (and later versions) and POSIX.1 use different mechanisms to handle caught signals.

Specifically, in UNIX System V.2 and earlier versions, when a signal is caught, the kernel will first reset the signal handler (for that signal) in the recipient process U-area, then call the user signal handling function specified for that signal. Thus, if there are multiple instances of a signal being sent to a process at different points, the process will catch only the first instance of the signal. All subsequent instances of the signal will be handled in the default manner.

For a process to continuously catch multiple occurrences of a signal, the process must reinstall the signal handler function every time the signal is caught. However, this is still not a guarantee that the process will catch the signal every time: between the time a signal handler is invoked for a caught signal X and the time the signal handler method is reestablished, the process is in a state of accepting the default action for signal X. If another instance of signal X is delivered to the process during that interval, the process will have to handle the signal in the default manner. This is a race condition, where two events occur simultaneously, and which event will take effect first is unpredictable.

To remedy the unreliability of signal handling in System V.2, BSD UNIX 4.2 (and later versions) and POSIX.1 use a different method: When a signal is caught, the kernel does not reset the signal handler, so there is no need for the process to reestablish the signal handling method. Furthermore, the kernel will block further delivery of the same signal to the process until the signal handler function has completed execution. This ensures that the signal handler function will not be invoked recursively for multiple instances of the same signal. System V.3 introduced the *sigset* API, which behaves in such a reliable manner also.

UNIX System V.4 has adopted the POSIX.1 signal handling method. However, users still have the option to instruct the kernel to use the System V.2 signal handling method on a per-signal basis. This is done via the *signal* APIs, as described next.

9.2   signal

All UNIX systems and ANSI-C support the *signal* API, which can be used to define the per-signal handling method. The function prototype of the *signal* API is:

```
#include <signal.h>

void (*signal ( int signal_num, void (*handler)(int) ) ) (int);
```

The formal arguments of the API are: *signal_num* is a signal identifier like SIGINT or SIGTERM, as defined in the <signal.h> header. The *handler* argument is the function pointer of a user-defined signal handler function. This function should take an integer formal argument and does not return any value.

The following example attempts to catch the SIGTERM signal, ignores the SIGINT signal, and accepts the default action of the SIGSEGV signal. The *pause* API suspends the calling process until it is interrupted by a signal and the corresponding signal handler does a return:

```
#include <iostream.h>
#include <signal.h>
/* Signal handler function */
void catch_sig( int sig_num )
{
      signal (sig_num, catch_sig);
      cout << "catch_sig: " << sig_nm << endl;
}
/* Main function */
int main()
{
      signal (SIGTERM, catch_sig);
      signal (SIGINT, SIG_IGN);
      signal (SIGSEGV, SIG_DFL);
      pause();                  /* wait for a signal interruption */
}
```

The SIG_IGN and SIG_DFL are manifest constants defined in the <signal.h> header:

```
#define SIG_DFL      void (*)(int)0
#define SIG_IGN      void (*)(int)1
```

The *SIG_IGN* specifies a signal is to be ignored, which means that if the signal is generated to the process, it will be discarded without any interruption of the process.

The *SIG_DFL* specifies to accept the default action of a signal.

The return value of the *signal* API is the previous signal handler for a signal. This can be used to restore the signal handler for a signal after it has been altered:

```
#include <signal.h>
int main()
{
```

```
        void (*old_handler)(int) = signal (SIGINT, SIG_IGN);
        /* do mission critical processing */
        signal (SIGINT, old_handler);   /* restore previous signal handling */
    }
```

The *signal* API is not a POSIX.1 standard. However, it is defined by ANSI-C and is available on all UNIX systems. Because the behavior of the *signal* API in System V.2 and earlier versions is different than that in BSD and POSIX.1 systems, it is not recommended to be used by portable applications.The BSD UNIX and the POSIX.1 define a new set of APIs for signal manipulation. The API's behavior is consistent in all UNIX and POSIX.1 systems that support them and they are described in the next two sections.

Note that UNIX System V.3 and V.4 support the *sigset* API, which has the same prototype and similar use as *signal*:

#include <signal.h>

void (*sigset (**int** signal_num, **void** (*handler)(**int**))) (**int**);

The *sigset* arguments and return value are the same as that of *signal*. Both functions set signal handling methods for any named signal. However, whereas the *signal* API is unreliable (as explained in Section 9.1), the *sigset* API is reliable. This means that when a signal is set to be caught by a signal handler via *sigset*, when multiple instances of the signal arrive one of them is handled while the other instances are blocked. Furthermore, the signal handler is not reset to SIG_DFT when the it is invoked.

9.3   Signal Mask

Each process in a UNIX (BSD 4.2 and later, and System V.4) or POSIX.1 system has a signal mask that defines which signals are blocked when generated to a process. A blocked signal depends on the recipient process to unblock it and handle it accordingly. If a signal is specified to be ignored and blocked, it is implementation-dependent on whether such a signal will be discarded or left pending when it is sent to the process.

A process initially inherits the parent's signal mask when it is created, but any pending signals for the parent process are not passed on. A process may query or set its signal mask via the *sigprocmask* API:

#include <signal.h>

int *sigprocmask* (**int** cmd, **const sigset_t** *new_mask, **sigset_t*** old_mask);

The *new_mask* argument defines a set of signals to be set or reset in a calling process signal mask, and the *cmd* argument specifies how the *new_mask* value is to be used by the API. The possible values of *cmd* and the corresponding use of the *new_mask* value are:

cmd value	Meaning
SIG_SETMASK	Overrides the calling process signal mask with the value specified in the *new_mask* argument
SIG_BLOCK	Adds the signals specified in the *new_mask* argument to the calling process signal mask
SIG_UNBLOCK	Removes the signals specified in the *new_mask* argument from the calling process signal mask

If the actual argument to *new_mask* argument is a NULL pointer, the *cmd* argument will be ignored, and the current process signal mask will not be altered.

The *old_mask* argument is the address of a *sigset_t* variable that will be assigned the calling process's original signal mask prior to a *sigprocmask* call. If the actual argument to *old_mask* is a NULL pointer, no previous signal mask will be returned.

The return value of a *sigprocmask* call is zero if it succeeds or -1 if it fails. Possible failure may occur because the *new_mask* and/or the *old_mask* actual arguments are invalid addresses.

The *sigset_t* is a data type defined in the <signal.h> header. It contains a collect of bit-flags, with each bit-flag representing one signal defined in a given system.

The BSD UNIX and POSIX.1 define a set of API known as *sigsetops* functions, which set, reset, and query the presence of signals in a *sigset_t*-typed variable:

```
#include <signal.h>

int sigemptyset ( sigset_t* sigmask );

int sigaddset ( sigset_t* sigmask, const int signal_num );

int sigdelset ( sigset_t* sigmask, const int signal_num);

int sigfillset ( sigset_t* sigmask );

int sigismember ( const sigset_t* sigmask, const int signal_num);
```

The *sigemptyset* API clears all signal flags in the *sigmask* argument.

The *sigaddset* API sets the flag corresponding to the *signal_num* signal in the *sigmask* argument.

The *sigdelset* API clears the flag corresponding to the *signal_num* signal in the *sigmask* argument.

The *sigfillset* API sets all the signal flags in the *sigmask* argument.

The return value of the *sigemptyset, sigaddset, sigdelset*, and *sigfillset* calls is zero if the calls succeed or -1 if they fail. Possible causes of failure may be that the *sigmask* and/or the *signal_num* arguments are invalid.

The *sigismember* API returns 1 if the flag corresponding to the *signal_num* signal in the *sigmask* argument is set, zero if it is not set, and -1 if the call fails.

The following example checks whether the SIGINT signal is present in a process signal mask and adds it to the mask if it is not there. Then it clears the SIGSEGV signal from the process signal mask:

```
#include <stdio.h>
#include <signal.h>
int main  ()
{
      sigset_t           sigmask;
      sigemptyset(&sigmask);                            /* initialize set */

      if (sigprocmask(0, 0, &sigmask)==-1) {   /* get current signal mask */
            perror("sigprocmask");
            exit(1);
      }
      else  sigaddset(&sigmask, SIGINT);        /* set SIGINT flag */

      sigdelset(&sigmask,SIGSEGV);                  /* clear SIGSEGV flag */
      if (sigprocmask(SIG_SETMASK,&sigmask,0)==-1)
            perror("sigprocmask");                     /* set a new signal mask */
}
```

When one or more signals are pending for a process and are unblocked via the *sigproc-mask* API, the signal handler methods for those signals that are in effect at the time of the *sig-procmask* call will be applied before the API is returned to the caller. If there are multiple instances of the same signal pending for the process, it is implementation-dependent whether one or all of those instances will be delivered to the process.

A process can query which signals are pending for it via the *sigpending* API:

```
#include <signal.h>
int sigpending ( sigset_t* sigmask );
```

The *sigmask* argument to the *sigpending* API is the address of a *sigset_t*-typed variable and is assigned the set of signals pending for the calling process by the API. The API returns a zero if it succeeds and a -1 value if it fails.

The *sigpending* API can be useful to find out whether one or more signals are pending for a process and to set up special signal handling methods for these signals before the process calls the *sigprocmask* API to unblock them.

The following example reports to the console whether the SIGTERM signal is pending for the process:

```
#include <iostream.h>
#include <stdio.h>
#include <signal.h>

int main()
{
        sigset_t          sigmask;
        sigemptyset(&sigmask);
        if (sigpending(&sigmask)==-1)
            perror( "sigpending");
        else cout << "SIGTERM signal is: "
            << (sigismember(&sigmask,SIGTERM) ? "Set" : "No Set" )
            << endl;
}
```

Note that, in addition to the above APIs, UNIX System V.3 and V.4 also support the following APIs as simplified means for signal mask manipulation:

```
#include <signal.h>

int sighold ( nt signal_num );
int sigrelse ( int signal_num );
int sigignore ( int signal_num);
int sigpause ( int signal_num );
```

The *sighold* API adds the named signal *signal_num* to the calling process signal mask. It is the same as using the *sigset* API with the SIG_HOLD action:

```
sigset ( <signal_num>, SIG_HOLD );
```

The *sigrelse* API removes the named signal *signal_num* for the calling process signal mask.

The *sigignore* API sets the signal handling method for the named signal *signal_num* to SIG_DFT.

Finally, the *sigpause* API removes the named *signal* signal_num from the calling process signal mask and suspends the process until it is interrupted by a signal.

9.4   sigaction

The *sigaction* API is a replacement for the signal API in the latest UNIX and POSIX. systems. Like the *signal* API, the *sigaction* API is called by a process to setup a signal handling method for each signal it wants to deal with. Both APIs pass back the previous signal handling method for a given signal. Furthermore, the *sigaction* API blocks the signal it is catching allowing a process to specify additional signals to be blocked when the API is handling a signal.

The *sigaction* API prototype is:

```
#include <signal.h>
int sigaction ( int signal_num, struct sigaction* action,
                           struct sigaction* old_action);
```

The *struct sigaction* data type is defined in the <signal.h> header as:

```
struct sigaction
{
        void            (*sa_handler) (int);
        sigset_t        sa_mask;
        int             sa_flag;
};
```

The *sa_handler* field corresponds to the second argument of the *signal* API. It can be set to SIG_IGN, SIG_DFL, or a user-defined signal handler function. The *sa_mask* field specifies additional signals that a process wishes to block (besides those signals currently specified in the process's signal mask and the *signal_num* signal) when it is handling the *signal_num* signal.

Putting all these together, the *signal_num* argument designates which signal handling action is defined in the *action* argument. The previous signal handling method for *signal_num* will be returned via the *old_action* argument if it is not a NULL pointer. If the *action* argument is a NULL pointer, the calling process's existing signal handling method for *signal_num* will be unchanged.

The following *sigaction.C* program illustrates uses of *sigaction*:

```
#include <iostream.h>
#include <stdio.h>
#include <unistd.h>
#include <signal.h>

void callme( int sig_num )
{
        cout << "catch signal: " << sig_num << endl;
}

int main( int argc, char* argv[] )
{
        sigset_t    sigmask;
        struct sigaction     action, old_action;

        sigemptyset(&sigmask);

        if (sigaddset( &sigmask, SIGTERM)==-1 ||
                sigprocmask(SIG_SETMASK, &sigmask,0)==-1)
            perror("set signal mask");

        sigemptyset(&action.sa_mask);
        sigaddset(&action.sa_mask,SIGSEGV);
```

```
            action.sa_handler = callme;
            action.sa_flags = 0;
            if (sigaction(SIGINT,&action,&old_action)==-1)

                perror( "sigaction");

            pause();                                    /* wait for signal interruption */

            cout << argv[0] << " exists\n";
            return 0;
    }
```

In the above example, the process signal mask is set with the SIGTERM signal. The process then defines a signal handler for the SIGINT signal and also specifies that the SIG-SEGV signal is to be blocked when the process is handling the SIGINT signal. The process then suspends its execution via the *pause* API.

The sample output of the program is:

```
%   CC sigaction.C -o sigaction
%   sigaction &
[1] 495
%   kill -INT 495
catch signal: 2
sigaction exits
[1]   Done              sigaction
```

If the SIGINT signal is generated to the process, the kernel first sets the process signal mask to block the SIGTERM, SIGINT, and SIGSEGV signals. It then arranges the process to execute the *callme* signal handler function. When the *callme* function returns, the process signal mask is restored to contain only the SIGTERM signal, and the process will continue to catch the SIGILL signal.

The *sa_flag* field of the *struct sigaction* is used to specify special handling for certain signals. POSIX.1 defines only two values for the *sa_flag*: zero or SA_NOCLDSTOP. The SA_NOCLDSTOP flag is an integer literal defined in the <signal.h> header and can be used when the *signal_num* is SIGCHLD. The effect of the SA_NOCLDSTOP flag is that the kernel will generate the SIGCHLD signal to a process when its child process has terminated, but not when the child process has been stopped. On the other hand, if the *sa_flag* value is zero in a *sigaction* call for SIGCHLD, the kernel will send the SIGCHLD signal to the calling process whenever its child process is either terminated or stopped.

UNIX System V.4 defines additional flags for the *sa_flag* field of *struct sigaction*. These flags can be used to specify the UNIX System V.3 style of signal handling method:

sa_flag value	**Effects on handling of *signal_num***
SA_RESETHAND	If *signal_num* is caught, the *sa_handler* is set to SIG_DFL before the signal handler function is called, and *signal_num* will not be added to the process signal mask when the signal handler function is executed
SA_RESTART	If a signal is caught while a process is executing a system call, the kernel will restart the system call after the signal handler returns. If this flag is not set in the *sa_flag,* after the signal handler returns, the system call will be aborted with a return value of -1 and will set *errno* to EINTR

9.5   The SIGCHLD Signal and the waitpid API

When a child process terminates or stops, the kernel will generate a SIGCHLD signal to its parent process. Depending on how the parent sets up the handling of the SIGCHLD signal, different events may occur:

1.   Parent accepts the default action of the SIGCHLD signal: Unlike most signals, the SIGCHLD signal does not terminate the parent process. It affects only the parent process if it arrives at the same time the parent process is suspended by the *waitpid* system call. If that is the case, the parent process will be awakened, the API will return the child's exist status and process ID to the parent, and the kernel will clear up the Process Table slot allocated for the child process. Thus, with this setup, a parent process can call the *waitpid* API repeatedly to wait for each child it created.

2.   Parent ignores the SIGCHLD signal: The SIGCHLD signal will be discarded, and the parent will not be disturbed, even if it is executing the *waitpid* system call. The effect of this setup is that if the parent calls the *waitpid* API, the API will suspend the parent until all its child processes have terminated. Furthermore, the child process table slots will be cleared up by the kernel, and the API will return a -1 value to the parent process.

3.   Process catches the SIGCHLD signal: The signal handler function will be called in the parent process whenever a child process terminates. Furthermore, if the SIGCHLD signal arrives while the parent process is executing the *waitpid* system call, after the signal handler function returns, the *waitpid* API may be restarted to

collect the child exit status and clear its Process Table slot. On the other hand, the API may be aborted and the child Process Table slot not freed, depending on the parent setup of the signal action for the SIGCHLD signal.

The interaction between SIGCHLD and the *wait* API is the same as that between SIGCHLD and the *waitpid* API. Furthermore, earlier versions of UNIX use the SIGCLD signal instead of SIGCHLD. The SIGCLD signal is now obsolete, but most of the latest UNIX systems have defined SIGCLD to be the same as SIGCHLD for backward compatibility.

9.6   The sigsetjmp and siglongjmp APIs

The *sigsetjmp* and *siglongjmp* APIs have similar functions as their corresponding *setjmp* and *longjmp* APIs. Specifically, both *setjmp* and *sigsetjmp* mark one or more locations in a user program. Later on, the program may call the *longjmp* or *siglongjmp* API to return to any of those marked location. Thus, these APIs provide interfunction *goto* capability.

The *sigsetjmp* and *siglongjmp* APIs are defined in POSIX.1 and on most UNIX systems that support signal masks. The function prototypes of the APIs are:

```
#include <setjmp.h>

int sigsetjmp ( sigjmpbuf env, int save_sigmask );
int siglongjmp ( sigjmpbuf env, int ret_val );
```

The *sigsetjmp* and *siglongjmp* are created to support signal mask processing. Specifically, it is implementation-dependent on whether a process signal mask is saved and restored when it invokes the *setjmp* and *longjmp* APIs, respectively.

The *sigsetjmp* API behaves similarly to the *setjmp* API, except that it has a second argument, *save_sigmask,* which allows a user to specify whether a calling process signal mask should be saved to the provided *env* argument. Specifically, if the *save_sigmask* argument is nonzero, the caller's signal mask is saved. Otherwise, the signal mask is not saved.

The *siglongjmp* API does all the operations as the *longjmp* API, but it also restores a calling process signal mask if the mask was saved in its *env* argument. The *ret_val* argument specifies the return value of the corresponding *sigsetjmp* API when it is called by *siglongjmp*. Its value should be a nonzero number, and if it is zero the *siglongjmp* API will reset it to 1.

The *siglongjmp* API is usually called from user-defined signal handling functions. This is because a process signal mask is modified when a signal handler is called, and *siglongjmp* should be called (if a user does not want to resume execution at the code where the signal interruption occurred) to ensure the process signal mask is restored properly when "jumping out" from a signal handling function.

The following *sigsetjmp.C* program illustrates the uses of *sigsetjmp* and *siglongjmp* APIs. The program is modified from the *sigaction.C* program, as depicted in Section 9.4. Specifically, the program sets its signal mask to contain SIGTERM, then sets up a signal trap for the SIGINT signal. The program then calls *sigsetjmp* to store its code location in the *env* global variable. Note that the *sigsetjmp* call returns a zero value when it is called directly in user program and not via *siglongjmp*. The program suspends its execution via the *pause* API. When a user interrupts the process from the keyboard, the *callme* function is called. The *callme* function calls the *siglongjmp* API to transfer program flow back to the *sigsetjmp* function (in the *main* function), which now returns a 2 value.

```
#include <iostream.h>
#include <stdio.h>
#include <unistd.h>
#include <signal.h>
#include <setjmp.h>

sigjmp_buf      env;

void callme( int sig_num )
{
      cout << "catch signal: " << sig_num << endl;
      siglongjmp( env, 2 );
}

int main()
{
      sigset_t    sigmask;
      struct sigaction    action, old_action;

      sigemptyset(&sigmask);

      if (sigaddset( &sigmask, SIGTERM)==-1 ||
            sigprocmask(SIG_SETMASK, &sigmask,0)==-1)
         perror("set signal mask");
      sigemptyset(&action.sa_mask);
      sigaddset(&action.sa_mask,SIGSEGV);
      action.sa_handler = (void (*)())callme;
      action.sa_flags = 0;

      if (sigaction(SIGINT,&action,&old_action)==-1)
         perror( "sigaction");
```

```
if (sigsetjmp( env, 1 ) != 0 )        {
                cerr << "Return from signal interruption\n";
                return 0;
}
else        cerr << "Return from first time sigsetjmp is called\n";

pause();                // wait for signal interruption (e.g., from keyboard)
}
```

The sample output of the above program is:

```
%   CC sigsetjmp.C
%   a.out &
[1] 377
Return from first time sigsetjmp is called
%   kill -INT 377
catch signal: 2
Return from signal interruption
[1]   Done              a.out
%
```

9.7   kill

A process can send a signal to a related process via the *kill* API. This is a simple means of interprocess communication or control. The sender and recipient processes must be related such that either the sender process real or effective user ID matches that of the recipient process, or the sender process has superuser privileges. For example, a parent and a child process can send signals to each other via the *kill* API.

The *kill* API is defined in most UNIX systems and is a POSIX.1 standard. The function prototype of the API is:

```
#include <signal.h>

int kill ( pid_t pid, int signal_num );
```

The *signal_num* argument is the integer value of a signal to be sent to one or more processes designated by *pid*. The possible values of *pid* and its use by the *kill* API are:

pid value	Effects on the *kill* API
a positive value	*pid* is a process ID. Sends *signal_num* to that process
0	Sends *signal_num* to all processes whose process group ID is the same as the calling process
-1	Sends *signal_num* to all processes whose real user ID is the same as the effective user ID of the calling process. If the calling process effective user ID is the superuser user ID, *signal_num* will be sent to all processes in the system (except processes-0 and 1). The latter case is used when the system is shutting down -- the kernel calls the *kill* API to terminate all processes except 0 and 1. Note that POSIX.1 does not specify the behavior of the *kill* API when the *pid* value is -1. The above effects are for UNIX systems only
a negative value	Sends *signal_num* to all processes whose process group ID matches the absolute value of *pid*

The return value of *kill* is zero if it succeeds or -1 if it fails.

The following *kill.C* program illustrates the implementation of the UNIX *kill* command using the *kill* API:

```
#include <iostream.h>
#include <stdio.h>
#include <unistd.h>
#include <string.h>
#include <signal.h>

int main( int argc, char** argv)
{
     int pid, sig = SIGTERM;
     if (argc==3)   {
       if (sscanf(argv[1],"%d",&sig)!=1)  {            /* get signal number */
          cerr << "Invalid number: " << argv[1] << endl;
          return -1;
       }
       argv++, argc--;
     }
     while (--argc > 0)
```

```
            if (sscanf(*++argv,"%d",&pid)==1)  {          /* get process ID */
                if (kill (pid, sig)==-1)
                        perror("kill");
            }
            else cerr << "Invalid pid: " << argv[0] << endl;
        return 0;
    }
```

The UNIX *kill* command invocation syntax is:

> *kill* [-<signal_num>] <Pid> ...

where *<signal_num>* can be an integer number or the symbolic name of a signal, as defined in the <signal.h> header. The *<Pid>* is the integer number of a process ID. There can be one or more *<Pid>* specified, and the *kill* command will send the signal *<signal_num>* to each process that corresponds to a *<Pid>*.

To simplify the above program, any signal specification at the command line must be a signal's integer value. It does not support signal symbolic names. If no signal number is specified, the program will use the default signal SIGTERM, which is the same for the UNIX *kill* command. The program calls the *kill* API to send a signal to each process whose process ID is specified at the command line. If a process ID is invalid or if the *kill* API fails, the program will flag an error message.

9.8   alarm

The *alarm* API can be called by a process to request the kernel to send the SIGALRM signal after a certain number of real clock seconds. This is like setting an alarm clock to remind someone to do something after a specified period of time.

The *alarm* API is defined in most UNIX systems and is a POSIX.1 standard. The function prototype of the API is:

#include <signal.h>

unsigned int *alarm* (**unsigned int** time_interval);

The *time_interval* argument is the number of CPU seconds elapse time, after which the kernel will send the SIGALRM signal to the calling process. If a *time_interval* value is zero, it turns off the alarm clock.

The return value of the *alarm* API is the number of CPU seconds left in the process timer, as set by a previous *alarm* system call. The effect of the previous *alarm* API call is canceled, and the process timer is reset with the new *alarm* call. A process alarm clock is not passed on to its forked child process, but an *exec*'ed process retains the same alarm clock value as was prior to the *exec* API call.

The *alarm* API can be used to implement the *sleep* API:

```
/* sleep.C */
#include <signal.h>
#include <stdio.h>
#include <unistd.h>
void wakeup()            {};

unsigned int sleep ( unsigned int timer )
{
        struct sigaction action;
        action.sa_handler = wakeup;
        action.sa_flags = 0;
        sigemptyset(&action.sa_mask);

        if (sigaction(SIGALRM, &action,0)==-1)  {
                perror("sigaction");
                return -1;
        }
        (void)alarm( timer );
        (void)pause();
        return 0;
}
```

The *sleep* API suspends a calling process for the specified number of CPU seconds. The process will be awakened by either the elapse time exceeding the *timer* value or when the process is interrupted by a signal.

In the above example, the *sleep* function sets up a signal handler for the SIGALRM, calls the *alarm* API to request the kernel to send the SIGALRM signal (after the *timer* interval), and finally, suspends its execution via the *pause* system call. The *wakeup* signal handler function is called when the SIGALRM signal is sent to the process. When it returns, the *pause* system call will be aborted, and the calling process will return from the *sleep* function.

BSD UNIX defines the *ualarm* function, which is the same function as the *alarm* API, except that the argument and return value of the *ualarm* function are in microsecond units. This is useful for some time-critical applications where the resolution of time must be in microsecond levels.

The *ualarm* function can be used to implement the BSD-specific *usleep* function, which is like the *sleep* function, except its argument is in microsecond units.

9.9   Interval Timers

The *sleep* function that suspends a process for a fixed amount of time is only one use of the *alarm* API. The more general use of the *alarm* API is to set up an interval timer in a process. The interval timer can be used to schedule a process to do some tasks at a fixed time interval, to time the execution of some operations, or to limit the time allowed for the execution of some tasks.

The following program, *timer.C*, illustrates how to set up a real-time clock interval timer using the *alarm* API.

```
#include <stdio.h>
#include <unistd.h>
#include <signal.h>
#define   INTERVAL   5

void callme( int sig_no )
{
        alarm( INTERVAL );
        /* do scheduled tasks */
}

int main()
{
    struct sigaction  action;
    sigemptyset(&action.sa_mask);
    action.sa_handler = (void (*)())callme;
    action.sa_flags = SA_RESTART;
    if ( sigaction( SIGALRM,&action,0 )==-1 )   {
       perror( "sigaction");
       return 1;
    }
    if (alarm( INTERVAL ) == -1)
       perror("alarm" );
    else while( 1 )   {
       /* do normal operation */
    }
    return 0;
}
```

In the above program, the *sigaction* API is called to set up *callme* as the signal handling function for the SIGALRM signal. The program then invokes the *alarm* API to send itself the

SIGALRM after 5 real clock seconds. The program then goes off to perform its normal operation in an infinite loop. When the timer expires, the *callme* function is invoked, which
restarts the alarm clock for another 5 seconds and then does the scheduled tasks. When the
callme function returns, the program continues its "normal" operation until another timer
expiration.

The above sample program may be useful in creating a clock synchronization program:
Every time the *callme* function is invoked, it polls a remote host for current time, then calls
the *stime* API to set the local system clock to be the same as the reference host.

In addition to using the *alarm* API to set up an interval timer in a process, BSD UNIX
invented the *setitimer* API, which provides capabilities additional to those of the *alarm* API:

* The *setitimer* resolution time is in microseconds, whereas the resolution time for
  alarm is in seconds

* The *alarm* API can be used to set up one real-time clock timer per process. The
  setitimer API can be used to define up to three different types of timers in a process:

  a.   Real time clock timer
  b.   Timer based on the user time spent by a process
  c.   Timer based on the total user and system times spent by a process

The *setitimer* API is also available in UNIX System V.3 and V.4. However, it is not
specified by POSIX. POSIX.1b defines a new set of APIs for interval timer manipulation.
These APIs are described in the next section.

The *getitimer* API is also defined in BSD and System V UNIX for users to query the
timer values that are set by the *setitimer* API.

The *setitimer* and *getitimer* function prototypes are:

```
#include <sys/time.h>

int setitimer ( int which, const struct itimerval *val, struct itimerval *old );
int getitimer ( int which, struct itimerval *old );
```

The *which* arguments to the above APIs specify which timer to process. Its possible
values and the corresponding timer types are:

which argument value	Timer type
ITIMER_REAL	Timer based on real-time clock. Generates a SIGALRM signal when it expires
ITIMER_VIRTUAL	Timer based on user-time spent by a process. Generates a SIGVTALRM signal when it expires
ITIMER_PROF	Timer based on total user and system times spent by a process. Generates a SIGPROF signal when it expires

The *struct itimerval* data type is defined in the <sys/time.h> header as:

```
struct itimeval
{
        struct timeval     it_interval;          // timer interval
        struct timeval     it_value;             // current value
};
```

For the *setitimer* API, the *val.it_value* is the time to set the named timer, and the *val.it_interval* is the time to reload the timer when it expires. The *val.it_interval* may be set to zero if the timer is to run once only. Furthermore, if the *val.it_value* value is set to zero, it stops the named timer if it is running.

For the *getitimer* API, the *old.it_value* and the *old.t_interval* return the named timer's remaining time (to expiration) and the reload time, respectively.

The *old* argument of the *setitimer* API is like the *old* argument of the *getitimer* API. If this is an address of a *struct itimeval*-typed variable, it returns the previous timer value. If the *old* argument is set to NULL, the old timer value will not be returned.

The ITIMER_VIRTUAL and ITIMER_PROF timers are primary useful in timing the total execution time of selected user functions, as the timer runs only while the user process is running (or the kernel is executing system functions on behalf of the user process for the ITIMER_PROF timer).

The *setitimer* and *getitimer* APIs return a zero value if they succeed or a -1 value if they fail. Moreover, timers set by the *setitimer* API in a parent process are not inherited by its child processes, but these timers are retained when a process *exec*'s a new program.

The following example program, *timer2.C*, is the same as the *timer.C* program, except that it uses the *setitimer* API instead of the *alarm* API. Also, there is no need to call the *setitimer* API inside the signal handling function, as the timer is specified to be reloaded automatically:

```
#include <stdio.h>
#include <unistd.h>
#include <sys/time.h>
#include <signal.h>
#define   INTERVAL   2

void callme( int sig_no )
{
      /* do some schedule tasks */
}

int main()
{
      struct itimerval val;
      struct sigaction  action;

      sigemptyset(&action.sa_mask);
      action.sa_handler = (void (*)())callme;
      action.sa_flags = SA_RESTART;
      if (sigactionSIGALRM,&action,0)==-1) {
         perror( "sigaction");
         return 1;
      }

      val.it_interval.tv_sec       = INTERVAL;
      val.it_interval.tv_usec      = 0;
      val.it_value.tv_sec          = INTERVAL;
      val.it_value.tv_usec         = 0;

      if (setitimer( ITIMER_REAL, &val, 0 ) == -1)
         perror("alarm" );
      else while( 1 )   {
         /* do normal operation */
      }
      return 0;
}
```

Note that the real time clock timer set by the *setitimer* API is different from that set by the *alarm* API. Thus, a process may set up two real-time clock timers using the two APIs. Furthermore, since the *alarm* and *setitimer* APIs require that users set up signal handling to catch timer expiration, they (when used to set up real-time clock timer) should not be used in conjunction with the *sleep* API. This is because the *sleep* API may modify the signal handling function for the SIGALRM signal.

9.10   POSIX.1b Timers

POSIX.1b defines a set of APIs for interval timer manipulation. The POSIX.1b timers are more flexible and powerful than are the UNIX timers in the following ways:

- Users may define multiple independent timers per system clock.
- The timer resolution is in nanoseconds.
- Users may specify, on a per-timer basis, the signal to be raised when a timer expires.
- The timer interval may be specified as either an absolute or a relative time.

There is a limit on how many POSIX timers can be created per process. This maximum limit is the TIMER_MAX constant, as defined in the <limits.h> header. Moreover, POSIX timers created by a process are not inherited by its child processes, but are retained across the *exec* system call. However, unlike the UNIX timers, if a POSIX.1 timer does not use the SIGALRM signal when it expires, it can be used safely with the *sleep* API in the same program.

The POSIX.1b APIs for timer manipulation are:

```
#include <signal.h>
#include <time.h>

int timer_create ( clockid_t clock, struct sigevent* spec, timer_t* timer_hdrp);
int timer_settime ( timer_t timer_hdr, int flag, struct itimrspec*val,
                                            struct itimerspec* old );
int timer_gettime ( timer_t timer_hdr, struct itimerspec*old );

int timer_getoverrun ( timer_t timer_hdr );

int timer_delete ( timer_t timer_hdr );
```

The *timer_create* API is used to dynamically create a timer and returns its handler. The *clock* argument specifies which system clock the new timer should be based on. The *clock* argument value may be CLOCK_REALTIME for creating a real time clock timer. This value is defined by POSIX.1b. Other values for the *clock* argument are system-dependent.

The *spec* argument defines what action to take when the timer expires. The *struct sigevent* data type is defined as:

```
struct sigevent
{
```

```
            int             sigev_notify;
            int             sigev_signo;
            union sigval    sigev_value;
    };
```

The *sigev_signo* field specifies a signal number to be raised at the timer expiration. It is valid only when the *sigev_notify* field is set to SIGEV_SIGNAL. If the *sigev_notify* field is set to SIGEV_NONE, no signal is raised by the timer when it expires. Because multiple timers may generate the same signal, the *sigev_value* field is used to contain any user-defined data to identify that a signal is raised by a specific timer. The data structure of the *sigev_value* field is:

```
    union sigval {
            int             sival_int;
            void            *sival_ptr;
    };
```

For example, a process may assign each timer an unique integer ID number. This number may then be assigned to the *spec->sigev_value.sival_int* field. Furthermore, to pass this data along with the signal (*spec->sigev_signo*) when it is raised, the SA_SIGINFO flag should be set in an *sigaction* call, which sets up the handling for the signal, and the signal handling function prototype should be:

void *<signal_handler>* (**int** signo, **siginfo_t*** evp, **void*** ucontext);

The data structure of the *siginfo_t* is defined in the <siginfo.h> header. When the signal handler is called, the *evp->si_value* contains the data of the *spec->sigev_value*.

If the *spec* argument is set to NULL and the timer is based on CLOCK_REALTIME, the SIGALRM signal is raised when the timer expires.

Finally, the *timer_hdrp* argument of the *timer_create* API is an address of a *timer_t*-typed variable to hold the handler of the newly generated timer. This argument should not be set to NULL, as the handler is used to call other POSIX.1b timer APIs.

The *timer_create* API, as well as all the following POSIX1.b timer APIs, return zero if they succeed and -1 if they fail.

The *timer_settime* starts or stops a timer running. The *timer_gettime* API is used to query the current values of a timer. Specifically, the *struct itimerpsec* data type is defined as:

```
    struct itimerspec {
            struct timespec     it_interval;
```

```
                    struct timespec          it_value;
        };
```
and the *struct timespec* data structure is defined as:

```
        struct timespec {
                time_t                  tv_sec;
                long                    tv_nsec;
        };
```

The *itimerspec::it_value* specifies the time remaining in the timer, and the *itimerspec::it_interval* specifies the new time to reload the timer after it expires. All times are specified in seconds (via the *timespec::tv_sec* field) and in nanoseconds (via the *timespec::tv_nsec* field).

In the *timer_settime* API, the *flag* argument value may be 0 or TIMER_RELTIME if the timer start time (as contained in the *val* argument) is relative to the current time. If the *flag* argument value is TIMER_ABSTIME, the timer start time is an absolute time. Note that the ANSI C *mktime* function may be used to generate the absolute time for setting a timer. Note that if the *val.it_value* is zero, it stops the timer from running. Furthermore, if the *val.it_interval* is zero, the timer will not restart after it expires. Finally, the *old* argument of the *timer_settime* API is used to obtain the previous timer values. The *old* argument value may be set to NULL, and no timer values are returned.

The *old* argument of the *timer_gettime* API returns the current values of the named timer.

The *timer_getoverrun* API returns the number of signals generated by a timer but was lost (overrun). Specifically, timer signals are not queued by the kernel if they are raised but are not being handled by their target processes (maybe they were busy handling other signals). Instead, the kernel records the number of these overrun signals per timer. The *timer_getoverrun* API can be used to determine the amount of time elapsed (between the timer started or handled to the present time), based on the overrun count of a named timer. Note that the overrun count in a timer is reset whenever a process handles the timer signal.

The *timer_destroy* API is used to destroy a timer created by the *timer_create* API.

The following program., *posix_timer_abs.C*, illustrates how to set up an absolute-time timer that will go off at 10:27 AM, April 20, 1996:

```
        #include <iostream.h>
        #include <stdio.h>
        #include <unistd.h>
        #include <signal.h>
```

```
#include <time.h>
#define    TIMER_TAG        12

void callme( int signo, siginfo_t* evp, void* ucontext )
{
     time_t tim = time(0);
     cerr  << "callme: " << evp->si_value.sival_int
           << ", signo: " << signo << ", " << ctime(&tim);
}
int main()
{
     struct sigaction       sigv;
     struct sigevent        sigx;
     struct itimerspec      val;
     struct tm              do_time;
     timer_t                t_id;

     sigemptyset( &sigv.sa_mask );
     sigv.sa_flags = SA_SIGINFO;
     sigv.sa_sigaction = callme;

     if (sigaction( SIGUSR1, &sigv, 0) == -1) {
          perror("sigaction");
          return 1;
     }

     sigx.sigev_notify = SIGEV_SIGNAL;
     sigx.sigev_signo  = SIGUSR1;
     sigx.sigev_value.sival_int = TIMER_TAG;

     if ( timer_create( CLOCK_REALTIME, &sigx, &t_id ) == -1) {
       perror("timer_create");
       return 1;
     }

     /* Set timer to go off at April 20, 1996, 10:27am */
     do_time.tm_hour     = 10;
     do_time.tm_min      = 27;
     do_time.tm_sec      = 30;
     do_time.tm_mon      = 3;
     do_time.tm_year     = 96;
     do_time.tm_mday     = 20;

     val.it_value.tv_sec    = mktime( &do_time );
     val.it_value.tv_nsec   = 0;
     val.it_interval.tv_sec = 15;
```

```
        val.it_interval.tv_nsec = 0;

        cerr << "timer will go off at: " << ctime(&val.it_value.tv_sec);

    if (timer_settime( t_id, TIMER_ABSTIME, &val, 0 ) == -1 ) {
        perror("timer_settime");
        return 2;
    }

    /* do something then wait for the timer to expire twice*/
    for (int i=0; i < 2; i++ )
        pause();

    if (timer_delete( t_id ) ==-1) {
        perror( "timer_delete" );
        return 3;
    }

        return 0;
}
```

The above program first sets up the *callme* function as the signal handler for the SIGUSR1 signal. It then creates a timer based on the system real-time clock. The program specifies that the timer should raise the SIGUSR1 signal whenever it expires, and the timer-specific data that should be sent along with the signal is TIMER_TAG. The timer handler returned by the *timer_create* API is stored in the *t_id* variable.

The next step is to set the timer to go off on April 20, 1996, at 10:27 AM and 30 seconds, and the timer should rerun for every 30 seconds thereafter. The absolute expiration data/time is specified in the *do_time* variable (of type *struct tm*) and is being converted to a *time_t*-type value via the *mktime* function. After these are all done, the *timer_settime* function is called to start the timer running. The program then waits for the timer to expire at the said date/time and expires again 30 seconds later. Finally, before the program terminates, it calls the *timer_delete* to free all system resources allocated for the timer.

The example output of the program is:

```
%     CC posix_timer_sbs.C  -o posix_timer_abs
%     posix_timer_abs
timer will go off at: Sat Apr 20 10:27:30 1996
callme: 12, signo: 16, Sat Apr 20 10:27:30 1996
callme: 12, signo: 16, Sat Apr 20 10:27:45 1996
```

Note that the above program can be modified to use a relative-time timer instead. For

example, to set the timer to go off 60 minutes from now and repeat every 120 seconds thereafter, the *main* function will be modified as in the following:

```
int main()
{
        /* set up sigaction for SIGUSR1 */
        ...

        /* Create a timer using timer_create */
        ...

        struct itimerspec      val;

        val.it_value.tv_sec    = 60;              /* expire 60 sec. from now */
        val.it_value.tv_nsec   = 0;
        val.it_interval.tv_sec  = 120;            /* repeat every 120 sec */
        val.it_interval.tv_nsec = 0;

        if (timer_settime( t_id, 0, &val, 0 ) == -1 ) {
            perror("timer_settime");
            return 2;
        }

        /* wait for timer expires */
        ...
}
```

The only differences in the modified *main* function from that in the *posix_timer_abc.C*
are: (1) the *do_time* variable and the *mktime* API are not being used; (2) the *val.it_value* is set
directly with the relative time (from the present) when the timer will first expire; and (3) the
second argument to the *timer_settime* call is set to 0 instead of to TIMER_ABSTIME.

9.11   *timer* Class

Along with the improved flexibility and accuracy offered by the POSIX.1b timers,
there is also considerably more code needed to create, use, and deallocate these timers. However, the APIs map nicely to a C++ timer class, and this class offers the following advantages
to users:

- It provides a high-level interface for manipulation of timers. This reduces the time in
  learning how to use timer, and in the programming and debug effort
- It encapsulates the interface codes to the APIs. These codes are being reused when
  multiple timers are created
- The class member functions may be altered to use the *setitimer* API on systems that

are not POSIX.1b-compliant. This reduces the porting efforts of user applications
• The timer class can be incorporated into other user classes that require built-in timers for their operations. For example, a bank ATM software may cancel a transaction when no user inputs are detected for 5 minutes

The timer class functions map to the POSIX.1b timer APIs in the following manner:

Timer class function	**POSIX.1b API**
constructor	timer_create
destructor	timer_delete
start or stop timer	timer_settime
get overrun statistics	timer_getoverrun
query timer values	timer_gettime

In addition to the above, the timer class constructor also sets up signal handling for the timer (via the *sigaction* API). The timer class declaration is specified in the *timer.h* and depicted below:

```
#ifndef TIMER_H
#define TIMER_H

#include <signal.h>
#include <time.h>
#include <errno.h>
typedef void (*SIGFUNC)(int, siginfo*, void*);

class timer
{
        timer_t            timer_id;
        int                status;
        struct itimerspec  val;
    public:
        /* constructor: setup a timer */
        timer( int signo, SIGFUNC action, int timer_tag,
                        clock_t sys_clock = CLOCK_REALTIME)
        {
            status = 0;

            struct sigaction sigv;;
            sigemptyset( &sigv.sa_mask );
            sigv.sa_flags = SA_SIGINFO;
            sigv.sa_sigaction = action;
```

```
              if (sigaction( signo, &sigv, 0 ) == -1) {
                     perror("sigaction");
                     status = errno;
              }
           else  {
                  struct sigevent sigx;
                  sigx.sigev_notify   = SIGEV_SIGNAL;
                  sigx.sigev_signo    = signo;
                  sigx.sigev_value.sival_int = timer_tag;

                  if (timer_create( sys_clock, &sigx, &timer_id ) == -1) {
                           perror("timer_create");
                           status = errno;
                  }
           }
     };

     /* destructor: discard a timer */
     ~timer()
     {
        if (status == 0)   {
              stop();
              if (timer_delete( timer_id ) == -1)
                     perror( "timer_delete" );
        }
     };

     /* Check timer status */
     int operator!()
     {
        return status ? 1 : 0;
     };

     /* setup a relative time timer */
     int run( long start_sec, long start_nsec, long reload_sec, long
              reload_nsec )
     {
        if (status) return -1;
        val.it_value.tv_sec         = start_sec;
        val.it_value.tv_nsec        = start_nsec;
        val.it_interval.tv_sec      = reload_sec;
        val.it_interval.tv_nsec     = reload_nsec;
        if (timer_settime( timer_id, 0, &val, 0 ) == -1 ) {
              perror("timer_settime");
              status = errno;
              return -1;
```

```
        }
        eturn 0;
    };

    /* setup an absolute time timer */
    int run( time_t start_time, long reload_sec, long reload_nsec )
    {
        if (status) return -1;
        val.it_value.tv_sec           = start_time;
        val.it_value.tv_nsec          = 0;
        val.it_interval.tv_sec        = reload_sec;
        val.it_interval.tv_nsec       = reload_nsec;
        if (timer_settime( timer_id, TIMER_ABSTIME, &val, 0 ) == -1 ) {
                perror("timer_settime");
                status = errno;
                return -1;
        }
        return 0;
    };

    /* Stop a timer from running */
    int stop()
    {
        if (status) return -1;
        val.it_value.tv_sec       = 0;
        val.it_value.tv_nsec      = 0;
        val.it_interval.tv_sec    = 0;
        val.it_interval.tv_nsec   = 0;
        if (timer_settime( timer_id, 0, &val, 0 ) == -1 ) {
                perror("timer_settime");
                status = errno;
                return -1;
        }
        return 0;
    };

    /* Get timer overrun statistic */
    int  overrun()
    {
        if (status) return -1;
        return timer_getoverrun( timer_id );
    };

    /* Get timer remaining time to expiration */
    int values( long& sec, long& nsec )
    {
```

```
            if (status) return -1;
            if (timer_gettime( timer_id, &val ) == -1) {
                perror(" timer_gettime" );
                status = errno;
                return -1;
            }
            sec  = val.it_value.tv_sec;
            nsec = val.it_value.tv_nsec;
            return 0;
        };
        /* Overload << operator for timer objects */
        friend ostream& operator<<( ostream& os, timer& obj)
        {
            long sec, nsec;
            obj.values( sec, nsec );
            double tval = sec + ((double)nsec/1000000000.0);
            os << " time left: " << tval ;
            return os;
        };
    };
    #endif
```

In the above class, the *timer::timer* constructor takes as argument the signal number of a signal to be raised when the new timer expires, the signal handler for the timer, and a timer tag. The last argument, *sys_clock*, is optional. It specifies that the new timer be based on a certain system clock. The constructor internally sets up signal handling for the named signal and creates a new timer, based on the *sys_clock*, and uses the named signal and *timer_tag*.

The *timer::run* and *timer::stop* starts and stops a timer running, respectively. They internally set up the *struct itimerspec* data to call the *timer_settime* API. Specifically, the *timer::run* function is overloaded, so that users may specify relative or absolute time for the initial run of the timer. If an absolute time is specified, the *start_time* argument value may be obtained via the *mktime* function, as shown in the *posix_timer.C* program (see last section).

In addition to the above, the *timer::overrun* function returns the overrun statistic of a timer object, and the *timer::values* function returns the remaining time until the next expiration of the timer. Finally, the "<<" operator is overloaded to print the *timer::values* results of a timer object.

Overall, the *timer* class member functions provide an abstract view of a POSIX.1b timer. Their interfaces are all the basic data required to set up and manipulate a timer. All the low-level code that interfaces with the POSIX.1b APIs are encapsulated and readily reusable for multiple timer objects.

The following sample program, *posix_timer2.C*, illustrates the advantages and ease of use of the timer class:

```
#include <iostream.h>
#include <stdio.h>
#include <stdlib.h>
#include <unistd.h>
#include "timer.h"

void callme( int signo, siginfo_t* evp, void* ucontext )
{
        long   sec, nsec;
        time_t tim = time(0);
        cerr  << "timer Id: " << evp->si_value.sival_int
                << ", signo: " << signo << ", " << ctime(&tim);
}
int main()
{
        timer t1 ( SIGINT,  callme,  1 );
        timer t2 ( SIGUSR1, callme,  2 );
        timer t3 ( SIGUSR2, callme,  3 );

        if (!t1 || !t2 || !t3 ) return 1;

        t1.run( 2, 0,  2, 0 );
        t2.run( 3, 500000000,  3, 500000000 );
        t3.run( 5, 0,  5, 0 );

        /* wait for timers to expire 10 times */
        for ( int i =0 ; i < 10; i++) {
            /* do some work and before timers expire */
            pause();

            /* show timers remaining time to expiration */
            cerr << "  t1: " << t1 << endl;
            cerr << "  t2: " << t2 << endl;
            cerr << "  t3: " << t3 << endl;
        }

        /* show timers overrun statistics */
        cerr << "t1 overrun: " << t1.overrun() << endl;
        cerr << "t2 overrun: " << t2.overrun() << endl;
        cerr << "t3 overrun: " << t3.overrun() << endl;

        return 0;
}
```

In the program, three timers are set up, such that the first timer expires every 2 seconds and raises the SIGINT signal. The second timer expires every 3.5 seconds and raises the SIGUSR1 signal. The third timer expires every 5 seconds and raises the SIGUSR2 signal. The signal handler for all the three signals is *callme* (users may use a different signal handling function per signal if they wish).

After the timer objects are created, the program goes into a loop and waits for 10 interruptions by any timer. For each interruption, it prints out (in the *callme* function) the timer that expires and the current date and time. Furthermore, it prints out (in the *main* function) the time remaining for all timer objects. After the 10 timer interruptions, the program prints out the timer object overrun statistics and then quits. The timer objects are destroyed implicitly via the *timer::~timer* function when the program terminates.

The sample output of the program is:

```
%     CC timer.C
%     a.out
timer Id: 1, signo: 2, Sat Apr 20 13:00:29 1996
        t1:  time left: 1.99944
        t2:  time left: 1.49698
        t3:  time left: 2.99601
timer Id: 2, signo: 16, Sat Apr 20 13:00:31 1996
        t1:  time left: 0.504464
        t2:  time left: 3.50374
        t3:  time left: 1.50304
timer Id: 1, signo: 2, Sat Apr 20 13:00:31 1996
        t1:  time left: 2.0047
        t2:  time left: 3.00398
        t3:  time left: 1.00327
timer Id: 3, signo: 17, Sat Apr 20 13:00:32 1996
        t1:  time left: 1.00468
        t2:  time left: 2.00397
        t3:  time left: 5.00326
timer Id: 1, signo: 2, Sat Apr 20 13:00:33 1996
        t1:  time left: 2.0047
        t2:  time left: 1.00398
        t3:  time left: 4.00251
timer Id: 2, signo: 16, Sat Apr 20 13:00:34 1996
        t1:  time left: 1.00467
        t2:  time left: 3.50385
        t3:  time left: 3.00313
timer Id: 1, signo: 2, Sat Apr 20 13:00:35 1996
        t1:  time left: 2.0047
        t2:  time left: 2.50399
        t3:  time left: 2.00328
```

```
timer Id: 3, signo: 17, Sat Apr 20 13:00:37 1996
timer Id: 1, signo: 2, Sat Apr 20 13:00:37 1996
      t1:  time left: 2.00309
      t2:  time left: 0.502374
      t3:  time left: 5.00143
timer Id: 2, signo: 16, Sat Apr 20 13:00:38 1996
      t1:  time left: 1.50468
      t2:  time left: 3.50396
      t3:  time left: 4.50325
timer Id: 1, signo: 2, Sat Apr 20 13:00:39 1996
      t1:  time left: 2.00468
      t2:  time left: 2.00385
      t3:  time left: 3.00313
t1 overrun: 0
t2 overrun: 0
t3 overrun: 0
```

9.12 Summary

This chapter described the signal handling methods in UNIX and POSIX.1 systems and the various means where a process could generate signals to other processes or to itself. The primary use of signals is for process controls, such that users, kernel, or processes can interrupt runaway processes via signals.

Furthermore, signals may be used to implement some simple means of interprocess communication. For an example, two processes can install signal handlers for the SIGUSR1 signal and synchronize their execution by sending each other the SIGUSR1 signal. In the next chapter, more elaborate methods for interprocess communication in the UNIX and POSIX.1 systems will be depicted.

Finally, signals can also be used to support the implementation of interval timers. Interval timers are useful in setting up scheduled tasks to be performed by processes, when those processes require timing or limiting of execution times of certain operations by processes. This chapter described the UNIX and POSIX.1b methods for implementing interval timers. A timer class is depicted to facilitate the use of timers in user applications. The specific advantages of the timer class are that it provides a simplified interface to timer creation and manipulation, promotes code reuse, and reduces porting efforts. Moreover, the timer class can be incorporated easily into other user classes for adding functionality to those classes.

Interprocess Communication

I nterprocess communication (IPC) is a mechanism whereby two or more processes communicate with each other to perform tasks. These processes may interact in a client/server manner (that is, one or more "client" processes send data to a central server process and the server process responds to each client) or in a peer-to-peer fashion (that is, any process may exchange data with others). Examples of applications that use interprocess communication are database servers and their associated client programs (using the client/server model) and electronic mail systems (using the peer-to-peer model), where a mailer process communicates with other remote mailer processes to send and receive electronic mails over the Internet.

Interprocess communication is supported by all UNIX systems. However, different UNIX systems implement different methods for IPC. Specifically, BSD UNIX provides sockets for processes running on different machines to communicate. UNIX System V.3 and V.4 support messages, semaphores, and shared memory for processes running on the same machine to communicate, and they provide Transport Level Interface (TLI) for intermachine communication. Furthermore, UNIX System V.4 supports sockets to facilitate porting of socket-based applications on to their system. Finally, both BSD and UNIX System V support memory map as an intramachine communication method.

This chapter examines the message, shared memory, memory map, and semaphore IPC methods. The next chapter will describe the socket and Transport Level Interface IPC methods.

10.1   POSIX.1b IPC Methods

IPC methods are not defined in POSIX.1 but are defined in POSIX.1b (the standard for a portable real-time operating system). The IPC methods defined in POSIX.1b are messages, shared memory, and semaphores. Although these POSIX.1b IPC methods have the same names as those of UNIX System V, their syntax is totally different from that of System V. This is done intentionally, due to the following drawbacks of the System V methods:

- The System V messages, shared memory, and semaphores use integer keys as identifiers (names). This creates a different name space from that of files that an operating system needs to support
- The integer identifiers of messages, shared memory, and semaphores are not unique across machines. Thus, these IPC methods inherently cannot be used by network-based applications for intermachine communication
- The System V messages, shared memory, and semaphores are implemented in the kernel space. This means that every operation on these IPC objects requires a process to do context switches from user-mode to kernel-mode to be able to access data kept in these IPC objects. Process performance is taxed using these methods

To overcome the above drawbacks, the POSIX.1b messages, shared memory, and semaphores are implemented differently, as follows:

- The POSIX.1b messages, shared memory, and semaphores use file name-like identifiers (e.g., */psx4_message*), which means that IPC objects can be referenced like any file object and no separate name space requires support by a kernel
- By defining network-wide unique textual names, IPC objects may support intermachine communication. POSIX.1b does not specify the naming convention for such purposes
- POSIX.1b IPC methods do not mandate kernel-level supports; thus, vendors may implement these IPC methods using library functions. Furthermore, IPC objects are created and manipulated in the process address space. All these minimize kernel involvement and improve the efficiency of these methods

Note that not many commercial UNIX systems currently support these IPC methods yet, but they will in future operating system releases.

This chapter describes both the UNIX System V and POSIX.1b message, shared memory, and semaphore IPC methods.

10.2   The UNIX System V IPC Methods

The IPC methods supported by UNIX System V are:

- *Messages*: allow processes on the same machine to exchange formatted data
- *Semaphores*: provide a set of system-wide variables that can be modified and used by processes on the same machine to synchronize their execution. Semaphores are commonly used with a shared memory to control the access of data in each shared memory region
- *Shared memory*: allows multiple processes on the same machine to share a common region of virtual memory, such that data written to a shared memory can be directly read and modified by other processes
- *Transport Level Interface:* allows two processes on different machines to set up a direct, two-way communication channel. This method uses STREAMS as the underlying data transport interface

In addition to the above, System V.4 also supports BSD sockets. This is to facilitate socket-based applications ported to that system, with minimum modification.

10.3   UNIX System V Messages

Messages allow multiple processes on the same UNIX machine to communicate by sending and receiving messages among themselves. This is like setting up a central mail box in a building, allowing people to deposit and retrieve mail from the mail box. Furthermore, just as all mail has a recipient address, each message has an integer message type assigned to it by a sender process, so that a recipient process can selectively receive messages based on a message type.

Messages were invented to overcome some of the deficiencies of pipes (named and un-named). One problem with pipes is that multiple processes can attach to the read and write ends of a pipe, but there are no mechanisms provided to promote selective communication between a reader and a writer process. For example, suppose there are processes, *A* and *B*, attached to the write end of a pipe and processes *C* and *D* attached to the read end of a pipe. If both *A* and *B* write data to the pipe, such that *A*'s data is read by *C* and *B*'s data is read by *D*, there is no easy way for *C* and *D* to selectively read data that are destined for them only. Another problem arises if data stored in a pipe is destroyed when both ends of the pipe have no process attached. Thus, pipes and their stored data are transient objects. They cannot be used by processes to exchange data reliably if they are not running in the same period of time.

Messages also allow multiple processes to access a central message queue. However, every process that deposits a message in the queue needs to specify an integer message type for the message. Thus, a recipient process can retrieve that message by specifying that same message type. Furthermore, messages stored in a message queue are persistent, even when there is no process referencing the queue. Messages are removed from a queue only when processes explicitly retrieve them. Thus, messages are more flexible for multiprocesses communication.

When multiple message queues exist in a UNIX system, each can be used by a set of applications for interprocess communication.

10.3.1 UNIX Kernel Support for Messages

The implementation of message queues in UNIX System V.3 and V.4 is analogous to the implementation of UNIX files. Specifically, there is a message queue table in a kernel address space that keeps track of all message queues created in a system. Each entry of the message tables stores the following data for one message queue:

- A name, which is an integer ID key assigned by the process that created the queue. Other processes may specify this key to "open" the queue and gets a descriptor for future access of the queue
- The creator user ID and group ID. A process whose effective user ID matches a message queue creator user ID may delete the queue and also change the queue control data
- The assigned owner user ID and group ID. These are normally the same as those of the creator, but a creator can set these values to reassign the queue owner and group membership
- Read-write access permission of the queue for owner, group members, or others. A process that has read permission to the queue may retrieve messages from the queue and query the assigned user and group IDs of the queue. A process that has write permission to a queue may send messages to the queue
- The time and process ID of the last process that sent a message to the queue
- The time and process ID of the last process that read a message from the queue
- The pointer to a linked list of message records in the queue. Each message record stores one message of data and its assigned message type

Figure 10.1 depicts the kernel data structure for messages.

When a process sends a message to a queue, the kernel creates a new message record and puts it at the end of the message record linked list for the specified queue. The message record stores the message type, the number of bytes of the message data, and the pointer to another kernel data region, where the actual message data is stored. The kernel copies the message data from the sender process's virtual address into this kernel data region, so that the sender process is free to terminate, and the message can still be read by another process in the future.

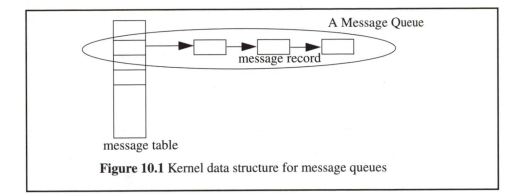

Figure 10.1 Kernel data structure for message queues

When a process retrieves a message from a queue, the kernel copies the message data from a message record to the process's virtual address and then discards the message record. The process can retrieve a message in a queue in the following manners:

- Retrieve the oldest message in the queue, regardless of its message type
- Retrieve a message whose message ID matches the one specified by the process. If there are multiple messages with the given message type existing in the queue, retrieve the oldest one among them
- Retrieve a message whose message type is the lowest among those that are less than or equal to the one specified by the process. If there are multiple messages that satisfy the same criteria, retrieve the oldest one among them

If a process attempts to read a message from a queue but no messages in the queue satisfy the retrieval criteria, then by default the process will be put to sleep by the kernel (until a message arrives in the queue that can be read by that process). However, the process can specify a nonblocking flag to the message receive system call that causes it to return a failure status instead of blocking the process.

Finally, there are several system-imposed limits on the manipulation of messages. These limits are defined in the <sys/msg.h> header:

System limit	Meaning
MSGMNI	The maximum number of message queues that may exist at any given time in a system
MSGMAX	The maximum number of bytes of data allowed for a message
MSGMNB	The maximum number of bytes of all messages allowed in a queue
MSGTQL	The maximum number of messages in all queues allowed in a system

The effects of these system-imposed limits on processes are:

- If the current number of message queues exist in the system is MSGMNI, any attempt to create a new message queue by a process will fail, until an existing queue is deleted by a process
- If a process attempts to send a message whose size is larger than MSGMAX, the system call will fail
- If a process attempts to send a message to a queue that will cause either the MSG-MNB or MSGTQL limit to be exceeded, then the process will be blocked until one or more messages are retrieved from the queue and the message can be inserted into the queue without violating both the MSGMNB and MSGTQL limits

10.3.2   The UNIX APIs for Messages

The <sys/ipc.h> header defines a *struct ipc_perm* data type that stores the owner and creator user and group IDs, the assigned name key, and the read-write permission of a message queue. This data type is also used by the UNIX System V semaphore and shared memory IPC methods.

The message table entry data type is *struct msqid_ds*, that is defined in the <sys/message.h> header. The data fields of the structure and the corresponding data it stores are:

Data field	Data stored
msg_perm	Data stored in a *struct ipc_perm* record
msg_first	Pointer to the first (oldest) message in the queue
msg_last	Pointer to the last (newest) message in the queue
msg_cbyte	Total number of bytes of all messages currently in the queue
msg_qnum	Total number of messages currently in the queue
msg_qbyte	Maximum number of bytes of all messages allowed in the queue. This is normally MSGMNB, but it can be set to a lower value by either the creator or the assigned owner of the queue
msg_lspid	Process ID of last process that sent a message to the queue
msg_lrpid	Process ID of the last process that read a message from the queue
msg_stime	Time when the latest message was sent to the queue
msg_rtime	Time when the latest message was read from the queue

Data field	Data stored
msg_ctime	Time when the message queue control data (the access permission and owner user ID and group ID) was last modified

The *struct msg* as defined in the <sys/msg.h> header is the data type of a message record. The data fields and the corresponding data stored are:

Data field	Data stored
msg_type	Assigned integer message type
msg_ts	Number of bytes of the message text
msg_spot	Pointer to the message text that is stored in a different kernel data region
msg_next	Pointer to the next message record, or NULL if this is the last record in a message queue

Figure 10.2 illustrates the uses of the aforementioned structures in the message table and message records.

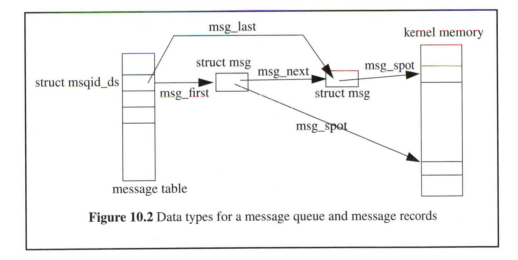

Figure 10.2 Data types for a message queue and message records

There are four APIs for message manipulation:

Messages API	Uses
msgget	Open and create if needed, a message queue for access
msgsnd	Send a message to a message queue
msgrcv	Receive a message from a message queue
msgctl	Manipulate the control data of a message queue

As stated earlier, message implementation is analogous to that of UNIX files, thus, the analogous APIs between messages and files are:

Messages API	Files API
msgget	open
msgsnd	write
msgrcv	read
msgctl	stat, unlink, chmod, chown

The header files needed for the messages APIs are:

```
#include <sys/types.h>
#include <sys/ipc.h>
#include <sys/msg.h>
```

10.3.3 msgget

The function prototype of the *msgget* API is:

```
#include <sys/types.h>
#include <sys/ipc.h>
#include <sys/message.h>

int msgget ( key_t key, int flag );
```

This function "opens" a message queue whose key ID matches the *key* actual value and returns a positive integer descriptor. This can be used in other message APIs to send and receive messages and to query and/or set control data for the queue.

If the value of the *key* argument is a positive integer, the API attempts to open a message queue whose key ID matches that value. However, if the *key* value is the manifested constant IPC_PRIVATE, the API allocates a new message queue to be used exclusively by the calling process.

If the *flag* argument is 0, the API aborts if there is no message queue whose key ID matches the given *key* value; otherwise, it returns a descriptor for that queue. If a process wishes to create a new queue (if none exists) with the given *key* ID, the *flag* value should contain the manifested constant IPC_CREAT and the read-write access permission (for owner, group and others) for the new queue.

For example, the following system call creates a message queue with the key ID of 15 and access permission of 0644 (that is, read-write for owner and read-only for group members and others), if such a queue does not preexist. The call also returns an integer descriptor for future queue references:

```
int   msgfdesc = msgget ( 15, IPC_CREATI0644 );
```

If a process wishes to guarantee the creation of a new message queue, it can specify the IPC_EXCL flag with the IPC_CREAT flag, and the API will succeed only if it creates a new queue with the given *key*.

The API returns -1 it if fails. Some possible causes of failure are:

Errno value	Cause of error
ENOSPC	The system-imposed limit MSGMNI has been reached
ENOENT	The *flag* value does not contain the IPC_CREAT flag, and no queue exists with the specified *key*
EEXIST	The IPC_EXCL and IPC_CREAT flags are set in the *flag* value, and a message queue with the specified *key* already exists
EACCESS	The queue with the specified *key* exists, but the calling process has no access permission to the queue

10.3.4 msgsnd

The function prototype of the *msgsnd* API is:

```
#include <sys/types.h>
#include <sys/ipc.h>
#include <sys/msg.h>

int msgsnd ( int  msgfd, const void* msgPtr, int len, int flag );
```

This API sends a message (pointed to by *msgPt)* to a message queue designated by the *msgfd* descriptor.

The *msgfd* value is obtained from a *msgget* function call.

The actual value of the *msgPtr* argument is the pointer of an object that contains the actual message text and a message type to be sent. The following data type can be used to define an object for such purpose:

```
struct msgbuf
{
        long  mtype;                   // message type
        char  mtext[MSGMAX];           // buffer to hold the message text
};
```

The *len* value is the size, in bytes, of the *mtext* field of the object pointed to by the *msgPtr* argument.

The *flag* value may be 0, which means the process can be blocked, if needed, until the function call completes successfully. If it is the IPC_NOWAIT flag, the function aborts if the process is to be blocked.

The return value of the API is 0 if it succeeds or -1 if it fails.

The following *test_msgsnd.C* program creates a new message queue with the key ID of 100 and sets the access permission of the queue to be read-write for owner, read-only for group members and write-only for others. If the *msgget* call succeeds, the process sends the message *Hello* of type 15 to the queue and specifies the call to be nonblocking. If either the *msgget* or the *msgsnd* call fails, the process calls *perror* to print out a diagnostic message.

```
#include <stdio.h>
#include <string.h>
#include <sys/ipc.h>
#include <sys/msg.h>

struct msgbuf
{
     long    mtype;
     char    mtext[MSGMAX];
} mobj = { 15, "Hello" };

int main()
{
   int fd = msgget (100, IPC_CREAT|IPC_EXCL|0642);
   if (fd==-1 || msgsnd(fd,&mobj,strlen(mobj.mtext)+1, IPC_NOWAIT))
      perror("message");
```

```
        return 0;
    }
```

10.3.5   msgrcv

The function prototype of the *msgrcv* API is:

```
#include <sys/types.h>
#include <sys/ipc.h>
#include <sys/msg.h>

int msgrcv ( int msgfd, const void* msgPtr, int len, int mtype, int flag );
```

This API receives a message of type *mtype* from a message queue designated by the *msgfd*. The message received is stored in the object pointed to by the *msgPtr* argument. The *len* argument specifies the maximum number of message text bytes that can be received by this call.

The *msgfd* value is obtained from a *msgget* function call.

The actual value of the *msgPtr* argument is the pointer to an object that has the *struct msgbuf*-like data structure.

The *mtype* value is the message type of the message to be received. The possible values and meaning of this argument are:

mtype value	Meaning
0	Receive the oldest message of any type in the queue
Positive integer	Receive the oldest message of the specified message type
Negative integer	Receive a message whose message type is less than or equal to the absolute value of the *mtype*. If there is more than one message in the queue meeting this criteria, receive the one that is the oldest and has the smallest message type value.

The *flag* value may be 0, which means the process may be blocked if no messages in the queue match the selection criteria specified by *mtype*. Furthermore, if there is a message in the queue that satisfies the *mtype* selection criteria but is larger than *len,* the function returns a failure status.

If a process specifies IPC_NOWAIT in the *flag* value, the call will be nonblocking. Also, if the MSG_NOERROR flag is set in the *flag* value, a message in the queue is selectable (if larger than *len)*. The function returns the first *len* byte of message text to the calling process and discards the rest of the data.

The *msgrcv* function returns the number of bytes written to the *mtext* buffer of the object pointed to by the *msgPtr* argument or -1 if it fails.

The following *test_msgrcv.C* program is the same one depicted in the last section, but after a message has been sent to the message queue, the process invokes the *msgrcv* API to wait and retrieve a message of type 20 from the queue. If the call succeeds, the process prints the retrieved message to the standard output; otherwise, it calls *perror* to print a diagnostic message.

```cpp
#include <iostream.h>
#include <stdio.h>
#include <string.h>
#include <sys/stat.h>
#include <sys/ipc.h>
#include <sys/msg.h>

/* data structure of one message */
struct mbuf
{
    long    mtype;
    char    mtext[MSGMAX];
} mobj = { 15, "Hello" };

int main()
{
    int perm = S_IRUSR|S_IWUSR|S_IRGRP|S_IWOTH;
    int fd = msgget (100, IPC_CREAT|IPC_EXCL|perm);

    if (fd==-1 || msgsnd(fd,&mobj,strlen(mobj.mtext)+1,IPC_NOWAIT))
        perror("message");
    else if (msgrcv(fd,&mobj,MSGMAX,20,MSG_NOERROR) > 0)
        cout << mobj.mtext << endl;
    else perror("msgrcv");
    return 0;
}
```

10.3.6 msgctl

The function prototype of the *msgctl* API is:

```
#include <sys/types.h>
#include <sys/ipc.h>
#include <sys/msg.h>

int msgctl ( int msgfd, int cmd, struct msqid_ds* mbufPtr );
```

This API can be used to query the control data of a message queue designated by the *msgfd* argument, to change the information within the control data of the queue, or to delete the queue from the system.

The *msgfd* value is obtained from a *msgget* function call.

The possible values of *cmd* and their meanings are:

cmd value	Meaning
IPC_STAT	Copy control data of the queue to the object pointed to by *mbufPtr*
IPC_SET	Change the control data of the queue by those specified in the object pointed to by *mbufPtr*. The calling process must be the superuser, creator, or the assigned owner of the queue to be able to perform this task. Furthermore, this API can only set the queue's owner user ID and group ID, access permissions and/or lower the *msg_qbyte* limit of the queue
IPC_RMID	Remove the queue from the system. The calling process must be the superuser, creator, or the assigned owner of the queue to be able to perform this task

This API returns 0 if it succeeds or -1 if it fails.

The following *test_msgctl.C* program "opens" a message queue with the key ID of 100 and calls *msgctl* to retrieve the control data of the queue. If both the *msgget* and *msgctl* calls succeed, the process prints to the standard output the number of messages currently in the queue,. It sets the queue owner user ID to be its own process ID via another *msgctl* call. Finally, the process invokes *msgctl* again to remove the queue.

```
#include <iostream.h>
#include <stdio.h>
#include <unistd.h>
#include <sys/ipc.h>
#include <sys/msg.h>
int main()
{
    struct msqid_ds mbuf;
    int fd = msgget (100, 0);
    if (fd>0 && msgctl(fd,IPC_STAT,&mbuf))     {
        cout << "#msg in queue: " << mbuf.msg_qnum << endl;
        mbuf.msg_perm.uid = getuid();   // change owner user ID
        if (msgctl(fd,IPC_SET,&mbuf)==-1)
                perror("msgctl");
    } else
            perror("msgctl");
    if (msgctl(fd,IPC_RMID,0)) perror("msgctl - IPC_RMID");
    return 0;
}
```

10.3.7 Client/Server Example

This section depicts a client/server application using messages. The first program *server.C* creates a daemon server process that runs in the background continuously to provide services to its client processes. The client processes are created by running the *client.C* program. The client processes post service requests to the daemon by sending messages to a message queue owned and managed by the daemon. The daemon responds to the client by sending messages to the same message queue.

Specifically, each service request message sent by a client process to the daemon server consists of:

Message data field	Meaning
message type	Integer service request command
message text	Client process ID in character string format (note that data stored in this field can be any arbitrary byte stream, including nonprintable characters)

The service request commands supported by the server are:

Service req. command	Service provided
1	Sends local date and time to client
2	Sends the Coordinated Universal Time (UTC) to client
3	Removes the message queue and terminates the daemon process. No response to client
4-99	Sends an error message back to client

Each response message sent by the server to a client consists of:

Message data field	Meaning
message type	Client process ID
message text	Service response data in character string format

Because both the server and its client interact through a common message queue, a message class can be defined to encapsulate all the message API interfacing from application programs. The following *message.h* header defines such a message class and is used by both the *server.C* and *client.C* programs:

```
/* The message.h header used by both the client.C and server.C */
#ifndef MESSAGE_H
#define MESSAGE_H
#include <stdio.h>
#include <stdlib.h>
#include <memory.h>
#include <unistd.h>
#include <sys/ipc.h>
#include <sys/msg.h>
#include <sys/wait.h>

/* common declarations for daemon/server process */
enum { MSGKEY= 176, MAX_LEN =256, ILLEGAL_CMD = 4 };
enum { LOCAL_TIME = 1, UTC_TIME = 2, QUIT_CMD = 3};

typedef struct mgbuf
{
    long        mtype;
    char        mtext[MAX_LEN];
} MSGBUF;

class message
{
  private:
```

```
      int    msgId;                 // message queue descriptor
      struct mgbuf mObj;
public:
   /* constructor. Get hold of a message queue */
   message ( int key )
   {
      if (msgId=msgget(key,IPC_CREAT|0666)==-1)
            perror("msgget");
   };

   /* destructor function. Do nothing */
    ~message () {};

   /* Check message queue open status */
   int good () { return (msgId >= 0) ? 1 : 0; };


   /* remove a message queue */
   int rmQ ()
   {
      int rc=msgctl(msgId,IPC_RMID,0);
      if (rc==-1) perror("msgctl");
      return rc;
   };

   /* send a message */
   int send ( const void* buf, int size, int type)
   {
      mObj.mtype = type;
      memcpy(mObj.mtext,buf,size);
      if (msgsnd(msgId,&mObj,size,0))         {
         perror("msgsnd"); return -1;
      };
      return 0;
   };

   /* receive a message */
   int rcv ( void* buf, int size, int type, int* rtype)
   {
      int len = msgrcv(msgId,&mObj,MAX_LEN,type,MSG_NOERROR);
      if (len==-1)    {
         perror("msgrcv"); return -1;
      }
      // Copy command or return data to buf and rtype
      memcpy(buf,mObj.mtext,len);
      if (rtype) *rtype = mObj.mtype;
```

```
            return len;
        };
    };
    #endif
```

The advantage of using the message class is that application programs do not need to use the underlying message APIs. They interface with a message object via a character buffer and a message type, using almost the same interface as do the *read* and *write* APIs for files. Thus, it reduces user programming effort. Furthermore, as will be seen in a later section, the message class implementation can be changed to use different IPC methods, with no changes required in the application code.

The following *server.C* program illustrates use of the *message.h* header:

```cpp
#include <strstream.h>
#include "message.h"
#include <string.h>
#include <signal.h>

int main()
{
    int     len, pid, cmdId, mypid = getpid();
    char    buf[256];
    time_t  tim;

    /* setup this process as a daemon */
    for (int i=0; i < 20; i++) sigset (i,SIG_IGN);
    setsid();

    cout << "server: start executing...\n" << flush;

    message mqueue(MSGKEY);                     // open a message queue
    if (!mqueue.good()) exit(1);                // quit if queue open fails

    /* wait for each request from a client */
    while (len=mqueue.rcv(buf,sizeof(buf),-99,&cmdId) > 0)
    {
        /* extract a client's PID and check the PID is valid */
        istrstream(buf,sizeof(buf)) >> pid;   // same as pid = atoi(buf);
        if (pid < 100)          // 0-100 are reserved for command IDs
        {
            cerr << "Illegal PID: " << buf << '/' << pid << endl;
            continue;
        }
```

```
                    /* Prepare response to a client */
                    cerr<<"server: receive cmd #" <<cmdId
                        <<", from client: "<<pid<<endl;
                    switch (cmdId)
                    {
                       case LOCAL_TIME:
                          tim = time(0);
                          strcpy(buf,ctime(&tim));
                          break;
                       case UTC_TIME:
                          tim = time(0);
                          strcpy(buf,asctime(gmtime(&tim)));
                          break;
                       case QUIT_CMD:
                          cerr << "server: deleting msg queue...\n";
                          return mqueue.rmQ();
                       default:                              /* send an error msg back */
                          ostrstream(buf,sizeof(buf)) << "Illegal cmd: " << cmdId << '\0';
                    }
                    /* send response to a client */
                    if (mqueue.send(buf,strlen(buf)+1,pid)==-1)
                       cerr << "Server: " << mypid << " send response fails\n";
                 };  /* loop forever */
                 return 0;
              }
```

The server process starts by setting itself up as a daemon process: It ignores all major signals and makes itself a session and process group leader. The process is now independent from its parent or sibling process.

The server process creates a message object with the key ID of 176 (this is chosen arbitrarily). The message constructor function creates a message queue if it does not preexist, with the assigned key ID and an access permission of read-write for all.

Once a message object is created, the server goes into a polling loop, where it waits for client processes to send service request messages to the message object. Specifically, since client service request commands are restricted to the range of 1-99, the server will poll messages whose message types are anything less than 100. Once a service request is read, the server checks that the client process ID is greater than 99 and sends a response message back to the client based on the service request command. However, if the service command is QUIT_CMD, the server deletes the message object and terminates itself.

One precaution in designing a program that uses messages is that a process should rarely need to read messages sent by itself. Thus, it is important that the process use a different set of message types for the outgoing and incoming messages. In the current example, the server response message types for clients are the clients' process IDs. These process IDs are always assumed to be larger than 100 (this is enforced in the *clent.C* program). Furthermore, the clients' service request message types are the service request commands (these commands are in the range of 1-99). Therefore, the server reads only clients' service request messages and not their response messages, and the clients only read the server's response messages and not its service request messages.

The *client.C* program is:

```
#include <strstream.h>
#include <string,h>
#include "message.h"

int main()
{
    int    cmdId, pid, mypid = getpid();
    while (getpid() < 100)
            switch (pid=fork())    {                   // make sure client PID > 99
                case -1: perror("fork"), exit(1);
                case 0:  break;
                default: waitpid(pid,0,0); exit(0);
            }
    cout << "client: start executing...\n";

    message mqueue(MSGKEY);              // create a message object
    if (!mqueue.good()) exit(1);         // quit if queue open fails
    char procId[256], buf2[256];
    ostrstream(procId,sizeof(procId)) << getpid() << '\0';
    do {
            /* Get a cmd from the standard input */
            cout << "cmd> " << flush;            // print an input prompt
            cin >> cmdId;                        // get a command from a user
            cout << endl;                        // force a <CR> at console
            if (cin.eof()) break;                // exit if EOF

            /* check cmd is valid */
            if (!cin.good() || cmdId < 0 || cmdId > 99)        {
                cerr << "Invalid input: " << cmdId << endl; continue;
            }
            /* send request to daemon */
            if (mqueue.send(procId,strlen(procId),cmdId))
                    cout << "client: " << getpid() << " msgsnd error\n";

            else if (cmdId==QUIT_CMD) break;       /* exit on QUIT_CMD */
```

```
/* receive data from daemon */
else if (mqueue.rcv(buf2,sizeof(buf2),mypid,0)==-1)
    cout << "client: " <<mypid << " msgrcv error\n";

/* print server's response data */
else cout << "client: " << mypid << " " << buf2 << endl;

} while (1);  /* loop until EOF */

cout << "client: " << mypid << " exiting...\n" << flush;
return 0;
}
```

The client program starts by first making sure its process ID is greater than or equal to 100. If this is not the case, it calls *fork* recursively until one of its child process IDs is greater than or equal to 100. In this process, all nonqualified "parent" processes simply wait for their child process to terminate before they terminate themselves. This is a simple way of guaranteeing that the client/server interaction condition (namely, that the client process ID be greater than 99) is met.

Once a client process is created, it "opens" a message object with the same key ID as the server. It then enters a loop, where it iteratively prompts users to enter a service request command from the standard input. For each command it receives, it checks whether the command is in the range of 1-99 then sends a service request message to the server process. After that, it reads the service response back from the server and prints the corresponding data to the standard output.

The client process terminates when EOF is encountered in the standard input (e.g., user presses <ctrl-D>) or an error is encountered in reading the standard input.

Some sample interaction of these client and server programs are:

> chp13 % server &
> *server: start executing...*
> *[1] 356*
> chp13 % client
> *client: start executing...*
> cmd> 1
> *server: receive cmd #1, from client: 357*
> *client: 357 Tue Jan 24 22:23:17 1995*
> cmd> 2
> *server: receive cmd #2, from client: 357*

client: 357 Wed Jan 25 06:23:19 1995

cmd> 4

server: receive cmd #4, from client: 357

client: 357 Illegal cmd: 4

cmd> 3

client: 357 exiting...

server: receive cmd #3, from client: 357

server: deleting msg queue...

[1]   Done   mserver

chp13 %

Although the above example shows only one client interacting with a server, there can be multiple client processes running simultaneously and interacting with the same server.

10.4   POSIX.1b Messages

POSIX.1b messages are created and manipulated in a manner similar to UNIX System V messages. Specifically, the POSIX.1b defines the <mqueue.h> header and a set of messages APIs:

```
#include <mqueue.h>

mqd_t     mq_open( char* name, int flags, mode_t mode,
                        struct mq_attr* attrp );

int       mq_send ( mqd_t mqid, const char* msg, size_t len,
                        unsigned priority );

int       mq_receive (mqd_t mqid, char* buf, size_t len, unsigned* prio );

int       mq_close ( mqd_t mqid );

int       mq_notify ( mqd_t mqid, const struct mq_sigevent* sigvp );

int       mq_getattr ( mqd_t mqid, struct mq_attr* atttrp );

int       mq_setattr ( mqd_t mqid, struct mq_attr* atttrp,
                        struct mq_attr* oattrp );
```

The *mq_open* API is like the *msgget* function: It returns a handle of type *mqd_t,* which designates a message queue. Note that *mqd_t* is not an integer descriptor.

The message queue "opened" by the *mq_open* function is given a name as specified in the *name* argument. The *name* value should be a UNIX path name-like character string and should always begin with the "/" character. It is implementation-dependent of whether additional "/" characters are allowed in the *name* value. Furthermore, users should not expect that a file with the same name is created by this call.

The *flags* argument specifies the access manner of the queue by a calling process. Its values may be O_RDONLY (the calling process can only receive messages), O_WRONLY (the calling process may only send messages), or O_RDWR (the calling process may send and receive messages). Furthermore, the O_CREAT flag may also be specified to indicate that if the named queue does not exist, it should be created. Moreover, if the O_EXCL flag is specified with the O_CREAT flag, it forces the function to abort if the named queue already exists.

Finally, the O_NONBLOCK flag may also be specified in an *oflag* value to indicate that future access of the message queue (via *mq_send* and *mq_receive* APIs) should be nonblocking.

The *mode* and *attrp* arguments are needed only if the O_CREAT flag is specified in the *oflag* argument. They specify read-write access permission and special attributes for a message queue created by this call. The *struct mq_attr* data type is defined in the <mqeue.h> header.

The function returns a *mqd_t*-type message queue handle if it succeeds or a *(mqd_t)*-1 value if it fails.

For example, the following opens and creates, if necessary, a message queue */foo* for read-write access. The access permission assigned to a newly create queue are read-write for the owner only. Furthermore, the new message queue may hold up to 200 messages, each message not to exceed 1024 bytes:

```
struct mq_attr attrv;          // contains attributes for a new queue
attrv.mq_maxmsg = 200;         // at most 200 msg may be in a queue
attrv.mq_msgsize = 1024;       // at most 1024 bytes per message
attrv.mq_flags = 0;

mqd_t mqid = mq_open( "/foo", O_RDWRIO_CREAT, S_IRWXU, &attrv);
if (mqid == (mqd_t)-1) perror("mq_open");
```

The *mq_send* API sends a message to a message queue referenced by the *mqid* argument. The *msg* argument value is the address of a buffer that contains a message text, and the *len* argument specifies the message text size in number of characters. The *len* value should be less than the message queue limit (maximum size per message); otherwise, the call will fail.

The *priority* argument value is an integer between 0 and MQ_PRIO_MAX. It is used to sort messages in a queue-messages with higher *priority* values are accessed earlier than those with lower *priority* values. Furthermore, if two or more messages have the same *priority* value in a queue, they are sorted in decreasing order, based on their duration in the queue. The older messages are retrieved before the newer ones.

The function returns 0 if it succeeds and -1 if it fails. Note that the function may block a calling process if the message queue is already full. However, if the queue was opened with the O_NONBLOCK flag, the function aborts and returns immediately with a -1 failure status.

The following example sends a message *Hello POSIX.1b* to a message queue, designated by *mqid*, with a priority value of 5:

```
char* msg = "Hello POSIX.1b";
if (mq_send( mqid, msg, strlen(msg)+1, 5)) perror("mq_send");
```

The *mq_receive* API receives the oldest and highest priority message from a message queue referenced by the *mqid* argument. The *buf* argument value is the address of a buffer containing the message text, and the *len* argument specifies the maximum size of the *buf* argument. If a message to be received is larger than *len* bytes, the function will return a failure status.

The *priop* argument is the address of an unsigned integer variable holding the priority value of the receiving message. If the argument value is given as NULL, the receiving message's priority value is a don't-care.

The function returns the number of message text bytes that has been put in the *buf* argument if it succeeds or -1 if it fails. Note that the function may block a calling process if the message queue is empty. However, if the queue was opened with the O_NONBLOCK flag, the function aborts and returns immediately with a -1 failure status.

If multiple processes are blocked on the *mq_receieve* call, then when a message arrives in the queue, the process with the highest priority and the longest waiting time gets the message.

The following example receives a message from a message queue designated by *mqid*:

```
char buf[256];
unsigned prio;
if (mq_receieve( mqid, buf , sizeof buf, &prio)==-1) perror("mq_receieve");
cerr << "receive msg: '" << buf << "', priority=" << prio << endl;
```

The *mq_close* API deallocates resources used to associate a message queue with a message handle, *mqid*. This function returns a 0 if succeeds or -1 if it fails.

The *mq_notify* API is used if a process wishes to receive asynchronous notification of a message's arrival at an empty queue, instead of being blocked by a *mq_receieve* call to wait for such an event. The *mqid* argument designates a message queue to monitor message arrival; the *sigvp* argument value is the address of a *struct sigevent*-type variable. The *struct sigevent* data type is defined in the <signal.h> header and contains the signal number which should be generated by the calling process when a message arrives at the designated message queue.

This function fails if there is a process that has already registered signal notification for the same message queue or is blocked by a *mq_receieve* call. Furthermore, even if a process succeeds with the *mq_notify* call and a notification signal is delivered (because a message has arrived at the message queue), it may still be unable to receive the message if another process issues a *mq_receieve* call before it does.

Finally, if the *sigvp* argument value is specified as NULL, the call unregisters signal notification for a specified message queue. The signal notification is also unregistered if the process already exists or calls the *mq_close* API on the message queue handle.

This function returns 0 if it succeeds or -1 if it fails.

The following example registers a SIGUSR1 signal to be delivered to the calling process if any message arrives at the message queue designated by the *mqid* variable:

```
struct sigevent sigv;
sigv.sigev_notify = SIGEV_SIGNAL;      // signal notification is requested
sigv.sigev_signo = SIGUSR1;            // send SIGUSR1 for notification
if (mq_notify(mqid, &sigv)==-1) perror("mq_notify");
```

The *mq_getattr* API queries attributes of a message queue designated by the *mqid* argument. The *attrp* is the address of a *struct mq_attr* type variable. The *struct mq_attr* data type is defined in the <mqeue.h> header. Some of its useful member fields and their meanings are:

Member Field	Meaning
mq_flags	Specifies whether the queue operation is blocking. Possible value is either 0 or O_NONBLOCK
mq_maxmsg	Maximum number of messages allowed in the queue at any one time
mq_msgsize	Maximum size, in bytes, allowed per message
mq_curmsgs	Number of messages currently in the queue

This function returns 0 if it succeeds or -1 if it fails.

The following example obtains attribute information for a message queue designated by the *mqid* variable:

```
struct mq_attr attrv;
if (mq_getattr(mqid, &attrv)==-1)
      perror("mq_getattr");
else  cout << "flags = " << attrv.mq_flags
            << ", cur no. msg: " << attrv.mq_curmsgs << endl;
```

The *mq_setattr* API sets the *mq_attr::mq_flags* attribute of a message queue designated by the *mqid* argument. The *attrp* is the address of a *struct mq_attr* type variable. This is the input argument to the function, and only the *attrp->mq_flags* value is used by the function. The legal value of this member field is either 0 (use blocking operation on the queue) or O_NONBLOCK (use nonblocking operation on the queue). The *oattrp* argument value, if specified as the address of a *struct mq_attr*-typed variable, returns the same information as the *mq_getattr* call prior to the *mq_setattr* call.

This function returns 0 if it succeeds or -1 if it fails.

The following example sets a message queue referenced by the *mqid* variable to use nonblocking operations. The old message queue attributes are ignored.

```
struct mq_attr attrv;
attrv.mq_flags = O_NONBLOCK;
if (mq_setattr(mqid, &attrv,0)==-1) perror("mq_setattr");
```

10.4.1 POSIX.1b Message Class

The message class defined in Section 10.3.7 is for UNIX System V messages only. The following *message2.h* header defines a new message class that uses POSIX.1b message APIs. Note that the new message class interface is the same as that in Section 10.3.7:

```
#ifndef MESSAGE2_H
#define MESSAGE2_H
#include <stdio.h>
#include <memory.h>
#include <sys/ipc.h>
#include <mqueue.h>                        // use POSIX.1b messages APIs

/* common declarations for daemon/server process */
enum { MSGKEY=186, MAX_LEN=256, ILLEGAL_CMD = 4};
enum { LOCAL_TIME = 1, UTC_TIME = 2, QUIT_CMD = 3 };
struct mgbuf
{
        long      mtype;
        char      mtext[MAX_LEN];
};

/* POSIX.1b message class */
class message
{
   private:
        mqd_t   msgId;                            // message queue handle
        struct mgbuf mObj;
   public:
        /* System V compatible constructor function */
        message( int key )
        {
           char name[80];
           sprintf(name,"/MQUEUE%d",key);
           if ((msgid=mq_open(name,O_RDWR|O_CREAT,0666,0))
                            == (mqd_r)-1)
              perror("mq_open");
        };

        /* POSIX.1b style constructor function */
        message( const char* name )
        {
           if (msgId=mq_open(name,O_RDWR|O_CREAT,0666,0))
                            == (mqd_r)-1)
              perror("mq_open");
        };

        /* destructor function */
        ~message() {  (void)mq_close( msgId); };

        /* check queue open status */
        int good() { return (msgId >= 0) ? 1 : 0; };
```

```
/* remove message queue */
int rmQ()
{
   return mq_close( msgId );
};

/* send a message */
int send( const void* buf, int size, int type)
{
   mObj.mtype = type;
   memcpy(mObj.mtext,buf,size);
   if (mq_send(msgId,(char*)&mObj,size,type)) {
      perror("mq_send");
      return -1;
   };
   return 0;
};

/* receive a message */
int rcv( void* buf, int size, int type, unsigned* rtype)
{
   struct mq_attr attrv;
   if (mq_getattr(msgId,&attrv)==-1)   {
      perror("mq_getattr");
      return -1;
   }
   if (!attrv.mq_curmsgs) return -1;     // no messages

   int len = mq_receive(msgId,(char*)&mObj,MAX_LEN,rtype);
   if (len < 0) {
      perror("mq_receieve");
      return -2;
   }

   if (type && ((type > 0 && type!=*rtype) ||
            (type < 0 && -type < *rtype)) )
      mq_send(msgId, (char*)&mObj, len, *rtype );
      return -3;                         // not the requested type
   }
   memcpy(buf,mObj.mtext,len);
   return len;
};
};
#endif                    /* MESSAGE2_H */
```

The POSIX.1b version of the message class, as shown above, can be used in the same manner as the System V version. Specifically, there are two *message::message* constructor functions, one is invoked with an integer key and the other with a message name. In either way, the *mq_open* function is called to open and create, if necessary, a message queue.

The *message::send, message::rcv* and *message::~message* functions have exactly the same interface as that of the System V message class. The only difference is that the POSIX.1b *message::rcv* function cannot really select messages based on a user's specified message type. Thus, the function gets the highest priority message from a queue. If the message type does not satisfy the user-defined message type, the function pushes the message back to the queue and returns a -1 failure status. A message type satisfies a user-defined type if: (1) the user-defined type is 0 (message type is don't-care); (2) the user-specified type matches the received message type exactly; or (3) the user-specified type is negative and the absolute value of that type is greater than or equal to the receiving message type.

The new *message2.h* header can be used in the same client and server programs as depicted in Section 13.3.7. The output of the newly compiled client and server programs should be identical to that of the System V version.

10.5   UNIX System V Semaphores

Semaphores provide a method to synchronize the execution of multiple processes. Semaphores are allocated in sets of one or more. A process can also use multiple semaphore sets. Semaphores are frequently used along with shared memory to establish an elaborate method for interprocess communication.

The UNIX System V semaphore APIs provide the following functions:

- Create a semaphore set
- "Open" a semaphore set and get a descriptor to reference the set
- Increase or decrease the integer values of one more semaphores in a set
- Query the values of one or more semaphores in a set
- Query or set control data of a semaphore set

Each semaphore has an unsigned short value. A process that has read permission for semaphores may query their values. A process that has write permission for semaphores can increase or decrease their values. If a process attempts to decrease a semaphore value such that the resultant value becomes negative, the operation, as well as the process, will be blocked until another process increases the semaphore's value to a number large enough that the blocked process's operation can succeed (i.e., the resultant semaphore value is 0 or a positive number). This forms the basis for multiprocess synchronization using semaphores:

- A process X that wishes to wait for another process Y decreases the value of one or more semaphores by some value such that it is blocked by the kernel
- When process Y is ready to let X resume execution, it increases the semaphores' values enough for X's semaphore operation to succeed. The kernel unblocks X

If a semaphore's value is a positive integer but a process explicitly queries its value as to whether it is zero, the process will be blocked until the semaphore's value is decreased to zero by another process.

If a process has access to a set of semaphores, it can perform operations on individual semaphores in the set or operate on two or more semaphores in the set simultaneously. In the latter case, if an operation cannot be performed on any of the selected semaphores, the entire operation fails, and the values of the semaphore set are unchanged. Thus, the semaphore operations are atomic at the set level. This is to ensure that when two or more processes attempt to read and write values on the same semaphore set, only one can perform operations at a given time.

10.5.1   UNIX Kernel Support for Semaphores

In UNIX System V.3 and V.4, there is a semaphore table in the kernel address space that keeps track of all semaphore sets created in the system. Each entry of the semaphore table stores the following data for one semaphore set:

- A name that is an integer ID key assigned by the process which created the set. Other processes may specify this key to "open" the set and get a descriptor for future access of the set
- The creator user ID and group ID. A process whose effective user ID matches a semaphore set creator user ID may delete the set and also change control data of the set
- The assigned owner user ID and group ID. These are normally the same as the creator user and group IDs, but a creator process can set these values to assign a different owner and group membership for the set
- Read-write access permission of the set for owner, group members, and others. A process that has read permission to the set may query values of the semaphores and queries the assigned users and group IDs of the set. A process that has write permission to a set may change the values of semaphores
- The number of semaphores in the set
- The time when the last process changed one or more semaphore values
- The time when the last process changed the control data of the set
- A pointer to an array of semaphores

Semaphores in a set are referenced by array indices, such that the first semaphore in the set has an index of zero; the second semaphore has an index of 1; and so on. Furthermore, each semaphore stores the following data:

- The semaphore's value
- The process ID of the last process that operated on the semaphore
- The number of processes that are currently blocked pending the increase of semaphore value
- The number of processes which are currently blocked pending the semaphor's value becoming zero

Figure 10.3 depicts the UNIX kernel data structure for semaphores.

Like messages, semaphores are stored in a kernel address space and are persistent, despite their creator process's termination. Furthermore, each semaphore set has an assigned owner, and only processes that have superuser, set creator, or assigned owner privileges may delete the set or change its control data. If a semaphore set is deleted, any processes that are blocked at that time due to the semaphores are awakened by the kernel - the system calls they invoked are aborted and return a -1 failure status.

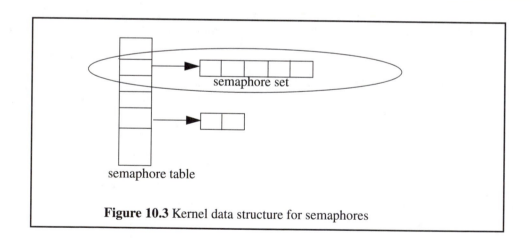

Figure 10.3 Kernel data structure for semaphores

Finally, there are several system-imposed limits on the manipulation of semaphores. These limits are defined in the <sys/sem.h> header:

System limit	Meaning
SEMMNI	The maximum number of semaphore sets that may exist at any given time in a system
SEMMNS	The maximum number of semaphores in all sets that may exist in a system at any one time

System limit	Meaning
SEMMSL	The maximum number of semaphores allowed per set
SEMOPM	The maximum number of semaphores in a set that may be operated on at any one time

The effects of these system-imposed limits on processes are:

- If a process attempts to create a new semaphore set that causes either the SEMMNI or the SEMMNS limit to be exceeded, the process will be blocked until one or more existing sets are deleted by a process.
- If a process attempts to create a semaphore set with more than SEMMSL semaphores, the system call fails.
- If a process attempts to operate on more than SEMOPM semaphores in a set in one operation, the system call fails.

10.5.2 The UNIX APIs for Semaphores

The <sys/ipc.h> header defines a *struct ipc_perm* data type, which stores the user ID, group ID, creator user ID and group ID, assigned name key, and the read-write permission of a semaphore set.

The semaphore table entry data type is *struct semid_ds*, which is defined in the <sys/sem.h> header. The data fields of the structure and the data stored are:

Data field	Data Stored
sem_perm	Data stored in a *struct ipc_perm* record
sem_nsems	Number of semaphores in the set
sem_base	Pointer to an array of semaphores
sem_otime	Time when last process operated on semaphores
sem_ctime	Time when last process changed control data of the set

In addition to the above, the *struct sem* data type, as defined in the <sys/sem.h> header, defines the data stored in a semaphore:

Data field	Data Stored
semval	Current semaphore's integer value
sempid	Process ID of the last process that operated on the semaphore
semncnt	Number of processes that are blocked waiting for

the semaphore's value to be increased

semzcnt   Number of processes that are blocked waiting for
                           the semaphore's value to become zero

Figure 10-4 illustrates uses of the aforementioned structures in the semaphore table and
semaphore records.

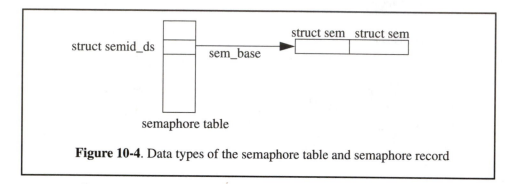

Figure 10-4. Data types of the semaphore table and semaphore record

The UNIX System V semaphore APIs are:

Semaphores API	Usages
semget	Open and create, if needed, a semaphore set
semop	Change or query semaphore value
semctl	Query or change control data of a semaphore set or delete a set

The header files needed for the semaphore APIs are:

```
#include <sys/types.h>
#include <sys/ipc.h>
#include <sys/sem.h>
```

10.5.3   semget

The function prototype of the *semget* API is:

```
#include <sys/types.h>
#include <sys/ipc.h>
#include <sys/sem.h>

int  semget ( key_t  key, int num_sem, int flag );
```

This function "opens" a semaphore set whose key ID is given in the *key* argument. The function returns a nonnegative integer descriptor that can be used in the other semaphore APIs to change or query semaphore value and to query and/or set control data for the semaphore set.

If the value of the *key* argument is a positive integer, the API attempts to open a semaphore set whose key ID matches that value. However, if the *key* value is the manifested constant IPC_PRIVATE, the API allocates a new semaphore set to be used exclusively by the calling process. Specifically, the "private" semaphores are usually allocated by a parent process which then forks one or more child processes. The parent and child processes then use the semaphores to synchronize their operations.

If the *flag* argument is 0, the API aborts when there is no semaphore set whose key ID matches the given *key* value. Otherwise, it returns a descriptor for that set. If a process wishes to create a new set with the given *key* ID (if none preexists), then the *flag* value should be the bitwise-OR of the manifested constant IPC_CREAT and the read-write access permissions for the new set.

The *num_sem* value may be 0 if the IPC_CREAT flag is not specified in the *flag* argument, or it is the number of semaphores to be allocated when a new set is to be created.

For example, the following system call creates a two-element semaphore set with the key ID of 15 and access permission of read-write for owner and read-only for group members and others (if such a set does not preexist). The call returns an integer descriptor for future references of the queue:

```
int perms = S_IRUSR | S_IWUSR | S_IRGRP | S_IROTH;
int semfdesc = semget ( 15, 2, IPC_CREAT | perms);
```

If a process wishes to guarantee creation of a new semaphore set, it can specify the IPC_EXCL flag with the IPC_CREAT flag, and the API will succeed only if it creates a new set with the given *key*.

The API returns a -1 value it if fails.

10.5.4   semop

The function prototype of the *semop* API is:

```
#include <sys/types.h>
#include <sys/ipc.h>
#include <sys/sem.h>
int  semop ( int semfd, struct sembuf* opPtr, int len );
```

This API may be used to change the value of one or more semaphores in a set (as designated by *semfd*) and/or to test whether their values are 0. The *opPtr* is the pointer to any array of *struct sembuf* objects, each of which specifies one operation (query or change value) for a semaphore. The *len* argument specifies how many entries are in the array pointed to by *opPtr*.

The *struct sembuf* data type is defined in the <sys/sem.h> header as:

```
struct sembuf
{
    short    sem_num;          // semaphore index
    short    sem_op;           // semaphore operation
    short    sem_flg;          // operation flag(s)
};
```

The possible values of *sem_op* and their meanings are:

sem_op value	Meaning
a positive number	Increase the indexed semaphore value by this amount
a negative number	Decrease the indexed semaphore value by this amount
a zero	Test whether the semaphore value is 0

If a *semop* call attempts to decrease a semaphore's value to a negative number, or if it tests a semaphore's value as 0 but it is not, then the calling process will be blocked by the kernel. This will occur unless the IPC_NOWAIT flag is specified in the *sem_flg* fields of the array entries where *sem_op* is a negative number or zero.

Another flag that may be specified in the *sem_flg* fields of the *struct sembuf* objects is SEM_UNDO. This instructs the kernel to keep track of the net semaphore value change on the indexed semaphore (due to the *semop* call). When the calling process terminates, the kernel will reverse these changes so that any other processes awaiting such changes will not be locked out indefinitely. This would occur because the exiting process forgot to undo the changes it made to the semaphore set.

The API returns a 0 if it succeeds or -1 if it fails.

```
#include <sys/types.h>
#include <sys/ipc.h>
#include <sys/sem.h>

/* decrease 1st semaphore value by 1, test 2nd semaphore value is zero */
struct semid_ds sbuf[2] = {{0, -1, SEM_UNDO|IPC_NOWAIT}, {1, 0, 0} };

int main()
{
    int perms = S_IRWXU | S_IRWXG | S_IRWXO;
    int fd = semget (100, 2, IPC_CREAT | perms);
    if (fd==-1) perror("semget"), exit(1);
    if (semop(fd,sbuf,2)==-1) perror("semop");
    return 0;
}
```

This example opens a two-element semaphore set with the key ID of 100, and it creates the set with read-write permission for all (if it does not preexist).

If the *semget* call succeeds, the process calls *semop* to decrease the first semaphore value by 1 and tests the second semaphore value as zero. Furthermore, it specifies the IPC_NOWAIT and SEM_UNDO flags when it operates on the first semaphore.

10.5.5   semctl

The function prototype of the *semctl* API is:

```
#include <sys/types.h>
#include <sys/ipc.h>
#include <sys/sem.h>

int semctl ( int  semfd, int num, int cmd, union semun arg );
```

This API can be used to query or change the control data of a semaphore set designated by the *semfd* argument or to delete the set altogether.

The *semfd* value is the semaphore set descriptor, as obtained from a *semget* function call.

The *num* value is a semaphore index where the next argument, *cmd,* specifies an operation to be performed on a specific semaphore within a set.

The *arg* argument is a union-typed object that may be used to specify or retrieve the control data of one or more semaphores in the set, as determined by the *cmd* argument. The *union semun* data type is defined in the <sys/sem.h> header as:

```
union semun
{
    int              val;       // a semaphore value
    struct semid_ds  *buf;      // control data of a semaphore set
    ushort           *array;    // an array of semaphore values
};
```

The possible values of *cmd* and their meanings are:

cmd **value**	**Meaning**
IPC_STAT	Copy control data of the semaphore to the object pointed to by *arg.buf.* The calling process must have read permission to the set
IPC_SET	Change the control data of the semaphore set by those data specified in the object pointed to by *arg.buf.* The calling process must be the supervisor, creator, or the assigned owner of the set to be able to perform this task. Furthermore, this API can establish only the set owner user and group IDs and access permission of the queue
IPC_RMID	Remove the semaphore from the system. The calling process must be the superuser, creator, or the assigned owner of the queue to be able to perform this task
GETALL	Copy all the semaphore values to the array pointed to by *arg.array*
SETALL	Set all the semaphore values by the corresponding values contained in an array pointed to by *arg.array*
GETVAL	Return the *num*-indexed semaphore value. *arg* is unused

cmd value	Meaning
SETVAL	Set the *num*-indexed semaphore value by the value specified in *arg.val*
GETPID	Return the process ID of the last process that operated on the *num*-indexed semaphore. *arg* is unused
GETNCNT	Return the number of processes that are currently blocked waiting for the *num*-indexed semaphore value to increase. *arg* is unused
GETZCNT	Return the number of processes that are currently blocked waiting for the *num*-indexed semaphore value to become zero. *arg* is unused

This API returns a *cmd*-specific value if it succeeds or -1 if it fails.

The following *test_sem.C* program "opens" a semaphore set with the key ID of 100 and calls *semctl* to retrieve the control data of the set. If both the *semget* and *semctl* calls are successful, the process prints to the standard output the number of semaphores in the set. It then sets the set owner user ID as its own process ID, via another *semctl* call. Finally, the process invokes *semctl* again to remove the set.

```
#include <iostream.h>
#include <stdio.h>
#include <unistd.h>
#include <sys/ipc.h>
#include <sys/sem.h>

union semun {
        int    val;
        struct semid_ds *mbuf;
        ushort *array;
} arg;

int main()
{
    struct semid_ds mbuf;
    arg.mbuf = &mbuf;
    int fd = semget (100, 0, 0);
    if (fd>0 && semctl(fd,0, IPC_STAT,arg))     {
        cout << "#semaphores in the set" << arg.mbuf->sem_nsems<< endl;
        arg.mbuf->sem_perm.uid = getuid(); // change owner user ID
```

```
        if (semctl(fd,0,IPC_SET,arg)==-1) perror("semctl");
    }
    else perror("semctl");
    if (semctl(fd,0,IPC_RMID,0)) perror("semctl - IPC_RMID");
    return 0;
}
```

10.6   POSIX.1b Semaphores

The POSIX.1b semaphores are created and manipulated in a manner similar to those in UNIX System V. Specifically, the <semaphore.h> header and the following APIs are defined by the POSIX.1b:

#include <semaphore.h>

sem_t*   *sem_open*(**char*** name, **int** flags, **mode_t** mode, **unsigned** init_value);

int   *sem_init* (**sem_t*** addr, **int** pshared, **unsigned** init_value);

int   *sem_getvalue* (**sem_t*** idp, **int*** valuep);

int   *sem_close* (**sem_t*** idp);

int   *sem_destroy* (**sem_t*** id);

int   *sem_unlink* (**char*** name);

int   *sem_wait* (**sem_t*** idp);

int   *sem_trywait* (**sem_t*** idp);

int   *sem_post* (**sem_t*** idp);

The POSIX.1b semaphores differ from those of UNIX System V in the following ways:

- POSIX.1b semaphores are either identified by a UNIX path name (as created via *sem_open*), or remain unnamed (but given a starting virtual address as created via *sem_init*). System V semaphores are identified by an integer key
- POSIX.1b creates one semaphore for each *sem_open* or *sem_init* call, whereas multiple System V semaphores can be created for each *semget* call
- A POSIX.1b semaphore value is increased or decreased by a value of 1 for each *sem_post* and *sem_wait* call, respectively. With System V semaphores, users can increase or decrease semaphore value by any integer value for each *semop* call

The *sem_open* function creates a semaphore whose name is given by the *name* argument. The syntax of the *name* argument value is the same as that for POSIX.1b messages. The *flags* argument value may be 0 if it knows that the named semaphore already exists. Otherwise, the O_CREAT flag specifies that a semaphore of the given name should be created. In addition, the O_EXCL flag may be specified with the O_CREAT flag to force the function to return a failure status if a semaphore of the given name already exists. The *mode* and *init_value* arguments are used for a newly create semaphore. Specifically, the *mode* argument value is the read-write permission for user, group, and others to be assigned to the new semaphore. The *init_value* argument value is an unsigned integer value to be assigned to the semaphore.

The function returns a *sem_t* pointer if it succeeds or -1 if it fails.

The *sem_init* function is an alternative to the *sem_open* function. A process that uses *sem_init* first allocates a memory region for the semaphore to be created. This memory region may be a shared memory if the semaphore is to be accessed by other processes. The memory region address is passed as value to the *addr* argument of *sem_init*. The *pshared* argument value is 1 if the semaphore is to be shared with other processes, 0 otherwise. The *init_value* argument specifies the initial integer value to be assigned to the semaphore. This value should not be a negative number.

The function returns a 0 value if it succeeds or -1 if it fails.

The *sem_getvalue* function returns the current value of a semaphore designated by the *idp* argument. The return value is passed via the *valuep* argument. The function returns 0 if it succeeds or -1 if it fails.

The *sem_post* function increases a semaphore value by 1, whether the *sem_wait* function decreases its value by 1. A semaphore is designated by the *idp* argument in both functions. If the value is already zero, the *sem_wait* function will block the calling process until it can succeed in its operation. The *sem_trywait* is similar to *sem_wait,* except that it is non-blocking and returns a -1 failure status (if it cannot decrease a specified semaphore value).

The *sem_close* and *sem_unlink* functions are used with semaphores created by the *sem_open* function. The *sem_close* function disassociates a semaphore from a process, and the *sem_unlink* function removes a semaphore from the system.

The *sem_destroy* function is used with semaphores that are created by the *sem_init* function. It deletes a semaphore from the system.

All the *sem_post, sem_wait, sem_trywait, sem_close, sem_unlink,* and *sem_destroy* functions return 0 if they succeed or -1 if they fail.

The following *test_semp.C* example creates a semaphore of the name */sem.0* and initializes it with a value of 1. If the semaphore is created successfully, the process does a *sem_wait* on it, bringing the semaphore value to 0, then performs a *sem_post* to increase the value back to 1. Finally, the process closes the semaphore handle via *sem_close* and removes the semaphore from the system via the *sem_unlink* API.

```
#include <stdio.h>
#include <sys/stat.h>
#include <semaphore.h>

int main()
{
    sem_t *semp = sem_open("/sem.0", O_CREAT, S_IRWXU, 1);
    if (semp==(sem_t*)-1)           { perror("sem_open"); return -1; }
    if (sem_wait(semp)==-1)         perror("sem_wait");
    if (sem_post(semp)==-1)         perror("sem_post");
    if (sem_close(semp)==-1)        perror("sem_close");
    if (sem_unlink("/sem.0") == -1) perror("sem_unlink");
    return 0;
}
```

The second example below, *test_semp2.C*, uses *sem_init* to create a semaphore at a dynamic address created by the process via *malloc*. The semaphore is specified as unshared (*pshare* value is zero), and its initial value is set to 1. If the semaphore is created, the *sem_getvalue* API is called to obtain the current value, and the process depicts the value to the standard output. Finally, the semaphore is destroyed from the system via the *sem_destroy* API.

```
#include <iostream.h>
#include <stdio.h>
#include <malloc.h>
#include <semaphore.h>

int main()
{
    int        val;
    sem_t      semval;
    if (sem_init ( &semval, 0, 1 )==-1) {
                perror("sem_init"); return 2;
    }
    if (sem_getvalue( &emval, &val)==0)
```

```
                      cout << "semaphore value: " << val << endl;
            if (sem_destroy(&semval) == -1)
                          perror("sem_destroy");
            return 0;
      }
```

10.7   UNIX System V Shared Memory

Shared memory allows multiple processes to map a portion of their virtual addresses to a common memory region. Thus, any process can write data to a shared memory region and the data are readily available to be read and modified by other processes.

Shared memory was invented to improve on the performance problem of messages: when a message is sent from a process to a message queue, the data are copied from the process virtual address space to a kernel data region. Then when another process receives this message, the kernel copies the message data from the region to the receiving process's virtual address space. Thus, message data are copied twice: From process to kernel and then to another process. Shared memory, on the other hand, does not have this data transfer overhead: Shared memory is allocated in the kernel virtual address when a process reads or writes data via a shared memory. The data is manipulated directly in the kernel memory region. However, shared memory does not provide any access control method for processes that use it. Therefore, it is a common practice to use semaphores, along with shared memory, to implement an interprocess communication media.

After a process attaches to a shared memory region, it gets a pointer to reference the shared memory. It can be used as if it was obtained via a dynamic memory allocator (i.e., *new*). The only difference is that data in a shared memory are persistent and do not go away, even if the process creating the shared memory region terminates.

There can be multiple shared memory regions existing in a given system at any one time.

10.7.1   UNIX Kernel Support for Shared Memory

In UNIX System V.3 and V.4, there is a shared memory table in the kernel address space that keeps track of all shared memory regions created in the system. Each entry of the table stores the following data for one shared memory region:

- A name that is an integer ID key assigned by the a process that created the shared memory. Other processes may specify this key to "open" the region and get a descriptor for future attachment to or detachment from the region

- The creator user and group IDs. A process whose effective user ID matches a shared memory region creator user ID may delete the region and may change control data of the region
- The assigned owner user and group IDs. These are normally the same as those of the creator user and group IDs, but a creator process can set these values to assign different owner and group membership for the region
- Read-write access permission of the region for owner, group members, and others. A process that has read permission to the region may read data from it and query the assigned user and group IDs of the region. A process that has write permission to a region may write data to it
- The size, in number of bytes, of the shared memory region
- The time when the last process attached to the region
- The time when the last process detached from the region
- The time when the last process changed control data of the region

Figure 10.5 depicts the kernel data structure for shared memory.

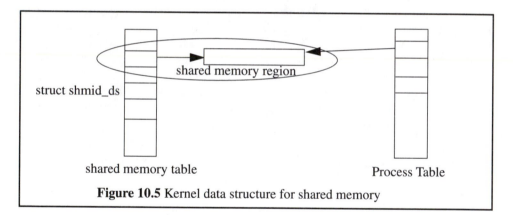

Figure 10.5 Kernel data structure for shared memory

Like messages and semaphores, shared memory is stored in kernel address space, and they are persistent, even if their creator processes no longer exist. Furthermore, each shared memory has an assigned owner, and only processes that have superuser, creator, or assigned owner privileges may delete the shared memory or change its control data.

Finally, there are several system-imposed limits on the manipulation of shared memory. These limits are defined in the <sys/shm.h> header:

System limit	Meaning
SHMMNI	The maximum number of shared memory regions that may exist at any given time in a system
SHMMIN	The minimum size, in number of bytes, of a shared memory region

System limit	Meaning
SHMMAX	The maximum size, in number of bytes, of a shared memory region

The effects of these system-imposed limits on processes are:

- If a process attempts to create a new shared memory, causing the SHMMNI limit to be exceeded, the process will be blocked until an existing region is deleted by another process
- If a process attempts to create a region whose size is less than SHMMIN or larger than SHMMAX, the system call will fail

10.7.2 The UNIX APIs for Shared Memory

The <sys/ipc.h> header defines a *struct ipc_perm* data type, which stores the owner user and group ID, creator user and group ID, assigned name key, and read-write permission of shared memory.

Each entry in the shared memory table is of type *struct shmid_ds*, which is defined in the <sys/shm.h> header. The data fields of the structure and the corresponding data it stores are:

Data field	Data Stored
shm_perm	Data stored in a *struct ipc_perm* record
shm_segsz	The shared memory region size, in number of bytes
shm_lpid	Process ID of the last process that attaches to the region
shm_cpid	Creator process ID
shm_nattch	Number of processes currently attached to the region
shm_atime	Time when the last process attached to the region
shm_dtime	Time when the last process detached from the region
shm_ctime	Time when the last process changed control data of the region

The UNIX System V shared memory APIs are:

Shared memory API	Uses
shmget	Open and create a shared memory
shmat	Attach a shared memory to a process virtual

	address space, so that the process can read and/or write data in the shared memory
shmdt	Detach a shared memory from the process virtual address space
shmctl	Query or change control data of a shared memory, or delete the memory

The header files needed for the shared memory APIs are:

```
#include <sys/types.h>
#include <sys/ipc.h>
#include <sys/shm.h>
```

10.7.3   shmget

The function prototype of the *shmget* API is:

```
#include <sys/types.h>
#include <sys/ipc.h>
#include <sys/shm.h>

int shmget ( key_t key, int size, int flag );
```

This function "opens" a shared memory whose key ID is given in the *key* argument. The function returns a nonnegative integer descriptor that can be used in other shared memory APIs.

If the value of the *key* argument is a positive integer, the API attempts to open a shared memory whose key ID matches that value. However, if the *key* value is the manifested constant IPC_PRIVATE, the API allocates a new shared memory to be used exclusively by the calling process. Specifically, the "private" shared memory is usually allocated by a parent process, which then forks one or more child processes. The parent and child processes then use the shared memory to exchange data.

The *size* argument defines the size of the shared memory region that may be attached to the calling process via the *shmat* API. If this function call creates a new shared memory, its size will be defined by the *size* argument. However, if this call "opens" a preexisting shared memory, the *size* argument may be less than or equal to the allocated size of the shared memory. In the latter case, if *size* is less than the actual size of the shared memory, the calling process can access only the first *size* bytes of the shared memory.

If the *flag* argument is zero, the API fails if there is no shared memory whose key ID matches the given *key* value. Otherwise, it returns the descriptor for that set. If a process wishes to create a new shared memory with the given *key* ID (if none preexists), then the *flag* value should be the bitwise-OR of the manifested constant IPC_CREAT and the read-write access permission for the new memory.

This function returns a positive descriptor if it succeeds or -1 if it fails.

10.7.4   shmat

The function prototype of the *shmat* API is:

```
#include <sys/types.h>
#include <sys/ipc.h>
#include <sys/shm.h>

void * shmat ( int  shmid, void* addr, int flag );
```

This function attaches a shared memory referenced by *shmid* to the calling process virtual address space. The process can then read/write data in that shared memory. Note that if this is a newly created shared memory, the kernel does not actually allocate the memory region until the first process calls this function to attach to it.

The *addr* argument specifies the desired starting virtual address in the calling process to which location the shared memory should be mapped. If this value is 0, the kernel is free to find an appropriate virtual address in the calling process to map to the shared memory. Most applications should set the *addr* value to zero, unless they explicitly store pointer or address references in the shared memory (e.g., keeping a linked list in the region). It becomes important for every process attached to the shared memory to specify the same virtual address (mapped to the shared memory).

The *flag* argument may contain the flag SHM_RND if the *addr* value is nonzero. The SHM_RND flag instructs the kernel that the virtual address specified in the *addr* argument may be rounded off to align with the page boundary. If the SHM_RND flag is not specified and the *addr* argument is not zero, the API fails (if the kernel cannot map the shared memory to the specified virtual address).

Another possible value of the *flag* argument is SHM_RDONLY, which means the calling process attaches to the shared memory for read-only. If this flag is not set, then by default the process may read and write data in the shared memory -- subject to permissions established by the creator of the shared memory region

The return value of this API is the mapped virtual address of the shared memory or -1 if it fails. Note that a process may call *shmat* multiple times to attach shared memory to multiple virtual addresses.

10.7.5 shmdt

The function prototype of the *shmdt* API is:

```
#include <sys/types.h>
#include <sys/ipc.h>
#include <sys/shm.h>

int shmdt ( void* addr );
```

This function detaches (or unmaps) shared memory from the specified *addr* virtual address of the calling process.

The *addr* value should be obtained from a *shmat* call prior to this function call.

The return value of the function is 0 if it succeeds or -1 if it fails.

The following *test_shm.C* program "opens" a shared memory with a size of 1024 bytes and the key ID value of 100. If the shared memory does not preexist, it is created by the *shmget* call, and its access permission is read-write for everyone.

After the shared memory is "opened," it is attached to the process virtual address via the *shmat* call. It then writes the message *Hello* to the beginning region of the memory and detaches from the memory. Any other process on the same system can now attach to that shared memory and read the message accordingly.

```
#include <iostream.h>
#include <stdio.h>
#include <stdlib.h>
#include <string.h>
#include <sys/stat.h>
#include <sys/ipc.h>
#include <sys/shm.h>

int main()
{
    int perms = S_IRWXU | S_IRWXG | S_IRWXO;
```

```
        int fd = shmget (100, 1024, IPC_CREAT | perms);
        if (fd==-1) perror("shmget"), exit(1);
        char* addr = (char*)shmat(fd, 0, 0);
        if (addr==(char*)-1) perror("shmat"), exit(1);
        strcpy( addr, "Hello");
        if (shmdt(addr)==-1) perror("shmdt");
        return 0;
    }
```

10.7.6 shmctl

The function prototype of the *shmctl* API is:

```
    #include <sys/types.h>
    #include <sys/ipc.h>
    #include <sys/shm.h>

    int  shmctl ( int shmid, int cmd, struct shmid_ds* buf );
```

This API can either query or change the control data of a shared memory designated by *shmid,* or delete the memory altogether.

The *shmid* value is the shared memory descriptor obtained from a *shmget* function call.

The *buf* argument is the address of a *struct shmid_ds*-type object that may be used to specify or retrieve the control data of a shared memory, as determined by the *cmd* argument. The possible values of *cmd* and their meanings are:

cmd value	Meaning
IPC_STAT	Copy control data of the shared memory to the object pointed to by *buf*. The calling process must have read permission to the set
IPC_SET	Change the control data of the shared memory by the data specified in the object pointed to by *buf*. The calling process must be the superuser, creator, or assigned owner of the shared memory to be able to perform this task. Furthermore, this API can set only the region's owner user and group IDs and access permission
IPC_RMID	Remove the shared memory from the system. The calling process must be the superuser, creator, or

assigned owner of the region to be able to perform this task. Note that if a shared memory to be removed has one or more processes attached to it, the removal operation will be delayed until these processes detach from it

SHM_LOCK   Lock the shared memory in memory. The calling process must have superuser privileges to perform this task

SHM_UNLOCK   Unlock the shared memory in memory. The calling process must have superuser privileges to perform this task

The function returns 0 if it succeeds or -1 if it fails.

The following *test_shm2.C* program "opens" a shared memory with the key ID of 100 and calls *shmctl* to retrieve the control data of the region. If both the *shmget* and *shmctl* calls are successful, the process prints to the standard output the size of the shared memory. It then sets the shared memory owner user ID as its owner user ID via another *shmctl* call. Finally, the process invokes *shmctl* again to remove the shared memory.

```cpp
#include <iostream.h>
#include <stdio.h>
#include <unistd.h>
#include <sys/ipc.h>
#include <sys/shm.h>

int main()
{
    struct shmid_ds sbuf;
    int fd = shmget (100, 1024, 0);
    if (fd>0 && shmctl(fd, IPC_STAT,&sbuf))    {
        cout << "shared memory size if: " << sbuf.shm_segsz << endl;
        sbuf.shm_perm.uid = getuid();        // change owner user ID
        if (shmctl(fd,IPC_SET,&sbuf)==-1) perror("shmctl");
    }
    else perror("shmctl");
    if (shmctl(fd,IPC_RMID,0)) perror("shmctl - IPC_RMID");
    return 0;
}
```

10.7.7   Semaphore and Shared Memory Example

This section depicts another version of the client/server application shown in Section 10.3.7. This new version uses semaphores and shared memory to implement the message queue instead of using messages. Thus, the *message.h* header needs to be changed significantly. However, the message class interface to the client and server programs, as well as the *client.C* and *server.C* modules, are exactly the same as those in Section 10.3.7. This is the benefit of C++ classes -- as long as the external interfaces of a class are unchanged, no applications that make use of that class need be modified, even if the internal implementation of the class has changed dramatically.

To implement a message queue using semaphores and shared memory, the shared memory provides a kernel memory region to store any messages sent to the queue. The semaphores control which process can access the shared memory (to read or write a message) at any one time. Specifically, there may be multiple client processes sending requests to the server process simultaneously, using the same *semop* system calls to manipulate the semaphores. The design of these *semop* calls must ensure that either they are all blocked while the server is actively accessing the shared memory or only one of the client processes is actively accessing the shared memory (all the other client processes and the server process are blocked). To meet these objective, two semaphores will be used. The assignment of these semaphore values, for various purposes, are:

Semaphore 0	Semaphore 1	Usage
0	1	Server is waiting for a client to send message
1	0	Client's message is ready for server to read
1	1	Server's response data are ready for a client

The interaction of client processes and the server process to the semaphore set is:

- The server initially creates the semaphore set and a shared memory. It initializes the semaphore set value to be 0, 1 (i.e., the first semaphore value is zero and the second semaphore's value is one)
- The server waits for a client to send a request to the shared memory by performing a *semop* call on the semaphore set with the supplied values of -1, 0. This blocks the server, as the current value of the set is 0,1 and none of the semaphores in the set can be changed by the *semop* call
- When one or more clients attempt to send a message to the shared memory, they all perform a *semop* call with the supplied values 0,-1. One of them will succeed, as the set value is 0,1 at that moment. However, as soon as a client process succeeds in its *semop* call, it immediately changes values to 0,0. This blocks all other clients that are performing the semop call of 0, -1 and continues blocking the server performing the *semop* call of -1,0
- The client process that succeeds in changing the semaphore set value can now write

a service request command and its PID to the shared memory. After it is done, it will perform a *semop* call with the value of 1,0. This unblocks the server process from its *semop* call, but the new value continues to block other client processes that are doing the *semop* call of 0,-1. If the service request command is not QUIT_CMD, the client process will perform *semop* call with the values of -1,-1 and block the client

- Once the server is unblocked it will read the client service request from the shared memory. If the command is QUIT_CMD, it will deallocate the shared memory and semaphore set, then terminate itself. However, if the command is not QUIT_CMD, the server writes the response data to the shared memory, then performs the *semop* call with the values of 1,1. This will unblock the client process that is performing the *semop* call of -1,-1. Other client processes which are performing the *semop* call of 0,-1 are still blocked by the new semaphore values. After the *semop* call, the server will go back to the state of (b) (to wait for a service request from a new client)

- The client that is unblocked by the server sets the semaphore set value to 0,0 and reads the server's response data. It prints the data to the standard output and then sets the semaphore values to 0,1 before it terminates itself. The last *semop* call sets the system back to the state of (c) above, and one of the clients will be unblocked and start interacting with the server via the shared memory and semaphores

The semaphore value transition, in the different stages of a client/server interaction, is shown in Figure 10.6 (the semaphore values are shown inside the ovals):

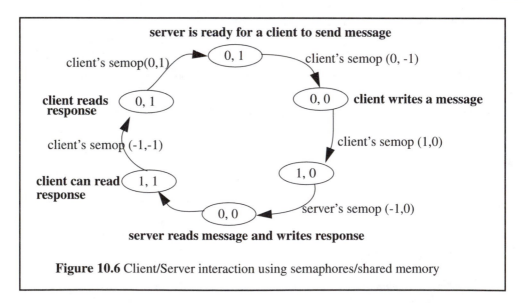

Figure 10.6 Client/Server interaction using semaphores/shared memory

The *message.h* header described in Section 10.3.7 is modified to use shared memory and semaphores instead of the message queue. The new message class is declared in the following *message3.h* header:

```
#ifndef MESSAGE3_H
#define MESSAGE3_H
#include <strstream.h>
#include <stdio.h>
#include <stdlib.h>
#include <memory.h>
#include <unistd.h>
#include <sys/ipc.h>
#include <sys/shm.h>
#include <sys/sem.h>
#include <sys/wait.h>
#include <sys/errno.h>

/* common declarations for daemon/server process */
enum { MSGKEY=186, MAX_LEN=256, SHMSIZE=1024, SEMSIZE=2 };
enum { LOCAL_TIME = 1, UTC_TIME = 2, QUIT_CMD = 3,
          ILLEGAL_CMD = 4, SEM_RD = 0, SEM_WR=1 };

struct mgbuf
{
   long     mtype;
   char     mtext[MAX_LEN];
};

class message
{
   private:
      int    shmId, semId;
      struct mgbuf *msgPtr;
      enum ipc_op {  RESET_SEM, CLIENT_GET_MEM,
                     CLIENT_SND_REQ, SERVER_RCV_REQ,
                     SERVER_GET_MEM, SERVER_SND_RPY,
                     CLIENT_RCV_RPY
                  };
   public:

      /* try to change semaphores' values */
      void getsem( enum ipc_op  opType )
      {
         static struct sembuf  args[2] = { {SEM_RD}, {SEM_WR} };
         switch (opType)     {
           case SERVER_GET_MEM:
                 return;
           case CLIENT_GET_MEM:
                 args[SEM_RD].sem_op = 0,
                 args[SEM_WR].sem_op = -1;
```

```
                break;
        case CLIENT_SND_REQ:
                args[SEM_RD].sem_op = 1,
                args[SEM_WR].sem_op = 0;
                break;
        case SERVER_RCV_REQ:
                args[SEM_RD].sem_op = -1,
                args[SEM_WR].sem_op = 0;
                break;
        case SERVER_SND_RPY:
                args[SEM_RD].sem_op = 1,
                args[SEM_WR].sem_op = 1;
                break;
        case CLIENT_RCV_RPY:
                args[SEM_RD].sem_op = -1,
                args[SEM_WR].sem_op = -1;
                break;
        case RESET_SEM:
                args[SEM_RD].sem_op = 0,
                args[SEM_WR].sem_op = 1;
    }
    if (semop(semId,args,SEMSIZE)==-1) perror("semop");
};

/* constructor function */
message( int key )
{
    if ((shmId=shmget(key, SHMSIZE, 0))==-1) {
        if (errno==ENOENT) {    // create a brand new message object
            if ((shmId= shmget(key, SHMSIZE, IPC_CREAT|0666)) ==-1)
                perror("shmget");
            else if ((semId=semget(key, SEMSIZE, IPC_CREAT|0666))
                        ==-1)
                perror("semget");
            else getsem(RESET_SEM);  // initialize a new semaphore set
        }
        else perror("shmget");
    }
    else if ((semId=semget(key,0,0))==-1)  /* get existing semaphores */
        perror("semget");

    if (shmId>=0 && !(msgPtr=(struct mgbuf*)shmat(shmId,0,0)))
        perror("shmat");
};
```

```
/* destructor function */
~message() {};

/* check message queue open status */
int good() { return (shmId >= 0 && semId>=0) ? 1 : 0; };

/* remove message queue */
int rmQ()
{
    if (shmdt((char*)msgPtr)<0) perror("semdt");
    if (!semctl(semId,0,IPC_RMID,0) && !shmctl(shmId,IPC_RMID,0))
        return 0;
    perror("shmctl or semctl");
    return -1;
};

/* send a message */
int send( const void* buf, int size, int type)
{
    int server = (type > 99);
    getsem(server ? SERVER_GET_MEM : CLIENT_GET_MEM);
    memcpy(msgPtr->mtext,buf,size);
    msgPtr->mtext[size] = '\0';
    msgPtr->mtype = type;
    getsem(server ? SERVER_SND_RPY : CLIENT_SND_REQ);
    return 0;
};

/* receive a message */
int rcv( void* buf, int size, int type, int* rtype)
{
    int server = (type < 0);
    getsem(server ? SERVER_RCV_REQ : CLIENT_RCV_RPY);
    memcpy(buf,msgPtr->mtext,strlen(msgPtr->mtext)+1);
    if (rtype) *rtype = msgPtr->mtype;
    if (!server) getsem(RESET_SEM);
    return strlen(msgPtr->mtext);
};
};  /* message */

#endif
```

In the new *message.h* header, *getsem* is a utility function that performs *semop* on a semaphore set based on the actual *opType* argument values (as assigned by either a server or a client process).

The *message* constructor function "opens" a shared memory and semaphore set with two elements. These two objects have the same key ID. If the semaphore set is a brand new object, it will be initialized to the initial values of 0, 1. This signifies that the first semaphore value is zero and the second semaphore value is 1.

The *send* function "sends" a message to the shared memory. Because the *semop* operations is different between a server and a client process, the function uses the *type* argument value to identify whether the calling process is a server or a client. If the *type* argument value is greater than 99, the function is called by a client process. Otherwise, it is called by a server process. The function blocks the *getsem* call until the process can complete its *semop* operation. After that it writes a message to the shared memory and calls *getsem* again to set semaphore values that unblock its counterpart process.

The *read* function works similarly: The *semop* operations which read a message from the shared memory are different between a server and a client process. Thus, it uses the *type* argument value to identify the calling process: If the *type* argument value is less than zero (actual is -99), the caller is a server process (otherwise, it is a client process). The function blocks the *getsem* call until the process can complete its *semop* operation. After that it reads a message from the shared memory and resets the semaphores to the initial values 0,1 (if the process is a client).

The *rmQ* function is called when a server process receives the QUIT_CMD from a client process. The function invokes the *semctl* and *shmctl* APIs to delete the semaphore set and the shared memory, respectively then to terminate the server process. This is necessary as semaphores and shared memory are persistent objects in kernel space, even after those processes that created them are terminated.

The output of the new server and client processes using the new *message.h* is similar to the one using messages, as seen in Section 10.3.7:

```
ch13 % mserver &
[1] 337
ch13 % server: start executing...
ch13 % mclient
client: start executing...
cmd> 1
server: receive cmd #1, from client: 338
client: 338  Thu Jan 26 21:50:59 1995
cmd> 2
server: receive cmd #2, from client: 338
client: 338  Fri Jan 27 05:51:01 1995
cmd> 4
```

server: receive cmd #4, from client: 338

client: 338 Illegal cmd: 4

cmd> 3

client: 338 exiting...

server: receive cmd #3, from client: 338

server: deleting msg queue...

[1]   Done   mserver

10.8   Memory Mapped I/O

Mmap is a creation of BSD UNIX. It allows a process to map its virtual address space directly to a file object memory page in a kernel space. The process can read and write data with the file object directly via the mapped memory. Furthermore, if more than one process maps to the same file object simultaneously, they share a mapped memory region. They can communicate with each other in a manner similar to that of using a shared memory.

Mmap differs from the regular UNIX file APIs in that after a file is opened for access (a process calls *read* to read data from the file), the kernel fetches one or more pages of the requested data from the file's hard disk storage. The data is then put into a kernel memory region and then copied into a buffer in the calling process's virtual address. The reverse situation applies to the *write* API: when a process calls *write* to write data to a file, the kernel copies the data from the process buffer into a kernel memory region. When the memory region is filled or the process requests to flush the buffer, the data are copied to the file's hard disk.

However, if the same process uses *mmap* instead, the kernel still fetches one or more pages of file data from its hard disk storage and puts them into a kernel memory region. In this case the process can directly access data in the memory region by referencing the virtual addresses mapped to the region. Thus, *mmap* is more efficient in manipulating file data. Any data written to a mapped region are stored in its corresponding file object automatically.

One application of *mmap* is to develop programs that can resume execution after being previously terminated. For example, a database management program can use *mmap* to map its virtual address to a database file, and all the data it manipulates are stored in the mapped region. When the process is terminated, the data are stored in the database file automatically. When its program is executed again, the new process maps to the database file and all previously written data are readily available for further use.

Another use of *mmap* is to emulate the shared memory function. Specifically, two or more processes that wish to perform interprocess communication can use *mmap* to map to the same file object. They can then read and write data to each other via their mapped virtual addresses. A later section will show how to use *mmap* to reimplement the client/server application, as depicted in the previous section.

10.8.1   Memory mapped I/O APIs

The <sys/mman.h> header declares all the *mmap* APIs:

API	Meaning
mmap	Maps a process virtual address space to a file object
munmap	Disassociates a process virtual address from a file object
msync	Synchronizes mapped memory region data with its corresponding file object data on a hard disk.

10.8.2   mmap

The function prototype of the *mmap* API is:

```
#include <sys/types.h>
#include <sys/mman.h>

caddr_t    mmap ( caddr_t addr, int size, int prot, int flags, int fd, off_t pos );
```

This function maps a file object designated by *fd* to the virtual address of a process starting at *addr*. If the *addr* value is zero, the kernel assigns a virtual address to map. The *pos* argument specifies the starting location in the file object that is mapped to *addr*. Its value should be either zero or a multiple of the memory page size (use the *getpagesize* or *sysconf* API to get the system memory page size value). The *prot* argument specifies the access permission of the mapped memory. Its possible values and meanings are:

prot value	Meaning
PROT_READ	The mapped region can be read
PROT_WRITE	The mapped region can be written
PROT_EXEC	The mapped region can be executed

The *flags* argument specifies mapping options. Its possible values and meanings are:

flags value	Meaning
MAP_SHARED	Data written to the mapped region are visible to other processes that are mapped to the same file object

MAP_PRIVATE	Data written to the mapped region are not visible to other processes that are mapped to the same file object
MAP_FIXED	The *addr* value must be the starting virtual address of the mapped region. The function fails if this cannot be accomplished. If this flag is not specified or if the MAP_VARIABLE flag is defined and specified by a system, the kernel can select a different virtual address than *addr* for the mapped region

The return value of the function is the actual virtual address where the mapped region starts or MAP_FAILED if the function fails.

The PROT_EXEC flag is used when the file object to be mapped is an executable file and the calling process has the superuser privilege. When a user invokes a command in a UNIX system, it is common for the kernel to perform a *mmap* of the command's executable file. This executes the instruction code of the program directly from the file's mapped memory.

The MAP_PRIVATE flag specifies that any data written to a mapped memory are not visible to other processes mapped to the same file object. However, this also disables written data in the mapped memory from being stored back into the object's disk file. Furthermore, suppose processes *A* and *B* both map to a file called *FOO*; process *A* specifies MAP_PRIVATE and *B* specifies MAP_SHARED. If process B writes data to the mapped memory before *A* does, the new data are seen by both processes. However, once *A* writes data to the shared memory, the kernel creates a private copy of the memory pages that *A* has modified, while *B* is still using the old page. From that point onward, any data written by *A* or *B* to their respective memory pages are not visible to each other.

MAP_PRIVATE is used by a debugger process to *mmap* a program for execution. The debugger often writes user-defined breakpoints to the instruction code of the debugged process. Those breakpoints should not be reflected in the executable file of the debugged program, nor should they be seen by other processes that are also mapping the same program.

Before a process can call *mmap* to map a file object, it must call the *open* API and assign the file descriptor to the *fd* argument. Furthermore, if the file object is newly created by the *open* call, the process should write at least *size* bytes of data to initialize the file. This is done because *mmap* does not allocate any memory region. It simply marks that the process's virtual address (from *addr* to *addr+size)* is legal to use. If the file size is less than that, there is no memory allocated by the kernel beyond the memory page that contains the virtual address *addr+<file_size>*. If the process attempts to access data anywhere between *addr+<file_size>* and *addr+size*, it may receive a SIGBUS signal.

The following *test_mmap.C* program "opens" a new file called FOO and initializes its size to SHMSIZE byte (with the data of "\0"). It then closes the file descriptor *fd*, as it is no longer needed. Finally, the process writes the string *Hello* to the mapped region and then terminates itself. If a user looks at the content of the file via the *cat* command, he or she would notice that the file contains the string *Hello*.

```
#include <strstream.h>
#include <stdio.h>
#include <stdlib.h>
#include <unistd.h>
#include <sys/types.h>
#include <sys/mman.h>
const int SHMSIZE = 1024;

int main()
{
    int ch='\0', fd = open ("FOO", O_CREAT | O_EXCL,0666);
    if (fd==-1) {
            perror("file exists"), exit(1);
    };
    for (int i=0; i < SHMSIZE; i++)              /* Initialize the file */
            write(fd, &ch, 1);
    caddr_t memP=mmap(0,SHMSIZE,PROT_READ|PROT_WRITE,
                        MAP_SHARED, fd, 0);
    if (memP==MAP_FAILED)    {
            perror("mmap");
            exit(2);
    }
    close(fd);                                  /* don't need this anymore */
    ostrstream(memP, SHMSIZE) << "Hello UNIX\n";
}
```

10.8.3 munmap

The function prototype of the *munmap* API is:

```
#include <sys/types.h>
#include <sys/mmap.h>

int      munmap ( caddr_t  addr, int size );
```

This function disassociates a mapped region from the process virtual address. The unmapped region starts at the *addr* virtual address and extends up to the memory page that contains the *addr+size* virtual address.

The function returns 0 if it succeeds or -1 if it fails.

10.8.4   msync

The function prototype of the *msync* API is:

```
#include <sys/types.h>
#include <sys/mmap.h>

int      msync ( caddr_t  addr, int size, int flags );
```

This function synchronizes data in a mapped region with its corresponding file object data on the hard disk. If *size* is 0, all modified pages in the region that contain *addr* are synchronized. If *size* is greater than 0, only the pages containing *addr* to *addr+size* are synchronized.

The *flags* argument specifies the synchronization method. Its possible values and meanings are:

flags value	Meaning
MS_SYNC	Flush data from mapped region to hard disk. Wait for data transfer to complete
MS_ASYNC	Flush data from mapped region to hard disk. Do not wait for the data transfer to complete
MS_INVALIDATE	Invalidate the data in the mapped region. Next reference to the region will cause new pages to be fetched from the hard disk.

The function returns 0 if it succeeds or -1 if it fails.

10.8.5   Client/Server Program Using Mmap

The client/server example, as depicted in Section 10.7.7, can be changed easily to use *mmap* instead of shared memory. Once again, the only changes required are in the *message.h* header. The *client.C* and *server.C* modules are unchanged, as shown in Section 10.3.7.

The new *message4.h* header which uses *semaphores* and *mmap* is as follows:

```
#ifndef MESSAGE4_H
#define MESSAGE4_H

#include <strstream.h>
#include <stdio.h>
#include <stdlib.h>
#include <string.h>
#include <fcntl.h>
#include <memory.h>
#include <unistd.h>
#include <sys/types.h>
#include <sys/ipc.h>
#include <sys/mman.h>
#include <sys/sem.h>
#include <sys/wait.h>
#include <sys/errno.h>
/* common declarations for daemon/server process */
enum { MSGKEY=186, MAX_LEN=256, SHMSIZE=1024, SEMSIZE=2 };
enum { LOCAL_TIME = 1, UTC_TIME = 2, QUIT_CMD = 3,
        ILLEGAL_CMD = 4, SEM_RD = 0, SEM_WR=1 };
struct mgbuf
{
    long     mtype;
    char     mtext[MAX_LEN];
};

class message
{
    private:
        int             semId;
        struct mgbuf  *msgPtr;
        enum ipc_op { RESET_SEM, CLIENT_GET_MEM,
                      CLIENT_SND_REQ, SERVER_RCV_REQ,
                      SERVER_GET_MEM, SERVER_SND_RPY,
                      CLIENT_RCV_RPY };
    public:
```

```
/* try to change semaphores' values */
void getsem( enum ipc_op  opType )
{
    static struct sembuf  args[2] = { {SEM_RD}, {SEM_WR} };
    switch (opType)     {
      case SERVER_GET_MEM:
            return;
      case CLIENT_GET_MEM:
            args[SEM_RD].sem_op = 0,
            args[SEM_WR].sem_op = -1;
            break;
      case CLIENT_SND_REQ:
            args[SEM_RD].sem_op = 1,
            args[SEM_WR].sem_op = 0;
            break;
      case SERVER_RCV_REQ:
            args[SEM_RD].sem_op = -1,
            args[SEM_WR].sem_op = 0;
            break;
      case SERVER_SND_RPY:
            args[SEM_RD].sem_op = 1,
            args[SEM_WR].sem_op = 1;
            break;
      case CLIENT_RCV_RPY:
            args[SEM_RD].sem_op = -1,
            args[SEM_WR].sem_op = -1;
            break;
      case RESET_SEM:
            args[SEM_RD].sem_op = 0,
            args[SEM_WR].sem_op = 1;
    }
    if (semop(semId,args,SEMSIZE)==-1) perror("semop");
};

/* constructor function */
message( int key )
{
    char mfile[256], fillchr='\0';
    ostrstream(mfile,sizeof mfile) << "FOO" << key << '\0';
    int fd =open(mfile,O_RDWR,0);
    if (fd==-1) {          /* a new file */
      if ((fd=open(mfile,O_RDWR|O_CREAT|O_TRUNC,0777))==-1)
          perror("open");
      else     {
```

```
                /* zero fill the file for mmap to work.
                   This is system dependent */
                for (int i=0; i < SHMSIZE; i++) write(fd, &fillchr, 1);
                if ((semId=semget(key, SEMSIZE, IPC_CREAT|0666))==-1)
                    perror("semget");
                else getsem(RESET_SEM);  // initialize a new semaphore set
            }
        }
        else {                    /* connect to an existing entry */
            if ((semId=semget(key, 0, 0))==-1) perror("semget");
                if ((msgPtr=(struct mgbuf*)mmap(0, SHMSIZE, PROT_READ |
                    PROT_WRITE, MAP_SHARED, fd,0))== MAP_FAILED)
                    perror("mmap");
                else close(fd);
        }
    };

    /* destructor function */
    ~message() {};

    /* check message queue creation status */
    int good() { return (semId>=0) ? 1 : 0; };

    /* remove message queue */
    int rmQ()
    {
        if (!semctl(semId,0,IPC_RMID,0) &&
                        !munmap((caddr_t)msgPtr,SHMSIZE))
            return 0;
        perror("shmctl or semctl");
        return -1;
    };

    /* send a message */
    int send( const void* buf, int size, int type)
    {
        int server = (type > 99);
        getsem(server ? SERVER_GET_MEM : CLIENT_GET_MEM);
        memcpy(msgPtr->mtext,buf,size);
        msgPtr->mtext[size] = '\0';
        msgPtr->mtype = type;
        getsem(server ? SERVER_SND_RPY : CLIENT_SND_REQ);
```

```
            return 0;
        };

        /* receive a message */
        int rcv( void* buf, int size, int type, int* rtype)
        {
            int server = (type < 0);
            getsem(server ? SERVER_RCV_REQ : CLIENT_RCV_RPY);
            memcpy(buf,msgPtr->mtext,strlen(msgPtr->mtext)+1);
            if (rtype) *rtype = msgPtr->mtype;
            if (!server) getsem(RESET_SEM);
            return strlen(msgPtr->mtext);
        };
    }; /* message */
    #endif      /* MESSAGE4_H */
```

The changes in the new *message.h* header are in the *message* constructor, where the *mmap* call replaces the *shmget* call. The map file name is constructed with a file name prefix of *FOO* (this is chosen arbitrarily) and followed by the given key ID. Note that if the file is newly created, it is initialized with SHMSIZE bytes of NULL characters. This is to ensure that the entire mapped memory region is allocated by the kernel to hold valid data.

Another change in the *message.h* header is in the *rmQ* function. This function is called when a server process is terminating and needs to delete its semaphore set and detach from the mapped memory.

The rest of the *message.h* code is the same as that in Section 10.7.7. The output of the new client/server program is similar to that in Section 10.7.7 also.

10.9   POSIX.1b Shared Memory

The POSIX.1b shared memory APIs are:

```
    #include <sys/mman.h>

    int        shm_open( char* name, int flags, mode_t mode );
    int        shm_unlink ( char* name );
```

The *shm_open* function creates a shared memory region whose name is given by the *name* argument. The syntax of the *name* argument value is the same as that for POSIX.1b messages. The *flags* argument contains the memory access flags (O_RDWR, O_RDONLY, or O_WRONLY) and any O_CREAT and O_EXCL flags. The *mode* argument is used if a new shared memory is created by this call. Its value is the read-write access permission (for user, group, and others) assigned to the new shared memory.

The function returns a -1 if it fails, or a nonnegative handle if it succeeds.

Note that unlike the System V *shmget* API, the *shm_open* API does not specify the size of the shared memory region, which is defined in a subsequent *ftruncate* call. The *ftruncate* function prototype is:

```
int     ftruncate ( int fd, off_t shared_memory_size );
```

where the *fd* argument value is a shared memory handle, as returned by a *shm_open* call. The *shared_memory_size* argument contains the size of the shared memory region to be allocated. Once a shared memory is allocated and its size defined, the *mmap* function should be called. This maps the shared memory region to the virtual address space of the calling process.

After a process finishes using a shared memory, it calls the *munmap* function to unmap the shared memory from its virtual address space. Then the *shm_unlink* function may be called to remove the shared memory from the system. The argument to the *shm_unlink* function is a UNIX path name for a shared memory region.

The following *test_shmp.C* program "opens" a read-write-accessible shared memory with the name */shm.0,* via the *shm_open* call and sets its size with the *ftruncate* function call. The shared memory is mapped to the process's virtual address space via the *mmap* call. The *memp* variable holds the starting address of the shared memory.

Once the shared memory is set up in the process, the *sem_init* function is called to create a semaphore at the beginning address of the shared memory. The process works with the semaphore and shared memory. After the process is done, it calls the *sem_destroy* function to remove the semaphore from the system. It finally calls the *shm_unlink* and *shm_unmap* functions to remove the shared memory from the system and to unmap the shared memory from the virtual address.

```
#include <stdio.h>
#include <unistd.h>
#include <errno.h>
#include <sys/stat.h>
#include <semaphore.h>
#include <sys/mman.h>
```

```
    int main()
    {
        long siz = sizeof(sem_t) + 1024;
        int shmfd = shm_open ("/shm.0", O_CREAT|O_RDWR, S_IRWXU);

        if (shmfd==-1)      { perror("shm_open"); return 1; }
        if (ftruncate(shmfd, siz)==-1)
                            { perror("ftruncate"); return 2; }

        char* memp = (char*)mmap(0, siz, PROT_READ |PROT_WRITE,
                                    MAP_SHARED, shmfd, 0L);
        if (!memp)          { perror("mmap"); return 3; }

        (void)close(shmfd);
        if (sem_init((sem_t*)memp,1,1) < 0) { perror("sem_init"); return 4; }
        /* do work with the shared memory and semaphore */
        if (sem_destroy((sem_t*)memp) < 0) { perror("sem_destroy"); return 5; }
        if (shm_unlink("/shm.0") < 0) { perror("shm_unlink"); return 6; }
        return shm_unmap( memp, sizeof(sem_t) + 1024);
    }
```

10.9.1 POSIX.1b Shared Memory and Semaphore Example

The client/server example depicted in Section 10.7.7 is rewritten using POSIX.1b shared memory and semaphore. Once again, the only changes required are in the *message.h* header. The *client.C* and *server.C* modules are unchanged, as shown in Section 10.3.7.

The new *messag5.h* header that contains a message class based on POSIX.1b shared memory and semaphore is:

```
    #ifndef MESSAGE5_H
    #define MESSAGE5_H

    /* specify the following source code is POSIX.1b compliant */
    #define   _POSIX_C_SOURCE        199309L
    #include <strstream.h>
    #include <stdio.h>
```

```
#include <memory.h>
#include <unistd.h>
#include <string.h>
#include <limits.h>
#include <sys/stat.h>
#include <semaphore.h>
#include <sys/mman.h>

/* common declarations for daemon/server process */
enum { MSGKEY=186, MAX_LEN=256, MAX_MSG=20 };
enum { LOCAL_TIME=1, UTC_TIME=2, QUIT_CMD=3
                                      , ILLEGAL_CMD=4 };
/* data record for one message */
struct mgbuf
{
    long          mtype;                    // msg type
    char          mtext[MAX_LEN];           // msg text
};

/* data record for one shared memory region */
struct shm_header
{
    sem_t         semaphore;                // semaphore
    struct  mgbuf     msgList[MAX_MSG];      // msg. list
};

/* message class */
class message
{
  private:
    struct shm_header    *memptr;
    sem_t                *sem_id;
    char                 mfile[256];
    enum ipc_op { GET_MEM, SND_RPY, RCV_REQ, RESET_SEM };
  public:
    /* constructor function */
    message( int key )
    {
       /* create a shared memory region */
```

```
ostrstream(mfile,sizeof mfile) << "FOO" << key << '\0';
int fd = shm_open(mfile, O_CREATIO_RDWR,
                        S_IRWXUIS_IRWXGIS_IRWXO);
if (fd==-1) { perror("shm_open"); return; }
(void)ftruncate(fd,sizeof(struct shm_header));

/* map shared memory to a process address space */
if ((memptr=(struct shm_header*)mmap(0,
                    sizeof(struct shm_header),
        PROT_READ | PROT_WRITE, MAP_SHARED, fd, 0))
        == MAP_FAILED)        {
    perror("mmap");
    return;
}

close(fd);

/* create a semaphore in the shared memory region */
sem_id = (sem_t*)&memptr->semaphore;
if ((sem_init(sem_id, 1, 1))==-1) perror("sem_init");

/* initialize msg list to be empty */
for (int i=0; i < MAX_MSG; i++)
    memptr->msgList[i].mtype = INT_MIN;
};

/* destructor function: unmap shared memory from process */
~message() { munmap(memptr, sizeof(struct shm_header)); };

/* check share memory creation status */
int good() { return (memptr) ? 1 : 0; };

/* remove shared memory and semaphore */
int rmQ()
{
    if (sem_destroy(sem_id)==-1) perror("sem_destroy");
    if (shm_unlink(mfile)==-1) perror("shm_unlink");
    return munmap(memptr, sizeof(struct shm_header));
};
```

```
                /* try to change semaphore's value */
                void getsem( enum ipc_op  opType )
                {
                   switch (opType)     {
                      case GET_MEM:
                      case RCV_REQ:
                          if (sem_wait(sem_id)==-1) perror("sem_wait");
                          break;
                      case SND_RPY:
                      case RESET_SEM:
                          if (sem_post(sem_id)==-1) perror("sem_post");
                          break;
                   }
                };  /* getsem */

                /* send a message to message queue*/
                int send( const void* buf, int size, int type)
                {
                   getsem(GET_MEM);                        // acquire semaphore
                   for (int i=0; i < MAX_MSG; i++)
                     if (memptr->msgList[i].mtype==INT_MIN)   {
                          /* find an empty slot in message queue to store msg */
                          memcpy(memptr->msgList[i].mtext, buf, size);
                          memptr->msgList[i].mtext[size] = '\0';
                          memptr->msgList[i].mtype      = type;
                          break;
                     }
                   if (i >= MAX_MSG)    {                  // msg queue is full
                     cerr <<  "Too many messages in the queue!\n";
                     return -1;                            // return failure
                   }
                   getsem(SND_RPY);                        // release semaphore
                   return 0;                               // return OK
                };  /* send */

                /* receive a message */
                int rcv( void* buf, int size, int type, int* rtype)
                {
                   do  {
```

```
            getsem(RCV_REQ);                        // acquire semaphore
            int lowest_type = -1;
            for (int i=0; i < MAX_MSG; i++)      {
                if (memptr->msgList[i].mtype==INT_MIN) continue;

                /* done if type==0 or type matches msg. type */
                if (!type || type==memptr->msgList[i].mtype) break;

                /* if type < 0 find the lowest msg type < type */
                if (type < 0 && -type >= memptr->msgList[i].mtype)
                    if (lowest_type==-1 || (memptr->msgList[i].mtype <
                                    memptr->msgList[lowest_type].mtype))
                        lowest_type = i;
            }
            if (i < MAX_MSG || lowest_type !=-1) {        // found one msg
                if (lowest_type!=-1) i = lowest_type;
                /* copy msg text and type to caller's variables */
                memcpy(buf,memptr->msgList[i].mtext,
                                strlen(memptr->msgList[i].mtext)+1);
                if (rtype) *rtype = memptr->msgList[i].mtype;
                /* mark queue slot as empty */
                memptr->msgList[i].mtype = INT_MIN;
                getsem(RESET_SEM);                  // release semaphore
                return strlen((char*)buf);          // return msg. size
            }
            getsem(RESET_SEM);                       // release semaphore
            sleep(1);                                // sleep for 1 second
        } while(1);                                  // check queue again
    };  /* rcv */
};  /* message */
#endif      /* MESSAGE5_H */
```

The new message class is different from that of Section 10.7.7. This is because the POSIX.1b semaphores are counting semaphores, and each semaphore value can be changed by 1 each time. Conversely, System V semaphore values can be altered by any integral value at a time. With this limitation, the new message class does not support a server and client engaging in private communication while other client processes are blocked by their *semop* call. This results in a new message class whose code is simpler: Each *send* or *receive* request is preceded by a *sem_wait* call to acquire a shared semaphore. The call is finished by a *sem_post* call which releases the acquired semaphore to unblock other processes (server or client) seeking access to the message queue. Furthermore, the message class now more truly implements System V and POSIX.1b message behavior.

The constructor function of the message class gets an integer key as argument and composes a textual name for the shared memory to be allocated. The shared memory is allocated via the *shm_open* call. It is read-write by the process, and the access permission assigned to user, group, and others is read-write-execute (in case this memory does not exist before the call).

Once a shared memory is allocated, its size is set to the size of the *struct shm_header* via the *ftruncate* call. The *struct shm_header* defines all the data fields for one shared memory region -- a shared semaphore variable and a list of message records to store server and client messages.

The shared memory region is mapped to the process virtual address space via *mmap*. The starting address of the mapped memory is determined by the kernel. After the *mmap* call, the file descriptor returned by the *shm_open* call is closed (it is no longer needed). Next, a semaphore is created via the *sem_open* call. The new semaphore is put at the starting address of the shared memory region designated as accessible by multiple processes, and its initial value is set to 1.

Finally, the message list is initialized by setting the message type of each message record in the list to INT_MIN (a large negative number) to indicate that they are unused.

When a message is sent to the message queue via the *message::send* function, the semaphore is first acquired via the *message::getsem* call (which, in turn, calls *sem_wait*). After this call, the process has acquired the semaphore and is allowed to access the message list in the queue. It scans every entry of the message list until it finds the first unused message record (whose message type is INT_MIN). It stores the message data (message text and type) in that record. When this is done, the process releases the semaphore via another *message::getsem* call (which, in turn, calls *sem_post*).

When a process tries to receive a message from the message queue via the *message::rcv* function, the semaphore is first acquired via the *message::getsem* call (which calls *sem_wait*). After this call, the process acquires the semaphore and is allowed to access the message list in the queue. It scans every entry of the message list until it finds a record whose type matches the message type specified by the calling process. It copies that record's message text and type to the input arguments of the function and releases the semaphore (via the *message::getsem* call). Finally, the function returns the message length to the caller. However, if no message in the queue matches the message type specified by a calling process, the function releases the semaphore, puts the process to sleep for 1 second, then repeats the entire message retrieval process. This is to block the calling process until a message arrives at the queue that satisfies process search criteria.

The *message::rmQ* function is called to destroy the shared memory and the semaphore. This is accomplished by calling *sem_destroy* to destroy the semaphore, *shm_unlink* to destroy the shared memory from the system, and finally, *munmap* to unmap the shared memory from the process virtual address space.

The new *message.h* header can be compiled with the client and server programs as shown in Section 10.3.7. The output of the new programs should be the same as that depicted in the Section 10.3.7.

10.10   Summary

This chapter examines UNIX System V.3, V.4, and POSIX.1b interprocess communication methods: messages, semaphores, shared memory, and *mmap*. The syntax of these APIs is explained in detail. Example programs that illustrate their use were also presented. A common drawback of these IPC methods is that there are no standards defined for their use be in intermachine communication. The next chapter will look at the BSD UNIX socket and UNIX System V.3 and V.4 Transport Level Interface (TLI) interprocess communication methods. Sockets and TLI can be used by processes running on different machines or on the same machine to communicate with each other.

Sockets and TLI

The previous chapter examined UNIX System V IPC methods using messages, shared memory, and semaphores. These methods are useful for processes communicating on the same machine, but they do not support processes running on different machines to communicate. The primary reason for this drawback is that message queues, shared memory regions and semaphore sets are identified by integer keys. These are guaranteed to be unique only on individual machines, not across multiple machines. Thus it is impossible for a process running on computer *A* to reference a message queue on machine *B* merely by using the message queue key. POSIX.1b IPC methods eliminate this problem by using textual names for their messages, semaphores, and shared memory. This standard leaves it up to computer vendors to define and interpret these names for IPC to work across their machines.

To support IPC over a local area network (LAN), BSD UNIX 4.2 developed sockets which provide protocol-independent network interface services. Specifically, sockets can run on either TCP (Transport Connect Protocol) or UDP (User Datagram Protocol). A socket can be addressed by a host Internet address and a port number. The address is guaranteed to be unique on the entire Internet, as each machine has an unique address and port number. Thus, two processes running on separate machines may communicate via sockets.

Since the introduction, sockets have been widely used in many network-based applications. Sockets are now available in BSD UNIX 4.3, 4.4, and even on UNIX System V.4. However, the implementation of sockets in UNIX System V.4 has some subtle differences from that of BSD UNIX. They are explained in later sections.

Transport Level Interface (TLI) was developed in UNIX System V.3. It was System V's answer to BSD UNIX sockets. Its use and APIs are similar to those of sockets. Furthermore, since TLI was developed based on STREAMS, it supports most transport protocols and is more flexible than sockets. TLI is available on both UNIX System V.3 and V4. Moreover, TLI is called XTI (X/Open Transport Interface) in the X/Open standard.

The following sections examine sockets and TLI APIs and show examples of socket-based and TLI-based applications. Note that sockets and TLI are not defined in POSIX.

11.1   Sockets

Sockets may be *connection-based* (i.e., sender and receiver socket addresses are pre-established before messages are passed between them) or *connectionless* (sender or receiver addresses must be passed along with each message sent from one process to another). There are different socket address formats, depending on the sockets' assigned domain. A domain defines the socket address format and the underlying transport protocol to be used. The common domains assigned to sockets are AF_UNIX (address format is a UNIX path name) and AF_INET (address format is the host name and port number).

Each socket has an assigned type, which determines the manner in which data is transmitted between two sockets. If a socket type is *virtual circuit*, data are transmitted sequentially in a reliable fashion and are nonduplicated. If a socket type is *datagram*, data are transmitted in a nonsequenced and unreliable fashion. Connection-based socket type is usually virtual circuit, whereas connectionless socket type is usually datagram. Datagram sockets are generally faster than are virtual circuit sockets and are used in applications where speed is more important than reliability.

Each socket type supports one or more transport protocols, but there is always a default protocol specified for each socket type on a given UNIX system. The virtual circuit default protocol is TCP and the datagram default protocol is UDP.

Sockets that are used to communicate with each other must be of the same type and belong to the same domain. Furthermore, connection-based sockets communicate in a client/ server manner: A server socket is assigned a "well-known" address and is constantly listening for client messages to arrive. A client process sends messages to the server via the server socket's advertised address. It is not necessary to assign an address to client sockets, as usually no process sends messages in this manner.

Connectionless sockets, on the other hand, communicate in a peer-to-peer manner: Each socket is assigned an address, and a process can send messages to other processes via their socket addresses.

The socket APIs are:

Socket APIS	Use
socket	Creates a socket of a given domain, type, and protocol
bind	Assigns a name to a socket
listen	Specifies the number of pending client messages that can be queued for a server socket.
accept	A server socket accepts a connection request from a client socket
connect	A client socket sends a connection request to a server socket
send, sendto	Sends a message to a remote socket
recv, recvfrom	Receives a message from a remote socket
shutdown	Shuts down a socket for read and/or write

The socket APIs' calling sequences that establish server and client virtual circuit connections are shown in Figure 11.1.

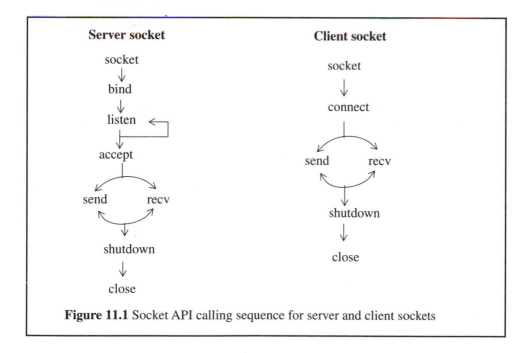

Figure 11.1 Socket API calling sequence for server and client sockets

To make sense of the use of these APIs, imagine that a socket is a telephone set. The *socket* API is to buy a phone from a shop. The *bind* API assigns a phone number to the phone. The *listen* API asks your phone company to set up a maximum allowance for Call Waiting on your phone. The *connect* API is to call someone, using your phone. The *accept* API answers a phone call. The *send* API speaks on the phone. The *recv* API listens to the caller through your phone. Finally, the *shutdown* API hangs up your phone after a call is finished. To discard the "phone," use the *close* API on the socket descriptor returned from a *socket* function call.

One the client's side, the process calls the *socket* function to set up a phone. It calls the *connect* function to dial a server's phone and uses the *send* and *recv* functions to communicate with the server. Once the conversation is over, it calls the *shutdown* function to hang up the phone and the *close* API to discard the "phone."

The calling sequences of socket APIs creating a datagram socket for interprocess communication are shown in Figure 11.2.

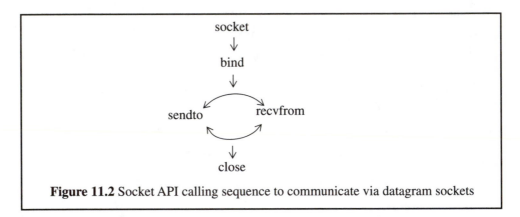

Figure 11.2 Socket API calling sequence to communicate via datagram sockets

The manipulation of datagram sockets is quite simple: A process calls *socket* to create a socket, then calls the *bind* function to assign a name to the socket. After that, the process calls the *sendto* function to send messages to other processes, and each message is tagged with the recipient's socket address. The process also receives messages from other processes via the *recvfrom* function. Each message received is tagged with the sender's socket address so that the process can reply via the same address.

Once the process finishes its IPC, it calls the *close* function to discard the socket. There is no need to call the *shutdown* function, as there is no virtual circuit established with other processes.

The following sections examine the socket APIs' syntax and use in more detail.

11.1.1   socket

The function prototype of the *socket* API is:

```
#include <sys/types.h>
#include <sys/socket.h>

int        socket (int  domain, int type, int protocol);
```

This function creates a socket of the given *domain, type, and protocol.*

The *domain* argument specifies the socket naming convention and the protocol address format. Some popular socket domains are AF_UNIX (UNIX domain) and AF_INET (Defense Advanced Research Project Agency Internet domain).

The *type* argument specifies a socket type. The possible values and their meanings are:

Socket type	Meaning
SOCK_STREAM	Establishes a virtual circuit for communication. Messages are sent in a sequenced, reliable, two-way, connection-based byte stream
SOCK_DGRAM	Establishes a datagram for communication. Messages are sent in a fast (usually connectionless) but unreliable fashion. Datagram messages are not guaranteed to be sent at all
SOCK_SEQPACKET	Provides a sequenced, reliable, two-way, connection-based message transmission with a fixed maximum message length

The *protocol* argument specifies a particular protocol to be used with the socket. Actual value is dependent on the *domain* argument. Usually, this is set to zero, and the kernel will choose an appropriate protocol for the specified domain.

The return value of the function is an integer socket descriptor if it succeeds or -1 if it fails. Note that a socket descriptor is the same as a file descriptor and uses up one file descriptor table slot in the calling process.

11.1.2   bind

The function prototype of the *bind* API is:

```
#include <sys/types.h>
#include <sys/socket.h>

int        bind ( int sid, struct sockaddr* addr_p, int len );
```

This function binds a name to a socket. The socket is referenced by *sid*, which is a socket descriptor, as returned by a *socket* function call. The *addr_p* argument points to a structure that contains the name to be assigned to the socket. The *len* argument specifies the size of the name structure pointed to by the *addr_p* argument.

The actual structure of the object pointed to by the *addr_p* argument is different for different domains. Specifically, for a UNIX domain socket, the name to be bound is a UNIX path name, and the structure of the object pointed to by the *addr_p* is:

```
struct sockaddr
{
    short    sun_family;
    char     sun_path[];
};
```

where the *sun_family* field should be assigned the value of AF_UNIX and the *sun_path* field should contain a UNIX path name. If the *bind* call succeeds, a file having a name specified in the *sun_path* field will be created in the file system. It should be deleted via the *unlink* API, once the socket is no longer needed.

For an Internet domain socket, the name to be bound consists of a machine host name and a port number. The structure of the object pointed to by the *addr_p* is:

```
struct sockaddr_in
{
    short          sin_family;
    u_short        sin_port;
    struct in_addr sin_addr;
};
```

where the *sin_family* field should be assigned the value of AF_INET. The *sin_port* field is a port number, and the *sin_addr* field is a host machine name where the socket resides. The *struct sockaddr_in* is defined in the <netinet/in.h> header.

This function returns a 0 if it succeeds or a -1 if it fails.

11.1.3   listen

The function prototype of the *listen* API is:

```
#include <sys/types.h>
#include <sys/socket.h>
int       listen ( int  sid, int size );
```

This is called in a server process to establish a connection-based socket (of type SOCK_STREAM or SOCK_SEQPACKET) for communication.

The *sid* argument is a socket descriptor, as returned by a *socket* function call. This is the socket that the *listen* API acts upon.

The *size* argument specifies the maximum (backlog) number of connection requests that may be queued for the socket. In most UNIX systems, the maximum allowed value for the *size* argument is 5.

The return value of the function is 0 if it succeeds or -1 if it fails.

11.1.4   connect

The function prototype of the *connect* API is:

```
#include <sys/types.h>
#include <sys/socket.h>
int       connect ( int  sid, struct sockaddr* addr_p, int len );
```

This is called in a client process in requesting a connection to a server socket.

The *sid* argument is a socket descriptor, as returned by a *socket* function call. In BSD 4.2 and 4.3, an unbound socket designated by *sid* is protocol-dependent as to whether it will be given a name. In System V.4, the socket is bound to the name assigned to it by the underlying transport provider.

The *addr_p* argument is a pointer to the address of a *sockaddr*-type object that holds the name of the server socket to be connected. The actual structure of the object is dependent on the domain of the server socket. The possible format is either *struct sockaddr* (for UNIX domain) or *struct sockaddr_in* (for Internet domain).

The *len* argument specifies the size, in number of bytes, of the object pointed to by the *addr_p* argument.

If *sid* designates a stream socket, a virtual circuit connection is established between the client and server sockets. The client's stream sockets may be connected only once. However, if *sid* designates a datagram socket, this establishes a default address for any subsequent *send* function calls via that socket. Datagram sockets may be "connected" multiple times to change their association with different default addresses. Datagram sockets may dissolve their association by connecting to a NULL address.

The function returns a 0 if it succeeds or a -1 if it fails.

11.1.5   accept

The function prototype of the *accept* API is:

```
#include <sys/types.h>
#include <sys/socket.h>

int      accept ( int  sid, struct sockaddr* addr_p, int* len_p );
```

This is called in a server process to establish a connection-based socket connection with a client socket (which calls *connect* to request connection establishment).

The *sid* argument is a socket descriptor, as returned by a *socket* function call. The *addr_p* argument is a pointer to the address of a *sockaddr*-typed object that holds the name of a client socket where the server socket is connected.

The *len_p* argument is initially set to the maximum size of the object pointed to by the *addr_p* argument. On return, it contains the size of the client socket name, as pointed to by the *addr_p* argument.

Note that if either the *addr_p* or the *len_p* argument is NULL, the function does not pass back the client's socket name to the calling process.

The function returns -1 if it fails; otherwise it returns a new socket descriptor that the server process can use to communicate with the client exclusively.

11.1.6   send

The function prototype of the *send* API is:

```
#include <sys/types.h>
#include <sys/socket.h>

int        send ( int  sid, const char* buf, int len, int flag );
```

This function sends a message, contained in *buf*, of size *len* bytes, to a socket that is connected to the socket, as designated by *sid*.

The *flag* argument is normally assigned a 0 value, but it can also be set to MSG_OOB, which means that the message contained in *buf* should be sent as an out-of-band message.

There are two types of messages that can be transmitted by sockets: regular messages and out-of-band messages. By default, every message sent by a socket is a regular message, unless it is explicitly tagged as out of band. If there is more than one messages of a given type sent from a socket, these are received by another socket in a FIFO order. The recipient socket may select which type of message it wishes to receive. Out-of-band messages should be used as emergency messages only.

If a process uses a connection-based socket or a connectionless socket that has a default recipient address established (via a *connect* function call), it can use either the *send* or *write* APIs to send regular messages via that socket. However, whereas *send* and *sendto* can be used to send zero-length messages, *write* should not be used in such operations. Furthermore, in BSD 4.2 and 4.3, a *write* function call fails if it is used on an unconnected socket. In System V.4, the same function call appears to succeed, but no data is actually sent.

The function returns -1 if it fails; otherwise it returns the number of data bytes sent.

11.1.7   sendto

The function prototype of the *sendto* API is:

```
#include <sys/types.h>
#include <sys/socket.h>

int   sendto ( int  sid, const char* buf, int len, int flag,
                            struct sockaddr* addr_p, int* len_p );
```

This function is the same as the *send* API, except that the calling process also specifies the address of the recipient socket name via the *addr_p* and *len_p* arguments.

The *sid, buf, len,* and *flag* arguments are the same as that of the *send* API. The *addr_p* is a pointer to the object that contains the name of a recipient socket. The *len_p* contains the number of bytes in the object pointed to by the a*ddr_p*.

The function returns -1 if it fails; otherwise, it returns the number of data bytes actually sent.

11.1.8   recv

The function prototype of the *recv* API is:

```
#include <sys/types.h>
#include <sys/socket.h>

int        recv ( int  sid, char* buf, int len, int flag );
```

This function receives a message via a socket designated by *sid*. The message received is copied to *buf,* and the maximum size of *buf* is specified in the *len* argument.

If the MSG_OOB flag is specified in the *flag* argument, an out-of-band message is to be received; otherwise, a regular message is wanted. Furthermore, the MSG_OOB flag may be specified in *flag*, which means that the process wishes to "peek" at the incoming message but does not want to remove it from the socket stream. It can call *recv* again later to receive the message.

If a process uses a connection-based socket or a connectionless socket that has a default recipient address established (via the *bind* API), it can use either the *recv* or the *read* API to receive regular messages via that socket. However, in BSD 4.2 and 4.3 *read* fails if it is used on an unconnected socket. In System V.4, however, *read* returns a zero value on an unconnected socket in blocking mode or returns a -1 value if the socket is nonblocking.

The function returns -1 if it fails: otherwise, it returns the number of data bytes received in *buf*.

11.1.9   recvfrom

The function prototype of the *recvfrom* API is:

```
#include <sys/types.h>
#include <sys/socket.h>

int   recvfrom (int  sid, const char* buf, int len, int flag,
                        struct sockaddr* addr_p, int* len_p);
```

This function is the same as the *recv* API, except that the calling process also specifies the *addr_p* and *len_p* arguments to receive the sender name.

The *sid, buf, len,* and *flag* arguments are the same as those of the *recv* API. The *addr_p* is a pointer to the object that contains the name of the sender socket. The *len_p* contains the number of bytes in the object pointed to by the *addr_p*.

The function returns -1 if it fails: otherwise, it returns the number of data bytes actually received.

11.1.10   shutdown

The function prototype of the *shutdown* API is:

```
#include <sys/types.h>
#include <sys/socket.h>

int   shutdown ( int  sid, int mode );
```

This function closes the a connection between a server and client socket.

The *sid* argument is a socket descriptor, as returned from a *socket* function call. This is the socket where the shutdown should occur.

The *mode* argument specifies the type of shutdown desired. Its possible values and meanings are:

Mode	Meaning
0	Closes the socket for reading. All further reading will return zero bytes (EOF)
1	Closes the socket for writing. Further attempts to send data to the socket will return a -1 failure code.
2	Closes the socket for reading and writing. Further attempts to send data to the socket will return a -1 failure code, and any attempt to read data from the socket will receive a zero value (EOF)

The function returns -1 if it fails, 0 if it succeeds.

11.2   a Stream Socket Example

This section depicts a pair of client/server programs that demonstrates how to set up stream sockets for IPC. The stream sockets used in the example may be UNIX domain sockets or Internet domain sockets. In the latter case, the client and server processes may run on the same machine or on two different machines.

To facilitate the implementation of socket-based applications, a *sock* class is defined to encapsulate the socket APIs from application programs. The advantages of this approach are: (1) it hides the low-level socket addresses set up from application programs. Users of this package manipulate socket addresses in terms of socket names or host names and port numbers only; and (2) the read and write member functions of the sock class are analogous to their equivalent UNIX file APIs. All these features reduce overhead in learning to use sockets, as well as the programming effort of users.

The *sock* class is defined in the *sock.h* header, as follows:

```
#ifndef SOCK_H
#define SOCK_H

#include <iostream.h>
```

```
#include <stdio.h>
#include <stdlib.h>
#include <unistd.h>
#include <memory.h>
#include <string.h>
#include <sys/types.h>
#include <sys/socket.h>
#include <arpa/inet.h>
#include <netinet/in.h>
#include <netdb.h>
#include <sys/systeminfo.h>
const int BACKLOG_NUM = 5;

class sock
{
    private:
       int sid;              // socket descriptor
       int domain;           // socket domain
       int socktype;         // socket type
       int rc;               // member function return status code

       /* Build a Internet socket name based on a hostname and a port no */
       int constr_name( struct sockaddr_in& addr, const char* hostnm,
                        int port )
       {
          addr.sin_family = domain;
           if (!hostnm)
             addr.sin_addr.s_addr = INADDR_ANY;
          else  {
             struct hostent *hp = gethostbyname(hostnm);
             if (hp==0)     {
                perror("gethostbyname");
                return -1;
             }
             memcpy((char*)&addr.sin_addr,(char*)hp->h_addr,
                        hp->h_length);
          }
          addr.sin_port = htons(port);
          return sizeof(addr);
       };

       /* Build a UNIX domain socket name based on a pathname */
       int constr_name( struct sockaddr& addr, const char* Pathnm )
       {
          addr.sa_family = domain;
          strcpy(addr.sa_data, Pathnm );
```

```
            return sizeof(addr.sa_family) + strlen(Pathnm) + 1;
        };

        /* Convert an IP address to a character string host name */
        char* ip2name( const struct in_addr in )
        {
            u_long laddr;
            if ((int)(laddr = inet_addr(inet_ntoa(in))) == -1) return 0;
            struct hostent *hp = gethostbyaddr((char*)&laddr,
                            sizeof (laddr), AF_INET);
            if (!hp) return 0;
            for (char **p = hp->h_addr_list; *p != 0; p++)        {
                (void) memcpy((char*)&in.s_addr, *p, sizeof (in.s_addr));
                if (hp->h_name) return hp->h_name;
            }
            return 0;
        };

public:
        /* sock object constructor function */
        sock( int dom, int type, int protocol=0 ) : domain(dom), socktype(type)
        {
            if ((sid=socket(dom, type,protocol))<0)  perror("socket");
        };

        /* sock object destructor function */
         ~sock()                { shutdown(); close(sid); }; // discard a socket

        int fd()                { return sid; };                    // return a socket's id

        int good()              { return sid >= 0; };              // check sock obj status

        /* assign a UNIX or an Internet name to a socket */
        int bind( const char* name, int port=-1 )
        {
            if (port == -1)    {                                // UNIX domain socket
                struct sockaddr addr;
                int len = constr_name( addr, name);
                if ((rc= ::bind(sid,&addr,len))<0) perror("bind");
            }
            else  {                                           // Internet domain socket
                struct sockaddr_in addr;
                int len = constr_name( addr, name, port);
                if ((rc= ::bind(sid, (struct sockaddr *)&addr, len))<0 ||
                    (rc=getsockname(sid, (struct sockaddr*)&addr, &len))<0)
                    perror("bind or getsockname");
```

```
            else cout << "Socket port: " << ntohs(addr.sin_port) << endl;
        }
        /* setup connection backlog threshold for a STREAM socket */
        if (rc!=-1 && socktype!=SOCK_DGRAM &&
                        (rc=listen(sid,BACKLOG_NUM)) < 0)
            perror("listen");
        return rc;
    };

    /* A server socket accepts a client connection request */
    int accept (char *name, int* port_p )
    {
        if (!name) return ::accept(sid, 0, 0);
        if (!port_p || *port_p == -1)    {              // UNIX domain socket
            struct sockaddr addr;
            int size = sizeof(addr);
            if ((rc = ::accept(sid, &addr, &size)) >-1)
            strncpy(name,addr.sa_data,size), name[size]='\0';
        }
        else {                                          // Internet domain socket
            struct sockaddr_in addr;
            int size = sizeof (addr);
            if ((rc = ::accept( sid, (struct sockaddr*)&addr, &size)) >-1)  {
                if (name) strcpy(name,ip2name(addr.sin_addr));
                if (port_p) *port_p = ntohs(addr.sin_port);
            }
        }
        return rc;
    };

    /* A client socket initiates a connection request to a server socket */
    int connect( const char* hostnm, int port=-1 )
    {
        if (port==-1)  {                                // UNIX domain socket
            struct sockaddr addr;
            int len = constr_name( addr, hostnm);
            if ((rc= ::connect(sid,&addr,len))<0) perror("bind");
        }
        else {                                          // Internet domain socket
            struct sockaddr_in addr;
            int len = constr_name( addr, hostnm, port);
            if ((rc= ::connect(sid,(struct sockaddr *)&addr,len))<0)
                perror("bind");
        }
        return rc;
    };
```

```
/* writes a message to a connected stream socket */
int write( const char* buf, int len, int flag=0, int nsid=-1 )
{
    return ::send(nsid==-1 ? sid : nsid, buf, len, flag );
};

/* reads a message from a connected stream socket */
int read( char* buf, int len, int flag=0, int nsid=-1 )  // read a msg
{
    return ::recv(nsid==-1 ? sid : nsid, buf, len, flag );
};

/* write to a socket of the given socket name */
int writeto( const char* buf, int len, int flag, const char* name,
                const int port, int nsid=-1 )
{
    if (port==-1)  {                              // UNIX domain socket
        struct sockaddr addr;
        int size = constr_name( addr, name);
        return ::sendto(nsid==-1 ? sid : nsid, buf, len, flag, &addr, size );
    }
    else  {                                       // Internet domain socket
        struct sockaddr_in addr;
        char buf1[80];
        if (!name)     {                          // use local host
            if (sysinfo(SI_HOSTNAME,buf1,sizeof buf1)==-1L)
                perror("sysinfo");
            name = buf1;
        }
        int size = constr_name( addr, name, port);
        return ::sendto(nsid==-1 ? sid : nsid, buf, len, flag,
                    (struct sockaddr*)&addr, size );
    }
};

/* Receive a message from a socket */
int readfrom( char* buf, int len, int flag, char* name, int *port_p,
                int nsid =-1)
{
    if (!port_p || *port_p == -1)      {          // UNIX domain socket
        struct sockaddr addr;
        int size = sizeof(addr);
        if ((rc=::recvfrom(nsid==-1 ? sid : nsid, buf, len, flag, &addr,
                    &size)) >-1 && name)
            strncpy(name,addr.sa_data,rc), name[rc]='\0';
    }
```

```
        else  {                                    // Internet domain socket
            struct sockaddr_in addr;
            int size = sizeof (addr);
             if ((rc = ::recvfrom(nsid==-1 ? sid : nsid, buf, len, flag,
                        (struct sockaddr*)&addr, &size)) >-1)        {
                if (name) strcpy(name,ip2name(addr.sin_addr));
                if (port_p) *port_p = ntohs(addr.sin_port);
            }
        }
        return rc;
    };

    /* shut down connection of a socket */
    int shutdown( int mode = 2 )
    {
        return ::shutdown (sid,mode);
    };
};     /* class sock */
```

The *sock* class is designed to hide the low-level socket API interface from application programs. Thus, an application that wishes to open a UNIX domain socket need only specify a UNIX path name to the *bind* or *connect* member functions. On the other hand, if an application wishes to open an Internet domain socket, it need only to specify the host name and port number. There is no need for an application to manipulate any *struct sockaddr*-typed objects. This saves programming time and reduces errors in setting up socket addresses.

The *sock* member functions are almost one-to-one correspondents with the socket APIs. This makes it easy for users who like to switch between using socket APIs and using the *sock* class objects. Furthermore, the *sock::read, sock::wirte, sock::readfrom,* and *sock::writeto* functions have a *nsid* argument that is assigned when a calling process is a server. It can communicate with a client process via the *nsid* socket descriptor, as obtained from an *sock::accept* function call.

A server program that makes use of the *sock* class to establish a stream socket connection with a client program is shown below:

```
/* sock_stream_srv.C */
#include "sock.h"

const char* MSG2 = "Hello MSG2";
const char* MSG4 = "Hello MSG4";

int main( int argc, char* argv[])
{
    char  buf[80], socknm[80];
```

```
        int  port=-1, nsid, rc;

        if (argc < 2)        {
           cerr << "usage: " << argv[0] << " <socknamelport> [<host>]\n";
           return 1;
        }

        /* check if port no. of a socket name is specified */
        (void)sscanf(argv[1],"%d",&port);

        /* create a stream socket */
        sock sp( port!=-1 ? AF_INET : AF_UNIX, SOCK_STREAM );
        if (!sp.good()) return 1;

        /* Bind a name to the server socket */
        if (sp.bind(port==-1 ? argv[1] : argv[2],port) < 0) return 2;

        /* accept a connection request from a client socket */
        if ((nsid = sp.accept(0, 0)) < 0) return 1;

        /* read MSG1 from a client socket */
        if ((rc=sp.read(buf, sizeof buf, 0, nsid)) < 0) return 5;
        cerr << "server: receive msg: '" << buf << "'\n";

        /* write MSG2 to a client socket */
        if (sp.write(MSG2,strlen(MSG2)+1,0,nsid)<0) return 6;

        /* read MSG3 from a client socket */
        if (sp.readfrom( buf, sizeof buf, 0, socknm, &port, nsid) > 0)
        cerr << "server: recvfrom '" << socknm << "' msg: '" << buf << "'\n";

        /* write MSG4 to a client socket */
        if (write(nsid,MSG4,strlen(MSG4)+1)==-1) return 7;
     }
```

The command line argument for this server program may be a UNIX path name for creating a UNIX domain socket. Conversely, it may be a port number and a host name (optional) for creating an Internet domain socket. In the latter case, if a host name is not specified, the host name of the local machine is used instead. Note that in the *sock::bind* function call, if an Internet domain socket is created, the function prints the assigned port number to the standard error port. This is so that a client process can reference that port number when creating a socket to communicate with the server's socket.

After a socket is created and assigned a name, the server process waits for a client connection to be established with its socket. After that, it receives the MSG1 message via the *sock::read* function from the client socket, prints the message, and sends the MSG2 message via the *sock::write* function to the client process. The server reads the MSG3 message from the client via the *sock::readfrom* function and replies to the client with the MSG4 message via the *write* API. Finally, the server process terminates, and the socket it allocated is discarded via the *sock::~sock* destructor function.

The client program that communicates with the above server is:

```
/* sock_stream_cls.C */
#include "sock.h"
const char* MSG1 = "Hello MSG1";
const char* MSG3 = "Hello MSG3";
int main( int argc, char* argv[])
{
    int  port=-1, rc;
    if (argc < 2)   {
       cerr << "usage: " << argv[0] << " <socknamelport> [<host>]\n";
       return 1;
    }

    /* check if port number of socket name is specified */
    (void)sscanf(argv[1],"%d",&port);

    /* 'host' may be a socket name or a host name */
    char buf[80], *host= (port==-1) ? argv[1] : argv[2], socknm[80];

    /* create a client socket */
    sock sp( port!=-1 ? AF_INET : AF_UNIX, SOCK_STREAM );
    if (!sp.good()) return 1;

    /* connect to a server socket */
    if (sp.connect(host,port) < 0) return 8;

    /* Send MGS1 to server */
    if (sp.write(MSG1, strlen(MSG1)+1) < 0) return 9;

    /* read MSG2 from server */
    if (sp.read(buf,sizeof buf) < 0) return 10;
    cerr << "client: recv '" << buf << "'\n";

    /* Send MGS3 to server */
    if ((rc=sp.writeto( MSG3, strlen(MSG3)+1, 0, host, port, -1)) < 0)
       return 11;
```

```
/* read MSG4 from server */
if ((rc=read(sp.fd(),buf,sizeof buf))==-1) return 12;
cerr << "client: read msg: '" << buf << "'\n";

/* shut down socket explicitly */
sp.shutdown();
}
```

The command line arguments for this client program are the same as those of the server program: a UNIX pathname or a port name followed by an optional host name. The program creates a UNIX domain socket or an Internet domain socket based on the command line arguments.

The client program calls the *sock::connect* function in connecting to the server socket. It writes the MSG1 message to the server via the *sock::write* function, then reads the MSG2 message via the *sock::read* function. After that, the client writes the MSG3 message to the server via the *sock::writeto* function and reads the reply MSG4 message via the *read* API. When the client process terminates, it explicitly shuts down the socket via the *sock::shutdown()* function call.

The above client/server can be run with UNIX domain sockets or Internet domain sockets. The following screen log depicts a sample interaction between server and client processes using UNIX domain sockets. The server socket name is arbitrarily set to SOCK:

```
% CC -o sock_stream_srv sock_stream_srv.C -lsocket -lnsl
% CC -o sock_stream_cls sock_stream_cls.C -lsocket -lnsl
% sock_stream_srv SOCK &
[1] 373
% sock_stream_cls SOCK
server: receive msg: 'Hello MSG1'
client: recv 'Hello MSG2'
server: recvfrom '' msg: 'Hello MSG3'
client: read msg: 'Hello MSG4'
[1]  + Done      sock_stream_srv SOCK
```

Note that in the above, when the server receives MSG3 from the client via the *sock::readfrom* function call, the *socknm* variable is assigned with a NULL string. This is because the client socket has not been bound with a name in the client process. In a client/server setup, it is generally allowed that only the server socket be named, so that client sockets can be connected to it (and not vice versa).

The following screen log depicts a sample interaction between server and client processes using Internet domain sockets. Here, the machine name that hosts both processes is *fruit*. It lets the system pick the available port number for the client and server sockets:

```
% sock_stream_srv 0 fruit &
[1] 374
Socket port: 32804
% sock_stream_cls 32804 fruit
server: receive msg: 'Hello MSG1'
client: recv 'Hello MSG2'
server: recvfrom 'fruit' msg: 'Hello MSG3'
client: read msg: 'Hello MSG4'
[1]  + Done        sock_stream_srv 0 fruit
```

Note that the same client/server programs are run, but with different command line arguments. The client/server processes are run with Internet domain sockets. The output of the programs are the same as in the UNIX domain sockets example. Furthermore, although the above example shows that the server and client processes are executed on the same machine, the result would be the same if run on separate machines. The only difference in running the two programs are: (1) execute the server program on one machine (for example, *fruit*); (2) execute the client program on a remote machine and specify the server socket port number and host name as command line arguments-the output message (i.e., re*ceive MSG1 and MSG3*) is displayed on its host machine, while the clients' output messages (i.e., *receive MSG2 and MSG4*) are displayed on their host machine.

The datagram socket-based programs also use the *sock.h* header, as above. The first program, *sock_datagram_srv.C* is:

```
#include "sock.h"
const char* MSG2 = "Hello MSG2";
const char* MSG4 = "Hello MSG4";

int main( int argc, char* argv[])
{
    int  port = -1, rc;
    char buf[80], socknm[80];

    if (argc < 2)  {
      cerr << "usage: " << argv[0]
           << " <socknamelport> [<remote-host>]\n";
      return 1;
    }
```

```
/* Check if port number or socket name is specified */
(void)sscanf( argv[1],"%d",&port);

/* Create a datagram socket */
sock sp( port==-1 ? AF_UNIX : AF_INET, SOCK_DGRAM );
if (!sp.good()) return 1;

/* assign a name to the socket */
if (sp.bind(port==-1 ? argv[1] : argv[2],port) < 0) return 2;

/* read MSG1 from peet */
if ((rc=sp.readfrom( buf, sizeof buf, 0, socknm, &port, -1)) < 0) return 1;
cerr << "server: recvfrom from '" << socknm << "' msg: " << buf << endl;

/* write MSG2 to peer */
if ((rc= sp.writeto( MSG2, strlen(MSG2)+1, 0, socknm, port, -1)) < 0)
    return 2;

/* establish a default client address */
if ((rc = sp.connect(socknm, port)) < 0) return 3;

/* read MSG3 from peer*/
if ((rc = sp.read(buf, sizeof buf, 0)) < 0) return 4;
cerr << "server: receive msg: '" << buf << "'\n";

/* write MSG4 to peer */
if (write(sp.fd(),MSG4,strlen(MSG4)+1)<0) return 5;
}
```

The above program is almost the same as the *sock_stream_srv.C*, except that the socket created here is declared to be SOCK_DGRAM (via the *sock::sock* function). The program is given its assigned socket name (for creating UNIX domain socket) or port number and/or host name (for creating an Internet domain socket) at the command line. This socket name is known by the peer that wishes to communicate with it. After the socket is created, the program reads a message from its peer via the *sock::readfrom* function, returning the peer's socket name. The program responds to its peer with the MSG2 message via the *sock::writeto* function. After that, the program establishes a default connection address with the peer socket via the *sock::connect* call. It then uses the *sock::read* function to read the peer's MSG3 message and, finally, replies with the MSG4 message via the *write* API.

The peer program, *sock_datagram_cls.C*, which communicates with the above program is:

```
#include "sock.h"
const char* MSG1 = "Hello MSG1";
```

```
const char* MSG3 = "Hello MSG3";
int main( int argc, char* argv[])
{
    char buf[80], socknm[80];
    int  nlen, port = -1, rc;
    if (argc < 2)   {
         cerr << "usage: " << argv[0]
              << " <sockname | port> [ <remote-host>]\n";
       return 1;
    }
    /* check if port number or socket name is specified */
    (void)sscanf(argv[1],"%d",&port);

    /* create a datagram socket */
    sock sp( port==-1 ? AF_UNIX : AF_INET, SOCK_DGRAM );
    if (!sp.good()) return 1;

    if (port==-1)   {                           // UNIX domain socket
       sprintf(buf,"%s%d", argv[1], getpid()); // construct client socket name
       if (sp.bind(buf,port) < 0) return 2;    // assign name to socket
    }
    else if (sp.bind(0,0) < 0) return 2;        // assign name to socket

    /* write MSG1 to peer */
    if ((rc=sp.writeto( MSG1, strlen(MSG1)+1, 0, port==-1? argv[1] :
argv[2],
              port, -1)) < 0)
       return 6;

    /* read MSG2 from peer */
    if ((rc=sp.readfrom( buf, sizeof buf, 0, socknm, &port, -1)) < 0) return 7;
    cerr << "client: recvfrom '" << socknm << "' msg: " << buf << endl;

    /* establish a default peer socket address */
    if (sp.connect(socknm,port) < 0) return 8;

    /* write MSG3 to peer */
    if (sp.write(MSG3, strlen(MSG3)+1) < 0) return 9;

    /* read MSG4 from peer */
    if ((rc=read(sp.fd(),buf,sizeof buf))==-1) return 10;
    cerr << "client: read msg: " << buf << endl;

    sp.shutdown();
}
```

The command line arguments for the above example are its peer's socket name or port number and/or host name. The program constructs its socket name (for UNIX domain socket) by taking its peer socket name and appending it with its own process ID. It could also let the system assign it a port number (for Internet domain socket) from the host machine. Once the program establishes its own datagram socket (via the *sock::sock* and *sock::bind* function calls), it sends an MSG1 message to the peer socket via the *sock::writeto* function and waits for the reply message MSG2 via the *sock::readfrom* function call. Continuing, the process sets up a default peer socket address via the *sock::connect* function. It then uses the *sock::write* function and the *read* API to send an MSG3 message to its peer process. These functions also allow it to receive the MSG4 message from the peer. Before the program terminates, it uses the *sock::shutdown* function to shut down the socket.

The sample output of these two programs on UNIX domain sockets is:

```
% CC -o sock_datagram_srv sock_datagram_srv.C -l socket -lnsl
% CC -o sock_datagram_cls sock_datagram_cls.C -lsocket -lnsl
% sock_datagram_srv SOCK_DG &
% sock_datagram_cls SOCK_DG
server: recvfrom from 'SOCK_DG572' msg: Hello MSG1
client: recvfrom 'SOCK_DG' msg: Hello MSG2
server: receive msg: 'Hello MSG3'
client: read msg: Hello MSG4
[1] + Done            sock_datagram_srv SOCK_DG
```

Notice in the above output that the first peer socket name is SOCK_DG and the counterpart socket name is SOCK_DG572. The output of these two programs is similar to that of the stream socket client/server programs.

The sample outputs of these two program on Internet domain sockets are:

```
% sock_datagram_srv 0 fruit &
Socket port: 32838
% sock_datagram_cls 32838 fruit
Socket port: 32840
server: recvfrom from 'fruit' msg: Hello MSG1
client: recvfrom 'fruit' msg: Hello MSG2
server: receive msg: 'Hello MSG3'
client: read msg: Hello MSG4
[1] + Done            sock_datagram_srv 0 fruit
```

In the above example, the first peer socket port number is 32838. It runs on a machine called *fruit*. The second process socket port number is 32840. It also runs on *fruit* (although it can be run on a different machine). The two processes interact in exactly the same fashion as when they were using UNIX domain sockets. The output is also identical, except for the printout of socket names.

11.3   Client/Server Message-Handling Example

This section depicts a new version of the client/server example shown in Chapter 10, Section 10.3.7. The new version uses stream sockets to set up a communication channel between the message server and each of its client processes. Furthermore, because the server is connected directly to each client process, each message sent from a client consists of a service command (e.g., LOCAL_TIME, GMT_TIME or QWUIT_CMD, etc.) encoded in character string format. The server also sends the service response to its client in a character string format.

The message server program, *sock_msg_srv.C*, is shown below:

```c
#include "sock.h"
#include <sys/times.h>
#include <sys/types.h>
#define MSG1 "Invalid cmd to message server"
typedef enum { LOCAL_TIME, GMT_TIME, QUIT_CMD,
                                ILLEGAL_CMD } CMDS;
/* process a client's commands */
int process_cmd (int fd )
{
   char    buf[80];
   time_t  tim;
   char*   cptr;

   /* read commands from a client until EOF or QUIT_CMD */
   while (read(fd, buf, sizeof buf) > 0)      {
      int    cmd = ILLEGAL_CMD;
      (void)sscanf(buf,"%d",&cmd);
      switch (cmd)         {
        case LOCAL_TIME:
           tim = time(0);
           cptr = ctime(&tim);
           write(fd, cptr, strlen(cptr)+1);
           break;
        case GMT_TIME:
           tim = time(0);
```

```
            cptr = asctime(gmtime(&tim));
            write(fd, cptr, strlen(cptr)+1);
            break;
        case QUIT_CMD:
            return cmd;
        default:
            write(fd, MSG1, sizeof MSG1);
    }
  }
  return 0;
}

int main( int argc, char* argv[])
{
   char  buf[80], socknm[80];
   int  port=-1, nsid, rc;
   fd_set  select_set;
   struct timeval timeRec;

   if (argc < 2)      {
      cerr << "usage: " << argv[0] << " <socknamelport> [<host>]\n";
      return 1;
   }

   /* check if port no. of a socket name is specified */
   (void)sscanf(argv[1],"%d",&port);

   /* create a stream socket */
   sock sp( port!=-1 ? AF_INET : AF_UNIX, SOCK_STREAM );
   if (!sp.good()) return 1;

   /* Bind a name to the server socket */
   if (sp.bind(port==-1 ? argv[1] : argv[2],port) < 0) return 2;

   for (;;)      {                        // Poll for client connections
      timeRec.tv_sec = 1;                 // polling time-out after one second
      timeRec.tv_usec= 0;
      FD_ZERO( &select_set );
      FD_SET( sp.fd(), &select_set );

       /* wait for time-out or a read event occurs for socket */
      rc = select(FD_SETSIZE, &select_set, 0, 0, &timeRec );
      if (rc > 0 && FD_ISSET(sp.fd(), &select_set))      {
         /* accept a connection request from a client socket */
         if ((nsid = sp.accept(0, 0)) < 0) return 1;
```

```
        /* process commands */
        if (process_cmd(nsid)==QUIT_CMD) break;

        close(nsid); /* recycle file descriptor */
      }
      /* else do something else */
    }
    sp.shutdown();
    return 0;
  }
```

The invocation syntax of a message server program is the same as that of the *sock_stream_srv.C* example. It allocates a stream socket and binds a name to it in the same manner. However, once the socket is set up, the server uses the *select* API to poll read events occurring on the socket. Each *select* polling time out after 1 second so that the server may be programmed to do something else, if needed.

When a client sends a service command to the server, it calls the *process_cmd* function to process all the service commands initiated by the client. The *process_cmd* function returns when the client sends either QUIT_CMD or a noninteger service command to the server. In either case, the server closes the *nsid* file descriptor that references the socket, as created by the *sock::accept* function call. After that, the server either continues to poll the stream socket for connection to another client or simply shuts down the stream socket and terminates itself.

The client program, *sock_msg_cls.C*, is:

```
#include "sock.h"
#define QUIT_CMD 2

int main( int argc, char* argv[])
{
   if (argc < 2)   {
      cerr << "usage: " << argv[0] << " <sockname | port> [<host>]\n";
      return 1;
   }
   int  port=-1, rc;

   /* check if port number of socket name is spceified */
   (void)sscanf(argv[1],"%d",&port);

   /* 'host' may be a socket name or a host name */
   char buf[80], *host= (port==-1) ? argv[1] : argv[2], socknm[80];
```

```
/* create a client socket */
sock sp( port!=-1 ? AF_INET : AF_UNIX, SOCK_STREAM );
if (!sp.good()) return 1;

/* connect to a server socket */
if (sp.connect(host,port) < 0) return 8;

/* Send cmds 0 -> 2 to server */
for (int cmd=0; cmd < 3; cmd++)     {
    /* compose a command to server */
    sprintf(buf,"%d",cmd);
    if (sp.write(buf,strlen(buf)+1) < 0) return 9;

    /* exit the loop if QUIT_CMD */
    if (cmd==QUIT_CMD) break;

    /* read reply from server */
    if (sp.read(buf,sizeof buf) < 0) return 10;
     cerr << "client: recv '" << buf << "'\n";
}
sp.shutdown();
return 0;
}
```

The client program's invocation syntax is the same as that of the *sock_stream_cls.C* example. It allocates a stream socket and connects it to the server socket in the same manner. However, once the socket is set up, the client sends the following service messages to the server: (1) tell local date/time; (2) tell GMT date/times; (3) quit command; and (4) solicit a warning message from the server.

For each service command sent by a client (except the QUIT_CMD), the client collects the server response and prints the results to the standard output. The client program terminates after it has sent the QUIT_CMD to the server.

The client and server programs are compiled as follows:

```
% CC -o sock_msg_srv sock_msg_srv.C -l socket -lnsl
% CC -o sock_msg_cls sock_msg_cls.C -lsocket -lnsl
```

A sample console log of the server/client program interaction is:

```
% sock_msg_srv 0 fruit &
[1] 441
```

```
Socket port: 32792
% sock_msg_cls 32792 fruit
client: recv 'Sun Feb 12 00:41:25 1995'
client: recv 'Sun Feb 12 08:41:25 1995'
[1]  + Done            sock_msg_srv 0 fruit
```

In the above, the client and server processes communicate using Internet domain stream sockets. The client collects only the server responses found on the LOCAL_TIME and UTC_TIME commands. Again, by using the Internet domain sockets, the above server and client processes can be run on separate machines.

The following console log shows the same client/server processes interacting in the same manner as the above, but using only UNIX domain sockets:

```
% sock_msg_srv SOCK_MSG &
[1] 446
% sock_msg_cls SOCK_MSG
client: recv 'Sun Feb 12 00:42:38 1995'
client: recv 'Sun Feb 12 08:42:38 1995'
[1]  + Done            sock_msg_srv SOCK_MSG
```

11.4   TLI

Transport Level Interface was developed in UNIX System V.3 as an alternative to sockets. TLI is more flexible than sockets and is based on STREAM, which supports most transport protocols. TLI creates transport end points whose behavior and function are similar to those of sockets. For example, TLI transport end points may communicate with each other in either a connection-based or a connectionless mode. Furthermore, processes running on different machines or on the same machine may communicate via their TLI transport end points. Both sockets and TLI transport end points are designated by file descriptors. Thus, a process may set the O_NONBLOCK flag on these file descriptors, either when they are assigned or via the *fcntl* function. This renders the execution of corresponding socket or TLI end point operations as nonblocking.

A TLI end point cannot communicate with a socket. When a TLI transport end point is created, a user must specify that a transport protocol be bound to that end point. In sockets, however, a user is not required to specify a transport protocol in creating a socket. The *socket* API will choose a default protocol based on the socket type. In addition to these differences, the address assigned to a socket for intramachine communication is different from that of a TLI end point. A TLI end point is assigned an integer port number for communicating with other transport end points on the same machine, whereas a socket is assigned a UNIX path name for the same function. For communication over the Internet, a TLI transport end point is assigned a machine name and a service port number (similar to that of *socket*). Finally, for connection-based communication, client sockets are usually not assigned addresses unless the client processes explicitly assign them. On the other hand, TLI transport end points are always assigned addresses, either by users or by the underlying transport protocol.

There is an almost one-to-one correspondence between TLI APIs and those of sockets. This makes it easy for socket-based applications to be converted to TLI. The next section gives an overview of TLI APIs and their comparison to socket APIs. The subsequent sections describe the syntax and use of TLI APIs in more detail. The final two sections depict two examples of TLI application: One is a rewrite of the client/server examples shown in Section 11.2, using TLI transport end point instead of sockets. The other example shows how to use TLI transport end points to send datagram messages.

11.4.1   TLI APIs

TLI system functions and their use are:

TLI API	Function
t_open	Creates a transport end point and specifies an underlying transport protocol
t_bind	Assigns a name to a transport end point. For a connection-based end point, this also specifies the maximum number of backlog connection requests allowed
t_listen	Waits for a connection request from a client transport end point
t_accept	Accepts a connection request from a remote transport end point
t_connect	Sends a connection request to a server transport end point
t_snd	For a connection-based transport end point only. Sends a message to a connected end point
t_rcv	For a connection-based transport end point only. Receives a message from a connected end point
t_sndudata	Sends a datagram message to a transport end point with a given address
t_rcvudata	Receives a datagram message and a sender address from a transport end point
t_snddis	Aborts a connection
t_rcvdis	Returns an abort connection indication with a reason

TLI API	Function
t_sndrel	Sends a request to a transport end point for orderly release of a connection
t_rcvrel	Returns an orderly connection release indication from a connected transport end point
t_error	Similar to *perror*, but prints TLI-specific error diagnostics if a TLI function call fails
t_alloc	Allocates dynamic memory for a transport end point
t_free	Deallocates dynamic memory of a transport end point
t_close	Closes a transport end point descriptor

The calling sequences of the above TLI APIs in establishing a server and client virtual circuit connection are shown in Figure 11.3.

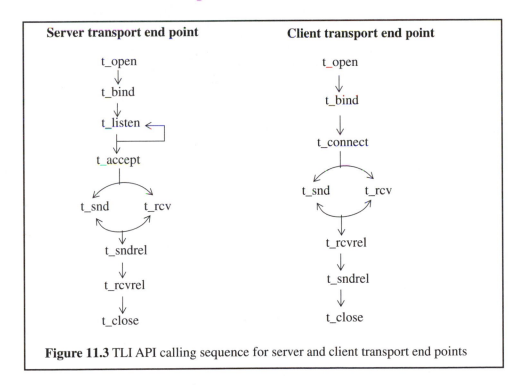

Figure 11.3 TLI API calling sequence for server and client transport end points

Notice the similarity of the calling sequences in the above to those depicted in Figure 11-1. Specifically, the *t_open* API is similar to the *socket* API, the *t_bind* is like the *bind* API, and the t_*snd* and *t_rcv* functions are similar to the *send* and *rcv* APIs, respectively. However, the *t_listen* API is not the same as the *listen* API. This is because the *listen* API sets the maximum number of pending connection requests allowed for a socket. For a transport end point, this information is set in the *t_bind* API instead. The *t_listen* API is actually like the socket's *accept* API, in that it causes the calling process to wait for a client connection request. Once a connection request is received, the *t_listen* function returns with the client transport end point address. The server may call either *t_accept* to accept the connection or the *t_snddis* function to abort the connection.

Like the *accept* API, the *t_accept* API may generate a new descriptor that designates a private transport end point for the server to communicate with a client process. The server process can continue to monitor further connection requests from other client processes via the original descriptor, as obtained from the *t_open* call.

Once a server and client process finish their communication, either one of them can call the *t_sndrel* function to send a disconnect notification request to their counterpart. The other process calls the *t_rcvrel* function to receive that notification and responds with a *sndrel* function call. Once the first process receives the reply notification via the *t_rcvrel* function, the transport end points are disconnected, and both processes may call the *t_close* function to dispose their transport end points.

As an alternative to the *t_sndrel* and *t_rcvrel* functions, a server and client process may call the *t_snddis* and *t_rcvdis* functions to abort a transport connection. The *t_snddis* function is abortive, and any data remaining to be sent over the transport end points are discarded immediately. The *t_sndrel* function, on the other hand, is nonabortive, and any remaining data to be passed between the transport connection are delivered before the connection is destroyed. All transport protocols used with TLI must support the *t_snddis* and *t_rcvdis* functions, but they are not required to support the *t_sndrel* and *t_rcvrel* functions.

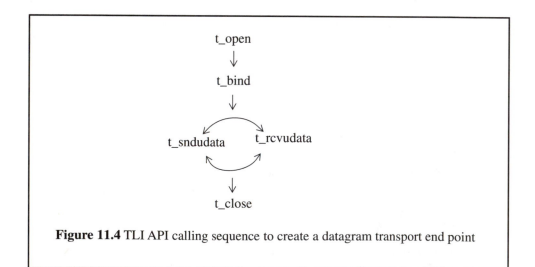

Figure 11.4 TLI API calling sequence to create a datagram transport end point

The TLI API calling sequence that creates a datagram transport end point is shown in Figure 11.4.

The manipulation of datagram transport end points is quite simple: A process calls *t_open* to create a transport end point, then calls the *t_bind* function to assign a name to the end point. After that, the process calls the *t_sndudata* function to send messages to other processes, and each message is tagged with a recipient transport end point address. The process also receives messages from other processes via the *t_rcvudata* function. Each message received is tagged with a sender transport end point address, so that the process can reply accordingly.

Once the process finishes its interprocess communication, it calls the *t_close* to discard the transport end point descriptor. There is no need to call the *t_snddis* or *t_sndrel* function here, as there is no virtual circuit established with other processes.

The following few sections examine TLI API syntax and use in more detail.

11.4.2   t_open

The function prototype of the *t_open* API is:

```
#include <tiuser.h>
#include <fcntl.h>

int        t_open (char*  path, int aflag, struct t_info* info);
```

This function creates a transport end point that uses a transport provider, as specified by *path*. The actual value to *path* may be the path name of a device file that designates the transport provider. For example, the */dev/ticlts* file designates a UDP transport provider, and the */dev/ticotsord* file designates a virtual circuit transport provider.

The *aflag* argument specifies the access mode of the transport end point by the calling process. Its value is defined in the <fcntl.h> header and is usually O_RDWR, which means that the calling process may send and receive messages via the transport end point. In addition, the O_NONBLOCK flag may also be specified with the O_RDWR flag, which renders the transport end point to perform nonblocking operations.

The *info* argument returns default characteristics of the underlying transport provider. This information is usually ignored and the actual value for *info* may be 0. However, if a user is interested in examining these default characteristics, the user can define a *struct t_info* typed variable and pass the address of that variable as actual value to the *info* argument.

When the function returns, he can look at the content of that variable. One interesting piece of data is contained in the *info->servtype* field. The possible values and meanings are:

servtype **value**	**Meaning**
T_COTS	The transport provider supports virtual circuit connection but not the orderly disconnection request
T_COTSORD	The transport provider supports virtual circuit connection and the orderly disconnection request
T_CLTS	The transport provider supports the passing of datagram messages

The above constants are declared in the <tiuser.h> header. The return value of the function is -1 if it fails. If it succeeds, the value is a descriptor that designates a transport end point created by the function.

The following statements create a connection-based transport end point that supports orderly release of connection. Furthermore, the transport end point operations are performed in nonblocking mode, and the transport default characteristic information is not wanted. The transport end point descriptor is assigned to the variable *fd*:

```
int fd = t_open( "/dev/ticotsord", O_RDWR|O_NONBLOCK,0);
if (fd == -1) t_error("t_open");
```

The following statements create a datagram transport end point. The transport end point operations are to be performed in the normal blocking mode, and the transport default characteristics are returned via the *info* variable. The transport end point descriptor is assigned to the variable *fd*:

```
struct t_info info;
int fd = t_open( "/dev/ticlts", O_RDWR, &info);
if (fd==-1) t_error("t_open");
```

Some transport end points have system-defined addresses, as specified in the */etc/services* file. For example, the following two lines in a */etc/services* file define two end points:

```
# /etc/services
test                      4045/tcp
utst1                     5001/udp
```

In the above, the first transport end point service name is *test* and it uses *TCP* as its transport provider. Thus, it is a connection-based end point. The second end point service name is *utst1* and it uses *UDP* as its transport provider. This makes it a datagram end point.

Given the above definitions in the */etc/services* file, one can determine the address of a transport end point address and its transport provider device file name as follows:

```
struct nd_hostserv hostserv;
struct netconfig    *nconf;
struct nd_addrlist  *addr;
void                *hp;
int                 type = NC_TPI_COTS_ORD;
if ((hp=setnetpath()) == 0)
{
      perror("Can't init network");
      exit(1);
}
hostserv.h_host = "fruit";           // assume the machine host name
hostserv.h_serv = "test";            // transport's service name
while ((nconf=getnetpath(hp)) != 0)
{
      if (nconf->nc_semantics == type
          && netdir_getbyname(nconf, &hostserv, &addr)==0)
          break;
}
endnetpath(hp);

if (nconf == 0 )
      cerr << "No transport found for service: 'test'\n";
else if ((tid=t_open(nconf->nc_device, O_RDWR, 0)) < 0)
      t_error("t_open fails");
else cerr << "transport end point's address is specified in addr\n";
```

In the above code segment, the machine name and the transport service name are assumed to be *fruit* and *test*, respectively. This information is stored in the *hostserv* variable. The *setnetpath, getnetpath,* and *endnetpath* functions are used to retrieve each entry in the /etc/netconfig file, where each entry contains a transport provider type and a corresponding device file name. In the above example, a transport provider of type NC_TPI_COTS_ORD (connection-based and support for orderly connection release) is sought. For each transport provider whose type matches the criteria, the *nconf* and *hostserv* variables are passed to the *netdir_getbyname* function. This finds the address of: (1) a transport end point on the specified machine (*fruit* in this example); and (2) the given service name (*test*). This function uses the specified transport provider.

The transport end point address is returned via the *addr* variable. This *addr* variable is used later on in the *t_bind* (server process) or *t_connect* (client process) function calls.

The above code can be modified as follows to get a datagram transport end point address. It is also the device file path name of the transport provider for *utst1* service:

* Assign the value NC_TPI_CLTS to the *type* variable instead of NC_TPI_COTS_ORD
* Assign the value *utst1* to the *hostserv.h_serv* data field

11.4.3   t_bind

The function prototype of the *t_bind* API is:

```
#include <tiuser.h>

int        t_bind (int fd, struct t_bind* inaddr, struct t_bind* outaddr);
```

This function binds an address (or a name) to a transport end point, as designated by the *fd* argument. The actual value of *fd* is obtained from a *t_open* call.

The *inaddr* argument contains the address assigned to the transport end point. Its actual value may be NULL, which means that the transport end point underlying the transport provider is to assign the necessary address.

The *struct t_bind* is declared as:

```
struct t_bind
{
        struct netbuf      addr;
        unsigned           qlen;
};
```

where the *qlen* field specifies the maximum number of connection requests that may be pending for the transport end point. This is set to a nonzero value for a server transport end point and a zero value for all other uses. The *addr* field contains the address to be assigned to the transport end point.

The *struct netbuf* is declared as:

```
struct netbuf
{
        unsigned int    maxlen;
        unsigned int    len;
        char*           buf;
};
```

where the *len* value specifies the number of characters in *buf* that contains the transport end point address. The *maxlen* field is a *don't-care* for *inaddr*.

The *outaddr* argument returns the actual address assigned to the transport end point by the underlying transport provider. This may be different from that specified in *inaddr*. If the transport provider fails to bind the address specified in *inaddr* to the end point, it will bind a different address to it instead. The actual value to *outaddr* may be NULL, which means that the calling process does not care what address is assigned to the transport end point. This is usually the case for a connection-based client transport end point.

If the actual value for *outaddr* is the address of a *struct t_bind* type variable, then, as input, the *outaddr->buf* is an address of a buffer defined by a calling process, and the *outaddr->maxlen* field specifies the maximum size of the *outaddr->buf* buffer. On return, the *outaddr->len* field contains the number of characters in the *outaddr->buf*, which stores the transport end point address, as assigned by the transport provider.

The function returns a -1 if it fails, a 0 if it succeeds.

The following sample code binds an address returned by the *netdir_getbyname* function (see the example in the last section) to a transport end point designated by *fd*. Furthermore, the end point may accept up to five client connection requests at any one time. Notice that *t_alloc* is used to allocate dynamic storage for the *struct t_bind*-typed object (as pointed to by *bind*). This guarantees that all the fields in the object are initialized properly.

```
struct t_bind *bind = t_alloc (fd, T_BIND, T_ALL);
if (!bind)
   t_error("t_alloc fails for T_BIND");
else {
   bind->qlen = 5;
   bind->addr = *(addr->n_addrs);
   if (t_bind(fd, bind, bind) < 0) t_error("t_bind");
}
```

A transport end point may be bound to an integer-type address, which is useful if the end point communicates with other transport end points on the same machine only. The following code binds an address of 2 to a transport end point designated by *fd*:

```
struct t_bind *bind = t_alloc (fd, T_BIND, T_ALL);
if (bind)     {
    bind->qlen = 5;
    bind->addr.len = sizeof(int);
    *(int*)bind->addr.buf = 2;
    if (t_bind(fd, bind, bind) < 0) t_error("t_bind");
} else t_error("t_alloc fails for T_BIND");
```

11.4.4   t_listen

The function prototype of the *t_listen* API is:

```
#include <tiuser.h>

int        t_listen ( int  fd, struct t_call* call );
```

This function waits for a client connection request to arrive at a transport end point as designated by *fd*. The client's transport end point address is returned via the *call* argument.

By default this function blocks the calling process until a client connection request is received. However, if *fd* is specified to be nonblocking (using the O_NONBLOCK flag in the *t_open* call or set via the *fcntl* function), the *t_listen* function returns immediately if no client connection request is detected by the function. The *t_errno* global variable will be set to TNODATA.

The *struct t_call* is declared as:

```
struct t_call
{
        struct             addr;
        struct netbuf      opt;
        struct netbuf      udata;
        int                sequence;
};
```

where the *addr* field contains the address of a client transport end point that initiates the connection request. The *opt* field contains any protocol-specific parameters. The *udata* field contains any optional user data to be sent along with the connection request. The *sequence* field contains an integer ID that is used to uniquely identify each connection.

The following code checks for a connection request in nonblocking mode. Notice that *t_alloc* is used to allocate the storage for the call variable. This is to ensure that the *maxlen* fields in the a*ddr, opt,* and *udata* are set to reflect the size of their *buf* member fields.

```
struct t_call *call = (struct t_call*)t_alloc (fd, T_CALL,T_ALL);
if (!call)
    t_error("t_alloc fails for T_CALL");
else do {
    if (t_listen(fd, call) == 0) break;        // got a connect request
    if (t_errmo!=TNODATA) {
        t_error("t_listen fails")
        exit(1);
    }
    /* do something else */
} while (1);
```

The above example first calls *t_alloc* to allocate dynamic storage for a *struct t_call* object and uses *call* to point to it. After that, the program goes into a loop where it calls *t_listen* to check for connection requests iteratively. If *t_listen* returns a zero value, a connection request is detected, and the program breaks out of the loop. However, if *t_listen* returns a nonzero value the *t_errno* global variable is checked. If *t_errno* is not set to TNODATA, some other error condition has occurred, and the program calls *t_error* to report a diagnostic message, then quits. Otherwise, a connection request is not yet available, and the program does something else, resuming the *t_listen* call afterward.

11.4.5   t_accept

The function prototype of the *t_accept* API is:

```
#include <tiuser.h>

int        t_accept ( int  fd, int newfd, struct t_call* call );
```

This function accepts a client connection request that is received via a *t_listen* call.

The *fd* value designates which server transport end point accepts the connection request. The *newfd* value designates a transport end point to be connected to the client transport end point. The *newfd* value may or may not be the same as *fd*. If they are the same, the transport end point must not have other connection requests pending, or this function will fail. On the other hand, if they are not the same value, the *newfd* must be allocated via a *t_open* call prior to its use in this function call. Then, after the *t_accept* call returns successfully, the *fd* can be used to accept more connection requests from other clients, and the *newfd* is used exclusively to communicate with the client whose transport address is specified in the *call* value. The *call* value is obtained from a *t_listen* call.

The function returns a -1 if it fails, a 0 value if it succeeds.

The following code spawns a child process to accept connection requests from one or more client processes. Note that the transport end point designated by *fd* is assumed to operate in blocking mode:

```
struct t_call *call = (struct t_call*)t_alloc (fd, T_CALL,T_ALL);
if (!call)
    t_error("t_alloc fails for T_CALL");
else while (t_listen(fd, call) == 0)        // got one connect request
    switch (fork())       {
        case -1: perror("fork"); break;      // parent process. fork fails
        default: break;                      // parent process. fork succeeds
        case 0:                              // child process to talk to client
            if ((newfd=t_open("/dev/ticotsord",O_RDWR,0))==-1 ||
                        t_bind(newfd,0,0)==-1)
                t_error("t_open or t_bind fails");
            else if (t_accept(fd, newfd, call)==-1)
                t_error("t_accept fails\n");
            else {
                t_close(fd);// don't need this anymore
                /* now communicate with a client via the newfd */
            }
    }
```

In the above example, *t_alloc* is called to allocate a dynamic storage for a *struct t_call* object to store a client transport address. The *struct t_call* object is referenced by the *call* variable. If the *t_alloc* call succeeds, the program goes into a loop, executing the *t_listen* function to wait for client connection requests to arrive. For each connection request received, the program creates a child process to deal with that client. Specifically, each child process creates a new transport end point that is of the same transport type as that designated by *fd*. The new transport end point is referenced by the *newfd* variable, and it is bound an arbitrary name (as assigned by the transport provider). After that, the child process calls the *t_accept* function to connect the *newfd* end point to the client's end point. If the *t_accept* call succeeds, the child process closes its copy of the *fd* descriptor, as it is no longer needed in that process and begins to communicate with the client.

11.4.6   t_connect

The function prototype of the *t_connect* API is:

```
#include <tiuser.h>

int       t_connect ( int fd, struct t_call* inaddr, struct t_call* outaddr );
```

This function sends a connect request to the server transport end point. The *fd* value designates which client transport end point is to be connected to that of the server. The server transport address is specified in the *inaddr* value. The address of the actual server transport end point bound is returned via the *outaddr* value.

The *inaddr* value must not be NULL, but the *outaddr* value may be NULL if the bound server transport address is a don't-care.

By default this function blocks the calling process until a server transport end point is connected or until a system error occurs. However, if *fd* is specified to be nonblocking, this function initiates a connection request and returns immediately (if a server transport end point is not connected right away). The *t_errno* global variable is set to TNODATA. The client can later call the *t_rcvconnect* function to check on the completion of the connect request. The function prototype of the *t_rcvconnect* function is:

```
#include <tiuser.h>

int       t_rcvconnect ( int fd, struct t_call* outaddr );
```

This function returns a -1 if it fails, a 0 value if it succeeds.

The following code sets a transport end point descriptor to be nonblocking via a *fcntl* call. It then attempts to connect to a server in a nonblocking manner. The server transport address is assumed to be 3.

```
struct t_call *call = (struct t_call*)t_alloc (fd, T_CALL, T_ALL);
if (!call) {
    t_error("t_alloc fails for T_CALL");
    exit(1);
}
call->addr.len = sizeof(int);              // set the server's transport address
*(int*)call->addr.buf = 3;
/* set the fd to be nonblocking. This can also be set at the t_open call */
if ((flg=fcntl(fd, F_GETFL,0)==-1 ||
            fcntl(fd,F_SETFL,flg|O_NONBLOCK)==-1) {
    perror("fcntl");
    exit(2);
}
if (t_connect(fd, call, call)==-1) {
    while (t_errno==TNODATA) {    // poll for connect request to complete
        /* do something else */
        if (t_rcvconnect(fd, call)==0) break;
    }
    if (t_errno!=TNODATA)     {
        t_error("t_connect or t_rcvconnect fails");
        exit(4);
    }
}  /* t_connect */
/* start communicating with a server transport end point */
```

In the above example, *fcntl* is called to set the transport end point designated by *fd* to be nonblocking. The program then calls *t_connect* to establish a connection with a server transport end point. The server transport address is assumed to be 3 (for local connection only). If *t_connect* does not succeed, the program goes into a loop where it does something else then calls *t_rcvconnect* to check on the completion of the connection request. The loop terminates when either *t_rcvconnect* returns a success status (return value is zero) or an error occurs, and *t_errno* is not set to TNODATA. If either the *t_connect* or the *t_rcvconnect* call succeeds, the program begins communicating with the server process.

11.4.7   t_snd, t_sndudata

The function prototypes of *t_snd* and *t_sndudata* APIs are:

```
#include <tiuser.h>

int        t_snd ( int fd, char* buf, unsigned len, int flags );
int        t_sndudata ( int fd, struct t_unitdata* udata );
```

The *t_snd* function sends a message of *len* bytes (contained in *buf*) to another process that is connected via the transport end point designated by *fd*. The transport end point must be a virtual circuit and has been connected to another end point via a *t_connect* (for a client process) or a *t_accept* (for a server process) call.

The *flags* value may be zero, which is the default, or it may be set with one or more of the following values, which are defined in the <tiuser.h> header:

flags value	Use
T_EXPEDITED	Tags the message as an urgent message. This is like the MSG_OOB flag in sockets. Note that the transport provider may or may not support this option. If it does not support this, the function fails, and the *t_errno* will be set to TNOTSUPPORT
T_MORE	Tells the recipient process that the message sent via the next *t_snd* call is a continuing message of the current message

The function returns a -1 if it fails or the number of characters in *buf* that were successfully sent. Note that if *fd* is specified to be nonblocking, the function returns immediately if the message in *buf* cannot be delivered to the recipient right away. The function return value is -1, and the *t_errno* is set to TFLOW.

The *t_sndudata* is used to send datagram messages via a connectionless transport end point. The *struct t_unitdata* is declared as:

```
struct t_unitdata
{
    struct netbuf     addr;
    struct netbuf     opt;
    struct netbuf     udata;
};
```

where *udata* contains the message to be sent to a peer transport end point and whose address is specified in *addr*. The *opt* value is any transport-specific options to be used in this message delivery.

Note that there are no *flags* values that can be set in a *t_sndudata* call to specify that the message sent is a T_EXPEDITED message.

The function returns a -1 if it fails or a 0 if it succeeds. Note that if *fd* is specified to be nonblocking, the function returns immediately if the message specified in *udata* cannot be delivered to the recipient right away. In this case, the function return value is -1, and the *t_errno* is set to TFLOW.

The following example sends an urgent message (MSG1) to a connected transport end point:

```
char* MSG1 = "Hello World";
if (t_snd( MSG1, strlen(MSG1)+1,T_EXPEDITED) < 0) t_error("t_snd");
```

The following example sends a datagram message (MSG1) to the peer transport end point whose address is 3 (a local connection):

```
char* MSG1 = "Hello World";
struct t_unitdata *t_ud =
                    (struct t_unitdata*)t_alloc(fd,T_UNITDATA,T_ALL);
if (!t_ud) {
    t_error("t_alloc for T_UNITDATA fails");
    exit(1);
}
t_ud->addr.len = sizeof(int);              // set recipient transport address
*(int*)t_ud->addr.buf = 3;
t_ud->udata.len = strlen(MSG1) + 1;   // set the message to be sent
t_ud->udata.buf = MSG1;
if (t_sndudata(fd, t_ud) < 0) t_error("t_sndudata");
```

11.4.8   t_rcv, t_rcvudata, t_rcvuderr

The function prototypes of *t_rcv, t_rcvudata* and *t_rcvuderr* APIs are:

```
#include <tiuser.h>

int      t_rcv ( int fd, char* buf, unsigned len, int* flags);

int      t_rcvudata ( int fd, struct t_unitdata* udata, int* flags);

int      t_rcvuderr ( int fd, struct t_uderr* uderr );
```

The *t_rcv* function receives a message that is put into *buf* by another process that is connected to the transport end point as designated by *fd*. The transport end point must be a virtual circuit and has been connected to another end point via a *t_connect* (for a client process) or a *t_accept* (for a server process) call.

The *len* value specifies the maximum size of the *buf* argument. The *flags* value is an address of an integer-typed variable. This variable holds the *flags* value that is sent along with the message via the *t_snd* function call. The possible values that may be returned in *flags* are 0, T_MORE, and/or T_EXPEDITED. These values are described in the last section.

The *t_rcv* function returns -1 if it fails or the number of data bytes that were put into *buf*. Note that if *fd* is specified to be nonblocking, the function returns immediately if no message can be received right away. In this case, the function return value is -1 and the *t_errno* is set to TNODATA.

The *t_rcvudata* is used to receive datagram messages via a connectionless transport end point. The *udata* value is an address of a *struct unitdata* typed variable and holds the datagram message received, as well as the sender's address.

The *flags* value is an address of an integer-typed variable. This variable is normally assigned a return value of 0. However, if the receiving buffer *udata->udata.buf* is too small to receive the entire incoming message, the returned *flags* value is set to T_MORE and the kernel copies only enough message text to fill up the *udata->udata.buf* buffer. The process should call *t_rcvudata* again to receive the rest of the message.

The *t_rcvudata* function returns -1 if it fails or 0 if it succeeds. Note that if *fd* is specified to be nonblocking, the function returns immediately if no message can be received right away. The function return value is -1, and the *t_errno* is set to TNODATA.

The *t_rcvuderr* is used to receive error diagnostics associated with a datagram message. This should be called only if a *t_rcvudata* call returns a failure status. The *struct t_uderr* is declared as:

```
struct t_uderr
{
    struct netbuf      addr;
    struct netbuf      opt;
    long               error;
};
```

where *addr* contains the destination transport address of the erroneous message, *opt* contains any transport-specific parameters to be used with the message delivery and *error* contains an error code.

The *uderr* value may be specified as NULL, which means no error diagnostic is wanted and the function simply clears the internal error status flag.

The *t_rcvuderr* function return -1 if it fails, or 0 if it succeeds.

The following example receives a message from a connected transport end point:

```
int       flags;
char      buf[80];
if (t_rcv( fd, buf, sizeof buf, &flags ) < 0) t_error("t_rcv");
```

The following example receives a datagram message from a peer transport end point and prints an error diagnostic if the *t_rcvudata* call fails:

```
struct t_unitdata *t_ud =
                    (struct t_unitdata*)t_alloc(fd,T_UNITDATA,T_ALL);
if (!t_ud) {
    t_error("t_alloc for T_UNITDATA fails");
    exit(1);
}
    int                flags;
char      buf[80];
t_ud->udata.len = sizeof (buf);           // setup a buffer to receive msg
t_ud->udata.buf = buf;

if (t_rcvudata(fd, t_ud, &flags)< 0) {    // receive a datagram message
    if (t_errno==TLOOK)     {
        struct t_uderr *uderr=
                    (struct t_uderr*)t_alloc(fd, T_UDERROR, T_ALL);
```

```
          if (!uderr)      {
             t_error("t_alloc for T_UDERROR fails");
             exit(2);
          }
          if (t_rcvuderr(fd, uderr) < 0)        // get error code
             t_error("t_uderr");
          else cerr << "Error code is: << uderr->error << endl;
          t_free(uderr, T_UDERROR);        // free error data record
       }
       else t_error("t_rcvudata");
    } else cout << "receive msg: '" << buf << "'\n";
```

11.4.9   t_sndrel , t_rcvrel

The function prototypes of *t_sndrel* and *t_rcvrel* APIs are:

```
    #include <tiuser.h>

    int      t_sndrel ( int  fd );
    int      t_rcvrel ( int  fd );
```

The *t_sndrel* function sends an orderly connection release request to the underlying transport provider. The process cannot send any further messages to the transport end point designated by *fd*, but it can continue to receive messages via *fd* until an orderly connection release indication is received.

The *sndrel* function returns -1 if it fails, 0 if it succeeds. If *fd* is set to be nonblocking and the orderly release request cannot be sent to the underlying transport provider immediately, the function returns a -1 value, and *t_errno* is set to TFLOW.

The *t_rcvrel* acknowledges the receipt of an orderly connection release indication. After this function is called, the process should not attempt to receive more messages via the transport end point designated by *fd*.

The *t_rcvrel* function returns -1 if it fails, 0 if it succeeds.

Note that not all transport providers support the *t_sndrel* and *t_rcvrel* functions. If a transport provider does not support these functions and they are called, they return a -1 value, and *t_errno* is set to TNOTSUPPORT.

The following example sends an orderly release request to a connected transport end point and waits for acknowledgment of the connection release indication:

```
if (sndrel(fd) < 0)
    t_error("sndrel");
else if (t_rcvrel(fd) < 0) t_error("rcvrel");
```

11.4.10   t_snddis, t_rcvdis

The function prototypes of *t_snddis* and *t_rcvdis* APIs are:

```
#include <tiuser.h>

int       t_snddis ( int  fd, struct t_call* call );
int       t_rcvdis ( int  fd, struct t_discon* conn );
```

The *t_snddis* function is used to abort an established transport connection or to reject a connection request by a client. When *t_snddis* is used to reject a connection request, the *call->sequence* field specifies which connection request to reject. When *t_snddis* is used to initiate an abortive release of a transport connection, *call* value may be NULL; otherwise, only the *call->udata* field is used. This field contains user data sent to the connected transport end point along with the abortive release indication.

The *t_snddis* function returns -1 if it fails, 0 if it succeeds.

The *t_rcvdis* function is used to retrieve an abortive release indication and any user data sent along with the indication. The *conn* value may be NULL if the process does not care about the user data or the reason for the abortive release. Otherwise, the *conn* value is the address of a *struct t_discon* typed variable. The *struct t_discon* is declared as:

```
struct t_discon
{
    struct netbuf    udata;
    int              reason;
    int              sequence;
};
```

The *conn->udata* contains any user data that are sent via a *t_snddis* call. The *conn->reason* contains a transport-specific reason code for the disconnection. The *conn->sequence* is meaningful only in a server process that has performed multiple *t_listen* calls and is used to determine which client process has initiated a *t_connect* and, finally, a *t_snddis* function call.

The *t_rcvdis* function returns -1 if it fails, 0 if it succeeds.

The following example sends an abortive release request to a connected transport end point:

```
if (t_snddis(fd) < 0) t_error("t_snddis");
```

The following example uses *t_rcvdis* to obtain a reason code for a rejection of a connection request:

```
if (t_connect(fd, call, call) < 0 && t_errno==TLOOK)
    if (t_look((fd)==T_DISCONNECT) {
        struct t_discon *conn = (struct t_discon*)t_alloc(fd,T_DIS,T_ALL);
        if (!conn)
            t_error("t_alloc for T_DIS fails");
        else if (t_rcvdis(fd,conn) < 0)
            t_error("t_rcvdis");
        else cout << "Disconnect reason code: " << conn->reason << endl;
    }
```

11.4.11   t_close

The function prototype of *t_close* APIs is:

```
#include <tiuser.h>

int        t_close ( int  fd );
```

The *t_close* function causes the transport provider to free all system resources that are allocated for the transport end point as designated by *fd,* and closes the device file associated with the transport provider. This should be called after the transport end point connection has been terminated via either the *t_sndrel* or the *t_snddis* call.

The *t_close* function returns a -1 if it fails or a 0 if it succeeds.

The following example closes a transport end point:

```
if (t_close(fd) < 0) t_error("t_close");
```

11.5   TLI Class

This section depicts the TLI class which performs functions similar to those in the sock class (see Section 11.2). Specifically, the TLI class encapsulates all low-level TLI system call interfaces and takes care of the dynamic memory management of the TLI-specific data structure (e.g., *struct t_call, struct t_bind,* etc.). These reduce the learning and programming time of users who wish to use TLI for IPC. Furthermore, the TLI class fosters maximum code reuse among all applications.

The TLI class is defined in the *tli.h* header as:

```
#ifndef TLI_H
#define TLI_H

/* TLI class definition */
#include <iostream.h>
#include <unistd.h>
#include <string.h>
#include <tiuser.h>
#include <stropts.h>
#include <fcntl.h>
#include <stdio.h>
#include <stdlib.h>
#include <signal.h>
#include <netdir.h>
#include <netconfig.h>
#define    UDP_TRANS      "/dev/ticlts"
#define    TCP_TRANS      "/dev/ticotsord"
#define    DISCONNECT     -1

class tli
{
    private:
        int            tid;          // transport descriptor
        int            local_addr;   // transport address for local IPC
        struct nd_addrlist *addr;     // transport address for Internet IPC
        struct netconfig   *nconf;    // transport provider device file
        int            rc;           // TLI functions return status code

        /* Allocate a structure to send a datagram message to an
```

```
        end point in Internet */
struct t_unitdata* alloc_ud ( int nsid, char* service, char* host )
{
    struct t_unitdata* ud=(struct t_unitdata*)t_alloc(
                nsid==-1 ? tid : nsid, T_UNITDATA, T_ALL);
    if (!ud)        {
        t_error("t_alloc of t_unitdata");
        return 0;
    }
    struct nd_hostserv      hostserv;
    struct netconfig        *ncf;
    struct nd_addrlist      *Addr;
    void                    *hp;
    if ((hp=setnetpath()) == 0)        {
        perror("Can't init network");
        return 0;
    }
    hostserv.h_host = host;
    hostserv.h_serv = service;
    while ((ncf=getnetpath(hp)) != 0)
        if (ncf->nc_semantics == NC_TPI_CLTS
                && netdir_getbyname(ncf, &hostserv, &Addr)==0)
            break;
    endnetpath(hp);
    if (!ncf)    {
        cerr << "Can't find transport for '" << service << "'\n";
        return 0;
    }
    ud->addr = *(Addr->n_addrs);
    return ud;
};

/* Allocate a structure to send a datagram message to an end point */
struct t_unitdata* alloc_ud ( int nsid, int port_no )
{
    struct t_unitdata* ud=(struct t_unitdata*)t_alloc(
                        nsid==-1 ? tid : nsid, (T_UNITDATA), (T_ALL));
    if (!ud)        {
        t_error("t_alloc of t_unitdata");
        return 0;
    }
    ud->addr.len = sizeof(int);
    *(int*)ud->addr.buf = port_no;
    return ud;
};
```

```
              /* Report a datagram message receive error */
              void report_uderr( int nsid )
              {
                 if ((t_errno) == (TLOOK))
                 {
                    struct t_uderr   *uderr;
                    if ((uderr=(struct t_uderr*)t_alloc(nsid==-1 ? tid : nsid,
                                      T_UDERROR,T_ALL))==0) {
                       t_error("t_alloc of t_uderr");
                       return;
                    }
                    if ((rc=t_rcvuderr(nsid==-1 ? tid : nsid, uderr)) < 0)
                       t_error("t_rcvuderr");
                    else cerr << "bad datagram. error=" << uderr->error << endl;
                    t_free((char*)uderr,T_UDERROR);
                 }
                 else t_error("t_rcvudata");
              };
      public:
           /* Constructor to create a transport end point for local IPC */
           tli( int srv_addr, int connless = 0 )
           {
              local_addr = srv_addr;
              nconf = 0;
              addr  = 0;
              if ((tid=t_open(connless ? UDP_TRANS : TCP_TRANS,
                                O_RDWR, 0)) < 0)
                 t_error("t_open fails");
           };


           /* Constructor to create a transport end point for Internet IPC */
           tli( char* hostname, char* service, int connless=0 )
           {
              struct nd_hostserv  hostserv;
              void  *hp;
              int type = connless ? NC_TPI_CLTS : NC_TPI_COTS_ORD;
              local_addr = 0;
              // find the transport provider for the specified host/service
              if ((hp=setnetpath()) == 0)     {
                 perror("Can't init network");
                 exit(1);
              }
              hostserv.h_host = hostname;
              hostserv.h_serv = service;
              while ((nconf=getnetpath(hp)) != 0)
                 if (nconf->nc_semantics == type
```

```
                    && netdir_getbyname(nconf, &hostserv, &addr)==0)
            break;
        endnetpath(hp);
        if (nconf == 0 )
            cerr << "No transport found for service: '" << service << "'\n";
        else if ((tid=t_open(nconf->nc_device, O_RDWR, 0)) < 0)
            t_error("t_open fails");
};

/* Destructor function */
~tli()                         { shutdown(); close(tid);  };

/* Check constructor success status */
int good()                     { return tid >= 0;  };

/* Let the transport provider  to bind a name to an end point */
int Bind_anonymous( )  { return t_bind(tid, 0, 0); };

/* Bind a name to a transport end point */
int Bind()
{
    struct t_bind  *bind;
    if ((bind= (struct t_bind*)t_alloc(tid, T_BIND, T_ALL))==0)       {
        t_error("t_alloc for t_bind");
        return -1;
    }
    bind->qlen = 1;        // max no of pending connect request
    if (nconf)  {              // Internet address
        bind->addr = *(addr->n_addrs);
    }
    else {                 // Local address
        ind->addr.len = sizeof(int);
        *(int*)bind->addr.buf = local_addr;
    }
    if ((rc = t_bind(tid, bind, bind)) < 0)
        t_error("t_bind");
    else                   // echo the actually bound address
        cerr << "server: t_bind: " << (*(int*)bind->addr.buf) << endl;
    return rc;
};
/* Wait for a connect request from a client transport end point */
int listen ( struct t_call*& call )
{
    if (!call && (call = (struct t_call*)t_alloc(tid, T_CALL, T_ALL))==0)
    {
        t_error("t_alloc");
```

```
                return -1;
             }
             if ((rc=t_listen(tid,call)) < 0) t_error("t_listen");
             return rc;
        };

        /* Accept a connect request from a client transport end point */
        int accept ( struct t_call * call )
        {
            /* create a new end point to communicate with client */
            int resfd;
            if (nconf)                    // Internet IPC
                resfd = t_open( nconf->nc_device, O_RDWR, 0);
            else                          // Local IPC, must be connection-based
                resfd = t_open(TCP_TRANS, O_RDWR, 0);
            if (resfd < 0)      {
                t_error("t_open for resfd");
                return -1;
            }
            // Bind an arbitrary name to the new end point
            if (t_bind(resfd,0,0) < 0)           {
                t_error("t_bind for resfd");
                return -2;
            }
            // Connect the new end point to the client
            if (t_accept(tid, resfd, call) < 0)        {
                if (t_errno == TLOOK)   {
                    if (t_rcvdis(tid, 0) < 0) {
                        t_error("t_rcvdis");
                        return -4;
                    }
                    if (t_close(resfd) < 0)      {
                        t_error("t_close");
                        return -5;
                    }
                    return DISCONNECT;
                }
                t_error("t_acept");
                return -6;
            }
            return resfd;
        };

        /* Initiate a connect request to a server's transport end point */
        int connect()
        {
```

```
        struct t_call *call;
        if ((call = (struct t_call*)t_alloc(tid, T_CALL, T_ALL))==0)    {
            t_error("t_alloc");
            return -1;
        }
        if (nconf)
            call->addr = *(addr->n_addrs);
        else {
            call->addr.len = sizeof(int);
            *(int*)call->addr.buf = local_addr;
        }
        cerr << "client: connect to addr=" << (*(int*)call->addr.buf) << endl;
        if ((rc=t_connect(tid,call,0)) < 0)    {
            t_error("client: t_connect"); return -2;
        }
        return rc;
};

/* Write a message to a connected remote transport end-pount */
int write( char* buf, int len, int nsid=-1 )
{
    if ((rc=t_snd(nsid==-1 ? tid : nsid, buf, len, 0)) < 0) t_error("t_snd");
    return rc;
};

/* Read a message from a connected remote transport end-pount */
int read( char* buf, int len, int& flags, int nsid=-1 )
{
    if ((rc=t_rcv(nsid==-1 ? tid : nsid, buf, len, &flags)) < 0)
        t_error("t_snd");
    return rc;
};

/* Write a datagram message to a remote end point in the Internet */
int writeto( char* buf, int len, int flag, char* service, char* host,
             int nsid=-1 )
{
    struct t_unitdata* ud = alloc_ud(nsid,service,host);
    ud->udata.len = len;
    ud->udata.buf = buf;
    if ((rc=t_sndudata(nsid==-1 ? tid : nsid, ud)) < 0)
        t_error("t_sndudata");
    return rc;
};
```

```
/* Write a datagram message to a remote end point on the
   same machine */
int writeto( char* buf, int len, int flag, int port_no, int nsid=-1 )
{
    struct t_unitdata* ud = alloc_ud(nsid,port_no);
    ud->udata.len = len;
    ud->udata.buf = buf;
    if ((rc=t_sndudata(nsid==-1 ? tid : nsid, ud)) < 0)
        t_error("t_sndudata");
    return rc;
};

/* Write a datagram msg to a end point whose address is specified
   in ud */
int writeto( char* buf, int len, int flag, struct t_unitdata* ud, int nsid=-1 )
{
    ud->udata.len = len;
    ud->udata.buf = buf;
    if ((rc=t_sndudata(nsid==-1 ? tid : nsid, ud)) < 0)
        t_error("t_sndudata");
    return rc;
};

/* Receive a datagram message from a remote end point */
int readfrom( char* buf, int len, int& flags, struct t_unitdata*& ud,
                        int nsid =-1)
{
    if (!ud && (ud=(struct t_unitdata*)t_alloc(nsid==-1 ? tid : nsid,
                    T_UNITDATA, T_ALL))==0)   {
        t_error("t_alloc of t_unitdata");
        return -1;
    }
    ud->udata.len = len;
    ud->udata.buf = buf;
    if ((rc=t_rcvudata(nsid==-1 ? tid : nsid, ud, &flags)) < 0)
        report_uderr(nsid);
    return rc;
};

/* Shutdown a transport connection using abortive release notification */
int shutdown( int nsid = -1 )
{
    return t_snddis( nsid==-1 ? tid : nsid, 0 );
};
};   /* class TLI */
#endif
```

The public member functions of the TLI class are on an almost one-to-one correspondence with those of the sock class. This is a reflection of the one-to-one correspondence of the TLI APIs and the socket APIs.

The major difference between the TLI class and the *sock* class is the naming convention assigned to each type of object. Specifically, a *sock* object name may be a UNIX path name (for UNIX domain socket) or a host name and a port name (for an Internet domain socket). A TLI object name may be an integer number (for local transport communication) or a host name and a service name (for Internet transport communication).

Another difference between the TLI class and the *sock* class is the *listen* function. Whereas the *sock::listen* sets only the maximum number of pending connection requests allowed for a *sock* object, the *TLI::listen* function actually waits for a client connection request to arrive. In fact, the *sock::accept* function actually combines the operation of the *TLI::listen* and *TLI::accept* functions.

The above TLI class does not support nonblocking operations, but it could easily be modified by users to support nonblocking operations. The following two sections depict two sample IPC applications that make use of the TLI class.

11.6   Client/Server Message Example

The first example that makes use of the TLI class is the client/server message passing example, as shown in Section 10.3.7. This new version uses connection-based transport end points to set up a communication channel between the message server and its client processes. Furthermore, because the server is connected directly to each client process, each message sent from a client consists of a service command (e.g., LOCAL_TIME, UTC_TIME, or QUIT_CMD, etc.) encoded in a character string. The server sends the service response to its client in a character string format also.

The message server program, *tli_msg_srv.C*, is shown below:

```
#include "tli.h"
#include <sys/times.h>
#include <sys/types.h>
#define MSG1 "Invalid cmd to message server"
typedef enum { LOCAL_TIME, GMT_TIME, QUIT_CMD,
                    ILLEGAL_CMD } CMDS;

/* create a child process to handle a client's commands */
void process_cmd (tli* sp, int fd )
{
    char    buf[80];
```

```
        time_t   tim;
        char*    cptr;
        int      flags;
        switch (fork())   {
           case -1:   perror("fork");  return;
           case 0:    break;
           default:   return;  // parent
        }
        /* read commands from a client until EOF or QUIT_CMD */
        while (sp->read(buf, sizeof buf, flags, fd) > 0)       {
           cerr << "server: read cmd: '" << buf << "'\n";
           int    cmd = ILLEGAL_CMD;
           (void)sscanf(buf,"%d",&cmd);
           switch (cmd)          {
              case LOCAL_TIME:
                 tim = time(0);
                 cptr = ctime(&tim);
                 sp->write(cptr, strlen(cptr)+1, fd);
                 break;
              case GMT_TIME:
                 tim = time(0);
                 cptr = asctime(gmtime(&tim));
                 sp->write(cptr, strlen(cptr)+1, fd);
                 break;
              case QUIT_CMD:
                 sp->shutdown(fd);                      // shutdown the connection
                 exit(0);
              default:
                 sp->write(MSG1, sizeof MSG1, fd);
           }
        }
        exit(0);
}
int main( int argc, char* argv[])
{
     char  buf[80], socknm[80];
     int  port=-1, nsid, rc;
     fd_set  select_set;
     struct timeval timeRec;
     if (argc < 2)      {
        cerr << "usage: " << argv[0] << " <serviceIno> <host>\n";
        return 1;
     }
     /* check if integer address no. or a service name is specified */
     (void)sscanf(argv[1],"%d",&port);
```

```
        /* create a connection-based transport end point */
        tli *sp;
        if (port==-1)
            sp = new tli( argv[2], argv[1] );
        else sp = new tli (port);

        if (!sp || !sp->good())        {
            cerr << "server: create transport endpoint object fails\n";
            return 1;
        }

        /* Bind a name to the server's transport end point */
        if (sp->Bind() < 0)            {
            cerr << "server: bind fails\n";
            return 2;
        }

        for (struct t_call *cal=0l; sp->listen(call)==0; )     {
            /* accept a connection request from a client socket */
            if ((nsid = sp->accept(call)) < 0)     {
                cerr << "server: accept fails\n";
                return 3;
            }
            cerr << "server: got one client connection. nsid=" << nsid << "\n";

            /* create a child process to process commands */
            process_cmd(sp,nsid);

            close(nsid); /* re-cycle file descriptor */
        }
        return sp->shutdown();
    }
```

The server program is invoked with either an integer address for local transport connection or a service and host name for Internet transport communication. The server begins execution by creating a transport end point and binds its name to it. It then enters a loop, where it listens for a connection request from client processes via the *tli::listen* function.

For each connection request received, the server calls the *tli::accept* function to connect with the client transport end point. The *tli::accept* function also returns a new transport descriptor (*nsid*) for the server to communicate exclusively with the connected client. The server calls the *process_cmd* function to process a connected client. The *process_cmd* function, in turn, forks a child process to deal with the client. It returns immediately to the server process, so that the server can continue to monitor other connect requests.

Each child process created in the *process_cmd* function calls the *tli::read* function to read each command from a connected client and then replies via the *tli::write* function. If the client sends the QUIT_CMD to the child process, the child process destroys the connection via the *tli::shutdown* call and terminates itself.

The client program that communicates with the server program via TLI class objects is *tli_msg_cls.C*:

```
#include "tli.h"
#define QUIT_CMD 2

int main( int argc, char* argv[])
{
    if (argc < 2)        {
        cerr << "usage: " << argv[0] << " <service|no> <host>\n";
        return 1;
    }
    char buf[80];
    int  port=-1, rc, flags;

    /* check if an integer address or a service name is spceified */
    (void)sscanf(argv[1],"%d",&port);

    tli  *sp;                            // create a transport end point
    if (port==-1)
        sp = new tli( argv[2], argv[1] );        // Internet transport
    else sp = new tli (port);                    // local transport
    if (!sp || !sp->good())        {
        cerr << "client: create transport endpoint object fails\n";
        return 1;
    }

    /* bind an arbitrary name to the transport end point */
    if (sp->Bind_anonymous() < 0)        {
        cerr << "client: bind fails\n";
        return 2;
    }

    /* connect to a server transport end point */
    if (sp->connect() < 0)        {
        cerr << "client: connect fails\n";
        return 3;
    }
```

```
        /* Send cmds 0 -> 2 to server */
        for (int cmd=0; cmd < 3; cmd++)        {
            /* compose a command to server */
            sprintf(buf,"%d",cmd);
            if (sp->write(buf,strlen(buf)+1) < 0) return 4;

            /* exit the loop if QUIT_CMD */
            if (cmd==QUIT_CMD) break;

            /* read reply from server */
            if (sp->read(buf,sizeof buf, flags) < 0) return 5;
            cout << "client: recv '" << buf << "'\n";
        }

        /* shutdown the transport connection */
        return sp->shutdown();

    } /* main */
```

The client program is invoked with a server address, which may be an integer address for local transport connection or a service and host name for Internet transport communication. The client begins execution by creating a transport end point and binds an anonymous name to it. A client does not need to have a well-defined name assigned to it because no other process initiates connection requests to the client process by address.

Once a transport end point is defined, the client calls the *tli::connect* function to establish a virtual circuit connection with the server transport end point. If this is accomplished successfully, the client sends a series of commands to the server via the *tli::write* function calls. The commands sent by the client, in their sending order, are LOCAL_TIME, UTC_TIME, and the QUIT_CMD. For each command sent (except the QUIT_CMD), the client waits for the server reply via the *tli::read* function and prints the server reply message to the standard output.

After the client sends the QUIT_CMD to the server, it shuts down the transport connect via the *tli::shutdown* function, then terminates itself.

The sample output of the client/server program execution is:

```
% CC -o tli_msg_srv tli_msg_srv.C -lnsl
% CC -o tli_msg_cls tli_msg_cls.C -lnsl
% tli_msg_srv 2 &
[1] 781
server: t_bind: 2
% tli_msg_cls 2
```

```
client: connect to addr=2
server: got one client connection. nsid=4
server: read cmd: '0'
client: recv 'Fri Feb 17 22:34:50 1995'
server: read cmd: '1'
client: recv 'Sat Feb 18 06:34:50 1995'
server: read cmd: '2'
[1]  + Done              tli_msg_srv 2
%
```

The same two programs can also be run unmodified but using an Internet transport connection instead. To enable this feature, a new entry, as shown below, is added to the */etc/services* file:

```
test                    4045/tcp
```

This new entry defines a new service call *test* which uses *TCP* as the transport provider, with the assigned port number of 4045. The following screen log shows the new run of the same client/server program, but here, the server transport address is *fruit* (host name) and *test* (service name):

```
% hostname
fruit
% tli_msg_srv test fruit &
[1] 776
server: t_bind: 135122
% tli_msg_cls test fruit
client: connect to addr=135122
server: got one client connection. nsid=4
server: read cmd: '0'
client: recv 'Fri Feb 17 22:34:04 1995'
server: read cmd: '1'
client: recv 'Sat Feb 18 06:34:04 1995'
server: read cmd: '2'
[1]  + Done              tli_msg_srv test fruit
```

11.7   Datagram Example

The second example shows two peer processes communicating via two datagram transport end points. These transport end points are created via the TLI class also. The two peer processes are *tli_clts1* and *tli_clts2*, as created from the *tli_clts1.C* and *tli_clts2.C* files, respectively.

The *tli_clts1.c* program is:

```c
#include <sys/systeminfo.h>
#include "tli.h"
#define MSG1 "Hello MSG1 from clts1"

/* get a host name */
int gethost( int argc, char* argv[], char host[], int len)
{
   if (argc!=3)      {
      if (sysinfo(SI_HOSTNAME,host,len)< 0)      {
         perror("sysinfo");
         return -1;
      }
   }  else strcpy(host,argv[2]);
   return 0;
}

int main( int argc, char* argv[])
{
   char  buf[80], host[80];
   int  port=-1, rc, flags=0;

   if (argc < 2)      {
      cerr << "usage: " << argv[0] << " <service|port_no> [<hostname>]\n";
      return 1;
   }

   /* check if port no. of a socket name is specified */
   (void)sscanf(argv[1],"%d",&port);
   /* Create a transport end point */
   tli  *sp;
   if (port==-1)      {
      if (gethost(argc, argv, host, sizeof host) < 0) return 2;
      sp = new tli( host, argv[1], 1 );
   } else sp = new tli (port, 1);

   if (!sp || !sp->good())      {
      cerr << "clts1: create transport endpoint object fails\n";
      return 3;
   }

   /* Bind a name to the transport end point */
   if (sp->Bind() < 0)      {
      cerr << "clts1: bind fails\n";
```

```
            return 4;
        }
        struct t_unitdata *ud = 0;
        if (sp->readfrom( buf, sizeof buf, flags, ud) < 0)        {
            cerr << "clts1: readfrom fails\n";
            return 5;
        }
        cerr << "clts1: read msg: '" << buf << "'\n";

        if (sp->writeto(MSG1, strlen(MSG1)+1, flags, ud) < 0)     {
            cerr << "clts1: writeto fails\n";
            return 6;
        }
        if (sp->readfrom(buf, sizeof buf, flags, ud) < 0)    {
            cerr << "clts: readfrom fails\n";
            return 7;
        }
        cerr << "clts1: read msg: '" << buf << "'\n";
        return 0;
    }
```

The *tli_clts1* program may be invoked with a single integer address (for local transport communication) or a service name, followed by an optional host name (for Internet transport communication). If a service name is specified, the name must also be defined in the */etc/services* file. If a host name is not specified with a service name, the host name of the machine on which the program is run is assumed.

The *tli_clts1* begins execution by creating a TLI object (a transport end point) based on the given command line arguments. If an Internet transport end point is to be created, the *gethost* function is called to retrieve the local host machine name from either the command line argument (if it is specified) or via the *sysinfo* function call.

After a TLI transport object is created, the process binds a name to the transport object, then reads a message (MSG2) to be sent by the *tli_clts2* process. Once the MSG2 message is received, the process prints that message to the standard output. It then writes a MSG1 message back to the *tli_clts2* process via the transport address contained in the *ud* variable. The *ud* variable is assigned by the *readfrom* call.

Finally, the process waits for the *tli_clts2* to send the last MSG3 message. Once that is received, the process prints that message to the standard output and terminates itself. The transport end point created by the process is discarded via the *TLI::~TLI* destructor function.

The *tli_clts2.c* program that communicates with the *tli_clts1* program is:

```
#include <sys/systeminfo.h>
#include "tli.h"
#define MSG2 "Hello MSG2 from clts2"
#define MSG3 "Hello MSG3 from clts2"

/* get a host name */
int gethost( int argc, char* argv[], char host[], int len)
{
    if (argc!=4)        {
        if (sysinfo(SI_HOSTNAME,host,len)< 0)     {
            perror("sysinfo");  return -1;
        }
    } else strcpy(host,argv[3]);
    return 0;
}

int main( int argc, char* argv[])
{
    char  buf[80], host[80];
    int  port=-1, clts1_port=-1, rc, flags=0;

    if (argc < 2)       {
        cerr << "usage: " << argv[0] <<
            " <service|port_no> <clts1_serviceno> [<host>]\n";
        return 1;
    }
    /* check if port no. of a socket name is specified */
    (void)sscanf(argv[1],"%d",&port);
    (void)sscanf(argv[2],"%d",&clts1_port);

    /* create a transport end point */
    tli  *sp;
    if (port==-1)       {                              // Internet transport
        if (gethost(argc, argv, host, sizeof host) < 0) return 2;
        sp = new tli( host, argv[1], 1 );
    } else sp = new tli (port, 1);               // local transport
    if (!sp || !sp->good())  {
        cerr << "clts2: create transport endpoint object fails\n";
        return 2;
    }

    /* Bind a name to the transport end point */
    if (sp->Bind() < 0)      {
        cerr << "clts2: bind fails\n";
        return 3;
    }
```

```
                    /* write MSG2 to the tli_clts1 process */
                     if (port==-1)
                        rc = sp->writeto(MSG2,strlen(MSG2)+1, 0, argv[2], host);
                     else rc = sp->writeto(MSG2, strlen(MSG2)+1, 0, clts1_port);
                     if (rc < 0)  {
                        cerr << "clts2: writeto fails\n";
                        return 4;
                     }

                    /* read MSG1 from the tli_clts1 process */
                     struct t_unitdata *ud = 0;
                     if (sp->readfrom(buf, sizeof buf, flags, ud) < 0)      {
                        cerr << "clts2: readfrom fails\n";
                        return 5;
                     }
                     cerr << "clts2: read msg: '" << buf << "'\n";

                    /* write MSG3 to the tli_clts1 process */
                     if (sp->writeto(MSG3, strlen(MSG3)+1, flags, ud) < 0) {
                        cerr << "clts2: writeto fails\n";
                        return 6;
                     }
                     return 0;
                  }
```

The *tli_clts2* program is very similar to the *tli_clts1* program. The difference is that it is invoked with either: (1) an assigned integer address and the integer address of the *tli_clts1* process (for local transport communication); or (2) its service name alone with that of *tli_clts1*, optionally followed by a machine host name (for Internet transport communication). If a service name is specified, the name must be defined in the */etc/services* file. If a host name is not specified with the service name, the host name is assumed.

The *tli_clts2* begins execution by creating a TLI object, based on the given command line arguments. If an Internet transport end point is created, the *gethost* function is called to retrieve the host machine name from either the command line argument (if it is specified) or via the *sysinfo* function call.

After a TLI transport object is created, the process binds a name to the transport object, then writes the MSG2 message (MSG2) to the *tli_clts1* process. Once the MSG2 message is sent, the process waits for the *tli_clts1* process to send it the MSG1 message. The process prints the MSG1 message to the standard output once it has been received.

Finally, the process writes the MSG3 message to the *tli_clts1* process before it terminates itself. The transport end point created by the process is discarded via the *TLI::~TLI* destructor function.

The following console log depicts the interaction of the *tli_clts1* and *tli_clts2* processes. The transport end points created here are based on integer addresses. The *tli_clts1*'s transport is assigned the integer address of 1, while that of the *tli_clts2* process is the address 2:

```
% CC -o tli_clts1 tli_clts1.C -lnsl
% CC -o tli_clts2 tli_clts2.C -lnsl
% tli_clts1 1 &
bind: 1
% tli_clts2 2 1
bind: 2
clts1: read msg: 'Hello MSG2 from clts2'
clts2: read msg: 'Hello MSG1 from clts1'
clts1: read msg: 'Hello MSG3 from clts2'
[1]  + Done              tli_clts1 1
```

To run the same programs again using host name/service names, the following two entries are added to the */etc/services* file:

```
utst1                    4046/udp
utst2                    4047/udp
```

The *utst*" is the service name assigned to the *tli_clts1* transport. The *utst2* is the service name for the *tli_clts2* transport. Both services use the *UDP* transport provider, which provides connectionless communication.

The following console log depicts the interaction of the same *tli_clts1* and *tli_clts2* processes, using Internet transport end points:

```
% tli_clts1 utst1 &
bind: 135123
% tli_clts2 utst2 utst1
bind: 135124
clts1: read msg: 'Hello MSG2 from clts2'
clts2: read msg: 'Hello MSG1 from clts1'
clts1: read msg: 'Hello MSG3 from clts2'
[1]  + Done              tli_clts1 utst1
```

Note that the output of the above session is identical to that of using local transport end points. No recompilation of the *tli_clts1.C* and *tli_clts2.C* programs is needed. The same two programs can also be run on different machines that are connected via an LAN. For example, suppose the *tli_clts1* program is run on a machine called *fruit* and the *tli_clts2* program is run on *apple*. The invocation syntax of the two programs is:

433

Run the *tli_clts1* program on the machine *fruit*:

```
fruit % tli_clts1 utst1 &
[1425]
```

Run the *tli_clts2* program on the machine *apple*:

```
apple % tli_clts2 utst2 utst1 fruit
...
```

Once the two programs are connected, the *tli_clts1* output messages are displayed on the machine *fruit*, while the *tli_clts2* messages are displayed on the machine *apple*.

11.8 Summary

This chapter examines BSD UNIX sockets and UNIX System V.3 and V.4 Transport Level Interface for interprocess communication. Sockets and TLI are better methods than are messages, shared memory, or semaphores, in that both sockets and TLI allow processes running on different machines to communicate. This is important for any serious client/server application, where a server is usually run on a power computer and client processes are run on end-user desktop computers.

The syntax of the sockets and TLI APIs are explained in detail in this chapter, as well as sample programs that illustrate their use. Furthermore, a *sock* class and a *tli* class are defined to encapsulate the API interface so as to reduce the learning and programming time of users who wish to use these constructs to create IPC applications.

Of the two IPC methods, TLI is more flexible than are sockets, in that it supports almost all transport protocols. Sockets support only a limited number of transport protocols for each socket type (this is controlled by hardware vendors who implement sockets on their computer systems). Also, TLI has more elaborate methods for transport-specific memory management (the *t_alloc* and *t_free* functions), transport error reporting (*t_error, t_rcvuderr,* and *t_look*), and connection release (*tli_snddis, tli_rcvdis, tli_sndrel* and *tli_rcvrel*). Thus, TLI allows users to create more sophisticated IPC applications.

However, TLI is available only in UNIX System V.3 and V.4, whereas sockets are available on all the latest UNIX systems (BSD 4.2, 4.3, 4.4, and UNIX System V.4). Furthermore, there is already a large volume of IPC applications existing today using sockets. Thus, if portability and interaction with existing socket-based applications are a concern to application developers, they should consider using sockets over TLI.

Remote Procedure Calls

Remote procedure call (RPC) is a mechanism by which a process on one machine invokes another process on either the same or a remote machine to execute a function on its behalf. It is like calling a local function in that the process makes a function call and passes data to the function, then waits for the function to return. What is special here is that the function will be executed by a different process. The RPC process interaction is invariably in a client/server manner, such that the process making an RPC call is a client process, and the process that executes an RPC function in response is a server process. A server process provides one or more service functions that can be invoked by its clients.

Remote procedure call is used in network-based applications to tap network resources on different machines. For example, in a distributed database system, the server process is a database management process, and it manages the data retrieval and storage of the database files. The client processes are the database front-end programs that allow users to input data inquiry and update commands. These user-issued commands are converted by the client processes into RPC calls to the server process. The return values of the RPC calls are depicted to the user by the client processes.

Another example of an RPC application is when a server process is running on a high-powered machine and the client processes are running on less powerful machines. Whenever a client process needs to do compute-intensive jobs, it uses RPC to direct the server to execute those jobs on the server machine. This balances the workloads of the two machines and also maintains an acceptable performance in the client machine.

Other advantages of using RPC are:

- It hides most of the network transport details from programmers. In this way, it allows programmers to develop and maintain their RPC-based programs more easily
- It uses a well-defined data representation format (e.g., XDR or external data representation) to represent data that is transmitted between server and client processes. The data format is machine architecture-independent. It allows machines of different architectures (e.g., Intel x86-based machines and SUN SPARC workstations) to communicate via RPC
- It supports all network transport protocols (connectionless and connection-based)
- Most advanced operating systems (e.g., UNIX, VMS, and Windows-NT) support RPC and are compatible with each other. This allows users to develop network-based applications that run across platforms and operating systems

The following sections examine the RPC programming techniques in more detail.

12.1   History of RPC

There were different implementations of RPC by different companies in the 1980s. Among them were Sun Microsystems's Open Network Computing (ONC) and Apollo Computers's Network Computing Architecture (NCA). Today, most commercial UNIX systems, such as Hewlett Packadd's HP-UX, International Business Machines's AIX, Sun Microsystems's Sun OS 4.1.x, and Santa Cruz Operation's SCO UNIX, all implement RPC based on the ONC method.

However, Sun's Solaris 2.x operating system and UNIX System V.4 implement RPC based on a modified version of the ONC method. The two methods are very similar, namely, they both use external data representation (XDR) format to transmit data across networks, and provide a *rpcgen* compiler to simplify the creation of RPC applications. The two methods differ, in that the ONC-based RPC APIs are based on sockets, whereas System V.4 RPC APIs can be based on sockets or on TLI.

This chapter examines the RPC programming techniques supported by both the ONC and UNIX Systems V.4 methods. In the following sections, unless stated explicitly, most descriptions are applicable to the ONC and System V.4 methods.

12.1   RPC Programming Interface Levels

There are different levels of RPC programming interface. They range from the very top level, where users invoke system-supplied RPC functions in the same manner as calling C library functions (e.g., *printf*), to the lowest level, where users create RPC programs using RPC APIs. These different programming interface levels are explained in detail in the rest of the chapter.

At the highest level, there are system-supplied RPC functions that users may call directly to collect remote system information. These functions can be used just like ordinary C library functions. The only special setup needed to use them are: (1) special header files that declare the function prototypes; and (2) links between the compiled programs with the -*lrpcsvc* switch. The *librpcsvc.a* library contains these RPC library function object codes.

The advantages of the RPC library functions are that they are easily used and impose little programming effort. However, there are only a few of these RPC library functions defined in a system. Thus, there is limited application for these functions.

The second level of RPC programming is to use the *rpcgen* compiler to generate RPC client and server stub routines automatically. Users write only the client *main* functions (which call the RPC functions) and the server RPC functions to create client and server programs. The *rpcgen* compiler can also generate XDR functions to convert any user-defined data types to XDR format for data transmission between client and server.

The advantage of using the *rpcgen* compiler is that users can focus on writing RPC functions and client main functions. There is no need to know the low-level RPC APIs. This saves programming effort and is less error prone. However, the drawbacks of this approach are that users have little control over any detailed attributes of the network transports used by the client and server programs created by *rpcgen*. They cannot manage the dynamic memory used by XDR functions.

The lowest level of RPC programming interface is to use the RPC APIs to create RPC client and server programs. The advantages of this are that users have direct control of the network transports used by the processes and the dynamic memory management in the XDR functions. However, this comes at the expense of more programming effort on the part of users.

12.2   RPC Library Functions

The RPC library function header is <rpcsvc.h>. Each header corresponds to a set of related RPC library functions and their XDR functions. The object code of these functions is stored in the *librpcsvc.a* library in the standard library directory (e.g., */usr/lib*).

The following are some common RPC library functions and their uses:

RPC library function	Uses
rusers	Gets the number of logged-in users on a remote system
rwall	Writes to a remote system
spray	Sends packets to a remote system
rstat	Gets performance data of a remote system

The following is an example program that makes use of the *rstat* RPC function to determine the up time of one or more remote systems. The up time is the elapsed time between system boot time and the current time. The *rstat* function also collects the average swap and paging statistics etc., of remote systems. The *rstat* function communicates with the *rc.rstatd* daemon running on a remote system via RPC:

```
/* rstat.C: get remote systems up time */
#include <iostream.h>
#include <rpcsvc/rstat.h>

extern "C" enum clnt_stat rstat(char *host, struct statstime *statp);
int main( int argc, char* argv[] )
{
    struct statstime statv;
    if (argc==1)   {
        cerr << "usage: " << argv[0] << " <host> ...\n";
        return 1;
    }
    while (--argc > 0)   {   /* do for each remote system specified */
        if (rstat(*++argv,&statv)==RPC_SUCCESS)   {
            int delta = statv.curtime.tv_sec - statv.boottime.tv_sec;
            int hour = delta / 3600;
            int min  = delta % 3600;
            cout << "'" << (*argv) << "' up " << hour << "hr. "
                 << (min/60) << " min. " << (min%60) << " sec."
                 << endl;
        }
        else perror("rstat");
    }
    return 0;
}
```

The above program accepts one or more remote system host names as command line argument. For each remote system specified, the process calls *rstat* to collect the remote system statistics. These data are put into the *statv* variable, and the up time of the remote system is computed by subtracting the *statv.boottime.tv_sec* value from that of the *statv.curtime.tv_sec*. The *struct statstime* data type is defined in the <rpcsvc/rstat.h> header.

A sample output of the program is:

```
%      CC rstat.C -o rstat -lrpcsvc -lnsl
%      rstat fruit lemon
'fruit' up 1 hr. 12 min. 31 sec.
'lemon' up 0 hr. 39 min. 24 sec.
%
```

As stated earlier, RPC functions are easy to use and provide the same programming interface as do C library functions. However, there are only a limited number of these functions provided by a system; thus, users need to use the *rpcgen* or the lowest RPC programming interface to create additional RPC functions for their own applications.

12.3   rpcgen

The *rpcgen* compiler is provided on most UNIX systems to support RPC-based application development. The input to the compiler is a user-written text file that describes the following information:

- An RPC program number
- One or more RPC program version numbers
- One or more RPC procedure numbers (in RPC, the term *function* and *procedure* are used interchangeably)
- Any user-defined data types that are used to pass data from and to RPC functions. The *rpcgen* creates XDR functions automatically for each of these data types
- Any optional C code that should be copied directly to the output files generated by the compiler

An RPC function is identified by a program number, a version number, and a procedure number.

An RPC program corresponds to one RPC server process, and the process is responsible for executing any of the defined procedures on a client's behalf. An RPC version specifies the revision level of a set of RPC functions. An RPC version number is an integer value and should start from 1. An RPC procedure number is an unique ID assigned to an RPC function. If there are multiple revisions of a function, the program and procedure numbers of that function are unchanged, only the RPC version number is different. All user-defined RPC function procedure numbers should start from 1. There is always an RPC function whose procedure number is zero in each RPC program. This function can be generated automatically by *rpcgen* or can be defined by users. This function takes no argument and returns nothing. Its purpose is for a client to "ping" the server to confirm the existence of the server process.

For example, given the following program, *print.c*:

```
/* print.C */
#include <iostream.h>
#include <fstream.h>

int print( char* msg )
{
        ofstream ofp( "/dev/console" );
        if (ofp) {
            ofp << msg << endl;
            ofp.close();
            return 1;
        }
        return 0;
}

int main( int argc, char* argv[] )
{
        while (--argc > 0)
            if (print(*++argv))
                    cout << "msg '" << (*argv) << "' delivered OK\n";
            else cout << " msg '" << (*argv) << "' delivered failed\n";
        return 0;
}
```

The program may be compiled and run as follow:

```
%      CC print.C -o print
%      print "Hello world" "Good-bye"
msg `Hello world` delivered OK
msg `Good-bye` delivered OK
```

the messages *Hello world* and *Good-bye* are displayed on the system console window of the machine where the *print* program is run.

To convert the *print* function to a remote procedure, a *print.x* file is created manually for it, as in the following:

```
/* print.x file: this is the input file for rpcgen */
program PRINTPROG
{
        version PRINTVER
```

```
{
    int PRINT ( string ) = 1;
} = 1;
} = 0x20000001;
```

In the *print.x* file, the assigned RPC program number, version number, and procedure number of the *print* function are 0x20000001, 1, and 1, respectively. The "program" and "version" are reserved key words for the *rpcgen*, and the PRINTPROG, PRINTVER, and PTINT are user-defined manifested constants for these assigned numbers in relation to the *print* function. By convention, these constants are specified in upper case, but they can be specified in lower case also.

Note the *print* function prototype declaration in *print.x*: the formal argument type of *print* is defined to be *string*, which is an RPC-defined data type for a NULL-terminated character string. Remote procedure call differentiates the data type of character pointers and NULL-terminated character arrays with the introduction of the *string* data type.

The *print.x* file is processed by *rpcgen* as:

```
%    ls
print.x
%    rpcgen print.x
%    ls
print.h    print.x    print_clnt.x    print_svc.x
```

There are three files generated by *rpcgen* from the *print.x* files. These files and their uses are:

File from *rpcgen*	Uses
print.h	Header file for the client and server program
print_svc.c	The server program without the RPC function definition
print_clnt.c	The client program stub. It contains all the interface functions to call the RPC server.

As a rule, if the input file to *rpcgen* is called *<name>.x*, the three corresponding output files generated by *rpcgen* are called: *<name>.h, <name>_svc.c,* and *<name>_clnt.c*.

The *print.h* header contains the declaration of the PRINTPROG, PRINTVER, and PRINT manifested constants, and the *print* function prototype. The *print.h* file for the above *print.x* file, as generated by *rpcgen* is:

```
#ifndef      _PRINT_H_RPCGEN
#define      _PRINT_H_RPCGEN
#include     <rpc/rpc.h>
#define      PRINTPROG              ((unsigned long)(0x20000001))
#define      PRINTVER               ((unsigned long)(1))
#define      PRINT                  ((unsigned long)(1))
extern  int * print_1( char**, CLIENT* );
#endif       /*!_PRINT_H_RPCGEN */
```

Note the *print* function declaration in *print.h*: the function name is the original followed by an underscore ("_") character and a procedure number. Thus, the RPC function name for the *print* function of version 1 is *print_1*. Furthermore, the return value of *print_1* is specified as *int** instead of *int*. This is typical of RPC functions: The argument and return value of each RPC function are passed by address, so if a local function accepts a *char**-typed argument, its RPC counterpart accepts a *char***-typed argument. The same is also true for return values: If a local function returns an *int*-typed value, its RPC counterpart returns an *int**-typed value.

The *print_1* function is created manually by a user from the *print* function. Its definition is specified in a separated *print_1.c* file as:

```
/* print_1.c file: server print function definition */
#include <stdio.h>
#include "print.h"

int* print_1( char** msg )
{
        static int result;
        FILE *ofp = fopen ( "/dev/console", "w");
        if (ofp)  {
                fprintf( ofp, "%s\n", *msg );
                fclose( ofp );
                result = 1;
        }
        else result = 0;
        return &result;
}
```

The major differences between the *print* and *print_1* definitions are that the argument and return values are pointer types. Thus, the *result* variable is defined as static in *print_1,* so that the function can return its address as a return value.

Once the *print_1.c* is defined, the server program can be compiled by a C compiler and run as follows:

```
%    cc -o print_server print_1.C print_svc.c -lnsl
%    print_server
```

There is no need to specify the ampersand ("&") symbol when running the server program, as it is specified in *print_svc.c* to be executed in the background automatically. The *-lnsl* option says that the server program requires linking with the *libnsl.so* or *libnsl.a* library to resolve all the RPC external library function references. This option is Sun Solaris-specific and may be replaced by a different option on a different platform.

The client program main function requires definition by the user. The main function calls the remote *print_1* function. The following *print_main.c* is modified from the *main* function in *print.C* to construct the main client program:

```
/* print_main.c: client main function */
#include <stdio.h>
#include "print.h"
int main( int argc, char* argv[] )
{
      int   *res, i;
      CLIENT *cl;
      if (argc<3)    {
            fprintf( stderr, "usage: %s <svc_host > msg ...\n" , argv[0] );
            return 1;
      }
      if (!(cl = clnt_create( argv[1], PRINTPROG, PRINTVER, "tcp"))) {
            clnt_pcreateerror( arhv[1] );
            return 2;
      }
      for (i=argc-1; i > 1; i--)    {
            if (!(res = print_1(&argv[i], cl)))   {
                  clnt_perror(cl, argv[1] );
                  return 3;
            }
            else if (*res==0)    {
                  fprintf( stderr, "print_1 fails\n" );
                  return 4;
            }
            else printf( "print_1 succeeds for %s\n", argv[i] );
      }
      return 0;
}
```

The command line arguments to the client program are: the host name of a *print* server and one or more messages to be sent to the server. The client program calls the *clnt_create* function to obtain a handle to communicate with the *print* server. The arguments to the *clnt_create* function are the server host machine name, the server program number, and version number. The last argument, *tcp,* specifies that the client and server processes will communicate via the TCP/IP transport protocol.

If the *clnt_create* call fails, it returns a NULL pointer, and the *clnt_pcreateerror* function is called to depict a diagnostic message for the error. On the other hand, if the *clnt_create* function succeeds, it returns a *CLIENT** handle, which is used as the second argument value in the subsequent *print_1* function call. The *print_1* function definition for the client program is defined in the *print_clnt.c* file. It is a stub, which in turn, calls the *print_1* function in the server program.

If the client's *print_1* function returns a NULL pointer, it means that the remote function call failed. In this case, the specified transport is not available or not working somehow, and the *clnt_perror* function is called to depict the reason of the failure. If *print_1* returns a non-NULL pointer value, the *res* pointer is consulted to obtain the returned status code of the *print_1* function. The possible values of the status code are application-defined and vary for different RPC functions.

The client program is generated by compiling the *print_main.c* and *print_clnt.c* modules together:

```
%    cc -o print_client print_clnt.c print_main.c -lnsl
```

Assume that the *print_server* program is running in the background on a machine called *fruit.* The *print_client* program can then be run as follows on any machine that is connected to *fruit* via a local or wide area network:

```
%    print_client   fruit  "Hello world"    "Good-bye"
print_1 succeeds for 'Hello world'
print_1 succeeds for 'Good-bye'
```

The system console window on *fruit* should display the following messages:

```
Hello world
Good-bye
```

12.3.1   clnt_create

The formal syntax of the *clnt_create* function is:

```
#include <rpc/rpc.h>

CLIENT*  clnt_create ( const char* hostname, const u_long prognum,
                       const u_long versnum, const char* nettype );
```

The *hostname* value is a NULL-terminated character string and specifies the name of a remote machine where the server process is run.

The *prognum* and *versnum* values are the program number and version number, respectively, of the remote function to be called.

The *nettype* value is a NULL-terminated character string that specifies what transport to use for communication between client and server. The possible values of *nettype* and their meanings are:

nettype value	Meaning
"netpath"	Choose a transport in the order specified in the NETPATH environment variable. If the NETPATH environment is not set, choose a "*visible*" transport, in the order specified in the */etc/netconfig* file
""	Same interpretation as "*netpath*"
"visible"	Choose a transport in the order specified in the */etc/netconfig* file, which has the "*v*" (visible) flag set
"circuit_v"	Same as "*visible*", but choose only connection-based transport
"datagram_v"	Same as "*visible*", but choose only connectionless transport
"circuit_n"	Same as "*netpath*", but choose only connection-based transport
"datagram_n"	Same as "*netpath*", but choose only connectionless transport
"udp"	Use the UDP transport
"tcp"	Use the TCP transport

If a *nettype* value is "*netpath*", "", "*circuit_n*", or "*datagram_n*", the client and server processes consult the NETPATH environment variable to determine which transport to use for RPC communication. The NETPATH environment variable is user-defined and contains a colon-delimited list of transports. The following is an example of a shell command defining the NETPATH environment variable:

%   setenv   NETPATH   tcp:udp

The return value of the function is NULL if it fails or a *CLIENT** pointer that is the handler for communication with a server process.

Note the *clnt_create* function is UNIX System V. 4-specific. The ONC functions to create RPC client handles are:

```
#include <rpc/rpc.h>

CLIENT*  clnttcp_create (struct sockaddr_in* svr_addr,
              const u_long prognum, const u_long versnum, int* sock_p,
              const u_long sendbuf_size, const u_long recvbuf_size);

CLIENT*  clntudp_create (struct sockaddr_in* svr_addr,
              const u_long prognum, const u_long versnum,
              struct timeval retry_timeout, int* sock_p);
```

The *clnttcp_create* and the *clntudp_create* functions are the TCP and UDP versions of the *clnt_create* function, respectively. These two functions use sockets as their underlying communication method, and the NETPATH environment variable is not used. Specifically, the *svc_addr* argument value is a pointer to the socket address of a server host name, and the *sock_p* argument value is the pointer to a socket port number of an RPC server. The socket port number may be specified as RPC_ANYSOCK, which means that it can be whatever port actually in use by the server.

Finally, the *retry_timeout* argument value specifies how long a client process should wait for a server response before it sends its request to the server again.

12.3.2   The rpcgen Program

The invocation syntax of the *rpcgen* program is:

```
rpcgen [<options>] <input_file>
```

The *input_file* argument is the path name of *a.x* file created by a user. This file specifies an RPC program number, a version number(s), and a procedure number(s). Furthermore, any user-defined data type used as an input argument and/or return value for RPC functions is also defined in this file.

The *rpcgen* program may take many options, but the following options are of most significance:

rpcgen option	Meaning
-K <time>	Specifies when a server process should exist after it has serviced a client request. If this option is not specified, the default *<time>* is 120 seconds. If *<time>* is set to -1, the server process will never terminate
-s <transport>	Specifies a transport to be used for the server process. The possible *<transport>* values are the same as those of the *nettype* values in a *clnt_create* call

For example. the following command invokes *rpcgen* to compile the *msg.x* file. The server program derived from the corresponding *msg_svc.c* file will exist 60 seconds after it has serviced a client request. It will use one of the connection-based and "*visible*" transports, as specified in the */etc/netconfig* file to communicate with its client process.

        %   rpcgen -K 60 -s circuit_v msg.x

12.3.3   A Directory Listing Example Using rpcgen

This section depicts another example of an RPC program generated via the *rpcgen*. The RPC function *scandir* gets a directory path name and an integer flag as input arguments. The function returns a linked list of file names that exist in the named directory. Furthermore, if the input flag value is nonzero, it also returns the UID and the last modification time stamp of each file found.

The *scan.x* input file to *rpcgen* is:

```
/* scan.x: directory listing service */
const MAXNLEN = 255;
typedef string name_t<MAXNLEN>;
```

```
/* input argument data type to scandir() */
typedef struct arg_rec *argPtr;
struct arg_rec
{
    name_t          dir_name;
    int             lflag;
};

/* The linked list record structure for one file info */
typedef struct dirinfo *infolist;
struct dirinfo
{
    name_t              name;       /* file name */
    u_int               uid;        /* UID         */
    u_long              modtime;    /* last modification time */
    infolist            next;       /* linked-list ptr */
};

/* return data type of scan() */
union res switch (int errno)
{
    case 0:             infolist  list;
    default:            void;
};

program SCANPROG
{
    version SCANVER
    {
            res SCANDIR(argPtr) = 1;
    } = 1;
} = 0x20000100;
```

The input argument type to the *scandir_1* RPC function is the address of a pointer to a *struct arg_rec* typed variable, which specifies a directory path name (the *struct arg_rec::dir_name* field) and an integer flag (the *struct arg_rec::lflag* field). The return data type of the function is nothing if the function fails. Otherwise, a linked list of records is produced, with each record of the type *struct dirinfo* specifying file information. The *name_t* definition states that it is a NULL-terminated character string with, at most, MAXNLEN characters.

The RPC program, version, and procedure numbers are specified as 0x20000100, 1, and 1, respectively.

The *scan.x* is compiled by the *rpcgen* as:

```
%     rpcgen scan.x
```

There are four files generated from this compilation: *scan.h, scan_svc.c, scan_clnt.c,* and *scan_xdr.c*. The *scan_xdr.c* file contains the XDR conversion functions for the *struct arg_rec* and the *struct dirinfo* data values.

The *scandir_1* function for the server program is defined in the *scandir.c* file:

```c
/* scan_1.c: server's scandir function definition */
#include <dirent.h>
#include <string.h>
#include <malloc.h>
#include <sys/stat.h>
#include "scan.h"

res* scandir_1(argPtr* darg)
{
    DIR *dirp;
    struct dirent *d;
    infolist nl, *nlp;
    struct stat statv;
    static res res;

    if !(dirp = opendir((*darg)->dir_name)))   {
        res.errno = errno;
        return &res;
    }
    xdr_free(xdr_res, &res);
    nlp = &res.res_u.list;
    while (d=readdir(dirp))        {
        nl = *nlp = (infolist)malloc(sizeof(struct dirinfo));
        nl->name = strdup(d->d_name);
        nlp = &nl->next;
        if ((*darg)->lflag)        {
            char pathnm[256];
            sprintf(pathnm,"%s/%s",(*darg)->dir_name,d->d_name);
            if (!stat(pathnm,&statv))     {
                nl->uid = statv.st_uid;
                nl->modtime = statv.st_mtime;
            }
        }
    }
    *nlp = NULL;
```

```
                res.errno = 0;
                closedir(dirp);
                return &res;
        }
```

The *scandir_1* function calls the *opendir* API to get a handler for scanning a directory file whose name is specified in the function input argument *(*darg)->dir_name*. If *opendir* fails, the *scandir_1* function returns the *errno* value via the *res.errno* field.

If the *opendir* call returns successfully, the function calls *readdir* repeatedly to get all files in the named directory. For each file obtained, a *struct dirinfo* record is allocated dynamically. The function stores the newly obtained file name and, possibly, the file UID and last modification time (if the *(*darg)->lflag* value is nonzero) in that record. The *struct dirinfo* records are chained together into a linked list, returned via the *res.res_u.list* field.

The server program is compiled and run as follows:

```
%    cc scan_1.c scan_xdr.c scan_svc.c -o scan_svc -lnsl
%    scan_svc
```

The client main program is specified in the *scan_main.c*:

```
/* scan_main.c: main function for the client program */
#include <stdio.h>
#include "scan.h"

int main( int argc, char* argv[])
{
    struct arg_rec  *iarg = (struct arg_rec*)malloc(sizeof(struct arg_rec));
    res    *result;
    infolist nl;

    if (argc!=4)        {
        fprintf( stderr, "usage: %s host directory <long>\n", argv[0] );
        return 1;
    }
    char *server = argv[1];
    iarg->dir_name = argv[2];
    iarg->lflag = 0;
    if (sscanf(argv[3],"%u",&(iarg->lflag))!=1) {
        fprintf( stderr, "Invalid argument: '%s'\n", argv[3] );
        return 2;
    }
```

```
CLIENT *cl = clnt_create(argv[1], SCANPROG, SCANVER, "visible");
if (!cl)   {
   clnt_pcreateerror(server);
   return 3;
}

iif (!(result = scandir_1(&iarg, cl)))  {          // RPC call fails
   clnt_perror(cl, server);
   return 4;
}

 if (result->errno)   {                  // function returns failure code
   errno = result->errno;
   perror(iarg->dir_name);
   return 5;
}

for (nl=result->res_u.list; nl; nl=nl->next)     {  // function succeeds
   if (iarg->lflag)
      printf( "...%s, uid=%d, mtime=%s\n" , nl->name, nl->uid,
              ctime(&nl->modtime) );
   else printf ( "...%s\n", nl->name);
}
return 0;
}
```

The client program is invoked with the host name of the server process, a remote directory name, and an integer flag that specifies whether the UID and last modification time
stamp of files in the specified directory are wanted (*lflag* value is nonzero) or not (*lflag* value
is zero).

The client *main* function calls the *clnt_create* to get a handler of the transport end point
that connects the specified server process. It then packs all the input argument data to the
dynamic memory (pointed to by the *iarg* variable) before it calls the *scandir_1* RPC function.
After the RPC function returns, the return value is checked to see whether the RPC call succeeded. If the call succeeded, the remote file information is printed to the standard output
accordingly. Otherwise, an appropriate error diagnostic is depicted to the user.

The client program is compiled and run as follows. It is assumed that the server is running on a machine called *fruit*.

```
%    cc scan_main.c scan_xdr.c scan_clnt.c -o scan_cls -lnsl
%    scan_cls  fruit    /etc    1
...magic, uid=2, mtime=Wed Aug  3 11:32:33 1994
...protocols, uid=10, mtime=Wed Aug  3 11:32:30 1994
```

12.3.4   rpcgen Limitations

The fact that *rpcgen* hides the low-level RPC APIs from users has both advantages and disadvantages.

rpcgen has the advantages of reducing programming effort and of being less error prone. Furthermore, users can concentrate more in coding RPC functions and client *main* functions, rather than RPC transport interface functions.

The disadvantages of *rpcgen*, however, are the following:

- Users have no direct control of the transport used by the server and client programs generated by *rpcgen*
- Users cannot manage the dynamic memory used by the XDR functions generated by *rpcgen*
- Most *rpcgen* compilers do not generate C++-compatible client and server stub functions. This may require manual modification of those stubs to make them acceptable for the C++ compiler (note that the *rpcgen* on Sun Microsystems workstations provides the -C option for generating C++-compatible files).

Given these limitations of *rpcgen*, users need to learn the lower level RPC APIs. This would allow users to work around the above *rpcgen* limitations if they become significant obstacles to application development.

12.4   Low-Level RPC Programming Interface

The low-level RPC APIs are declared in the <rpc/rpc.h> header. These APIs include the creation of client and server handles with user-specified transports, the registration of RPC functions to the *rpcbind* daemon, and the calling of remote RPC functions from client processes. Furthermore, client processes can specify authentication methods via these APIs to establish secure connections with server processes.

Before the low-level RPC APIs are presented, the methods to create XDR functions for user-defined data types are covered. This is because some lower level RPC APIs require users to specify the actual data and their corresponding XDR functions for RPC function arguments and return values. By writing their own XDR functions, users also have direct control over dynamic memory allocation and deallocation in those functions.

12.4.1   XDR Conversion Functions

An XDR function is called twice whenever a piece of data is passed between a client process and a server process. For example, when a client passes some data to an RPC function, the data are converted to XDR format before being transmitted to the network. This conversion process is called *serializing*. Then, before the target RPC function receives the data, the same XDR function is called on the server side to convert the data from XDR format to the data format of the host machine. This process is called *deserializing*. There are built-in basic XDR conversion functions for most RPC basic data types. These basic functions are capable of performing both serializing and deserializing. Furthermore, user-defined XDR functions (which, in turn, call the basic XDR functions) automatically inherit the serializing and deserializing capability. These built-in basic XDR functions are:

RPC data type	XDR function
int	xdr_int
long	xdr_long
short	xdr_short
char	xdr_char
u_int	xdr_u_int
u_long	xdr_u_long
u_short	xdr_u_short
u_char	xdr_u_char
float	xdr_float
double	xdr_double
enum	xdr_enum
bool	xdr_bool
string	xdr_string
union	xdr_union
opaque	xdr_opaque

The *u_int, u_long*, etc. data types are the unsigned counterparts of the data types *int, long*, etc. The *bool* data type is converted to the *bool_t* data type by the *rpcgen*, and the *boot_t* data type is defined in C as:

```
typedef enum { TRUE=1, FALSE=0 }      bool_t;
```

The *opaque* data type stands for a sequence of arbitrary bytes. It may be used to declare fixed-size arrays or variable-size arrays, such as the following:

```
opaque    x[56];
opaque    vx<56>;
```

The above definitions are converted to C definitions by *rpcgen* as:

```
char x[56];
struct
{
     u_int    xv_len;          /* actual length of the xc_val array */
     char     *xc_val;         /* dynamic array */
} xv;
```

If users define their own data types, they can use either *rpcgen* to generate the XDR functions for these data types or write their own XDR conversion functions. For example, if the user defines the following data type *struct complex*:

```
struct complex
{
     unsigned      uval;
     char          ary[80];
     int           *ptr;
     long          lval;
     double        dval;
};
```

the XDR function for the *struct complex* is:

```
bool_t xdr_complex ( XDR *xdrs, struct complex* objp)
{
     if (!xdr_u_int(xdrs, &objp->uval)) return FALSE;
     if (!xdr_vector(xdrs, objp->ary, 80,
         sizeof(char), (xdrproc_t)xdr_char))
              return FALSE;
     if (!xdr_pointer(xdrs, &objp->ptr, sizeof(int), (xdrproc_t)xdr_int))
              return FALSE;
     if (!xdr_long(xdrs, &objp->lval)) return FALSE;
     if (!xdr_double(xdrs,&objp->dval)) return FALSE;
     return TRUE;
}
```

All XDR function return values are of type *bool_t*, which is TRUE if a function succeeds, FALSE otherwise. The XDR function for *complex* consists of calling basic XDR functions to convert each field member of the *complex* record. Note that the fixed-size array *complex::ary* is converted by the RPC built-in function *xdr_vector*. The arguments of the *xdr_vector* function are: an XDR pointer that points to a buffer holding the converted data, the fixed-size array address, the number of elements in the array, the size of each array element, and the XDR function converting each array element.

The *comples::ptr* member is converted by another RPC built-in XDR function *xdr_pointer*. The arguments to the *xdr_pointer* function are: an XDR pointer that points to a buffer holding the converted data, the address of the pointer, the size of the data that the pointer points to, and the XDR function for those same data.

12.4.2   Lower Level RPC APIs

To create RPC-based client and server programs, there are two sets of RPC APIs (one for each). These APIs and their calling sequences in the client and server processes are shown in Figure 12.1.

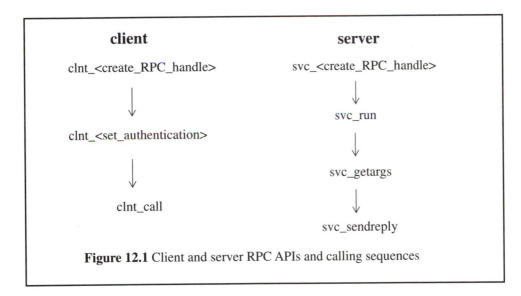

Figure 12.1 Client and server RPC APIs and calling sequences

The *clnt_<create_RPC_handle>* stands for a set of RPC APIs, each of which creates a client handle that can be used to communicate with an RPC server for specified RPC program and a version numbers. These APIs differ in their level of detail in specifying the network transport protocol used in communicating with an RPC server. These APIs are:

Client API	Use
clnt_create	Specifies a generic class of transport to be selected at run time
clnt_tp_create	Specifies a specific transport to be used

Client API	Use
clnt_tli_create	Specifies a TLI transport end point to be used, and the sending and receiving buffer size for RPC communication. The TLI handle is created in the client program

The *clnt_<create_authentication>* stands for a set of RPC APIs, each of which creates an authentication data record to be used by an RPC server to authenticate a client. These APIs are optional and are needed only if an RPC server requires security control. Furthermore, users may create their own RPC client/server authentication schemes and their own RPC authentication functions for their programs. The standard RPC authentication functions for client programs are:

Client API	Use
authnone_create	Creates a NULL authentication data record. The calling RPC server should not require client authentication
authsys_create_default	Creates an authentication record based on System V process access control method
authdes_seccreate	Creates an authentication record whose data is encrypted using the DES encryption method

The *clnt_call* API calls an RPC server to execute an RPC program of a given procedure number. The function call includes the input argument and its XDR function, as well as the address of the variable that receives the return value and its XDR function.

On the server side, the *svc_<create_RPC_handle>* stands for a set of RPC APIs, each of which creates a server handle that can be used to respond to client RPC requests. These APIs differ in their level of detail specifying the network transport protocol used in communicating with RPC clients. These APIs are:

Server API	Use
svc_create	Specifies a generic class of transport to be selected at run time
svc_tp_create	Specifies a specific transport to be used
svc_tli_create	Specifies a TLI transport end point to be used, and the sending and receiving buffer size for RPC communication. The TLI handle is created in the server program

The *svc_run* API is called after a server creates an RPC handle. This function goes into an infinite loop waiting for client RPC requests to arrive and calls a user-defined dispatcher function to service each call. This function may be replaced by a user-defined function, particularly if users want the server to do something else whenever it is not servicing requests.

The dispatcher function calls the *svc_getargs* API to extract any RPC function arguments sent from a client process. It then calls the requested RPC function and uses the *svc_sendreply* API to send the function return value to the client.

The syntax of these APIs is discussed in later sections. The next section introduces two RPC classes that encapsulate low-level RPC API interfacing. These RPC classes provide a simplified RPC programming interface for users, while allowing user control over RPC transport specification and memory management of XDR function data.

12.5   RPC Classes

The section defines two RPC classes: One for constructing a RPC server, and one for construction a RPC client. The main use of these classes is to provide a high-level RPC interface to application developers, so that they don't have to know the details of the ONC or UNIX System V RPC APIs. Furthermore, users may derive their own subclasses from these RPC classes, such that their subclass objects store more data than do the RPC server or client handles, as well as provide additional functions (for example, predefined callback and broadcast functions).

In summary, the advantages of the RPC classes are:

* They hide the differences in APIs between the ONC and System V.4 methods. This makes applications that use these classes portable on most commercial UNIX systems
* They reduce the learning time and programming effort of users in creating RPC applications
* These classes enable users to focus their programming efforts in developing their core client and server functions. This provides the same advantage as does *rpcgen*
* The RPC classes can be modified by users to control RPC transports and the authentication methods used, as well as any dynamic memory management of XDR function data

The following *RPC.h* header defines two RPC classes that encapsulate the RPC client and server APIs.

```
#ifndef RPC_H
#define RPC_H
```

```
#include <iostream.h>
#include <stdio.h>
#include <stdlib.h>
#include <string.h>
#include <unistd.h>
#include <time.h>
#include <sys/types.h>
#include <rpc/rpc.h>
#include <utmp.h>

#ifdef    SYSV4
#include <rpc/svc_soc.h>
#include <rpc/pmap_clnt.h>
#include <netconfig.h>

#else                    /* ONC */
#include <rpc/pmap_clnt.h>
#include <sys/socket.h>
#include <netdb.h>
#define AUTH_SYS   AUTH_UNIX
#endif

#define UNDEF_PROGNUM     0x0
#define TCP_BUFSIZ          4098
typedef int (*rpcprog)(SVCXPRT*);

typedef struct
{
     unsigned       prgnum;
     unsigned       vernum;
     unsigned       prcnum;
     rpcprog        func;
} RPCPROG_INFO;

/* RPC server class                              */
class RPC_svc
{
        int              rc;
        unsigned         prgnum, vernum;
        static RPCPROG_INFO* progList;
        static int       numProg;
        SVCXPRT          *svcp;
     public:
        /* Dispatch routine */
        static void dispatch( struct svc_req* rqstp, SVCXPRT  *xport )
        {
```

```
            if (rqstp->rq_proc==NULLPROC) {
                    svc_sendreply(xport, (xdrproc_t)xdr_void, 0);
                    return ;
            }
            uid_t  uid = 0;
            gid_t  gid = 0, gids[20];
            short  len = 0;
            switch (rqstp->rq_cred.oa_flavor)    {
               case AUTH_NONE:
                    break;
               case AUTH_SYS: {
#ifdef SYSV4
                    struct authsys_parms* authp;
                    authp = (struct authsys_parms*)rqstp->rq_clntcred;
#else
                    struct authunix_parms* authp;
                    authp = (struct authunix_parms*)rqstp->rq_clntcred;
#endif
                    uid   = authp->aup_uid;
                    gid   = authp->aup_gid;
            }    break;
#ifdef SYSV4
                case AUTH_DES: {
                    if (!authdes_getucred(
                            (struct authdes_cred*)rqstp->rq_clntcred,
                            &uid, &gid, &len, (int*)gids)) {
                            svcerr_systemerr(xport);
                            return;
                    }
            }    break;
    #endif
                default:
                    svcerr_weakauth(xport);
                    return;
            }

            if (uid != getuid() && uid!=(uid_t)0) {
               svcerr_weakauth(xport);
               return;
            }

            for ( int i=0; i < RPC_svc::numProg; i++ )
               if (RPC_svc::progList[i].prcnum==rqstp->rq_proc &&
                    RPC_svc::progList[i].vernum==rqstp->rq_vers &&
                    RPC_svc::progList[i].prgnum==rqstp->rq_prog)
               {
```

```
                    if ((*RPC_svc::progList[i].func)(xport)
                            !=RPC_SUCCESS)
                        cerr << "rpc server execute prog "
                                << rqstp->rq_proc << " fails\n";
                    break;
                }
            if (i >= RPC_svc::numProg) svcerr_noproc(xport);
};


    /* Constructor function. Create an RPC server object for the
        given prognum/version
    */
    RPC_svc( unsigned prognum, unsigned versnum,
                    const char* nettype)
    {
#ifdef SYSV4
            rc=svc_create(dispatch, prognum, versnum, nettype);
            if (!rc)
                cerr << "Can't create RPC server for prog: "
                        << prognum << endl;
            else prgnum = prognum, vernum = versnum;
            svcp = 0;
#else
            int proto = 0;
            if (nettype && !strcmp(nettype,"tcp")) {
                svcp=svctcp_create(RPC_ANYSOCK, TCP_BUFSIZ,
                                    TCP_BUFSIZ);
                proto = IPPROTO_TCP;
            } else {
                svcp=svcudp_create(RPC_ANYSOCK);
                proto = IPPROTO_UDP;
            }

            if (!svcp) {
                rc = 0;
                cerr << "Can't create RPC server for prog: "
                        << prognum << endl;
            } else {
                rc = 1;
                prgnum = prognum, vernum = versnum;
            }
            pmap_unset( prognum, versnum );
            if (!svc_register(svcp, prognum, versnum, dispatch, proto))
            {
                cerr << "could not register RPC program/ver: "
                        << prognum << '/' << versnum << endl;
```

```
                      rc = 0;
               }
#endif
   };

   /* create a server handle for call back */
   RPC_svc( int fd, char* transport, u_long progno, u_long versno )
   {
#ifdef SYSV4
            struct netconfig *nconf = getnetconfigent(transport);
            if (!nconf) {
               cerr << "invalid transport: " << transport << endl;
               rc = 0;
               return;
            }
            svcp = svc_tli_create( fd, nconf, 0, 0, 0);
            if (!svcp) {
               cerr << "create server handle fails\n";
               rc = 0;
               return;
            }
            if (progno == UNDEF_PROGNUM)
               progno = gen_progNum( versno, nconf,
                                     &svcp->xp_ltaddr);
            if (svc_reg(svcp, progno, versno, dispatch, nconf)==FALSE)
            {
               cerr << "register prognum failed\n";
               rc = 0;
            }
            freenetconfigent( nconf );
#else
            /* fd should be a socket desc. which may be
               RPC_ANYSOCK */
            if (progno == UNDEF_PROGNUM) {
               progno = gen_progNum ( versno, &fd, transport );
            }
            int    proto = 0;
            if (!strcmp(transport,"tcp")) {
               svcp = svctcp_create( fd, TCP_BUFSIZ, TCP_BUFSIZ );
               if (fd) proto = IPPROTO_TCP;
            }
            else {
               svcp = svcudp_create ( fd );
               if (fd) proto = IPPROTO_UDP;
            }
            if (!svcp) {
```

461

```
                              cerr << "create server handle fails\n";
                              rc = 0;
                              return;
                      }
                      if (fd) pmap_unset( progno, versno );
                      if (!svc_register(svcp, progno, versno, dispatch, proto)) {
                          cerr << "could not register RPC program/ver: "
                                  << progno << '/' << versno << endl;
                          rc = 0;
                          return;
                      }
#endif
                      prgnum = progno, vernum = versno;
                      rc = 1;
              };

              /* return program number */
              u_long progno()   { return prgnum;    };

              /* destructor function */
              ~RPC_svc()
              {
                      pmap_unset( prgnum, vernum );
                      svc_unregister( prgnum, vernum );
                      if (svcp) svc_destroy(svcp);
              };

              /* Check if a server object is created successfully */
              int good()       {   return rc;     };

              /* server pool RPC request from clients */
              static void run() {   svc_run();      };


              /* poll for RPC requests. This is for asynchornous RPC call-back */
              static int  poll( time_t  timeout )
              {
                      int  read_fds = svc_fds;
                      struct timeval  stry;
                      stry.tv_sec = timeout;
                      stry.tv_usec = 0;
                      switch (select(32, &read_fds, 0, 0, &stry)) {
                         case -1:    return -1;
                         case  0:    return 0;  /* no event */
                         default:    svc_getreq( read_fds );
                      }
```

```
                return 1;
};

/* register an RPC function and start servicing RPC requests */
int run_func( int procnum, rpcprog func )
{
        if (good()) {
            if (func) add_proc( procnum, func );
            run();        /* this willl never return */
        }
        return -1;
};

/* register a new RPC function */
void add_proc( unsigned procnum, rpcprog func )
{
        for (int i=0; i < numProg; i++)
            if (progList[i].func==func) return;
        if (++numProg == 1)
            progList = (RPCPROG_INFO*)malloc(
                                sizeof(RPCPROG_INFO));
        else
            progList = (RPCPROG_INFO*)realloc((void*)progList,
                            sizeof(RPCPROG_INFO)*numProg);
        progList[numProg-1].func = func;
        progList[numProg-1].prgnum = prgnum;
        progList[numProg-1].vernum = vernum;
        progList[numProg-1].prcnum = procnum;
};

/* Called by an RPC function to get argument value from a client */
int getargs( SVCXPRT* transp, xdrproc_t func, caddr_t argp )
{
        if (!svc_getargs( transp, func, argp))   {
            svcerr_decode(transp);
            return -1;
        } else return RPC_SUCCESS;
};

/* Called by an RPC function to send reply to a client */
int reply( SVCXPRT* transp, xdrproc_t func, caddr_t argp )
{
        if (!svc_sendreply(transp, func, argp)) {
            svcerr_systemerr(transp);
            return -1;
        }
```

```
                else return RPC_SUCCESS;
        };

    #ifdef SYSV4
        /* Generate a transient RPC program no. */
        static unsigned long gen_progNum( unsigned long versnum,
                                struct netconfig* nconf, struct netbuf* addr)
        {
                static unsigned long transient_prognum = 0x5FFFFFFF;
                while (!rpcb_set( transient_prognum++, versnum,
                        nconf, addr))
                    continue;
                return transient_prognum -1;
        };
    #endif

        static unsigned long gen_progNum ( unsigned long versnum,
                                    int* sockp, char* nettype )
        {
                static unsigned long transient_prognum = 0x5FFFFFFF;
                int     s, len, proto = IPPROTO_UDP;
                int     socktype = SOCK_DGRAM;
                struct sockaddr_in  addr;

                if (!strcmp(nettype,"tcp")) {
                    socktype = SOCK_STREAM;
                    proto   = IPPROTO_TCP;
                }

                if (*sockp== RPC_ANYSOCK) {
                    if ((s = socket(AF_INET, socktype, 0)) < 0) {
                            perror("socket");
                            return 0;
                    }
                    *sockp = s;
                }
                else s = *sockp;

                addr.sin_addr.s_addr = 0;
                addr.sin_family     = AF_INET;
                addr.sin_port       = 0;
                len                 = sizeof(addr);

                (void)bind( s, (struct sockaddr*)&addr, len );
                if (getsockname( s, (struct sockaddr*)&addr, &len ) < 0)
                {
```

```
                    perror("getsockname");
                    return 0;
              }
              while (!pmap_set( transient_prognum--, versnum, proto,
                                          addr.sin_port))
                     continue;
              return transient_prognum -1;
       };

}; /* RPC_svc */

/* RPC client class                                    */
class RPC_cls
{
       CLIENT  *clntp;
       char    *server;
    public:
       /*  Constructor function. Create an RPC client object for
           the given server/prognum/version */
       RPC_cls( char* hostname, unsigned prognum, unsigned vernum,
                 char* nettype)
       {
#ifdef SYSV4
              if (!(clntp=clnt_create(hostname,prognum,vernum,nettype)))
                 clnt_pcreateerror(hostname);
              else {
                 server = new char[strlen(hostname)+1];
                 strcpy(server,hostname);
              }
#else
              struct hostent* hp = gethostbyname(hostname);
              struct sockaddr_in  server_addr;
              int    addrlen, sock = RPC_ANYSOCK;

              if (!hp)
                 cerr << "Invalid host name: '" << hostname << "'\n";
              else {
                 addrlen = sizeof(struct sockaddr_in);
                 bcopy( hp->h_addr, (caddr_t)&server_addr.sin_addr,
                                  hp->h_length);

                 server_addr.sin_family = AF_INET;
                 server_addr.sin_port = 0;

                 if (nettype && !strcmp(nettype,"tcp"))
                     clntp=clnttcp_create(&server_addr, prognum, vernum,
```

465

```
                                              &sock, TCP_BUFSIZ, TCP_BUFSIZ);
                    else {
                        struct timeval  stry;
                        stry.tv_sec = 3;
                        stry.tv_usec = 0;
                        clntp=clntudp_create(&server_addr, prognum,
                                                    vernum, stry, &sock);
                    }

                    if (!clntp)
                        clnt_pcreateerror(hostname);
                    else {
                        server = new char[strlen(hostname)+1];
                        strcpy(server,hostname);
                    }
                }
#endif
                if (clntp) set_auth ( AUTH_NONE );
        };

        /* destructor function */
        ~RPC_cls()  { (void)clnt_destroy( clntp ); };

        /* Check if a client object is created successfully */
        int  good() { return clntp ? 1 : 0; };

        /* set authentication data */
        void set_auth( int choice, unsigned timeout = 60 )
        {
                    switch (choice) {
                        case AUTH_NONE:
                            clntp->cl_auth = authnone_create();
                            break;
                        case AUTH_SYS:
                        case AUTH_SHORT:
#ifdef SYSV4
                            clntp->cl_auth = authsys_create_default();
#else
                            clntp->cl_auth = authunix_create_default();
#endif
                            break;
                        case AUTH_DES: {
                            char netname[MAXNETNAMELEN+1];
                            des_block  ckey;
                            if (key_gendes(&ckey))  perror("key_gendes");
                            if (!user2netname(netname, getuid(), "netcom.com"))
```

```
                              clnt_perror(clntp,server);
                          else clntp->cl_auth = authdes_seccreate(netname,
                                           timeout, server, &ckey);
                          if (!(clntp->cl_auth)) {
                              cerr << "client authentication setup fails\n";
                              perror("authdes_seccreate");
                              clnt_perror(clntp,server);
                              clntp->cl_auth = authnone_create();
                          }
                      }  break;
                      default:
                          cerr << "authentication method '" << (int)choice
                                << "' not yet supported\n";
                          clntp->cl_auth = authnone_create();
                  }
        };

        /* Call an RPC function */
        int call( unsigned procnum, xdrproc_t xdr_ifunc, caddr_t argp,
                xdrproc_t xdr_ofunc, caddr_t rsltp, unsigned timeout = 20 )
        {
                  if (!clntp) return -1;
                  struct timeval timv;
                  timv.tv_sec  = timeout;
                  timv.tv_usec = 0;
                  if (clnt_call(clntp, procnum, xdr_ifunc, argp,
                          xdr_ofunc, rsltp, timv)!=RPC_SUCCESS) {
                      clnt_perror(clntp, server);
                      return -2;
                  }
                  return RPC_SUCCESS;
        };

        /* Support RPC broadcast */
        static int broadcast( unsigned prognum, unsigned versnum,
                      unsigned procnum, resultproc_t callback,
                      xdrproc_t xdr_ifunc, caddr_t argp,
                      xdrproc_t xdr_ofunc, caddr_t rsltp,
                      char* nettype = "datagram_v")
        {
#ifdef SYSV4
                  return rpc_broadcast(prognum, versnum, procnum,
                          xdr_ifunc, argp, xdr_ofunc, rsltp, callback, nettype);
#else
                  return clnt_broadcast(prognum, versnum, procnum,
                          xdr_ifunc, argp, xdr_ofunc, rsltp, callback);
```

```
#endif
};
/* set client time-out period */
int set_timeout( long usec )
{
        if (!clntp) return -1;
        struct timeval timv;
        timv.tv_sec = 0;
        timv.tv_usec = usec;
        return clnt_control( clntp, CLSET_TIMEOUT, (char*)&timv);
};
/* get client time-out period */
long get_timeout()
{
        if (!clntp) return -1;
        struct timeval timv;
        if (clnt_control( clntp, CLGET_TIMEOUT, (char*)&timv)==-1)
        {
            perror("clnt_control");
            return -1;
        }
        return timv.tv_usec;
};
};
#endif /* _RPC_H */
```

The calling sequences of these RPC member functions in a typical client and server are shown in Figure 12.2.

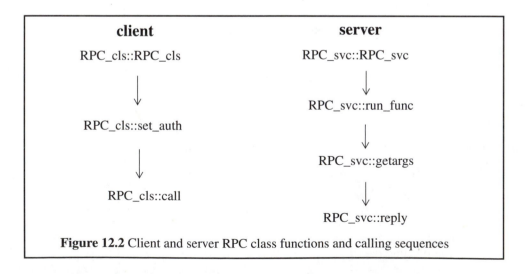

Figure 12.2 Client and server RPC class functions and calling sequences

The *RPC_svc::RPC_svc* constructor function creates a server RPC handle for the given RPC program and version numbers. Furthermore, this function registers a user-defined dispatcher function that is called when a client calls an RPC function managed by the server. The last argument to *RPC_svc::RPC_svc* is the *nettype* value, which defines the transport protocol to be used between the server and its clients. This function internally calls the *svc_create* API to create the server handle. However, users can easily modify the *RPC_svc::RPC_svc* function to call the *svc_tp_create* or *svc_tli_create* API instead.

The *RPC_svc::run_func* is called to register an RPC function and its assigned procedure number to the server, then causes the server to block and wait for client RPC calls (via the *svc_run* API). Note that if a user wishes to register more than one RPC function on a server, the server program will be changed accordingly, as follows:

```
RPC_svc svcp = new RPC_svc(....);
if (!svcp || !svcp->good()) return 1;
svcp->add_func( <procnum1>, prog1 );
...
svcp->add_func( <procnumN-1>, progN-1);
svcp->run_func( <procnumN>, progN);
```

When a client RPC request arrives, the dispatcher function registered via the *RPC_svc::RPC_svc* function is called to service the client request. The dispatcher function does the following:

- Checks that the client-requested RPC number is 0. If it is, the client is simply pinging the server, and it simply sends a reply to the client with a NULL return value
- If the client specifies any authentication data, the function validates the data and flags an authentication error if the validation fails. Note that in the current function, the client authentication is optional. This may need to be changed for secure RPC transactions. The server should always insist that clients send authentication data in each RPC call. The RPC authentication method is discussed in a latter section
- After the client authentication succeeds, the dispatcher function calls the RPC function requested by the client

Each RPC function called by the *RPC_svc::dispatch* function should have the function prototype of:

```
int <function_name> ( SVCXPRT* );
```

where the argument is a transport handler for communication with a client's transport end point. The function return value is zero (RPC_SUCCESS) if it succeeds, nonzero otherwise. In addition to these, the RPC function should expect a global *RPC_svc** pointer (whose variable name is application-defined) that holds the address of the RPC server handle. The function should call *RPC_svc::getargs* to extract any arguments from the calling client and use the *RPC_svc::reply* to send a return value to the client.

In a client program, the client handle for specified RPC program and version numbers is obtained via the *RPC_cls::RPC_cls* constructor function. The constructor function internally calls the *clnt_create* API to acquire the client handle. Like the *RPC_svc* constructor function, the *RPC_cls::RPC_cls* function may be changed by users to use the *clnt_tp_create* or *clnt_tli_create* API instead.

Client authentication data may be set via the *RPC_cls::set_auth* call. The *RPC_cls* class currently supports the AUTH_NONE, AUTH_SYS, and AUTH_DES methods, but users may modify the *RPC_cls::set_auth* function to implement their own authentication methods. The AUTH_NONE, AUTH_SYS, and AUTH_DES authentication methods are described in a later section. Note that ONC uses AUTH_UNIX instead of the AUTH_SYS.

The client calls an RPC function via the *RPC_cls::call* function. The arguments to the *RPC_cls::call* function are: an RPC procedure number, an XDR function to convert input arguments to the XDR format, the address of a variable that holds the input arguments, an XDR function to convert the RPC function return value (from XDR format to local machine format), and the address of a variable holding the RPC function return value. This *RPC_cls::call* returns RPC_SUCCESS if it succeeds, a nonzero value otherwise.

The static *RPC_cls::broadcast* function supports RPC broadcast requests from a client process to all server processes on a network. This function is described in detail in Section 12.8.

Finally, applications that use the RPC classes should be compiled with the following options on different commercial UNIX systems:

UNIX system	CC compile options
Solaris 2.x	-DSYSV -lsocket -lnsl
Sun OS 4.1.x	-lnsl
HP-UX 9.0.x	None
IBM AIX 3.x and 4.x	-lrpcsvc
SCO 3.x	-lsocket

The above compile options specify which RPC system libraries to be linked with user applications on the various UNIX systems. The *-DSYSV4* option is needed on Sun's Solaris 2.x system, so that UNIX System V.4 RPC APIs are used instead of the ONC APIs.

To illustrate the use of RPC classes, the remote message printing programs, as shown in Section 12.3, are rewritten as follows. Note that the new client and server programs are simpler than their previous versions, which use *rpcgen*:

The client program *msg_cls2.C* is:

```
/* client program: using low-level RPC APIs */
#include "msg2.h"
#include "RPC.h"

int main(int argc, char* argv[])
{
    int res;
    if (argc<3)    {
       cerr << "usage: " << argv[0] << " host msg <nettype>\n";
       return 1;
    }

    /* create a client handler to an RPC server */
    RPC_cls cl( argv[1], MSGPROG, MSGVER,
                      argc>=4 ? argv[3] : "netpath");
    if (!cl.good()) return 1;

    /* call the printmsg RPC function. return value is set to res */
    if (cl.call( PRINTMSG, (xdrproc_t)xdr_string, (caddr_t)&argv[2],
             (xdrproc_t)xdr_int, (caddr_t)&res) != RPC_SUCCESS)
       return 3;

    /* check RPC function's return value */
    if (res!=0)
       cerr << "clnt: call printmsg fails\n";
    else cout << "clnt: call printmsg succeeds\n";

    return 0;
}
```

The client program is invoked with two or three arguments. The first argument is the host name of the machine where the RPC server is running. This may be a local machine name if the client and server are both running on the same machine. The second argument to the client program is a character string message sent to the RPC server for printout. The optional third argument is the transport to be used by the client to communicate with the server. If the third argument is not specified, the default is "*netpath*". The legal values for the third argument and their meanings are the same as that for the *nettype* argument of the *clnt_create* API, as described in Section 12.3.1.

The *msg2.h* is user-defined and contains only the declaration of the *printmsg* function RPC program, version, and procedure numbers:

```
/* msg2.h */
#ifndef MSG2_H
#define MSG2_H

#include <rpc/rpc.h>

#define MSGPROG ((unsigned long)(0x20000001))
#define MSGVER ((unsigned long)(1))
#define PRINTMSG ((unsigned long)(1))

#endif /* !MSG_H */
```

The RPC server program that corresponds to the client program is *msg_svc2.C*:

```
/* server program: low-level RPC APIs */
/*   usage: msg_svc2 <transport> */
#include <iostream.h>
#include <fstream.h>
#include "msg2.h"
#include "RPC.h"
static RPC_svc *svcp = 0;                 // RPC server handle
/* the RPC function */
int printmsg( SVCXPRT* xtrp )
{
    int     res  = 0;                     // holds the return status code
    char    *msg = 0;                     // hold client's function argument

    /* get function argument from client */
    if (svcp->getargs( xtrp, (xdrproc_t)xdr_wrapstring,(caddr_t)&msg) !=
              RPC_SUCCESS)
        return -1;

    /* get argument successful. Open the system console for output */
    ofstream ofs ("/dev/console");
    if (ofs)
        ofs << "server:' " << msg << "'\n";
    else res = -1;

    /* send return status code to client */
    if (svcp->reply(xtrp, (xdrproc_t)xdr_int, (caddr_t)&res)
            !=RPC_SUCCESS)
        res = -1;
```

```
            /* RPC function completes. Send a success return code to dispatch */
            return res;
    }

    /* main server function */
    int main(int argc, char* argv[])
    {
            /* create a server for the given program number and version number */
            svcp = new RPC_svc( MSGPROG, MSGVER,
                                argc==2 ? argv[1] : "netpath");

            /* register the given RPC function and then waits for clients' RPC
               requests */
            if (svcp && svcp->run_func( PRINTMSG, printmsg )) ;

            return 0; /* shouldn't get here unless the server handle creation failed */
    }
```

The server program is invoked with either no argument or a *nettype* specification. If no *nettype* argument is specified, the *"netpath"* value is used as the default.

The server process calls the *RPC_svc::RPC_svc* function to create a server handle for the given RPC program number, version number, and *nettype* value. After that, the server calls the *RPC_svc::run_func* to register the *printmsg* function as a client-callable RPC function, then calls the *svc_run* to poll client RPC requests.

When a client's RPC request arrives, the *svc_run* function calls the *RPC_svc::dispatch* function to handle the request. The *RPC_svc::dispatch* function is responsible for checking that the client RPC procedure number is correct and that the client authentication, if specified, is valid. The RPC function is then called.

The RPC function, as invoked by the *RPC_svc::dispatch* function, calls the *RPC_svc::getargs* function to get the client's argument data. When the RPC function returns, it sends its return value back to the client via the *RPC_svc::reply* function.

The final piece of the source code needed for this example is a separate C file. *RPC.C* contains definitions of the *RPC_svc::numProg* and *RPC_svc::progList* static variables. The *RPC_svc::progList* is a pointer to a dynamic array that keeps track of each RPC function corresponding to a unique combination of a program number, version number, and procedure number. The *RPC_svc::numProg* contains the number of valid entries in the *RPC_svc::progList* array.

The *RPC.C* file content is:

```
#include "RPC.h"
int        RPC_svc::numProg = 0;
RPCPROG_INFO *RPC_svc::progList = 0;
```

The *printmsg* client and server programs are compiled (on a Sun's Solaris 2.x system) and run as follows:

```
%    CC -DSYSV4 -c RPC.C
%    CC -DSYSV4 msg_cls2.C RPC.o -o msg_cls2 -lsocket -lnsl
%    CC -DSYSV4 msg_svc2.C RPC.o -o msg_svc2 -lsocket -lnsl
%    msg_svc2 &
[135]
%    msg_cls2 fruit "Hello RPC world"
clnt: call printmsg succeeds
```

In the above sample execution, both the client and server processes are run on a machine called *fruit*. The server is run explicitly in the background, and the client is invoked with the message string *Hello RPC world*. After the client runs, the server prints the message *server: 'Hello RPC world'* to the system console of *fruit*.

To aid users in better understanding the operation of RPC classes, the low-level RPC APIs are presented in the next few sections.

12.5.1   svc_create

The syntax of the *svc_create* function is:

```
#include <rpc/rpc.h>

int      svc_create (void (*dispatch)(struct svc_req*, SVCXPRT *),
                     u_long prognum, u_long versnum, char* nettype);
```

The *svc_create* function creates a transport end point for the given *nettype* value in a server process. The server monitors all RPC calls to the given program and version numbers. Furthermore, for each of these RPC requests, the *dispatch* function is called to respond to it.

The possible values and their meanings for the *nettype* argument are shown in Section 12.3.1.

The *dispatch* function is user-defined and takes two arguments. The first argument contains client RPC call information that is useful when the server responds to the call. Specifically, the *struct svc_req* data type is defined by the <rpc/svc.h> header as:

```
struct svc_req
{
    u_long              rq_prog;        /* service program number */
    u_long              rq_vers;        /* service protocol version */
    u_long              rq_proc;        /* the desired procedure */
    struct opaque_auth rq_cred;         /* raw cred. from the wire */
    caddr_t             rq_clntcred;    /* read only cooked cred. */
    struct __svcxprt *  rq_xprt;        /* associated transport */
};
```

where the *rq_prog, rq_vers,* and *rq_proc* fields contain the RPC function's program, version, and procedure numbers, respectively, that a client wishes to invoke. The *rq_cred* and *rq_clntcred* fields contain client authentication data accessible by the *dispatch* function to authenticate the client. The *rq_xprt* field contains the client transport information and is generally ignored by the *dispatch* function.

The second argument of the *svc_create* is the transport end-point handle. It is passed to the RPC function, which then uses it to get the function argument values from a client. It is also used to send return values to the client.

The return value of the function is a nonzero server handle if it succeeds, zero if it fails.

The ONC functions to create RPC server handles are:

```
#include <rpc/rpc.h>

SVCXPRT* svctcp_create ( int svr_addr,  const u_long sendbuf_size,
                                        const u_long recvbuf_size);


SVCXPRT* svcudp_create ( int svr_addr );
```

The *svctcp_create* and the *svcudp_create* functions are the TCP and UDP versions of the *svc_create* function, respectively. Furthermore, these two functions use sockets as their underlying communication method. Specifically, the *svc_addr* argument value is a socket port number used by an RPC server to communicate with its clients. The socket port number may be specified as RPC_ANYSOCK, which means it can be any port number assigned by the host system.

Finally, the *sendbuf_size* and *recvbuf_size* argument values specify buffer sizes to send and receive data between a server and its clients.

12.5.2   svc_run

The syntax of the *svc_run* function is:

```
#include <rpc/rpc.h>

void     svc_run (void );
```

This function is called by an RPC server to wait for client RPC calls to arrive. When an RPC call arrives, the function calls a *dispatch* function that was registered via the *svc_create, svc_tp_create,* or *svc_tli_create* APIs to service the request.

This function does not return.

12.5.3   svc_getargs

The syntax of the *svc_getargs* function is:

```
#include <rpc/rpc.h>

boot_t   svc_getargs (SVCXPRT* xprt, xdrproc_t* func, caddr_t argp);
```

This function is called by the RPC function in a server process. It is called to retrieve function arguments that are sent by a client process. The *xprt* argument is a transport handle that is connected to a client process. The *argp* argument holds the address of a variable where client argument data are placed. Finally, the *func* argument is a pointer to an XDR function that is used to deserialize client argument data to the server's host machine data format.

This function returns TRUE if it succeeds, FALSE otherwise.

12.5.4   svc_sendreply

The syntax of the *svc_sendreply* function is:

```
#include <rpc/rpc.h>

boot_t   svc_sendreply (SVCXPRT* xprt, xdrproc_t* func, caddr_t resultp);
```

This function is called by an RPC function in a server process. It is called to send return values to a client process. The *xprt* argument is a transport handle that connected to a client process. The *resultp* argument holds the address of a variable where the function return values are placed. Finally, the *func* argument is a pointer to an XDR function used to serialize the return value to XDR format.

This function returns TRUE if it succeeds, or FALSE otherwise.

12.5.5   clnt_create

The syntax of the *clnt_create* function is:

```
#include <rpc/rpc.h>

CLIENT*   clnt_create (char* hostnm, u_long prognum, u_long versnum,
                       const char* nettype);
```

This function creates a handle to communicate with an RPC server. The *hostnm* argument is the name of the machine where the RPC server is running. The *prognum* and *versnum* arguments identify the RPC server by the RPC program and version numbers. The *nettype* argument specifies the transport used in connecting to the server process.

The possible values and meanings of the *nettype* argument are shown in Section 12.3.1.

The function return value is a nonzero client handle if it succeeds, NULL if it fails. If the function fails, users may call the *clnt_pcreateerror* API to print a more detailed error diagnostic message to the standard output. The function prototype of the *clnt_pcreateerror* API is:

```
void clnt_pcreateerror( const char* msg_prefix_string );
```

The *msg_prefix_string* argument is a user-defined message string that is depicted, along with the diagnostic message from the *clnt_pcreateerror* function.

12.5.6   clnt_call

The syntax of the *clnt_call* function is:

```
#include <rpc/rpc.h>

enum clnt_stat
    clnt_call (CLIENT* clntp, u_long funcnum, xdrproc_t argfunc,
               caddr_t argp, xdrproc_t resfunc, caddr_t resp,
               struct timeval timv );
```

This function is called in a client process to invoke an RPC function. The *clntp* argument is the client handle obtained from a *clnt_create, clnt_tp_create,* or *clnt_tli_create* API. The *funcnum* argument is the RPC function procedure number. The *argfunc* argument is the address of an XDR function used to serialize the client input argument data to XDR format before they are sent to the RPC function. The *resfunc* argument is the address of an XDR function used to deserialize RPC function return values to the client's data format. Finally, the *timv* argument specifies the time-out limit (in CPU seconds or microseconds) for this call.

The function return value is RPC_SUCCESS if it succeeds, a nonzero return code if it fails. If it fails, the client process may call *clnt_perror* to print a more detailed error diagnostic message to the standard output. The function prototype of the *clnt_perror* API is:

```
void clnt_perror( const CLIENT* clntp, const char* msg_prefix );
```

The *prefix_string* argument is a user-defined character string that is depicted along with the diagnostic message from the *clnt_pcreateerror* function. The *clntp* argument is the client handle identifying the calling process.

12.6   Managing Multiple RPC Programs and Versions

The RPC classes can be used to create a server process that manages multiple RPC programs. Each program may contain one or more versions of a set of RPC functions. The following example illustrates how this is done.

The server program in this example maintains two RPC programs: The first program number is PROG1NUM, the second is PROG2NUM. PROG1NUM contains two versions (VERS1NUM and VERS2NUM) of an RPC function whose procedure number is FUNC1NUM. The program also contains another RPC function whose version and program numbers are VERS1NUM and FUNC2NUM, respectively. The second program

(PROG2NUM) consists of one RPC function whose version and procedure numbers are VERS1NUM and FUNC2NUM, respectively. The declarations of these RPC program, version, and procedure numbers are contained in the *test.h* header:

```
#ifndef TEST_H
#define TEST_H

#define PROG1NUM    0x20000010
#define PROG2NUM    0x20000015

#define VERS1NUM    0x1
#define VERS2NUM    0x2

#define FUNC1NUM    0x1
#define FUNC2NUM    0x2

#endif
```

The RPC server program is *test_svc.C*:

```
#include "RPC.h"
#include "test.h"

RPC_svc *svc1p, *svc2p, *svc3p;

/* RPC function: prog_no=1, vers_no=1, proc_no=1 */
int func1_1_1 (SVCXPRT* xprt)
{
    cerr << "*** func1_1_1 called\n";
    svc1p->reply(xprt, (xdrproc_t)xdr_void, 0);
    return RPC_SUCCESS;
}

/* RPC function: prog_no=1, vers_no=1, proc_no=2 */
int func1_1_2 (SVCXPRT* xprt)
{
    cerr << "*** func1_1_2 called\n";
    svc1p->reply(xprt, (xdrproc_t)xdr_void, 0);
    return RPC_SUCCESS;
}

/* RPC function: prog_no=1, vers_no=2, proc_no=1 */
int func1_2_1 (SVCXPRT* xprt)
{
    cerr << "*** func1_2_1 called\n";
```

```
      svc2p->reply(xprt, (xdrproc_t)xdr_void, 0);
      return RPC_SUCCESS;
}

/* RPC function: prog_no=2, vers_no=1, proc_no=1 */
int func2_1_1 (SVCXPRT* xprt)
{
   cerr << "*** func2_1_1 called\n";
   svc3p->reply(xprt, (xdrproc_t)xdr_void, 0);
   return RPC_SUCCESS;
}

/* server main function */
int main(int argc, char* argv[])
{
   char* nettype = (argc>1) ? argv[1] : "netpath";

   /* create server handle for prog_no=1, vers=1 */
   svc1p = new RPC_svc ( PROG1NUM, VERS1NUM, nettype );

   /* create server handle for prog_no=1, vers=2 */
   svc2p = new RPC_svc ( PROG1NUM, VERS2NUM, nettype );

   /* create server handle for prog_no=2, vers=1 */
   svc3p = new RPC_svc ( PROG2NUM, VERS1NUM, nettype );

   if (!svc1p->good() || !svc2p->good() || !svc3p->good())    {
      cerr << "create server handle(s) failed\n";
      return 1;
   }
   /* register a function: prog_no=1, vers_no=1, proc_no=1,
         func=func1_1_1*/
   svc1p->add_func( FUNC1NUM, func1_1_1 );

    /* register a function: prog_no=1, vers_no=1, proc_no=2,
         func=func1_1_2*/
   svc1p->add_func( FUNC2NUM, func1_1_2 );

    /* register a function: prog_no=1, vers_no=2, proc_no=1,
         func=func1_2_1*/
   svc2p->add_func( FUNC1NUM, func1_2_1 );

    /* register a function: prog_no=2, vers_no=1, proc_no=1,
         func=func2_1_1*/
   svc3p->add_func( FUNC1NUM, func2_1_1 );
```

```
        /* wait for clients' RPC requests for all servers */
        RPC_svc::run();
        return 0;
    }
```

The server program takes an optional argument from the command line, which specifies the correct transport type to use. If this is not specified, the default *nettype* value is "*netpath*".

The server creates three *RPC_svc* objects, one for each version of the RPC program it manages:

RPC_svc	Program Managed	Version Managed
svc1p	PROG1NUM	VERS1NUM
svc2p	PROG1NUM	VERS2NUM
svc3p	PROG2NUM	VERS1NUM

Once all three *RPC_svc* objects are created successfully, the server registers the RPC functions via *RPC_svc* objects. The name of each RPC function is constructed as: the prefix string *func,* followed by a program number, an underscore, a version number, another underscore, and finally, a procedure number. Thus, a function named *func1_2_1* means the function is version 2 of procedure 1 in RPC program 1.

After all the RPC functions are registered, the server calls the *RPC_svc::run* function to wait for client RPC requests to arrive. When any one of these requests arrives, the *RPC_svc::dispatch* function is called, which, in turn, calls one of the registered RPC functions (according to the client's specified program, version, and procedure numbers).

The client program for this example is *test_cls.C*:

```
#include "RPC.h"
#include "test.h"

int main(int argc, char* argv[])
{
    if (argc < 2)  {
        cerr << "usage: " << argv[0] << " <server-host> [<nettype>]\n";
        return 1;
    }

    char* nettype = (argc > 2) ? argv[2] : "netpath";

    while (1)  {
```

```
          unsigned progid, progno, verno, procno;
          /* get desire RPC program no, version no, and function no */
          do {
              cout << "Enter prog#, ver#, func#: " << flush;
              cin >> progno >> verno >> procno;
              if (cin.eof()) return 0;
          } while (!cin.good());

           /* translate user program no to internal number */
          progid = (progno==1) ? PROG1NUM : PROG2NUM;

          /* create a client handle to the requested RPC server */
          RPC_cls *clsp = new RPC_cls ( argv[1], progid, verno, nettype);
          if (!clsp->good())   {
              cerr << "create client handle(s) failed\n";
              return 2;
          }

          /* call the user-requested RPC function */
          if (clsp->call( procno, (xdrproc_t)xdr_void, 0, (xdrproc_t)xdr_void, 0 )
                    != RPC_SUCCESS)
              cerr << "client call RPC function fails\n";

          delete clsp;
      }
      return 0;
  }
```

The client program is invoked with the server host machine name, and optionally, a *nettype* value. If no *nettype* value is specified, it defaults to "*netpath*".

The client program is an interactive program and prompts a user to enter the program, version, and procedure numbers for each RPC function called. For each set of numbers obtained the client process creates a *RPC_cls* object and calls the requested function via that object. The client process terminates when EOF is encountered in the input stream.

The server and client programs are compiled and run as shown below. In the example, both the server and client are run on a machine called *fruit*.

```
%    CC -DSYSV4 test_cls.C RPC.C -o test_cls -lsocket -lnsl
%    CC -DSYSV4 test_svc.C RPC.C -o test_svc -lsocket -lnsl
%    test_svc &
[1235]
%    test_cls fruit
Enter prog#, ver#, func#: 1 1 1
```

```
***f unc1_1_1 called
Enter prog#, ver#, func#: 1 1 2
*** func1_1_2 called
Enter prog#, ver#, func#: 1 2 1
*** func1_2_1 called
Enter prog#, ver#, func#: 2 1 1
*** func2_1_1 called
Enter prog#, ver#, func#: 1 1 0
Enter prog#, ver#, func#: 4 1 2
fruit: RPC: Procedure unavailable
client call RPC function fails
Enter prog#, ver#, func#: ^D
```

In the above sample run, the RPC functions were called in this order: *func1_1_1, func1_1_2, func1_2_1,* and *func2_1_1*. The user input *1 1 0* causes the client to ping the RPC server for the program PROG1NUM (version VERS1NUM). There is no response message depicted for this ping operation. Finally, the user inputs *4 1 2* in an attempt to call a nonexistent RPC function, and error messages are flagged from both the *RPC_cls::call* function and the client *test_cls.C* program.

12.7   Authentication

Some RPC services are restricted to designated classes of users who can make use of them. This requires client processes to authenticate themselves to the servers before requested RPC functions can be called. UNIX systems provide a few basic authentication methods for users and allow users to define their own authentication methods.

The UNIX System V.4 RPC built-in authentication methods are: AUTH_NONE, AUTH_SYS, AUTH_SHORT, and AUTH_DES. The ONC RPC authentication methods are: AUTH_NONE, AUTH_UNIX (equivalent to AUTH_SYS), and AUTH_DES. These authentication methods are described in more detail in the following sections.

To support authentication, (whether it is a system-supplied or user-defined method) the *struct svc_req* argument data passed from a client to an RPC server dispatch function specifies the target function's numbers (program, version, and procedure) and client authentication data. Specifically, the *struct svc_req* type is declared as:

```
struct svc_req
{
    u_long              rq_prog;        /* service program number */
    u_long              rq_vers;        /* service protocol version */
    u_long              rq_proc;        /* the desired procedure */
    struct opaque_auth  rq_cred;        /* raw cred. from the wire */
```

483

```
    caddr_t                    rq_clntcred;        /* read only cooked cred */
    struct __svcxprt *         rq_xprt;            /* associated transport */
};
```

where the *struct opaque_auth* data type is declared in the <rpc/auth.h> header as:

```
struct opaque_auth
{
    enum_t          oa_flavor;      /* authentication method */
    caddr_t         oa_base;        /* pointer to custom auth. data */
    u_int           oa_length;      /* size of the data pt. by oa_base */
};
```

The *opaque_auth::oa_flavor* field specifies which authentication method is used by the client. If the argument value is AUTH_NONE, AUTH_SYS, AUTH_SHORT, or AUTH_DES, the *opaque_auth::oa_base* and *opaque_auth::oa_length* fields are don't-care. The *svc_req::rq_clntcred* field points to a data record that contains the corresponding authentication data.

However, if the *opaque_auth::oa_flavor* field value is one of the AUTH_xxx, the *opaque_auth::oa_base* field points to a user-defined authentication data record, and the *opaque_auth::oa_length* field contains the size of the data record referenced by the *opaque_auth::oa_base* field.

The following three sections examine the UNIX system built-in RPC authentication methods. Users can create their own authentication methods based on these.

12.7.1   AUTH_NONE

This is the default UNIX System V RPC authentication method, which actually does not use any authentication at all. A client can explicitly set this authentication method by calling the *authnone_create* API, as follows:

```
CLIENT* clntp = clnt_create( ... );
if (clntp)    {
    clntp->cl_auth = authnone_create();
    clnt_call (clntp, ...);
}
```

After a client calls the *authnone_create* function, any RPC dispatch functions called by this client receive the *svc_req::rq_cred.oa_flavor* value as AUTH_NONE. These functions should ignore the *svc_req::rq_cred.oa_base,* *svc_req::rq_cred.oa_length,* and the *svc_req::rq_clntcred* values.

12.7.2   AUTH_SYS (or AUTH_UNIX)

This method uses the UNIX system process access control method, which is based on process user ID and group GID to authenticate clients. A client can explicitly set this authentication method by calling the *authsys_create_default* API, as follows:

```
CLIENT* clntp = clnt_create( ... );
if (clntp) {
    clntp->cl_auth = authsys_create_default();
    clnt_call (clntp, ...);
}
```

After a client calls the *authsys_create_default* function, any RPC dispatch functions called by this client will receive the *svc_req::rq_cred.oa_flavor* value as AUTH_SYS, and the *svc_req::rq_clntcred* field will point to a data record with the following structure:

```
struct aythsys_parms
{
    u_long       aup_time;        /* auth. data creation time */
    char*        *aup_machname;   /* client's machine name */
    uid_t        aup_uid;         /* client's effective UID */
    gid_t        aup_guid;        /* client's effective GID */
    u_int        aup_len          /* no. of entry in aup_gids */
    gid_t *      aup_gids;        /* client's supplemental GIDs */
};
```

An example of a server dispatch function that checks client authentication is:

```
int diaptch ( struct svc_req* rqstp, SVCXPRT* xtrp )
{
    struct authsys_parms* ptr
    switch (rqstp->oa_flavor)   {
      case AUTH_NONE:
        break;
      case AUTH_SYS:
        ptr = (struct authsys_parms*)rqstp->rq_clntcred;
        if (ptr->aup_uid != 0) {
            svcerr_systemerr(xtrp);
```

```
            return;
        }
        break;
    case AUTH_DES:
        ...
        break;
    default:
        svcerr_weakauth( xtrp );
        return;
    }
    /* perform or call the actual RPC function */
    ...
}
```

In the above example, the RPC server skips checking client authentication if it is specified as AUTH_NONE in the *rqstp->rq_cred.oa_flavor*. However, if the client's selected authentication method is AUTH_SYS, the server checks whether the client effective UID is superuser, (via the *rqstp->rq_clntcred.aup_uid* argument). If it is not, the *svcerr_systemerr* API is called by it to print a system error message. This is just an example, and real user applications may authenticate client UIDs and/or GIDs in any way they desire.

If a client authentication is none of the system default methods, the server calls the *svcerr_weakauth* API to send an "unsupported" authentication error to the client.

The function prototypes of the *svcerr_weakauth* and *svcerr_systemerr* APIs are:

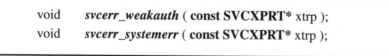

```
void    svcerr_weakauth ( const SVCXPRT* xtrp );
void    svcerr_systemerr ( const SVCXPRT* xtrp );
```

The *xtrp* argument to both of the above functions is a transport handle for communication with a client process. This argument value is passed as the second argument to an RPC server's dispatch function.

Note that ONC provides the *authunix_create_default* API instead of *authsys_create_default,* and that the AUTH_SYS and AUTH_SHORT constants are replaced by the AUTH_UNIX constant. However, the underlying authentication method based on process UIDs and GIDs are the same on all UNIX systems.

12.7.3   AUTH_DES

The AUTH_SYS authentication method is simple to use but is not secured because client identification, namely, UID and GID, are not guaranteed unique on the Internet. Furthermore, a client can easily alter the *cl->cl_auth* data to change its identity to someone else before it makes an RPC call. To remedy these defects, the AUTH_DES was created to provide a more sophisticated authentication method for RPC applications.

To use the AUTH_DES method, a client process first needs to call the *user2netname* API to get a *"netname"* that is guaranteed to be unique on the entire Internet. This *netname* is constructed by taking the domain name of the client process and prepending it with the name of the process operating system and effective UID. For example, if a process is running on a UNIX machine in the domain *TJSys.com* and the process's effective UID is 125, its *netname* is *unix.125@TJS.yscom*. This *netname* is unique because a domain name is always unique on the Internet. Furthermore, within a domain, each UID should be unique among all machines running the same operating system. Thus, if the *TJSys.com* domain contains VMS machines that also have a user with the UID of 125, the *netname* of any process created by that user is *vms.125@TJSys.com*. This differentiates it from the UNIX process with the same UID and domain.

As an alternative to the *user2netname* API, a process may call the *host2netname* API to get a *netname* for the machine on which it is running. This *netname* is guaranteed to be unique on the Internet, but it refers to a machine and not a user. In the above example, if the process is running on a UNIX machine called *fruit*, the *netname* returned by *host2netname* is *unix.fruit@TJSys.com*. The choice of which API (*user2netname* or *host2netname*) to use depends on whether users want their RPC applications to check authentication at the user level or at the machine level.

The syntax of the *user2netname* and *host2netname* APIs are:

```
#include <rpc/rpc.h>

int     user2netname (char netname[MAXNETNAMELEN+1],
                      uid_t eUID, const char* domain );

int     host2netname (char netname[MAXNETNAMELEN+1],
                      const char* hostnm, const char* domain );
```

The first argument of both functions is a character buffer of at least MAXNET-NAME+1 size. This is to hold the returned unique name of the process. The second argument of the *user2netname* is the effective UID of the process, whereas the second argument to the *host2netname* is the host machine name. The third argument to both functions is the process domain name. If the *domain* argument value is passed as NULL, local domain name is assumed.

These functions return 1 if they succeed, 0 if they fail.

To create an AUTH_DES data record in a client process, the *authdes_seccreate* API is called. The function prototype of this API is:

```
#include <rpc/rpc.h>

int    authdes_seccreate (char netname[MAXNETNAMELEN+1],
              unsigned window, const char* time_host, const des_block* ckey);
```

The *netname* argument value is either the calling process *netname* or its host machine *netname*. This specifies the identity of the client process.

The *window* argument specifies a time period, in seconds, when the client credential as established, by this call will expire. If an RPC server receives an RPC call from a client that was authenticated more than *window* seconds later, the server will reject the request.

The *time_host* argument specifies a machine name upon which the authentication time stamp is based. This is usually the target RPC server's machine name. If this argument is specified as NULL, there is no need to synchronize client and server time.

The *ckey* argument is a DES key that is used to encrypt the client credential. This key is used by the target server to decrypt the credential. If this argument is specified as NULL, the operating system generates a random DES key for it. A client can explicitly get a DES key via the *key_gendes* API.

The *authdes_seccreate* API returns an *AUTH** pointer that points to the encrypted client credential if it succeeds, NULL if it fails.

The *key_gendes* API creates a DES key for a calling process. Its function prototype is:

```
int key_gendes( des_block* ckey );
```

The argument of the *key_gendes* function is the address of a *des_bloc-* typed variable. This is to hold the generated DES key. The function returns 0 it succeeds, -1 if it fails.

On an RPC server side, a server can retrieve a client's DES credential via either the *authdes_getucred* or the *netname2host* API. Specifically, the *authdes_getucred* is used if the credential is a user *netname* (obtained via the *user2netname* API). This API decrypts the credential and returns the client UID and GID(s) to the server. On the other hand, if the client credential is a machine *netname* (obtained via the *host2netname* API), the *netname2host* API is called to extract the client host machine name accordingly.

The function prototypes of these APIs are:

```
#include <rpc/rpc.h>

int    authdes_getucred (const struct authdes_cred* adc,
              uid_t* uid_p, gid_t* gid_p, short* len_p, gid_t* gidArray);

int    netname2host (const char* netname, char* hostname, int len);
```

For the *authdes_getucred* API, the *adc* argument value is obtained via the *rqstp* argument of the server dispatch function. Specifically, the *rqstp->rq_clntcred* field is the value for the *adc* argument. This argument points to the client's encrypted credential.

The *uid_p* and *gid_p* arguments are addresses of variables that hold the returned UID and GID of a client, respectively.

The *gidArray* and *len* arguments are address of variables that hold the returned array of supplemental GIDs and the number of client entries, respectively.

For the *netname2host* API, the *netname* argument value is obtained via the *rqstp* argument of the server dispatch function. Specifically, the *rqstp->rq_clntcred->adc_fullname.name* field is the value for the *netname* argument.

The *hostname* argument is the address of a character buffer that holds the returned client host machine name. The *len* argument specified the maximum size of the buffer pointed to by the *hostname* argument.

Both the *authdes_getucred* and *netname2host* functions return 1 if they succeed, 0 if they fail. Note that in the RPC classes defined in Section 12.5, the *RPC_cls::set_auth* may be called by a client process to set the AUTH_SYS or AUTH_DES credential. If the AUTH_DES method is used, the client's credential is based on its effective UID and GID.

On the server side, the *RPC_svc::dispatch* function checks each client credential according to the authentication method used. If a client uses the AUTH_NONE method, the dispatch function simply skips the credential check. This may not be allowed in real life secured RPC applications. The users may change the dispatch function to flag an error and refuse to execute the requested RPC function if the client specifies the AUTH_NONE method. Furthermore, if a client uses the AUTH_DES method, the dispatch function calls the *authdes_getucred* API to extract client UID and GID(s). This is acceptable as long as the *RPC_cls::set_auth* calls the *user2netanme* API only (and not *host2netname*) to create the client's credential. However, if a user's application uses *host2netname* and/or *user2netname* to generate client credentials, the *RPC_svc::dispatch* function should be changed accordingly.

12.7.4   Directory Listing Example with Authentication

This directory listing example is shown in Section 12.3.3 is shown again below, but rewritten with the following changes:

* It uses RPC classes instead of *rpcgen*
* It illustrates how a client process pings a server process
* It illustrates RPC authentication mechanism

The *RPC.h* and *RPC.C* files are as shown in Section 12.5. The *scan2.h* file is created manually as follows:

```
#ifndef SCAN2_H
#define SCAN2_H

#include <rpc/rpc.h>
#define MAXNLEN 255
typedef char *name_t;
typedef struct arg_rec *argPtr;

struct arg_rec
{
    name_t    dir_name;
    int       lflag;
};

typedef struct arg_rec arg_rec;
typedef struct dirinfo *infolist;

struct dirinfo
{
    name_t    name;
    u_int     uid;
    long      modtime;
```

```
        infolist      next;
};
typedef struct dirinfo dirinfo;

struct res
{
    int           errno;
    union
    {
        infolist      list;
    } res_u;
};
typedef struct res res;

#define SCANPROG ((unsigned long)(0x20000100))
#define SCANVER ((unsigned long)(1))
#define SCANDIR ((unsigned long)(1))

extern "C" bool_t xdr_name_t(XDR *, name_t*);
extern "C" bool_t xdr_argPtr(XDR *, argPtr*);
extern "C" bool_t xdr_arg_rec(XDR *, arg_rec*);
extern "C" bool_t xdr_infolist(XDR *, infolist*);
extern "C" bool_t xdr_dirinfo(XDR *, dirinfo*);
extern "C" bool_t xdr_res(XDR *, res*);

#endif /* !SCAN_H */
```

The client program *scan_cls2.C* is:

```
#include <errno.h>
#include "scan2.h"
#include "RPC.h"

int main( int argc, char* argv[])
{
    static res result;
    infolist nl;

    if (argc<3) {
        cerr << "usage: " << argv[0] << " host directory [<long>]\n";
        return 1;
    }

    /* create a client RPC hanlde */
    RPC_cls cl( argv[1], SCANPROG, SCANVER, "netpath");
```

```
   if (!cl.good()) return 1;

   /* set authentication credential base on DES encryption method */
   cl.set_auth( AUTH_DES );

   /* ping the RPC server to make sure it is alive */
   if (cl.call( 0, (xdrproc_t)xdr_void, 0, (xdrproc_t)xdr_void, 0 ) ==
         RPC_SUCCESS)
      cout << "Prog " << SCANPROG << " /" << SCANVER << ") is alive\n";
   else {
      cerr << "Prog " << SCANPROG << "/" << SCANVER << " is dead!\n";
      return 2;
   }

   /* allocate memory to hold the return directory listing */
   struct arg_rec *iarg = (struct arg_rec*)malloc(sizeof(struct arg_rec));

   iarg->dir_name = argv[2];         // set remote directory name
   iarg->lflag = 0;                  // set long listing flag
   if (argc==4 && sscanf(argv[3],"%u",&(iarg->lflag))!=1)  {
      cerr << "Invalid argument: " << argv[3] << endl;
      return 3;
   }

   /* Call the RPC function */
   if (cl.call( SCANDIR, (xdrproc_t)xdr_argPtr, (caddr_t)&iarg,
            (xdrproc_t)xdr_res, (caddr_t)&result) != RPC_SUCCESS)
   {
      cerr << "client: call RPC fails\n";
      return 4;
   }

   /* RPC call completed. Check the function's return code */
   if (result.errno)  {
      errno = result.errno;
      perror(iarg->dir_name);
      return 5;
   }

   /* RPC function completes successfully. Now list remote dir content */
   for (nl=result.res_u.list; nl; nl=nl->next)   {
      if (iarg->lflag)
         cout << "..." << nl->name << ", uid=" << nl->uid << ",mtime="
               << ctime(&nl->modtime) << endl;
      else cout << "..." << nl->name << "\n";
   }
```

```
        return 0;
    }
```

The client program is invoked with the server host machine name, a remote directory name, and possibly, an integer flag. The remote directory name is the directory whose content is to be returned by the RPC function. The optional integer flag specifies whether the returned directory listing should be in detailed (*lflag*=1) format or with file names (*lflag*=0) only.

If a client program is invoked with the correct arguments, it creates a *RPC_cls* object for connection with a server via the *RPC_cls::RPC_cls* constructor function. The RPC server is identified by the SCANPROG, SCANVER, and SCANFUNC constants (the RPC program, version, and procedure numbers).

Once the client *RPC_cls* object is created, the client process calls the *RPC_cls::set_auth* function to generate a client credential using the AUTH_DES method. The *RPC_cls::set_auth* function can create authentication credentials by using AUTH_NONE, AUTH_SYS, or AUTH_DES can hide all low-level RPC authentication APIs from users.

After the client credential is set up, the client calls the RPC server with a procedure number of 0. This is to ping the RPC server to make sure it is alive. If the *RPC_cls::call* function fails, the client prints an error message to that effect and quits; otherwise, client execution continues.

The client allocates dynamic memory for the *iarg* variable to store the input argument in the RPC function: a remote directory name and a long listing flag. The client calls the RPC function via the *RPC_cls::call* function and specifies that its return value be stored in the *result* variable. Furthermore, the XDR functions for the input argument and return value are the user-defined *xdr_argPtr* and *xdr_res* functions, respectively.

If the RPC function returns a success status code, the client program prints the RPC function return value (the remote directory content listing) to the standard output. Note that if the directory listing format flag is 1, the printout for each file consists of the file name, UID, and last modification time. If, however, the directory listing format flag is zero, only the name of each file in the remote directory is shown.

The server program that provides the remote directory listing service is in the *scan_svc2.C* file:

```
        #include <stdio.h>
        #include <stdlib.h>
        #include <dirent.h>
        #include <string.h>
```

```
#include <malloc.h>
#include <errno.h>
#include <sys/stat.h>
#include "scan2.h"
#include "RPC.h"
static RPC_svc *svcp = 0;

/* The RPC function */
int scandir( SVCXPRT* xtrp )
{
    DIR *dirp;
    struct dirent *d;
    infolist  nl, *nlp;
    struct stat statv;
    res res;
    argPtr darg = 0;

    /* Get function argument from a client */
    if (svcp->getargs( xtrp, (xdrproc_t)xdr_argPtr,
                  (caddr_t)&darg)!=RPC_SUCCESS)
        return -1;

    /* start scaning the requested directory */
    if (!(dirp = opendir(darg->dir_name)))     {
        res.errno = errno;
        (void)svcp->reply(xtrp, (xdrproc_t)xdr_res, (caddr_t)&res);
        return -2;
    }

    /* free memoryallocated from a previous RPC call */
    xdr_free((xdrproc_t)xdr_res, (char*)&res);
    /* store files' informaton to res as the return values */
    nlp = &res.res_u.list;
    while (d=readdir(dirp))   {
        nl = *nlp = (infolist)malloc(sizeof(struct dirinfo));
        nl->name = strdup(d->d_name);
        nlp = &nl->next;
        if (darg->lflag)   {
            char pathnm[256];
            sprintf(pathnm,"%s/%s",darg->dir_name,d->d_name);
            if (!stat(pathnm,&statv))     {
                nl->uid = statv.st_uid;
                nl->modtime = statv.st_mtime;
            }
        }
    }
```

```
            *nlp = 0;
            res.errno = 0;
            closedir(dirp);

            /* Send directory listing to client */
            if (svcp->reply(xtrp, (xdrproc_t)xdr_res,
                        (caddr_t)&res)!=RPC_SUCCESS)
                return -2;

            return RPC_SUCCESS;
        }

        /* RPC server's main function */
        int main(int argc, char* argv[])
        {
            svcp = new RPC_svc( SCANPROG, SCANVER, "netpath");
            if (svcp->run_func( SCANDIR, scandir )) return 1;
             return 0; /* shouldn't get here */
        }
```

The above program creates an RPC server that provides a directory listing service. There is no command line argument needed to invoke the program.

The process creates a *RPC_svc* object via the *RPC_svc::RPC_svc* constructor function. After this is done, the server calls the *RPC_svc::run_func* function to register the *scandir* RPC function to the *RPC_svc* object and waits for client RPC calls to arrive.

When a client RPC call arrives, the *RPC_svc::dispatch* function is called. This function first checks whether the requested RPC procedure number is zero. If the client is pinging the server, this function simply returns with a NULL reply. This completes the server response to a ping request.

If a client is not pinging the server, the dispatch function checks the client credential according to the authentication method specified. If the authentication check fails, the dispatch function raises an RPC system error and quits. The current *RPC_svc::dispatch* function accepts only clients whose UIDs are either zero (superuser) or the same as that of the server process.

After the client credential is verified as correct, the dispatch function finds the requested RPC function and invokes it. In this example, the only RPC function is *printmsg*; which performs the following operations when invoked:

- It obtains function arguments from a client process
- It frees any dynamic memory allocated for the *res* variable in a previous call

- It scans the requested directory and puts information from all files in that directory to the *res* variable
- It sends the *res* variable as return value to the calling client

The final pieces of code in this example are the XDR functions for user-defined data types (e.g., *struct arg_rec, argPtr, infolist*, etc.). These XDR functions are defined in the *scan2_xdr.c* file:

```c
#include "scan2.h"

/* XDR function for the name_t data type */
bool_t xdr_name_t(register XDR *xdrs, name_t *objp)
{
    register long *buf;
    if (!xdr_string(xdrs, objp, MAXNLEN)) return (FALSE);
    return (TRUE);
}

/* XDR function for the argPtr data type */
bool_t xdr_argPtr(register XDR *xdrs, argPtr *objp)
{
    register long *buf;
    if (!xdr_pointer(xdrs, (char **)objp, sizeof (struct arg_rec), (xdrproc_t)
                xdr_arg_rec))
        return (FALSE);
    return (TRUE);
}

/* XDR function for the arg_rec data type */
bool_t xdr_arg_rec(register XDR *xdrs, arg_rec *objp)
{
    register long *buf;
    if (!xdr_name_t(xdrs, &objp->dir_name)) return (FALSE);
    if (!xdr_int(xdrs, &objp->lflag)) return (FALSE);
    return (TRUE);
}

/* XDR function for the infolist data type */
bool_t xdr_infolist(register XDR *xdrs, infolist *objp)
{
    register long *buf;
    if (!xdr_pointer(xdrs, (char **)objp, sizeof (struct dirinfo), (xdrproc_t)
                xdr_dirinfo))
        return (FALSE);
```

```
        return (TRUE);
    }

    /* XDR function for the dirinfo data type */
    bool_t xdr_dirinfo(register XDR *xdrs, dirinfo *objp)
    {
        register long *buf;
        if (!xdr_name_t(xdrs, &objp->name)) return (FALSE);
        if (!xdr_u_int(xdrs, &objp->uid)) return (FALSE);
        if (!xdr_long(xdrs, &objp->modtime)) return (FALSE);
        if (!xdr_infolist(xdrs, &objp->next)) return (FALSE);
        return (TRUE);
    }

    /* XDR function for the res data type */
    bool_t xdr_res(register XDR *xdrs, res *objp)
    {
        register long *buf;
        if (!xdr_int(xdrs, &objp->errno)) return (FALSE);
        if (objp->errno==0) {
            if (!xdr_infolist(xdrs, &objp->res_u.list)) return (FALSE);
        }
        return (TRUE);
    }
```

The above XDR functions should be self-explanatory. These XDR functions can be generated manually or via the *rpcgen*. For the latter, users need to declare their data types in a *rpcgen* .x file and use *rpcgen*-specific data types, such as *string,* where applicable.

The above client and server programs are created by the following shell commands:

```
    %   CC -c scan2_xdr.c RPC.C
    %   CC -DSYSV4 -o scan_svc2 scan_svc2.C scan2_xdr.o \
                RPC.o -lsocket -lnsl
    %   CC -DSYSV4 -o scan_cls2 scan_cls2.C scan2_xdr.o \
                RPC.o -lsocket -lnsl
```

The sample run of the client and server programs are shown below. The server program is run on a machine called *fruit*, whereas the client program may be run on any machine that is connected to *fruit*:

```
    %   scan_svc2 &
    [1] 955
```

```
%    scan_cls2 fruit .
....
.....
...scan_cls2.C
...scan_svc2.C
...RPC.C
...RPC.h
...scan2_xdr.c
...scan2.h
...scan_svc2
...scan_cls2
Prog 536871168 (version 1) is alive
```

12.8   RPC Broadcast

Some RPC requests may require a response from all servers on the network that provides the requested services. For example, a client process may wish to set the system clock of all machines on the LAN. Assume there is an RPC server running on each machine and that its effective user ID is the superuser. The client process broadcasts the new clock time to all these servers with one RPC call, and each server updates its system clock accordingly.

To use RPC broadcasting, a process can use the *RPC_cls::broadcast* member function. This is a static function and does not require an *RPC_cls* object be created prior to making the call. This function, in turn, calls the *rpc_broadcast* API to implement the broadcast. The function prototype of the *rpc_broadcast* API is:

#include <rpc/rpc.h>

enum clnt_stat **rpc_broadcast** (**unsiged** prognum, **unsigned** versnum,
      unsigned funcnum, **xdrproc_t** argfunc, **caddr_t** argp,
      xdrproc_t resfunc, **caddr_t** resp, **resultproc_t** callme, **char*** nettype);

The *prognum, versnum,* and *funcnum* arguments are the numbers of an RPC function to be invoked.

The *argfunc* argument is the address of an XDR function used to serialize/de-serialize the RPC function argument as specified in the *argp* argument. Similarly, the *resfunc* argument is the address of an XDR function used to serialize/deserialize the RPC function return value to be placed in the *resp* argument.

The *nettype* argument specifies the transport to be used for the RPC broadcast call. This must be a connectionless transport protocol, such as UDP. The default value for *nettype* in the *RPC_cls::broadcast* function is "*datagram_v*", which can use any "*visible*" datagram transport as specified in the */etc/netconfig* file. Two other *rpc_braodcast* restrictions are: (1) a broadcast request may not exceed the MTU (maximum transfer unit) limits of its host machine (for Ethernet-based machines, the MTU limit is 1500 bytes); and (2) only servers that are registered with the *rpcbind* daemon can respond to RPC broadcasts. This is the case if a server is created via the *svc_create* or *svc_tp_create* APIs.

The *callme* argument is a user-defined function that is called for each RPC server response. The function prototype of the *callme* function is:

int callme (caddr_t resp, struct netbuf* server_addr, struct netconf* nconf);

where the *resp* argument is the same *resp* value specified in the *rpc_broadcast* call. This is the address of a variable defined in the client process that holds the server return value. The *server_addr* argument contains a responding server address. The *nconf* argument contains the network transport information used by the server.

Once the *rpc_braodcast* function is called, it blocks the calling process to wait for server responses. For each RPC server response, the function calls the *callme* function to service the response. It the *callme* function returns a 0 value, the *rpc_broadcast* waits for another server response to arrive. On the other hand, if the *callme* function returns a nonzero value, the *rpc_braodcast* function terminates and returns control to the calling process.

The *rpc_broadcast* function returns an RPC_TIMEDOUT value if it has waited and tried the broadcast several times without getting any server response. It returns an RPC_SUCCESS value if the *callme* function returned TRUE; otherwise, it returns a nonzero value to indicate an error.

The *rpc_broadcast* function uses the AUTH_SYS method to authenticate the calling process to all RPC server processes that receive the broadcast call.

Note that in ONC, the *rpc_broadcast* API is replaced by the *clnt_broadcast* API. The two functions have almost the same signature and return value, except that the *clnt_broadcast* API does not use the *nettype* argument.

```
#include <rpc/rpc.h>

enum clnt_stat   clnt_broadcast (unsiged prognum, unsigned versnum,
        unsigned funcnum, xdrproc_t argfunc, caddr_t argp,
        xdrproc_t resfunc, caddr_t resp, resultproc_t callme );
```

Furthermore, the *callback* function prototype for the *clnt_broadcast* API is:

```
int callme ( caddr_t resp, struct sockaddr_in* server_addr );
```

where the *resp* argument is the same *resp* value as specified in the *clnt_broadcast* call. This is the address of a variable defined in the client process that holds the server return value. The *server_addr* argument contains a responding server address. Its data type is a pointer to a socket address.

12.8.1   RPC Broadcast Example

The *msg_cls2.C* program shown in Section 12.5. is rewritten below using RPC broadcast. Only the client program is changed. The new client program *msg_cls3.C* is:

```
/* client program: use broadcast to print msg on server's system console */
#include "msg2.h"
#include "RPC.h"

static unsigned int num_responses = 0;


/* client's broadcast call back function */
bool_t callme (caddr_t res_p, struct netbuf* addr, struct netconfig *nconf)
{
    num_responses++;                    // keep track of no.of server responded

    if (res_p==0 || *((int*)res_p)!=0)  {
        cerr << "clnt: call printmsg fails\n";
        return TRUE; /* stop broadcast due to error */
    }
    cout << "clnt: call printmsg succeeds\n";
    return FALSE; /*wait for more response */
}

/* client main function */
int main(int argc, char* argv[])
{
    int   res;
    if (argc<2)   {
        cerr << "usage: " << argv[0] << " msg <transport>\n";
```

```
            return 1;
        }
        /* client sends a broadcast request and waits for responses */
        int rc = RPC_cls::broadcast( MSGPROG, MSGVER, PRINTMSG,
                (resultproc_t)callme, (xdrproc_t)xdr_string, (caddr_t)&argv[1],
                (xdrproc_t)xdr_int, (caddr_t)&res);

        switch (rc)    {
            case RPC_SUCCESS:        break;
            case RPC_TIMEDOUT:       if (num_responses) break;
            default:                 cerr << "RPC broadcast failed\n";
                                     return 2;
        }
        cout << "RPC broadcast done. No reponses: " < <num_responses
            << endl;
        return 0;
    }
```

The new *printmsg* client program takes one command line argument and broadcasts it as the message. It calls the *RPC_cls::broadcast* function to broadcast the message. In the *RPC_cls::broadcast* call, the client process specifies *callme* as the function to be called by the *rpc_broadcast* API for each server response. Furthermore, the *printmsg*'s argument and XDR function, as well as the variable holding the *printmsg* return value and XDR function, are set in the *RPC_cls::broadcast* function call in the same manner as in an *RPC_cls::call* function call.

The *callme* function is called for each server response to the broadcast. The function simply checks that the return value succeeds or does not. The function returns TRUE to stop the broadcast if the server return value is a failure or FALSE to continue receiving more server responses. The *callme* function increments the global variable *num_responses* to keep track of the number of servers actually responding to the broadcast.

After the *RPC_cls::broadcast* call returns, the client program checks the function return status code. If the status code is RPC_SUCCESS, the broadcast was terminated by the *callme* function and all is well. However, if the status code is RPC_TIMEDOUT, then the *num_responses* variable is checked to see whether any server responded to the broadcast. If there are none (the *num_responses* value is zero), the RPC broadcast failed, and an error message is flagged to the user. On the other hand, if the *num_responses* variable value is nonzero, it means that the RPC broadcast was successful. The *rpc_broadcast* function returns because all servers responded to the broadcast.

The sample run of the server program, *msg_svc2* (as shown in Section 12.5) and the new client program, *msg_cls3*, which runs in RPC broadcast mode, is:

```
%     CC -DSYSV4 -o msg_cls3 msg_cls3.C RPC.C -lsocket -lnsl
%     msg_cls3 "Testing RPC broadcast feature"
clnt: call printmsg succeeds
clnt: call printmsg succeeds
...
```

The system consoles on all machines running the *msg_svc2* daemon print the message *Testing RPC broadcast feature*.

12.9   RPC Call Back

In some RPC applications, it may be desirable for a server to call a client process back after some period of time. This allows the client process to do some other work in the mean-time. An example of this is when a client process requests an RPC server process to execute a time-consuming function but does not wish to wait for the RPC function to finish before continuing execution. Instead, the client specifies an RPC function that the server can call when it is ready to send results back to the client. Thus, the client and server can both be doing useful work concurrently, improving overall system efficiency.

For an RPC server to call a client back, the client must define an RPC program number, a version number, and a procedure number for the callback function. In a sense, the client is acting as both an RPC client and a server.

The following example programs illustrate how this is done. In the example, the RPC server provides an alarm clock service to processes on the LAN. A client process that desires this service sends an RPC call to the server and specifies the following information:

* The client process host machine name
* The client's callback RPC function program, version, and procedure numbers
* The alarm clock period, in seconds

When the RPC server receives a request from a client, it forks a child to set up an alarm signal, which is sent to the child process after the client-specified alarm clock period expires. When the alarm period does expire, the child process makes an RPC call to the client call-back function to inform it of that fact and afterward terminates itself. During all this processing, the RPC server is continuously monitoring for other client alarm service requests. The original client process is working on something else during the alarm clock period.

The header file, *aclock.h*, is shared by the client and server programs:

```
#ifndef ACLOCK_H
#define ACLOCK_H

#include <rpc/rpc.h>
#define    MAXNLEN       255

typedef char *name_t;

/* client's call-back information to the RPC server */
struct arg_rec
{
    name_t    hostname;            // client's host machine name
    u_long    prognum;             // client's RPC function program no.
    u_long    versnum;             // client's RPC function version no.
    u_long    funcnum;             // client's RPC function procedure no.
    u_long    atime;               // alarm clock time
};

/* client's call-back RPC functions' version no. and procedure no. */
#define    CLNTVERNUM          1
#define    CLNTFUNCNUM         1

/* server's RPC function's program number, version no., and function no. */
#define    ACLKPROG            ((unsigned long)(0x20000100))
#define    ACLKVER             ((unsigned long)(1))
#define    ACLKFUNC            ((unsigned long)(1))
/* XDR functions for conversion of client's call-back data */
extern  bool_t xdr_name_t(XDR *, name_t*);
extern  bool_t xdr_arg_rec(XDR *, arg_rec*);

#endif /* !ACLOCK_H */
```

The RPC server program, *aclk_svc.C,* is:

```
#include <signal.h>
#include "aclock.h"
#include "RPC.h"

RPC_svc *svcp;                     // the RPC server handle
static struct arg_rec argRec;      // contains a client's call-back info

/* make an RPC call to a client's call-back function */
void call_client( int signum )
{
    u_long timv= alarm(0); /* alarm time remaining */
```

```
        RPC_cls cls( argRec.hostname, argRec.prognum,
                                      argRec.versnum, "netpath");
        if (!cls.good())   {
           cerr << "call_client: create RPC_cls object failed\n";
           exit(1);
        }

        if (cls.call( argRec.funcnum, (xdrproc_t)xdr_u_long, (caddr_t)&timv,
                      (xdrproc_t)xdr_void, 0 )!=RPC_SUCCESS)
           cerr << "call_client: call client failed\n";

        exit(0); /* kill the child process */
}

/* server's RPC function. Invoked by a client to setup an alarm service */
int set_alarm( SVCXPRT* xtrp )
{
    /* Get client's info: host name, RPC call-back function's program no,
       version no, and procedure number
    */
    if (svcp->getargs( xtrp, (xdrproc_t)xdr_arg_rec, (caddr_t)&argRec)
              !=RPC_SUCCESS)
       return -1;

    /* send a dummy reply to client */
    if (svcp->reply( xtrp, (xdrproc_t)xdr_void, 0)!=RPC_SUCCESS) {
       cerr << "printmsg: sendreply failed\n";
       return -2;
    }

    /* create a child process to handle this client */
    switch (fork()) {
        case -1:   perror("can't fork");
                   break;
        case 0:    /* child process */
                   alarm(argRec.atime);
                   signal(SIGALRM, call_client);
                   pause();              // wait for alarm to expire
    }

    /* parent process. Return to main loop to service other clients*/
    return RPC_SUCCESS;
}

int main(int argc, char* argv[])
{
```

```
/* create a server handle to wait for RPC calls to the set_alarm func*/
RPC_svc *svcp = new RPC_svc( ACLKPROG, ACLKVER, "netpath");

/* register the RPC function and wait for RPC calls */
if (svcp->run_func( ACLKFUNC, set_alarm )) ;

return 1; /* the server process shouldn't never get here */
}
```

The server program starts by creating an *RPC_svc* object to initiate the *set_alarm* RPC function. The program number, version number, and procedure number of this *set_alarm* RPC function are ACLKPROG, ACLKVER, and ACLKFUNC, respectively. The server calls the *RPC_svc::run* function to wait for client RPC requests to arrive.

When a client RPC request arrives, the *set_alarm* RPC function is called. The *set_alarm* function, in turn, calls the *RPC_svc::getargs* function to extract the RPC call-back information. This information is stored in the *argRec* variable. After the *RPC_svc::getargs* call succeeds, the server calls the *RPC_svc::reply* to send a dummy reply to the client. This finishes the RPC call, and the client can now go on to do something else.

After the *RPC_svc::reply* call, the server forks a child process to deal with the client, and the parent (the parent process) returns to the polling loop to wait for other client RPC requests.

The child process calls the *alarm* API to set up a SIGALRM signal to be sent to it after the client-specified alarm clock period elapses. It also calls the *signal* API to catch the SIGALRM signal when it is delivered to the child process. Finally, the child process calls the *pause* API to suspend its execution until the SIGALRM signal arrives.

When the SIGALRM signal is delivered to the child process, the *call_client* function is called. This function sets up an *RPC_cls* object to connect with the client RPC call-back function and sends the remaining alarm clock time (which should be zero) as argument to the client RPC function. After the RPC call completes, the function calls the *exit* function to terminate the child process.

The client program for this example is *aclk_cls.C*:

```
#include <netconfig.h>
#include "aclock.h"
#include "RPC.h"

#define CLNTPROGNUM 0x20000105
RPC_svc *svcp = 0;
```

```
/* client's RPC call-back function */
int callback( SVCXPRT* xtrp )
{
    u_long timv;
    /* get server's alarm remaining time */
    if (svcp->getargs( xtrp, (xdrproc_t)xdr_u_long, (caddr_t)&timv)
            !=RPC_SUCCESS)
    {
        cerr << "client: get alarm time fails\n";
        return -1;
    }
    cerr << "client: alarm time left is: " << timv << endl;

    /* send a dummy reply to server */
    if (svcp->reply(xtrp, (xdrproc_t)xdr_void, 0)!=RPC_SUCCESS) {
        cerr << "client: send reply failed\n";
        return -2;
    }
    /* do other work, then terminates the client process */
    exit(0);
}

/* register a call back with an RPC server */
int register_callback( char* local_host, char* svc_host, u_long alarm_time)
{
    /* tell remote server the process's host name, prog no, vers. no,
        func. no, and the alarm time
    */
    struct arg_rec argRec;
    argRec.hostname = local_host;
    argRec.prognum  = svcp->progno();
    argRec.versnum  = CLNTVERNUM;
    argRec.funcnum  = CLNTFUNCNUM;
    argRec.atime    = alarm_time;

    /* setup a client object to connect to the RPC server */
    RPC_cls clnt( svc_host, ACLKPROG, ACLKVER, "netpath");
    if (!clnt.good()) return 1;

    /* call the server's RPC function (set_alarm) */
    if (clnt.call( ACLKFUNC, (xdrproc_t)xdr_arg_rec, (caddr_t)&argRec,
            (xdrproc_t)xdr_void, (caddr_t)0 ) !=RPC_SUCCESS)
        return 2;
    cerr << "client: " << getpid() <<": RPC call done\n";
    return 0;
}
```

```
/* client main function */
int main (int argc, char* argv[])
{
    if (argc!=4)   {
        cerr << "usage: " << argv[0] << " <local-host> <svc-host> "
              << "<transport>\n";
        return 1;
    }

    /* create a server object to receieve call back from a remote server */
    if (!(svcp= new RPC_svc( CLNTPROGNUM, CLNTVERNUM, argv[3])))
        return 2;

    /* define the callback function */
    svcp->add_func( CLNTFUNCNUM, callback );

    /* register the callback with a remote server */
    if (register_callback( argv[1], argv[2], 10)) return 3;

    /* do other work here .... */

    svcp->run(); /* wait for alarm to expire */
    return 0;
}
```

The client process begins by creating an *RPC_svc* object to register its call-back RPC function, *callback*, with the *rpcbind* (via the *svc_create* API). The call-back function program, version, and procedure numbers are CLNTPROGNUM, CLNTVERNUM, and CLNT-FUNCNUM, respectively. After the *RPC_svc* object is created, the client calls the *register_callback* function to inform the alarm server of the alarm clock period and the call-back information. Upon return of the *register_callback* function, the client proceeds to do other work. It then calls the *RPC_svc::run* function at the end to wait for the server call-back to arrive.

The *register_callback* function creates an *RPC_cls* object to connect to the alarm server RPC function. It calls the server RPC function and passes a record of data containing: (1) the client's host machine name; (2) the call-back function program, version, and procedure numbers; and (3) the alarm clock period. This information is needed by the server to call the client RPC function when the alarm period expires.

The client's *callback* RPC function is called by the alarm server when the alarm period expires. The *callback* function calls the *RPC_svc::getargs* to extract the server argument (the remaining alarm clock time). It then sends a dummy reply to the server via the *RPC_svc::reply* function. Finally, the function calls *exit* to terminate the client process.

The XDR conversion functions of the above program are contained in the *ack_xdr.c*:

```
#include "aclock.h"
bool_t xdr_name_t(register XDR *xdrs, name_t *objp)
{
    register long *buf;
    return (!xdr_string(xdrs, objp, MAXNLEN)) ? FALSE : TRUE;
}

bool_t xdr_arg_rec(register XDR *xdrs, arg_rec *objp)
{
    register long *buf;
    if  (!xdr_name_t( xdrs, &objp->hostname ))      return (FALSE);
    if  (!xdr_u_long( xdrs, &objp->prognum ))       return (FALSE);
    if  (!xdr_u_long( xdrs, &objp->versnum ))       return (FALSE);
    if  (!xdr_u_long( xdrs, &objp->funcnum ))       return (FALSE);
    if  (!xdr_u_long( xdrs, &objp->atime ))         return (FALSE);
    return (TRUE);
}
```

The XDR functions translate the client's call-back information, as specified in a *struct arg_rec* record, which is sent to the alarm server in the *set_time* RPC call.

The above programs are compiled and run as shown below. It is assumed that the server is running on a machine called *saturn*, while the client process is running on a machine called *fruit*:

On machine *saturn*:

```
saturn %   CC -DSYSV4 -o aclk_svc aclk_svc.C RPC.C aclk_xdr.c \
               -lsocket -lnsl
saturn %   aclk_svc &
```

On machine *fruit*:

```
fruit %      CC -DSYSV4 -o aclk_cls aclk_cls.C RPC.C aclk_xdr.c \
                 -lsocket -lnsl
fruit %      aclk_cls fruit saturn netpath
client: 1567: RPC call done
client: alarm time left is: 0
```

12.10   Transient RPC Program Number

In the above example, the client RPC function has a predefined program number, version number, and procedure number. This restricts the client process in running more than one process at any one time on the network. One solution to this restriction is to create different versions of the client program, each with a different assigned RPC program number. However, this makes it hard to maintain the programs. A better solution is for each client process to generate a transient RPC program number at run time, so that multiple instances of the client processes may be active concurrently on a LAN (the server can differentiate them by their unique RPC program numbers). Note that the following discussion is based on the UNIX System V release 4 version of RPC. Not all UNIX systems support the transient port number generation method.

The RPC program numbers 0x40000000 -- 0x5fffffff are reserved for transient use. This allows any process to dynamically contact the *rpcbind* daemon to reserve one or more of these values as its RPC program number(s); as long as the number is not being used by other processes,. When the process terminates, the transient RPC program numbers that it claimed are made available again for use by other processes.

The *RPC_svc::gen_progNum* static function can be used to allocate a transient RPC program number. This function calls the *rpcb_set* API, for each number in the 0x40000000 and 0x5fffffff range, to query the *rpcbind* daemon whether a number is currently assigned to any process. The function stops at the first lowest available transient program number, and the *rpcb_set* registers that program number and the specified version number with the *rpcbind*.

The function prototype of the *rpcb_set* API is:

```
#include <rpc/rpc.h>

bool_t  rpcb_set (const u_long prognum, const u_long versnum,
                  const struct netconfig* netconf, const struct netbuf* addr);
```

The *prognum* and *versnum* arguments are the requested RPC program and version numbers to be assigned to the calling process. The *netconf* argument contains the transport information of the calling process. Finally, the *addr* argument is the network address of the calling process.

The function returns TRUE if it succeeds, and the requested program and version numbers are registered with *rpcbind* for the process with the specified address and transport. This function returns FALSE if it fails.

The *netconf* and *addr* arguments of the *RPC_svc::gen_progNum* are a bit tricky to get, particularly if a server handle is created via the *svc_create* API. However, if one uses the *svc_tli_create* API instead to create a server handle, the *netconf* and *addr* values of the server are readily available.

To accommodate the use of transient program numbers, the following overloaded *RPC_svc::RPC_svc* constructor function can be added to the *RPC_svc* class:

```
RPC_svc( int fd, char* transport, u_long progno, u_long versno )
{
    rc = 0;                                    /* assume failure status */

    struct netconfig *nconf = getnetconfigent(transport);
    if (!nconf) {
        cerr << "invalid transport: " << transport << endl;
        return;
    }

    /* create a server handle */
    SVCXPRT *xprt =svc_tli_create( fd, nconf, 0, 0, 0);
    if (!xprt) {
        cerr << "create server handle fails\n";
        return;
    }

    if (!progno)   {              /* generate a transient one */
        progno = gen_progNum( versno, nconf, &xprt->xp_ltaddr);
        nconf = 0;                 /* tell svc_reg don't talk to rpcbind */
    }

    if (svc_reg(xprt, progno, versno, dispatch, nconf)==FALSE)
        cerr << "register prognum failed\n";
    else  {
        prgnum = progno, vernum = versno;
        rc = 1;
    }
    freenetconfigent( nconf );
};
```

In the above overloaded constructor function, the *getnetconfigent* function, is called to return a pointer to a *struct netconf* data record that contains the network transport information for the given function argument. Once the transport handle contained in the *nconf* variable is obtained, the *svc_tli_create* API is called to create a server handle and a default address for the given transport. The *netconf* variable is freed via the *freenetconfigent* function.

The function prototype of the *svc_tli_create* API is:

```
#include <rpc/rpc.h>

SVCXPRT*  svc_tli_create (const int fd, const struct netconfig* netconf,
            const struct t_bind* baddr, const u_int sendsz, const u_int recvsz);
```

The *fd* argument is a file descriptor referencing a transport device file. If its value is specified as RPC_ANYFD, a transport device file determined by the *netconf* argument is used. The address assigned to the server is determined by the *baddr* argument if it is not NULL; otherwise, a default address chosen by a given transport is used. The *sendsz* and *recvsz* arguments specify the desired sending and receiving buffer size for the server handle. If their values are zero, the default buffer sizes determined by the transport will be used.

The *svc_tli_create* API returns NULL if it fails; otherwise, it returns a server handle.

If the *svc_tli_create* succeeds and a given *progno* argument value is 0, the *RPC_svc::gen_progNum* function is called to generate a transient program number. After that, the *svc_reg* API is called to associate an RPC program number and version number with their dispatch function.

The function prototype of the *svc_reg* API is:

```
#include <rpc/rpc.h>

int    svc_reg (const SVCXPRT* xprt, const u_long prognum,
                const u_long versnum, const void (*diaptch)(...),
                const struct netconfig* netconf);
```

The *xprt* argument is a server handle. The *prognum* and *versnum* arguments are the RPC program and version numbers associated with a dispatch function, as given in the *dispatch* argument. The *netconf* argument specifies a network transport that can be used to register the RPC function and dispatch function with the *rpcbind* daemon. If the *netconf* argument is NULL, no such registration is needed.

In the *RPC_svc* constructor function, the *svc_reg* is called with the *netconf* argument set to zero (if the *RPC_svc::gen_progNum* has been called). This is because the *RPC_svc::gen_progNum* function automatically registers the RPC function with the *rpcbind* daemon.

511

The *svc_reg* function returns FALSE if it fails; otherwise, it returns TRUE, and an RPC server is set up successfully.

The *aclk_cls.C* program can be rewritten to use the overloaded *RPC_svc::RPC_svc* constructor function, which creates a transient program number. The new *aclk_cls2.C* program is:

```
#include <netconfig.h>
#include "aclock.h"
#include "RPC.h"
#define CLNTPROGNUM 0x20000105
RPC_svc *svcp = 0;

/* client's RPC call-back function */
int callback( SVCXPRT* xtrp )
{
    u_long timv;
    /* get server's alarm remaining time */
    if (svcp->getargs( xtrp, (xdrproc_t)xdr_u_long, (caddr_t)&timv)
            !=RPC_SUCCESS) {
        cerr << "client: get alarm time fails\n";
        return -1;
    }
    cerr << "client: alarm time left is: " << timv << endl;

    /* send a dummy reply to server */
    if (svcp->reply(xtrp, (xdrproc_t)xdr_void, 0)!=RPC_SUCCESS) {
        cerr << "client: send reply failed\n";
        return -2;
    }
    /* do other work, then terminates the client process */
    exit(0);
}

/* register a call back with an RPC server */
int register_callback( char* local_host, char* svc_host, u_long alarm_time)
{
    /* tell remote server the process's hostname, prog no, vers. no, func. no,
       and the alarm time
    */
    struct arg_rec argRec;
    argRec.hostname = local_host;
    argRec.prognum  = svcp->progno();
    argRec.versnum  = CLNTVERNUM;
    argRec.funcnum  = CLNTFUNCNUM;
```

```
        argRec.atime    = alarm_time;

        /* setup a client object to connect to the RPC server */
        RPC_cls clnt( svc_host, ACLKPROG, ACLKVER, "netpath");
        if (!clnt.good()) return 1;

        /* call the server's RPC function (set_alarm) */
        if (clnt.call( ACLKFUNC, (xdrproc_t)xdr_arg_rec, (caddr_t)&argRec,
                (xdrproc_t)xdr_void, (caddr_t)0 ) !=RPC_SUCCESS)
            return 2;

        cerr << "client: " << getpid() <<": RPC call done\n";
        return 0;
    }

/* client main function */
int main (int argc, char* argv[])
{
    if (argc!=4) {
        cerr << "usage: " << argv[0] << " <local-host> <svc-host> "
                << "<transport>\n";
        return 1;
    }

    /* create a server object to receieve call back from a remote server */
    if (!(svcp= new RPC_svc( RPC_ANYFD, argv[3], 0, CLNTVERNUM )))
        return 2;

    /* define the callback function */
    svcp->add_func( CLNTFUNCNUM, callback );

    /* register the callback with a remote server */
    if (register_callback( argv[1], argv[2], 10)) return 3;

    /* do other work here .... */

    svcp->run(); /* wait for alarm to expire */
    return 0;
}
```

Notice that the only difference between the new *aclk_cls.C* and the one depicted in Section 12.9 is on one line: the creation of the *RPC_svc* handle via the *new* operator in the main function.

The program can be compiled and run as in Section 12.9. The output of the old and new client/server programs is the same.

12.11 RPC Services Using Inetd

RPC servers are commonly daemon processes that run continuously, waiting for RPC calls from their clients. This has the disadvantage that system resources allocated for these processes (e.g., the Process Table slots) cannot be used by other processes, even when the daemons are idle. To improve system resource utilization, port monitors such as *inetd* may be used to monitor network addresses for RPC services, while the RPC servers are not run at all. However, when an RPC request arrives, the port monitor spawns an RPC server to respond to that request, and the server terminates itself after the service is performed. Thus, system resources are allocated to an RPC server only for the duration when it is responding to a client request.

Most commercial UNIX systems use *inetd* as the port monitor. *inetd* is started at system boot, and it consults the */etc/inetd.conf* file for network addresses to monitor. Specifically, each entry of the */etc/inetd.conf* file has the following syntax:

<service> <transport> <protocol> <wait> <uid> <program> <arg>

The various fields in the entry state that if a request for <service> arrives, *inetd* should execute <program> and supply <arg> as its argument. The effective user ID of the executed process should be <uid>, and it uses <transport>/<protocol> to communicate with its client process. The commonly used <transport> and corresponding <protocol> values are:

Transport	Protocol
stream	tcp
dgram	udp

For socket-based services, the <wait> field should be specified as *nowait* for connection-based (tcp) transport and *wait* for connectionless (udp) transport. For TLI-based services, the <wait> field is commonly set as *wait*.

The port address for a <service> is defined in the */etc/services* file as:

<service>   <port>/<protocol>

For example, given the following entry in a */etc/inetd.conf* file:

login   stream   tcp   nowait   root   /etc/in.rlogind   in.rlogind when a remote user attempts to login to the local host, *inetd* should execute the */etc/in.rlogind* program as *root*. The *rlogin* process will use TCP/IP transport. The port address that the *rlogin* process uses is 513, as stated in the */etc/services* file:

```
login                513/tcp
```

To instruct *inetd* to monitor a particular RPC request, the */etc/inetd.conf* file should contain an entry for the RPC server as:

```
<prog_num>/<vers_num>    <transport>  <protocol>   <wait> \
           <uid>            <program>       <arg>
```

Here, <prog_num> and <vers_num> are the RPC server's program and version numbers. The other fields can be the same as before for ONC-based RPC. However, in UNIX System V.4, the <transport> may be *tli* if the RPC server handle is created based on TLI, and the <protocol> values may be *rpc/tcp, rpc/udp*, or *rpc/**. The protocol value of *rpc/** means that the server may use any TLI-supported transport.

For example, the directory listing program as shown in Section 12.7.4 uses 0x200100 and 1 as the RPC program and version numbers. To make *inetd* support the service, the following entry should be added to the */etc/inetd.conf* file (here the executable file of the RPC server is assumed to be */proj/scan_svc3*):

For ONC:

```
# 536871168 is same as 0x20000100
536871168/1    stream    tcp   wait     root  /proj/scan_svc3    scan_svc3
```

For System V.4:

```
536871168/1    tli    rpc/*   wait    root    /proj/scan_svc3    scan_svc3
```

In addition to configuring *inetd*, the RPC server should create its *RPC_svc* (the *RPC_svc* class is described in Section 12.5) handle using the constructor:

```
RPC_svc::RPC_svc( int fd, char* transport, unsigned long progno,
                  unsigned long versnum);
```

Furthermore, the *fd* argument value for the *RPC_svc* constructor should be zero, as this is assigned by *inetd* to correspond to the incoming RPC request. In the above example, the directory listing server should create its *RPC_svc* handle as:

RPC_svc *svcp = new RPC_svc(0, "tcp", 0x20000100, 1);

When the *RPC_svc::RPC_svc* constructor is called, it creates the *RPC_svc* handle using the following RPC APIs:

For ONC:

- Call *svctcp_create* (for stream transport) or *svcudp_create* (for datagram transport) to create a server handle
- Call *svc_reg* to register a dispatch function to be invoked when an RPC call arrives

For System V.4:

- Call *getnetconfigent* to obtain a *struct netconfig* object for the transport (*tcp* or *udp*) desired
- Call *svc_tli_create* to create a server handle
- Call *svc_reg* to register a dispatch function to be invoked when an RPC call arrives

Readers who are interested in the detail calling sequence of the above APIs should consult the *RPC_svc* constructor code as shown in Section 12.5.

The above works are all the necessary changes for using *inetd* to monitoring RPC service requests. The rest of the server code is the same as if it were not using *inetd*. Furthermore, there are no change at all in the XDR functions and the client programs that make RPC calls.

As the final example, the remote directory listing program shown in Section 12.7.4 is rewritten below so that the server uses *inetd* to monitor RPC requests on its behalf. The client program (*scan_cls2.C*) and the XDR functions (*scan_xdr.c*) are the same as in Section 12.7.4 and, thus, are not depicted again. The modified server program is *scan_svc3*.C and is shown below:

```
#include <stdio.h>
#include <stdlib.h>
#include <dirent.h>
#include <string.h>
#include <malloc.h>
#include <errno.h>
#include <sys/stat.h>
#include <sys/resource.h>
#include "scan2.h"
```

```
#include "RPC.h"
static    RPC_svc *svcp = 0;
static    int    work_in_progrss = 0;
static    int    ttl = 60;                    /* time-to-live: 60 seconds */
/* The RPC function */
int scandir( SVCXPRT* xtrp )
{
    DIR             *dirp;
    struct dirent   *d;
    infolist        nl, *nlp;
    struct stat     statv;
    res             res;
    argPtr          darg = 0;
    work_in_progress = 1;                     /* process not killed by alarm */

    /* Get function argument from a client */
    if (svcp->getargs( xtrp, (xdrproc_t)xdr_argPtr,
                  (caddr_t)&darg)!=RPC_SUCCESS)
        return -1;

    /* start scaning the requested directory */
    if (!(dirp = opendir(darg->dir_name)))      {
        res.errno = errno;
        (void)svcp->reply(xtrp, (xdrproc_t)xdr_res, (caddr_t)&res);
        return -2;
    }

    /* free memoryallocated from a previous RPC call */
    xdr_free((xdrproc_t)xdr_res, (char*)&res);

    /* store files' informaton to res as the return values */
    nlp = &res.res_u.list;
    while (d=readdir(dirp))   {
        nl = *nlp = (infolist)malloc(sizeof(struct dirinfo));
        nl->name = strdup(d->d_name);
        nlp = &nl->next;
        if (darg->lflag)   {
            char pathnm[256];
            sprintf(pathnm,"%s/%s",darg->dir_name,d->d_name);
            if (!stat(pathnm,&statv))     {
                nl->uid = statv.st_uid;
                nl->modtime = statv.st_mtime;
            }
        }
    }
    *nlp = 0;
```

```
        res.errno = 0;
        closedir(dirp);

        /* Send directory listing to client */
        int    rc = svcp->reply(xtrp, (xdrproc_t)xdr_res,(caddr_t)&res);
        work_in_progess = 0;              /* process can be killed by alarm */
        return rc;
    }

/* signal handling routine */
static void done ( int signo )
{
        if (!work_in_progress) exit(0);
        signal( SIGALRM, (void(*)(int)) exit );
        alarm( ttl );
}

int main(int argc, char* argv[])
{
        struct rlimit rls;
        switch (fork()) {
            case  0:    break;
            case -1:    perror( "fork");
            default:    return errno;
        }

        /* close all I/O streams, except descriptor 0 */
        rls.rlim_max = 0;
        getrlimit(RLIMIT_NOFILE, &rls);
        if (rls.rlim_max == 0)  {
                fprintf( fp, "getrlimit failed\n");
                return 1;
        }

        for (int i = 1; i < rls.rlim_max; i++)    (void) close(i);

        /* all output messages redirected to the system console */
        int fd = open("/dev/console", 2);
        (void) dup2(fd, 1);
        (void) dup2(fd, 2);
        setsid();

        /* Now create the RPC server handle */
        svcp = new RPC_svc( 0, "tcp", SCANPROG, SCANVER );
        if (!svcp || !svcp->good()) {
                fprintf( stderr, "create RPC_svc object failed\n" );
```

```
        exit( 1 );
    }

    svcp->add_proc( SCANDIR, scandir );

    /* terminate daemon after alive for 60 seconds */
    signal( SIGALRM, done );
    alarm( ttl );

    svcp->run();

    return 0;
}
```

In the above program, the server creates an *RPC_svc* handle for the file descriptor zero and the transport used is *tcp*. It registers the *scandir* function to be callable by clients, then sets up the SIGALRM signal to be sent to itself. The latter is done because *inetd* does not spawn a new process for a service request if there is already a server process running (this is done to avoid creating too many redundant processes). Thus, it is common practice for a server spawned by *inetd* to remain blocked for a set period of time after it has serviced a request, so that it may catch the next service call that comes shortly.

After registering the *done* function as the signal handler for SIGALRM, the server program calls *RPC_svc::run*. This causes the *scandir* function to be called immediate, as there is already a pending request. When the *scandir* function returns, the server is blocked in the *RPC_svc::run* function waiting for the next RPC call. The server lives, at most, 60 seconds, unless a new RPC call arrives before the time is up. If that happens the *done* function will reset the alarm clock so that the process can run for another 60 seconds. The *work_in_progress* global variable is set whenever the *scandir* function is called, and it is reset when the *scandir* function returns. This variable is used by the *done* function to decide whether to terminate the process or to restart the alarm clock.

The client and server programs are compiled on a UNIX System V.4 system, as follows (on ONC systems, compile them without the -DSYSV4 option):

```
    %   CC -c scan2_xdr.c RPC.C
    %   CC -DSYSV4 -o scan_svc3 scan_svc3.C scan2_xdr.o \
                RPC.o -lsocket -lnsl
    %   CC -DSYSV4 -o scan_cls2 scan_cls2.C scan2_xdr.o RPC.o \
                -lsocket -lnsl
```

The */etc/inetd.conf* file entry for the *scan_svc3* server is (using System V.4 format):

```
536871168/1tli    rpc/* wait    root    /proj/scan_svc3 scan_svc3
```

Finally, the sample run of the client and server programs is shown below. The server program is resided on a machine called *fruit*, while the client program may be run on any machine that is connected to *fruit*. Only the client program needs to be started manually, while the server program is executed by *inetd*:

```
%    scan_cls2 fruit .
....
.....
...scan_cls2.C
...scan_svc2.C
...RPC.C
...RPC.h
...scan2_xdr.c
...scan2.h
...scan_svc2
...scan_cls2
Prog 536871168 (version 1) is alive
```

12.12   Summary

This chapter describes three methods of creating RPC programs: (1) using the system-supplied RPC library functions; (2) using the *rpcgen* compiler to create custom RPC function and client main programs; and (3) using the RPC classes to create full custom client and server RPC programs.

Of the three approaches, the last one, which uses RPC classes, is most flexible, in that users have complete control over the content of the client and server programs, and they can also control the transport properties used by their applications. Furthermore, the RPC classes encapsulate most of the low-level RPC API interface. Thus, programming effort is not much more time-consuming than when using the *rpcgen* compiler.

Finally, numerous examples are depicted in the chapter to illustrate various RPC programming techniques. These include RPC broadcast, asynchronous call-backs (from clients to servers), authentication, transient RPC program number generation, and using *inetd* to monitor RPC requests. Users may use these example programs as starting points and may modify them to create their own RPC-based applications.

Multithreaded Programming

A thread is a piece of program code executed in a serial fashion. Most UNIX applications are single-threaded programs, as each of them executes only one piece of program code at any one time. For example, a single-threaded process may get a command from a user, execute the command, display the results to the user, then wait for a next command. While the process is executing a command, the user must wait for it to finish before entering subsequent commands.

A multithreaded program, on the other hand, can have several pieces of its code executed "concurrently" at any one time. Each piece of the code is executed by one thread of control. Thus, in the previous example, if the process were multithreaded, the user could enter commands immediately, one after the other, and the process executed all commands concurrently.

Multithreaded programming can be used to develop concurrent applications. These applications can be run on any multiprocessor systems and make good use of hardware resources. Specifically, if a multithreaded application runs on a system with M processors, each of its threads may be run on a separate processor simultaneously. Thus, the performance of the application may be improved by N times, where N is the maximum number of processors available at any one time, and N is less than or equal to M.

If a multithreaded application is run on a uniprocessor system, its performance may still be improved. For example, if one of its threads is blocked in a system call (e.g., waiting for data to be transferred to a tape device), another thread can be run on the processor right away. Thus, the overall execution time of the application is reduced.

In addition to the above benefits, multithreaded programming is also a good compliment to object-oriented programming. This is because each object-oriented application consists of a collection of objects interacting with each other to perform tasks. Each of these objects is an independent entity and can be executed by a thread and run in parallel with other objects. This results in significantly improvement in performance for these applications. For example, in a multithreaded, object-oriented, window system, each menu, button, text field, and scrolled window may be executed by a thread. Thus, any of these window objects may be activated, one right after the other, without waiting for other objects to finish their execution.This makes the entire GUI application more responsive ("interactive") to users than its single-threaded counterpart.

Threads differ from child processes created by the *fork* API in the following ways:

- Threads may be managed by either user-level library functions or the operating system kernel. Child processes as created by the *fork* system call are managed by the operating system kernel. In general, threads is more efficient, and require much less kernel attention, to create and manage than do child processes
- All threads in a process share the same data and code segments. A child process has its own copy of virtual address space that is separate from its parent process. Thus, threads use much less system resources than do child processes
- If a thread calls the *exit* or *exec* function, it terminates all the threads in the same process. If a child process calls the *exit* or *exec* function, its parent process is not affected
- If a thread modifies a global variable in a process, the changes are visible to other threads in the same process. Thus, some synchronization methods are needed for threads accessing shared data. This problem does not exist between child and parent processes

All in all, the benefits of using multithreaded programming are:

- It improves process throughput and responsiveness to users
- It allows a process to make use of any available multiprocessor hardware on any system it is run on
- It allows programmers to structure their code into independently executable units and maximize concurrency
- Threads reduce the need to use *fork* to create child processes, thus improving each process performance (less context switching). Also, less kernel involvement is needed in managing their execution
- It is the natural choice for multiprocessing, object-oriented, applications to enhance their performance

The drawback of multithreaded programming is users must be careful in designing thread synchronization in each program. This is to ensure that threads do not accidentally mis-read/write shared data or destroy their process via the *exit* or *exec* system call.

Multithreaded programming has been in development since the mid-1980s. Different versions of multithreaded programming interfaces were offered by different UNIX vendors. The POSIX committee has developed a set of multithreaded APIs, which is now part of the POSIX.1c standard. This chapter describes both the Sun Microsystems Solaris 2.x and POSIX1.c multithreaded APIs, with emphasis on the Sun APIs. The Sun multithreaded APIs are described because the POSIX.1c standard is new and not many UNIX vendors are supporting it yet. On the other hand, the Sun multithreaded APIs have been available for application programmers for quite some time. Furthermore, the Sun multithreaded APIs closely resemblance those of the POSIX.1c APIs, and there is almost a one-to-one correspondence of the Sun multithreaded APIs to the POSIX.1c APIs. Thus applications which are based on the Sun multithreaded APIs can be easily converted to the POSIX.1c standard.

13.1   Thread Structure and Uses

A thread consists of the following data structures:

- A thread ID
- A run-time stack
- A set of registers (e.g., program counter and stack pointer)
- A signal mask
- A schedule priority
- A thread-specific storage

A thread is created by the *thr_create* function (or the *pthread_create* in POSIX.1c). Each thread is assigned a thread ID that is unique among all threads in a process. A newly created thread inherits the process signal mask and is assigned a run-time stack, a schedule priority, and a set of registers. The run-time stack and registers (program counter and stack pointer) enable the thread to run independently of other threads. The schedule priority is used to schedule the execution of threads. A thread may change its inherited signal mask and allocate dynamic storage to store its own private data.

When a thread is created, it is assigned a function to execute. The thread terminates when that assigned function returns or when the thread calls the *thr_exit* (*pthread_exit* in POSIX.1c) function. When the first thread is created in a process, two threads are actually created: One to execute a specified function and the other to carry on the execution of the process. The latter thread terminates when the *main* function returns or when it calls the *thr_exit* function.

All threads in a process share the same data and code segments. If a thread writes data to global variables in the process, those changes are seen by other threads immediately. Furthermore, if a thread calls the *exit* or *exec* API, the containing process and all its threads are terminated. Thus, a terminating thread that does not want to destroy its containing process should call the *thr_exit* function instead.

A thread can change its signal mask via the *thr_sigsetmask* (*pthread_sigmask* in POSIX.1c) function. If a signal is delivered to a process, then any thread which has not masked the signal will receive it. A thread can send signals to other threads in the same process via the *thr_kill* (*pthread_kill* in POSIX.1c) function, but it cannot send signals to specific threads in a different process, as thread IDs are not unique among different processes. A thread may use the *signal* or *sigaction* API to set up per-thread signal handling.

A thread is assigned an integer thread schedule priority number. The larger the priority number the more frequently a thread is scheduled to run. A thread schedule priority number can be inquired and changed by the *thr_getprio* and *thr_setprio* (*pthread_attr_getschedparam* and *pthread_attr_setschedparam* in POSIX.1c) functions, respectively. In addition to these, a thread can deliberately yield its execution to other threads of the same priority via the *thr_yield* (*sched_yield* in POSIX.1c) function. Moreover, a thread can wait for the termination of another thread and get its exit status code with the *thr_join* (*pthread_join* in POSIX.1c) function.

Note that in Sun a thread can suspend and resume execution of another thread via the *thr_suspend* and *thr_continue* functions. Furthermore, if a function is executed by multiple threads and uses static or global variables to which data is assigned and used on a per-thread basis, it needs to create thread-specific storage to store these actual data for each thread. A thread-specific storage is allocated via the *thr_keycreate, thr_setspecific and thr_getspecific* functions.

13.2   Threads and Lightweight Processes

The Sun thread library functions create objects called lightweight processes (LWPs), which are scheduled by the kernel for execution. LWPs are like virtual processors in that the thread library functions schedule threads in a process to be bound to LWPs and be executed. If a thread bound to an LWP gets suspended (e.g., via the *thr_yield* or *thr_suspend* function), the LWP is assigned to bind to another thread and executes that thread's function. If an LWP makes a system call on behalf of a thread, it remains bound to that thread until the system call returns. If all LWPs are bound to threads and are blocked at system calls, the thread library functions create new LWPs to bind unbound threads that are waiting for execution. This ensures that a process is constantly executing. Finally, if there are more LWPs than threads existing in a process, the thread library functions remove idle LWPs to conserve system resources.

Most threads are unbound and can be scheduled to bind to any available LWP. However, a process may create one or more threads that are permanently bound to LWPs. These are called *bound threads*. They are used primarily if they need:

- To be scheduled by the kernel for real-time processing
- To have their own alternate signal stacks
- To have their own alarms and timer

The relationships of threads, LWPs, and hardware processors are depicted in Figure 13.1.

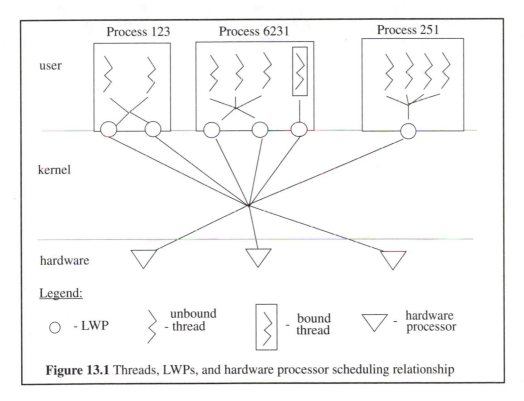

Figure 13.1 Threads, LWPs, and hardware processor scheduling relationship

In Figure 13-1, the process 123 has two unbound threads that are scheduled on two LWPs. The process 6231 has three unbound threads that are scheduled on two LWPs and one bound thread that is executed by another LWP. The process 251 has four unbound threads that are scheduled on one LWP. The unbound threads on each process are scheduled by the thread library functions to be bound and run on LWPs in that process. The LWPs of all processes are, in turn, scheduled by the kernel to run on the three existing hardware processors.

In POSIX.1c, threads have an attribute known as *scheduling contention scope*. If a thread contention scope attribute is set to PTHREAD_SCOPE_PROCESS, the thread is managed by user-level library functions and is an "unbound" thread. All threads with this same attribute share processor resources that are available to their containing process. On the other hand, if a thread contention scope attribute is set to PTHREAD_SCOPE_SYSTEM, then the thread is managed by the operating system kernel and is considered "bound". POSIX.1c does not specify how a "bound" thread should be handled by the kernel.

13.3   Sun Thread APIs

This section describes only the Sun thread APIs. The POSIX.1c thread APIs are described in the Section 13.4. This is done so as to avoid confusing readers of the two different sets of APIs. The various sub-sections in Section 13.4 list the corresponding APIs between Sun to the POSIX.1c standard. These can be used for converting multithreaded applications from Sun to the POSIX.1c standard.

To use the Sun thread APIs, users should do the following:

- Include the <thread.h> header in their programs
- Compile and link their programs with the *-lthread* option. If the *-lC* option is specified also, then the *-lthread* option should be specified before the *-lC* switch. For example, the following compiles a multithreaded C++ program call *x.C*:

        %   CC x.C -o x -lthread -lC

Unless otherwise stated, most of the thread APIs depicted below return a 0 value if they succeed or a -1 value if they fail. In case they fail, *perror* may be called to print error diagnostic messages.

13.3.1   thr_create

The *thr_create* function prototype is:

```
#include <thread.h>
int         thr_create (void* stackp, size_t stack_size, void* (*funcp)(void*),
                        void* argp, long flags, thread_t* tid_p);
```

The function creates a new thread to execute a function whose address is given in the *funcp* argument. The function specified in *funcp* should accept one *void**-typed input argument and return a *void** data. The actual argument to be passed to the *funcp* function, when the new thread starts executing, is specified in the *argp* argument.

The *stackp* and *stack_size* arguments contain the address of a user-defined memory region and its size in number of bytes, respectively. This memory is used as the new thread run-time stack. If the *stackp* value is NULL, the function allocates a stack region of *stack_size* bytes. If the *stack_size* value is 0, the function uses a system default value that is one megabyte of virtual memory. Users rarely need to supply their own memory region for a thread stack. Thus, the normal values to *stackp* and *stack_size* arguments are NULL and zero, respectively.

In addition to the above, the *flags* argument value may be zero, meaning that no special attributes are assigned to the new thread. On the other hand, the *flags* value may consist of one or more of the following bit-flags:

flags value	Meaning
THR_DETACHED	Creates a detached thread. This means that when the thread terminates, all its resources and assigned thread ID can be reused for another thread. No thread should wait for it (via the *thr_join* function)
THR_SUSPENDED	Suspends the execution of the new thread until another thread calls the *thr_continue* function to enable it to execute
THR_BOUND	Creates a permanently bound thread
THR_NEW_LWP	Creates a new LWP along with the new thread
THR_DAEMON	Makes the new thread a daemon thread. Normally a multithreaded process terminates when all its threads are terminated. However, if the process contains one or more daemon threads, the process terminates immediately when all nondaemon threads are terminated.

The new thread ID is returned via the *tid_p* argument. If the actual value of the *tid_p* argument is assigned NULL, no thread ID is returned. The thread ID data type is *thread_t*.

The *thr_create* function may fail if there is not enough system memory to create a new thread, the *stackp* argument contains an invalid address, or the *stack_size* argument value is nonzero and less than the system-imposed minimum limit. The system-imposed minimum stack size limit for a thread is obtained from the *thr_min_stack* function:

```
size_t      thr_min_stack ( void );
```

A thread can find out its thread ID via the *thr_self* function:

```
thread_t    thr_self    ( void );
```

The following sample code creates a new detached and bound thread to execute a function called *do_it*. The argument passed to *do_it* d is the address of the *pInt* variable. The new thread's ID is assigned to the *tid* variable, and its stack is allocated by the function with the system default size:

```
extern void* do_it (void* ptr);
int         *pInt;
thread_t    tid;
if (thr_create( 0, 0, do_it, (void*)&pInt,
                        THR_DETACHEDITHR_BOUND, &tid) < 0)
        perror("thr_create");
```

13.3.2   thr_suspend, thr_continue

The function prototypes of the *thr_suspend* and *thr_continue* functions are:

```
#include <thread.h>

int         thr_suspend ( thread_t tid );
int         thr_continue ( thread_t tid );
```

The *thr_suspend* function suspends the execution of a thread whose ID is designated by the *tid* argument value.

The *thr_continue* function resumes the execution of a thread whose ID is designated by the *tid* argument value.

These functions may fail if the *tid* value is invalid.

13.3.3   thr_exit, thr_join

The function prototypes of the *thr_exit* and *thr_join* functions are:

```
#include <thread.h>

int        thr_exit ( void* statusp);
int        thr_join ( thread_t tid, thread_t* dead_tidp, void** statusp);
```

The *thr_exit* function terminates a thread. The actual argument value to the *statusp* argument is the address of a static variable that contains the exit status code of the terminating thread. If no other thread is expected to retrieve the terminating thread exit status code (e.g., the thread is detached), the *statusp* argument value may be specified as NULL.

The *thr_join* function is called to wait for the termination of a nondetached thread. If the *tid* argument value is zero, the function waits for any thread to terminate. The *dead_tidp* and *statusp* argument values are addresses of variables that hold the terminated thread's ID and exit status value, respectively. The actual values to these arguments may be NULL, which means those data are unwanted.

The following example waits for all nondetached threads in a process to terminate, then terminates the current thread:

```
status int   *rc, rval=0;
thread_t   tid;
while (!thr_join(0, &tid, &rc))
    cout << "thread: " << (int)tid << ", exits, rc=" << (*rc) << endl;
thr_exit( (void*)&rval );
```

13.3.4   thr_sigsetmask, thr_kill

Each thread has its own signal mask which is inherited from its creating thread. A thread may modify its signal mask via the *thr_sigsetmask* API. When a signal is delivered to a multithreaded process, a thread in that process which has the signal unblocked will receive the signal. If there are multiple threads in the process with the signal unblocked, the system will arbitrarily pick any one of them as the target for the signal. Thus to simplify the implementation of multithreaded programs, it is recommended that a process elects a dedicated thread to handle one or more signals for the entire process, while other threads in the same process block those signals.

In addition to the above, a thread may also send a signal to another thread in the same process via the *thr_kill* API. The *thr_sigsetmask* and *thr_kill* function prototypes are:

```
#include <thread.h>
#include <signal.h>

int        thr_sigsetmask ( int mode, sigset_t *sigsetp, sigset_t *oldsetp);
int        thr_kill ( thread_t tid, int signum);
```

The *thr_sigsetmask* function sets the signal mask of a calling thread. The *sigsetp* argument contains one or more of the signal numbers applied to the calling thread. The *mode* argument specifies how the signal(s) specified in the *sigsetp* argument is to be used. The possible values of the *mode* argument are declared in the <signal.h> header. These values and their meanings are:

mode value	Meaning
SIG_BLOCK	Adds signals contained in the *sigsetp* argument to the thread signal mask
SIG_UNBLOCK	Removes signals contained in the *sigsetp* argument from the thread signal mask
SIG_SETMASK	Replaces the thread signal mask with the signal(s) specified in the *sigsetp* argument

If the *sigsetp* argument value is NULL, the *mode* argument value is ignored.

The *oldsetp* argument value should be the address of a *sigset_t*-typed variable returning the old signal mask. If the *oldsetp* argument value is NULL, the old signal mask is ignored.

The *thr_kill* function sends the signal as given in the *signum* argument to a thread whose ID is given by the *tid* argument. The sending and receiving threads must be in the same process.

The following example adds the SIGINT signal to a thread signal mask, then sends the SIGTERM signal to a thread whose ID is 15:

```
sigset_t    set, oldset;
sigemptyset( &set );
sigaddset( &set, SIGINT );
if (thr_setsigmask( SIG_BLOCK, &set, &oldset)) perror("thr_sigsetmask");
if (thr_kill((thread_t)15, SIGTERM)) perror("thr_kill");
```

13.3.5   thr_setprio, thr_getprio, thr_yield

The prototypes of the *thr_setprio, thr_getprio and thr_yield* functions are:

```
#include <thread.h>

int        thr_setprio ( thread_t tid, int prio);
int        thr_getprio ( thread_t tid, int* priop);
void       thr_yield ( void );
```

The *thr_setprio* function sets the scheduling priority of a thread, as designated by the *tid* argument, to the *prio* value. Threads with higher priority values are scheduled more often than are those with lower values.

The *thr_getprio* function returns a thread's current priority value via the *priop* argument. The thread is designated by the *tid* argument.

The *thr_yield* function is called by a thread to yield its execution to other threads with the same priority. This function always succeeds and does not return any value.

Thread scheduling is done via thread library functions, not by the kernel. Threads are scheduled to bind to LWPs, which, in turn, are scheduled by the kernel to be executed on a hardware processor.

13.3.6   thr_setconcurrency, thr_getconcurrency

The function prototypes of the *thr_setconcurrency* and *thr_getconcurrency* functions are:

```
#include <thread.h>

int        thr_setconcurrency ( int amount );
int        thr_getconcurrency ( void );
```

The *thr_setconcurrency* function specifies the minimum number of LWPs that should be kept in a process. This ensures that a minimum number of threads are executing concurrently at any time. Note that the system takes the *amount* argument value as a hint, but it honors this concurrency request based on the availability of system resources.

The *thr_getconcurency* function returns the current concurrency level of a process.

13.3.7   Multithreaded Program Example

The following program is a rewrite of the RPC-based client and server programs shown in Section 12.5 of Chapter 12. The client program gets a message string from a user, issues an RPC call to the server *printmsg* function, which prints the message on the server system console.

The changes made in this version are in the client program (*msg_cls.C*) only: The client repeatedly prompts a user for a server host name and a message. For each host name and message data received from the user, the client process calls a function to allocate a dynamic memory region to hold the data. It then creates a thread to make an RPC call to a server running on the specified host, and requests that the user message be printed on the server system console.

The new *msg_cls2.C* client program is:

```
#include <thread.h>
#include <signal.h>
#include "msg2.h"
#include "RPC.h"

/* Record to hold one host name and message data for one thread */
typedef struct
{
    char      *host;
    char      *msg;
} MSGREC;

#define    MAX_THREAD       200
thread_t thread_list[ MAX_THREAD ];               // stores all threads' IDs

/* Function executed by a thread to send a message */
void* send_msg( void* ptr )
{
    int              res;
    MSGREC           *pRec = (MSGREC*)ptr;

    /* Set thread's signal mask to everything except SIGHUP */
    sigset_t   setv;
    sigfillset(&setv);
    sigdelset(&setv, SIGHUP);
    if (thr_sigsetmask(SIG_SETMASK,&setv,0)) perror("thr_setsigmask");

    /* Create a client handle to communicate with a host */
    RPC_cls cl( pRec->host, MSGPROG, MSGVER, "netpath");
```

```
      if (!cl.good()) thr_exit( &res );

      /* Call the remote host to print the message to its system console */
      (void)cl.call( PRINTMSG, (xdrproc_t)xdr_string, (caddr_t)&(pRec->msg),
                          (xdrproc_t)xdr_int, (caddr_t)&res);

      /* Delete dynamic memory */
      delete pRec->msg;
      delete pRec->host;
      delete pRec;

      /* Check RPC function execution status */
      if (res!=0) cerr << "clnt: call printmsg fails\n";
      int *rcp = new int(res);
      thr_exit( rcp );
      return 0;
}


/* Function to create a thread for a user message */
int add_thread( int& num_thread )
{
   char host[60], msg[256];
   thread_t tid;
   int res;

   /* Get remote host name and message from a user */
   cin >> host >> msg;
   if (cin.eof()) return RPC_FAILED;   /* normal return */
   if (!cin.good())   {                /* I/O error detected */
      perror("cin");
      return RPC_FAILED;
   }

   /* Create dynamic memory for message text and host name */
   MSGREC *pRec = new MSGREC;
   pRec->host = new char[strlen(host)+1];
   pRec->msg = new char[strlen(msg)+1];
   strcpy(pRec->host,host);
   strcpy(pRec->msg,msg);

   /* Create a suspended thread to process the message */
   if (thr_create( 0, 0, send_msg, pRec, THR_SUSPENDED, &tid )) {
      perror("thr_create");
      return RPC_FAILED;
   }
```

```
        else if (num_thread>= MAX_THREAD)      {
            cerr << "Too many threads created!\n";
            return RPC_FAILED;
        }
        else {                      /* Create a thread successfully */
            thread_list[num_thread++] = tid;
            cout << "Thread: " << (int)tid << " created for msg: '"
                 << msg << " [" << host << "]'\n";
        }
        return RPC_SUCCESS;
}

/* Client main function */
int main(int argc, char* argv[])
{
    int                 num_thread=0;
    thread_t            tid;
    int                 *res;

    /* Set concurrency level */
    if (thr_setconcurrency(5)) perror("thr_setoncurrency");
    cout      << "No. LPWs: " << thr_getconcurrency() << endl;

    /* Create a thread to send each mesg input by a user */
    while (add_thread(num_thread)==RPC_SUCCESS) ;

    /* Set each thread's priority and launch it */
    for (int i=0; i < num_thread; i++)
    {
        thr_setprio(thread_list[i],i);
        thr_continue(thread_list[i]);
    }

    /* Wait for every thread to terminate */
    while (!thr_join(0,&tid,(void**)&res))
    {
        cerr << "thread: " << (int)tid << ", exited. rc=" << (*res) << endl;
        delete res;
    }

    /* Terminate the main tread */
    thr_exit(0);
    return 0;
}
```

In the above program, the client process starts up by calling the *thr_setconcurrency* function to set the number of available LWPs to five. This specifies that at least five threads can run concurrently at any one time. The process finds out the number of actual LWPs created via the *thr_getconcurrency* function and prints that information to the standard output.

The process next calls the *add_thread* function repeatedly until it returns a zero return value. Each time the *add_thread* function is called, it gets a host name and a message from a user via the standard input. If end-of-file or an input error occurs, the function returns a zero value to *main* to indicate the end of user input. If the input data is retrieved successfully, the *add_thread* function allocates a dynamic memory to store the user-specified host name and message into a MSGREC-typed record. The function then calls the *thr_create* function to create a thread to execute the *send_msg* function. The *send_msg* function input argument is the address of a MSGREC-typed variable just allocated. The thread is created with a system-allocated stack, and it is suspended immediately after being created. The newly created thread's ID is stored in a global array *thread_list,* and the *add_thread* function returns a 1 value to *main* to indicate a successful execution status. If, however, the thread is not created successfully or MAX_THREAD threads have already been created, the function returns a zero value to *main* to signal the error.

After the *add_thread* function has created all the threads needed to handle all user input data, the *main* function (the main thread) scans the *thread_list* array and sets the schedule priority of each thread. The thread ID is stored in the array with a value related to the thread's position (index) in the array. Thus, the first thread in the array has the lowest priority, the next one has the second-lowest priority, and so on. The *main* function launches each suspended thread to run via the *thr_continue* function. After all this, the *main* function waits for each thread to terminate and prints the thread ID and exit status code to the standard output.

Each thread launched executes the *send_msg* function. The thread first sets its signal mask to include everything except the SIGHUP signal. It then creates an RPC client handle to be connected to the *printmsg* server whose host name is given in the *send_msg* function input argument. If the RPC client handle is created successfully, the thread calls the *RPC_cls::call* function to send the user message to the *printmsg* server. This prints the message to the server's system console. Finally, the thread deletes the dynamic memory that stores the host name and message, then creates a dynamic memory to store the return status value, and returns this dynamic data to the *main* function via the *thr_exit* call. The reason that the exit code is stored in a dynamic memory is because the *send_msg* function is executed by multiple threads, and each thread must return its own status code. Thus, the return value cannot be stored in an automatic or a static variable, but must be put in a dynamic variable that is unique for each thread.

The *printmsg* server program (*msg_svc2.C)* and the *RPC_cls* class definition as specified in the *RPC.h* header are shown in Section 12.5 of Chapter 12. The new *msg_cls2.C* client program is compiled as follows:

%   CC -DSYSV4 msg_cls2.C -o msg_cls2 -lthread -lnsl

The *-lthread* and *-lnsl* options tell the link editor to link the *msg_cls2.o* object file with the thread (*libthread.so*) and network (*libnsl.so*) libraries, respectively. The *libthread.so* library contains all the thread API object codes, and the *libnsl.so* library contains the RPC-related codes.

The sample run and output of the client program is shown below. The words in italic are input data entered by a user from the standard input.

```
%    msg_cls2
No. LPWs: 5
fruit    happy_day
Thread: 4 created for msg: 'happy_day [fruit]'
fruit    easter_sunday
Thread: 5 created for msg: 'easter_sunday [fruit]'
fruit    Good_bye
Thread: 6 created for msg: 'Good_bye [fruit]'
thread: 5, exited. rc=139424
thread: 6, exited. rc=139424
thread: 4, exited. rc=139424
%
```

The system console of the machine *fruit* shows the following for the above run:

```
server: 'easter_sunday'
server: 'Good_bye'
server: 'happy_day'
```

13.4   POSIX.1c Thread APIs

This section describes the POSIX.1c thread APIs for basic thread manipulation. The corresponding POSIX.1c and Sun thread APIs are:

Sun thread API	POSIX.1c thread API
thr_create	pthread_create
thr_self	pthread_self
thr_exit	pthread_exit
thr_kill	pthread_kill
thr_join	pthread_join

To use these APIs, application program should include the <pthread.h> header which declares all the POSIX.1c multithreaded function prototypes. Furthermore, if a program manipulates threads scheduling priority, then the <sched.h> header should be included also.

Unless otherwise stated, most of the thread APIs depicted below return a 0 value if they succeed, or a -1 value if they fail. In case they fail *perror* may be called to print error diagnostic messages.

13.4.1   pthread_create

The *pthread_create* function prototype is:

```
#include <pthread.h>

int        pthread_create ( pthread_t* tid_p, const pthread_attr_t* attr,
                            void* (*funcp)(void*),  void* argp );
```

The API creates a new thread to execute a function whose address is given in the *funcp* argument. The function specified in *funcp* should accept a *void**-typed input argument and return a *void** data. The actual argument to be passed to the *funcp* function, when the new thread starts execution, is specified in the *argp* argument.

The new thread ID is returned via the *tid_p* argument. If the actual value of the *tid_p* argument is assigned NULL, then no thread ID is returned. The thread ID data type is *pthread_t*.

The *attr* argument contains properties to be assigned to the newly created thread. The *attr* argument value may be NULL, if the new thread is to use the system default property values, or it is the address of an attribute object. POSIX.1c defines a set of APIs to create, destroy, inquire or set attribute objects. An attribute object may be associated with multiple threads, so that whenever an attribute object's properties are updated, all threads associated with that object will be affected by the changes. This is different from Sun threads where properties are specified for each thread individually.

The *pthread_attr_init* and *pthread_attr_destroy* APIs creates and destroys, respectively, an attribute object:

```
#include <pthread.h>
int        pthread_attr_init ( pthread_attr_ t* attr_p );
int        pthread_attr_destroy ( pthread_attr_ t* attr_p );
```

Once an attribute object is created via the *pthread_attr_init* function, its properties may be checked or set via the *pthread_attr_get* and *pthread_attr_set* APIs, respectively. The possible properties which may be contained in an attribute object and the associated APIs to check and set them are:

Property	API to check	API to set
Contention scope	pthread_attr_getscope	pthread_attr_setscope
Stack size	pthread_attr_getstacksize	pthread_attr_setstacksize
Stack address	pthread_attr_getstackaddr	pthread_attr_setstackaddr
Detach State	pthread_attr_getdetachstate	pthread_attr_setdetachstate
Schedule policy	pthread_attr_getschedpolicy	pthread_attr_setschedpolicy
Schedule Parameters	pthread_attr_getschedparam	pthread_attr_setschedparam

All the above *pthread_attr_get* APIs take two arguments: The first argument is the pointer to an attribute object, and the second argument is the address of a variable to hold the inquired property value. Similarly, all the above *pthread_attr_set* APIs also take two arguments:The first argument is the pointer to an attribute object, and the second argument is either a new property value or the pointer to a variable which holds the new property value.

The thread scheduling contention scope has been explained in Section 13.2. The possible values to set this property are PTHREAD_SCOPE_PROCESS or PTHREAD_SCOPE_SYSTEM.

A thread detach state specifies if a thread is created detached or joinable. The possible values for this property are PTHREAD_CREATE_DETACHED or PTHREAD_CREATE_JOINABLE.

A thread scheduling policy specifies, among other things, the scheduling priority of a thread. The second argument to the *pthread_attr_getschedparam* and *pthread_attr_setschedparam* APIs is the address of a *struct sched_param*-typed variable. In this variable there is an integer-typed *shced_priority* field, which specifies the scheduling priority of any thread that owns this property.

Finally, a newly created thread's run-time stack size and address may be set in a similar fashion as the *stack_size* and *stackp* arguments to the *thr_create* call (see Section 13.3.1). The difference here is that *pthread_attr_setstacksize* and *pthread_attr_setstackaddr* APIs are used to set these properties for one or more threads.

The following sample code creates a new detached and bound thread with a scheduling priority of five. The thread executes a function called *do_it* with an argument specified by the *pInt* variable. The new thread's ID is assigned to the *tid* variable and its stack is allocated by the function with the system default size:

```
extern void* do_it (void* ptr);
int                        *pInt;
pthread_t                  tid;
pthread_attr_t             attr, *attrPtr = &attr;
struct sched_param         sched;

if (pthread_attr_init( attrPtr ) == -1) {
    perror("pthread_attr_init");
    attrPtr = 0;
}
else {
    pthread_attr_setdetachstate( attrPtr,PTHREAD_CREATE_DETACH);
    pthread_attr_setscope( attrPtr, PTHREAD_SCOPE_SYSTEM);
    if (pthread_attr_getschedparam(attrPtr,&sched)==0) {
        param.sched_priority = 5;
        pthread_attr_setschedparam(attrPtr, &sched );
    }
}
if ([thread_create( &tid, &attr, do_it, (void*)&pInt ) == -1)
    perror("pthread_create");
```

13.4.2   pthread_exit,   pthread_detach,
        pthread_join

The prototypes of the *pthread_exit, pthread_detach* and *pthread_join* functions are:

```
#include <pthread.h>

int        pthread_exit ( void* status );
int        pthread_detach ( void* status );
int        pthread_join ( pthread_t tid, void** statusp);
```

Both the *pthread_exit* and *pthread_detach* functions terminate a thread. The *pthread_exit* function may be used by a non-detached thread, while the *pthread_detach* function is used by a detached thread. The actual argument value to the *statusp* argument is the address of a static variable which contains the exit status code of the terminating thread. The *statusp* argument value may be specified as NULL, if no other thread is expected to retrieve the terminating thread exit status code.

The *pthread_join* function is called to wait for the termination of a non-detached thread and returns the thread's exit status value as passed via a *pthread_exit* call.

The following example waits for a non-detached threads to terminate, then terminates the current thread:

```
status int      *rc, rval=0;
thread_t        tid;
if (!pthread_join(tid, &rc))
        cout << "thread: " << (int)tid << ", exits, rc=" << (*rc) << endl;
pthread_exit( (void*)&rval );
```

13.4.3   pthread_sigmask, pthread_kill

The prototypes of the *pthread_sigmask* and *pthread_kill* functions are:

```
#include <pthread.h>
#include <signal.h>

int          pthread_sigmask ( int mode, sigset_t *sigsetp, sigset_t *oldsetp);
int          pthread_kill ( pthread_t tid, int signum);
```

The *pthread_sigmask* function sets the signal mask of a calling thread. The *sigsetp* argument contains one or more of the signal numbers to be applied to the calling thread. The *mode* argument specifies how the signal(s) specified in the *sigsetp* argument is to be used. The possible values of the *mode* argument, as declared in the <signal.h> header, and their meanings are:

mode value	Meaning
SIG_BLOCK	Adds signals contained in the *sigsetp* argument to the thread signal mask
SIG_UNBLOCK	Removes signals contained in the *sigsetp* argument from the thread signal mask
SIG_SETMASK	Replaces the thread signal mask with the signal(s) specified in the *sigsetp* argument

If the *sigsetp* argument value is NULL, the *mode* argument value is don't-care.

The *oldsetp* argument value should be the address of a *sigset_t**-typed variable return-ing the old signal mask. If the *oldsetp* argument value is NULL, then the old signal mask is ignored.

The *pthread_kill* function sends a signal, as specified in the *signum* argument, to a thread whose ID is given by the *tid* argument. The sending and receiving threads must be in the same process.

The following example adds the SIGINT signal to a thread signal mask, then sends the SIGTERM signal to a thread whose ID is 15:

```
sigset_t    set, oldset;
sigemptyset( &set );
sigaddset( &set, SIGINT );
if (pthread_setmask( SIG_BLOCK, &set ,&oldset ))
            perror("thr_sigsetmask");
if (pthread_kill((thread_t)15, SIGTERM)) perror("pthread_kill");
```

13.4.4   sched_yield

The function prototype of the *sched_yield* API is:

```
#include <pthread.h>
int         sched_yield ( void );
```

The *sched_yield* function is called by a thread to yield its execution to other threads with the same priority. This function returns 0 on success and -1 when fails. This API is the POSIX.1c counterpart to the Sun's *thr_yield* API.

13.5   Thread Synchronization Objects

Threads in a process share the same address space as the process. This means that glo-bal and static variables in the process are accessible by all its threads. To ensure the correct manipulation of these variables, threads must use some methods to synchronize their opera-tions. Specifically, no thread should access a variable while its value is being changed by a thread. Furthermore, no thread should change a variable value while other threads are reading that variable value.

Thread synchronization is also needed when two or more threads are doing I/O operations on a common stream. For example, if two threads are writing to a stream simultaneously, it is unpredictable as to which data is output to that stream. Also, a similar problem occurs when two threads are reading data from a stream simultaneously.

To solve these thread synchronization problems, Sun and POSIX.1c provide the following objects to control thread operations on shared data and I/O streams in a process:

- Mutually exclusive locks (mutex locks)
- Condition variables
- Semaphores

Of the above objects, mutex locks are the most primitive and efficient to use. They are used to serialize the access of shared data or execution of code segments.

Condition variables are the second most efficient method after mutex locks. They are commonly used with mutex locks to control asynchronous access of shared data.

Semaphores are more complex than mutex locks and condition variables. They are used in the similar manner as the UNIX System V and POSIX.1b semaphores.

In addition to the above, Sun provides read-write locks as one more means for threads synchronization. Specifically, read-write locks allow multiple read-access and single write-access to any shared data. This capability is not provided by the aforementioned objects. Read-write locks are commonly used to guard data that are read frequently, but changed infrequently, by multiple threads.

Processes that use any one of these synchronization objects need to define storage for them in their virtual address space. If these objects are defined in shared memory regions that are accessible by multiple processes, they can be used to synchronize threads in these different processes.

The following sections describe these objects in more detail.

13.5.1   Mutually Exclusive Locks (mutex Locks)

Mutex locks serialize the execution of threads, such that when multiple threads try to acquire a mutex lock, only one of them can succeed and continue its execution. The other threads are blocked until the lock is released (unlocked) by its owner thread. When a mutex lock is released, it is unpredictable as to which pending thread is freed to acquire the lock.

The following table lists the corresponding Sun and POSIX.1c APIs for mutex locks manipulation:

Sun APIs	POSIX.1c API
mutex_init	pthread_mutex_init
mutex_destroy	pthread_mutex_destroy
mutex_lock	pthread_mutex_lock
mutex_trylock	pthread_mutex_trylock
mutex_unlock	pthread_mutex_unlock

The following two sub-sections describe these Sun and POSIX.1c mutex lock APIs in more detail.

13.5.1.1   Sun Mutex Locks

The Sun thread library functions for mutex lock operations are:

Function	Use
mutex_init	Initializes a mutex lock
mutex_lock	Sets a lock on a mutex lock
mutex_unlock	Unlocks a mutex lock
mutex_trylock	Like *mutex_lock*, except it is nonblocking
mutex_destroy	Discards a mutex lock

The prototypes of these functions are:

```
#include <thread.h>

int     mutex_init ( mutex_t *mutxp, int type, void* argp );
int     mutex_lock( mutex_t* mutxp );
int     mutex_trylock ( mutex_t* mutxp );
int     mutex_unlock ( mutex_t* mutxp );
int     mutex_destroy ( mutex_t* mutxp );
```

The *mutxp* argument value is the address of a *mutex_t*-typed variable. This variable is defined by the calling thread and is set to reference a mutex lock via the *mutex_init* function. The *type* argument of the *mutex_init* function specifies whether the mutex lock is accessible by threads in different processes. Its possible values and meanings are:

type value	Meaning
USYNC_PROCESS	The mutex lock can be used by threads in different processes
USYNC_THREAD	The mutex lock can be used by threads in the calling process only

The *argp* argument of the *mutex_init* function is currently unused. Its value should be specified as 0.

A mutex lock should be initialized only once in a process. It is discarded by the *mutex_destroy* function.

A mutex lock is acquired (or locked) by a thread via the *mutex_lock* function and released (unlocked) via the *mutex_unlock* function. The *mutex_lock* function blocks a calling thread if the lock has already been acquired by another thread. The thread is unblocked when the mutex lock is unlocked, and the thread is allowed to acquire it.

The *mutex_trylock* function is similar to the *mutex_lock* function except that if a requested lock is already acquired by another thread, the function returns an error status to the calling thread, rather than blocking it.

13.5.1.2 POSIX.1c Mutex Locks

The POSIX.1c APIs for mutex lock operations are similar to that of Sun:

Function	Use
pthread_mutex_initI	Initializes a mutex lock
pthread_mutex_lock	Sets a lock on a mutex lock
pthread_mutex_unlock	Unlocks a mutex lock
pthread_mutex_trylock	Like *mutex_lock*, except it is nonblocking
pthread_mutex_destroy	Discards a mutex lock

The prototypes of these functions are:

```
#include <pthread.h>

int      pthread_mutex_init ( pthread_mutex_t *mutxp,
                              pthread_mutexattr_t* attrp);

int      pthread_mutex_lock( pthread_mutex_t* mutxp );

int      pthread_mutex_trylock ( pthread_mutex_t* mutxp );
```

```
#include <pthread.h>

int        pthread_mutex_unlock ( pthread_mutex_t* mutxp );

int        pthread_mutex_destroy ( pthread_mutex_t* mutxp );
```

The *mutxp* argument value is the address of a *pthread_mutex_t*-typed variable. This variable is defined by the calling thread and is set to reference a mutex lock via the *pthread_mutex_init* function. The *attrp* argument is a pointer to an attribute object for the new mutex lock. This value may be NULL, if a mutex lock is to use default property values; otherwise, it is a pointer to a *pthread_mutexattr_t*-typed object that contains property values for the new mutex lock.

As an alternative of calling the *pthread_mutex_init* API, a mutex lock may also be initialized via the PTHREAD_MUTEX_INITIALIZER static initializer. Thus, the following code:

```
pthread_mutex_t        lockx;
(void)pthread_mutex_init( &lockx, 0 );
```

is the same as this statement:

```
pthread_mutex_t        lockx = PTHREAD_MUTEX_INITIALIZER;
```

The *pthread_mutex_lock, pthread_mutex_trylock, pthread_mutex_unlock,* and *pthread_mutex_destroy* have the similar invocation syntax and the same corresponding function as the Sun *mutex_lock, mutex_trylock, _mutex_unlock,* and *_mutex_destroy* APIs, respectively.

13.5.1.3 Mutex Lock Examples

The following *printmsg* function may be called by any thread to print messages to the standard output. This function ensures that only one thread can print a message to the standard output at a time. The *main* function is a sample application to test the *printmsg* function:

```
/* printmsg.C */
static mutex_t lockx;                    // define the lock storage
void* printmsg (void* msg )
{
    /* acquire the lock */
    if (mutex_lock(&lockx))
        perror("mutex_lock");
```

```
        else  {
            /* print the msg */
            cout << (char*)msg << endl << flush;

            /* release the lock */
            if (mutex_unlock(&lockx)) perror("mutex_unlock");
        }
    }

    int main(int argc, char* argv[])
    {
        /* initialize the mutex lock */
        if (mutex_init(&lockx, USYNC_THREAD,NULL)) perror("mutex_lock");

        /* create threads which call printmsg */
        while (--argc > 0)
            if (thr_create(0,0,printmsg,argv[argc],0, 0)) perror("thr_create");

        /* wait for all threads to terminate */
        while (!thjr_join(0,0,0)) ;

        /* discard the mutex lock */
        if (mutex_destroy(&lockx)) perror("mutex_destroy");
        return 0;
    }
```

In the above example, the *main* function initializes the mutex lock *lockx* to be used by all threads in the same process. It then creates multiple threads, one per command line argument, to call the *printmsg* function and display the command argument strings to the standard output. It does not matter how many threads call the *printmsg* function simultaneously, as the function serves only one thread at a time.

A sample run of the *printmsg.C* program and its output is:

```
% CC printmsg.C -lthread -o printmsg
% printmsg  "1"  "2"  "3"
3
2
1
```

As another example, the following *glob_dat* class defines a data type for variables that can be accessed by multiple threads simultaneously. This class is defined in a *glob_dat.h* header:

```
#ifndef GLOB_DAT_H
#define GLOB_DAT_H

#include <iostream.h>
#include <thread.h>
#include <stdio.h>

class glob_dat
{
   private:
      int        val;
      mutex_t    lockx;
   public:
      // constructor function
      glob_dat( int a )
      {
         val = a;
         if (mutex_init(&lockx, USYNC_THREAD,0)) perror("mutex_init");
      };
      // destructor function
      ~glob_dat() { if (mutex_destroy(&lockx)) perror("mutex_destroy"); };

      // set new value
      glob_dat& operator=( int new_val )
      {
         if (!mutex_lock(&lockx)) {
            val = new_val;
            if (mutex_unlock(&lockx)) perror("mutex_unlock");
         }else perror("mutex_unlock");
         return *this;
      };
      // retrieve value
      int getval( int* valp )
      {
         if (!mutex_lock(&lockx)) {
            *valp= val;
            if (!mutex_unlock(&lockx)) return 0;
            perror("mutex_unlock");
         } else perror("mutex_lock");
         return -1;
      };

      // show value to an output stream
      friend ostream& operator<<( ostream& os glob_dat& gx)
      {
```

```
        if (!mutex_lock(&gx.lockx)) {
            os << gx.val;
            if (mutex_unlock(&gx.lockx)) perror("mutex_lock");
        } else perror("mutex_lock");
        return os;
    };
};        /* glob_dat */
#endif
```

The actual value of a *glob_dat*-type variable is stored in the *glob_dat::val* data field. The *glob_dat::lockx* mutex lock is used to serialize the access of the *glob_dat::val* by multiple threads. The *glob_dat::lockx* and *glob_dat::val* members are initialized when a variable of this type is defined. The *glob_dat::lockx* mutex lock is discarded when the *glob_dat::~glob_dat* destructor function is called.

The *glob_dat::getval, glob_dat::show,* and *glob_dat::operator=* member functions allow threads to retrieve, show, and set any *glob_dat-typed* variable value. By using the mutex lock, these functions are MT (multithreaded) -safe, meaning they can be called by multiple threads simultaneously to operate on the same variable without causing problems.

The following example program, *glob_dat.C*, illustrates how a *glob_dat*-typed variable, *globx* is accessed by multiple threads:

```
#include <strstream.h>
#include "glob_dat.h"
glob_dat globx (0);                              // define globx

void* mod_val (void* np )
{
    int old_val, new_val;
    istrstream((char*)np) >> new_val;
    if (!globx.getval(&old_val))     {           // get current value
        globx = old_val + new_val;               // add new value
        cout  << (int)thr_self() << ": arg=" << (char*)np
            << "' -> " << globx << endl;         // show result
    }
    return 0;
}

int main(int argc, char* argv[])
{
    thread_t tid;
    while (--argc > 0)                  // for each command line argument
```

```
     if (thr_create(0,0,mod_val,argv[argc],0,&tid)) perror("thr_create");
     while (!thr_join(0,0,0)) ;            // wait for threads to terminate
     return 0;
}
```

The *main* function creates the *globx* variable with an initial value of zero. It then creates a thread for each command line argument to execute the *mod_val* function. The actual argument value passed to each *mod_val* function call is a command line argument. It is made up of an integer value text string (e.g., *"51"*). The *mod_val* function converts its argument to an integer value, gets the current value of the *globx* value and adds the new integer value to the current value. The resultant value is assigned to the *globx* variable, which is then printed to the standard output.

A sample run of the above program and its output is:

```
% CC glob_dat.C -lthread -o glob_dat
% glob_dat "1" "2" "3"
4: arg='3' -> 3
5: arg='2' -> 5
6: arg='1' -> 6
```

One problem to avoid in using mutex locks is in creating a dead-lock condition within a process. This may occur when a process uses multiple mutex locks and two or more threads in that process attempt to acquire these locks in random order. For example, suppose two mutex locks (*A* and *B*) are initialized in a process and two threads (*X* and *Y*) in the process use these locks. Suppose thread *X* has acquired lock *B*, and thread *Y* has acquired lock *B*. When X attempts to acquire lock *B*, it is blocked because lock *B* is owned by thread *Y*. If thread *Y* then attempts to acquire lock *A*, it is also blocked. This creates a dead-lock condition: both *X* and *Y* are blocked as each of them tries to acquire a lock owned by the other. Neither of these threads can proceed any further, as the owner of the lock is blocked and unable to release the lock.

To prevent dead-lock conditions, threads that use mutex locks should always acquire them in the same order and/or use the *thr_trywait* function instead of *thr_wait* to acquire locks. In the first method, because all threads acquire locks in the same order, it is impossible for a thread to attempt acquiring a lock that is owned by a blocked thread. In the second method, if a thread uses the *thr_trywait* function to acquire a lock, the function returns a non-zero value immediately (if the lock is owned by another thread). Thus, the thread is not blocked and can perform some other work and try to acquire the lock again later.

13.5.2   Condition Variables

Condition variables are used to block threads until certain conditions become true. Condition variables are usually used with mutex locks so that multiple threads can wait on the same condition variable. This is done as follows: First, a thread acquires a mutex lock, but is blocked by a condition variable, pending the occurrence of a specific condition. While the thread is blocked, the mutex lock it acquires is released automatically. When another thread modifies the state of the specific condition, it signals the condition variable to unblock the thread. When the thread is unblocked, the mutex lock is reacquired automatically, and the thread tests the condition again. If the condition remains false, the thread is again blocked by the condition variable. On the other hand, if the condition is now true, the thread releases the mutex lock and proceeds with its execution.

13.5.2.1   Sun Condition Variables

The Sun thread library functions for condition variable operation are:

Function	Use
cond_init	Initializes a condition variable
cond_wait	Blocks on a condition variable
cond_timedwait	Same as *cond_wait*, except that a time out period for the block duration is specified
cond_signal	Unblocks a thread that is waiting on a condition variable
cond_broadcast	Unblocks all threads that are waiting on a condition variable
cond_destroy	Discards a condition variable

The prototypes of these functions are:

```
#include <thread.h>

int      cond_init ( cond_t *condp, int type, int argp );
int      cond_wait ( cond_t* condp, mutex_t *mutxp);
int      cond_timedwait ( cond_t* condp, mutex_t* mutxp, timestruct_t * timp );
int      cond_signal ( cond_t* condp );
int      cond_broadcast ( cond_t* condp );
int      cond_destroy ( cond_t* condp );
```

The *condp* argument value is the address of a *cond_t*-typed variable. This variable is set to reference a condition variable via the *cond_init* function. The *type* argument of the *cond_init* function specifies whether the condition variable is accessible by different processes. Its possible values and meanings are:

type value	Meaning
USYNC_PROCESS	The condition variable can be used by threads in different processes
USYNC_THREAD	The condition variable can be used by threads in the calling process only

The *arg* argument of the *cond_init* function is currently unused. Its value should be specified as zero.

The *cond_wait* function blocks the calling thread to wait for the condition variable to change state as specified by the *condp* argument. It also releases the mutex lock as specified by the *mutxp* argument.

When another thread calls the *cond_signal* function on the same condition variable, the mutex lock is reacquired for a pending thread. That thread is unblocked and resumes execution at the return of the *cond_wait* function call. If there are multiple threads blocked by the same condition variable, they should all use the same mutex lock. When the condition variable is signaled, only one of the blocked threads can succeed in acquiring the mutex lock and proceed with execution. The other threads continue to be blocked by the same mutex lock.

The *cond_timewait* function is similar to the *cond_wait* function, except that it has a third argument *timp* which specifies that the calling thread should not be blocked past the time-of-day as specified in that argument.

The *cond_signal* signals a condition variable, as specified by the *condp* argument and unblocks the thread waiting on that variable. The *cond_broadcast* signals a condition variable and unblocks all threads that are waiting. If there is no thread waiting on a signaled condition variable, the *cond_signal* or *cond_broadcast* call on that variable has no effect.

13.5.2.2 Condition Variable Example

The following example illustrates the uses of a mutex lock and a condition variable. The program, *pipe.C*, creates a reader thread and a writer thread. The reader thread reads data from a user and passes them to a writer thread via a global array *msgbuf*. The writer thread prints messages contained in the *msgbuf* to the standard output. The two threads terminate when end-of-file is encountered from the user. The reader and writer threads synchronize their access of *msgbuf* via a mutex lock and a condition variable.

The *pipe.C* program is:

```
#include <iostream.h>
#include <thread.h>
#include <string.h>
#include <stdio.h>
#include <signal.h>

#define FINISH()   { cerr << (int)thr_self() << " exits\n"; \
        mutex_unlock(&mutx); thr_exit(0); return 0; }

mutex_t mutx;
cond_t  condx;
int     msglen, done;
char    msgbuf[256];


/* write messages sent from the reader thread to the standard output */
void* writer (void* argp )
{
   do   {
      mutex_lock(&mutx);                        // acquire the mutex lock
      while (!msglen)    {                      // loop if no message
           cond_wait(&condx,&mutx);             // wait on the cond. variable
         if (done) FINISH();                    // kill thread if done
      }
      cout << "*> " << msgbuf << endl;          // print mesg to std output
      msglen = 0;                               // reset msg buffer size
      mutex_unlock(&mutx);                      // release the mutex lock
   } while (1);

    FINISH();                                   // clean up and exit
}

/* read messages from user and send them to the writer thread */
void* reader (void* argp )
{
   do   {
      mutex_lock(&mutx);                        // acquire the mutex lock
      if (!msglen)   {                          // check buffer is empty
        if (!cin.getline(msgbuf,256)) break;    // get input from user
        msglen = strlen(msgbuf)+1;              // set msg length
        cond_signal(&condx);                    // signal writer to read msg
      }
      mutex_unlock(&mutx);                      // release the mutex lock
```

```
        } while (1);

        FINISH();                                    // clean up and exit
}

/* main thread to control the reader and writer threads */
main()
{
    thread_t wtid, rtid, tid;

    /* initialize mutex lock and condition variable */
    mutex_init(&mutx, USYNC_PROCESS, 0);
    cond_init(&condx, USYNC_PROCESS, 0);

    /* create a writer thread */
    if (thr_create(0,0,writer,0,0,&wtid)) perror("thr_create");


    /* create a read thread */
    if (thr_create(0,0,reader,0,0,&rtid)) perror("thr_create");

    /* wait for the read thread to exit */
    if (!thr_join(rtid,&tid,0))  {
        done = 1;
        cond_signal(&condx);
    }

    /* clean up */
    mutex_destroy(&mutx);
    cond_destroy(&condx);
    thr_exit(0);
}
```

The *main* function initializes the *mutx* mutex lock and the *condx* condition variable. It then creates the writer thread and reader thread to execute the *writer* and *reader* functions. The main thread then waits for the reader thread to terminate via the *thr_join* function and signals the write thread to terminate via the *done* global variable. After the reader and writer threads are terminated, the main thread discards the mutex lock and the condition variable via the *mutex_destroy* and *cond_destroy* functions, respectively.

The reader thread reads one or more input lines from a user from the standard input. For each line it reads, it first acquires the mutex lock to make sure it can access the *msgbuf* and *msglen* global variables. When the mutex lock is acquired successfully, the thread puts the user message into the *msgbuf* array and sets the *msglen* variable to be the size of the message text. It then uses the *cond_signal* and *mutex_unlock* functions to signal the writer process to check the *msglen* variable. The reader thread terminates when it cannot read an input text from the user. In that case, it releases the mutex lock and terminates itself via the *thr_exit* function.

The writer thread constantly polls the *msglen* global variable. If the *msglen* value is not zero, a message is available in the *msgbuf* array and can be printed to the standard output. To process each message, the thread first acquires the mutex lock to make sure it can access the *msglen* and *msgbuf* variables exclusively. If that succeeds, it blocks the *cond_wait* function call until the reader thread or main thread calls the *cond_signal* function to unblock it. When the writer thread is unblocked, it checks whether the *done* variable value is nonzero. If so, the main thread signals the writer thread to exit. However, if the *done* variable is zero and the *msglen* variable value is not zero, the thread prints the message contained in *msgbuf* to the standard output. Otherwise, it goes back to the *cond_wait* loop to wait for a message to arrive. Note that when the writer thread is blocked in the *cond_wait* call, the *mutx* mutex lock is released so that the reader or main thread can acquire it. The *cond_wait* function automatically reacquires the mutex lock before unblocking the writer thread when the reader or main thread calls the *cond_signal* function on the *condx* variable.

A sample run of the *pipe.C* program and its output is:

```
%     CC pipe.C -lthread -o pipe
%     pipe
Have a good day
*> Have a good day
Bye-Bye
*> Bye-Bye
5 exists
4 exists
```

13.5.2.3   POSIX.1c Condition Variables

The corresponding POSIX.1c APIs to the Sun APIs for condition variable manipulation are:

POSIX.1c API	Sun API
pthread_cond_init	cond_init
pthread_cond_wait	cond_wait
pthread_cond_timedwait	cond_timedwait
pthread_cond_signal	cond_signal
pthread_cond_broadcast	cond_broadcast
pthread_cond_destroy	cond_destroy

The function prototypes of these POSIX.1c APIs are:

```
#include <pthread.h>

int      pthread_cond_init ( pthread_cond_t *condp, pthread_condattr_t *attr );
int      pthread_cond_wait ( pthread_cond_t* condp, pthread_mutex_t *mutxp);
int      pthread_cond_timedwait (pthread_cond_t* condp,
                            pthread_mutex_t* mutxp, struct timespec* timp );
int      pthread_cond_signal ( pthread_cond_t* condp );
int      pthread_cond_broadcast ( pthread_cond_t* condp );
int      pthread_cond_destroy ( pthread_cond_t* condp );
```

The *condp* argument value is the address of a *pthread_cond_t*-typed variable which references an allocated condition variable. The *attr* argument of the *pthread_cond_init* function is a pointer to an attribute object which specifies properties for the condition variable. The actual argument for *attr* may be 0 if the condition variable is to use default property values.

Note that a POSIX.1c condition variable may be initialized via the static initializer PTHREAD_COND_INITIALIZER. Thus the following code:

```
pthread_cond_t    cond_var;
(void) pthread_cond_init( &cond_var, 0 );
```

is the same as this statement:

```
pthread_cond_t    cond_var = PTHREAD_COND_INITIALIZER;
```

The *pthread_cond_wait, pthread_cond_timedwait, pthread_cond_signal, pthread_cond_broadcast* and *pthread_cond_destroy* have the same function as the Sun *cond_wait, cond_timedwait, cond_signal, cond_broadcast* and *cond_destroy* APIs, respectively. Please refer to Section 13.5.2.1 for description of these APIs.

13.5.3   Sun Read-Write Locks

Read-write locks are like mutex locks, except that these locks can be acquired for read-only and write-only. One or more threads can hold a read lock on a read-write lock simultaneously. A thread that wishes to set a write lock on a read-write lock is blocked until all read locks are released. On the other hand, if a thread acquires a write lock on a read-write lock, no other threads can set any read or write lock on it until the former thread releases its write lock. If two threads attempt to acquire a read-write lock at the same time, one for read and the other for write, the write lock will be granted. Read-write locks are not as efficient as mutex locks, but they can be used to permit simultaneous read access of data by multiple threads.

Read-write locks are not defined in POSIX.1c, so they are Sun-specific. The Sun thread library functions for read-write locks operations are:

Function	Use
rw_init	Initializes a read-write lock
rw_rdlock	Acquires a read lock
rw_tryrdlock	Acquires a read lock, in nonblocking mode
rw_wrlock	Acquires a write lock
rw_trywrlock	Acquires a write lock, in nonblocking mode
rw_unlock	Unlocks a read-write lock
rw_destroy	Discards a read-write lock

The prototypes of these functions are:

```
#include <thread.h>

int      rw_init ( rwlock_t *rwp, int type, void* argp );
int      rw_rdlock ( rwlock_t* rwp);
int      rw_tryrdlock ( rwlock_t* rwp );
int      rw_wrlock ( rwlock_t * rwp);
int       rw_trywrlock( rwlock_t* rwp );
int      rw_unlock ( rwlock_t* rwp );
int      rw_destroy ( rwlock_t* rwp );
```

The *rwp* argument value is the address of a *rwlock_t*-typed variable. This variable is set to reference a read-write lock via the *rw_init* function. The *type* argument of the *rw_init* function specifies whether or not the read-write lock is accessible by different processes. Its possible values and meanings are:

type value	Meaning
USYNC_PROCESS	The read-write lock can be used by threads in different processes
USYNC_THREAD	The read-write lock can be used by threads in the calling process only

The *argp* argument of the *rw_init* function is currently unused. Its value should be specified as zero.

The *rw_rdlock* function attempts to acquire a read lock on a read-write lock as specified by the *rwp* argument. This function blocks the calling thread until the operation succeeds.

The *rw_tryrdlock* function is like the *rw_rdlock* function, except that it is non-blocking. If the function aborts because the requested lock has been set as write-only by another thread, it returns a non-zero value and sets the *errno* to EBUSY.

The *rw_wrlock* function attempts to acquire a write lock on a read-write lock as specified by the *rwp* argument. This function blocks the calling thread until the operation succeeds.

The rw_*trywrlock* function is like the *rw_wrlock* function, except that it is nonblocking. If the function aborts because the requested lock is owned by another thread, it returns a nonzero value and sets the *errno* to EBUSY.

The *rw_unlock* and *rw_destroy* functions unlock and discard, respectively, a read-write lock as specified by the *rwp* argument.

The following *pipe2.C* program is a rewrite of the *pipe.C* program presented in the last section. The new program uses a read-write lock instead of a mutex lock and a condition variable to synchronize the reader and writer threads.

```
/* pipe2.C */
#include <iostream.h>
#include <thread.h>
#include <string.h>
#include <stdio.h>
#include <signal.h>

rwlock_t rwlk;
int     msglen, done = 0;
char    msgbuf[256];

/* writer thread function */
void* writer (void* argp )
{
   while (!done)   {
      if (rw_rdlock(&rwlk)) perror("rw_rdlock");      // set a read lock
      if (msglen)   {                                 // check mesg. exits
         cout << "> " << msgbuf << endl;              // print a message
```

```
            msglen = 0;                                    // reset msg. buffer
          }
          if (rw_unlock(&rwlk)) perror("rw_unlock(1)");    // unlock rw lock
          thr_yield();                                     // yield to other thread
        }
        /* clean up and exit thread */
        cerr << "write thread (" << (int)thr_self() << ") exits\n";
        thr_exit(0);
        return 0;
}

/* reader thread function */
void* reader (void* argp )
{
      do {
         if (rw_wrlock(&rwlk)) perror("rw_wrlock");        // set a write lock
         if (!msglen)   {                                  // empty buffer ?
            if (!cin.getline(msgbuf,256)) break;           // get a mesg from a user
            msglen = strlen(msgbuf)+1;                     // set mesg size
         }
         if (rw_unlock(&rwlk)) perror("rw_unlock(2)");     // unlock rw lock
         thr_yield();                                      // yield to other thread
      } while (1);

      /* clean up and exit thread */
      cerr << "read thread (" << (int)thr_self() << ") exits\n";
      if (rw_unlock(&rwlk)) perror("rw_unlock(3)");
      thr_exit(0);
      return 0;
}

/* main thread function */
main()
{
      thread_t wtid, rtid, tid;
      (void)rw_init(&rwlk, USYNC_PROCESS, 0);

      /* create a writer thread */
      if (thr_create(0,0,writer,0,0,&wtid)) perror("thr_create");

      /* create a read thread */
      if (thr_create(0,0,reader,0,0,&rtid)) perror("thr_create");

       /* wait for read process to exit */
      if (!thr_join(rtid,&tid,0)) done = 1;
```

```
        /* clean up */
        rwlock_destroy(&rwlk);
        thr_exit(0);
    }
```

The *main* function initializes a read-write lock, then creates reader and writer threads to work together. The main thread waits for the reader thread to exit, then signals the writer thread to terminate via the *done* variable. After that, the main thread discards the read-write lock and exits.

The reader thread executes the *read* function. It gets one or more lines of text from a user. For each input message line, it acquires a read-write lock for write access. This ensures that it has exclusive use of the *msgbuf* and *msglen* variables. When the write lock is acquired, the thread writes the message text to the *msgbuf* array, sets the *msglen* to the size of the message text, and releases the read-write lock. The thread then yields its execution to the writer thread, so that the latter can access the lock and *msgbuf* variable. After that, it gets the next message from the user and repeats the above process. The thread exits when it cannot read any text from a user. When that happens, it unlocks the read-write lock and exits via the *thr_exit* function.

The writer thread executes the *write* function. It reads one message at a time from the reader thread and prints the message to the standard output. For each message it processes, it first acquires a read lock on the read-write lock and checks that the *msglen* variable value is greater than zero. If a message is present in the *msgbuf* variable, the thread prints the message to the standard output and resets the *msglen* to zero. After these procedures, the thread unlocks the read-write lock and yields its execution to the reader thread so that the latter can access the lock and put the next message into the *msgbuf* buffer. The thread terminates when the global variable *done* is set to nonzero by the main thread. This means that no more messages are available, and the thread exits via the *thr_exit* function.

A sample run of the *pipe2.C* program and its output is:

```
%    CC pipe2.C -lthread -o pipe2
%    pipe2
Have a good day
*> Have a good day
Bye-Bye
*> Bye-Bye
^D
read thread (5 )exists
write thread (4) exists
%
```

13.5.4   Semaphores

Both the Sun thread library and POSIX.1c provide APIs for semaphore manipulation of. These thread-based semaphores are similar to System V semaphores in that each semaphore has an integer value that must be either zero or a positive number. A semaphore value may be set by any thread that has access to it. If a thread attempts to decrement a semaphore value that will result in a negative number, the thread is blocked. It remains this way until another thread increases the semaphore value to a large enough number for the blocked thread's operation on the semaphore to result in a zero or positive value.

The blocking features of semaphores can be used to synchronize the execution of certain code segments or the access of shared data by multiple threads. Before accessing a shared resource, each thread attempts to decrement a semaphore value by 1. Only one of them succeeds, while the rest are blocked. Once the successful thread finishes using the shared resource, it increments the semaphore value to its previous value so that another thread can be unblocked and proceed with accessing the shared resource.

Semaphores can be used in place of mutex locks and condition variables. However, whereas mutex locks can be released only by the threads holding them, any thread can increment or decrement a semaphore to which they have access. To ensure program reliability, additional programming effort is needed by users to keep track of what each thread is doing in regard to a semaphore.

POSIX.1c uses the same semaphore APIs as in POSIX.1b for thread synchronization. Please refer to Chapter 10, Section 10.6 for a description of these APIs. Sun Microsystems, on the other hand, defines a different set of semaphore APIs for thread synchronization. These APIs and their correspondence to the POSIX.1b semaphore APIs are:

Sun API	POSIX.1b API	Use
sema_init	sem_init	Initializes a semaphore
sema_post	sem_post	Increases a semaphore value by 1
sema_wait	sem_wait	Decreases a semaphore value by 1
sema_trywait	sem_trywait	Decreases a semaphore value by 1, but nonblocking
sema_destroy	sem_destroy	Discards a semaphore

The prototypes of the Sun semaphore APIs are:

```
#include <synch.h>

int      sema_init ( sema_t *svp, int init_val, int type, void* argp );
int      sema_wait ( sema_t* rvp );
```

```
#include <synch.h>

int      sema_trywait ( sema_t* rvp );
int      sema_post ( sema_t * svp);
int      sema_destroy ( sema_t* svp );
```

The *svp* argument value is the address of a *sema_t*-typed variable. This variable is set to reference a semaphore via the *sema_init* function. The new semaphore is set to an initial value as specified by the *init_val* argument. The *type* argument of the *sema_init* function specifies whether or not the semaphore is accessible by different processes. Its possible values and meanings are:

type value	Meaning
USYNC_PROCESS	The read-write lock can be used by threads in different processes
USYNC_THREAD	The read-write lock can be used by threads in the calling process only

The *argp* argument of the *sema_init* function is currently unused. Its value should be specified as zero.

The *sema_wait* function attempts to decrement the value of a semaphore as specified by the *svp* argument. This function blocks the calling thread until the operation succeeds.

The *sema_trywait* function is like the *sema_wait* function, except that it is non-blocking. If the function aborts because the requested semaphore value cannot be decreased, it returns a nonzero value and sets the *errno* to EBUSY.

The *sema_post* function increases the value of a semaphore as specified by the *svp* argument.

The *sema_destroy* function discards a semaphore as specified by the *svp* argument.

The following *pipe3.C* program is a rewrite of the *pipe.C* program presented in the last section. The new program uses a semaphore instead of a read-write lock to synchronize the reader and writer threads.

```
/* pipe3.C */
#include <iostream.h>
#include <thread.h>
```

```cpp
#include <string.h>
#include <stdio.h>
#include <signal.h>
#define FINISH()   { cerr << (int)thr_self() << " exits\n";  thr_exit(0); return 0; }
sema_t  semx;
int     msglen, done;
char    msgbuf[256];

/* a write thread function */
void* writer (void* argp )
{
   do   {
      sema_wait(&semx);                      // acquire a semaphore
      if (msglen)   {                        // if a message is in buffer
         cut << "*> " << msgbuf << endl;     // print out the message
         msglen = 0;                         // reset message buffer size
      }
      sema_post(&semx);                      // release a semaphore
      thr_yield();                           // let other threads run
   } while (!done);                          // do until no more messages
   FINISH();                                 // clean-up and terminate
}
/* a reader thread function */
void* reader (void* argp )
{
   do   {
      sema_wait(&semx);                      // acquire a semaphore
      if (!msglen)   {                       // check buffer is empty
         if (cin.getline(msgbuf,256))        // get a new message
            msglen = strlen(msgbuf)+1;       // set message size to msglen
         else done = 1;                      // no more input messages
      }
      sema_post(&semx);                      // release the semaphore
      thr_yield();                           // let other threads run
   } while (!done);                          // do until no more messages
   FINISH();                                 // clean-up and terminate
}

/* main thread function */
main()
{
   thread_t wtid, rtid;
   /* initialize a semaphore with an initial value of 1 */
   sema_init(&semx, 1, USYNC_PROCESS, 0);
```

```
        /* create a writer thread */
        if (thr_create(0,0,writer,0,0,&wtid)) perror("thr_create");
        /* create a reader thread */
        if (thr_create(0,0,reader,0,0,&rtid)) perror("thr_create");

        /* wait for all threads to exit */
        while (!thr_join(0,0,0)) ;

        /* clean up */
        sema_destroy(&semx);
        thr_exit(0);
    }
```

The above program is similar to the last two examples. The difference here is that a semaphore is used instead of a mutex lock, condition variable, or read-write lock. Specifically, a *semx* semaphore is initialized in the main thread with an initial value of 1. When the reader and writer threads are run, both try to acquire the semaphore via the *sema_wait* function call. Only one of them can succeed.

If the writer thread acquires the semaphore before the reader thread does, it finds the message buffer empty and releases the semaphore. This yields its execution to the reader thread. When the reader thread acquires the semaphore, it reads a message from the user and puts it into the *msgbuf* array. This sets the *msglen* to be the size of the message text. It then releases the semaphore and yields its execution to the writer thread.

When the writer thread is unblocked by the semaphore, it finds that the *msgbuf* is not empty and prints the message contained in it to the standard output. It then resets the *msglen* variable and releases the semaphore. This starts the next round of message processing by the reader and writer threads.

When a reader thread cannot read a message from the standard input (may be due to end-of-file), it sets the *done* variable to 1. This signals both itself and the writer thread to terminate via the *thr_exit* function call.

A sample run of the *pipe3.C* program and its output is:

```
%    CC pipe3.C -lthread -o pipe3
%    pipe3
Have a good day
*> Have a good day
Bye-Bye
*> Bye-Bye
^D
```

5 exists

4 exists

13.6   Thread-Specific Data

Automatic variables and dynamic memory allocated within a function are owned by each thread that executes that function. Global and static variables can be shared by multiple threads, but they must use mutex locks, conditional variables, etc. to synchronize their access of shared data. Some other global variables, however, cannot be synchronized to maintain a minimum level of concurrency within multithreaded programs. For example, the *errno* variables defined in the C library are set by each system call. Thus, if multiple threads make system calls concurrently, the *errno* variable must be set to different values for different threads. This problem can be worked around by requiring that only one thread at a time make a system call. This renders multithreaded programs to run in single-threaded mode.

The *errno* problem is resolved by the thread library, which automatically creates a private copy of *errno* for each thread that makes system calls. Thus, multiple threads can make system calls and check their *errno* values at the same time.

Another similar problem is when functions contain static variables concurrently accessible by multiple threads. For example, the C library function *ctime* returns the character string of a local date and time. This string is stored in the internal static buffer of the *ctime* function:

```
const char* ctime ( const time_t *timval )
{
        static char timbuf[...];
        /* convert timval to local date/time and store result to timbuf */
        return timbuf;
}
```

Thus, if several threads call the above *ctime* function simultaneously, the function must somehow be able to return different results for different threads. One could resolve the above problem by allocating dynamic buffers to store the requested date/time in each call. However, this causes several problems:

- The function takes more time and memory to execute. This taxes the performance and memory requirement of programs that use this function
- Existing programs that use this function need to be changed to deallocate the dynamic memory returned by this function
- Unchanged single-threaded programs cannot be used in the multithreaded environment.

To solve the above problem, both POSIX.1c and Sun define "re-entrance" versions of popular library functions. These new functions can be called by multiple threads concurrently with no side effects, and their performance is the same as or better than their single-threaded counterparts. The names of these re-entrance functions are the same as their counterparts but with a _r suffix. Thus, the re-entrance version of the *ctime* function is called *ctime_r*. All these new functions take one additional argument, which is the address of a variable that holds the returned value. The variable is defined by the calling threads. Thus, multiple threads may call the same function simultaneously and each receives its answer via its supplied variable. Existing or single-threaded programs may continue to use the old library functions and are not affected by the multithreaded environment. New multithreaded programs should use the re-entrance versions of library functions.

The new *ctime_r* function definition is as follows:

```
char* ctime_r (const time_t* timval, char buf[])
{
    /* convert timval to local date/time and store the result to buf */
    ....
    return buf;
}
```

Note that the *ctime_r* function uses its input argument *buf* to store the caller's requested date and time stamp and returns the *buf* address to the caller.

Sun provides re-entrance versions of C, math, and socket library functions.

Even with re-entrance functions and thread library-supported global variables that are defined dynamically for each thread, there may still be a need to have user-defined thread-specific data. For example, users who develop a utility package (for example, a new GUI package) that can be used by other programmers may wish to define their own versions of *errno*. This would allow their users to check *errno* for any error code returned by the utility functions. However, their package functions may be called by multiple threads concurrently, creating a need for their functions to define a per-thread-specific *errno*. Before showing how this is done, the following functions are defined in the Sun thread library for manipulation of thread-specific data:

Function	Use
thr_keycreate	Defines a common key for all threads
thr_setspecific	Store sa thread value to a key
thr_getspecific	Retrieves a thread value from a key

The prototypes of these functions are:

```
#include <thread.h>

int      thr_keycreate( thread_key_t * keyp, void (* destr)(void*) );
int      thr_setspecific ( thread_key_t key, void* valuep);
int      thr_setspecific( thread_key_t key, void** valuep);
```

The *keyp* argument value is the address of a *thread_key_t*-typed variable. This variable is initialized by the *thr_keycreate* function. The optional *destr* argument is the address of a user-defined function that may be called to discard a thread value. This occurs when a thread that has registered a value with the **keyp* variable terminates. The argument value passed to the *destr* function is the address of a terminating thread value that is registered with the **keyp* via the *thr_setepecific* function.

The *thr_setspecific* function is called by a thread to register a value with a key. The *key* argument specifies which key with which to register. The *valuep* argument contains the address of the thread value. A key may maintain multiple values at any one time, but only one per thread.

The *thr_getspecific* function is called to retrieve the value of a calling that which has been registered with a key designated by the *key* argument. The thread value is returned via the *valuep* argument.

The following *pkg.h* header defines a data class that can be used by multiple threads simultaneously. Specifically, the class defines an *errno* and an *ofstream* object for each thread so that there are no conflicts among threads calling the same class functions. The *pkg.h* file content is:

```
#ifndef PKG_H
#define PKG_H
#include <fstream.h>
#include <stdio.h>
#include <thread.h>

/* record to store a set of thread-specific data */
class thr_data
{
        int          errno;          // errno for a thread
        ofstream&    ofs;            // output stream for a thread
        /* other stuffs */
    public:
        /* constructor */
```

```
        thr_data( int errval, ofstream& os) : errno(errval), ofs(os) {};

         /* destructor */
         ~thr_data()           { ofs.close();  };

         /* return a thread's errno */
         int& errval()         { return errno; };

         /* return a thread's ostream handle */
         ofstream& os()     { return ofs;   };

         /* other member functions */
};

/* Utility package class */
class Xpackage
{
        thread_key_t        key;                     // key for all threads
        ofstream            ocerr;                   // default output stream
        /* other package data */

     public:

        /* called when a thread dies. Discard a thread-specific data */
        friend void destr( void* valueP )
        {
           thr_data  *pDat = (thr_data*)valueP;
           delete pDat;
        };

        /* constructor */
        Xpackage() : ocerr("err.log")
        {
           if (thr_keycreate(&key,destr)) perror("thr_create");
        };

        /* destructor */
        ~Xpackage()        { ocerr.close(); };
        /* called when each thread starts */
        void new_thread( int errval,  ofstream& os )
        {
           thr_data      *pDat;
           pDat = new thr_data(errval, os);          // alloc a thread-specific data
           if (thr_setspecific(key,pDat)) perror( "thr_setspecific");
        };
```

```
/* set a thread's errno and return a value */
int set_errno( int rc )
{
    thr_data      *pDat;
    if (thr_getspecific(key,(void**)&pDat))
        perror("thr_getspecific");
    else pDat->errval() = rc;
    return rc==0 ? 0 : -1;
};

/* return current errno value for a thread */
int errno()
{
    thr_data      *pDat;
    if (!thr_getspecific(key,(void**)&pDat))
        return pDat->errval();
    else perror("thr_getspecific");
    return -1;
};

/* return a thread's outstream handle */
ofstream& os()
{
    thr_data      *pDat;
    if (!thr_getspecific(key,(void**)&pDat)) return pDat->os();
    perror("thr_getspecific");
    return ocerr;
};

/* a sample package function */
int chgErrno(int new_val )
{
        return set_errno( new_val +int(thr_self()) );
};
/* other package functions */
};
#endif /* PKG_H */
```

All thread-specific data are stored in a *thr_data*-typed record. The record stores *errno* and *ofstream* objects that are private for each thread. Users may redefine the *thr_data* class to contain additional thread-specific data if desired.

There should be a *Xpackage*-typed variable defined globally in every user program. When the program starts up, the *Xpackage::Xpackage()* constructor is called, which initializes the *Xpackage::key* variable shared by all threads in the process. The *Xpackage::ocerr* variable references a default output stream in case a thread-defined output stream cannot be opened. If a user wants to store different types of thread-specific data in a process, he or she may define multiple *Xpackage*-typed variables, one for each type of thread-specific data.

The *Xpackage::set_errno()* is called by the package functions to set the *errno* value for a calling thread. The *Xpackage::errno()* is called by a thread to retrieve its private *errno* value. The *Xpackage::os()* is called to return an output stream object for a thread.

The *Xpackage::chgErrno()* is a sample package function that performs useful tasks. In this example, however, the *Xpackage::chgErrno()* function does nothing but set the per-thread *errno* value to be the thread ID plus 100. Like all other defined package functions, it returns a 0 value if succeeds or a -1 value otherwise (the thread-specific *errno* is set with an error code accordingly).

The *destr* function is called whenever a thread terminates. The *destr* function discards thread-specific *thr_data*-typed data. If a thread has registered multiple *thr_data*-typed records with multiple *Xpackage*-typed variables, then the *destr* function is called multiple times, once for each *thr_data*-typed data belonging to the terminating thread.

The following *thr_errno.C* file depicts a sample user program that makes use of the *Xpackage* class. The file content is:

```
#include "pkg.h"
Xpackage pkgObj;                              /* a package object */

/* function executed by each thread */
void* func1( void* argp )
{
    int *rcp = new int(1);

    /* open a thread's outstream */
    ofstream ofs ((char*)argp);
    if (!ofs) thr_exit((void**)&rcp);

    /* initialize a thread-specific data */
    pkgObj.new_thread( 0, ofs );

    /* do work with package functions here */
    pkgObj.chgErrno( 100 );  /* change a thread's errno */

    /* write some data to a thread's outstream */
    pkgObj.os() << (char*)argp << " [" << (int)thr_self() << "] finishes\n";
```

```
        /* thread terminates, set exit code */
        *rcp = pkgObj.errno();
        thr_exit(rcp);
        return 0;
    }

    /* main thread's function */
    int main(int argc, char** argv)
    {
        thread_t    tid;
        int         *rc;

        /* create a thread for each command line argument */
        while (--argc > 0)
            if (thr_create(0,0,func1,(void*)argv[argc],0,&tid)) perror("thr_create");

        /* wait for all threads to terminate */
        while (!thr_join(0,&tid,(void**)&rc))    {
            cerr << "thread: " << (int)tid << " exists. rc=" << *rc << endl;
            delete rc;                              // delete thread's dynamic mem
        }

        /* terminate the main thread */
        thr_exit(0);
        return 0;
    }
```

The program is invoked with one or more file names as command line arguments. Each argument is the file name of a thread output stream. For each argument, the main thread creates a new thread to execute the *func1* function. The argument to the *func1* function is the new thread's output stream file name. After all the threads are created, the main thread waits for them to exit and then terminates.

When a thread starts executing the *func1* function, it defines an *ofstream* object to reference the given output file. It then calls the *pkgObj.new_thread()* to allocate its thread-specific data storage, which stores the *ofstream* object and initializes the *errno* value to zero. When these are done, the thread calls the package functions to perform actual work. At the end it calls the *pkgObj.chgErrno()* function to set its *errno* value to 100 plus its thread ID value. This causes the *errno* value of each thread that executes the *func1* function to be unique for each thread. The thread then calls the *pkgObj.os()* function to return its output stream object and also prints the stream object output file name and thread ID. The thread terminates by specifying its private *errno* value as the actual argument to the *thr_exit* function call.

The sample run of the *thr_errno* program and its output is:

```
%     CC thr_errno.C -o thr_errno -lthread
%     thr_errno     a     b
thread: 5 exists. rc=105
thread: 4 exists. rc=104
%     cat a
a [5] finishes
%     cat b
b [4] finishes
```

In the above sample run, the *thr_errno* program is invoked with two file names: *a* and *b*. Two threads are created to execute the *func1* functions. The first thread ID is 5 and it creates an output file called *a* with the content of *a [5] finishes*. The thread terminates with an exit value of 104. The second thread ID is 4. It creates a file called *b* with the content of *b [5] finishes* and its exit value is 105.

13.7   The Multithreaded Programming Environment

To support multithreaded programming, Sun Solaris provides a thread library for users to create and manipulate threads in their programs. There are also modifications in the standard libraries such that there are re-entrance versions of many popular library functions. Global variables (e.g., *errno*) that are exported from standard libraries are defined dynamically for each thread that uses them. All of these ensure that multiple threads make use of standard libraries concurrently with reliable results.

Besides all the above, Sun Solaris also modifies the kernel to support symmetrical multi-processing and LWP scheduling. There is also a multithreaded version of the *debugger* and *truss* commands which debug and trace individual thread activities in a process. All of these features are expected to be provided by other vendors that support multithreaded programming environments on their systems.

13.8   Distributed Multithreaded Application Example

This section describes a multithreaded distributed program. This is an interactive program that executes user shell commands on any machine on a LAN. The program uses RPC to communicate with dedicated RPC servers running on remote hosts. When a user issues a shell command, the program creates a thread to connect with an RPC server on a user-specified host. The server executes the user command on that host, and its return status code is checked by the thread to flag any error code to the user.

By using a thread to handle each user command, the program can accept a new command while it is executing one or more previous commands by other threads. Thus users do not have to wait for each command to finish execution before issuing another one. This makes the program more "interactive" than an equivalent program that is single-threaded. Furthermore, the program can readily make use of any multi-processor resources that may be available on its the host machine.

By using RPC, the program can distribute its work loads to other computers on the network. This greatly enhances the performance and flexibility of the program. Furthermore, by using the RPC broadcasting technique, the program can automatically determine which hosts have its RPC servers running for communication purposes. Thus, the only setup required for users is to load the RPC servers on host machines of their choice (which may be heterogeneous platforms such as UNIX workstations, VMS machines and Windows-NT machines) and run the program on a host machine that supports multithreaded programs (e.g., a Sun Solaris workstation).

The RPC server that communicates with the interactive program and executes user shell commands is contained in the *shell_svc.C* program. This program uses the RPC classes as defined in Chapter 12 to create a *RPC_svc* object for RPC operations. The *shell_svc.C* file is:

```
#include "mshell.h"
#include "RPC.h"
RPC_svc *svcp;                                  // RPC server object pointer

/* RPC function to execute one user's shell command */
int execshell( SVCXPRT* xtrp )
{
    static int   res=0, rc= RPC_SUCCESS;
    char  *shell_cmd = 0;

    /* get user's shell command from a RPC client */
    if (svcp->getargs( xtrp, (xdrproc_t)xdr_string, (caddr_t)&shell_cmd)
            !=RPC_SUCCESS)
      return -1;

    /* execute the command via the system function */
    res = system(shell_cmd);

    /* send execution result to the RPC client */
    if (svcp->reply(xtrp, (xdrproc_t)xdr_int, (caddr_t)&res)!=RPC_SUCCESS)
        rc =  -2;

    return rc;
}
```

```
/* RPC server main function */
int main(int argc, char* argv[])
{
    /* create a RPC server object for the execshell function */
    RPC_svc *svcp = new RPC_svc( SHELLPROG, SHELLVER,
                    argc==2 ? argv[1] : "netpath");
    if (!svcp || !svcp->good()) return 1;
    /* wait for RPC clients' requests */
    if (svcp->run_func( EXECSHELL, execshell )) return 3;
    return 0;                              /* shouldn't get here */
}
```

The RPC server program creates an *RPC_svc* object to execute the *execshell* function when requested by a RPC client. The *execshell* function takes a NULL-terminated character string from a client that contains a UNIX shell command. It calls the *system* function to execute that shell command. The return value of the *system* function call is returned to the RPC client via the *RPC_svc::reply* function. The RPC server process is a daemon and is run in the background until the system is shut down or is explicitly killed by a user.

The RPC.h header and its companion RPC.C files are defined in Section 12.5 of Chapter 12. The following *mshell.h* header defines the RPC program number, version number, and function number for the *execshell* function:

```
#ifndef MSHELL_H
#define MSHELL_H
#include <rpc/rpc.h>

#defineSHELLPROG ((unsigned long)(0x20000001))
#defineSHELLVER  ((unsigned long)(1))
#defineEXECSHELL ((unsigned long)(1))

#endif /* !MSHELL_H */
```

The RPC server program is compiled and run as follows on any computer that supports UNIX System V Release 4-style RPC functions:

```
%    CC -DSYSV4 shell_svc.C RPC.C -o shell_svc -lnsl
%    shell_svc &
```

The interactive main program is *main_shell.C*. It is a menu-driven program that repeatedly displays a menu of selections to the standard output. A user enters a selection by the menu index, and the program executes that selection via a thread. The *main_shell.C* program is:

```
#include <strstream.h>
#include <thread.h>
#include <string.h>
#include <stdio.h>
#include "mshell.h"
#include "shellObj.h"

/* collect remote hosts that have server running on it */
extern void* collect_hosts( void* argp );
extern void* display_hosts( void* argp );
extern void* exec_shell( void* argp );

shellObj *funcList[4];                       // dispatch table
int   numFunc = sizeof(funcList)/sizeof(funcList[0]);
rwlock_t   rwlck;                            // read-write lock

/* Quit program */
void* quit_prog( void* argp )
{
    return (void*)0;
}

/* Execute one shell command on a host */
void* getcmd( void* argp )
{
    char host[20], cmd[256], cmd2[256];
    cout << "shell cmd> " << flush;
    cin >> cmd;
    cin.getline(cmd2,256);
    cout << "host: " << flush;
    cin >> host;
    if (!cin)
        cout << "Inavlid input\n" << flush;
    else
    {
        if (strlen(cmd2)) strcat(strcat(cmd," "),cmd2);
        strcat(strcat(cmd,"/"),host);
        char* ptr = new char[strlen(cmd)+1];
        ostrstream(ptr,strlen(cmd)+1) << cmd;
        if (thr_create(0,0,exec_shell,ptr,THR_DETACHED,0)) per-
ror("thr_create");
    }
    return (void*)1;
}
```

```
/* Get an user input selection and execute it */
int exec_cmd()
{
    char buf[256];
    cout << "Selection> " << flush;
    cin >> buf;
    cout << endl;
    if (cin)
    {
        int  idx = -1;
        istrstream(buf) >> idx;
        if (idx >=0 && idx < numFunc)
            return funcList[idx]->doit(0);
        else cerr << "Invalid input\n";
    }
    return 0;
}

/* display menu to user */
void display_menu(ostream& os)
{
    for (int i=0; i < numFunc; i++)
        (void)funcList[i]->usage(os,i);
}

/* initialize read-write lock and dispatch table */
int init_all()
{
    /* initialize the read-write lock */
    if (rw_init (&rwlck, USYNC_THREAD, 0))
    {
        perror("rwlock_init");
        return -1;
    }
    /* initialize the dispatch table */
    funcList[0] = new shellObj( "Collect host names", collect_hosts);
    funcList[1] = new shellObj( "Display host names", display_hosts);
    funcList[2] = new shellObj( "Execute a shell command", getcmd, 0);
    funcList[3] = new shellObj( "Quit", quit_prog, 0);
    return 0;
}

/* main routine */
int main()
{
    if (init_all() == 0)
```

```
      do   {
         display_menu(cerr);
         if (!exec_cmd()) break;
      } while (1);
   thr_exit(0);
}
```

In this interactive program, there are four menu selection to users:

Index	Function	Usage
0	*collect_hosts*	Finds all hosts running the RPC server
1	*display_hosts*	Displays all host names running the RPC server
2	*getcmd*	Execute some shell command
3	*quit_prog*	Quits the interactive program

The above four functions' addresses are stored in a dispatch table *funcList*. When a user enters a selection, that integer value is used to index the dispatcher table and to invoke the function for that entry. For example, if a user enters a selection of zero, the *collect_hosts* function is invoked.

Each entry of the *funclist* table is a pointer to a *shellObj* object. The *shellObj* class is defined in the *shellObj.h* header as:

```
#ifndef SHELLOBJ_H
#define SHELLOBJ_H

#include <iostream.h>
#include <thread.h>
#include <string.h>
typedef void* (*FNPTR)( void *);

class shellObj
{
      char*        help_msg;
      FNPTR        action;
      void*        (*fnptr)( void* );
      int          create_thread;
   public:
      // constructor. Set help msg, action func and errno
      shellObj( const char* msg, FNPTR func, int thr_ok=1)
      {
         help_msg = new char[strlen(msg)+1];
         strcpy(help_msg,msg);
```

```
         action  = func;
         create_thread = thr_ok;
      };
      // destructor function
      ~shellObj() { delete help_msg; };

      // print object usage
      ostream& usage( ostream& os, int idx)
      {
         os << idx << ": " << help_msg << endl;
         return os;
      };

      // do action
      int doit( void* argp )
      {
         if (create_thread) {
            thread_t  tid;
            if (thr_create(0,0,action,argp,THR_DETACHED,&tid))
               perror("thr_create");
            return (int)tid;
         }
         else return (int)action(argp);
      };
   };
   #endif /* !SHELLOBJ_H */
```

Each *shellObj* object contains a help message that explains its use, a function pointer to a user-defined function (which may be called to do the actual work of the object), and a flag to specify whether or not the user-defined function should be invoked via a thread when it is called. The four *shellObj* objects for the four functions *collect_hosts*, *display_hosts*, *getcmd* and *quit_prog* are created and referenced via the *funcList* table entry 0, 1, 2, and 3, respectively.

The *main* function of the interactive program first calls the *init_all* function to initialize: (1) the read-write lock *rwlck*; and (2) the *funcList* dispatch table with four *shellObj* objects. After that, the main function goes into a loop, calling the *display_menu* function to display a selection menu to a user. It next calls the *exec_cmd* function to prompt a user for a menu selection and invokes a function for that selection. The loop exits when the *exec_cmd* returns a zero value and the *main* function terminates via the *thr_exit* function.

The *display_menu* function scans through the *funcList* dispatch table and invokes the *shellObj::usage()* function of each *shellObj* object addressed by table entry. This causes each *shellObj* object to print out its use and dispatch table index to the output stream *cerr*.

Each user selection to the menu is obtained via the *exec_cmd* function. The function checks that the user input index is in the range of zero to 3 and flags an error if this is not true. If user input is valid, the *exec_cmd* function uses that number as an index to the *funcList* table to obtain a pointer to a *shellObj* object. It then invokes the *shellObj::doit()* function of that object. The *exec_cmd* function returns either a zero value, if it cannot obtain data from a user, or the return value of the *shellObj::doit()* function that it invoked.

The *exec_cmd* function passes the 0 argument value to each *shellObj::doit()* function it invokes. For the menu selection of 0 and 1, the corresponding *collect_hosts* and *display_hosts* functions are executed by detached threads immediately. However, for the menu selections of 2 and 3, the corresponding *getcmd* and *quit_prog* functions are not executed by detached threads. Each of these four functions returns a nonzero value if its execution is successful, a zero value if it fails.

The threads created to execute the *collect_hosts* and *display_hosts* functions are detached from the main threads. This means that as soon as they terminate, their resource and thread IDs can be reused by other new threads. This is so because the interactive program may run for a long time and must maintain its responsiveness to user inputs. It cannot afford to suspend itself in any *thr_join* function call to wait for other threads to exit.

There is no argument value passed to any *collect_hosts* and *display_hosts* function calls. The *getcmd* function gets an input shell command and a host name from a user. It then creates a thread to execute the *exec_shell* function. The actual value passed to the *exec_shell* function is a NULL-terminated character string that contains a shell command, followed by a "/" and finally a host name where the command is to be executed. Thus, if an actual argument passed to an *exec_shell* function is:

"cal 1995 > foo/fruit"

it asks to execute the *cal 1995 > foo* shell command on the host *fruit*. The list of available hosts that have the *shell_svc* daemon installed are collected by the *collect_hosts* functions, and the list is displayed to the user via the *display_hosts* function.

The *collect_hosts, display_hosts,* and *exec_shell* function definitions are contained in the *shell_cls.C* file:

```
#include <fstream.h>
#include <strstream.h>
#include <stdio.h>
#include <netdir.h>
#include <string.h>
#include <thread.h>
#include "mshell.h"
#include "RPC.h"
```

```
#define TMPFILE    "/tmp/hosts"

/* read-write lock to synchronize the access to the hostlist table by threads */
extern rwlock_t rwlck;              // defined and initialized in main_shell.C

/* maintain a list of available hosts */
#define MAXHOSTS   30
static char  *hostlist[MAXHOSTS];          // list of host names
static int   numhosts;                     // actual no. of hosts

/* make a RPC call to a server to execute one shell command */
int exec_host( const char* cmd, char* host )
{
    int   res=0;
    /* create a client handle to connect to the RPC server */
    RPC_cls cl( host, SHELLPROG, SHELLVER, "netpath");
    if (!cl.good()) return 1;
    /* authenticate client tothe RPC server */
    cl.set_auth( AUTH_SYS );

    /* call the execshell function on the server */
    if (cl.call( EXECSHELL, (xdrproc_t)xdr_string, (caddr_t)&cmd,
                (xdrproc_t)xdr_int, (caddr_t)&res) != RPC_SUCCESS)
        return 2;

    // flag an error if execshell fails
    if (res!=0)  cerr << "clnt: exec cmd fails\n";
    return res;
}

/* check if a named host is in the hostlist table */
int check_host( const char* hostnm )
{
    if (rw_rdlock(&rwlck)) perror("rw_rdlock");          // acquire lock for read

    for (int i=0; i < numhosts; i++)
        if (!strcmp(hostlist[i],hostnm)) break;          // break if name found

    if (rw_unlock(&rwlck)) perror("rw_unlock");          // release read lock

    return  (i < numhosts) ? 1 : 0;                      // return 1 is name is OK
}

/* Executed by a thread created by func3: exec one command on a host */
void* exec_shell( void* argp )
{
```

```
      int rc = 0;
      char* cmd = (char*)argp;
      char* host = strrchr(cmd,'/');
      *host++ = '\0';
      if (!check_host(host))        {                      // check host name is OK
         cout << "Invalid host: '" << host << "'\n" << flush;
         rc = 1;
         thr_exit(&rc);                                    // exit with an error
      }
      rc = exec_host( cmd, host );
      thr_exit(&rc);                                       // exit thread
      return 0;
   }

   /* Executed by a thread called by func2: display all available hosts */
   void* display_hosts( void* argp )
   {
      int rc = 0;
      char buf[256], cmd[256];

      if (rw_rdlock(&rwlck)) perror("rw_rdlock");          // acquire a read lock

      if (!numhosts)                                       // NOP if no hosts
         rc = -1;
      else {
         /* store the hosts listing to a temporary file */
         ostrstream(buf,256) << TMPFILE << "." << thr_self();
         ofstream ofs (buf);
          if (!ofs)
            cerr << "Create temp file '" << buf << "' failed\n";
         else      {
            for (int i=0; i < numhosts; i++)
               ofs << i << ":  " <<  hostlist[i] << endl;
            ofs.close();

            /* pop-up a xterm to display the host listing */
            ostrstream(cmd,256) << "xterm -title Hosts -e view " << buf;
            if (system(cmd)) perror("system");

            /* remove the temporary file */
            if (unlink(buf)) perror("unlink");
         }
      }

      if (rw_unlock(&rwlck)) perror("rw_unlock");          // release the read lock
      thr_exit(&rc);                                       // terminate the thread
```

```
        return 0;
    }

    /* record a remote host name to the hostlist table */
    int add_host( const char* hostnm )
    {
        int new_entry = 1;                              // success return code
        if (rw_wrlock(&rwlck)) perror("rw_wrlock");     // acquire write lock

        for (int i=0; i < numhosts; i++)                // is name in table?
            if (!strcmp(hostlist[i],hostnm)) break;

        if (i >= numhosts)      {                       // name not in list
            if (numhosts >= MAXHOSTS)
                cerr << "Too many remote hosts detected\n";
            else    {                                   // add a new entry
                hostlist[numhosts] = new char[strlen(hostnm)+1];
                strcpy(hostlist[numhosts++],hostnm);
            }
        }
        else new_entry = 0;                             // failure return code
        if (rw_unlock(&rwlck)) perror("rw_unlock");     // release write lock
        return new_entry;
    }


    /* client's broadcast call back function */
    bool_t callme (caddr_t res_p, struct netbuf* addr, struct netconfig *nconf)
    {
        struct nd_hostservlist *servp;

        /* extract server's hostname(s) from the addr argument */
        if (netdir_getbyaddr(nconf,&servp,addr))
            perror("netdir_getbyaddr");

        else for (int i=0; i < servp->h_cnt; i++) // add host names to hostlist table
            if (!add_host( servp->h_hostservs[i].h_host ))
                return TRUE;                    /* end broadcast if found a host twice */

        return FALSE; /                          // get more servers' responses
    }

    /* Executed by a thread created by func1: collect hosts that have server on it */
    void* collect_hosts( void* argp )
    {
        /* Sends a broadcast request and waits for servers' responses */
```

```
int rc = RPC_cls::broadcast( SHELLPROG, SHELLVER, 0,
             (resultproc_t)callme,              (xdrproc_t)xdr_void,
             (caddr_t)NULL, (xdrproc_t)xdr_void, (caddr_t)NULL);

/* check broadcast results */
switch (rc) {
  case RPC_SUCCESS:                          // successful
    break;
  case RPC_TIMEDOUT:                         // time-out
    if (numhosts) break;
  default:            /* flag an error if no hosts responded */
    cerr << "RPC broadcast failed\n";        // fail
    rc = 1;
}
thr_exit(&rc);                               // terminate the thread
return 0;
}
```

When the *collect_hosts* function is invoked, it makes an RPC broadcast call to ping all *shell_svc* daemons on the network. Each daemon response to the RPC broadcast is registered by the *callme* function. This function extracts the daemon's host name via the *netdir_getbyaddr* function and adds that host name to the *hostlist* table via the *add_host* function. The *add_host* function returns a value of 1 if it successfully adds a new host name to the *hostlist* table, a zero value otherwise. The *callme* function terminates the RPC broadcast if it sees that the same host responds to the broadcast twice. This would indicate that the RPC broadcast has not received any new responses and is in the rebroadcast process.

Once the RPC broadcast is finished, the *collect_hosts* function checks the broadcast result and terminates its thread with a return value of RPC_SUCCESS for success and a non-zero value for failure.

Note that access to the *hostlist* table is guarded by the read-write lock *rwlck*. This is needed as the *hostlist* table is accessed by all threads created to execute the *collect_hosts, display_hosts,* and *exec_shell* functions. It is important to ensure that the writer threads (executing the *collect_hosts* function) do not access the *hostlist* table simultaneously with the reader threads (executing the *display_hosts* and *exec_shell* functions)

When the *display_hosts* function is invoked, it displays all the host names in the *hostlist* table. These are the hosts running the *shell_svc* daemon. The function acquires and releases the read-write lock before and after it accesses the *hostlist* table. This is to ensure that the *collect_host* threads do not modify the table while reading it.

To make the host listing output separate from the main thread menu display, the *display_hosts* function stores the host listing to a temporary file and invokes an *xterm* to execute the *view* *<temp_file>* command on a separate window. The window disappears when a user quits the *view* command and the temporary file is discarded. The function terminates the thread with a exit value of 0 if it succeeds, a nonzero value if it fails.

When the *exec_shell* command is invoked, its input argument is a NULL-terminated character string that contains a user-defined shell command and a host name. The function calls the *check_host* command to make sure that the user-specified host name is in the *hostlist* table. If it is not, the thread terminates with a 1 value (failure). On the other hand, if a user-specified host name is valid, the function calls the *exec_host* function, which, in turn, creates an *RPC_cls* object to connect to the *shell_svc* daemon on the given host. Furthermore, the *exec_host* function calls the *execshell* RPC function via the *RPC_cls* object to execute the user shell command on that host. The *exec_host* and the *exec_shell* thread terminate with a zero value if the remote shell execution is successful or a nonzero value otherwise.

The interactive program is made up of the *main_shell.C* and *shell_cls.C* files. They are compiled as follows and the sample output of its execution is shown below. For this example, the hosts that have the *shell_svc* daemon installed are *fruit* and *veggie*.

```
%    CC -DSYSV4 shell_cls.C main_shell.C -o shell_cls -lthread -lnsl
%    shell_cls
0: Collect hosts names
1: Display hosts names
2: Execute a command
3: Quit
Selection> 0

0: Collect hosts names
1: Display hosts names
2: Execute a command
3: Quit
Selection> 1
< output shown in a xterm window: 0: fruit 1: veggie >

0: Collect hosts names
1: Display hosts names
2: Execute a command
3: Quit
Selection> 2

shell cmd> cal 1995 > foo
host> fruit
```

0: Collect hosts names
1: Display hosts names
2: Execute a command
3: Quit
Selection> 3

13.9   Summary

This chapter described multithreaded programming techniques based on the Sun Microsystems Solaris thread library and the POSIX.1c standard. Specifically, both Sun and POSIX1.c provide a set of thread library functions for users to create and manipulate threads in their applications. Various synchronization objects like mutex locks, condition variables and semaphores are also provided for users to synchronize thread access of shared data in the same process.

Other system support of multithreaded programs include special APIs for modifying per-thread base signal mask and provide re-entrance versions of major library functions. All of these thread-specific environment supports are also expected to be available in other platforms that support multithreaded programs.

Multithreaded programming is particularly useful for multiprocessing and object-oriented applications. This is demonstrated in the last section, where a distribution and multithreaded interactive program is depicted. This example program provides a framework for users to create their own applications, making use of any multiprocessing or network computing resources available on the machines running their applications.

N

O

R